The Gentle Art of Walking

A Compilation from The New York Times

Introduction by **Hal Borland**

Edited by **George D. Trent**

Arno Press/Random House
1971

TABLE OF CONTENTS

INTRODUCTION: The Longest Walk . . . Not Always Gentle v
CHAPTER ONE: The Gentle Art of Walking 1
    Legislation to Preserve Amenities 27
    Walking Clubs 29
    New York Walk Book 32
    President Kennedy and the 50-Mile Walk 35
    Famous Walkers 41
        John H. Finley 43
        The Leather Man 47
        Barbara Moore 48
        Edward Payson Weston 52
CHAPTER TWO: Country Walking in The United States 80
    The Backpacking Boom 83
    Winter Woods in North and South 91
    The Appalachian Trail 94
    North From New York 105
    Northward to Whiteface 108
    Northeast to Katahdin 137
    South From New York 150
    Some Westward Touch-Points 158
CHAPTER THREE: City Walking in The United States 175
    Annapolis 177
    Boston 180
    Hartford 185
    Miami Beach 188
    New Orleans 189
    New York 192
    Philadelphia 200
    San Francisco 203
    Washington 206
CHAPTER FOUR: Walking Abroad 211
    Austria (Vienna) 213
    Belgium (Bruges, Brussels) 216
    Canada (Ontario) 221
    Denmark (Copenhagen) 224
    France (Paris) 227
    Great Britain (London, Wales, Cambridge, Edinburgh, Oxford, Salisbury) 230
    Greece (Athens) 251
    Holland (Amsterdam) 253
    Ireland (Dublin) 256
    Israel (Jerusalem) 260
    Italy (Florence, Milan, Rome, Venice) 266
    Nepal (Katmandu) 277
    Puerto Rico (San Juan) 278
    Spain (Barcelona, Madrid, Segovia, Toledo) 281
    Switzerland 291
SUGGESTED ADDITIONAL READING 301
INDEX 303

The Longest Walk . . . Not Always Gentle

Hal Borland

FROM THAT DAY WHEN THE BABY HAULS HIMSELF UP OFF all fours and takes his first few tottery steps till the octogenarian shuffles through his final doorway, we walk. Some walk as little as they can manage, others as much as they can find time for; but we all have that unique ability to stand erect and walk on two feet. In a very real sense, man's tenancy on this planet is a consequence of his ability to travel on foot. It has been a long, long walk.

The really great events in mankind's history, most of them recorded only in rocks and bones, were migrations of families and tribes from one place to another, and they were all accomplished on foot. The horse and the wheel, after all, are relatively new means of travel, only a few thousand years in man's service. Before that, men walked wherever they went. And they went, almost literally, to the ends of the earth. Whether Africa or Asia was the birthplace of the species, man began spreading over the land, down through Africa, out across Asia deep into China and Mongolia, all the way down to Java. Then westward through Russia and the Balkans, until he had made all Europe his own, too. There the remarkable Cro Magnons left not only their footsteps but their splendid stone tools and their incredible cave art. Generation by short generation, men spread over the habitable land of this earth. And eventually, rather late, they reached the Americas.

That chapter, which I think of as one of the longest walks of all, is hidden in a very foggy past. It is a story I shall return to a little later. Meanwhile, families were evolving into tribes, tribes were becoming community groups, and men were slowly evolving from hunters to farmers. As primitive hunters they had been nomads, following the herds that provided their food. They had lived on foot, in the chase, forever on the move. But eventually some tribes found ways to encourage the growth of plants from which they could harvest a food supply that did not have to be hunted down and slaughtered and that would not soon spoil in storage. They became crude farmers, and they became relatively sedentary.

Rivalries, of course, were inevitable, between hunters and farmers and between competing tribes of hunters. There was competition for hunting territory, and there was competition for arable land, for water, for a hospitable climate. Among the earliest records we have of Northern Africa, on the Middle East, of Asia, are accounts of armed men marching forth to combat, of armies marching up and down the land. And armies, right down to the present day, consisted of armed men on foot. The wheel and the horse were reserved for the leaders. Even when the barbarian hordes came swarming out of the East and down across Europe, most of them were on foot.

So the earliest stories we have are of armies marching, forever marching. Often they were borne to the scene of battle in ships, and often there were primitive naval battles. But the man on foot was the one who bore the brunt, who did the crucial fighting, and who marched back to his camps in triumph or defeat. Homer sang of men who went to war in ships but marched to battle on foot. Caesar's classic account is the story of Roman legions marching across Europe in a tide of conquest. They went on foot all the way to the Channel and by sea across the Channel into England. The Romans built roads, remarkably durable roads, but not for their legions to be carted anywhere. Those roads were for the wagons that hauled their impedimenta, their gear and supplies, while the legions marched out to take and hold the provinces from which the wagons took back to Rome the farm-stuffs, food and wine for wealthy citizens who wouldn't walk a mile if they could avoid it.

Eventually the "barbarians," as they were called, the outlanders who were still sturdy in leg and strong in forearm, burst through the outer defenses and came down on Rome. Foot-soldiers, hungry for ease and wealth, they lived off the land like the primitives who were there so long before them, and they fought like them too. The Goths, the Visigoths, the Vandals and the Huns eventually marched to victory and carved up the Roman Empire.

The Middle Ages was a restless time of wandering, with friars and beggars, peasants and thieves on every road. Populations were increasing, Western Europe was prospering, the nobles were rich, the common people were poor, and there was a yearning for change, for adventure, for new and unknown places. The climax of this era came with the Crusades, which began in the eleventh century. The religious purpose was to reclaim Jerusalem from the Infidels, and all the Church from the pope down to the least of the wandering mendicant friars, preached that purpose. But there was also the lure for merchants of increased trade with the Middle East. For the nobles there was the lure of both military and religious honors. For the peasants there was the lure of travel, adventure, a footloose life such as they had never known. Hordes of restless, rootless people gathered around such leaders as

Peter the Hermit and Walter the Penniless. These rabble crusaders swarmed down across Europe like locusts, living on the countryside, undisciplined mobs rather than armies, hungry for adventure as well as food, welcoming violence, They finally reached Constantinople, where Alexis I, forewarned of their coming, quickly arranged to have them taken across the Bosporus, out of his domain. In Asia Minor they advanced to meet the Turks and were defeated in the first of countless battles between Crusaders and Infidels. Some survivors turned back. Others remained to join later Crusaders. The holy pilgrimages and the war with the Infidels dragged on and on for two hundred years.

Meanwhile, European men had begun to follow up their curiosity about the scope of the world. They had begun to comprehend the general outlines of all except what we know today as the Western Hemisphere. By ship, by caravan and on foot, men had established travel and trade routes down around Africa, north into Russia, east all the way to China. Before the end of the thirteenth century, Prior John of Pian de Carpine had traveled across Bohemia to Tartary, across the Russian steppes and all the way across China to the court of the Chinese emperor. Friar William of Rubruck had gone by way of the Danube and the Black Sea into Tartary and thence on foot—quite a walk by any standards—all the way into Tibet, the first European there and the last one there for several hundred years. And Marco Polo, who set out with his father and uncle from Venice on a trading expedition to Constantinople, went on from there all the way to Peking. He came home, was caught in one of those minor wars of the time, between Venice and Genoa, and was imprisoned three years. He whiled away the time writing an account of his travels, which we still read, fascinated.

There was much going to and fro in the next two centuries. Most of it was by water, but when a man wanted to get somewhere by land there were only two ways to travel, afoot or on horseback. Only the rich could afford horses, and the poor far outnumbered the rich. Most travelers went afoot. Then came the late years of the fifteenth century and the voyages of Columbus. A whole new world, the lands that would be known as the Americas, was discovered. And now I must go back and take up the story I spoke of earlier: that long walk which led to the peopling of those Americas.

THE AMERICAN STORY HAD ITS BEGINNINGS IN WHAT WE speak of as the Pleistocene epoch, or the Ice Age. As geologists measure time, it began about a million and a half years ago. At least four times great ice masses were formed by relatively minor changes in climate, and each time the ice came slicing down across the land from the north. Each massive ice sheet, millions of square miles in extent and in many places more than a mile thick, locked up immense quantities of water, shrinking the oceans in their beds. The surface of the Pacific was lowered, according to geological evidence, by at least 150 feet. When that happened, vast areas of what we now know as continental shelves and submerged land bridges were left

well above water. One such land bridge, an isthmus at least 300 miles wide, connected Siberia and Alaska. Because the great masses of ice in America were east of the Alaskan mountains, and because this land bridge blocked the flow of Arctic water southward, western Alaska and eastern Siberia had temperate climates. And since each of the Ice Ages came gradually and retreated slowly, taking between 10,000 and 20,000 years to come and to go, there was ample time for that isthmus to become a vast, rolling plain with lush grass and bushes and trees along its ponds and slow streams of fresh water.

During those land-bridge intervals, particularly the later ones, Pleistocene animals such as the big-horned bison, the mammoth, the camel and the horse fed there, ranging freely from Siberia to Alaska and down the American coast. Tribesmen who had spread north and east long before, Asiatic nomads who lived by the chase, followed those meat animals out across that hospitable isthmus, not in a mass migration but in a gradual movement, and began to spread out on the American mainland. Their movement was southward, then east below the foot of the ice sheet; and in time they went far south, and far east. They came on foot, perhaps with domesticated dogs but certainly not with domesticated horses or cattle. Dates are wholly speculative, but their coming could have been 40,000 or 50,000 years ago. Granting the possibility of such dates, in the next 25,000 to 35,000 years man had walked and carried seeds of his culture more than 10,000 miles, all the way to Cape Horn.

And that is why I speak of that migration, the arrival of man in Alaska and his subsequent journeying and colonization all the way to Tierra del Fuego, as one of the longest walks of all. Most of the other mass migrations of prehistoric man were gradual, the slow spread of hunting tribes into virgin territory, usually prompted by tribal growth and the decimation of food animals. But here, in a relatively short time, the newcomers spread over and largely occupied the greater part of two vast continents. Even more remarkable, out of this swift migration and settlement rose three cultural achievements of such high quality that they must be called civilizations. These were the cultures of the Incas of Peru, the Aztecs of Mexico, and the Iroquois of northeastern United States. And elsewhere, particularly in North America, dozens of lesser cultures evolved.

All this was done on foot, as it were, without horse or wheel for conveyance. The wild horse, in fact, was doomed to extinction here long before historic times, and did not return to this continent until the Spaniards arrived in the sixteenth century. Meanwhile, man walked where he would go, unless there was a water route. Then he traveled by dugout or bark canoe.

It was the Spanish conquistadors who changed this by bringing the horse back to America. But that change came gradually, not all at once. Hernando Cortez conquered Montezuma and took the Aztec capital, partly because the Aztecs first thought he and his mounted men were centaur-like gods. They even thought the Spanish arquebuses were somehow a part of the horses and breathed dragon-like fire that could kill. They learned, of course, that the horse was just another animal with edible flesh, and they killed a great many of them. Other horses escaped or were stolen and were the start of the mustangs that eventually put hoofs under the Plains Indians and made them not only far-ranging nomads but mounted warriors, often rated equal to the best the world has ever known.

But meanwhile, the early Spaniards did a great deal of walking on this newly discovered continent. Their expeditions to the mainland included horses, at least enough for the leaders and their top assistants, but, as always and elsewhere in those days, the rank and file were on foot. And when an expedition penetrated inland any distance the whole company traveled at the foot soldier's pace. The Spanish foot soldier, burdened with his arms and cumbersome equipment, was essentially a slow traveler, far slower than the Indians. As the Indians soon developed a taste for horse flesh, every Spanish expedition that ventured far inland eventually reached the point where everyone, leaders included, was on foot. Consequently, those early Spanish explorers walked and walked and walked, many of them to their death. Even those who undertook to explore by water, particularly along the shores of the Gulf of Mexico, were often set afoot in strange, unfriendly places.

Cabeza de Vaca is sometimes called the first man to walk across America. Actually, he walked only from the Gulf of Mexico to the Gulf of California, but it took him six years, thanks to the Indians. And he had three companions. They were members of one of the most ill-fated of the early expeditions, which was led by Panfilo de Naravaez, and wrecked by a hurricane. The survivors of the expedition reached the Florida shore and made their way to the site of Tallahassee. There they built boats and skirted the coast to the vicinity of Galveston Bay, where they were wrecked again. De Vaca, with two other Spaniards and black Esteban, set out for Mexico on foot. Nobody knows how far they traveled in the next six years, but bee-line it was only about 1,000 miles to the Spanish settlement, where they told tall tales of "The Seven Cities of Cibola," gleaming with emeralds set in the walls and crusted with gold. They said the Indians declared Cibola was only a few days travel to the north, in the land of "hunchback cows."

The Spanish viceroy of Mexico sent Fray Marcos, with black Esteban as a guide, to find this Indian Golconda. The party went north into present New Mexico, found only the Zuni pueblos, and turned back. But Fray Marcos' report did not settle anything. Francisco Vasquez Coronado was sent, with 300 mounted lancers and 700 infantrymen, to find those fabulous cities. They went from Culiacan, Mexico, all the way to central Kansas, almost as far as Cabeza de Vaca and his companions had walked. Along the way most of the mounted lancers became foot soldiers because the Indians killed or stole their horses. So

that long walk in search of a chimera led only to a bootyless return with nearly all the company on foot.

Meanwhile Hernando de Soto had been named governor of Cuba with the right to conquer "Florida," meaning the American mainland. De Soto, who had served under Pizzaro in Peru, led an expedition that landed near present St. Petersburg in 1539. They marched north and west, through the future Gulf states, finally crossed the Mississippi near Memphis, pushed on to present Little Rock, then went down the Ouchita and Red rivers to the Mississippi again. There de Soto, sick and worn-out, died of fever and privation. The man who succeeded him, Luis de Moscoso, then led the forlorn remnant of the expedition back and forth through the swamps and canebrakes another year before he took them back to the Mississippi, built crude boats and eventually got down the river and across the gulf to Tampico.

Various Spanish expeditions followed into the Southwest. Padre Augustin Rodriguez led a handful of foot soldiers north to the vicinity of Albuquerque, where the Indians killed the friar and most of his party. Don Antonio de Espejo took an expedition north to rescue the friar, not knowing his fate, and explored a good part of New Mexico. Caspar Castano de Sosa, lieutenant governor of Nuevo Leon, led a party up the Pecos to Taos and beyond. Captain Leyva Bonilla and Juan de Humana set out northward in 1595 in search of Quivira and probably reached southern Colorado. But there the Indians attacked and killed all but one of the party. Finally Juan de Onyate was authorized by the viceroy to go on a campaign of conquest and settlement, and in 1598, he established a settlement about 25 miles north of Santa Fe. By 1600 New Mexico was a Spanish colony, and the Spaniards, foot soldiers and friars mostly, had walked over almost every area of the Southwest. Many Spanish bones were buried there, and many Spanish horses were butchered or set free to roam the hills and multiply. Santa Fe was founded in 1609.

Meanwhile, the French were taking the measure of the eastern half of the continent. Whereas Spaniards thought in paces and leagues, the French thought in days of canoe travel and days of portage. By preference, the French chose the waterways. When they had to engage in overland travel, it usually was on foot, for they were not the horsemen that the Spaniards were. Consequently, the native Indians of Northeast America, foot and canoe travelers themselves, never became horsemen.

The early French were seamen who explored the coasts and inlets. They did not penetrate inland until late in the sixteenth century, and Quebec was not founded until 1608. It was 1634 before Jean Nicolet, the first white man there, reached Lake Superior. That journey was primarily a voyage up the lakes, and not for another 60-odd years did the French explorers go much further. Then Louis Jolliet and Father Jacques Marquette, with five companions, went by canoe from the lakes down the Wisconsin to the Mississippi and on down to the mouth of the Arkansas. Ten years later, Sieur de la Salle and Henri de Tonti, with an escort of foot soldiers, went from the mouth of the Illinois all the way to the mouth of the Mississippi and claimed for France all the area drained by the big river. He called it *La Louisiane,* honoring Louis XIV. Thus were laid the foundations for French claims to the vast Louisiana Territory.

So the Spanish gained their foothold and made the land their own, for another century at least, with the imprint of their footsteps on the soil. So the French gained their foothold and measured their claims by river drainage, by canoe travel, by proclamation. And meanwhile a few groups of Englishmen were cutting little clearings along the Atlantic coast and making brief, tentative trips inland. FOR THE MOST PART, THE FIRST ENGLISH COLONISTS were villagers and small farmers, not venturers or horizon-dreamers. That breed had to wait a generation or two. But there was something about this land, the vastness of its woodlands and rivers and savannahs, its mountains and prairies and huge interior valleys, that would call forth the wide-ranging, restless urgency that was to mark so many later Americans.

A scattering of settlements, clearings within sight and sound of the roll and boom of Atlantic surf, was the beginning. Before long, however, there was an occasional young man with itching feet and a roving heart. Such men became hunters and fur trappers and traders, and they gloried in their knowledge of the backwoods. They knew the game trails and the Indian paths, and they became familiar with the Indians themselves. Before 1700 they had marked almost every valley and hilltop in the back-country, and some had gone as far as mid-Ohio and Kentucky. And they were being followed by settlers, who carved farms and backwater communities out of the big woods, who drove their hogs and cattle to market in the coastal cities and walked right back home, shaking the city dust off their feet as soon as they could. They went afoot because most of the backwoods trails were footpaths and because a man on foot could travel quietly as a deer, could vanish into the shadows like a bobcat or a fox. The horse was a part of the falderal of life among merchants and plantation folk, like linen shirts and polished boots. Backwoods folk had few horses. Oxen pulled their plows and carts, and a man traveled on shank's mare.

It was foot-travel time and foot-travel country, and that backwoods fringe kept widening out and settling up, reaching into Tennessee and Kentucky, into the Ohio Country, always westward, toward the Big River. In 1732 George Washington was born in Virginia tidewater country. In 1734 Daniel Boone was born in a cup of red hills in the Schuylkill valley of Pennsylvania. Far-travelers, both of them were to be. At 17, Boone turned his back on the hills of home and went south and west across the Alleghenies till he came to the Yadkin Valley. Boone opened the way to interior Kentucky, and before he was 25 he knew more backwoods trails and backwoods lore than anyone else in those shadowy woodlands. At 21, George Washington was sent by Governor Dinwiddie to warn the French up on Lake Erie to stay out of the Ohio Country. With Christopher Gist, he went almost 500 winter miles and found and warned sour, one-eyed Legardeur St. Pierre. On the way back, caught in a year-end storm, he almost drowned rafting across the ice-filled Ohio.

From the little farms, from the seashore villages, from the big plantations, they went, packs on their backs, rifles in their hands, dreams in their heads. They had left footprints all the way to the Mississippi before the Colonies became a Union. And after that war, while the statesmen argued and the politicians haggled a settlement and a brand new government, those men in moccasins, those far travelers with horizons in their eyes, were leading the way westward. All the way to the Big River, and to the vast Louisiana Territory beyond.

France had ceded *La Louisiane* to Spain in 1762, under pressure from the French and Indian War, but it was ceded back to France in 1800, in complex European political maneuvers. But by 1803 Napoleon was in urgent need of money and sold the whole of Louisiana Territory west of the Mississippi to the United States for $15,000,-000. President Jefferson already had quietly set about organizing an expedition to explore at least a part of that area. Now those plans quickly matured. On May 14, 1804, the Lewis and Clark Expedition left St. Louis on one of the great explorations of all history. The company was gone two years; it traveled approximately 5,000 miles, and brought back the first informed report on the northern half of the area west of the Mississippi, and its plant and animal life. The company's equipment and supplies were carried by boat or packhorse, but the able-bodied men walked most of the way, and they towed their 55-foot keelboat a good part of the way up the Missouri river. It was an astonishing feat.

In the expedition was a man named John Colter, who left the party on the upper Missouri on the return trip, to remain there as a trapper. With two other men—trappers already were working in the area for Spanish trader Manuel Lisa—Colter reached the valley of the Yellowstone the following year, 1807. There he discovered the fantastic gysers and hot springs of present Yellowstone Park. The next year while trapping with one companion he was surprised by hostile Blackfoot Indians. His companion was killed and Colter was stripped and told to run for his life, a form of torture. He ran six miles across a thorny upland, outdistanced all but one Indian, killed him barehanded, and reached Jefferson Fork in time to hide under a raft of driftwood. The Indians gave him up for drowned and Colter walked, naked and unarmed, living on roots, for seven days till he reached Lisa's trapping headquarters. Rested and equipped with a new outfit, he then went back to trapping beaver.

By 1820 the fur trade of the West had expanded into the far mountain country. The Mountain Men, trappers and explorers who were equally at home on horseback or afoot, were moving into the vast, unmapped, virtually unknown wilderness. It was they who explored those mountains, those rivers and deserts and fertile valleys. It was they who guided the official explorers when they finally arrived: men like Jim Bridger, Tom Fitzpatrick, the Sublettes, Dave Jackson, Old Bill Williams, Jedediah Smith, Kit Carson, Hugh Glass.

Pause a moment for Hugh Glass's story. He went up the Missouri with Andrew Henry's party in 1823 to trap beaver and establish a fort on the upper river. Far up the Grand, Glass was attacked by a grizzly with cubs and mauled fearfully. His companions killed the bear but despaired of Glass's life. Leaving two men to tend him till he died and then bury him, the party went on. The two, after a couple of days, decided Glass was as good as dead and left him. When they caught up with the main party they reported Glass dead and buried. But Hugh Glass was too tough to die that way. He crawled to a nearby spring, slowly recovered enough to begin an incredible crawl to Fort Kiowa a hundred miles down the river. Living on berries and wolf-killed buffalo calves, without knife or flint or gun, he kept going. Finally, he was able to get to his feet and walk a mile or so a day. He reached the fort, healed himself, and eventually set out again on foot to find his original party. He found them, a living ghost, whose revenge was the remorse of those two who had deserted him for dead.

Those Mountain Men lived mountainous legends. Did you ever hear of Jedediah Strong Smith?

'Diah Smith was one of the few really literate Mountain Men. He carried a Bible and Shakespeare in his pack. He went up the river early, became a master trapper of beavers, and finally bought a partnership in the leading fur company there. Curious about far places, he traveled all over the West, twice went all the way to California and back, once crossed the Sierra when the snow was deep enough to bury a horse, and went afoot from the Sierra all the way back to Great Salt Lake. He traveled up and down the Pacific Coast, from San Diego to Vancouver, trapped beaver on the Sacramento, was repeatedly attacked by Indians and harassed by the Spanish. At least twice he crossed the Mojave desert. And finally he sold his share of the fur business, returned to St. Louis and set up as a Santa Fe trader. On his first trip to Sante Fe he was waylaid and killed by Indians. He had lived only 32 years. On each of his trips to the Pacific he had traveled afoot at least 3,200 miles, at least as far as he rode in a saddle.

They lived tall tales, taller than the tales they told. Kit Carson? You've heard of him. Old Bill Williams? No. Both Carson and Williams guided Fremont, showed him what to discover, how to get there, and how to get back safely. Jim Bridger? Tom Fitzpatrick? Look them up.

But eventually someone in London found a way to make high hats out of silk, and the beaver trade went to pieces. The trappers sat around their remote campfires and growled, "Hell's full o' high silk hats!" And the settlers came up the rivers, over the long trails west, settlers and traders with Conestoga wagons and six-span ox teams, and bullwhackers who walked every step of the way, over the California Trail, the Oregon Trail, the Mormon Trail. And when the settlers came, even the women walked beside the wagons.

MEANWHILE, BACK ON THE EAST COAST ANOTHER BREED of far-wanderers had appeared, men less interested in far places than in what lived there, in the birds, the beasts, the trees and the flowers. The American naturalists had begun to explore, observe, and report. John Bartram was the first of them. Born in 1699 near Philadelphia, he studied plants because he wanted to be a doctor. Instead he became a farmer, and then a botanist, America's first botanist. Self-taught, he collected specimens and slowly developed a botanical garden on his own farm. His reputation spread to England, and he acquired patrons to whom he sent seeds and plants. He made botanical trips, on foot, to Lake Erie, to the Carolina mountains, to Florida. He lived to be 78, and he passed his knowledge on to his son, William, our first naturalist-artist, whose work still commands respect. An ornithologist as well as a botanist, William traveled far, wrote well, observed accurately. His principal book, a classic now known as *Bartram's Travels,* was published in 1791. The full title tells a good deal about the man and what he did: *Travels through North and South Carolina, Georgia, East and West Florida, the Cherokee Country, the Extensive Territories of the Muscogulges, or Creek Confederacy, and the Country of the Choctaws.*

William Bartram was adviser and teacher to Alexander Wilson, Scotch-born weaver-teacher-naturalist who published the first American ornithology. He wrote the text and painted the pictures, and they were published in seven volumes between 1808 and 1813. Wilson covered the United States east of the Mississippi and north of Florida, and his work was so comprehensive that only 23 indigenous birds were added to his list in the next hundred years. He spent ten years preparing his *Ornithology,* and he must have left his footprints on more of the eastern half of this country than anyone except the Bartrams had seen till then.

John James Audubon came to American from France in 1804, at the age of 19, and about ten years later, perhaps inspired by Wilson's *Ornithology,* was painting birds himself. Audubon spent the better part of twenty years roaming the wilderness, largely afoot, and painting birds. His pictures were first published in Scotland in 1827, and three years later he collaborated with William MacGillivray on text to go with them. Audubon later made other trips, including one to the West, and published a volume on American animals. He was a far-walker in his youth, a far-talker in his later years.

Henry David Thoreau was a boy of 10 in Concord, Massachusett, the year Audubon's first volume of bird pictures was published. Perhaps he eventually saw Audubon's pictures, but, they were not his inspiration. He seems to have been born with it. And with the necessity to walk, to go places afoot. The two years he lived in the cabin on Walden Pond were constant walking years—miles and miles of travel afoot—during which he puzzled out his thoughts to set down in his journals, and eventually published in the two books brought out during his lifetime. He walked, one time and another, all over Cape Cod, over a good many Massachusetts mountains, through the Maine woods. A social critic and something of a philosopher, he was primarily a naturalist, a far-walker and a splendid observer.

John Burroughs was 8 years old and John Muir was 7 when Thoreau built his cabin in the woods. Burroughs was born in New York state, Muir in Scotland. Burroughs, after a time as a government clerk, returned to the land, became a farmer, a naturalist, a writer, a notable foot-traveler. His feet came to know a great deal about his native hills. He walked, and led others walking, well into the twentieth century.

John Muir was brought to this country at the age of 11, grew up in Wisconsin with a deep interest in botany. He made several long walking trips, studying botany, before he went to California in 1868, settled there and became a naturalist and a conservationist. John Muir probably walked more miles of the Sierra country than any other man ever did, and he was largely responsible for the creation of Yosemite National Park and the preservation of the redwood groves.

By the time Muir died, in 1914, and Burroughs, in 1921, the old breed of far-wanderers, both east and west, had thinned out. Most of the remote places had been explored except the polar regions. They still held their challenge, and until the airplane was "polarized," so to speak, the explorers who went there had only their two legs for transportation after they reached the ice, with dog sleds for emergencies. But polar travel is not exactly what most of us think of when we speak of taking a walk or even going on a hike. However, there are memorable names among those who made their difficult way on foot across those forbidding white wastes. In the Arctic there were Franklin, Beechy, Ross, Rae, Macmillan, Stefansson, Perry, Nansen. In the Antarctic were Weddell, Wilkes, Ross, Scott, Shackleton, Amundsen. I once talked with Bob Bartlett, who captained the ship on several Arctic expeditions, and he said, in that foghorn voice of his, "A polar trip isn't too bad, really, till you have to get out and walk." He said it with a grin, but there was the look in his hooded, light blue eyes of a man who had walked in the Arctic and wanted no more of it.

Not many of us walk nowadays as they used to. There isn't the necessity, for one thing. Even the farmer rides a tractor now and no longer walks his furrows. Children no longer walk to school; the school bus now is ubiquitous. When I was young we not only walked to school, sometimes several miles, but we walked for fun, as much as fifteen or twenty miles a day. Now if I walk twenty miles a week I am doing well. We grew up and, like everyone else, took to cars and trains and buses and jet planes simply to keep up with our clock-harried selves. For too many of us, walking became a therapeutic exercise recommended by the doctor, something we could approximate on a jog-pad at home or a treadmill at the club gym.

Is the long, long walk over? Not quite, but its pace and its objectives have changed. Having asserted his tenancy by leaving his footprints on nearly all this planet's exposed land, man now has found ways to walk the mysterious depths of the oceans and has penetrated space far enough to leave fabulous footprints on the moon. Weekend hikes on the moon or the ocean's floor will not soon depopulate terrestrial golf courses, but a daring few, like those of the past who had to see the far side of the mountains, undoubtedly will extend the long walk down a tenuous path into the future. Meanwhile, millions of others will walk the well-marked, familiar paths that so many have walked before them. Many will be pavement walkers, by choice or circumstance, but many more will take to the open country. They are the ones who cannot accept technology as the be-all and end-all of life. They must find trees and grass and flowing water, the enduring things of this earth.

So they will continue to walk, not trying to make big discoveries, but looking for little discoveries and big satisfactions, where paths are well trodden. Looking for the clean, clear view down a rural valley in upstate New York an hour after sunrise. For the vista from Mount Monadnock on an early autumn afternoon. For the blaze of sunset from Kit Carson Hill on the High Plains of eastern Colorado. For the cool, pine-scented summer evening in a high Sierra valley. For the surge and beat of surf and the feel of sand on the Great Beach at Cape Cod, the long beach at Hatteras, or at Padre Island, or on the lonely Pacific beach above the mouth of the Quillayute. You have to walk to know such things intimately, to be a part of them, and a great many people have such an inner necessity.

I live within a few miles of the Appalachian Trail, and I often see walkers there, brown with weather, serene with a sense of reality, self-sufficient. They make me think of those early colonists who had to get away from the settled towns and cities, had to go and find—well, first to find themselves. I think of the other trails, and of those walking them today, for the same reason. The Potomac Heritage Trail, the Continental Divide Trail down the backbone of the Rockies, the Pacific Crest Trail down the Cascades and the Sierra Nevada. The historic trails where men still walk, the Natchez Trace, the Santa Fe and Oregon and Lewis and Clark Trails, the North Country Trail. I think of Justice William O. Douglas, a naturalist in the direct line from the Bartrams through Wilson and Muir, who has walked more miles of these and other trails than anyone else I know.

The inner necessity persists, and the memories guide us, the race memories, though we know footprints themselves are as evanescent as dew. Wind or water or grass will wipe them out. But meanwhile we have the peculiar privilege of mankind, the freedom to walk this earth, see its beauties, taste its sweetness, partake of its enduring strength.

Chapter One

THE GENTLE ART OF WALKING

The Gentle Art of Walking

Travelers by shank's mare use a special technique; they sometimes even have their own philosophy of walking. Here is what they say.

By H. I. Brock

WHEN man became man and a biped he learned to use shanks' mare to go places. Still his first step on his own is his first accomplishment toward independence. On his two legs he performed all his land journeys for centuries. He kept on walking most of the time even when he had tamed a four-footed fellow-creature to carry him on his longer and speedier journeys. He invented wheels—and still he walked on most of his affairs. Only when he mounted those wheels on air cushions and hitched them to a gas engine did he get the notion in his head that he could not get anywhere by walking.

Now that war, which used to depend on foot soldiers, has gone in for tanks and airplanes, the civilian finds himself grounded—more or less—with the prospect that, as the days pass, it will be rather more than less.

Whether more or less, he's got to make the best of it. Very well. Because the centuries have formed the human body for walking, the doctors agree that, take it all in all, to use the body for walking is one of the best ways to keep it fit. The natural play of the muscles and the joints promotes a healthy circulation of the blood, is good for the nerves, assists the brain and dissipates humors—or eliminates poisons, if you prefer the modern way of putting it. You get much better exercise swinging along on your two feet than you do sitting on the back of your lap behind the steering wheel of a motor car.

Poets have gone tramping time out of mind to invoke the muse. Statesmen have used that simple method of getting down to earth and escaping the welter of words which is politics. Philosophers have been peripatetics—walkers about. Einstein pursues relativity afoot across the rolling country around Princeton. Which means that you can walk while you think—and, if the thinking you do while you walk seems more like ruminating, the conclusion that comes out of the proceeding is sometimes all the clearer. Dr. John Huston Finley, apostle of pedestrianism, said that "the land of our better selves is most surely reached by walking."

People who have continued to walk from choice include other notable persons of our time: college presidents, authors, editors, critics of the drama and doctors of divinity. Some of them treat walking as a sport—walk for the glory of walking and the record of mileage covered; some of them go walking to explore the world or the city or the neighborhood. Explorers generally, when they do not go upon ocean voyages, have gone on foot—witness the encounter between Stanley and Dr. Livingstone in the heart of Africa.

Sentimental journeys have been made on the legs that God gave us, and pilgrimages by treading the highways and byways with the staff that is the comforter. But walking for its own sake, like riding on a horse for its own sake—not merely to ketch a fox or to fly fences, or to get where you are going—is what counts with many walkers. There is the feel of the thing—the way you get into the swing of it after you have fallen into your stride and the rhythm of the movement gets into you the way, one long-legged footman said, it does when you dance. This chap, who writes for a living, said he liked a four-mile gait and ten or fifteen miles to go, but he could do a day's journey and climb mountains as well.

Naturally he was interested in the "technique" of walking—the body forward, the shoulders back, the free swing of the legs from the hips with the swing of the arms to help. He had been doing some civilian drill and he noticed that the doughboys' stride, posture and rhythm, as the drill sergeant's manual was applied, produced a tonic effect. He illustrated his point by marching up and down in cadence.

As a matter of fact, each fighting nation has developed a marching technique of its own. The British on the march are looser-jointed than we are, with freer knee action, and the French go at a long loping swing that seems to use the shoulders to push ahead with. It is a technique, anyway, that uses the whole body and carries

you over the ground at a great pace—on the level particularly. Perhaps it is not so good for hill climbing. (The German goose-step, so-called, is of course a parade march, not a ground-covering gait; on the road the Herrenfolk, when they are not motorized, slog along not so differently from the rest of us.)

GENERALLY speaking—aside from hikers who go across country singly or in packs, and mountain climbers who have an itch to get to the top of high places the hard way—the principle holds good of dividing into two kinds the people who make a serious business or recreation of walking. They are those who walk to be walking and those who walk to look at things.

The first kind take up walking, in the beginning, perhaps, for the sake of the exercise and then fall in love with walking and pursue it as a passion. They are prone to carry machines that clock their miles for them and to accumulate "centuries"— hundred-mile credits. They talk about walking as horsy folk talk about riding.

The other sort are really explorers— curious people who love the scenery of the country: woods, fields and streams, the road over the hill, lanes winding among farmsteads, mountain trails, either tame land or wild; or who love the sights of the city and like an intimate view of the goings-on, and the habitations of men packed together. Some walkers combine the passion for walking with the curiosity of the sight-seer.

I KNOW a critic of the drama who says he walks to lose himself, to become (as he puts it) one of the missing men of a great city, and thus capture freedom. Nobody can find him at home, or in the office, or get him on the telephone. At heart this man is no less an explorer than Amundsen. Part of the kick of going off to the ends of the earth is getting away from things gone stale and drab through custom.

Our critic, playing truant, has poked around the waterfront of New York for years. He knows the North River roustabouts, the loafers on the East River piers. He knows the Jersey shores where the ships are berthed, the harbor front under Staten Island's hills, the docks and shipyards and yacht basins that fringe Brooklyn's long and smudgy reach along the

river and the bay. One of the great advantages of walking here in New York is that you can take ferries at small expense, rest while you cross the water, watch the panorama of the port and have th sense of disembarking in a strange country. Each of our islands is strange to the other. And many parts of this big town are strange to every other part of it.

Like the wise Ulysses, though your ship is only a ferryboat, you are a seafarer and a collector of men and cities. The prescription for that sort of walking, our modern Ulysses says (and he has seen many strange places scattered around the globe), is to put on old clothes, from shoes to hat, and leave your everyday self behind you with your white-collar suit.

UNFORTUNATELY the waterfront is not, in these days, for inquisitive strangers or amateur vagrants, the happy hunting ground it used to be. The Coast Guard has taken over. But New York remains a city which holds within it many cities. And some of them are interior cities. Even in walking through Central Park you can visit in effect three continents—Europe, Africa and South America—besides encountering the soldiers of all the United Nations.

If you stroll through the lovely gardens where the park faces the Jeffersonian façade of the Museum of the City of New York you will be in the West Indies and hear little but Spanish spoken. And, though strolling is not walking, if you have walked all the way up there from the

Plaza, you have had a walk not beneath the contempt of any but the most fanatical pedestrian.

Our 22,000-odd acres of parks, it may be noted, offer admirable walking terrain whether for exercise or exploration, with the problem of getting to the distant ones by subway or bus an additional challenge to the spirit of adventure. If you are not adventurous the nearest park will serve perfectly well.

However, the subways and the ferries and the trains take you out of the city not inconveniently. There is rough country on the Palisades right across the Hudson, with climbing effects if your taste runs to clambering over rocks— pedestrian steeplechasing instead of flat walking. The path on top of the Croton Aqueduct is good going for those who choose the country but had liefer follow the open trail than emulate the mountain goat.

But above all, if you have mastered the art of walking pavements without pain to your feet, there are all the streets of New York open to you. If you have never walked the streets of New York except in the beaten track of your affairs they offer ample room for exercise and clocking records and a field of exploration that is matched by hardly any city in the world. If you have walked the streets of New York in days gone by and think you know the little old town, do not let that stop you. So many parts of it have been so changed in a decade that the men who think they know the city best will find almost any walk a voyage of discovery.

July 12, 1942

WALKING AS A FINE ART

PLEASURES ATTENDING A TRAMP THROUGH THE COUNTRY.

THE PROPER SEASON FOR PEDESTRIAN TOURS—THE ROUTES TO BE SELECTED AND OUTFIT REQUIRED.

Pedestrian tours are more common in England and on the Continent than in this country. It may be remarked in passing that this is the traveling system of the tramp and the broken-down thespian in this country. To those with health and strength for a long day's walk and an eye for the picturesque in nature a pedestrian tour possesses many attractions; and it is not likely that our athletes will fail to Americanize this custom of their transatlantic friends. The veteran humorist, Josh Billings, has been in the habit for years of making a long provincia tour in a buggy with his wife, traveling by day and sleeping at night at the roadside inns, and he declares that this is the only way to see a country properly.

The pedestrian tour, which to those able to endure the walk is only a healthful exercise, possesses many advantages over the riding tour. Like the bird, one can cut across fields or through woods. Not being compelled to keep to the road, the pedestrian may linger among sweet-scented wild flowers, while the driver is plodding in the dust under the broiling sun.

The outfit for a tour afoot, as the Continental journals call these little pedestrian excursions, is a walking or sack suit of stout black or blue flannel or other material. The country people, through croquet and lawn tennis, have become familiar with knickerbockers, and so the hardy pedestrian may now wear this style of clothes and find them very convenient. The trousers should be supported by a belt rather than by suspenders, as affording free action for exercise. If the weather is warm the vest can be left off, but it is better to be a little inconvenienced by the heat than to suffer from chill in the morning and evening and in passing through the cool and shady recesses of the forest. The underclothing should be a light flannel, and the hose of light wool. Stout brogans, with the soles following the shape of the feet, should be worn, or canvas baseball shoes—without the spikes, of course. A derby or felt hat will be more comfortable and durable than a straw or a cloth headgear. In the waterproof knapsack carried on the back in military fashion should be a gossamer waterproof cloak or surtout, a change of underclothing, toilet articles, but few other articles, as after one or two days' traveling every ounce of additional weight will seem a pound. A pocket flask, containing whisky or brandy, should always be carried for medical purposes (to temper the water with, or in case of snake bites.) A stout but not too heavy walking stick will be found a great convenience. In the pocket carry a small compass. This outfit need not be expensive, but may be in accordance with the means of the purchaser. And so, too, the expenses along the route depend entirely upon the tastes and resources of the party. Only first-class hotels can be patronized and the best of everything demanded, or the happy medium in all things may be sought with entire comfort and less expense. The expenses may be reduced a trifle by stopping for meals and lodgings at farm houses instead of roadside inns; but except in the interior country this will not always be feasible, as the hostlery will be suggested by the folk, who will sometimes hesitate to take strangers under their roof. About $2 a day is a safe estimate for a pedestrian tour on the plan indicated. A knowledge of the country roads can always be obtained from the local or county maps generally to be found hanging in the sitting room or barroom of the cross-roads inn.

For a pedestrian tour two is company, three being generally one too many. To the strong and hearty, to whom the mere exercise of walking is a sufficient attraction in being able to cover so many miles a day without fatigue or overexertion, it is very pleasant and easy to walk along the road or across the field in such pure air, with a gentle breeze tempered by the genial sun, charming landscapes opening up at almost each step, but to students in botany, or ornithology, or geology, one of these tours possesses manifold interest. It is astonishing how the almost forgotten schoolday knowledge comes out, or rather into the head, on these tours; and instead of being mere pedestrians the tourists may be said to become wanderers. As Bacon said, "knowledge is power," and the power soon asserts itself and makes the owner properly proud when he finds he knows more than the others about the sweet-voiced feathery songsters that populate the surrounding woods; or can tell the history of the stones composing a stratum in yonder landslide; the family relations of this little slip of herbage; or the origin of the gamey little fish that swims by in the pellucid brook. The country boy will stare in amazement at the magic work of the photographer, but will evince his cleverness in working what to him appears to be a marvel to the fact that he is a city chap; he is dumfounded when this city chap manifests a superior knowledge about the birds, fields, and wild flowers to that of the boy who has been among them all his life. Comparatively few, except scientific students, however, possess sufficient botanical or ornithological knowledge to make a tour of this kind specially interesting, and it is to the larger class, seeking a change from the conventional mode of passing the Summer, that this article is addressed, and to those to whom the tour afoot through the interior counties would be a novelty and a charm. Weak and sickly youths, who would not be able to endure the journey, or those to whom the exercise of walking is not pleasant, should never think of taking one of these tours. One of the first and indeed the most requisite qualification for a pedestrian tour is a love of walking. Walking is an art, and an art which is to be acquired only through a predilection or a natural love for the exercise. Some people never like to walk; never enjoy an exercise which is exhilarating and glorious to others who feel better the further they go. It is obvious that those for whom walking possesses no charm should not find one of these tours enjoyable. The change of scene and air—and there is no better way to see the country or to enjoy its fresh air—would not compensate one who does not enjoy walking for the effort of exercise and perseverance that he would be required to make on one of these tours. On the other hand, it is not easy to portray the keen physical and intellectual enjoyment of those who, throwing their shoulders back, start out with strong and nimble step for a day's walk. The air inhaled seems to partake of the component parts of the surrounding sights, the verdure of the fields, the fragrance of the flowers, the coolness of the breeze, and even the sensation of existence is a greater realization seemingly than ever before. It is a trite saying that the shoemaker must love his last; hunters, fishermen, and woodsmen must be born with an innate love for the sport, and so those who would indulge in athletic exercises must be trained for it, and without a predilection for them they will never succeed. Given, therefore, a man who is walking for the sake of the exercise, and start him on a pedestrian tour such as we have indicated, and he is invested with a new life. The excitement and bustle of a promenade on the crowded street in the city is supplied by the activity of nature which is visible on every hand; by the chatter of the birds or the lowing of the cattle; while the eye is never so much attracted by any display in a store window as by the constant change of scene—this village now affording a charming vista of forest and hamlet, this mountain unfolding a curious panorama of waving green, this road unwinding in a most picturesque way. No one who enjoys walking can fail to appreciate the charms of the country and the scenery. It is true that the athlete is seldom a poet; on the contrary he is a muscular Christian, with none of the aspirations of the poet; but the strong and healthy always enjoy outdoor exercise and the free scenes of nature, and sometimes understand them in native homely language better than the poet, who is very apt to be lazy or weak, and beyond the glorious resuscitation of one of these grand runs across country on foot. In rainy weather the tourist is storm-bound at the hostlery at which he happens to be stopping. It is seldom, however, that protracted rainstorms occur in the Summer months. The light showers that come on suddenly he is protected from by the waterproof coat carried in his knapsack, and it serves to settle the dust without making the road muddy. A day stormbound in one of the country inns may be passed pleasantly enough by the two friends in social chat with the other inmates, but several days under these circumstances become very dreary. The best period for a pedestrian tour is the late Spring or the early Autumn. In the middle of the Summer the sun and the air are too warm for enjoyable day walking and the roads are likely to be dusty and the fields suffering from drought. In the late Spring vegetation is in an interesting state and the roads and air are equally agreeable, while in the early Autumn the later decay produced by the approaching Winter is indicated in the fading condition of growth and earth.

One does not feel inclined to be active and bothering himself when all nature seems determined to repose under the lethargic influences of a warm atmosphere and a molten sky, the leaves and vegetation drooping, while the cows and horses lie lazily in the shade, while the invigorated and hearty condition in the other periods inspires the tourist in his work, or to speak more correctly, the pleasure of his pedestrian exercise. The pleasure of the tour may be increased by the tourist's carrying a gun and fishing rod, one or the other of which when not in use can be swung over the shoulder. The stroll through the forest will offer many an attractive shot, and a period of rest by the brookside will be rendered pleasanter by casting the line. One important thing to be constantly borne in mind by the pedestrian tourist is the weight of his outfit, and he should, therefore, be sure of his carrying ability in regard to taking along his gun and rod or they may eventually become a burden to him, and the inclination to throw them away or express them home will become very strong. The idea, however, should be to make the tour a diversion rather than a journey over a given route, and the rod and gun will afford much wayside sport. Those who have never made one of these tours can form no idea of the constant pleasurable excitement of the journey, in the passing incidents of meeting tramps and teams and interesting old farmhouses, the now-you-see-it-and-now-you-don't-see-it deceptions of the wandering road in regard to the approach to the village, as indicated by the church steeple, and finally in the various characters encountered in the houses and hotels. Those who are respectful and well-behaved may always be sure of a cordial reception at the farmhouses and will enjoy the acquaintances thus made. It may be different if pedestrian touring should become common, though as the pedestrian pays his way like any other traveler there is no reason why there should be any change in this respect.

The tour or route, of course, depends on the time at the disposal of the tourist. A good short tour for 10 days or a fortnight is Long Island—down one side, up the other side. The south shore is low and marshy, with a sea breeze. The great south road is good walking, and extends all the way to Montauk Point. The north shore is high woodland, overlooking the Sound, and the forest roads lead through some fine landscapes. The old turnpike up the Hudson River is a good tour for several weeks; indeed, it will be hard to find a more interesting route than this, which can be followed, if desirable, for hundreds of miles through one of the most charming sections of landscapes that can be found anywhere. The neighboring counties in New-Jersey afford several very attractive routes for the pedestrian tourist. It is always well to keep near railroad towns in case of sickness and for communication with those left at home, and the course of the West Shore Railroad is a beautiful country for a pedestrian tour. Another good route is up the Sound shore in Connecticut, with several branches into the interior manufacturing districts, which will prove very interesting. Solitary roads through a thinly inhabited country lacking interest, and thickly settled roads with frequent traveling, are alike to be avoided for obvious reasons. The objects of the tour, of course, must influence its selection, whether the idea is simply exercise and travel, or whether it is desirable to secure also some sport with the rod and gun. Any of the routes indicated will enable the tourist to have a little sport with the rod and gun while strolling along some of the finest roadways with some of the most expansive and charming landscapes to be found anywhere. The route of the canals winds through a picturesque country and offers many attractions to the tourist, especially to the student of character. Indeed, there is hardly any section of this or the surrounding States that they would be likely to visit that is not sufficiently thickly settled on the main roads to afford accommodation and safety to a couple of pedestrian tourists. If the expense is admissible, the tourists might add a pedometer to the outfit as a source of amusement to themselves in recording their mileage and as a source of wonder to the country bumpkins. The pedometer will be found serviceable in regulating the travel, as a great danger is, that, led on by the exhilarating atmosphere, one may go more one day than proper, and be laid up or be "seedy" the next day; while by judicious regulation of the miles at starting, increasing each day until the desired maximum is attained, overexertion may be avoided.

May 31, 1885

LONG HIGHROAD BECKONS TO THE WALKER

Three Miles a Day, or a Thousand a Year, Is the Goal Set for American Pilgrims

By JOHN H. FINLEY

IT is in the month of April, said "learned Chaucer" in "The Canterbury Tales," that folk long to go on pilgrimages and to seek strange strands. And it has occurred to me that April is quite the best month in all the year in which to begin the thousand-mile pilgrimages which I am proposing; for in April the weather begins to invite even the most torpid out-of-doors ("its showres swoote the droughte of March hath perced to the roote,") and the New Year resolutions to take daily exercise in the open are tempted to put forth the vernal buds of new vows.

The pilgrimages I propose do not, however, require the pilgrims actually to set out for any distant land or strange strand. They may walk their thousand miles without going a hundred miles from their homes. If, for example, President Coolidge were to join this company of pilgrims, walking three miles a day about Washington, he would in the four years of his new administration walk in distance across the United States with side journeys along the way. Or a youth or young man or woman might in the course of a lifetime, (which such daily walks should lengthen), walk across all the lands in one zone around the globe.

And while exercise in the open air would be the first purpose in these pilgrimages for urban folk, a second objective might be the journey in imagination over a like distance of some country, chosen for travel, either one's own country or some foreign land, the "pilgrims" to become acquainted through "collateral reading" and pictures with the landscapes and historic associations through which each one travels at the pace of three miles a day. Thus one might, while walking to and from one's office or daily work, in the course of a month of Spring walk a hundred miles in the south of France with Felix Gras's Reds of the Midi from Marseilles up through Avignon and Orange, or traverse the Côte d'Azure by the red rocks and the blue sea, or walk across the Campagna from the Eternal City up through Tivoli and out to Horace's Sabine farm and look upon the snow-capped Soracte, or up among the Tuscan hills with Howells's "Tuscan Cities" in one's pocket.

Imagined Journeys

In midsummer, even though kept at one's work in the city, one might in the early mornings and late evenings make a journey on foot in one or another of the Scandinavian countries, or up in the lake region of England, or one might let one's mind, in the midst of the fiery heat, think "on the frosty Caucasus" and make one's way with Lord Bryce (when he was only young James Bryce) down to Ararat or wander among the heathered moors or the Highlands of Scotland. In the Autumn one might play the troubadour through the Côte d'Or in France or meander among the hills in Greece. And in the Winter make a pilgrimage to the Holy Land.

Indeed, the medal which I designed several years ago to give to those who walked certain distances bears beneath the figure of a walker the legend "à la Sainte Terre"—to the Holy Land. I am indebted for this legend to Thoreau, who, after deriving the word "saunterer" from Sainte-Terrer, a Holy Lander, adds: "They who never go to the Holy Land in their walks * * * are indeed idlers and vagabonds." A real pilgrim is no idler or vagabond or aimless vagrant; he is a destinated person, a walker, a "hiker," a wanderer or even a "saunterer" with a goal, but with an ever-changing prospect. There should ever be a Carcassonne in one's itinerary, even if we never get beyond Narbonne or Perpignan, a Sainte Terre in our purpose, even if we perish before reaching it, as did the soldiers whose graves I saw in Palestine at the foot of the last hill on their crusader way to the Holy City which they never saw but helped to recover.

"The wealth of the world is so unbounded," adds Thoreau, "and each man's Holy Land lies in so different a direction that it is difficult to say whither his path will lead."

When I award the "à la Sainte Terre" medal I translate the legend freely as meaning "to our better selves"—the "better" meaning both physical and spiritual health, which is reached by most people most certainly by keeping their feet on what that beloved philosopher of the out of doors, Liberty Bailey, has called "the holy earth." The crusaders in the Middle Ages used to call every road which led "à la Sainte Terre" the Via Dei, the way of God. It is often difficult for a pedestrian in this age to think of a city street or even a country highway in this definition, for in the one he is in daily peril of the taxis and in the other he is pushed off into the gutter or roadside by the automobiles. There has just come a gratifying bit of news that in one community at least a pedestrian is given by law the right of way, except in the congested districts, and may by holding up his hand have all the authority of a traffic policeman.

It is a great injury to public health (and also to spiritual welfare) that is done through the monopolizing of streets and roads by cars that discourage walking. It isn't merely that men and women, even youth, are tempted to softness by the comfort of the automobile. There is the incidental discouraging menace of the "machine" and the driver who regards contemptuously the person on foot.

But in spite of all this, walking is to be persistently practiced as a way to our better selves in health. Even the city street and the country road, requiring alertness of the walker, may become, in spite of their perils and inconveniences, every one of them a Via Dei, and we must do our best to make and keep them not only highways of democracy, where even the humblest pedestrian has an equality of right with the single paunchy passenger in a high-power

motor car, but also highways to health.

Walking in City Streets

And there is something to be said even for city streets. They are walkable nearly every day in the year for one thing, if the walker is properly clothed and shod. Then, as the author of "Shanks' Mare" says, there are joys on the pavements which even the loneliest of roads cannot offer. "The kaleidoscope changes so often that even one's beaten paths never become monotonous. * * * No dream of Arabian Nights ever imagined a more dazzling array of jewels than the mazes of streets with their myriad lights afford [by night]. And a stroll by day along the busy waterfront, where great ships from every clime lie at anchor, will give a more intimate idea of the world's commerce than all the books and market reports ever written."

Three miles a day—a thousand miles a year in the open and on foot! These foot-miles will save many gallons of gasoline, lengthen the life of tires (and incidentally that of the walker), save street car fare (incidentally relieve subway congestion), and, best of all, promote the health of him or her who takes this free fresh-air medicine for mind and body. Who would not walk a thousand miles for such a God-given preventive or remedy?

Thoreau said that he could not preserve his health and spirits unless he spent four hours at least in the open. The suggested "three miles" do not require in time more than a quarter of Thoreau's minimum, and perhaps they are not enough for both health and spirits, but one may keep open windows and find other means of preserving one's "spirits." An authority whose book "Going Afoot" I commend to all walkers (Bayard H. Christy), makes the following sensible observations about daily walking:

"The Daily Walk." Walking is to be commended, not as a holiday pastime merely, but as part of the routine of life, in season and out. Particularly to city dwellers, to men whose occupations are sedentary, is walking to be commended as recreation. Will a man assert himself too busy? His neighbor plays a game of golf a week; he himself, perhaps, if he will admit it, is giving half a day a week to some pastime—maybe a less wholesome one.

It is worth a man's while to reckon on his walking every day in the week. It may well be to his advantage, in health and happiness, to extend his daily routine afoot—perhaps by dispensing with the services of a "jitney" from the suburban station to his residence, perhaps by leaving the train or street car a station further from home, perhaps by walking downtown to his office each morning.

It is, however, not only the daily walks over familiar ground that complete these proposed pilgrimages. In addition to these there should be occasional and frequent long walks, for which the daily exercise prepares us and at least one real "hike" a year. Incidentally these longer walks and longest "hikes" will make up the average for the days when the short three-mile walk was impossible for one reason or another. When President of the College of the City of New York I used to make this suggestion to the students at the beginning of every holiday period, long or short:

> Take a long walk,
> Read a good book,
> Make a new friend.

It is the best bit of counsel for a holiday, and during a real vacation should be taken repeatedly. A long walk ought when possible to lead us into the country, where one can actually touch the ground, as did the old Antaeus, the wrestler, to renew his strength; but it may also be taken in the city.

Around Manhattan Island

For myself, I have been accustomed to walk around Manhattan Island once a year, partly for the rigorous and testing exercise, partly to keep the whole island with its variegated life in my consciousness and partly just for the sake of doing it. And one does touch the ground, too, up just this side of Spuyten Duyvil, where one has to make one's way by a trail through the woods as wild as a bit of New Hampshire. Moreover, such feats as this furnish one not only with agreeable memories, but with the satisfaction of achievement. I should feel that I had lost some of the most pleasurable and thrilling memories of my life if I had not had the forty-mile walk in France, the night which dawned into the day that waked all Europe to war, or the sixty-mile walk in one day and night across the Holy Land, or the seventy-mile walk across New Hampshire. One ought to have every year some long walk to keep in memory—and it should include the night with the day.

I once said to Dean Liberty Bailey that there was one more club that I'd like to form—one with no dues on the part of the members except the obligation to walk—*a league of walkers that might reach around world in time.* It is in effect such a company that I here and now invite to accompany one another in a pilgrimage of a thousand miles to "sundry lands" while staying of necessity at home. All who wish to join in such a pilgrimage may do so without recording their resolutions or vows to do so (though the writer would be pleased to have word of their purpose). It would give a sense of companionship to know that there were other travelers who might perhaps share their experiences on the journey. But to each of the first thousand who complete the thousand miles by April 1 in 1926 and send a log—that is, an authentic record of the daily walks making a total of a thousand miles, including one single day's "hike" of at least twenty-six miles—the writer engages to send the medal, in bronze, described above (and pictured in the large in the accompanying illustration, the medal being somewhat more than an inch in length) as a souvenir of the journey together, to testify, as Chaucer would say:

That I was of their fellowship anon

April 12, 1925

Emblem of the League of Walkers—a la Sainte Terre (to the Holy Land) is a Phrase of Thoreau's Newly Applied—Drawn by S. J. Woolf.

THE ART OF WALKING.

Any one who persuades his country-men to make a practice of walking as a daily exercise two miles for one he walked before is as great a benefactor as the grower of two blades of grass for one. A nation of walkers will be a nation of hardy and enduring people. " The great thing about walking," says the veteran WESTON in an article in The Saturday Evening Post, " is that it is Nature's " remedy. It isn't exercise in the ordi-" nary meaning of the word. If you do " it regularly and easily it is more like a " perfect massage." But he bids his disciples " not to overdo it." Still he would have them walk as far as they can comfortably, not trying to break records. Distance will come with practice.

A former Health Officer of the Port of New York, Dr. ALVAH H. DOTY, has prepared a book, small enough to slip into the pocket, on walking for health. It is so wise and sweet that if only one copy were extant the bibliophiles would be scrambling for it. Dr. DOTY makes a point of explaining that if the vascular system is to be in good order, the heart sound and regular, one must step out so many miles a day. Good walkers always have good hearts if they start with one, and the not entirely sound heart is the better for walking in moderation. But to return to Mr. WESTON. He maintains that " if you walk wisely and regularly " you'll miss the aches and pains of rheu-" matism." He gives some practical advice. Each man to his own gait. The heel-and-toe he declares unnatural. Go slowly and easily, but keep going, with periods for rest and contemplation. Then if you are cursed with sleeplessness it will vanish, and rugged health will be yours. " The shoulders should be " allowed to swing free, with the muscles " relaxed." Carry a short stick, swing it and change from one hand to the other. The feet should be lifted only enough to advance the body with every step. " As " a consequence the heel and ball of the " foot land almost simultaneously, and

" the shock is distributed over the whole " mechanism of the foot." For bathing the feet " a couple of fistfuls of rock salt in six or eight quarts of water " is prescribed. The veteran wears lisle thread socks, never wool, but he has walked on roads and pavements, not on rough mountain trails where wool saves the feet from bruising. A pair of leggins is recommended. Walking, he declares, keeps " a man always in condition without overtraining." At 71 he walked 4,000 miles across the continent to the Pacific.

Physicians and trainers have told WESTON that he was a born walker. He walked to walk, not to look at the scenery or " for to admire." To get over the ground was luxury to him. It was attainment like the mountain climber's winning " the top of the world." WESTON does not profess to be a botanist or an epicure in sunsets. The road is his comrade, not Nature. He has not been the Sainte-Terrer, Saunterer, or Holy-Lander, whom THOREAU celebrates. HAZLITT wanted the clear blue sky over his head and the green turf under his feet, to march three hours to dinner, " and then to thinking." Our grand old man of the road preferred to walk for twenty-four hours, " and then to sleeping." If he ever wanted to be alone, which was STEVENSON's preference, the dear public would not let him. Such a celebrity had his " gallery," willing or not. " 'Tis the best of humanity that goes out to walk," observed EMERSON to his countrymen who elected to ride in buggies or in sleighs. But nowadays walking clubs abound in spite of the automobile. Youth of both sexes are on the road in knicker-bockers. Their elders buckle on knap-sacks and take the staff from the corner. It must be admitted, however, that automobile addicts walk less and less, and, except those who pace the golf links, they need to savor WESTON's precepts and shake a leg on the heath or stalk the wild.

August 1, 1926

The Joy of Walking

By DONALD CULROSS PEATTIE

AMERICA, land of the motor car, land of the rubber tire, is going off wheels and learning to walk.

Of this I sing.

If ever you complained of a speed-mad America and extolled the charms of the horse-and-buggy age, if ever you jeered that wheels had made us a nation of tenderfeet and groaned that our highways kill more than the bombing of London, your prayers are answered and your fears made groundless. For America is finding its feet again.

Yesterday I moved from a house eleven miles from my children's school to a new home, where, by walking three-quarters of a mile, they can board the school bus. So I save rubber. But this morning I discovered that to get the morning mail I must also go down to the highway, making a mile-and-a-half round trip during which I climb back up a 300-foot hill.

I set out, my mind full of the usual Monday morning humdrums and problems, complaining to myself that in this way I missed the morning news broadcast and consumed a valuable half-hour of my freshest energies, in order to get the post. I was even "noble" about it, assuring myself that it was just one of countless inconveniences that we were all facing.

But I came back to my desk with my blood tingling, with every stale and mundane concern washed out of my head and all self-pity jeered out of me by jays and crows, frisking, scolding squirrels and errant Spring winds.

I had heard the titmouse calling his merry song of peet-o, peet-o, and song sparrows tuning up on the alder bushes where the catkins were hanging out all pollen-dusty and fertile. I had heard the brook gurgling among its boulders, and smelled fresh loam, lichen wet with dew, spawn of toadstool. I had seen the mountains in long shafts of early light and a flight of band-tailed pigeons flashing white wings as they crossed a little valley on important pigeon business. The oats were shooting, pale green and tender, out of the fine black earth in the fields, and I heard a plowman shout at his old white horse as he turned at the end of the velvety furrow and set the blade in the next row.

HAD I taken my car to run down to the mailbox I should have had only a fleeting glimpse, or none, of all these fine sights. Of all these fragrances I should have caught not a whiff, but only gasoline fumes. Above the noise of the wheels how should I have heard the sea-dirge of the pines, or the chuckling of the linnets, or the jolly scampering of lizards on old leaves?

True, I should have "saved" about twenty-five minutes of my priceless time. For what? For the sake of a more sluggish digestion, of a wider girth beneath my belt, staler air in my lungs, duller thoughts in my head, a posture grown by that much older. I should have lopped off half an hour of fresh and living experience. For, after all, time is not money; time is an opportunity to live before you die. So a man who walks, and lives and sees and thinks as he walks, has lengthened his life.

It was Thoreau, himself one of the most inveterate of walkers, who insisted that if you took the train from Concord to Fitchburg, and he took shanks' mare, he would arrive first. For, he reasoned, you would have to stop and work till you had earned the price of a ticket. While you were doing that he would be in Scotland afore ye. And have seen enough sights and had

> Forget your car; leave the highroad, take the byroad; don't chatter; get acquainted with yourself and the world.

enough encounters to write another immortal chapter.

All the great naturalists have been habitual walkers, for no laboratory, no book, car, train or plane takes the place of honest footwork for this calling, be it amateur's or professional's. Gilbert White and Izaak Walton were devotees of the art and tireless exponents of its charms. W. H. Hudson in England was practically a tramp, and so was John Muir in this country. John thought nothing of walking from one end of the Sierra to the other,

just to see a tree or a flower; he once walked from Wisconsin to the Gulf of Mexico! Asked what preparations he made for these famous treks, he replied: "I throw a loaf of bread and a pound of tea in an old sack and jump over the back fence."

THERE spake the true walker, as contrasted with those persons with overdeveloped thyroids who walk to set records, who add stones to their packs when climbing mountains and count their steps to calculate how far they have come. Not thus did John Burroughs walk, or Richard Jefferies or Alexander Wilson. John James Audubon could and often did walk a hundred miles in two days. It sounds like a startling record, but on one of my own walks, along the old Roman Road from Canterbury to London, I was overtaken by a little Welsh soldier, though I was walking fast; he had come thirty-five miles that day, and hoped to make it fifty before he slept—in some hedge. He slowed to my pace for ten miles, while he told me his adventures in many parts of the world. Then he had to leave me because he could not wait.

He was quite a philosopher, that fellow, and indeed all walkers become philosophers. Didn't Plato and Socrates pace up and down in the stoas of the Acropolis while they pulled their beards and unriddled the universe? Robert Louis Stevenson and Ralph Waldo Emerson were Peripatetics too, as you can easily tell by the kind of philosophy they expounded, one peculiarly kindly, reasonable, hopeful, cheerful and refreshing.

SOMETHING happens to the walker who knows how to think and observe as he goes. In the first place he is physically prevented from wasting his time and cluttering his mind in a great many ways that, we get to imagining, are inevitable or even pleasant or important. While you are walking you cannot be reached by telephone or telegraph, and you cannot reach anybody in those ways. That in itself is a great blessing. You cannot put out a hand, as you do even in an automobile, and twiddle the radio and so let in the war and the stock market, a flood of soda-pop and chewing-gum spiels, and all the quizzes and jazzes that wrangle on the in-

nocent airs. You cannot play bridge or consult an astrologer, bet on a horse or go to a movie. In the compensation for these keen deprivations, walking offers you health, happiness and an escape from civilization's many madnesses.

I have often started off on a walk in the state called mad—mad in the sense of sore-headed, or mad with tedium or confusion; I have set forth dull, null and even thoroughly discouraged. But I never came back in such a frame of mind, and I never met a human being whose humor was not the better for a walk. It is the sovereign remedy for the hot-tempered and the low-spirited—provided, of course, that you know how to walk.

When I was about 8 years old I was actually taught to walk by an elderly man who was a master of the art. He showed me how to carry that good companion, a stick, without tiring of it; how to climb without getting winded, slanting your body forward, going on the balls of your feet and respecting the hill ahead of you. From him I learned that you should never take a highroad if you can find a byroad or a footpath. He taught me not to chatter; he instructed me to quench thirst well before I started out, to go stoutly shod and lightly clad.

True, that was country walking. Later I learned, by myself, the joys of circum-ambulating city streets—at their most magical in the dusk and early in the morning. No American city, with its checker-board street plan, is the equal in fascination, for the pedestrian, of London and Paris. Yet New York, Boston, Washington and San Francisco, to mention only some cities I know, have their charms for the foot passenger. To enjoy city walking to the utmost you have to throw yourself into a mood of loving humanity. For a whistling boy must be your bird song, girls' faces your wayside flowers, the flow and roar of the street your clattering, swirling streams, and tall buildings your sun-smitten crags. And by night you have the spattered office lights above for your winking constellations.

BUT alas, as our rubber heels wear off and cannot be replaced, curb-trotting is going to jar and tire us more than in the past. And so I think we shall for pleasure be riding out again to the end of the bus or trolley line or taking the old plush-and-varnish suburban trains to some outlying point, and there we'll alight and step forth amid country sights and sounds. We shall smell again the bitter-sweet reek of leaf fires where people on the edge of the village are raking their lawns and watching for the first crocuses.

We shall hunt again for spicebush, and set our teeth in the thin sweet bark just to taste and smell again that tingling aromatic principle.

We shall be carrying bird glasses and cameras (light ones in both cases, if we are wise) and snacks of lunch. Personally, I'm down on sandwiches. Far rather would I take a mixture of shelled pecans and sweet dried currants, with dark chocolate for dessert, and in warm weather, cider preferred or apple juice, since they are refreshing even if not iced. But rather than carry too much heavy liquid, I'd chance buttermilk from some old spring-house, or just nice, wet, well-water, tasting a little, with a cool astringent tang, of iron from the pump and tin from the dipper.

So, good luck to you fellow-hiker, wherever you go! May you never run out of tobacco or songs; may the trees be great and old and the girls young and comely. May the sun shine upon your cheek and the shade lie upon the back of your neck. May you find wood and strawberries and sassafras. But he who flingeth away the bottle and hindereth not the picnic paper, he that carveth the beech bole and she that expects others to carry her coat, camera and pack, may their socks be lumpy, and farm dogs bite their calves!

April 5, 1942

OUT OF THE CITY, INTO THE OPEN
Even in Winter New York's Army of Week-End Hikers Flees From the Pavements To Hills and Valleys, There to Find Abundant Rewards for Body and Soul

By JOHN KIERAN

ANOTHER Sunday has arrived. Out they scatter from the big city, popping up out of the subway, down off the elevated, piling out of trolley cars, headed for Westchester or the open country across the Hudson, the week-end walkers with their knapsacks on their backs. They have stout shoes and stout hearts. They roam the hills, climb the cliffs and their voices come echoing up from the valley. Spring calls them; Summer lures them; Autumn entrances them; Winter does not deter them.

As Wamba, the son of Witless, the son of an Alderman, said to the Black Knight at the siege of Torquilstone: "Nomen est legio." Their name is legion. They go forth in groups, bands, regiments.

There are platoons of Boy Scouts. There are hiking clubs out for enjoyment and exercise. There are campers, even at this time of year. There are amateur naturalists inspecting the private lives of birds, beasts and reptiles, peering at shrubs and trees, finding sermons in stones and books in the running brooks.

In short, there are all sorts of walkers, as there are all sorts of walks. Some pessimists assert that our race is whirling to perdition on balloon tires. But even such pessimists must make an exception in favor of the walkers. The exception, however, should not include that species of pest known as the hitch-hiker. Away with that fraud who has sullied the fair name of

the sturdy hiker and the honest walker! The glorious landscape is nothing to him. He scans not the sky, but the paved road. He loves not the quiet silence of the woods. He longs for the hum of a motor, the clash of gears, the whine of brakes. He disdains the caress of the clean breeze on his cheek and sniffs the air like a hound for the scent of gasoline.

But those other folk who roam afoot over the highways and the hills, across the fields and down the valleys, they are of the elect. To them Thoreau would extend his greeting: "Children come aberry-ing, railroad men taking their Sunday walk in clean shirts, fishermen and hunters, poets and philosophers —in short all honest pilgrims, who

came out to the woods for freedom's sake and really left the village behind—I was ready to greet with, 'Welcome, Englishmen! Welcome, Englishmen!' for I had communication with that race." Thus spoke the poet-philosopher-naturalist of Walden Pond.

There are so many varieties of walk that it is impossible to classify them. To name a few:

1. *The Escape.* The burst into the open on foot as a relief from the life of wheels within wheels in a crowded city.

2. *The Constitutional.* An upper-class kind of strolling or walking, p r o b a b l y r e c o m m e n d e d by an expensive doctor.

3. *The Hike.* U n d e r t a k e n alone or with any number of companions, a trip from one point to another w i t h stopover privileges.

4. *The Walk for Distance.* A deliberate a t - tempt to cover ground on foot, mile after mile. While this can be recommended as good for the body, it is not p a r t i c u l a r l y g o o d f o r t h e soul. It induces a certain superior attitude, an air of c o n d e - scension toward those who cover lesser distances or not distance at all. It becomes a game, like golf, and the d i s t a n c e walker, boasting of the miles he has put behind him, may be quite as boring as the golfer going over his strokes before an audience that wishes him in Gehenna.

5 *The Daily Jaunt.* The rush to the train in the morning and the stroll home from the station in the evening, or the walk from the hotel or apartment to the office along the paved streets. Some lucky fellows may have a route that takes them through one of the city parks.

6. *The Moonlight Stroll.* Favored by young people and poets and frowned upon by owls and other suspicious folk.

7. *The Walking Tour.* A vacation on foot extending for days, weeks or months. Much to be recommended, either at home or abroad. But this is a seasonal sport. A walking tour of England, the Black Forest, the Tyrol, the Marne Valley and the White Mountains would be fine from the late Spring to the early Fall, but in the cold and snow of Winter there would be handicaps, drawbacks, hardships and barriers.

8. *The Winter Walk.* Differs from the walk at any other season of the year. Sometimes becomes

"The Quiet Silence of the Woods."

Photo by Rittase.

a competition with nature, a defiance of the north wind, a conquest of the cold, a refusal to bow the knee and crouch by the fireside. At other times and on bright, calm Winter days, an enjoyment of life and nature at its keen, sparkling crispness. Everything is clear, definitely outlined. There are no secrets. A man comes in from a Winter walk feeling that he has completed an achievement; he has shown his strength.

But all this is a mere mechanical classification. It misses the finer points, the real flavor of walking. It was Bliss Carman who wrote:

Now the joys of the road are chiefly these:
A crimson touch on the hard-wood trees;
A vagrant's morning, wide and blue,
In early Fall, when the wind walks, too;
A shadowy highway, cool and brown,
Alluring up and enticing down

From rippled water to dappled swamp,
The outward eye, the quiet will,
From purple glory to scarlet pomp;
And the strident heart from hill to hill.

This should be the marching song of the walking brigade. It is too long to print here, but too good to be neglected by those who can appreciate it most. Just a few more excerpts are offered in evidence:

An open hand, an easy shoe
And a hope to make the day go through, * * *
The resonant far-listening morn
And the hoarse whisper of the corn, * * *
The racy smell of the forest loam
When the stealthy, sad-heart leaves go home.

Perhaps it would be worth while to gather a Walker's Anthology of Verse. Tennyson, Wordsworth, Thomson, Shakespeare, Bryant, Keats and Swinburne would be distinguished contributors. There would be Bryant's musings on a walk through the Autumn woods:

Ah! 'twere a lot too blest
Forever in thy colored shades to stray;
Amid the kisses of the soft southwest
To roam and dream for aye;

And leave the vain low strife
That makes men mad—the tug for wealth and power—
The passions and the cares that wither life,
And waste its little hour.

This leads to additions to the category of walks. To wit:

9. *The walk contemplative*— Can be leisurely or taken at a fairly brisk pace. Out in the open, striding past trees a century old, climbing hills that once knew the tread of the Indian, bathed in the same sunlight that has been pouring down on the earth for countless ages, a man can weigh and consider things at their proper value. Emerson was an advocate of the contemplative walk. So was Wordsworth. Thoreau tells how he sometimes returned by night through the woods to his hut by Walden Pond and, reaching for the latch, suddenly realized that he had no recollection of the walk through the darkness at all, so engrossed had he been in his thoughts.

10. *The walk for relaxation*— Lengthy or brief, as the case may be, taken as a relief by the man who has been tied to a desk or a machine. The hum of the machine fades out of the ear. The tedium of deskwork is relieved by this excursion into the open. The brain rests while the muscles work. The walkers obtain a measure of "respite; respite and Nepenthe" from carking cares and the chains of civilized slavery.

11. *The companionate walk*— The saunter with friends for the sake of friendship and a few hours in the open, a perambulating chat in a stimulating setting.

Sometimes the narrow walls of a house cramp a man's thoughts and feelings. His vision widens with the horizon. It may even occur to him that the sun overhead is 93,000,000 miles away. In that light he can afford to be broadminded.

12. *The questing walk*—An expedition on foot in search of something, whether it be a shrub, a tree, Indian relics, a migrant bird or a favorite flower. This is more properly a hunt than a walk but it leads men far afield on foot and carries them through many days in the open. The questing walk is one of the best

"The Questing Walk Is One of the Best Walks."

Photo by Matzdorff From Nesmith.

walks. It calls for sharp eyes as well as sturdy legs. It requires patience and persistance. Each such walk adds to the store of knowledge and kindles an enthusiasm for further expeditions; for the puzzling paradox is that the more a man knows, the more he wishes to know. The dullard remains smugly content "in the glorious assurance of impenetrable ignorance."

The pomp and glory of Autumn have departed. The Winter is at hand. But no road is closed to the walker and no weather can balk him. The first thing a walker learns is that the weather is never so bad as it looks through a window. The snow whirls down. The wind whips around the corners. The house is cold. The inmates gaze out timorously and "pity the poor sailors on a night like this!" But the chap out in it with proper clothing strides along cheerfully, warm as a cricket on a hearth, his blood circulating rapidly from the labor of plowing through the snow, his lungs filling deeply with fresh air and his whole being suffused with a deep satisfaction. It's fun, a walk in a snowstorm. It makes a man a boy again. It recalls schooldays, youthful expeditions, Christmas festivities. And it puts a new complexion on the world for the time being.

"In the dead of Winter" is a misleading phrase. There is plenty of life in Winter and the man who walks abroad in the time of cold and snow knows it well. The trees

are sleeping but the buds, tightly wrapped, are a promise of another awakening. The walker meets his feathered friends, the Winter birds; the fluttering junco, the businesslike nuthatch, the lively chickadee and the industrious woodpecker. There may be distinguished visitors from the northward regions, such as a flock of redpolls riding in on the wings of the storm. Man builds himself insulated houses, puts in steam heat, tightens the weather strips and practically seals himself up at the approach of Winter, and out in the woods and the thickets, in the hail, the rain and the snow, with a cold wind rushing down out of the north, the sturdy walker on his tramp will find these lively little feathered fellows twittering valiantly and going merrily through a storm that will "Paralyze New York and New England," as the headlines frequently have it.

. . .

THERE are some things that the Winter walker learns by experience. Snow itself, coming down or already on the ground, is a source of more enjoyment than trouble. If the walking is a bit heavy, the walker will find it that much easier to keep warm. With proper clothing and footwear, the temperature does not matter much.

But the wind is an important factor. On a still, cold day a fellow can climb the hills and roam the ridges, enjoying the wintry landscape to the full. But the wind whipping down, especially if the country is covered with snow and the temperature is low, is the arch enemy. It cuts like the edge of a razor. Then is the time to stick to the valleys, to walk under the protection of cliffs, to take the lee side of the bare woods and to avoid, wherever possible, meeting the onslaught of Boreas face to face.

Still, there are those hardy souls who fare forth from the heated apartments of Manhattan in midwinter to walk miles along the sand at Long Beach, where an icy blast always seems to be wandering up and down. A contrary wind, too. In a walk down to the point it buffets the adventurer full in the face. He has to grit his teeth, bend forward and plunge to gain ground. Up in one of the sand hollows, with the surf crashing

near at hand, a fire is made from driftwood and the luncheon coffee and sandwiches out of the knapsack are consumed.

Then comes the trip back along the beach. This should be easy. The wind will be at his back, of course. But it never is. It buffets him in the face again. The walk back is as much a battle as the outward journey. No wonder the weary walker suspects that the shriek of the wheeling gulls overhead is laughter at his expense.

But it's all worth while and plenty of fun. Any walk is beneficial, good for body and soul. Apart from the exercise, time spent on such trips clears the mind as the opening of windows clears the air in overcrowded rooms. Wordsworth mourned that

*The world is too much with us;
    late and soon,
Getting and spending, we lay
    waste our powers;
Little we see in nature that is
    ours.*

But the thousands of sturdy walkers setting out from the paved streets for the open country whenever opportunity offers are proof that many hearts still yearn for more than a touch of Nature and many feet are on the right trail.

December 6, 1931

To Own the Streets and Fields

The man who walks, says a peripatetic philosopher, can take title to the world he sees around him.

By HAL BORLAND

HE was about 10 years old, sandy-haired, stocky, deeply tanned. A car stopped and offered him a ride, but he declined and went on walking resolutely up the country road. So I quickened my step and caught up with him. We exchanged greetings. We discussed the weather. He spoke his mind, diplomatically. Obviously, he was a possibility for the campaign of 1988 or '92, so I asked, "Are you walking, by any chance, to fit yourself for the Presidency?"

"What?" he asked.

"Do you expect to be President of the United States? President Truman is quite a walker, you know."

He looked at me with a suspicious smile. "Are you kiddin'?" He picked up a stone and shied it at a tree, and I asked, "Just why are you walking, then?"

He became very serious. "To get tough," he said. "I want to be quarterback on our team, and I got to get tough."

A few minutes later he left me and took a short cut through the orchard to his house, singing "Sioux City Sue" at the top of his lungs. And I continued my walk, down past the hollow where the cattails were turning brown and over the ridge where scarlet mottled the sumac. I didn't care to play quarterback; I merely wanted to walk.

QUARTERBACK or President, we are scarcely out of the cradle before we try to walk; some instinct lies there within us to get up on our hind legs and take one step after another. We learn to talk largely by imitation; but we learn to walk, to stand and move from one place to another, because of that inner compulsion to get up off all-fours and assert our manhood. We stand, and a new world is spread before us. We walk, and we can explore that world. The more we walk, the more we learn.

You can rate a man's curiosity about his world and his fellow men by his walking habits. Certainly the one who walks isn't the kind that expects all things to come to him. I suspect that it would be possible, if one were to study the matter systematically, to gauge a man's mental breadth and depth by examining his attitude toward walking; whether he likes to walk, and where he walks, and how, and why.

Is it possible to walk without some stimulus to thought? I doubt it. The very movement seems to stir the mind into action. The jolt of even the smoothest gait tends to loosen ideas, give them a chance to rub against each other and mingle and find new proportion and arrangement. The physiologist, of course, will explain this by saying that exercise and fresh air improve the circulation and stimulate the brain by feeding it more oxygen. But I doubt the sufficiency of that explanation. It reduces walking to the status of premeditated exercise; and whoever generated a great thought, or even an enduring one, by doing calisthenics in front of an open window?

HALF the benefit, and even more of the satisfaction, of walking comes from the leisurely change of scene. It may be only from one city block to another, or it may be from one hilltop to the next, but it is change, and it is stimulating. Even if you walk substantially the same route day after day, there is change in the familiar things you see. This is more noticeable in the country, where the wind, the clouds, the light, the growing things are never twice the same. But there is change, too, even in a city street, in the shop windows and the dooryards, in the people you meet.

And there is a leisure about walking, no matter what pace you set, that lets down the tension. It is your own pace, be it an amble, a saunter, a stroll, a promenade, a jog, a hike or a trot. If you have set yourself a distance you can take it fast or slow, and if you have set yourself a time you can hurry or dawdle. The decision is yours, and so is the world for a little while.

Some prefer to walk alone, aloof with their thoughts, or open to passing companionship. I am one who prefers to walk with a companion whose ways and words are mine, who is in step with me and I with her. But any walker's companion should be his own choice. As a general rule, the chatterer should be left behind. One needs a walking companion who understands economy of words as well as of energy. I suspect that at least some of those who prefer a dog's company on a walk have walked once too often with a person who must keep up a continuous rattle of conversation. Such a talker is no walker; he—or she—is a perambulating egotist afraid to let the world's immensity shrink him to his proper size.

WALKING can shrink the biggest of us, give us that sense of proportion which we all need on occasion. In an automobile you feel that miles are of no consequence and that all hills are low. In an airplane you lose your sense of both time and distance. In both cases you feel that you, not the machine, have altered reality. But on foot you soon learn how high is a hill and how long is a mile. And when you have walked the same road through all the seasons, you know how certain is change and how gradual.

WALKERS acquire a special ownership of roads and streets and parks and fields. I shall forever own certain parts of a dozen cities, because I walked their streets, a stranger, and became familiar with their sights and sounds and smells and knew their people, even though they did not know me. Even though I met those people later and they showed me the city that they knew, my ownership was in no way changed. I had made my own discoveries.

All walking is discovery. On foot we take the time to see things whole. We see trees as well as forests, people as well as crowds. When the mood is right—and walking provokes such a mood when we are most in need of it—we can even see ourselves with particular clarity. We get our feet back on the ground.

The man on horseback may be a symbol of leadership in a particular cause, but I prefer the man afoot for my leader—at least the man who has not forgotten the virtues of walking. He has a sense of time and proportion,

and if he lacks patience he can and will quickly acquire or renew it. He knows, from experience afoot, that if he hurries beyond need or reason he will wear himself out before he has reached his destination; that if he travels at a steady pace he will arrive where he is headed and get there fit for whatever awaits him. So doing, he will also have had an intimate look at the world around him. He will have had time for discovery and appraisal.

IT is all very well to know the whole world, but breadth of knowledge calls for depth of understanding. He knows most about the world who knows best that world which is within reach of his own footsteps. Not all hills and valleys are alike, but unless a man knows his own hills and valleys he is not likely to understand those of another man a thousand miles away. And I am not at all sure that he even understands himself.

He who walks may see and understand. You can study all America from one hilltop, if your eyes are open and your mind is willing to reach. But first you must walk to that hill.

October 6, 1946

Animal Man Needs To Hike

By WILLIAM O. DOUGLAS

RECENTLY in New Mexico, I went for a hike on snowshoes, dropping 6,000 feet down La Luz Canyon on the western slopes of Sandia Mountain. We met ice conditions that extended our journey from four hours to over eight. A nervous press sent alarming stories across the country. But those knowledgeable in hiking, including cross-country travel on skis, would have had a calmer attitude. Hikers are usually injured only when they walk our streets and thread their way through traffic. Hiking the hills is man's safest adventure.

A trail along a ridge or through a valley or down an old country road is an exciting gymnasium. Most gyms are dingy and crowded, filled with the odor of sweat. The trail leading through woods or across meadows is filled with the fresh fragrance of the outdoors. There are no weights to pull, no bicycles to ride, no oars to exercise. But the ups and downs of the average trail exercise most of the muscles and man ends his hike tired but renewed.

Hiking or walking is man's most natural exercise. We were biological beings before our intellectual or spiritual powers matured. The cells and protoplasm, the blood vessels and tissues, the muscular and circulatory systems have not changed since the days of the cave man. The veneer of progress and civilization is a thin one. The intellectual man and spirit-

---

WILLIAM O. DOUGLAS, an Associate Justice of the Supreme Court since 1939, has written several books about the outdoors, including "My Wilderness" and "Of Men and Mountains."

ual man can dominate the animal man. But the animal man needs constant renewal. His health is indeed a prerequisite to complete well-being.

HIKING or walking is exercise for a whole life span. One hundred and fifty-nine people joined us on a recent back-pack trip of three days along the Olympic Beach in the State of Washington. Of these there were 26 over 60, four over 70 years old and four under 10.

Though the teen-ager can walk competitively, the oldster must set his own pace. That is why hiking outlasts tennis, squash, touch football and other sports. At the age of 66, I cannot keep up with the 26-year-old hiker. It would be foolish to try. But I can finish the 30 miles before dark—if I set my own pace.

A stroll is not a hike. Strolling indeed is tiring. Why, I am not sure. But a bracing hike is invigorating, and while one comes in weary, a 30-mile hike will give his body a tone good for several days.

REGULAR hiking is necessary if sore muscles are to be avoided. American hiking shoes are hard to come by, for we are no longer a nation of hikers. The average outdoor boot will "kill" a person in 20 miles, not to mention 30 miles. It does not have adequate arch support; nor does the heel fit snugly. The GI boot is the best available, although those who hike year-after-year will end up having their shoes made to order. Mine came from Lobb in London and Peter Limmer in Intervale, N. H. There are other good shoemakers. But one must have a perfect fit to cover long distances, day after day.

Moreover, if blisters are to be avoided, two pairs of socks must be worn—a light cotton next to the skin and a heavy wool one on the outside. Any friction is then absorbed by the two layers.

THE outdoors is filled with wonders for those who walk with knowing eyes. The world of botany is there to explore, winter as well as summer. The bird migrations offer endless change, while the nonmigrants become regular objects of study. Their calls in time become familiar, and the other animals, from squirrels to deer, come into fascinating focus, week after week.

I have friends who mostly disregard the flora and fauna on their hikes. Their eyes are glued to the earth looking for rocks—rocks which, cut in two, will make attractive jewelry, vases or ashtrays.

Whatever the hobby may be, it relieves the hike of any monotony. The mind is lost in a world far from office or professional routine. As a result, magical things happen.

The subconscious carries a heavy burden of our worries, concerns and problems. On a long hike it functions free of additional tensions and pressures. And somehow or other it seems to unravel many a tangled skein of problems during a six-to-eight-hour hike. The process is a mystery, though I have experienced it again and again.

While writing a book or a lecture, I have come to a cul-de-sac, the next terminal being hidden from view. Or an argued case has projected difficult questions that loom so large that no opinion can be written until they are resolved. While my conscious processes are engaged in searching

out the wild persimmon tree or a sassafras bush or in listening for the pileated woodpecker or in detecting the abode of muskrats, the subconscious is solving my professional or personal problems. It is seldom that all perplexities are not clarified by the end of 20 miles. Answers and solutions, previously bothersome, become clear as day.

Yes, hiking sloughs off cares in mysterious ways. It also is wonderful exercise and stimulating to the mind. I recommend it for those marching toward 80 as well as for those not yet 10.

March 21, 1965

'Out Of Shoes Come New Feet'

Above them are boy and summer sky; beneath is a good earth to explore.

Photographs and text by WRIGHT MORRIS

MAYBE you've wondered, over the years, why we do our best to put shoes on a real boy, but we like bare feet on the one we see on the summer calendar. Maybe our feet remember what our minds forget. Every summer, out of an old pair of shoes, a boy takes a new pair of feet. Any boy can tell you there are just two seasons — the open season, when he takes his feet out of cold storage, and the closed season, when he washes his feet, puts them away. The open season is when he discovers the world. All he needs is a pair of bare feet, his own, at the end of the right length of leg.

Where the world begins.

What is the right length of leg? It was Abe Lincoln's notion, as you know, that a man's legs should be long enough to reach the ground, but the ground is not an easy thing to reach these days. There are small fry who have never set eyes on it. Their legs will reach to the floor

or the sidewalk, or down the street to the movie lobby, but they don't reach back to where the world began. Now, a leg that won't do that is not leg enough. The proper length of a boy's legs is about knee high to a grasshopper. Leg enough to get him into trouble—and then to get him out again.

The poet who said that the grass was a flag, out of some kind of green stuff woven, would know that the figure in a small fry's carpet is there underfoot. It is there in the yard like the tracks of the chickens, the fresh smell of mint, and the drone of flies on hot summer afternoons.

Perhaps *when he was a boy* is just a way of saying that, though some things pass, other things are like the snowy castle in the glass ball on the sewing machine. They are there forever. And they will spring to life whenever a small fry summons them.

From the house to the yard is just a step—but how far is it from the house to the pump? That depends, as any boy will tell you, on whether the pail is empty or full of water. And that depends a good deal on whether there are one or two pairs of feet.

The text for the day, and for every day, is right there at his feet. The three R's and something to boot—history, biography, and quite a bit of fiction, are there in the chicken tracks, and the piece of rotting whiffletree, wearing a nosegay of mint.

The new world begins along the creek bank, right after the flood has washed the old world away. Any barefoot boy is apt to discover it. The part that nothing will wash away is the earth that he remembers—the world that comes home, forever, on his feet.

In the beginning you have the earth and the sky, a pair of bare feet, and perhaps a barn. In the barn you have some pigs, a horse, a cow and a Model T Ford with some bicycle wheels. And sooner or later, there on the oil drum, you have a Leghorn egg.

That wagon wheel that you see over the well is meant to keep the big feet out—and let the small feet in. Also marbles, echoes, and the creatures that inhabit wells. But it's the small pebble, and the long, far fall that makes the everlasting plop.

June 11, 1950

HAVE PEDESTRIANS RIGHTS ?—Clearly not as against city railroads, if the insane manner in which the track of the East Broadway railroad is laid from the point where it strikes the City Hall Park until it reaches the lower end of the route at Ann-street, is lawful. The roadway, as we have pointed out before, infringes so close upon the sidewalk that the cars in passing almost overhang the pavement. Over this dangerous piece of road the car-drivers still continue to urge their horses at the rate of six or seven miles an hour, sweeping apparently at extra speed around the curve opposite the Astor House, and bringing up at Barnum's Museum, to again overlap the walk at Ann-street, and for a considerable distance up Park-row. Passengers attempting to enter the Third and Fourth avenue cars at the stand near where the East Broadway curve traverses the flagging on the easterly side of Broadway, do so at great risk of life and limb, on account of this reckless driving. Any day from our office windows we expect to see some person, more likely a woman with ample crinoline, who may be waiting for an up-town car, whisked off the sidewalk, to be mangled, perhaps killed, by these dangerous vehicles. It would perhaps be folly to hope that these tracks will be taken up and relaid at a safe distance from the sidewalk, but surely it is not too much once again to ask the Superintendent of the East Broadway road to instruct his drivers to pass these points where accidents must sooner or later happen, at a moderate rather than increased speed.

March 31, 1865

Walking Tours.

Not long since a foreign tourist landed at Boston and announced his intention of walking to Chicago, and possibly to San Francisco. In this way he rightly judged he could see far more of the country, in the same space of time, than by whirling through it in the cars. The feat, even if accomplished, is not unprecedented, though we doubt if it has often been performed under the disadvantage of a fifty pound knapsack, with which this English gentleman has chosen to burden himself. But the attempt furnishes a hint which pleasure-travelers might well consider.

It is astonishing how little pedestrian tours are resorted to in this country. Even the short stretch of two or three miles between home and office is shirked by the majority of people. The long walks of twelve and fourteen miles, which elsewhere are thought nothing of, we should regard with dismay. In the country, people simply do not walk at all. If a farmer has to go but half a mile to visit his neighbor, the inevitable buggy must be hitched up for the purpose.

Of late years there has been some change in this respect. Athletic sports of all sorts have come more into vogue, and the result is perceptible in the increased vigor and robustness of our youth. Yet, walking still ranks lower in popular favor than any other form of exercise, although it is certainly the cheapest of all, and quite as beneficial and attractive as any. The walking tours so common in Wales and Switzerland, and the Highlands of Scotland, are here so uncommon as to be fairly called unknown. Not one American in a thousand knows any section of his own country with that minuteness which only a pedestrian tour can give. Of course something of this is chargeable to the vastness of our area. In walking through Wales and Switzerland, one can see, as it were, to the end of one's journey. But to stroll over the whole "boundless continent," where distances are so excessive, and objective points so remote, is a damper on the sturdiest energy.

Yet, even this objection may be obviated by properly limiting one's ambition. It is not necessary that everybody should walk from Boston to Chicago. But a two weeks' vacation might be spent much worse than in walking leisurely from New-York to Boston. In those quaint old central Massachusetts villages, some of them, like Deerfield, shaded by miles of peerless elms, that waved over Indian massacres centuries ago, there is a life utterly unknown to most of our town-folk, and which can be thoroughly appreciated only by the wayside rambler. Up the valley of the Connecticut, too, from its mouth to its source in the Vermont hills, the tourist might walk for days with lovely sights to cheer him at every step. Cape Cod might furnish a shorter trip of unflagging interest, while the attractions of the White Mountain country are well understood. And in our own State, a walk from New-York to Albany, or from Albany to Buffalo, would reveal to the observant pedestrian many unsuspected phases of national life, and a charming and ever varying series of natural landscapes.

These are hints which might be indefinitely extended. From such a trip as one of these, the tourist would return invigorated in body and refreshed in mind, and with expanded notions of men and things. Nor would he find the enjoyment costly. His baggage might be carried on his back in a knapsack weighing considerably less than fifty pounds. A change of linen and toilet articles, compose the whole of his necessary outfit. So equipped, clad in a serviceable suit of some coarse dark cloth, with stout, easy shoes, and a good pilgrim's staff, he may tramp over half the State of New-York for the price of a week's stay at a fashionable watering-place. And the pleasure and instruction so obtained would be cheap at almost any cost. Not the least charm of the walking tour, is its utter freedom, its independence of all those irksome exactions that most annoy the traveler. No anxieties about train or boat break the pedestrian's slumber or spoil his meals. The tyranny of punctuality for a while he is able to forswear, and he can taste the sweets of that delightful vagrancy which some latent touch of the gypsy or the savage in human blood, sometimes makes all of us long for. Pedestrians know these and a hundred other pleasures, and they can only wonder at the blindness that persistently refuses to share so inexhaustible and various a form of recreation.

August 18, 1871

15

THE PEDOMETER.

It is naturally a source of satisfaction to a man to know that he is healthy and strong, and he is entitled to feel pride in his ability to outrun, outwalk, or outswim his fellows; but why should any one care to have his physical points measured mathematically, as we measure the horse-power of a steam-engine? Yet, there are multitudes of men in whom this desire is very strong. In old days, the Coney Island beach was lined with the itinerant owners of odd-looking machines, who greeted visitors with the cry: "Here you are! Test your lungs for ten cents," or, "Walk right up, now, and try your strength for a quarter." In response to these invitations, hundreds of human beings would walk right up, or concede that they were there, and thereupon blow through unsavory tubes, or strain themselves by lifting heavy weights, in order to obtain certificates setting forth their lung or limb power. That this should have been a satisfaction to anybody, except the machine owners, is incomprehensible, but it was a manifestation of a passion deeply implanted in nearly every human heart.

To this passion the inventor of a new pedometer which has recently been brought out appeals. It is his belief that if every man learns that by carrying a small instrument in his pocket he can know at the end of each day just how far he has walked, he will instantly go and buy that instrument. Undoubtedly the inventor is right. There are thousands of men who are ready to buy pedometers the moment their attention is called to the existence of such devices. If you ask them why they want pedometers, they will say that it is in order to know how many miles they may have walked within any given period. If you press the matter, and ask them why they want this knowledge, they will straightway be stricken dumb, or, forgetting the dignity of their sex, will effeminately and irritably reply: "Oh! because." There probably never lived any honest man except a professional pedestrian or an explorer, who really felt that it would do him any good to know the precise length of his daily walk. A wicked man may, indeed, pervert a pedometer to the service of vice, by exhibiting it to his wife whenever the latter requests him to go on an errand for her, and calling her attention to its carefully falsified record, which shows that he has walked forty-three miles, and is consequently utterly tired out. In this case, however, the value of the pedometer would be in proportion to its ability to lie. A truthful and trustworthy pedometer would be as worthless to the wicked as to the just. Nevertheless, man is born with a yearning to reduce himself to figures, and as the pedometer panders to this desire, he buys it.

The particular pedometer to which reference is here made is put in motion by the jar communicated to the human pocket whenever the owner of the pocket in which the instrument is carried takes a step. As a matter of fact, a man seldom alters the length of his step when walking, and hence, if at the end of a day he divides the whole number of steps recorded by the pedometer by the number which are equal to a mile, he can find how many miles he has walked. When Mr. Mahoney, of Clinton, Ill., read the advertisement detailing the manner in which the pedometer worked, he said to himself that it was a most simple and beautiful instrument, and that he would send for one without delay. Mr. Mahoney is a slight, consumptive, and peaceful man, and is married to a most excellent and energetic woman, who is described by her female acquaintances as "a great two-footed thing,"—it being their opinion that no woman can with any self-respect own more than one foot. On the day when he received his pedometer he put it in his pocket, and walked a mile down the railroad track and a mile back again. An examination of the pedometer told him that he had walked precisely two miles, and he was accordingly delighted with it.

That evening the baby cried, and when Mr. Mahoney was ordered by his wife to give it his watch to play with, he gave it the pedometer by mistake. The infant rather approved of it, but still persisted in occasionally bewailing its want of judgment in being born in Illinois, and Mr. Mahoney was, therefore, compelled to get up and rock the cradle. He was a patient man, and he rocked the cradle for nearly two hours before he fell asleep. He had reason to regret that he had suffered sleep to overpower him, for about 3 o'clock in the morning Mrs. Mahoney, justly exasperated at the unnatural wretch who preferred sleep to rocking the infant, threw a shoe at him and woke him up. He had just replaced the pedometer in his pocket, when his wife, feeling that forbearance was no longer a virtue, rose up and shook him for ten minutes without cessation.

The next morning at breakfast Mr. Mahoney, with a view of propitiating his affectionate wife, showed her the pedometer and explained its operation. "Yesterday, my dear," he remarked, "I walked exactly two miles—one mile down the track and one mile back. No! I give you my solemn word, I did not go any where else, and I didn't see her or any other girl. Now, if you will open the pedometer you will see that the index stands at the figure 2, which proves that I walked two miles only." What was his horror when Mrs. Mahoney requested him to take notice that the index pointed to "17," and that it thus convicted him of having walked to and from the residence of an objectionable young woman with red hair, who lived just eight miles and a half from the Mahoney mansion. The scene that followed need not be described. Betrayed and libeled by his own pedometer, Mr. Mahoney could make no coherent defense, and it was not until he found himself lying in a dark room and subjected to the soothing influences of arnica and brown paper that he remembered that he must have rocked the baby at least six miles, and that Mrs. Mahoney must have shaken him fully nine miles on the previous evening. He no longer puts faith in pedometers operated by the jarring of the human body, and has given the instrument, which so nearly proved his ruin, to the baby as an aid in the development of teeth.

August 18, 1878

TOURIST STEPS OUT TO THE BEAT OF A PEDOMETER

By PHYLLIS MERAS

IN three weeks of touring in Europe, I walked 51 miles a week for a total of 153 miles. I knew it was not a record, but I thought it was an accomplishment until I came home and compared notes with a friend who told me that, in four weeks abroad, he had walked 294.5 miles (73.6 miles a week). We both know precisely how far we walked because we both used pedometers.

I got the pedometer idea on my previous trip to Europe. Aboard the ship was a German tourist who took daily constitutionals, always methodically measuring his route.

This inspired a curious interest into how much walking I was doing incidental to traveling, and so I bought a pedometer for myself. They are available at cutlery stores, sporting-goods shops and better toy stores for about $7.

A pedometer resembles an old-fashioned dollar pocketwatch in diameter and thickness. It must be attached to the waist, the hip or the leg, or whatever part of the anatomy moves forcefully to and fro when one walks.

A tiny pendulum inside the pedometer swings as the leg swings, and each swing clicks a wheel escape, as in a clock hand, and moves to show the mileage. The pedometer can be adjusted for the length of one's step; the average stride, according to the directions that came with my pedometer, is 25 to 27 inches.

Easy for Men

For men, wearing a pedometer poses no problem. It can be clipped to a side pocket or easily suspended from a belt and camouflaged under a jacket. But what does a woman do?

Suspend it from a garter or tuck it into a stocking? Let it hang lumpily from a half-slip? Or wear only shirtwaist dresses because they have belts?

I chose the last-named attire and, because the weather was warm and I was coatless, the pedometer proved quite an attraction. It kept swinging back and forth at my waist, and I was frequently tapped on the shoulder and asked the time in strange tongues.

My habit was to put the pedometer on when I left my hotel in the morning, and take it off at dinner time. When one is dressed for dinner in silk, one feels awkward with a pedometer dangling from one's waist.

I have always walked extensively while on vacation, but never kept track of my distances. I like exploring on foot because it is a good way to make friends. The traveler who is walking invites friendship from townspeople in a way that tourists in sleek cars or on bulging buses never can — or do.

In Lisbon, for example, I was feted with cold codfish cakes by a couple of whom I asked walking directions. In Yugoslavia, while tramping through wintry streets, I was invited to, and accepted, a plum-brandy breakfast. In Hungary, a chance curbstone encounter led to a rollicking country picnic at a Communist workers rest camp.

Exasperated Solution

In some cities, I have walked simply from exasperation: in Cairo, because bearded men hanging out of tram windows intimidated me, and in London, because I got claustrophobia on the Underground.

But, until this most recent vacation, my approach to walking was not scientific. I just walked and walked. This time, however, inspired by the stalking German, I decided to keep track of the miles.

The first day in Paris, I covered two miles through the Louvre. If I had been in really fine fettle, I suppose I could have covered all six miles.

Two-Hour Walk

At least I think it is six miles. Guidebooks say it takes two hours to visit all the galleries nonstop. At three miles

an hour—the average pedestrian's rate—that makes six miles.

When I got tired of walking inside, I went outside and wandered about the Tuileries Gardens for awhile. There are 60 acres (3,018 feet by 1,065 feet) there.

I reconnoitered back and forth a mile's worth, and I also rambled up the mile-and-two-tenths Champs Elysées and visited Napoleon's tomb. The pedometer registered eight miles by dinnertime.

The second day in Paris, I puffed vertically up 190 feet to the Eiffel Tower's first level (the top is almost 1,000 feet). Going vertically apparently upset my pedometer, for, by the time I got down, I had shaken loose the hook that attaches the apparatus. It did not operate properly again until I got to an English-speaking repair shop in London.

There, pedometer reinstated, I wandered about Hampstead one day, climbing up hills that Keats is supposed to have climbed. Keats was an indefatigable pacer, I learned from my reading; he once walked 600 miles to Scotland, although without a pedometer.

Cabbie on Foot

I got lost in Hampstead and hopped a taxi to take me to the nearby Highgate Cemetery, where, my guidebook said, there were Egyptian sarcophagi and Karl Marx's flower-bedecked tomb. When we reached the cemetery, the cabbie wanted to know if he could not visit it with me, too.

He said he had never before heard of just taking a walk in a cemetery. "Fancy that, I'd like to tell the Mum about it," he said. So we walked together among the yews.

That day, the pedometer registered nine miles.

Another day in London, I walked along the Embankment, nodding to the Chelsea pensioners who wear red uniforms and live in old men's

homes there, and I visited the Tate Gallery and the National Gallery. That was a nine-mile day, too.

Stonehenge Trudge

A third day, I took a train to Salisbury, but missed the bus to Stonehenge. And so I trudged that distance—nine and one-half miles worth.

When I got back home to the United States, I telephoned my walking friend to tell him proudly how well I had done. (When I called, all I knew was that he liked to walk, too. I had no idea that he had embarked once on a similar experiment.)

He listened sympathetically. Then he produced his figures, although kindly prefacing his remarks by saying that he did 20 push-ups daily.

One day in London, he said, his pedometer registered 21.5 miles. In Brussels another day, he had walked 15.3 miles, and in Copenhagen one Saturday, 14 miles. He said he frequently took a trolley to the end of the line and then followed the car tracks back. In this country, he went on, he averages about five miles a day.

I promptly donned my pedometer again to see how well I compared with him in United States walking. My domestic experiments show I average three miles on an average American working-walking day.

Those Extra Steps

In Europe, of course, there are all those extra feet one takes in stepping back to cock the camera for a better shot of Notre Dame, or just meandering across a street to examine a carnation bouquet decorating a side of beef in a butcher's window.

Not only friends, but also fun and physical fitness are the satisfying results for those who choose to walk while abroad. For those with gastronomy in mind, there is perhaps no better way to work up an appetite for pasta than 10 miles on foot on Roman cobblestones. And what could make frogs' legs more succulent than a climb up the 225 steps to Sacré Coeur?

December 4, 1966

A Modest Proposal to Let Pedestrians Survive

By ROBERT L. DUFFUS

NOBODY can say: Pedestrians of the world unite, you have nothing to lose but your chains. Pedestrians have no chains— these are reserved for automobilists caught in the snow. Furthermore, the pedestrian is not a class, he is a situation.

Almost everybody drives or rides, at least at times. When he is doing this he hates pedestrians. They get in the way. They walk too slowly. They sneer. They cost money if killed or injured.

But even the former and occasional driver or rider turns at times into a pedestrian. For instance, the most hardened motorist walks from his easy chair in the living room to whatever spot it is where he takes the wheel, steps on the starter and goes hunting. And sometimes he walks a little in his daily rounds—the half block from his office to his favorite gorging place, the fifteen blocks from his office to where he has been able to park.

Democracy Forever

All I intend to say is that although the pedestrian is not a class he is at any given time more numerous than the fellow citizens who are driving or riding in cars and who believe there is a constitutional amendment—though there is not and never was—that says nobody on foot shall ever be allowed to impede the movements of anybody in an automobile.

What I do mean to assert, in addition to the above, is that in a democracy the majority ought to rule, and that in any city, town or street the majority is always on foot, not behind a gasoline-driven metallic beetle. This may be called the John B. Sniggins Law, because as far as I know no such person ever existed and if he did he did not invent such a theorem. (I did it myself, in case anybody wonders.)

In what I am glad is not my native city and sometimes am glad I live in, the Sniggins Law is honored in the non-observance.

Justice vs. Tyranny

There is, for example, a detestable cat named Tweets on a sign that says I must not start to cross a street on a green light unless the light has just turned green. If I could catch Tweets out after dark I would dye her green all over, attach a small and harmless firecracker to her tail, and set her loose on Fifth Avenue at the rush hour.

For what is Tweets really saying? She is really saying that an automobile on a one-way avenue or street may continue to run on a red light while I twiddle—or rather tweetle—my thumbs on the curb because

my green light may eventually turn red. Tweets is all for moving automobiles. What the hell is an automobile compared with one or more human beings? Don't ask Tweets. Tweets is the slave of the Traffic Commissioner.

What is my solution for the traffic problem? I have toyed with the idea of abolishing traffic altogether. A less drastic measure would be to stop all private automobiles ten miles from the center of New York City, or any big town, and let the drivers and passengers get in on foot—this would teach them to respect pedestrianism.

Still less sweeping, and I am a reasonable man in some respects, would be to require any automobile entering the heart of a big city to have at least five passengers, not counting, of course, an occasional pregnant mother on her way to the hospital in a taxi driven by a chauffeur who has had nursing training in an Army hospital.

I do not see the sense of a car occupied by one or two persons bullying its way around town in contemptuous disregard of the rights of anywhere from five to ten persons who are going on their lawful errands on foot.

What is the matter with feet? Will Detroit tell me that?

I am not against Detroit, though I have been there several times and have talked with

fairly young men who used to hunt prairie dogs where the tall apartment houses now stand.

A Pedestrian's Creed

For Detroit's benefit as well as for the benefit of all those countless human beings (I always go to sleep before I get them counted) who sometimes walk on city streets I urge that the rights of the pedestrian be recognized, defined and respected.

In New York City Tweets stands for the calm arrogance of the driver (which he will forget and regret when he is even temporarily a walker) who thinks jaywalking is a capital crime. Jaywalking isn't a crime at all; and each and every pedestrian who starts on a green light has a God-given right to finish on his own feet and not in a hospital or a funeral parlor. This is my creed.

In California a pedestrian *always* has the right of way, so I have been told and so I have found, if he starts on the green light, or maybe even if he doesn't. It is not lawful to kill pedestrians in California simply because they are pedestrians— there must be other charges, murder, for instance.

I'd like to see the California law applied everywhere. Why not? Who's boss—humanity or the machine?

———

Mr. Duffus was born a pedestrian.

April 2, 1961

GIANTS IN THOSE DAYS.

We all know that the Victorians were a fat, lifeless and stodgy lot, but still there were great walkers among them. Recently there was celebrated in London the fiftieth anniversary of " The Sunday Tramps." This was an organization of valiant pedestrians founded by LESLIE STEPHEN in 1879. It numbered in its membership many men well known in literary or university or public life. Reminiscences concerning them have been coming into print, either through survivors of the early group or their descendants. The feats of some of the walkers of that day are amazing considering their occupation and lack of special physical training. LESLIE STEPHEN himself was good any afternoon for a stroll of twenty miles, and was on record as having walked from Cambridge to London in twelve hours, without any particular effort or fatigue. He simply had had a notice that the Alpine Club was to have a dinner that night, " so I " called for my boots, breakfasted, " went out of the hall and on to " London." It was STEPHEN who spoke of his long friendship for FAWCETT, partly because that gentleman " had always been a regular and vigorous walker." The founder of " The Sunday Tramps " once wrote: " I am much inclined to " measure a man's moral excellence " by his love of walking."

What these trampers of other days along the roads of England would do under modern conditions, when motor cars and char-à-bancs make life miserable for pedestrians, it is hard to say. Even in the old days they were accustomed to leave the highway when they could, to walk along sylvan paths, or to make short cuts through private property so as to come into touch with the most attractive bits of the countryside. For these latter excursions, through grounds where the public was forbidden to enter, they had the advantage of the advice of a legal member, Sir FREDERICK POLLOCK. He had devised a formula which they employed whenever they had to deal with a troublesome gamekeeper or an indignant owner warning them off. It ran as follows: " We hereby " give you notice that we do not, " nor doth any of us, claim any " right of way or other easement " into or over these lands, and we " tender you this shilling by way of

"amends." Whether the existing Sunday Tramps, of whom a saving remnant remains to this day, take advantage of this lawful defense, or incantation, is not stated. But they continue to walk, even if at a lessened pace and over shorter stretches, in order to continue what might be called the apostolic succession of peripatetic philosophers.

February 6, 1930

THE WALKER

In The New Statesman and Nation some whimsical humorist deplores such walkers for walking's sake as HAZLITT and STEVENSON and confesses himself a stroller who gets his pleasure from what he hears and sees on his stroll. Yet isn't this stroller with his dilettante legs a distant relation of the saunterer, the perfect and rare walker, only one or two specimens of which THOREAU had ever seen? Of the true transcendental walker, the crusader HENRY was perhaps the sole example. " You must walk," he says, " like the " camel, which is said to be the only " beast which ruminates while walk- " ing." ROUSSEAU, a solitary jogger, never thought so much—at least he says so—as when he trudged over the fields and through the forests during his sojourn in England.

CARLYLE, a stout lad on his shanks, may be supposed to have thought cloudily and apocalyptically as he strode over the heather. According to DE QUINCEY, no friend of understatement, WORDSWORTH'S pedal communion with nature covered a distance equal to seven trips around the world. The effect of this prolonged pedestrianism on his poetic feet is an ancient joke. But rumination is a vexation. Abstraction makes us mad. We can't all be BELLOCS, BRYCES, LESLIE STEPHENSES.

DICKENS, an incurable walker, was on the road for fun. Those who are eccentric enough to linger as Jeffersonians after Mr. HAMILTON'S recent and final victory may be cheered to remember that the all-accomplished Monticellian was a non-ruminant ambulator. This is his advice to PETER CARR:

The object of walking is to relax the mind. You should therefore not permit yourself even to think while you're walking; but divert yourself by the objects surrounding you.

Old reliable Dr. FRANKLIN is impitiably practical. He tells son WILLIAM that

there is more exercise in one mile's riding on horseback than five in a coach; and more in one mile's walking on foot than five on horseback; to which I may add that there is more in walking one mile up and down stairs than five on a level floor.

Did old Mr. BRYANT have this advice in mind when he practiced walking or running upstairs in the old Evening Post Building? At any rate, it won't do to think, however appropriate the thought, of " Thanatopsis " when you are breasting or skirting the automobilious torrent. Only the non-ruminants survive.

June 2, 1937

HIKING

A member of the rare tribe of voluntary walkers, fresh from a trip on the hoof, pack on back, through the Green Mountains (though the White Mountains, the Rockies or the Sierras would doubtless have done as well), writes to say that what this country needs most is a revival of pedestrianism. Let (he says) the noble principle of the Appalachian Trail be applied the country over, so that those who will may travel from the Gulf of Mexico to the Bay of Fundy and from Chatham Head to Point Pinos without getting in the way of a single motor car. Then educate people to use those trails.

What good does pedestrianism do (he asks) except to wear out shoes? It teaches us (he answers) the virtue of patience. It compels us to see the shapes of things as we cannot when we wear the winged heels of modern travel. We go, on foot, a shorter distance but we see and experience more —more, indeed, by the hour than under any other system of locomotion. Walking gives us the supreme satisfaction, of which civilized man has been nearly deprived, of doing things for ourselves. This is the more true if we carry, as not all can do but many can, our bed and board with us.

He remembers (he asserts) adventures money cannot buy—that can be bought only by sweat, by weariness, by struggles for breath, even by moments of disgust when he would throw up the whole enterprise of walking if he could. A fondness for nature (he states) is like a healthy and enduring marriage—beyond sentimentality, characterized by occasional quarrels, by mutual recrimina-

tions and by happy reconciliations. He does not see how this is to be achieved unless one pits one's naked strength against the inanimate obstacle.

In conclusion (or almost so), he points his argument with a day on Vermont's Long Trail—a day of stumbling hard work over rugged paths that rose and fell precipitously, barking shins, almost wrenching ankles, winding where no trails seemingly ought to go, cajoling with blueberries and distant vistas, snarling with twisted roots, slippery ledges and sliding stones. But the day closed with arrival at one of the cabins kept up by the Green Mountain Club, a bunk in which to lay a sleeping bag, a stove on which to cook a Lucullian banquet of bacon, rice and coffee, a westward view over the lovely intervale of Underhill to Lake Champlain and the misty Adirondacks, a tasteful if not opulent sunset, a profiled moon, the Big Dipper swinging under the cliffs, the winking of homelike gleams in the valley below, from which those in the cabin were cut off by night, as completely as willing castaways on an island, by the nocturnal occlusion of the trails.

After that the Northern Lights appeared, fanwise, great streamers shooting over the pine-etched cliffs. In the morning the reflected sunrise, under a slowly lifting curtain of mountain fog, was a vision of impossible glory in the great ranges across the lake, golden, fantastic, hardly of this earth.

Our correspondent went to the beginning of the trail in an automobile —so much he admits. But these things, at their best (he stoutly maintains) are to be had only by hard walking. That is the manner in which one approaches the abodes of the gods. He adds that most of the events that are unfortunate in our time arose with the decline of pedestrianism. A walking nation (he insists) never decays— unless, of course, it walks with man-killing weapons in its hands. He is not sure that that ever did any one any good.

September 26, 1937

THE REDISCOVERY OF FEET

One of the good things the Army is doing for those who are fortunate enough to be young and healthy enough to be in it is to remind them what feet and legs are for. One reads of "hardening hikes" in which troops march seven or eight miles the first day, ten the second, and fifteen the third. This is enough to horrify some of the stay-at-homes, including those toothy youngsters with upraised thumbs who would rather stand for an hour on a corner waiting for a lift than walk two miles.

Yet most of us, with transportation almost always at our disposal, probably underestimate our walking powers as well as the pure joys of walking. We can hardly equal the achievements of the Chinese guerrillas, who make nothing of forty to fifty miles a day on foot, of such professionals as the late Edward Payson Weston, who once walked 100 miles in a little under twenty-two hours and a half, or of such distinguished amateurs as the late Dr. John H. Finley, who modestly acknowledged a record of seventy miles in twenty-four hours.

Such strolls call for long training, skill (for there is skill in walking well) and fortitude. Almost any one with sound legs and normal feet can walk up to ten or fifteen miles a day and enjoy the experience. There are still many dirt roads for the American walker and thousands of miles of mountain trails for the adventurous. If the Army "hardening," plus a not too serious gasoline shortage, encourages this ancient and healthy sport we can write that result down on the credit side of our "unlimited emergency" ledger.

July 8, 1941

THE DECLINE OF WALKING.

The former Health Officer of the Port of New York, Dr. ALVAH H. DOTY, who likes to see panoramas unrolled from a seat in an automobile as well as another man, has produced a book entitled "Walking for Health." It may not have the charm or fancifulness of STEVENSON'S "Walking Tours," or of HAZLITT'S "On Going a Journey," or of GEORGE OTTO TREVELYAN'S essay on vagabondizing, but it serves a useful purpose in drawing attention to the decline of walking. Dr. DOTY compares it with other forms of stretching the muscles and expanding the lungs in the open air, and pronounces it better than any of them. A strong walker, a good heart! No other outdoor recreation does so much for the vascular system. If you want to stave off arterio-sclerosis, keep walking. That is the message of Dr. DOTY.

It is intended for the motormaniacs as well as for the sedentary. All the world is riding now and losing the use of its legs. Commuters who once made light of walking a mile from the railway station to their homes today have their cars carry them home. When there is something going on at the suburban club, members who live two blocks away get out their automobiles. Some nice people would as soon be seen carrying a parcel, or with hands ungloved, as to be seen proceeding anywhere on foot when the car could be used. As a consequence there is a growing demand for books on taking off flesh by dieting.

HERBERT W. GLEASON, author of "Through the Year With Thoreau," has written, in the form of a letter to an automobile-smitten friend, a delightful skit on the man who rides and won't walk. Congratulating his friend on acquiring a new model, he responds to an inquiry about his own car. It is evidently a miracle of efficiency. While "it does not have disc wheels, nor a de-"tachable spot light, nor an automatic "squeegee on the windshield," it never has an overheated engine nor a clogged carburetor, and climbs hills with a 50 per cent. grade. Tire troubles never occur. No road is too rough for it. "The "design is one that was made by an "Eminent Architect a great many years "ago, and it has never been improved "upon." No license is required, it may be parked anywhere, and no garage is needed, "for," concludes Mr. GLEASON, "I take it to bed with me." One is reminded of HAZLITT'S:

Give me the clear blue sky over my head and the green turf beneath my feet, a winding road before me and a three hours' march to dinner—and then to thinking! It is hard if I cannot start some game on these lone heaths. I laugh, I run, I leap, I sing for joy.

All this being said, there is no reason why a wise man shouldn't tool about the country in his car to see the scenery and keep up his walking, too.

April 13, 1924

Topics of The Times

WALK, doctors say. Walk for exercise, for stimulation or for relaxation. Walk to improve muscle tone, circulation and to get fresh air in your lungs. Walk for a better figure and for color in your cheeks. Walk for health and walk for fun—in the city, in the country.

Walking is excellent exercise, but only when it is done correctly. First of all, your standing posture must be right from the soles of the feet to the top of the head. Stand with the weight on the balls of the feet, the knees relaxed but not bent. Pull the hips down in back, pull the abdomen up and in. Pull the ribs up out of the waist so that the chest is held high. Pull the shoulders back and down as though you were carrying two heavy suitcases. Push up with the top of the head to straighten out the curves of the neck and spine. Don't tilt the head up, or push the chin forward. The chin line should be parallel to the ground:

When you walk, maintain this standing posture. There should be little movement from the shoulders to the hips. Swing the legs from the hips in long purposeful strides. (Never walk from the knees—this will make you seem to shuffle.) Swing the arms from the shoulders, with the palms turned in toward the body. Keep the shoulders still. Don't twist them from side to side, and don't move them up and down in a see-saw motion. Keep your hips smooth—don't let them sway. Don't let your head wobble—hold it straight and high. And *walk,* don't stroll.

If you follow these instructions, not only will your posture improve, and, of course, your figure too in the process, but your walk as well. It will begin to take on a new easy, gliding grace.

So that you won't fall into sloppy posture habits, check up on your posture every once in a while. Every time you stop for a traffic light, for instance, think . . . abdomen in, chest high, head up. Learn to take longer, deeper breaths, too, as you walk.

Clothes have a great effect on the amount of fun and exercise you get from walking. Comfortable, low-heeled shoes are a must. A skirt with enough fullness to give walking freedom is important, too. Take along a scarf so that you will have something for your throat if it turns chilly. If you wear a hat, wear one that will stay on in a stiff breeze. Either leave your handbag at home or wear one with a shoulder strap that will leave your arms free.

April 23, 1944

A Time for All Things This peak season for most outdoor activities is the off-season for walking. As a general rule, the walker is not one who is in need of the excellent advice which the doctors give us annually at the time; "Don't overdo it." His name rarely if ever figures in the list of summer casualties under sunstroke, heat prostration or third-degree sunburn. On his days-off at this time of year the seasoned walker is not a-walking; he can usually be found sitting under a tree in some cool spot, probably with a book which he has brought along with some vague notion of improving his mind.

He may find that just sitting under a tree is so pleasant—he very soon abandons any idea of trying to improve his mind in this weather—that he asks himself why he ever takes the trouble to walk at all. "Were it not better done as others use," he begins but breaks off there, for he knows from years of experience that when the first cool week-ends of September arrive he will again be tramping over the back roads of Westchester or Rockland County or along the reaches of the lordly Hudson.

One Foot on the Ground For the present it seems more profitable to think about walking than to walk. It is time to pay heed to the ancient wisdom of the East: "It is better to walk than to run, it is better to stand than to walk, it is better to sit than to stand, it is better to lie than to sit."

The first thing that strikes one about walking is that the word is directly related to the idea of progress, of getting somewhere. Says the Concise Oxford Dictionary:

Walk, v. i. & t. (Of men) progress by advancing each foot alternately never having both off ground at once.

You are required to make progress when you walk and you are required to keep at least one foot on the ground. Those are two very wholesome requirements for these times.

From the French The French word for walking has some remarkable connotations. The Latin language, from which French is almost wholely derived, had half a dozen words for walking, depending on what kind of walking it was, but the French took their verb *marcher* from the same root as *marteau,* meaning hammer. It was "pounding" along the old Roman roads

which probably fixed the word in the language.

Today *marcher* means "to walk," "to function" or "to make progress." A Frenchman, *marching* cross-country, may note with annoyance that his watch has ceased to *march,* but he may think with satisfaction that his business is *marching* very well. He will greet a friend with a cheery "That marches?"

Soul of a Journey The reason why the walker continues to walk in the face of all the difficulties that modern means of locomotion have put in his way has been well stated by William Hazlitt, who wrote his essay "On Going a Journey" 124 years ago, in the heyday of the stage coach. The title is significant; the real walker is always "going a journey," from Here to There. That distinguishes him from the man who is out for a "constitutional," on the one hand, and the "hiker," who follows a rough trail to a high place for the sake of view, on the other.

The walker "going a journey" alone will probably wish to be written down like Abou Ben Adhem as one who loves his fellow-men, but he is bound to agree with Hazlitt:

"Give me the clear blue sky over my head, and the green turf beneath my feet, a winding road before me, and a three hours' march to dinner—and then to thinking! It is hard if I cannot start some game on these lone heaths."

Black Care Rides That is the whole business in a nutshell: the walker "goes a journey" in order to think, "to start some game," to refresh his stock of shopworn ideas—perhaps on occasion to give the slip to a certain dark lady known to the ancients as Atra Cura or Black Care.

It was the Roman poet who left a monument more enduring than bronze who wrote, "Behind the horseman sits Black Care." In the Augustan Age Black Care rode behind the Roman knight on his horse and with the Roman senator in his litter. Black Care rides today in a luxurious limousine. She slips aboard the great plane about to start a dash to the other side of the world. Without an advance reservation she travels on any trip of the Twentieth Century Limited.

Black Care is essentially a rider, not a walker. She may set out with the walker "going a journey" but after an hour or so she usually gets discouraged and disappears somewhere in the woods.

July 29, 1946

WALKING WEATHER

When the last few leaves are dropping from maples, beeches, elms and birches, when the slow-flowing woodland brooks are no longer concealed by a moist carpet of golds, reds and browns, comes the year's best walking weather. In the hill country of the northland the pasture oaks cling to their faded-brown leathery foliage, but sidehill groves and hardwood ridges are temple groves for a brief time each sunny day.

Between leaf-dropping time and Indian summer comes an interlude of bracing days and tingling nights. Each morning white hoarfrost lies on meadows and fields. The fall plowing is a mass of little icy crinkles and ravines. As the late-rising reluctant sun sends its slanting rays over a chilled world the light calls forth miniature jewel gleamings for a few moments. Small ponds of mist gather in the lowlands and hesitatingly dissolve into nothingness as the morning wears on. Wisps of mist play over the dark, damp wooden shingles on weathered spring houses and gray-boarded barns.

It's good to walk on the land in late October. There's a crispness in the air whether sun be shining or stratus clouds cast a gray hue over the valleys and mountains. Now that leaves have fallen from alders and sumacs and the goldenrod and asters half droop toward the ground, one can see the etched lichen pictures on the stone walls; the great heaps of stones in the corners of upland fields look like piles of big gray apples. The yellow-tan soil before woodchuck dens makes dots by the pasture fence. From an upland lookout one can see far. White church spires make exclamation points among village elms; the river winding through the brown valley floor is a crooked silver thread. On a clear night when the countryman climbs to the top of the steep pasture it seems as if the sky were an inverted bowl flecked with golden dots. This is the season of walking weather, and he who traverses the lowlands and uplands feels in closer touch with verities that offer solace in a troubled world.

October 24, 1946

Topics of The Times

Well to Left of Center When Cicero wrote to his friend Atticus, "Utor via," he was saying literally, "I use the highway," but what he meant was: "As for me, I am playing safe by keeping in the middle of the road." Poor old Cicero tried so hard to keep in the middle of the road that he has been harshly called a trimmer—a cruel fate for a great man who was always anxious about his reputation with posterity. Possibly he was a bit too anxious. History often minimizes those who play safe.

Many politicians still prefer the middle of the road, but the pedestrian who starts out to use the highway (in the literal sense), if he values life and limb, avoids it. No matter how conservative his inclinations he keeps well to the left, facing traffic, and he does not venture into the middle of the road even to cross to the other side until he has taken a good look in both directions. Those are the rules of the road for the pedestrian. They tend to keep him from becoming a non-pedestrian in an ambulance.

Another Forgotten Man One who clings to walking as "the only way to see the country" must find himself in the category of forgotten men. In all the road building and road repairing that has been going on no thought has been given to him. If he is very lucky, he may find an old dirt road running in his direction. He can do pretty well with a smooth shoulder on a hard road or some turf beside the concrete. But he must be prepared to put up with the hardships which are reserved for forgotten men.

He may use an automobile map, but he uses it "in reverse." Heavy red lines, which tell the motorist the quickest and best routes, he avoids. He looks for thin, dark lines, which reveal old, neglected country roads, or at least secondary roads where the traffic is lighter. Preferably he does not start a trip on a week-end or a Sunday. It is best to choose a day when the Sunday drivers are hard at work trying to earn the money to meet the impending next installment on the car, say a Monday.

Roads That Grew If the walker is fortunate in choosing his road, he becomes more and more convinced that walking is "the only way to see the country." The old narrow country road with its twisting and turning, so maddening to the motorists, has the greatest charm for the walker. It is as much a part of the landscape as the brook, for it never knew the compass or the ruler of the engineer. It never existed on a blueprint; it grew there as a road.

Every twist and turn had its reason for being—a hill here, a bog there, the corner of someone's farm there, or even the presence at some farmhouse of a dog people were afraid of. These are some of the special advantages that the scientifically engineered superhighway has to do without and the motorist must forego.

***

Walkers and Riders

One fact of considerable social significance is impressed upon one who walks along the roads. That is that we have become a nation of riders. The few walkers one meets are usually hitch-hikers watching for their chance to leave the walkers and join the riders. The village children coming home from school, who used to look in at the open door to see the smith at work, now pass in a huge contraption labeled "School Bus."

It was quite different on the great roads across the mountains which opened the interior of this country for settlement. We read that along with a stream of wagons passed countless pioneers on foot, carrying huge packs on their backs. They must have been a particularly hardy race of pioneers. Their descendants are probably riding round today in the most expensive cars.

***

Indiana and Athens

One remembers young Abe Lincoln of Indiana. Carl Sandburg tells us that he walked everywhere within fifty miles of his father's farm. He thought nothing of walking twenty or thirty miles in a day—to hear a lawyer make a speech, to do an errand at the store. He would walk much further if he heard of anyone who would lend him a book. Those long walks through the woods must have had a great influence on Lincoln's character. It was then perhaps that he began that practice of restating every "proposition" in his own words—that habit which left its mark on all the thoughts of his great mind.

One remembers young Henry Thoreau of Concord, who thought nothing of walking twelve miles to Boston to hear Emerson lecture—and after the lecture walking back to Concord. Later in life he was to recall, "I have traveled a good deal in Concord"—and, of course, always on foot. His friend Emerson also believed that walking was the only exercise for a philosopher, and regretted the time wasted in tending his garden.

For there does seem to be some mystical relation between walking and thinking. At Athens there were the "peripatetic philosophers," who walked with their pupils as they lectured. Socrates seems to have been always walking about the city. One day he walked the four miles to Piraeus to see a religious festival. In the evening he started to walk back to the city. Some friends overtook him and invited him to the home of one of them. There the conversation started which Plato made into "Politeia," or "The Republic." If Socrates had taken a taxi that evening there would obviously have been no "Politeia."

July 6, 1947

Topics of The Times

New Definition Needed?

There was a time when a pedestrian was simply a person who journeyed or moved from place to place on foot, hence a walker. More recently we wheel-mad creatures have come to think of "pedestrian" more particularly in connection with someone who has been hit by an automobile. Who knows? Perhaps in a thousand years (or less) the dictionary will define pedestrian as "one who, while afoot, is struck, injured or put to death by an automobile or other gasoline or jet propelled vehicle."

Today's newspapers indicate that a change in definition may not be too far off. It is rare that the word pedestrian occurs in our daily journals detached from news of an accident. "Pedestrian Hit by Speeding Car" and similar headlines accenting the grim hazards of life afoot are so common that it is small wonder our mental picture of a pedestrian is changing.

***

Again On Foot

Today a pedestrian, thanks to the crisis in parking space, is a journeying person who is compelled to walk from his car to his destination, or from his car to the subway which will bring him closest to his destination. Thus the automobile, which once saved man the trouble of placing one foot before the other in order to go from one place to another, is forcing him back on his feet.

We are assured that this is but a temporary inconvenience, but the situation serves to remind us that civilization in its forward march has delicate ways of snarling men in the coils of their own labors. These occasional curiosities of progress may only be pauses in man's advance inspired by the Fates, who wish to see if men still retain a sense of humor. The Fates probably reason that if a man can see the humor represented by the vast distance between where he must leave his car and where he wants to go, then he still must be fundamentally sound.

***

A Lost Art

There are too few pedestrians in the mold of the late Dr. John Finley, who did so much to further walking as an art. His annual trek around Manhattan was not a stunt, but rather a friendly perambulation. In him was the spirit of the true walker. Today many inhabitants of cities and suburbs know their own immediate neighborhoods only as seen over a chromium radiator ornament. The only path they tread is between front door and car door; the peculiarities of the pavement and the low reach of a tree's branches in the next block, or the break in a hedge down the street, through which a garden peeks, are unknown to them.

***

The Forgotten Trails

We suspect that this desertion of the feet is not confined to the motorist, but that the disease has spread to his children. A young friend who recently visited the woods and fields, near a large city, where he played twenty years ago as a boy, returns a significant report. In those days, he said, a stream flowed through the woods and on each side of the water there was a deep-trodden path, worn by boys like himself bent on exploration, games of cowboys and Indians and other noisy adventures. He reports that the stream is still there, as lovely as ever (strangely enough), but that the paths are now so faint that he found them with difficulty. Although the city has moved nearer to the woods, and children are still growing up in it, several visits to his old haunts failed to disclose youngsters scuffling on the once well-worn trails. He concludes that the automobile in two decades has made casual expeditions into the woods, and hence the accompanying pedestrian exertions things of the past.

***

A Fad Again?

To be sure, he added, he found "hiking clubs" whose members climb into cars and ride for thirty or forty miles in order to walk five or ten, then drive home again. But what he seemed to regret was the virtual absence of children "out for a walk," where in years past there were

dozens. His theory is that one of these days walking will suddenly become a fad, like miniature golf, and that for a whole summer men, women and children will be swarming everywhere on foot. Their slogan will be taken from Charles Dickens: "* * * walk and be happy; walk and be healthy." (It was Dickens who also wrote of "certain ancients, far gone in years, who have staved off infirmities and dissolution by earnest walking—hale fellows, close upon ninety, but brisk as boys.") Shoe manufacturers, cobblers and chiropodists suddenly will find their trades thriving. Then, he says, the bubble will burst, and we'll be back where we are—driving the two blocks to the drug store for a quart of ice cream.

December 11, 1947

Topics of The Times

Walking for Recreation
There seems to be a healthful trend toward more walking for recreation. It may be that as time goes on we shall learn to use leisure time for leisurely pursuits. This is not to say that crowded ball parks, massive stadia filled with roaring humanity and radio comedians who suffer barbed gibes for a few thousand per week have not earned a place in the contemporary scene.

It was only a few years ago that sincere individuals were deeply concerned about the "leisure problem." Some sociologists, educators and laymen believed that a man was a safer unit of society if he were engaged nine hours a day for six days a week at a vocational pursuit. Eventually the social order adjusted itself to five and a half days of labor. Then a few vocations experimented with the five-day week. Today the idea of a forty-hour week is solidly entrenched.

Seven Days on the Farm
The countryman who works six days a week and does his chores on Sunday is not very much worried about the problem of leisure-time activities. The tools of production are constantly growing more efficient. He reflects that a generation ago it required six or eight times as many hours to grow an acre of corn with horse power as it does today with mechanical power. It was a day's labor to buck a cord of wood that a power saw whirs through in an hour. Electricity milks the cows, pumps the water and turns the grindstone. The change means that the farmer's wife does not have to fill kerosene lamps or stoke a woodburning range. The farmer reflects on these matters, though he realizes that only 52 per cent of the nation's 5,800,000 farms have electricity, as compared with 96 per cent of the urban homes. But time will remedy lags and the 28 per cent of farmsteads that now have running water will soon increase in number.

Knowing the Land
Walking is the countryman's recreation, and as he rambles in the field, meadow, upland pasture and through the woodland he has evolved in his mind a set of principles that may be of interest to others. The first principle is one of Thoreau's basic philosophies. He, you will recall, traveled "widely in Concord." An intimate knowledge of a smaller area engenders an anticipation that one does not feel if he attempts to explore too extensive an area. It is difficult to specify amounts in acres, but considerable experience leads to the conclusion that 100 acres of varied terrain is the most rewarding size.

Second, unless one is walking just for exercise, it is wise to stake out an area of diverse countryside. There are things to watch and to study in a brook-traversed meadow that one cannot find on a thin-soiled pasture hillside. A low-lying woodland of evergreens is a different world from a rocky ridge covered with beeches.

Courses in Nature Study
The walking program can well be correlated with a program of study regarding a specific field of interest. There is much to be said in favor of adult education courses where people gather to ponder the cross-currents of international problems, pursue studies in the maze of economics or work together thumping out pewter bowls and copper trays. The countryman, however, prefers to organize his own courses. During one period he specializes in studying the bark patterns of the different species of trees. After he has observed the species of his farm and filled a notebook with writing he will have difficulty deciphering months and years hence, he purchases a book on geology and spends a period studying rocks. In turn he delves into the flora of the swamps, observes toadstools and mushrooms, considers ferns and mosses and puts in a period on marine life along the brook.

Walking Plus Study
Walking is a pleasant and rewarding way to use leisure hours if one combines countryside rambling with a learning process. This last principle is important. Walking, plus study, gives an avocation that is year round and weatherproof. When the Weather Man is too cantankerous one has books and notebooks and plans. With stout shoes, old clothes, a few books and a pencil, an area of land and an inquiring mind one has a leisure time activity that insures a quiet, satisfying interest in an unquiet society.

Not for the City Man
Walking, however, is not an urban avocation, though our endless sidewalks provide a convenient means of perambulation. There are few who, like the late Dr. Finley, enjoy circumnavigating the borders of Manhattan Island during the course of a brisk winter day. The philosopher has said indeed that "the proper study of Mankind is Man," and that is plentiful on a congested city street. But such studies can be even more comfortably pursued sitting in a taxicab while talking with the driver.

There are no sidewalks in the country. One has to make his way as best he can against the stream of motor traffic on the highways. But there are plenty of secluded by-paths where moving feet fall softly. Bordered in beauty, they give space in which to loaf and invite one's soul. It comes like a silent and meditative companion to consider the humble life scuttling through the underbrush, the slow passage of the seasons, the opening bud and the falling leaf. But the soul of the walker is a shy thing. It comes closest in complete solitude.

February 15, 1948

They're Killing Us

Truth about feet is, we're killing them!

By Beatrice Oppenheim

TO hear the chiropodists tell it, our feet are killing us. The New York State Podiatry Society reports that 80 per cent of Americans old enough to vote have something wrong with their feet. And though 95 per cent of babies are born with good feet, 8 per cent of them have some sort of incipient foot trouble as early as the end of their first year.

FOOT TROUBLE—

If you think that bunions, corns, calluses, fallen arches, arthritis, clubfoot and athlete's foot comprise the list of pedal ailments, you don't know the half of it. The Journal of the American Medical Association once listed fifty-three varieties of foot ills. Industrial podiatrists estimate that foot ailments and accidents cost workers and employers in the United States $100,000,000 annually. And that doesn't cover all the backache, headache, premature wrinkles, general fatigue, irritability, anxiety, neuroses, domestic and personality troubles traced to unhappy feet.

PEDESTRIANISM—

We all use our feet more than we realize. Even a house-

wife treads 8½ miles in an ordinary day. Her son of school age romps 15 miles a day, her little girl 11½ miles. If her husband is a business man, he may take only 12,000 steps in a working day. But, assuming his weight to be 165 pounds, even that represents nearly 1,000 tons of jolts on his soles. His stenographer, whose job is sedentary, nevertheless averages 43 miles of walking a week.

All that is mere mincing, however, alongside a real, pedestrial occupation. The city patrolman pounding a beat paces off 14 miles a day. The postman hauls our bills and billets-doux 22 miles on his appointed rounds. The plowman homeward plods his weary way, after following his horse for 25 miles since sunrise.

HELPFUL HINTS—

Do you know how to walk? The toes should point straight ahead or even slant a little inward. The heel strikes first,

then the foot rocks forward on its outer border until the toes grip. The ball comes down last, and push-off for the next step comes from the big toe. If your heels wear down first on the outer, rear corner, you are doing all right.

The next time the boss catches you with your feet on the desk, explain you are resting. Podiatrists recommend it. A restful position when you are not sitting at a desk is with the ankles crossed, weight on the outer edges of the feet.

With the increasing use of "loafers" the time is approaching when men will be able, with the utmost convenience, to exercise the privilege which

women have long enjoyed, of slipping their feet out of their shoes at the movies or at dinner. All the better.

MILADY'S SLIPPER—

Fifteen times as many women as men have foot trouble, and podiatry clinics have three times as many women

patients as men.

One glance into the show window of a women's shoe store tells the story. Of all the ancient style mutilations surviving in the civilized world, the French heel is probably the worst. The woman in high heels is continually walking downhill, Dr. Morton explains. Her foot cannot slide forward in the shoe because the vamp is so small and tight. In trying to compensate for the excessive forward lean, she throws her whole posture out of line and invites strains in other parts of her body.

PEDITHERAPY—

The barber, whose red and white striped pole is a vestige of ye olden times when he was the poor man's surgeon, used to trim corns as well as beards a century ago.

What is believed to be the first specialized chiropodist's parlor in this country was opened near the Old South Meeting House in Boston in 1840 by Nehemiah and Andrew Jackson Kenison, brothers, with their cousin, Parker Kenison.

Twenty years later President Lincoln summoned a podiatrist, Dr. Isachaar Zacharie, to the White House to treat his feet. Raw-boned Abe's left foot was 12 inches and his right 12¼, and neither was friendly. They were so much on his mind that he became the first Commander in Chief to commission a chiropodist to the Federal Army.

September 19, 1948

Observer: Using the Man-Stunner Tonight, Sis?

By RUSSELL BAKER

WASHINGTON, March 22— It is becoming dangerous for a man to walk the streets alone at night. A solitary male nightwalker tells of a harrowing experience on a lonely street within three blocks of his home recently, and his story illustrates the refinements of peril that result from the national crime-mindedness.

Strolling the Sidewalk

Subject was strolling the

sidewalk of his upper-middle class residential neighborhood at approximately 10 P.M. and musing absently, as is his wont, on the transience of life and the onset of gray at the temples.

Absorbed in his thoughts, he failed to notice that he was being approached by a short, squat woman who, he now swears, looked exactly like George Zucco. Within perhaps twenty feet of her, he reached absent-mindedly for his pipe.

At this gesture, he heard the woman cry, "Get him, Killer!" and saw her unleash an enormous hound whose jaws dripped blue fire. The beast caught him before he had made four strides of panicked retreat, hurled him to the sidewalk and expertly seized his pipe wrist in poisonous jaws.

In a trice the woman was upon him. She wielded a baseball bat. "Thought you'd try something funny against a defenseless woman, eh?" she

crowed. "Come across with that pistol."

Solitary male nightwalker surrendered his pipe and submitted to a humiliating frisking before the woman agreed to listen to his explanation that he was merely an innocent neighbor out for a stroll, and to escort him to his house to be identified by his wife.

Preconceived Notions

This man was a victim of

25

the general conviction among the women of America that it is no longer safe for a woman to walk the streets alone at night. Hereafter, if he ever walks the streets alone at night again, he will give women pedestrians a wide berth, for he knows the chances are excellent that they will be armed to the teeth and quick on the trigger.

Now it is fairly easy to spot a woman who is carrying a baseball bat and leading a monstrous hound and to avoid her by crossing the street or running up an alley. The difficulty for men arises from women who are carrying only small arms such as the dirks, snubnosed .38's and gas guns with which the munitions lobby is arming the ladies for self-defense.

Feelings of Security

Thoughtlessly reaching for a pipe while passing a nervous woman with a dirk can be an agonizing mental lapse. The problem facing society is how to give our women a feeling of security on the streets without imperiling the lives of men who also like a nightly stroll.

In an effort to solve this problem, American industry has come up with the Protect-U aerosol spray can. Basically, it works like spray-on deodorant. The lady lifts the can, squeezes the cap and aims for the man's eyes. The spray is said to stun the man momentarily, "permitting the woman to escape."

It also bathes the victim in a peculiar odor which marks him for easy arrest and identification. It is hard to see how Protect-U can be anything but a social disaster. Consider the nervous woman who sees a hulking silhouette reaching for its pipe. If armed only with conventional military hardware, she will think twice before acting.

With her harmless but effective aerosol spray, however, she will have the easy option of spraying first and asking questions afterward. By momentarily stunning every male pedestrian who makes a nervous gesture, she may have time to check the bodies for weapons and, if she finds none, to make her escape without having to answer to the police.

The men, on the other hand, though suffering only a momentary stunning, are going to have to go around for several days exuding a peculiar and easily identifiable odor.

How Explain It?

The problems of explaining this peculiar and easily identifiable odor to a wife upon returning from a nocturnal walk need not be dwelt upon. ("Well, you see, I was passing this woman with a momentary-stunning can when I reached for my pipe. . . .")

Something has to be done to make those streets just as safe for men at night as they are for women.

March 23, 1965

In Step

Footnotes on walking these brisk fall days.

❝To enjoy a countryside it is essential to make a direct contact with it, and this is only to be accomplished by walking over it."—*F. S. Smythe.*

❝Unhappy business men, I am convinced, would increase their happiness more by walking six miles every day than by any conceivable change of philosophy." — *Bertrand Russell.*

❝Walkers are not intelligent, and do not think ahead; they walk themselves weary, and develop all manner of ailments in the process. A good walk, you say, is worth them all? Very true."—*Rose Macaulay.*

❝Never did I think so much, exist so much, be myself so much as in the journeys I have made alone and on foot. Walking has something about it which animates and enlivens my ideas. I can hardly think while I am still; my body must be in motion to move my mind."—*Rousseau.*

❝I cannot see the wit of walking and talking at the same time. When I am in the country I wish to vegetate like the country." — *William Hazlitt.*

❝Walking brings out the true character of a man. The devil never yet asked his victims to take a walk with him. You will not be long in finding your companion out. All disguises will fall away from him."—*John Burroughs.*

❝Experience teaches me that whatever a fellow-guest may have of power to instruct or to amuse when he is sitting on a chair, or standing on a hearthrug, quickly leaves him when he takes one out for a walk." —*Max Beerbohm.*

❝I have a remedy which I borrowed of a Scotch professor. He taught me to pour whisky into my socks instead of down my throat, making the foot, shoe, and sock yielding and pliable. I give this as a sovereign preventive of sore feet."—*A. N. Cooper.*

**Compiled by
EDWARD F. MURPHY**

October 16, 1960

The Walk

A man can muster a variety of reasons when he goes for a walk. It's a nice day. He needs the exercise. He hasn't been out in the park, or the fields, or the woods, for quite a while. He wants a breath of fresh air, needs to stretch his legs.

Excuses, all of them, and good enough. But they aren't reasons. The reasons are both personal and complicated. How can you explain that you need to know that the trees are still there, and the hills and the sky? Anyone knows they are. How can you say it is time your pulse responded to another rhythm, the rhythm of the day and the season instead of the hour and the minute? No, you cannot explain. So you walk.

There are the trees, bigger than a man, smaller than a mountain. There are the hills, the enduring hills. There is the sky, where birds fly and white cloud-galleons sail, the vast blue bowl of sky with the certainty of day and night, the infinity of stars.

There is the earth, the sun, the wind—the turning earth, the blazing sun, the restless wind that knows the farthest ocean, the highest hill. You walk, stretch your legs, refresh your lungs. You see and feel and know some of the things a man must know about this deliberately spinning earth where man came to being, where man still lives

October 25, 1967

Legislation to Preserve Amenities

4 TRAILS SOUGHT AS SCENIC AREAS

Report Urges Creation of New National System

By WILLIAM M. BLAIR
Special to The New York Times

WASHINGTON, Jan. 14—The Administration is expected to call on Congress soon to create four national scenic trails as the initial units of a nationwide system of trails for hikers, bicyclists and casual visitors to historic points.

Last year the Administration asked Congress only to designate the Appalachian Trail, from Maine to Georgia, as the first national trail while studies were made on 10 others. Now however, the Administration will seek immediate recognition in a new bill of these trails:

¶The Appalachian Trail, extending 2,000 miles from Mount Katahdin, Me., to Springer Mountain, Ga.

¶Potomac Heritage Trail, 825 miles from the mouth of the Potomac River to its source in Pennsylvania, including the 170-mile Chesapeake and Ohio canal towpath.

¶The Continental Divide Trail, 3,082 miles from the Montana-Canadian border to Glacier National Park, along the Rocky Mountains to Silver City, N.M.

¶The Pacific Crest Trail, 2,300 miles from the Washington-Canadian border down the backbone of the Cascade and Sierra Nevadas to the California-Mexican border.

Easements Necessary

No estimate was available on the cost of these outdoor recreation projects. Parts of nearly all the trails are in Federal or state domain but some rights-of-way or scenic easements would have to be negotiated for private land.

The Bureau of Outdoor Recreation made public today a new report of 155 pages, recommending a system of metropolitan, park and forest and long national scenic trails. It estimated the cost of acquiring private land or easements on private land along the Appalachian Trail at about $4.6-million. New construction and maintenance over a 10-year period, the report estimated, would push the total bill to $9.1-million.

The report, prepared by Interior and Agriculture Department officials, recommended prompt detailed studies on five other major trails, the Lewis and Clark, Oregon, North Country, Natchez Trace and Santa Fe. A number of other proposed trails were deferred for future consideration.

The report stemmed from a request by President Johnson in his natural beauty message to Congress in 1965. It found that the most urgent need was for trails in or near metropolitan areas and suggested that new trails might be constructed on public utility rights-of-way, abandoned railroad lands and along river and canal banks.

"The task of providing adequately for metropolitan trail needs can be handled best through the cooperation and integrated efforts of the various public and private interests involved," the report said.

Some Federal money and other aid is available, it said, adding:

"Major responsibility for planning, acquisition, development and maintenance of metropolitan trail systems, however, properly devolves upon the municipal and county parks departments."

Simple Pleasures

"Walking, hiking and bicycling are simple pleasures within the economic reach of virtually all citizens," the report said. "Horseback riding, even though increasingly expensive for urban dwellers, is available to a large proportion of Americans."

Opportunities to enjoy these "basic activities have become increasingly limited for the American people as the society has urbanized and as economic development has preempted areas which earlier had been devoted to outdoor recreation uses."

Walking, it noted, ranked second only to driving for pleasure among Americans.

In a section on trail needs in the Washington area, the report took up the jet noise from National Airport opposite the capital on the Virginia side of the Potomac. Jet noise, it said, "adversely affects trail use and other outdoor recreation activity in and near the area."

This is especially true along the Chesapeake and Ohio Canal, a favorite walking place for area residents, and the Potomac River, which the jets follow in their approach and departure

FOR A TRAIL UP MOUNT MARCY
Proposition to Build a Bridle Path to Near the Top of the Peak.

ALBANY, Aug. 5.—A committee consisting of Charles Monroe Holt, Chief Forester; Addison W. Baird, Treasurer; Martin Bohler, and Solomon Kelley has undertaken the plan to open up a bridle path and trail to the summit of Mount Marcy, the highest peak in New-York State and the second highest east of the Mississippi, and has asked the assistance of the State Fisheries, Game, and Forest Commissioners in the undertaking.

It is proposed to run this path by the way of John's Brook Valley, from Keene Valley, Essex County. The plan is to extend the bridle path eight miles, and the trail to the summit, two miles, making the entire distance ten miles. There are to be a camp and a stable at the head of the bridle path.

It is the intention of the projectors to open the trail during the present season and to build a good bridle path as fast as the funds will permit. The estimated expense is $250, which it is hoped to raise by subscription. A little State aid would not go amiss, but cannot be secured save by legislative enactment. A few years since the State voted $500 for a trail up Slide Mountain, in the Catskills, and now it is possible to drive to the highest mountain in the Catskills with ease.

The present trail up Mount Marcy, the king of the Adirondack hills, is almost impassable in places. There is a good grade to the top, and an excellent trail could be opened. The surveyors ran the line seven miles to-day.

August 6, 1895

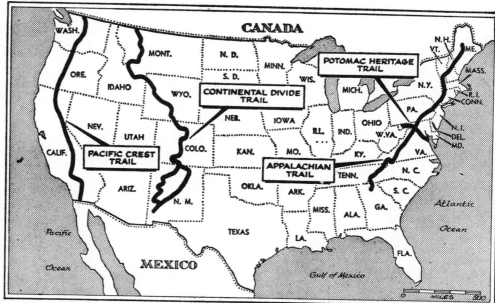

The New York Times   Jan. 15, 1967

PROPOSED NATIONAL TRAILS: Heavy lines show the four national scenic trails that the Johnson Administration is expected to ask the Congress to create this year.

27

from National Airport, the report said. It continued:

"The Federal Aviation Agency should be required to solicit and consider the views of the Secretary of the Interior on effects of proposed changes in the use of National Airport, involving possible increases in frequency of air traffic, increases in noise level and duration and related developments which might adversely affect use and enjoyment of Washington metropolitan area recreation facilities."

This recomendation came only two days after Secretary of the Interior Stewart L. Udall had complained that sonic booms created by military jet aircraft had caused damage in two and possibly three national parks in Western states. The shock waves set up by the sonic boom caused dirt and rock slides, damaging prehistoric cliff dwellings in Arizona, he said.

Mr. Udall also is known to have been disturbed that the Federal Aviation Agency had not consulted with the Interior Department before permitting jets to use National Airport, beginning in April, 1966.

January 15, 1967

4 NEW LAWS ADD TO PUBLIC LANDS

Johnson Signs Bills Making National Parks and Trails

By WILLIAM M. BLAIR
Special to The New York Times

WASHINGTON, Oct. 2—Two new national parks and a system of scenic rivers and trails were added to the nation's outdoor public preserve today.

President Johnson signed four bills to add, as he told witnesses to the ceremony in the East Room of the White House, "still more to the scenic wealth of our country."

The signing raised to an even dozen the number of national parks, national seashores and national lakeshores created in the Kennedy and Johnson Administrations since 1961.

It also marked the passage by Congress this year of more than a dozen major conservation bills. Some of them had long and bitter histories, such as the 58,000 acre Redwood National Park, which was established today.

In addition to the Redwood park, Mr. Johnson approved a North Cascades National Park in the state of Washington, two adjacent recreation areas and an adjacent wilderness area.

This area covers 1.1 million acres in what has been described as the American Alps, close to the populous areas of the Pacific Northwest.

The scenic trails measure provides for a system of urban and rural trails. The first components of the system are the Appalachian Trail in the East and the Pacific Coast Trail in the West.

The legislation also calls for a study of 14 other trails for possible inclusion in the system.

Wild Scenic Rivers System

The first Wild Scenic Rivers System, which also has had a stormy background, provides for preserving all or parts of eight rivers. The aim is to preserve the unspoiled sections.

The measure also names 27 rivers as potential additions to the system.

Mr. Johnson hailed the adoption of the Redwood park as one that "will stand for all time as a monument to the wisdom of our generation." He also said that it would be "remembered as one of the great conservation achievements of the 90th Congress."

However, in an offhand remark, he gave recognition to the hard fact that a long struggle still is ahead to round out the parks and other outdoor preserves. The Redwood park, for example, will not be completed until the process of acquiring private land within the park boundaries and obtaining title to state-owned land, including three state parks is completed.

Looking over a map marked with outdoor areas authorized since 1961, the President asked: "Is there a member of the Appropriations Committee in the House?"

California to Trade

Political consideration also will play a part in the new park. Redwood timber companies will seek to make the best bargain they can under provisions involving the exchange of their holdings for Government-owned land near the park.

California will seek to make the best trades it can because the park bill provides that the Federal Government can acquire only by donation the three state redwood parks within the national park boundaries.

The three state redwood parks are the Jedidiah Smith and Del Norte, which make up the northern unit of the national preserve and Prairie State Park in a southern unit. The two sections are connected by a narrow strip of land along the Pacific Ocean. South of Prairie Creek State Park is still another section of land to be acquired. In this area, along Redwood Creek, are some of the world's tallest trees.

The measure authorizes the appropriation of $92-million from the Land and Water Conservation Fund, a congressionally approved law to help pay for conservation projects.

Congress tapped off-shore oil revenues this session to build up the fund, which has lagged in providing the funds needed for park acquisitions. The fund started with park and other public recreation admission fees and the tax on motorboat fuels.

The $92-million is more than the cost of all the other national parks combined. The Redwood and North Cascades National Parks are the 34th and 35th national parks.

October 3, 1968

ART OF WALKING SAVED BY THE HIKING CLUBS

Their Members Lay Trails and Erect Shelters in Wild Spots That Motor Cars Cannot Reach—Appalachian Club Is Fifty Years Old

By RAYMOND H. TORREY.

THE imminent extermination of the pedestrian by the automobile is one of the stock subjects of the humorist. Many of them seem fo think that the only place where the use of the feet for locomotion is still safe is within doors or perhaps on a golf course. But walking, and for pleasure, is still practiced; in fact, it is increasing. And the automobile has had a direct effect in making it more enjoyable, in that it has driven the pedestrian off the highways to the woodland trails, where the pleasant scents of earth and trees and flowers have no competition from gasoline exhaust.

Take any suburban train on Sunday mornings, or on holidays, and you will find a considerable proportion of the passengers made up of men and women, boys and girls in hiking clothes. Some of them may be veterans, whose worn but sturdy outdoor clothes show a briar-rent or spot of camp-fire grease, and whose knapsacks have long ago lost all newness. Others may be beginners, such as the girls who combine their brothers' olive-drab breeches with high-heeled thin soled shoes—but they have the idea, and if they keep on they will learn to don shoes that will stand rocks and mud and swamps.

The hikers will include lone individuals who prefer to tramp by themselves; small parties, a man and wife or two or three men or women; and large groups of a dozen or more, sometimes as many as fifty on a fine Spring or Autumn day. In the Winter accoutrements will include snowshoes and skis. There may be a group going out for a day of volunteer trail-making in Harriman Park armed with hatchets and huge pruning shears and a load of metal markers.

Build Trails and Shelters.

These larger groups are the walking clubs, which have developed to such extent that their activities constitute an important outlet to the need for outdoor recreaion. They have grown up with little coddling, without stimulus or support from any philanthropic agencies, simply by cooperation for mutual interests. Some of them do a great deal for the public in general in the way of providing trail and shelter facilities, issuing guidebooks and in other ways making the woodlands, to which the pedestrian is now driven by the motor car, more accessible and less fearsome to the beginner.

Almost all of these clubs centre in large cities. Their members include many who were born in the country, came to the city to work, and, as soon as they could, established relations with groups that would take them back into the fields and woods for holidays. Not all are country folk by birth. Many of them were born and have always lived in cities, and among such are large numbers of persons, mostly young, of our recent immigrant stocks. There is no better way of Americanizing them, and it is interesting to see how quickly they adopt the ways and the equipment of Americans of older stocks, whose great-grandfathers did their hiking as pioneers—through hostile Indian territory.

Some of the clubs are now past their first half century in age; others may not be a year old; new groups are formed every Spring and may last only for the season, or be merged in others or renewed when the open weather comes around again. The more stable groups are not governed by the seasons. Their program lasts all the year, except for a recess in July and August when their members take heavy packs for long hikes in the Adirondacks. Their best months are those of frosty weather and snow, when the Winter winds feel cold and clean on one's face and the Autumn haze goes out of the sky and one can see the Catskills, blue in the north, from any of the tops of the Hudson Highlands.

Boston's Famous Club.

Boston and New York were the earliest centres for the establishment of these outdoor clubs. The Appalachian Mountain Club of Boston celebrated its fiftieth anniversary last Fall. It has a splendid history of service, not only to its 3,500 members but to the public at large. It now has spacious headquarters in Joy Street, just off Beacon, where it maintains a library of outdoor literature. It has made and maintains over 300 miles of trails, with huts and shelters, for the public in the White Mountains of New Hampshire. It is chartered by three States—Massachusetts, New Hampshire and Maine—to hold areas of scenic or scientific interest as public preserves, received by gift, and so holds in trust fifteen such areas. Its guidebook of the White Mountains is a model of its kind and the demand for it and the frequent improvements in the trail and shelter system require almost yearly revisions.

The New York section of the Appalachian Mountain Club, which has been in existence for fifteen years, unites over 300 members living in New York and vicinity for the purpose of Saturday and Sunday walks, holiday week-end excursions and social affairs. Its outdoor territory covers a circle a hundred miles about New York. It also maintains a Summer camp on the south shore of Long Island.

The oldest walking group in New York is the Fresh Air Club, now in its fifty-second year. It prides itself on its "hard boiled" character and its wide knowledge of the region about the city, to many points of which it has given whimsical names based on amusing incidents of hikes, or in some

cases as memorials to deceased members. Its membership includes men of diverse character, business standing and wealth, all united in their outdoor pursuits. One of its memories is of the death of two members, Ormsbee and "Father Bill" Curtis, in a July snowstorm on the summit of Mount Washington. In memory of them, the club built, for the use of all climbers, a new trail up Slide Mountain, in the Catskills, the beginning of which was marked by a monument erected by former Supreme Court Justice Harrington Putnam of Brooklyn, one of the earliest members and still active.

The Long Trail.

Another group past the half century mark in age, which devotes its walks, long or short, to a definite scientific pursuit, is the Torrey Botanical Club, established in 1870, and named for John Torrey then Professor of Botany at Columbia University. Its program includes Saturday and Sunday walks for the study of some phase of botany, under the guidance of experts, and longer trips to regions of particular interest between April and October. It also conducts bi-monthly trips for Winter botanizing in the other months.

A club of recent origin, which has already given large service to its members and to the public, is the Green Mountain Club. It was organized about fifteen years ago to promote the development of the Long Trail, a hikers path over the Vermont ranges, and to equip it with shelters for overnight use. The Long Trail now extends from the Massachusetts boundary, near North Adams, 250 miles north to Jay Peak, from which one can look down upon Quebec, to the boundary of which the trail will eventually be carried. More than thirty shelters have been built, some by gift funds, some out of club dues, along the trail, often at altitudes above 3,000 feet. A commodious clubhouse was built for the organization by its President, Mortimer R. Proctor, in Sherburne Pass, between Rutland and Woodstock, and another overnight stop on the trail is the hotel on Mount Mansfield.

Of the total membership of about 1,200, the New York section comprises about 350. In addition to its support of the Long Trail it maintains varied activities in the vicinity of New York, including Saturday and Sunday hikes, week-end excursions, nature guidance outings, lectures and social affairs. It leases a Winter and Summer camp on one of the highest points of the Harriman section of the Palisades Interstate Park. The organization of this group was due to Dr. Will S. Monroe, formerly a teacher in Montclair (N. J.) Normal School. He is now living on a farm he has purchased under the east foot of Couching Lion,

as he is trying to make Vermonters call what they persist in naming Camel's Hump.

Adirondack Facilities.

Dr. Monroe contends that Samuel de Champlain called it Couching Lion in 1602. He manages the yearly clearing and improvement of the Monroe section of the Long Trail, from Bolton to the Lincoln-Warren Pass, forty miles, with funds provided by the New York section, and it is the model section of the trail. To his interest in natural science was due the establishment of special walks and meetings called "nature guidance outings." These have proved popular and now centre about Dr. Monroe's old camp, Wyanokie Lodge, in Northern Passaic County, N. J.

A still newer club, modeled after the Appalachian and Green Mountain Clubs, with a general sphere of work supplemented by outings near New York, is the Adirondack Mountain Club, organized three years ago to cooperate with the State Conservation Commission and other agencies in adding to the trail and shelter facilities in the Adirondacks. It has built a through trail, 135 miles long, from Northville to Lake Placid, with half a dozen log shelters, the gift of George D. Pratt, former Conservation Commissioner and now honorary President of the club. Mr. Pratt also financed the erection of a commodious camp, on property given to the club by a lumber company on John's Brook, on the trail from Keene Valley to Mount Marcy. The club proposes soon to add to its Adirondack facilities a centre for climbers near Elk Lake.

Women's and Young People's Clubs.

The club has an active New York chapter of more than 300 members; it offers Saturday and Sunday and holiday outings like the others and has leased for the past two Winters a camp on Upper Twin Lake in Harriman Park, from which it will move this Spring into a new camp constructed by the Commissioners of the Palisades Interstate Park on the large new Lake Sebago, recently constructed by damming Stony Brook in the Ramapo section of the park.

An outdoor group that is limited to women as members, but includes men as guests on its outings, is the Inkowa Club of New York, organized eight years ago, largely through the interest of Mrs. E. H. Harriman, Miss Anne Morgan, Mrs. Daniel Guggenheim and others. It has a city house at Spuyten Duyvil and a country house on Greenwood Lake. Its national organization, the Inkowa Club of America, is now open to both men and women, and a membership of 1,500 is sought to make it possible to keep the Greenwood Lake house open all the year.

Some of the other groups in and about New York are the New York Ramblers, a club of young people of both sexes who are more recent adventurers into our near-by wilds; the New York Hiking Club, of similar character; the Shore and Mountain Club, which has not yet admitted women, because it wants to keep its walks long and hard—although there are some women hikers who could outlast men; the Paterson Ramblers, who devote much attention to Indian relics and botany; the Westchester Trails Association, an outgrowth of the work of the Westchester County Recreation Commission, and the Staten Island Bird Club, connected with the public museum in that borough.

Field excursions for the study of different forms of outdoor science are in the programs of the educational departments of the city's museums. City College has a geology group that hikes under the leadership of Professor B. T. Butler. The New York-New Jersey Trail Conference draws volunteers from many groups to work on the trails in the Harriman section of the Interstate Park.

Every Spring one hears of some new group being organized to promote hiking programs. It is simple enough, if one can find volunteer officers who will give time to the routine and good hike leaders who will make up interesting schedules. Dues of a dollar upward support the scheme. In the groups like the Green Mountain and Adirondack Mountain Clubs the camping feature has been made successful by having volunteer hosts, usually a married couple, who manage and chaperon the house parties. The tendency in all the well-established outdoor clubs is to increase the variety of services offered, and an immense amount of unselfish and capable volunteer work is given.

Where Motors Can't Follow.

Similar outdoor groups can be found in many large American cities. Chicago has its Prairie Club, with walking parties so large that they require a special train and three country camps; Minneapolis has a large hiking club fostered by the city Park Department; Cleveland, Omaha and Kansas City have such groups. The Rocky Mountain Club of Denver has a fine record of alpinism; the Wasatch Hiking Club of Salt Lake City includes a basketball and bowling team in addition to its outdoor program.

So the hiking club appears to have come to stay and its members expect to keep the use of their legs and not to allow them to become atrophied because of the automobile; they know where they can escape to woods and swamps and ledges and hilltops where the gas buggy can't follow—not even

a Ford. Such refuges for the pedestrian can be found in places an hour or so out by rail, where one can climb a hill and see the towers of Manhattan shining thirty to forty miles away. Hiking is increasing—and there is no end of wild places left within a hundred miles of New York if one leaves the roads and adventures a little.

April 25, 1926

WALKING CLUBS.

The American hiker was a lonely figure until walking clubs were organized, and that did not occur before large tracts of mountain and forest land invited exploration. New England, with its White Mountains, Green Mountains and the Katahdin region, excluded no one from its beauties by trespass signs. As a matter of fact, the New England farmer was hospitable to the sojourner who invaded his woodlots and rock pastures. Most people are not like HAZLITT and ROUSSEAU, who preferred solitary walking to company on the path. Companionship is as necessary to many roamers as fresh air and a trail to follow. As ERNEST A. DENCH says in the June Nature Magazine, hiking has become a national pastime. In recent years walking clubs have sprung up everywhere, as he points out. The growing interest in them can be accounted for by the opening of more and more national and State parks or reservations. This is especially so in the South, where within a few years the Great Smoky Mountains Park, of almost 500,000 acres, was set aside for recreation.

The distinction of being the pioneer outdoor organization is claimed by the Appalachian Mountain Club of Boston, which was formed in 1876. It has been a true leader in blazing the way for the health-giving exercise, for its own sake and to cultivate a love of nature. One year later was incorporated the Fresh Air Club of New York, whose playground has always been the Highlands of the Hudson and the Ramapos. The Paterson Rambling Club has hiked for thirty years in the hill and forest country along the New Jersey-New York boundary. One of the most stalwart groups of walkers is the Green Mountain Club of Vermont, to which thousands of vacationists owe the pleasures of the Green Mountain Trail from Jay Peak, near the Canadian line, to the highlands of Northern Massachusetts. Together with a trail from Katahdin, it is to be extended through the Appalachians to the Great Smokies. Chicago has its Prairie Club, Minneapolis its Minnehikers, while Cincinnati, Cleveland, Omaha, Milwaukee, Indianapolis and Pacific Coast cities are also on the list.

May 22, 1934

New York Walk Book

NEAR AND FAR WALKS.

The more intimate and alluring service of geography, which is popularly supposed to have only a scientific and impersonal interest, is illustrated in the little book just published by the American Geographical Society (at Broadway and 156th Street, New York). It is called the " New York Walk Book " and gives inviting information not only concerning trails and paths and scenery amid the enchanting environs of New York City for the "country-footed," but also concerning urban shrines for the feet of urban pilgrims. It has been compiled and composed by men who are practiced out-of-doors men, rugged men in whom the artist tents with the scientist—" saunterers " in the etymology which THOREAU gave to the word, going afoot à la sainte terre, inhabitants of L. H. BAILEY'S " holy earth."

It is a book that should be in the hands of thousands of New Yorkers, as a light unto their feet, whether they walk in the " steep-walled canyons of finance " or seek the "sweetness of the " tops of old mountains or the dainties " of the hills that last forever," or try to find the by-paths and trails beyond the reach of the honking motor car, the sputtering motorcycle, or even the stealthy bicycle. There are maps and carefully prepared notes to give accurate guidance for excursions afoot within a radius of fifty or a hundred miles of the city, including Westchester County, the Highlands of the Hudson and the Ramapos, Northern and Central New Jersey and the New Jersey pine barrens, Long Island, the Shawangunk Range, the Catskills and the Taconics. As a centre of exercise on foot, New York City may claim (upon the authority of the learned Geographical Society, which knows the whole earth and the fullness thereof) " variety and " advantage and adventure surpassed by " few cities." Nothing like this little book, which also contains valuable local historical and geological information, " has appeared in the world before," says the Director, Dr. BOWMAN.

Moreover, through the vistas of these nearer trails, one catches glimpses of " The Long Trail," which is now projected the length of the Appalachian Range from Maine down to Georgia. It is to be hoped that the Geographical Society will some day lead on with like handbooks the feet of many that have become inured to the nearer trails and teach the enchanting geography of America to increasing numbers. HENRY JAMES, in one of his delightfully interminable sentences, describes some of the scenery along that trail: " A cluster of promon- " tories, or the lost classic elegance, over- " hanging vast, receding reaches of river, " mountain-guarded and dim, which take " their place in the geography of the " ideal, in the long perspective of the " poetry of association, rather than in " those of the State of New York."

This scene is, after all, in the geography of the real, even if it had come to seem to him in the distance as a landscape of the ideal. The American Geographical Society can give no better service, in the midst of all its scientific researches, than to help Americans to become acquainted at first hand and as far as possible on foot with the land they live in, from Maine, girded by " bays resplendent, starred and gemmed by a thousand isles," to the " gilded portal " on the western coast " for sailing toward the Island of the Blest."

November 18, 1923

Topics of The Times

Book of Walkers

The third edition of the "New York Walk Book" appears at a time when there are more than forty million automobiles in America. When the first edition was published back in 1923 there were only fifteen million cars. There are now so many cars that every man, woman and child in the country could go out motoring this week-end. It is surprising, therefore, that there is any need for a "Walk Book," for it means that there must be some walkers left. Many walkers, it is true, have joined the ranks of the riders, and a good many who persisted in walking have been maimed or otherwise removed from the highways. Judging solely by the "Walk Book," one would say that the number of walkers abroad in the land had actually increased, for this third edition has been expanded and refined over the first edition. It is a handsome volume of more than 300 pages, with new maps, more of the excellent drawings of the original edition, and an exhaustive commentary on all the interesting country around New York.

Walkers and Riders

About the time that the original "Walk Book" was published there was a tendency among the walkers to look scornfully upon the riders, to set apart the walkers from the riders, like the sheep from the goats. Many of the walkers of that period have grown older and perhaps wiser, for they have long since joined the riders with a particular affinity for big handsome cars. They travel on white-wall tires instead of worn boots, and use the parkways rather than the back roads. And most walking itself has changed during the same period. Walking is now "organized"; it is done by groups rather than by individuals or pairs. Trips have to be carefully planned in advance and led by guides who know the country to be traversed. Walking as practiced by such famous walkers as Thoreau, Emerson, Wordsworth and Hazlitt is pretty much out for dwellers in this thickly populated area. Far out in the country such superior walkers may still be found, and it is to them that we shall have to look for the last word on walking.

Henry Versus Henry

The ideal of Henry Ford, that every American family should have a means of convenient, cheap and swift locomotion, has been fulfilled, with the elimination of the factor of cheapness. At the opposite side of the American scheme of things one might place Henry Thoreau, who would dispense with all such gadgets as motor cars and cultivate the spirit with cultivating the bean patch. Henry Ford's idea has now swept the country, but Henry Thoreau's idea also persists in deep American undercurrents. It may be seen in this "Walk Book," which assumes no sentimental interest in nature but suggests a sturdy approach and a willingness to undergo hardship in order to arrive at the heart of things.

It is for this reason that the "Walk Book" is such an excellent guide to all the regions around New York. No automobile guide would attempt to do what the walking guide does and no general guide would receive so much care from so many hands. It all goes to show that really to know the country one has to. get very close to it. The "Walk Book" knows old roads and abandoned roads that lead to long-forgotten places of interest with odd bits of history attached to them. Its maps reverse the accepted order of things by showing the trails in broad red lines, like the through roads on automobile maps.

Stars mark the best views, not the larger towns, along the route. Contours are important, too. Hills, valleys, streams and springs recover the significance they had for the first settlers in these parts. To arrive at the real America one has to go back to the days before the motor age, for the motor car has not only changed ways of living but also the very appearance of the country, which is scarcely seen as it really is as one speeds along a modern highway in a motor car.

The "Walk Book" also recalls one fact worth recording in world history—namely, that never before has a great city and a host of satellite towns appeared on the map in such varied and interesting terrain. Great cities usually spread out over level plains—like London, Paris, Berlin and Chicago. New York leaps great rivers and bays to reach out into what was and still is very rugged country. A good part of the near-by country has never been tamed. From the top of Bear Mountain, forty miles up the Hudson, you can see the towers of Manhattan. No foot-slogger is going to climb Bear Mountain just to look at the towers of Manhattan, but that view does reveal this strange phenomenon—millions of people living between lofty towers and virgin hills.

June 3, 1951

GUIDE FOR HIKERS IN THE EMPIRE STATE

By CHARLES POORE

ANYONE who likes to dance, and knows how to do so—these are not necessarily clashing ideas—can enjoy the holiday pleasures lavishly set out in the "New York Walk Book," (American Geographical Society, $3.50) a remarkably appealing guide to a thousand trails in the plains and valleys and hills beyond Manhattan's windowed mountain ranges.

For there is not much in the way of walking that is more strenuous than modern dancing. Indeed, walking along the Palisades or on the shores of Long Island or what the bandanna-size map at the end of the guide majestically calls "Bear Mountain and Adjacent Areas," may be a shade the easier sport, since you can wear sensible shoes, as comfortable as old cliches.

You can sit right down when you get tired without having to fight your way through thickets of malevolent elbows. You can breathe rich, authentic air. And your rations will not only be more nourishing than the memorabilia you find on night club plates but identifiable at a glance, like as not.

There are thoughtful authorities who hold that a man or a girl who has survived the rugged rigors of a New York night club dance floor can outpace the hardiest mountaineer on the rockiest stretch of the Appalachian Trail with laughable ease.

This, of course, is an undersimplification. You must never forget that the true walker also likes to intimate that he has Been Through a Lot when he comes back after a day's or a week's horizontal and perpendicular strolling. He may merely have been on safari through the city's peculiarly varied parks, or he may have spent a couple of nights on the cold, Torquemada grills of Appalachian Trail shelters. In either case, you must humor him. You must soothingly agree that he probably has the biggest blister on his right toe since Bikini. If he claims he saw a cougar in the Ramapos, the least you can do is to suggest, alternatively, that it was a wild Jersey leopard searching hungrily for its young.

Stopping Dodges

And when he wrathfully denounces the scandalous conservatism of the guide's mileage estimates, all you can do is play variations on the word Amen. "Look at this!" he will say. "Look at this! The 'New York Walk Book' claims it's only seven miles from the place where I got off the train to the top of this ridge. Why, it's three times as far, if it's an inch. I'll bet I covered forty miles today."

Later on, after he has had a bath and meditated and been medicated with martini, he will tell you about the magnificent views he saw, and the colors of the wildflowers along the way, and the earlier drink from a brook, and deer he heard crashing through the trees, and the waterfall, and the poison ivy patch, berries he wanted to eat but wasn't quite sure whether they were poisonous, and the lost pond where he'd like to build a house some day.

First, however, you'd better resign yourself to hearing a brisk speech on what liars contour lines

on maps are. He's absolutely right, too. The poets and dreamers of the American Geographical Society who made these maps may think that they have done their duty when they have made one squiggly little brown line and marked it 600 feet and put another right on top of it marked 700 feet, and so on.

But have they in any slightest degree begun to indicate what it means to a human being, to the human spirit, to human fortitude and endurance, to the flesh and sinew and pounding heart of a man, to climb up those lines? Certainly not! You try climbing Jug End Mountain in southern Massachusetts on a fair summer's day (Yes, Jug End is in the "New York Guide"; we're not called the Empire State for nothing) and you'll say a thousand bahs to the sheltered cartographers and their bottles of brown ink and their contour lines. The view from the top is worth it though. After that, of course, you are honor bound to go on and climb Mount Everett and Mount Race.

Roaming in Prospect Park

In a less extravagantly virile mood, it is more appropriate to pick out some of the less stupendous trails offered in the guide. You can start with a cheerfully amphibious operation in Prospect Park, say, where, soon after you pass through Battle Pass, the Zoo

and the Lefferts Homestead, the book suggests that "to the right ¼ mile is the winding narrow section of the lake on which rowboats can be hired or a launch ride taken for a two-mile circuit."

Or take the Independent subway to 190th Street and explore Jeffrey's Hook near the base of the George Washington Bridge, or go over to Staten Island, or up into Westchester. You'll soon find that there are all sorts of trails where you least expected to find them— or, shall we say, to find yourself looking for them?

Always remember, though, that the guide has packed the wisdom of the walking ages into one magnificently gnomic observation. "As soon as any uphill work has to be done, the speed of walking falls off rapidly." And just how swiftly walking gets slower under those circumstances every walker knows.

But protocol and etiquette require you to observe certain formalities when you are thoroughly winded and want to stop but don't like to say so bluntly. "What a superb panorama!" will do, if there's anything that can possibly pass for a view in sight, as you pause and glance keenly at the horizon. If there's no view whatsoever, you'll just have to say, "I wonder where I put that notebook I meant to bring along," or stoop and tie your shoelace, or say: "I'm

tired" and sit down. After all, that's one of the purposes of walking.

"The walker," the guide says, "should plan his trips sitting at home in his armchair with maps and guide at hand." He can, thus, decide whether he has time to take a train to the starting point of his walking trip, or whether he'd better drive up; how much time to allow, what food to take along, what flowers and trees and historic sites to observe, and so forth.

Updegraff's Law

As a matter of fact, one of the best ways to use the guide is to follow what is known in walking circles as Updegraff's Law, which states that the best walks are those that are never taken, and was named by an early Times Square settler who read guides all day long and never stirred out of his armchair.

The "New York Walk Book" is excellently suited to that. It is full of wonderful historic lore, so that you get a full education on the region around New York as you read. It identifies all the flora and fauna far better than anyone else could do it this side of Brooks Atkinson or John Kieran. Best of all, it gives you a chance to rest up in case you might want to go for a spot of really strenuous dancing that evening.

July 15, 1951

President Kennedy and the 50-Mile Walk

50-Mile Marine Hike Revived by Old Order

WASHINGTON, Feb. 5 (AP) — At President's Kennedy's suggestion, 20 Marine officers will attempt a 50-mile hike next week.

The exercise, to be conducted at Camp Lejune, N.C., was suggested by the recent discovery of a long-forgotten Executive Order.

Gen. David M. Shoup, the Marine Commandant, sent the 54-year-old document to Mr. Kennedy. The President responded with a proposal that General Shoup find out "how well our present-day officers perform the test."

At least 10 captains and 10 lieutenants, selected to provide a sample of personnel, will take this test: walk 50 miles within three days (some officers of 1908 covered the course in a day). Upon reaching the final half-mile, the officers must double-time 200 yards, rest 30 seconds; double-time for 300 yards, rest a minute, and sprint 200 yards to the finish line.

February 6, 1963

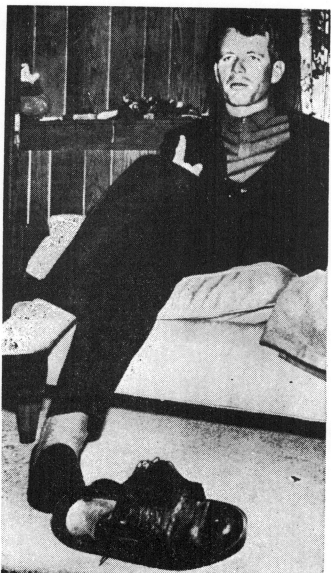

United Press International Telephoto

JOURNEY'S END: Shoes that Attorney General Robert F. Kennedy wore on 50-mile hike Saturday lie on floor as he relaxes in loafers at Camp David, Md. He walked from Washington to Camp David in 17 hours, three hours less than the standard suggested recently by President Kennedy, as an ideal test for military personnel.

February 11, 1963

In The Nation

Earlier Links Between Presidents and Hiking

By ARTHUR KROCK

WASHINGTON, Feb. 11—By one of those mysterious workings of chance that are epitomized by the word "fortuitous," the 1963 celebration of the birth date of Abraham Lincoln coincides with a fad started by his current successor that was American daily routine in Lincoln's time. And of all the Presidents, his practice of this routine was perhaps the most indicative of his possession of one of the qualities which a President must demonstrate to become established in history, not only as a "great" man, but as a man of character.

The current craze which seems to be spreading out of Washington into the rest of the nation on this Lincoln's birthday is, of course, hiking. As on numerous prior occasions, this fad was created by a passing remark of the President in office.

Someone reminded Mr. Kennedy of Theodore Roosevelt's 1908 executive order to test whether U.S. Marine Corps officers could prove, by marching 50 miles in 20 hours, that they were in the state of fitness he thought they should be. Mr. Kennedy repeated this in words viewed as a challenge by the Marines in particular and as a stunt by people in general. And this evoked a response far more tangible than the President's previous organized and frequently-articulated public fitness program.

Roads Are Crowded

Onto the roads of Maryland,

Virginia, Nebraska, California, Kentucky, South Carolina and who knows where else, there immediately swarmed an assorted collection of members of the armed forces, Federal officials bursting to prove their devotion to their chief, and fad-prone citizens (who are as countless as the sands of the sea). Mr. and Mrs. Kennedy last night walked a couple of hundred yards they usually cover by motor in their journeys from Washington airports to the White House. It was first-page news this morning. And the hike of his brother, the Attorney General, over the 50 miles T. R. prescribed for the Marines was a much-more publicized Federal case than the one the A. G. argued before the Supreme Court, though this was his first appearance as a trial lawyer.

The late Dr. John H. Finley, once the editor of The New York Times, hiked annually around Manhattan Island. Ambassador Keith Officer of Australia, when he was No. 2 in his country's embassy here, frequently walked the 45 miles between his house in Georgetown and a Sunday luncheon-table near Middleburg, Va. To these the publicity now being given to hiking would have been disturbing, more, however, as a suggestion of the scope of the sheep-type mentality in the United States than as an indication that the ability to take a long hike is abnormal among its citizens.

But if, by some means beyond the comprehension of the finite man, consciousness of the present can be communicated to the past, the shade in our national Pantheon that is most disturbed by the publicity of the current fad must be Lincoln's. His neighbors in Indiana and Illinois well recalled "he used to trudge miles to borrow a book." As a boy he walked eight miles daily, for months, back and forth to school in Spencer County, Ind. During the winter of 1830-1831 he covered six miles a day to cut rails for a Major Warnick.

12 Miles for Book

The next winter, when Lincoln was 23, in pursuance of his ambition to learn grammar, he walked the round-trip of 12 miles to borrow a copy of Kirkham's treatise on this subject and return it the same day.

The young Captain Lincoln may have soldiered on horseback part of the time during the Black Hawk War. But the marching span of his troop ranged from 20 to 25 miles every day in May, 1832. And when Lincoln was mustered out, after having "fit, bled and come away," he covered on foot most of the 200 miles between Dixon's Ferry, Ill., and his home near Peoria. In March, 1837, on the adjournment at Vandalia of the Illinois Legislature to which he had been elected, his horse having been stolen, the country Jake whose life and presidency the nation and the world again will honor with reverence tomorrow, hiked the 100 miles back home to New Salem, attended by jeers from the town smartalecks at the dust-covered, gangling, six-foot seven, gaunt traveler with the skinny neck and the uncomely face.

The concurrence of this year's Lincoln's birthday with the hiking fad inspired by Mr. Kennedy, also evokes the thought that Presidential preaching apparently must be joined to active practice to start a silly season of national emulation. This is probably why the American people never took for their athletic example President Truman's brisk, long walks every morning.

February 12, 1963

United Press International Telephoto

EVERYBODY'S DOING IT. Bamboo cane in hand, Brig. Gen. R. McC. Tompkins steps out ahead of 31 Marine officers on a 50-mile march about sprawling Camp Lejeune, N.C. He's assistant commander of the 2d Marine Division.

February 13, 1963

GENERAL PLACES 9TH IN HIKE OF 50 MILES

CAMP LEJEUNE, N.C., Feb. 13 (AP) — President Kennedy had his answer today. From the general on down, the Marines are physically fit.

They laughed when Brig. Gen. Rathvlyn McClure Thompkins, carrying a walking stick, set off to prove that he, too, could trudge 50 miles.

But the laugh soon faded.

General Thompkins began walking at 8 A.M. yesterday and strutted across the finish line at 2:02 A.M. today.

WASRINGTON, Feb. 13 (AP) —President Kennedy, who started the current hiking fad, received today a special "50-miler Award" from the Boy Scouts of America. The award is to be passed on to his younger brother, Robert, the family's current hiking champion.

The delegation of 12 scouts who called on Mr. Kennedy also left some manuals on how to win hiking merit badges. There was a special copy for Pierre Salinger, the press secretary, who decided yesterday it would not be healthy for him to lead White House workers on a long walk.

February 14, 1963

Washington

Drinkers of the World, Unite!

By JAMES RESTON

WASHINGTON, Feb. 14 — President Kennedy is a puzzle. One day he pleads with the country to sacrifice, and the next he pleads with it to accept a tax cut. One day he venerates brains, and the next he tries to popularize walking.

Trying to popularize walking in America is like trying to popularize prohibition in Kentucky. Asking a citizen to walk instead of ride in America is like asking a Frenchman to drink milk instead of wine. And the last French premier who did *that*, Pierre Mendes France, was booted out of office.

President Kennedy himself is a living symbol of the dangers of exercise. So long as he concentrated on history, literature and politics, he was all right. But the minute he picked up a spade and started digging a hole for that Arbor Day tree in Canada, his back buckled and he's been a rocking-chair case ever since.

Now the poor man is on doctor's order not to pick up his own son or play golf, and he's complaining. Actually, if he were wise, he would be grateful. President Eisenhower's problem was that he was a golfer, and it stands to reason that no man can endure the agonies of both the Presidency and golf, especially when he's a lousy putter.

There are great advantages to the sedentary life, particularly around the White House. President Franklin D. Roosevelt survived and succeeded in office at least partly because he was a victim of polio. He wasn't always mounting horses or airplanes or promoting 50-mile hikes. He had to sit still and think, and he survived four Presidential elections and lived 63 years 72 days, whereas Theodore Roosevelt, the champion of the strenuous life, only got through one and a half terms and died at 60.

Prime Examples

This is very dubious advice, living on Metrecal and hiking for publicity into the Blue Ridge mountains. Look at President Taft. When they sprung him from Yale in the class of 1878, the average weight of his classmates was 151 pounds. Taft weighed in on graduation day at 225 and kept going up from there to around 300. Meanwhile, he endured long sentences in the War Department, the Philippines, Cuba, the Presidency, the Yale Law School and the Supreme Court before he finally died here in Washington at the age of 72.

In contrast, Calvin Coolidge, that skinny symbol of austerity, died at 60, probably because, after he left the White House, he took up the reckless and strenuous craft of writing a newspaper column.

The political implications of this walking binge could be even more serious than the physical. President Kennedy survived the anti-Catholic vote in the election of 1960, but the anti-walking vote in America is infinitely larger.

For example, as soon as the President started urging people to take to the hills, an anti-exercise organization in Washington, previously partial to President Kennedy, held an emergency protest meeting here in Hall's saloon.

The name of the organization is "Athletics Anonymous." It is composed of men who have previously suffered from exercise, most of them heart cases, and it works roughly on the same principle as "Alcoholics Anonymous." Only in "Athletics Anonymous," when a member hears about somebody who begins to get a compulsion to walk or ride a horse, or run around the Lincoln Memorial, he goes to the poor fellow, puts a drink in his hand and talks him into staying home.

Bobby's the Villain

Bobby Kennedy, of course, is the villain of this whole silly business. Bobby is an athletic delinquent. He bats his kids over volley-ball nets from birth just to toughen them up, and it was no surprise that he was the first New Frontiersman to hike the 50 miles.

He should study the life of Winston Churchill, the greatest man of the age. Winnie trifled with exercise in Africa during his youth and later built brick walls, but later he reformed and most of the time thereafter preferred smoking and drinking to hiking.

What this capital needs is not the 50-mile hike but the 50-minute "think." It could easily be arranged. The National Security Council, for example, could have been summoned to think for 50 minutes before sending out that rocket at Canada the other day.

Even Theodore Roosevelt, who is being blamed for the official hiking craze, wasn't all "Rough Rider." He made his daughter Alice learn something new out of a book every night before she went to bed, and tell him what it was at breakfast every morning, no matter how late she was out the night before. The device worked too. She has been following his advice ever since, and bless her, she was 79 this week.

February 15, 1963

Random Notes in Washington: Anyone for Not Taking a Walk?

Special to The New York Times.

WASHINGTON, Feb. 17 — This was hiking week in Washington.

Attorney General Robert F. Kennedy walked 50 miles, dropping his assistants behind him.

Defense Secretary Robert S. McNamara's immediate staff went on a 20-mile hike today.

Five secretaries on Capitol Hill walked 33 miles for the honor of Congress — they said.

If all this becomes a competition between the branches of Government, the Supreme Court could be a surprise winner. It has some of the healthiest hikers in town.

Justice William O. Douglas is a well-known climber of mountains. Chief Justice Earl Warren and Justice Tom Clark often walk several miles to work, and the newest member of the court, Arthur J. Goldberg, has taken to joining them. Byron R. White, a one-time all-American is still in good shape. And William J. Brennan Jr. walks four to six miles every day before breakfast.

And here's a note for Pierre Salinger, the White House press secretary who gave up his hike: the Supreme Court's press officer, Banning E. Whittington, walked 18 miles last Sunday just for fun.

*

Cloak of Secrecy

Even President Kennedy did a little walking last week.

After a reception for civil rights leaders he and Mrs. Kennedy took a stroll outside the White House grounds, right on the public sidewalk. A Secret Service car trailed discreetly behind.

The couple passed a number of Washington pedestrians, but no one seemed to recognize them. Which probably shows again that you don't see what you're not looking for.

February 18, 1963

GOVERNOR IN STEP: Gov. Grant Sawyer of Nevada hits the road on a 25-mile hike from Carson City. It is one of many long walks occasioned by the President's fitness program. At the right is Mrs. Lucille Redd, of Salt Lake City, Utah, member of the Democratic National Committee.

Science

'Physically Fit' — but for What?

By HOWARD A. RUSK, M.D.
NEW YORK.

A few weeks ago President Kennedy called attention to a directive issued by President Theodore Roosevelt that Marines should be able to march 50 miles in three days, spending no more than 20 hours on their feet.

In citing this order, President Kennedy unwittingly touched off the biggest craze in hiking since Cold Cash Pyle sponsored his coast to coast Bunion Derby in the 20's.

During the last few weeks the Fifty Mile Madness has joined the ranks of swallowing goldfish, the hula hoop, and other national crazes.

Supposedly all this nonsense is an indication of the physical fitness and the health of the hikers. But during this hullabaloo, we have failed to define physical fitness or ask ourselves the question—physically fit for what?

Physical fitness has always ranked along with happiness, security and success as one of the major objectives of life that most people desire.

But like its companion goals, physical fitness itself is a vague term that lacks definition and concrete standards.

Physical fitness advocates imply that there is a strong correlation between a high degree of physical or muscular fitness and health, social success and ability to work. The facts, however, do not bear this out.

Draft Rejection Figures

Draft rejection figures are frequently cited as a strong indication that too many of our young men are not physically fit. This is misleading.

First, draft rejection figures include rejections based on mental ability, educational attainment and psychological and social adjustment as well as physical health.

Acceptance or rejection by the draft may indicate the presence or absence of some pathological process or chronic disability, but it does not mean an individual is either "healthy" or "unhealthy" or "physically fit"

Story About Walking

The walking craze that has seized some fitness-minded occupants of the Whhte House draws only mild contempt from Vermont's rugged senior Senator George Aiken.

He told his Senate colleagues last week about two Vermont cows, Alice and Tomboy by name, who some years ago walked the 1,200 miles from Brandon, Vt., to St. Louis, Mo., in 90 days. Of course, he added, that averaged to only about 13 miles a day, but along with the walking the cows gave an average of 40 pounds of milk a day, too.

"If it were not for that," Farmer Aiken said, "I would be tempted to challenge— on behalf of the Vermont cows—the Write House staff to a walk of any distance of two miles or more.

"But inasmuch as the production of 40 pounds of milk daily would present an insurmountable obstacle to the White House staff, I shall forego issuing the challenge at this time.."

February 25, 1963

or "physically unfit" except within the specific context of military service.

Failure of American school children to achieve as good scores as European and Japanese children on certain physical performance tests has also been frequently cited as evidence that our children are below par in physical fitness and health.

But as Dr. Ernest Jokl, University of Kentucky, has said, "Few erroneous ideas are so deeply rooted among the public as that of physical training to promote health. Physical training is a procedure capable of improving efficiency, but incapable of improving health."

Dr. Peter Karpovich, Springfield College, who is one of our leading authorities in the physiology of exercises, has commented: "There are two main stumbling blocks to the definition of physical fitness; one, the relation of physical fitness to health; and the other, the consideration of what constitutes a physical fitness test."

He defines physical fitness as a "fitness to perform some specified task requiring muscular effort."

Dr. George Silver, Montefiore Hospital, New York City, has pointed out that British investigators tend to be critical of the classical tests of physical fitness because the training is not comparable to what is done in life.

The Baruch Report

About 15 years ago, the Baruch Committee on Physical Medicine and Rehabilitation sponsored by Bernard M. Baruch, issued a report in which it called attention to the danger of over-simplification and misapplication of the term "physical fitness."

Existing tests to determine physical fitness have been based largely on pre-employment examinations and studies involving military personnel, athletes and school children. As the Baruch Committee stated, "Physical fitness describes the functional capacity of an individual for a task. It has no real meaning unless the task or job for which fitness is to be judged is specific. Physical fitness for a task depends on the physical equipment and physiological competence of the individual for the stress which the task imposes, together with the complex psychological factors grouped together under the term—motivation."

When President Kennedy cited Theodore Roosevelt's directives, he was "telling it to the Marines," not to the faddists who have been caught up in this latest swirl of exhibitionism.

Times have changed but the popular concept of physical fitness has not. Today, our civilization demands mental ability and technological skill rather than undue emphasis on muscular strength. When we talk about physical fitness, we should always ask the question—physically fit for what?

March 1, 1963

Walking Craze: It Was Fun While It Lasted

Hikers from Redwood High School at Larkspur, Calif., as they neared the end of their 50-mile cross-country trek

Walking Challenge Creates Fad for 50-Mile Hikes

By ROBERT M. LIPSYTE

Walking was once a pastime for British vegetarians, pickets for peace, political candidates and persons with disabled cars. But for two glorious weeks last month, a sedentary nation took to the open road.

Most of the nation, footsore and spent, already has sunk back into soft chairs, or remounted. But the latest fad, created by Presidential suggestion, may have started a new American sport.

New York department stores have reported a rush on pedometers, and the State Podiatry Society claims a 10 per cent increase in patients. And if business and health weren't enough, the Russians added their needle to national pride. Said Gabriel Korobkov, head track and field coach of the Soviet Olympic team:

"So a man walks 50 miles in one day—what of it? Tomorrow, he catches a taxicab again to go four blocks."

A Blistering Response

The epic of shank's nightmare began when President Kennedy wondered if present-day marines

Open Road Leads to Offices of the Foot Doctors

were fit enough to hike 50 miles in 20 hours, a requirement set for marine officers during President Theodore Roosevelt's term of office. The response was blistering.

Marines by the platoon, Boy Scouts by the troop, and bun-

ion-loads of teen-agers, government workers and Sunday drivers went and took a walk. Most of the marines and Boy Scouts, and some of the federal government workers (including Attorney General Robert F. Kennedy) made it. Pierre Salinger, the portly White House press aide, settled for a 6.5-mile workout.

"I may be plucky but I'm not stupid," he said.

The nation, sitting comfortably, chuckled indulgently at Salinger's comment. But to physicians, experienced walkers and physical training specialists, there was more stupidity than pluck in the entire business. Walking was wonderful, they agreed, but setting out on a 50-mile hike without proper training was insane.

Dr. Paul Dudley White, the 76-year-old heart specialist who chops wood, rides bicycles and walks daily, said it was a "silly stunt."

Like Dancing the Twist

"People can endanger themselves," warned the American Medical Association. "Walking 50 miles is like dancing the twist or jumping on a reverse tumbling apparatus without proper training. We get distressed when people go out and strain themselves."

And the National Recreation Association, whose first honorary president was Theodore Roosevelt, was mildly horrified.

"The 50-mile hike verges on insanity," said a spokesman. "Walking is a pleasure, but not when you're checking off the miles like an automaton."

But out of the shin splints, the corns and the blisters may yet come a healthful renascence, the experts agree. Walking is considered the easiest and healthiest exercise, and increased interest in it can only be for the good.

Medical authorities, however, agree that persons should work up to long hikes gradually. A middle-aged man of sedentary occupation would do well to begin with one or two miles a day, moving up to five miles and 10 miles over a period of time.

Evan (Doc) Corns, a Los Angeles physical training specialist, has suggested that the walker take long, deep breaths, inhaling for six steps and exhaling for six steps, gradually increasing the steps per breath to 15.

Corns advises that the walker's weight be equally distributed on both feet, principally along the outer edge of the feet. Walk on the entire foot, keep spine straight and abdomen pulled in, he says. Let the legs swing from the hips and arms swing freely in opposition.

Other rules are simpler: Dr. Lester W. Bluhm, president of the State Podiatry Society, suggests well-broken in, all-leather shoes and two pairs of socks. The National Recreation Association suggests walking with a goal rather than aimless ambling.

The bona-fide walker, whether he is out for a moonlight stroll, a daily constitutional or pure escape, joins a band of noted walkers, such as:

Former President Truman, who walks a mile before breakfast; the late Dr. John Huston Finley who walked 70 miles to celebrate his seventieth birthday (signposts honoring him were erected by the city on the East River Drive); Thomas Wolfe who gained literary inspiration on the streets of Brooklyn, and the average American housewife, who, for reasons having nothing to do with health, contemplation, or the White House logs nine miles a day.

April 1, 1963

Blisters for Publicity

Aided and abetted by all possible publicity media, and then some, hiking has suddenly become the national fad. The attention accorded to those who appear to be making use of their legs for the first time is perverse testimony to our enslavement by the automobile. The very fact that walking is placed in the same jejune category as goldfish swallowing or dancing the twist suggests that it is considered a craze with a limited life span.

There is a spirit of adventure in walking across fields, down untrodden ways or strolling through city streets, something not apparent from the hiking jag that is now in vogue. Those who are using shoe leather simply because it has come into fashion and may possibly provide a news item are collecting only bunions, blisters and publicity. But they are missing the real joys provided by walking, which cannot possibly be appreciated by the publicity seekers partaking in the current hiking fad.

February 23, 1963

Famous Walkers

John H. Finley

DR. FINLEY HAILED ON 70TH BIRTHDAY

Educator Celebrates Day by Working After Annual Walk Around Manhattan.

SKETCH OF CAREER ISSUED

Teachers Are Reminded of His Varied Services to Schools —Many Send Messages.

Dr. John H. Finley, former president of Knox and City Colleges, observed his seventieth birthday quietly yesterday, spending a large part of the day at his desk.

As has been his custom for many years, Dr. Finley observed the occasion Wednesday night, devoting the hours of 8 P. M. to 4 A. M. to a walk around Manhattan Island. He recalled yesterday that he has taken this walk, in celebration of his birthday, with the exception of a few years when he was out of the city, every year since 1910.

A pedometer he carried indicated that the route he followed this year measured thirty-two miles. Walking, in recent years, has been Dr. Finley's principal exercise.

His walk took him from mid-Manhattan to the waterfront of the West Side. After following the waterfront to the Battery, he continued up the East Side waterfront to the Harlem River, and from there followed the West Side waterfront to his starting point before going to his home near Gramercy Park.

Sketch of Career Distributed.

Letters and telegrams of congratulation arrived in great numbers at Dr. Finley's office in The New York Times Annex. Since 1921 he has been associate editor of THE NEW YORK TIMES. Dr. William J. O'Shea, Superintendent of Schools, made public a sketch of Dr. Finley's career. This had been prepared for

distribution among the teaching and student bodies in the New York schools, to familiarize them with Dr. Finley's work. The sketch read:

"Exercises will be held at the College of the City of New York on Oct. 26, 1933, in honor of Dr. John H. Finley, who has just passed his seventieth birthday.

"Dr. Finley's life has been one of service to the cause of education, not only of children but of adults as well. In recent years Dr. Finley gave freely of his time to the Board of Education, acting as chairman of the Advisory Board on Industrial Education.

"His boyhood was spent on the Illinois prairie, where he attended a one-room country school. Later he was a teacher in one of these schools before working his way through Knox College, of which he became the president at the age of 29.

"When he was chosen as president of the City College just thirty years ago, he was no stranger to our city and State, for in the position of secretary of the New York State Charities Aid Association he had become familiar with many of its problems. After serving the college as its president for ten years, Dr. Finley became State Commissioner of Education.

His Aid to Education Hailed.

"As head of the State Education Department, he aided in the enactment of considerable legislation to improve the schools of the State. He strove to secure the best educational opportunities for all children of the State.

"Although Dr. Finley relinquished a salaried public office in 1921, his interest and zeal in welfare work has not lessened. He has been closely identified with the work of the Boy Scouts of America, the National Child Welfare Association, the New York Council of Adult Education, the National Recreation Association, the Junior Red Cross and numerous other welfare organizations. He was also instrumental in organizing committees for the extension of good-will and tolerance throughout the world.

"Dr. Finley has kept himself in fine bodily condition for his many activities by athletics and exercise. His habit of taking long walks might very well be followed more generally by Americans. His advice to the students of the City College at the beginning of a vacation period was to 'read a book, make a friend, and take a walk.'"

James Byrne, Chancellor of the University of the State of New York, is to be the principal speaker at the City College exercises.

October 20, 1933

John H. Finley Dead

Times Editor Emeritus

He Succumbs at 76 in His Sleep—Had Long and Distinguished Career as Educator and Journalist

Dr. John Huston Finley, editor emeritus of THE NEW YORK TIMES, died early yesterday morning in his home, 1 Lexington Avenue. He was 76 years old.

Death came peacefully to the noted editor and educator, who was stricken with a coronary embolism while asleep. He apparently died about 5 A. M., but the fact was not known until shortly after 7 A. M., when Mrs. Finley entered his room to awaken him.

Although Dr. Finley had been seriously ill during the Spring of 1938, he had been in good health recently and active in his many interests. On Wednesday he visited his office at THE TIMES, where he wrote an editorial. He then dined and spent a quiet evening at home, retiring early.

Dr. Finley, who was internationally known in the spheres of education, arts and letters, and journalism, joined THE NEW YORK TIMES as associate editor in 1921, when Charles Ransom Miller was editor and Rollo Ogden an associate editor. Mr. Miller died in 1922 and Mr. Ogden became editor. Mr. Ogden died Feb. 22, 1937, and Dr. Finley became acting editor.

On April 21, 1937, THE TIMES announced Dr. Finley's appointment as editor. He held that post until Nov. 16, 1938, when, because of ill health, he took the title of editor emeritus, being succeeded by Charles Merz.

Dr. Finley's death occasioned many expressions of sorrow when the news became known. Mayor La Guardia last night directed that all flags in the city be flown at half-staff for ten days. Dr. Nelson P. Mead, acting president of City College, of which Dr. Finley had been president for ten years, had previously ordered that the flags on that institution be half-staffed for ten days.

A man of wide interests, Dr. Finley had a long and distinguished career and it brought him many honors. His activities were manifold, ranging from pedestrianism to the restoration of the Parthenon and from studying the Bible to active and intimate association with many philanthropies.

He was an educator, a writer, a lecturer, and he was unusually interested in the promotion of the arts.

During the World War he headed the Red Cross Commission in Palestine. For several years he was New York Commissioner of Education. Up to his death he was connected with many civic and charitable organizations. He received honorary degrees from more than thirty colleges and universities, and twelve governments bestowed thirteen decorations on him.

Thousands of persons knew Dr. Finley as a versatile speaker of scholarly charm and as a master of ceremonies at dinners both formal and informal. His writings, which abounded in deep knowledge of the classics, made him known to innumerable others. He once won the appellation of one of the ten most cultured men in the United States.

Besides the widow, the former Miss Martha Ford Boyden, Dr. Finley is survived by a daughter, Mrs. William H. Kiser Jr., the former Ellen Boyden Finley, of Atlanta, Ga.; two sons, Robert Lawrence Finley of New York and Dr. John Huston Finley Jr., Associate Professor of Greek and Latin at Harvard University, and eight grandchildren.

Funeral services will be held at 10:30 A. M. tomorrow at the First Presbyterian Church, Fifth Avenue and Eleventh Street. Burial, which will be private, will be in the family plot at Princeton, N. J.

March 8, 1940

From a drawing by Feodor Zakharov.

John Huston Finley

As He Was Seen by Members of The New York Times Staff

It will be a long time before Dr. Finley's associates on THE TIMES—and that means, as he looked at it, printers, office boys, editors, reporters, elevator men and every one concerned with getting out the paper—grow used to the thought that he won't be coming in again. It seems as though he must be off on a trip somewhere.

His empty office on the southeast corner of the tenth floor has so much in it that speaks of him, and for him, that a person can't look into it without seeing him there, across the desk from the little bust of Dante. One could pretty nearly write his biography from what is in that room.

He loved people. He loved walking. He loved the art of printing. The room says these things right away. The portraits of some of the people are there, usually with a grateful or affectionate inscription: Allenby, Lawrence of Arabia, Amundsen, Nansen, Grover Cleveland, Cardinal Mercier among others.

On the desk lies the short stick—maybe twenty

inches long—that he carried on his walks to keep his hands from swelling. There are names carved on it, mostly but not always place names: "Albania—London—Roma—Monastir—Paris—Tyre—Sidon—Sinai—Jaffa—Beersheba—Jerusalem—Jericho."

One remembers how he used to like to talk about that walk through Palestine, when he was wartime head of the Red Cross Commission to that country. He wanted to walk the whole length of the country but he came to the British front line and had to stop. He mentioned his difficulty to Allenby. "We'll push the line up for you," said Allenby, and he did, and Dr. Finley finished his stroll.

A "Magnificent Success"

To hear Dr. Finley tell the story, one wouldn't have guessed there was danger in the trip, though there was. Nor would one guess what Lord Allenby called the "magnificent success" of Dr. Finley's work in Palestine.

He was born to walking like a bird to flying. He probably would have been satisfied to go everywhere he went on foot, if it hadn't been for oceans getting in the way and the shortness of time. Once he walked seventy-two miles in a day. He was telling of this a year or so ago, when some one observed that that must be as much as could be done in a day. A shade of regret crossed his face and he shook his head. No, he said, 100 miles was about the record.

For about thirty years he walked around the island of Manhattan on his birthday, pausing at his office to do his day's work. Once he attended an educational conference at Princeton, which lasted till the last train had left for New York. The other conferees went to bed. He said he guessed he would walk home, and did. Next day he was at his desk at THE TIMES, looking a little tired but not admitting it. Sometimes when he had a lecture to give somewhere out of town, he would take an early train, get off short of his destination and walk the rest of the way.

Striding Along

After his serious illness in 1938 his friends could not believe that he would ever be active again, but he was. Some of his younger colleagues have been encountering him on the street this Winter, on pretty cold days. He would be striding along with a stoop that did not seem old age or weariness so much as an eagerness to get somewhere. He would not wear an overcoat, but he did wear over his shoulders a muffler woven in the Finley plaid.

He had a printer's case and a font of type on a stand under the south window of his office. He had been a printer in his youth and he never forgot the case nor did he get the ink off his fingers—as the saying goes. Before one member of the editorial staff was assigned regularly to the night make-up the staff members used to take turns staying late and putting the page to bed. Dr. Finley not only took his turn with the rest but insisted on taking other people's turns when some one was ill or absent.

He would go down to the composing room on the fourth floor and stand side by side with the make-up man while the type was fitted into the form. He could read type as fast as any printer. Every one in the composing room came to know him, and he had a smile and a joke for them all. When the fore-

man had pneumonia Dr. Finley showed up at the hospital not once but three times. When Dr. Finley was made editor one of his composing room friends set up a complimentary message and sent the type up to him—a dozen lines neatly bolted together. Dr. Finley carried the keepsake in his pocket until it began to wear holes and thereafter kept it on his desk where he could show it to visitors.

He had a string of academic and other honors as long as his arm, but he always identified himself as "Mr. Finley"—never, in the manner of the rest of the world, as "Dr. Finley." What tickled him most in the matter of honors, perhaps, was a friendly message from one of his heroes (and he was a great hero-worshiper, never suspecting that there was anything heroic in himself); or perhaps the fact that Sir Hubert Wilkins named some islands in the Weddell Sea after him and Admiral Byrd put his name on a 15,000-foot Antarctic mountain.

He had the gentleness and kindliness that one sometimes finds in explorers and other outdoor men of the naturally fearless type. In all his official and professional positions he had to put up with bores, but his patience was endless. Once his secretary came in to tell him, "That irrepressible woman is here again." He nodded and went on for a few moments with his work. Then he called to the secretary. "And now," he said, "what about that—that *energetic* woman?"

A True Interest in Youth

He was really interested in young people. More than one young reporter on THE TIMES staff has had a sincerely encouraging word from him. He would hunt up a man who had done what he thought a good piece of work and tell him how much he liked it. He adopted the daughters of several of his colleagues as his "nieces" and would send them books and advise them about their studies. He took an interest in the office boys, and he was delighted and proud when those on the tenth floor once sent him a birthday message in Greek.

He must have known almost every eminent American of his time, as well as foreigners of distinction, but he was just as simple with famous people as with the run of humanity. Sometimes a visitor whose name was in the news would come to the office for lunch or drop in for a chat with Dr. Finley. He let others talk politics or economics or statecraft with them and asked them about their friends and families, as though they were old neighbors from home.

He wore the garment of his vast experience and his notable achievements with unaffected modesty. He kept a youthfulness, almost an ingenuousness, all his life. He never seemed an old man—the boy in him was always visible. One had to read his editorials or other writings or listen to his speeches—and he made hundreds and hundreds of them, ranging from inspiring lectures to introductions or graceful after-dinner talks, in which he was past master—to realize how wise he was and how much he knew.

The Loss of a Friend

The morning he died his associates knew as soon as they stepped inside the building that something had happened. The elevator men had no smiles that morning, and on every floor there were sad faces. Every one, it seemed, had lost a friend.

But every one knew that Dr. Finley wouldn't want

his passing to cast too heavy a shadow over others. He showed how he thought of death in six lines of verse he wrote for a memorial meeting for Century Club members who had died during 1938:

When we're pegged out for good upon our board,
And pegs of red and white no more record
Our comings and our goings here below,
May Pegasus, who bears aloft our fames,
Then peg us in with stars against our names
Where all the Century's immortals go.

It is hard to say good-bye to him. People will go on listening for his step along the corridor, and for the cheery sound of his voice. It will be long before his associates will be sure that he isn't sitting at his desk, smiling across at the bust of Dante. When he doesn't come they will half believe that he is off presenting a medal or dedicating something or putting courage into an audience of puzzled young folks. They will half-believe that he will soon return, with a triumphant gleam in his eye, from some long walk, or with a story of the beauty of airplane flight through clouds and thunder, unafraid.

And they may wholly believe that he is still walking, somewhere, staff in hand, listening to the sound of rivers by night, as vigorous as he was when he strode the forty miles from Lausanne to Geneva in eight hours, but never walking too fast to see beauty in Nature and comradeship in the humblest of his fellow-beings.

No, one can't think of Dr. Finley and death together. He loved life too much. He has walked beyond our vision—that is all.

March 10, 1940

Pedestrian

Special to THE NEW YORK TIMES.

SUFFERN, N. Y., March 7—Daniel Carter Beard, National Scout Commissioner, expressed deep sorrow today at his home, Brooklands, near here, when he heard a radio announcement of the death of Dr. John H. Finley. He recalled Dr. Finley's interests and in Boy Scout work and many hours passed with the editor in discussing a mutual favorite pastime of hiking.

At executive board meetings of Boy Scout directors Dr. Finley would relax from a knotty problem to discuss hiking, Mr. Beard recalled. Continuing, he said: "Dr. Finley was my idea of a real pedestrian. He was as thrilled by the sights in a walk through a congested district as by the beautiful scenic effects afforded in the open country. Several years ago I became enthralled as I listened to Dr. Finley recount his experiences of a day's hike around the edge of Manhattan Island.

"He mentioned briefly the sections of Manhattan he passed through, but he detailed his account about the people he saw. The longshoremen, truck drivers, hurrying commuters along West Street, the idle seamen and visitors to the Battery and along South Street. The foreign districts of the lower East Side—he described at least thirty persons he saw on that trip.

"When I asked him if he saw nothing but people, he told me he also was delighted to find potato patches, small gardens of cabbages, lettuce and other vegetables tucked away in the most unexpected places near the shoreline. He appeared pleased when I told him that while everybody considered him a good editor I knew he was a good reporter, as he had proved it from his account of that trip.

"Dr. Finley could tell more about little known facts concerning New York City than any person I have met. He gathered all this knowledge from walks through the city.

"Ten years ago Dr. Finley came here on my birthday. He wore his Scottish kilts, as we had told him all visitors must appear in uniform. He liked to walk through the Ramapo Mountains back of here and also claimed Bear Mountain Park was one of the best walking districts in the world.

"There was not a Revolutionary iron mine in this section or point of interest he had missed, but like his jaunts through the city, he featured his accounts with experiences with mountaineers, Jackson whites, and others."

March 8, 1940

DR. FINLEY'S CITY: AN ENDLESS WALK

Daily Ramblings Recalled as City College Gives Medal Named in His Honor

CARS WERE HIS ENEMY

They Shut Out Sounds and Smells, but He Seldom Missed a Detail

By GAY TALESE

Were he within walking distance yesterday, John Huston Finley would probably have spent the crisp, sunny New York morning strolling along the East River—his long legs moving a mile every 12 minutes, his plaid scarf fluttering in the breeze, his blue-gray eyes ever-curious about the city around him.

Although Dr. Finley, who was the third president of City College and later the editor of The New York Times, has been dead since 1940, he left an impression that would not have been more lasting had he walked all those miles over fresh concrete.

Men still talk about Dr. Finley's walks through New York, which sometimes exceeded 60 miles a day and circled Manhattan.

Birthday Commemorated

He was especially remembered last night at the Astor Hotel, where the City College Alumni Association held its annual dinner in commemoration of his 100th birthday.

Dr. Finley was born on an Illinois farm where, as a plowboy, he would fasten his copy of Horace to the plow handle so as not to waste time while his horse rested in the shade.

Even in New York there remained in him the country boy's way of wandering, and he despised automobiles until his dying day.

He lived at 1 Lexington Avenue, near Gramercy Park at 21st Street. There was a different doorman there yesterday, but the building and the street are unchanged.

Walk Named for Him

Dr. Finley would stride down the steps, turn right, then right again toward the East River, where signs mark a walk named for him. Yesterday he would have seen a bird-like woman feeding pigeons on Third Avenue, heard the squeaks from children's swings inside Peter Cooper Village, then probably been stopped by the whiskered panhandler on Second Avenue.

The path along Franklin D. Roosevelt Drive, cutting between the river and the bumper-to-bumper traffic, was deserted yesterday morning. Dr. Finley would have been offended.

"If only they were not tempted by the wheel of the street car or motor," he once wrote. "I suppose, those cliff-dwellers had become enslaved by wheels, just like the old mythical Ixion, who was tied to one."

Dr. Finley could have heard the squawks of gulls following the sea churned up behind ships. He could also smell the fish from Teddy's market, where early each morning 50,000 pounds of fish are delivered—attracting every stray cat within the Second Assembly District.

Along South Street, he would have passed Yuen Roys' live poultry market and Ludwig Pollak's warehouse, stuffed with 1.5 million bars of Baby Ruth candy bars for Manila, 200,000 yards of cotton for California, and a calculating machine for Milan.

Then, past the Manhattan Bridge, past the Brooklyn Bridge, walking around the curved path toward South Ferry. There, he would have heard the clangs of the horse-shoe pitchers outside the Seamen's Church Institute, not far from the Staten Island ferries.

Then up the West Side Highway, where, outside the Downtown Athletic Club, lines of black limousines wait for Very Important People.

Dr. Finley would have heard and seen them all—the important and unimportant sights and sounds of New York.

November 21, 1963

(An article by Dr. Finley appears on page 4.)

The Leather Man

HIS LIFE A PENANCE.

THE STRANGE STORY OF THE FAMOUS VAGRANT, THE LEATHER MAN.

The Leather Man, found dead in a cave near Sing Sing on Sunday, had tramped for nearly 40 years over the country roads in Westchester County, in this State, and in New-Haven, Fairfield, and Litchfield Counties in Connecticut. His suit of clothes, patched and repatched with leather, made him a unique figure among tramps and gave him his name. Caves scattered about the country he frequented were his chosen abiding places, and when remote from these he readily found shelter in the barns of the farmers, who never feared that he would do their property injury. Farmer's wives willingly fed him, and vainly tried to get him to talk. Country school children gave him pennies and sweetmeats, and no one seemed to fear him. The long staff he carried was never used, save as an aid to locomotion.

Thousands of Connecticut-born boys and girls have gazed after the strange figure and wondered what he carried in the huge leather sack that was always slung across his shoulder. Two years ago, when the old fellow was found lying ill in a cave near Woodbury, Conn., the secrets of the old sack were discovered by the young men who found and nursed him back to life. They were a French Prayer Book printed in 1844, a pipe of his own make, a hatchet, a small tin pail, a jackknife, and an awl, the lot constituting his library and housekeeping utensils. Suspended about his neck was a crucifix and the usual scapular worn by Catholics. His only underclothing was a knit woolen jacket.

He could rarely be induced to speak to any one, but when he did speak it was in the patois of Southern France, of which he was a native. A romance there certainly was in his life, for he was free to confess that his method of life was a penance. Something less than a decade ago an emissary from his relatives in France overtook the old man on his tramp near Wilton, Conn., and tried to induce him to return to his native country. This agent refused to reveal the old man's personality, saying only that his people in France were very wealthy and well born. Partly from words dropped by the Leather Man to a Professor at Yale College, who once got him to talk, and partly from an old Frenchman in Bridgeport who claimed to know his relatives, this story of his life was formulated and has been commonly accepted:

While a young man he fell in love with a girl employed in a leather manufactory near Marseilles, owned by his father. The father opposed the match; the girl rejected the proposals of a dishonorable alliance with the son made by the parent; the girl disappeared. The young man became convinced there had been foul play, and eventually that the girl had been murdered through the machinations of his parents. He then left home and his country, and never let his friends hear from him. Frequent publications in American papers of the man and his wanderings, which were always scheduled so that he appeared at certain places at regularly-recurring periods, brought the attention of his brothers to him. His identity was absolutely established. But the Leather Man refused to quit the vagrant life he followed persistently as a sort of expiation for the crime he believed his father had either personally committed or had hired some one to commit.

Coroner Sutton held an inquest at Sing Sing yesterday and heard how Henry Miller, an employe on the aqueduct, had on Sunday taken his wife to see the cave on George Dell's farm and had discovered the old man's body under the shelving rock which served him as a shelter. Mr. Dell and Reuben and Walter Whitson testified that they had known the Leather Man for 30 years. The Whitsons had last seen him two weeks ago. He was then very ill and hardly able to walk, but he declined to accept assistance. Drs. Madden and Collins testified that death was due to blood poisoning resulting from a cancer, which had eaten away part of the lower jaw. The verdict of the Coroner's jury was:

"That the Leather Man came to his death from cancer and inability to obtain or take food."

The body was buried yesterday afternoon in the Sparta Cemetery. The Coroner has two books, which were found in the cave, made of brown paper and full of figures and hieroglyphics which could not be deciphered.

March 26, 1889

WANDERER'S GRAVE IS MARKED AT LAST

'Leather Man' Died in '89 Near Ossining in Cave—Honored by Historical Groups

Special to THE NEW YORK TIMES.

OSSINING, N. Y., May 16— Historically minded residents of Westchester and western Connecticut remedied today a sixty-four-year oversight by placing a bronze marker on the pauper's grave of "the Leather Man" in Sparta Cemetery on Albany Post Road between this village and Briarcliff Manor.

The Leather Man had been identified as Jules Bourglay after he died of cancer of the mouth in a cave on a Briarcliff farm in 1889. He was a Frenchman from Lyons or Marseilles who maintained a remarkably regular schedule of foot-loose wandering in the sparsely settled territory between the Hudson and Connecticut Rivers from about 1858 until his death.

He made his own suit, cap and traveling bag from the tops of discarded leather boots. He infrequently earned small sums for odd jobs but depended mostly on the bounty of the rural folk he visited on a schedule usually thirty-four days apart.

Silent on Wandering Motive

His friends in New York's Westchester and Dutchess Counties and in western Connecticut bedded him in their barns and nursed him when illness laid him low. He loved children, and they loved him.

He never revealed the story of his past, but it was rumored that a great personal tragedy had prompted him to forsake his native France for anonymity as the Leather Man in this area.

The placing of a small plaque at the Leather Man's grave was arranged by the Ossining Historical Society and the Westchester County Historical Society at a brief ceremony attended by fifty persons, among them a few whose parents had told them of the dark-haired, clean-shaven wanderer and the caves in which he camped when not "in residence" at a farmhouse.

Speakers included Thomas J. Price of Astoria, Queens, donor of the grave marker. A cave near the Yonkers property of his parents had been frequently used by the transient.

Also figuring in the ceremony were Leroy W. Foote of Middlebury, Conn., whose interviews with 400 old-timers produced a lengthy dossier on the Leather Man; Elliot Baldwin Hunt, president of the Westchester County Historical Society; Allison Albee, a society trustee and Leather Man authority, and the Rev. Robert B. Pattison, pastor emeritus of the First Baptist Church of Ossining, representing the Ossining Historical Society.

May 17, 1953

Barbara Moore

Walking Sergeants Here From Coast; Meanwhile—

The New York Times

Sgts. Patrick Moloney, left, and Mervyn Evans leave the Lincoln Tunnel upon arriving here from San Francisco.

United Press International Telephoto

Dr. Barbara Moore at Indianapolis, on her way here.

Woman Finishes Walk Over Length of Britain

Special to The New York Times.

LONDON, Feb. 4—Dr. Barbara Moore, 56-year-old dietitian, arrived at Land's End tonight after having tramped the length of Britain. The thousand-mile journey from John o'Groat's House, a point in far northern Scotland, took her twenty-three days.

She was followed on the last fifty-seven-mile leg of her walk today from Bodmin, Cornwall, by a crowd on foot and in automobiles that swelled to several thousand. At Penzance, with only ten miles to go, she told reporters:

"I have proved, I hope, that we women can do all that man can."

Dr. Moore, who, as far as is known, is the first woman to have walked the route, averaged nearly four miles an hour, eleven hours a day, on a diet consisting mainly of raw vegetables, fruits, nuts, fruit juices, honey and milk.

February 5, 1960

BRITISH WOMAN SETS A WALK ACROSS U. S.

Special to The New York Times.

LONDON, March 1—Blisters, trickery and the weather have eliminated hundreds of contestants in a walking race the length of Britain. But the doughty 56-year-old woman who started it all is looking for longer roads to conquer.

Dr. Barbara Moore, whose walking exploits have made her a national figure, said today she planned to leave within the next few weeks for the United States to walk from San Francisco to New York.

Expecting to complete the trip in forty-five days, she will walk from west to east in the hope that weather conditions will be improving as she enters the second half of her journey.

Earlier this month the Russian-born dietitian completed the 1,000-mile walk from John o'Groats, at the northern tip of Scotland, to Land's End, the extreme southwestern point of England, in twenty-three days.

Billy Butlin, operator of vacation camps, then offered £5,000 ($14,000) for the winners of a walking race over the same route.

At the start last Friday there were about 715 entries. Tonight about 200 were scattered over the course, some many miles behind the leaders.

Complaints that some contestants were hitching rides led Mr. Butlin to set up check points and more than 100 persons were soon disqualified.

In the lead tonight was David Robinson, 35-year-old research student and former cross-country runner. He was thirty-three miles ahead of John Grundy, 26, a marathon runner.

March 2, 1960

2 Britons Hike From San Francisco to Coliseum

Sergeants Claim Record: 66 Days 4 Hours 17 Minutes

Two British sergeants yesterday completed a hike from the Golden Gate Bridge in San Francisco to New York's Coliseum.

Their time was 66 days 4 hours 17 minutes. They said the adventure had cured them of further trans-continental walking ambitions.

By extraordinary discipline, the men kept themselves to an average pace of nearly forty-six miles a day through every condition of terrain and weather in eleven states.

They laid immediate claim to a record for the distance. In 1909, Edward Weston walked from Los Angeles to New York in seventy-two days. In 1927, Abraham L. Monteverde made it in the opposite direction in 79 days 10 hours 10 minutes.

Dr. Barbara Moore of Britain, who has resumed her own cross-country hike in Indiana follow-

46 Miles a Day Averaged— Dr. Moore Plods On

ing an accident, charged that the pair had accepted rides.

The men denied this and pointed out that American Legion posts had spot-checked them all across the country, by appointment to the British War Office.

The members of the present tandem are:

Royal Air Force Sgt. Patrick Molony, 34 years old, of Limerick, Ireland. He is 5 feet 7 inches tall, weighs 147 pounds and wears a size 7 walking boot.

Army Sgt. Mervyn Evans, 33, of Trefriw, Wales. He is 5 feet 8 inches tall, weighs 150 pounds and wears a 7-large boot.

Sergeant Moloney left two pounds and his partner four pounds somewhere in the heartland of the nation. They had nothing to spare when they started, they said.

The sergeants' faces were a

deep crimson from 3,022 miles of exposure to the weather, but neither man complained of inordinate fatigue.

The pair looked, in fact, like athletes at the peak of their condition.

But they agreed that it had been "a gruelling test of endurance" on a seemingly endless desert of asphalt.

A third man, Sgt. Roy Rogers of Harrow in Middlesex, followed them in a jeep attached to a rented trailer in which the men slept. They walked from 5 A. M. to 8 P. M. daily.

Suffering only occasional nausea, melancholy and tiny foot blisters (which they treated and bathed in antiseptic), tne pair walked through wind and rain, hail and snow, a blizzard in Nevada, the cruel hills of southwestern Pennsylvania and the catwalk of the Lincoln Tunnel.

"The feet are the most important thing in the world," Sergeant Evans said at the end. "It doesn't matter how fit you are or how strong—if you haven't got a good pair of feet, you haven't got a thing." The men wore out two pairs of shoe heels each on the way.

June 18, 1960

Hail, Conquering Heroine Comes!

The New York Times

Dr. Barbara Moore, the British physician who walked from San Francisco, is received in triumph in Times Square.

Dr. Moore Ends 85-Day Hike From California to Times Sq.

By McCANDLISH PHILLIPS

Dr. Barbara Moore of Britain, the walking vegetarian, limped briskly into Times Square last night after having hiked 3,387 miles from San Francisco in eighty-five days.

"I did it to prove my theories about eating," she said.

The 56 - year - old physician entered the square at 6:18 P. M. A howling crowd immediately closed in, briefly cutting off traffic on Seventh Avenue and on Forty-third Street.

For almost a minute Dr. Moore enjoyed roughly the privileges of a cork in mid-sea, but ten policemen dived into the crowd to join hands, forming a ring around her.

But for the bright red bandana that covered her long honey-colored locks, Dr. Moore, who is 5 feet 3 inches tall, would have been lost to the sight of all but a handful.

Her transcontinental trip was not yet entirely finished. The New Jersey police had driven her more than five miles to the mouth of the Holland Tunnel late yesterday so that she could reach the city before dark. She will pace off that distance today in Central Park.

Replies in Verse

Dr. Moore was reminded immediately on her arrival here that two British sergeants, who had left San Francisco a day earlier than she, on April 12, had made a similar hike in 66 days 4 hours 17 minutes. Royal Air Force Sgt. Patrick Maloney, 34, and Army Sgt. Mervyn Evans, 32, reached here June 17.

Dr. Moore replied with a couplet:

The dirty take the 30,
But 40's for the sporty.

U. S. Route 30, which the sergeants followed part of the way, was "just a joke," she said —level and practically curveless.

But on Route 40, which she followed most of the way, there were manifold hazards; deserts, dust storms, deep snow, tornadoes, roaring truck traffic.

In Colorado, she said, she had had to walk twenty miles through drifts on snowshoes. In Utah she stepped into a hole and twisted her left ankle. In Missouri and Illinois she was badly sunburned In Indiana she was struck by a car and hospitalized three days.

Dr. Moore emerged from the Holland Tunnel at 5:17 P. M. yesterday. The police led her along Canal Street to Broadway, where she was directed to use the sidewalk. The police then left her at the mercy of the press and others.

Kept to Sidewalk

Dr. Moore took long strides up Broadway, dodging pedestrians and twice rubuffing Symon Gould, the American Vegetarian Party's candidate for President. At Herald Square she tired of the sidewalk and, there being no police to stop her, took a center lane of Broadway for her own. Ignoring "Don't Walk" signs and stop-lights, she went north against southbound traffic into Times Square, where 2,000 people waited.

After she was in the Square ten minutes, the police formed a flying wedge and moved her to the Astor Hotel, where she told a press conference, "I just want sleep, lots of sleep."

There was not much prospect of that, however. She was scheduled to appear on a television show at midnight. Before being shown to the Astor's Bridal Suite, she sipped champagne and ate diced carrots, white turnips and broccoli, passing up watercress, cole slaw, sliced tomatoes and fresh fruit salad.

Kept On Sidewalk

Five persons in turn, the last Lee Bauer, a vegetarian from St. Louis, had escorted her in automobiles laden with fruits and vegetables.

Her first escort, a man she remembered only as Hodges, had taken her as far as Topeka, Kans., Mr. Bauer said, "but he ate meat and drank" and Dr. Moore severed the association.

Mr. Bauer said that Dr. Moore was no longer a practicing physician, but that she did research on geriatrics and nutrition, using herself "as a sort of laboratory."

The most important item of her attire was ankle-length seamless white wool athletic socks. She carried eight pairs of shoes, of which she used only three and wore out none.

The credit for her endurance in her six-mile-an-hour pace, she made clear, must go to her meatless diet. Along the way she imbibed grass juice, orange juice and water. She ate powdered cashews, cucumbers, sunflower seeds, sesame seeds, soya "meatburgers," nectarines and other uncooked foods "that come out of the ground or grow on trees."

Dr. Moore noted that there were two kinds of vegetarians —"mixed vegetarians and extreme vegetarians." She put herself in the latter class. She eschews meat, not only because of her convictions about health, but also because of her feelings toward animals.

It was painful to Mr. Bauer to see her drink milk on the last three days of her long journey. The Russian-born physician knew "all the arguments against milk," Mr. Bauer said sadly, but she had lost twenty pounds and was down to 116, so she put caution aside and drank it.

As was her custom on most days, Dr. Moore started out yesterday at 3 A. M. after four hours' sleep. She was eleven miles south of New Brunswick, N. J., and headed north on U. S. Route 1, walking against the traffic. At 4:17 P. M. she stopped

on the Newark side of the Passaic River Bridge on the Old Lincoln Highway.

A reception at the Astor Hotel awaited her and time was growing short. After much discussion, Dr. Moore asked the Hudson County Police to drive her to the entrance to the Holland Tunnel, a distance of five and one-half miles.

Dr. Moore's total walking distance yesterday was 37.1 miles. One day in Utah, she said, she walked 109 miles from 2:30 A. M. to 8 P. M. And once years ago, in India, she said she fasted ninety days.

Mr. Gould, the vegetarian candidate later denied Dr. Moore had rebuffed him. He said that he had told Dr. Moore there were 300,000 vegetarians in this country and they were "most proud of her feat, spelled f-e-a-t."

She lived near Stalingrad for her first twenty-five years, gaining a medical degree there and in Great Britain. Her home now is Eastlea Court, Old Bisley Road, Fromley, Aldershot, Hants, England. Her husband, Harry, is a sculptor and a vegetarian. They have no children.

July 7, 1960

DR. MOORE STRIDES HER LAST LAP HERE

British Woman Makes Up a 5-Mile Ride by Walking Central Park Circuit

Dr. Barbara Moore, Britain's walking exponent of vegetarianism, took a constitutional around Central Park yesterday.

It wasn't just to keep her hand, or rather foot, in. She had to hike five miles to make up on an auto ride she had taken Wednesday to reach New York before dark after having hoofed 3,387 miles from San Francisco in eighty-five days.

With a police car pacing her and a group of reporters and cameramen puffing to keep within sight, the 56-year-old physician entered the park at Central Park South, walked up the East Drive to near 110th Street and down the West Drive to a point a block from her starting point. She did the route, a little more than six miles, between 9:51 and 11:24 A. M.

Arms swinging briskly and feet moving lithely in her long heel-and-toe stride, she maintained all the way what she called her "moderate" pace, to favor her injured left ankle. Her preferred pace is faster, she confided to an interviewer running alongside.

Had Slept 5½ Hours

Dr. Moore wore her usual red bandana, black knitted sweater, black toreador pants, white socks and rib-rubber-soled men's walking shoes. She looked the picture of vitality, although she had only five and a half hours' sleep, and had limited breakfast to a small cantaloupe and water.

She stopped only once, near the Tavern on the Green, where Ed Meagher, a doorman, delivered a pitcher of orange juice. She quaffed two glasses, spurning ice. Returning to the Astor Hotel to wash, she ate a handful of raisins for lunch. "That's why I lost weight," she explained. "No time to eat."

In the afternoon she went to the Australian Consulate General at 636 Fifth Avenue. At her request, W. H. Bray, deputy consul general, cabled the municipality of Blacktown to find out if it wanted her to make a 400-mile hike ending July 17 or one of 1,163 miles from Adelaide to the town, which is near Sydney, in September. Blacktown is celebrating its railroad's centennial.

She expects a reply this morning. In any event, she intends to go right back to Britain, where her husband, a sculptor, is awaiting her.

July 8, 1960

50

Dr. Moore's Little Walk

Dr. Barbara Moore's eighty-five-day walk from San Francisco has come to an end with a final stroll in Central Park. The British vegetarian lady averaged a little under forty miles a day, although, on occasion, she could clip off as much as one hundred and nine miles when the going was good. Her average speed was nearly three times that of the old-fashioned covered wagon and her maximum day's journey was about half that of the Pony Express.

This achievement may have proved, as Dr. Moore thinks it did, that vegetarians can work up a good deal of energy. It has also been proved by such Arctic explorers as Vilhjalmur Stefansson that a diet consisting exclusively of meat will do the same thing. One thing, at least, Dr. Moore's trip did demonstrate—and this is that in her middle fifties she is a woman of spirit and determination.

She revealed a diplomatic quality, except in some of her references to two British Air Force sergeants who recently crossed the continent in a little over sixty-six days. The diplomatic quality showed in her response to a greeting from one of our Presidential candidates. Scrupulously refusing to interfere in American politics, she did not state whether, if she were an American, she would vote for a Vegetarian President or a candidate of a major party.

July 8, 1960

GLASS WORKER WINS 891-MILE FOOT RACE

Special to The New York Times.

LONDON, March 13 — Jim Musgrave, a 38-year-old glass worker from Doncaster, Yorkshire, finshed first early today in the 891-mile foot race from John o'Groats House in Scotland to Land's End at the southwest tip of England.

It took him 15 days 14 hours 32 minutes to cover the distance and win a first prize of £1,000 ($2,800).

Mr. Musgrave, whose previous athletic career had been limited to what he described as "a four or five-mile merchant seaman's race in Africa," ran and walked the last 100 miles in twenty-seven sleepless hours.

Ninety minutes behind him came John Grundy, 26, a marathon runner from Wakefield, Yorkshire. He won the second prize of £500 ($1,400).

The race has attracted wide attention since it began Feb. 26. At the start 715 men and women were entered; but by this morning only a handful of contestants remained.

Mr. Murgrave, a stocky man only five feet tall, made the race during his annual two-week vacation. The race was sponsored by Billy Butlin, an operator of vacation camps, who offered £5,000 ($14,000) in prizes.

March 14, 1960

Edward Payson Weston

The Great Pedestrian Feat.

PORTLAND, Me., Tuesday, Oct. 29.

WESTON, the pedestrian, started to-day, at noon precisely, on his walk to Chicago, amid enthusiastic cheers from a vast crowd assembled at the Post-office to see him start. He struck an easy five-mile gait, and is now pushing up Congress-street with a large crowd in his train.

PORTLAND, Me., Tuesday, Oct. 29.

WESTON arrived at North Berwick at 12 o'clock midnight. He missed the road twice and went three miles out of his way. He is bright and lively.

October 30, 1867

Arrival of Weston at Chicago.

CHICAGO, Thursday, Nov. 28.

WESTON arrived here at 10 o'clock this morning. The street, through which he passed to the Sherman House, was lined with interested spectators. He appears at the Opera House this afternoon and evening.

November 29, 1867

The Pedestrian Mania.

A kind of pedestrian mania seems to afflict this country just now. We hear of erratic pedestrians rushing across this continent in every direction, just as the recent meteors traversed the heavens. Side by side with telegrams announcing the progress of events in Italy we find, day after day, telegrams announcing that of a pedestrian walking so many miles a day for so many thousand dollars. Mayors greet him, roughs assail him, Police protect him, children are kissed by him, and every detail is telegraphed with pre-Raphaelite minuteness. Another would-be rival of the possessor of the seven-leagued boots has started for San Francisco on foot, but he is "taking notes, and faith, he'll print them," so he scarcely comes within the category to which we refer, having a motive somewhat above that of gaining money for himself or losing it for others. A third worthy recently started to walk a given distance round a fixed course in a certain time,

but after accomplishing a small portion of it, appears to have been carried away by centrifugal force, and to have gone off at a tangent, leaving his speculative supporters in the lurch.

Of course, there is a certain amount of interest attaching to these performances, or attempted performances, just in the same degree that there is to any exceptional physical feats; to those of the circus acrobat as well as to those of the professional pedestrian. WESTON, the most notable of the class to which we refer, has not accomplished the great feat of walking one hundred miles in twenty-four hours which he attempted, but he has displayed an amount of muscular power and endurance which place him on a par with the man who can hold so many pounds weight at arm's length for a longer time than any one else. It is simply impossible to claim for such feats as those of WESTON any of the credit attaching to athletic sports, properly so-called. In many respects his performance closely resembles prize fighting. He has displayed great pluck and endurance, at the cost of great personal discomfort, and possible risk to his life. And at what advantage to the public? An opportunity for betting to professional gamblers, who would just as soon have bet on two raindrops running down a pane of glass, or on the length of two straws drawn from a wheatstack, and the gratification of a few curiosity-hunting sight-seers. There is nothing in common in such a feat with genuine athletic sports. There is little, if any, skill involved in walking, from which amateurs may learn. The great end of athletic sports is to fully develop, without injuring, the physical powers of people whom sedentary pursuits compel to take the exercise necessary to health in a concentrated and suitable form. But walking so many miles a day for so many days, fails to satisfy any one of the conditions required. It is simply a test of dogged endurance, which must necessarily be confined to contests among professional athletes. It is by necessity out of the reach of amateurs, and must consequently lack all the incentives of honorable emulation which give the great charm to rowing, base-ball and cricket—recreations in which daily indulgence is compatible with hard mental exertion or diligent attention to business. Let all due credit be given to WESTON and his humbler imitators for their prowess and pluck, but do not let them attempt to confound these sensational performances with true and health-giving physical education. That no form of muscular effort is more likely to be injurious than the attempt, without the long necessary training, to undertake similar feats, is illustrated by the death of an amateur, who, for a very short time, essayed to keep up with the great pedestrian on his journey.

December 1, 1867

PEDESTRIAN FEATS.

The following is a summary of the fastest and most successful feats of pedestrianism on record: In 1809 a man named Barclay, England, walked 1,000 miles in 1,000 consecutive hours. In 1806 he walked from Wry to Crathynaird and back, a distance of twenty-eight miles, in four hours. In 1830 Newsam, of Philadelphia, walked 1,000 miles in eighteen days; and in 1847 Joseph Eaton, aged seventy years, of Boston, walked 100 quarter miles in 100 consecutive quarter hours. In the same year he walked 1,000 miles in Canada in 1,000 consecutive hours. In 1856 William Spooner, London, walked seven miles in fifty-two minutes, and in 1858. Charles Westhall, London, walked half a mile in three minutes and ten seconds. In the same year Wm. H. Boyd, Charleston, S. C., walked one mile in six minutes and fifty-two seconds. Hill, of Brooklyn, walked half a mile backward in seven minutes in 1865, and in the same year John Brighton, Liverpool, walked eleven and a half miles in one hour and thirty-one minutes. George Topley, of New-York, walked seven and a half miles in fifty-six minutes and ten seconds in 1868. About the same time M. Westley, Troy, N. Y., went over fifty miles of a country road in nine hours and twenty-two minutes, including thirty-six minutes in rests. Shortly after this performance a man named Payne, of Saratoga, walked fifty miles in ten hours and fifty-seven minutes. In 1869, George Davison, of England, walked fifteen miles in one hour fifty-seven minutes and forty-one seconds, and I. De Witt, Chicago, walked 1,000 miles in 1,000 consecutive hours. In 1870 E. P. Weston, Skating Rink, New-York, performed a feat in pedestrianism by walking 100 miles in twenty-one hours, thirty-eight and fifteen seconds, inclusive of rests. The last remarkable feat of pedestrianism was in 1871, when Jas. Redfern, England, walked twenty-five miles in four hours, thirty-three minutes, and twenty-seven seconds, and also fifty miles in nine hours, thirty-four minutes, and three seconds, resting eight minutes and thirty seconds. In August, 1870, J. Griffiths, Leeds, England, walked one mile in six minutes and forty-eight seconds, and two miles, in 1872, in fourteen minutes and twenty seconds. Last September W. J. Morgan, London, England, walked three miles in twenty-two minutes and thirty-four seconds, and seven miles in fifty-four minutes and fifty-seven seconds. In May, 1873, J. Stockwell, London, England, walked one mile in six minutes and twenty-five seconds, two miles in fourteen minutes and fourteen seconds, and seven miles in fifty-four minutes and ten seconds.

May 6, 1874

THE WALKING TORTURE.

The quickness with which anything of a popular sort, if it happens to amuse, takes root here is very remarkable. For example, two seasons ago a popular magazine made a decided hit in publishing an article on the use of the bow, and immediately that charming and commendable sport became the subject of scores of clubs. Little had been known of the bow except as an implement with which the small boy misses birds and breaks windows; but immediately the appropriate stores blossomed into a profusion of long-bows, of lance-wood, cam-wood, rose-wood, snake-wood, and all the other woods, with targets, finger-tips, quivers, and arrows so many that the new thing was as if it had always been. The genial "Autocrat" was moved to say, some years ago, that he believed, if it should become necessary to revive burning at the stake, somebody would be found who understood disposing the fagots, securing the chains, and all the other details.

The walking craze is another illustration. It began not many months ago—for the old-time performances of WESTON, the Great Failer, need not be reckoned—and since then there has been a surfeit of matches. The most singular feature, beyond the insatiability of the depraved taste which supports it, is the rapidity with which the standard of walk-ability has worked upward. Thus, an unknown woman commenced, in Brooklyn, the task of walking 2,700 quarter miles in as many consecutive quarter hours, and plodded on until the incredulous indifference with which she was regarded gave way to vivid curiosity that followed her to the end of her four weeks' task. She had the inevitable "ovation"; something or other was presented to her by the first citizens, and the local papers published elaborate articles about her, explaining how her wonderful stomach had brought her through. Soon came another woman, and, in the same building, walked 4,000 quarters instead of 2,700, but attracted scarcely any attention. Her stomach was not made the subject of even a paragraph. Had the woman walked—or hopped—a much less distance upon one leg, the unipedal performance might have been unique enough to affect a palate already well strung by sensation spice; but the public had seen *that* once, and preferred the Gilmore arena. There appeared the Bridgeport champion, whose hobble ended his fame as suddenly as it began; then the still-remembered six-days' contest; then the painful female exhibition; and then the attempt of the forty, the notable fact being that of the ten who held out, two beat ENNIS and three beat HARRIMAN.

Still the fever rages. Pedestrian vies with pedestrienne, but it is the latter who jauntily challenges attention on the bill-boards, and whose "cuts" are freely offered for sale or hire in advertising columns. The pedestrienne is the favorite attraction, for since the first pomological transaction in the first garden, woman has had a peculiar drawing power. So, and because she is the weaker vessel, men go to see her strain her frame against time, and women, imagining somehow that they honor their sex, go in pride that a woman can do things. But the unnaturalness of these performances is proved by the fact that, unlike all rational entertainments of either the senses or the intellect, mere repetition will not satisfy; what has been done several times becomes common—the strain and the marvel must go on increasing. The walkers must, therefore, go into the country tent, with the two-headed and other monstrosities which nature flings out now and then to show what could be done if she willed irregularity, and thus the craze must expend itself, or else it must add new attempts. The 4,000 quarter-miles must be increased by successive thousands; the quarters must become halves; the contestants must go on one, three, four, or more or less legs than are given; or in some way the appetite for the morbidly unnatural must be stimulated. Ingenuity will not be put at fault. Let there be a match to hop furthest, or stand longest on one leg, feathered bipeds not excluded; squealing, miaouwing, crowing and similar contests, no discrimination exercised on account of age, sex, skin, number of legs, presence or absence of caudal appendices, or otherwise; wrestling matches for old women; crutch combats for old men; tongue-lashings for termagants; lick-jackets for small-boys; ecclesiastical trials for Presbyters; bill-posting, on Mondays, for Representatives in Congress; and so on, for six days, ending with a grand performance of everybody's doing what he conceives himself to do best, the audience being requested to rise and join. Olympian games, revived in this manner, would thrill this decorative age and be a grand restoration of the classic days when no woman wore a trail. When these palled on the public taste, some new tests of endurance could be offered—holding the breath, or holding the head under water; doing without food or sleep; listening to the reading of TALMAGE'S sermons; or, best of all, the rack. That would be a mediæval revival; persons who know exactly how to construct and use it could be readily found; and it would make the most drawing exhibition ever known, unless it should find a rival in the thrilling performance once known as "pressing." Both these are simple. One sketches the arms and legs; the other lays you on your back, with weights on your chest. One gives suppleness to the sinews; the other exercises important muscles; both stimulate the memory and give clearness to theological views. Both would draw superbly and would hit the prevailing taste. Nor could there be any consistent objection. After a number of thin, half-starved women, in the hope of gaining from the custom of the hour a comfortable subsistence, have been found to immolate themselves in walking, there could be no difficulty in finding contestants of each sex for the rack; as for the spectators, their eagerness would be insatiable and their numbers embarrassing. As for the performance, if the rack is torture and is demoralizing, what is walking? The thing is a provoking of nature to interpose—a deliberate attempt to see how much abuse the human frame will endure. The interest lies in watching that attempt, for while the alertness of the stride and the physical beauty of the work are at their best the interest is least. People go to see the thing after it becomes torture, as they do to see the acrobat walk on a high wire and the trainer put his head in the lion's mouth—in the half-hope of seeing the one fall and the other lose his head. Horse-racing has its demerits, but it is not repulsive. It is not cruelty; the horse acts naturally and willingly, without getting any injury, and the scene is not necessarily a defiled one. But saw-dust rings, foul air, weary assistants and spectators, and worn-out trampers, abusing their bodies because a depraved appetite enjoys it, form a scene in which all elements of athletic interest and real manhood are wanting. The excess is the faulty thing, but the end is nothing but excess. In the form of gymnastic exercise—of pitching quoits, of wrestling, of running, or even of walking, in short times—it would be as unobjectionable as the rowing match; in its long-time form it is repulsive and degrading. The incidental stimulus it may possibly give to genuine pedestrianism is a small compensation. For the sake of consistency, we should naturalize bull-fighting and stop repressing the cockpit, the dog-pen, and the pugilistic ring, or else repress all performances which consist in putting human endurance to strain.

May 4, 1879

WALKING-MATCHES.

Mr. VANDERBILT has lately announced that he will not permit the international walking-match to take place at the Madison-Square Garden. It is Mr. VANDERBILT's opinion that people walk too much already, and that man's real mission in life is to ride on the railways in which Mr. VANDERBILT is interested. If WESTON and his rivals will encourage the manly sport of riding on the Hudson River Railroad, Mr. VANDERBILT will gladly see that they have every opportunity of buying tickets and of riding a thousand miles in a thousand hours. As for pedestrianism, however, he regards it as a sinful waste of time and a wicked neglect of the railway privileges which a beneficent railway king has provided.

Whatever may be Mr. VANDERBILT's motive, it is to be hoped that his opposition to the contemplated walking-match will be successful. There was a time when Mr. WESTON succeeded in partially convincing his fellow-countrymen that he was a new kind of evangelist, who, in some mysterious way, promoted the cause of religion and morality by taking long walks. That conviction long ago faded away, and the public now regards Mr. WESTON as a tedious and wholly unnecessary person. The mere fact that he was engaged at any specified time in drearily walking round and round a track in some part of this City has of late years been sufficient to cast a gloom over the whole community. Now that he has taken to himself seven or more other pedestrians, with whom he proposes to walk at the Madison-Square Garden, there is a general feeling that this is too much. The only kind of pedestrianism in which Mr. WESTON could engage, with the entire approval of the public, would be that exciting feat in connection with a plank which so many involuntary pedestrians successfully performed in the days when piracy was one of the most popular of athletic sports.

There are two salient objections to public walking-matches. One is their horrible dreariness. The spectacle of a number of men plodding over a race-track is depressing to the last degree. Few men can witness the spectacle without the aid of artificial stimulants, and hence a walking-match inevitably leads to a vast consumption of alcoholic drinks. It may be said that this is all wrong, and that there are certain features of a walking-match that are very cheering. For example, one or more of the contestants is sure to become lame before the match is ended, and to suffer an amount of pain as he hobbles over the course which must consume vitality and shorten his life. This sounds plausible, but the fact is that no pedestrian has yet died on the track. If Mr. WESTON would pledge himself to die in the course of his next match, there are thousands of people who would be ready to witness the performance, and to show their appreciation of his good taste, but we all know that neither he nor his companions will do anything of the sort. They will become exhausted, giddy, and faint. They will suffer a degree of physical anguish that a heathen Roman audience would recognize as being not out of place in a first-class gladiatorial show, but they will stoutly refuse to die and so put a stop to the match. Mr. WESTON, in particular, will survive the international walking-match, and will live to make a dozen more pedestrian failures before he retires from public life. There is no class of people who are so insensible to what is rightfully expected of them as are professional pedestrians.

The other chief objection to walking-matches is the interminable disputes to which they give rise. Everybody knows that after the contemplated international match is over, the contestants will write a series of letters showing that the winner bought his victory, and that every one of them is, in the opinion of all the others, a mean, disreputable fellow. As soon as the noise of this inevitable quarrel has ceased, new and previously-unheard-of pedestrians will challenge the victor, and we shall then have to undergo a new match. If the pedestrian is dreary when walking, he is a positive nuisance when his walk is over and he begins to wrange with his rivals.

What is gained by these international walking-matches no one can find out. What if Mr. WESTON does demonstrate that he can walk further than any other man? What of it, so long as he declines to utilize his powers by walking a thousand miles away from civilization and never coming back again? Suppose that there are vicious persons who take pleasure in witnessing the tortures which beaten pedestrians frequently undergo while trying to walk " for a record." Their pleasure is precisely of the same nature as the pleasure which they would receive in witnessing a prize-fight, and inasmuch as the brief pain suffered by the pugilist is much less than the prolonged agony which some of the beaten pedestrians suffered during the last days of the recent London walking-match, it seems silly for the authorities to prohibit prize-fighting while they find no fault with walking-matches. If Mr. VANDERBILT is correctly reported as having said that an international walking-match is a low and demoralizing exhibition, he was entirely right, however much his opinion may have been due to his railway prejudices. There is not one interesting or redeeming feature in walking-matches as they are usually conducted. They are dreary, demoralizing, and useless, and, in comparison with them, a bull-fight or a bear-baiting exhibition is a rational and improving pastime. The only walking-matches which could command intelligent approval are now out of fashion. They formerly took place in English prisons and were closely connected with an ingenious mechanical device known as the tread-mill.

August 29, 1879

FROM PHILADELPHIA ON FOOT IN 23 HOURS

Weston, the Aged Pedestrian, Beats His Own Record.

HE MADE IT 43 YEARS AGO

Every Little Town Had a Cheering Throng Out as the Old Man Passed By.

Edward Payson Weston, the sixty-seven-year-old pedestrian, walked from Philadelphia to this city yesterday in 23 hours and 31 minutes, thus beating by twenty-five minutes his record of 23 hours and 49 minutes made forty-three years ago. He was in good condition after his journey and talked freely with his friends and admirers.

Weston arrived at the City Hall at 11:31 P. M. and walked to the Fifth Avenue Hotel, where he was expected at midnight. He arrived there at 12:07. A crowd that had gathered at the hotel cheered vociferously.

With Weston came a procession, which was headed by a mounted policeman. Then came the old man with his walking cane in one hand, a swinging lantern in the other. He walked up and down the block in front of the hotel several times as if to make sure that he had arrived.

Then he was caught up by his friends, and fairly carried on the shoulders of the crowd into the hotel. He hastened to his room, where he gathered a crowd about him, and, growing reminiscent, told of his past performances. His good humor was the best index to his condition, which was excellent.

Weston's walking tour from Philadelphia to this city to equal or break his record of 23 hours and 49 minutes in 1863 was for him a triumphal march through all the towns along the route. His coming was heralded hours before his arrival, and the appearance of the old man in his shirt sleeves, knee breeches, and gaiters, swinging the inevitable cane, was a signal for bursts of cheering.

There were many among those who thronged to give him a send-off or a pass-over who had waited forty-three years ago to do the same thing. The old man, they said, walked with the same firm gait and defiant shoulders. The last few miles of the road found him a little fatigued, but not a whit daunted.

"I feel tired," he said, "but not nearly beaten. Oh, dear, no!"

The most trying part of his trip was between Kingston and New Brunswick, N. J. Here, in the hot sun after midday, a seven-mile hill was encountered. Weston tackled it with a laugh, but he had not counted on the dust, which got into his lungs and started a cough.

When he arrived at New Brunswick he was fairly done up, although he himself wouldn't admit it. Drs. Lee and Taylor, the two physicians who had accompanied him from Philadelphia, had previously arranged for a room at a hotel in New Brunswick. Weston took advantage of it, although, owing to the possibility of muscular reaction, he was not allowed to walk upstairs. He had a room on the ground floor.

Here he rested for twenty-five minutes. The time allowed for rest at this point was thirty minutes, but the aged pedestrian was too anxious to remain quiet. He was behind time. The shifting of the City Hall in Philadelphia four miles west of where it stood when he made his record in 1863, had set him back in his calculations. He had made up time, however, at every town he passed through, although as far north as Newark he was still a little behind time.

His start was made from the City Hall, Philadelphia, at 12:05 yesterday morning. At Frankford, Penn., owing to the increased distance, he was twenty minutes late. He kept decreasing this loss until at Trenton, N. J., through which he passed at 7:30 A. M., he was twenty minutes ahead of his schedule.

Owing to the severe conditions between Kingston and New Brunswick, however, Weston's arrival at the latter place was ten minutes behind his schedule. Considering the altered distance of the starting point, however, he was still ahead of his own record. At no stage in the march did he show the slightest variation from his soldierly toe and heel gait.

At Elizabeth, N. J., where Weston arrived about 8 P. M., he was enthusiastically received. Many trotted beside the old pedestrian as far as Newark. Many more, however, changed their minds after going a short distance. In spite of Weston's 67 years, he kept most of his followers running, and Drs. Lee and Taylor had to keep their horse trotting nearly all the way from Philadelphia. They were compelled to change their horse at Trenton.

Weston's biggest reception before his arrival here was at Newark, where a great crowd assembled to see the old man pass through the city at 9:03 P. M. He received several congratulatory telegrams there. Weston was seven minutes late at Newark, but the pace at which he was going promised a gain of time on the Plank Road, into which he swung at 9:15 o'clock with a cheery cry of:

"Last lap, gentlemen."

Drs. Lee and Taylor traveled with Weston, one to study his condition and the general effect of the long march on a man of his age, and the other to haul out the best food at the most advantageous moments. The food consisted mainly of liquids, egg and milk, and hot coffee. These Weston consumed without stopping, except at New Brunswick, where he took advantage of the rest to eat a little. The food was all weighed for scientific purposes.

May 24, 1906

WESTON WILL WALK TO BEAT OLD TIME

Veteran to Duplicate Remarkable Feat He Accomplished Just Forty Years Ago.

THOUGH NOW 69 YEARS OLD

Leaves for Portland, Where He Will Start Tuesday for Chicago—Secret of His Wonderful Preservation.

Edward Payson Weston, the veteran pedestrian, now in his sixty-ninth year, started yesterday from this city by steamer for Portland, Me., where he will start on Tuesday next to duplicate the remarkable walking feat which he undertook and completed just forty years ago, when he was 29 years old, going from Portland to Chicago, a distance of a shade over 1,235 miles, in thirty days, without walking on Sundays. The actual time which Weston occupied in making the trip in 1867 was 25 days and 23 hours. He caluculates to better that time in this trip, in spite of his advanced years, in just 24 hours better time—24 days and 23 hours.

The feat, which was remarkable enough in a man of 29 years of age, is wonderful for a man of 69 years. Few men of 30 could average fifty miles a day for a week to-day, yet this man in his advanced years proposes to maintain that average for nearly a month. Weston is convinced that he can do the trick without distressing himself, and believes he will leave the road at Chicago in better condition than when he takes it at Portland. The doctors and attendants who are with him to-day believe that he can do it without difficulty, and his successful accomplishment of the feat of walking from Philadelphia to New York in 24 hours one year ago would seem to argue that he is perfectly capable of accomplishing it.

Weston, in spite of his gray hairs, gives one the impression of much less an age than he really is, and his vitality and wiry vigor are astonishing. He stands about 5 feet 7 inches in height, weight less than 150 pounds, but is as hard as nails. The usual deterioration which is noticeable in men of 70 years of age, in the tissues and blood vessels, is entirely lacking in him, according to the reports of experienced and well-known physicians who have examined him, and he came off the road a year ago, after his walk from Philadelphia to New York, with no acceleration of pulse and with a perfectly normal temperature, as though the feat were an ordinary every day stroll. And such he asserts such undertakings are.

Weston has made no preparation for his long walk to Chicago, in the ordinary sense. He believes that training is most artificial and unnecessary, and that in the

Weston Confident of Repeating His Long Walk of Forty Years Ago.

AS WESTON APPEARED IN 1867

FROM PORTLAND ME. TO CHICAGO, ILL. OCT. 29TH TO NOV 28TH 30 DAYS.

WESTON'S STRIKING RAINY DAY COSTUME

AS HE APPEARS AT PRESENT

main it is harmful. It creates, he says, a condition which is unnatural, because it is not sustained, that when followed by the usual lapses at the completion of the given task, injures the body very seriously, not to speak of the excessive exercise which one takes in the undue hardships imposed by the athlete upon himself in his preparations. He declares that for the man who takes uniformly good care of himself there is not the slightest need for training, and that in the course of all his long career in which he has engaged in many long-distance walking feats he has never trained for a single day.

The explanation of his superb condition lies simply in the regularity of his habits and the simplicity of the fare that he eats. While not a total abstainer either from liquor or tobacco, he is an excessively temperate man. He has never in his life, he declares, taken a drink over a bar. He uses no stimulants whatever during the contests in which he engages, nor for a brief time before he undertakes a contest, and eats regularly the same food during what would ordinarily be the training period that he eats ordinarily. This consists of two eggs, four slices of bread, and two cups of coffee for breakfast, no luncheon, and a dinner of meat, about a quarter pound, two potatoes, and such vegetables and fruit as are in season. He drinks at night a single cup of tea. He eats fish and poultry at times, but game rarely, and never lobsters or other rich foods that tend to upset the stomach by giving it extraordinary work to do. He especially avoids pastries.

He rises in the morning at 8 o'clock and goes to bed at 2, holding that six hours' sleep is ample for any one, and that more tends to lethargic action of the bodily functions. He invariably takes an hour and a half's nap after dinner. In his life he has had a single illness, an attack of typhoid in 1871, and such minor

ailments as he has had, like colds, he has invariably sweated out with exercise and cured in a day. Rain or shine, day by day, he walks from twelve to fifteen miles, except on Sunday, when he never takes exercise. He declares that it is with great difficulty that he shakes off the consequent torpor on Monday morning.

This is the life that Weston has been living always, and he believes it accounts entirely for his condition and exceptional vitality. He says that it costs less in bodily fatigue and is less harmful to walk 100 miles in twenty-four hours than it costs the athlete to run 100 yards in ten seconds. He calls attention to the accelerated heart action and unnatural breathing that succeeds such unusual exertion, and declares they are harmful.

Weston proposes to make his present walk according to a given schedule which he has already prepared. He crosses ten States and over 300 cities and towns, and has so laid out his itinerary that it will bring him to Chicago just twenty-four hours ahead of his former time. He will run ahead of this schedule as much as possible to be prepared for an exceptional mishap that may befall him, but his excesses in this way will be gradual. His time table calls for a start from Portland at 5 o'clock on the afternoon of Oct. 29, and the following stops are to be made:

Date.	Place.	Dist.	Total
Oct. 29	Kennebunk, Me.	22	22
Oct. 30	Hampton, N. H.	46	68
Oct. 31	Jamaica Plain, Mass.	53	121

Nov. 1	Natick, R. I.	48	169
Nov. 2	Andover, Conn.	59	228
	Sunday.		
Nov. 4	Waterbury, Conn.	58	286
Nov. 5	Great Barrington, Mass.	59	335
Nov. 6	Troy, N. Y.	53	388
Nov. 7	Fonda, N. Y.	43	431
Nov. 8	Utica, N. Y.	53	484
Nov. 9	Syracuse, N. Y.	55	539
	Sunday.		
Nov. 11	Palmyra, N. Y.	59	598
Nov. 12	Batavia, N. Y.	55	653
Nov. 13	Buffalo, N. Y.	37	690
Nov. 14	Silver Creek, N. Y.	32	722
Nov. 15	Northeast, Penn.	54	776
Nov. 16	Ashtabula, Ohio.	58	834
	Sunday.		
Nov. 18	Cleveland, Ohio.	57	891
Nov. 19	Wakeman, Ohio.	59	940
Nov. 20	Tremont, Ohio.	41	981
Nov. 21	Springfield, Ohio.	45	1,026
Nov. 22	Byron, Ohio.	42	1,068
Nov. 23	Ligonier, Ind.	62	1,130
	Sunday.		
Nov. 25	La Porte, Ind.	70	1,200
Nov. 26	Calumet, Ind.	22	1,222
Nov. 27	Chicago, Ill.	13	1,235

Weston is undoubtedly the greatest pedestrian that ever walked, and had a tremendous vogue some years ago. As his present walk to Chicago is a duplication of a feat of forty years ago, so his walk from Philadelphia to New York in twenty-four hours last year was a duplication of his feat of thirty-three years before. He walked from the early sixties to the late eighties almost continuously in public exhibitions, and in his day made a lot of money. He had the patronage abroad, where pedestrianism was much more popular than at any time in this country, of such men as Lord Rosebery, Lord Charles Beresford, the Duke of Montrose, Lord Algernon Lenox, Sir John Astley, Dr. Pavey, physician to King Edward, then Prince of Wales, and the interest of the Prince himself. In 1877 he made a match with Dan O'Leary, then regarded as the greatest of pedestrians for a belt given by Sir John Astley. He was some twenty-six miles

behind O'Leary nearing the end of the race, and pulled up eighteen miles on him, when he was induced to leave the track for two hours. Afterward it was learned that O'Leary was ready to give up the race had Weston kept on at the time, but the retirement gave O'Leary a chance to recover some of the lost distance, and they finished O'Leary, 520 miles, and Weston, 510, at the end of 142 hours, the time of the race.

Two years later he walked 2,000 miles in 1,000 hours, and in the same year broke the record for a six-day walk and won the Astley belt by doing 550 miles in 141 hours and 58 minutes, winning easily from Blower Brown. Two weeks before, in practice, he walked 562 miles in a trial in the same time. In 1884 he walked about England 5,000 miles in 100 days, 50 miles each day, and delivered a temperance lecture every night, and in 1886 he walked again against O'Leary in a match and drove the latter from the track. His greatest distance walked in a day in a match is 115 miles, though he did 127 in practice. The fastest miles he has ever walked were two miles in the match with Brown on the last day, when he made the five hundredth mile in 7 minutes 51 seconds, and the next in 7 minutes 50 seconds. He has walked 58 miles in 12 hours and 400 miles in 5 days repeatedly.

Weston declares the last day of a six-day race is easier than the first, and the second day the hardest of all. He says more than two hours' sleep in such a race is a detriment, as the muscles become cramped after that. Care of the feet he regards as an essential of success, and uses rock salt baths for this purpose. He walks down hills backward to relieve the strain of tense muscles and avoids the heel and toe method religiously.

Though some of his notions are undoubtedly fanatical, his methods are based on a common sense regard for laws of nature and his wonderful physical qualities to-day are the result of nothing else than careful regular living and the observance of these natural laws. He is a most interesting old man.

October 27, 1907

WESTON STARTS LONG WALK.

Veteran Pedestrian Leaves Portland for Chicago Amid Cheers of Crowd.

PORTLAND, Me., Oct. 29.—Planning to duplicate his feat of forty years ago of walking to Chicago, a distance of 1,230 miles, in twenty-six days, Edward Payson Weston started at 5 o'clock to-night from the Portland Post Office amid the cheers and good wishes of fully one thousand persons, who had gathered to see him start. He is 69 years of age.

Mr. Weston was greeted by a number of friends, including former Mayor James P. Baxter, who watched his departure forty years ago, and was accompanied to the south Portland city line by Joseph C. Sterling, who, as a police officer, escorted him over the same route on the first walk. Mayor Clifford witnessed his departure and administered an oath that the conditions of the feat should be complied with.

Mr. Weston expects to arrive at Chicago Post Office at 2 P. M. Thursday, Nov. 28, averaging 50 miles a day. He will go by way of Boston, Troy, Utica, Syracuse, Buffalo, Toledo, and Cleveland. There was an arrangement for Henry S. Chmehl of Chicago to start at the same time for Portland.

October 30, 1907

WESTON THE WALKER.

Old EDWARD PAYSON WESTON, footing it from Portland, Me., to Chicago, Ill., carries pleasant memories with him to every stopping place. Forty years ago he walked over the same route, and covered the whole distance, 1,326 miles, in 24 days 22 hours and 40 minutes. He is allowing himself 26 days this time.

In 1868 WESTON walked 100 miles in 22 hours and 20 minutes, and eleven years later he still held the championship among long-distance walkers, winning the Astley belt at the international contest in Agricultural Hall, Islington, London.

WESTON was the originator of the walking contests, the inciter of the six-day-go-as-you-please contests in the old Madison Square Garden, and now, in the era of the motor car he sticks to his excellent legs as a means of locomotion, and has started in bravely to demonstrate anew the merit of his carefully preserved gait. With WESTON the art of walking was revived. Every schoolboy in the land began to emulate him. Professional walkers became as numerous as jockeys and circus tumblers. ROWELL, the Englishman, with his easy jog-trot, soon cast WESTON'S long-distance records in the shade, but WESTON clings to this day to his old steady manner of putting one foot before the other. He walks as the wandering friars of Mediaeval Europe may have walked from the towns of Italy to the crude cities of the north, as Tannhäuser and his comrades may have walked in their long pilgrimage to Rome.

The bicycle races, and later, the automobile races, have supplanted the popular walking matches of long ago. The age is more rapid in every way, and athletic sports are more common and varied. WESTON'S triumphs, however, live in the memory, and he is now walking over his old ground like the amiable ghost of a simpler age.

November 1, 1907

WESTON FINISHES HIS LONG WALK

Asserts That He Has Broken His Former Record by 40 Hours.

CHALLENGES THE WORLD

Owing to a Misunderstanding Chicago's Official Reception Plans Were Not Carried Out.

Edward Payson Weston finished his walk from Portland, Me., to Chicago, yesterday, arriving at the Chicago Post Office at 12:10, beating his record made forty years ago by 40 hours.

Special to The New York Times.

CHICAGO, Nov. 27.—I am now resting up after the most triumphal walk I have ever made, one series of ovations from Portland, Me., to Chicago, Ill.

It has been ended by a demonstration greater than I ever imagined could be given any man, much less my humble self. Chicago afforded me a welcome which will be a treasure to my memory for the rest of my life.

On entering Chicago at 12:30 A. M. I was met by the Police Department and members of the new Illinois Athletic Club, together with numerous automobile parties, and hundreds on foot. Being so late we decided to stop for the night at Chicago Beach, which is about eight miles from the Post Office.

It was very late before I retired, as there were so many people who had stayed up to meet me that I could not sleep until I had met them all.

I was called at 8 A. M. We left the hotel at 10 o'clock, and amid the cheers of thousands began the march to the Post Office.

William Hale Thompson, President; George Lytton, Secretary, and E. C. Racey, Chairman of the new Illinois Athletic Club, met me, and invited me to partake of the hospitality of their club, of which I am now a guest, at the Chicago Beach Hotel.

The following morning, during the entire trip to the Post Office, their members, either in motor cars or on foot, were in constant attendance, doing the best that in them lay for the comfort and assistance of me and mine, and it is perhaps as much due to the efforts of their President and those with him as to Chicago's splendid police that the course was so well taken care of.

A finer body of the men than the Chicago police it has never been my great fortune to meet. I was entirely surrounded by mounted officers, who kept the streets clear before me, and although as we turned into Michigan Avenue we found the street literally packed with people, they soon cleared a passage, and I never had to hesitate in my walk. All along the

route the sidewalks were filled to the edge with the cheering thousands, and every window was full of people.

The cheering was deafening. The nearer I got to the Post Office the denser the crowd became, and only the great precaution the Police Department had taken prevented accidents in the surrounding crowd. Shortly after starting I was met by Chief of Police Shippy, Fire Marshal Horan, and Alderman Badenoch, who were my personal escort and walked the entire route with me.

Denser and denser became the crowds until the Post Office was reached, and where Mayor Busse of Chicago, with Postmaster Campbell, were waiting to meet me. Here my walk officially ended, but I continued on to the Illinois Athletic Club through the closely packed streets.

It is my trust that in the little talk I gave from the balcony of the clubhouse I was able to tell them how sensible I was of their kindness. After luncheon with their President and Mr. Racey, the Chairman of the Reception Committee, and an inspection of their quarters, one hour's rest and supper, I found myself much interested in the evening's sports and especially enjoyed a few moments' bowling, though I fear my skill at that pastime is less than my walking ability.

This is perhaps the most appropriate place for me to express my heartfelt appreciation of the splendid reception accorded me by the Illinois Athletic Club.

It will scarcely be necessary, in the light of the above, to comment at length upon my physical condition, save to say that at this hour of 11 P. M. I am convinced more than ever before that there is that in the American nature, which places it above all other nations, for it is this true spirit that is ever present, be it upon the field of sports or the field of battle.

I conclude by congratulating them upon their victory and thanking Providence that I was permitted for a short time to be that spirit's incarnation.
EDWARD PAYSON WESTON.

COULD REPEAT WALK SOON.

Weston Wants to Meet a Walker from Some Other Country.

CHICAGO, Nov. 27.—Edward Payson Weston completed his 1,288-mile walk from Portland, Me., at 12:15 o'clock to-day.

The finish to-day was a triumphal march from the Chicago Beach Hotel through the South Side boulevards at a pace which taxed the powers of endurance of several city officials and others who essayed to walk beside the aged pedestrian.

While the trip officially ended at the Federal Building, an unfortunate circumstance and Weston's pride operated to change the reception plans at the last moment.

At the Federal Building Weston, flushed with victory, approached the Jackson Boulevard entrance, used only by employes and to which the public is not admitted. At the door a uniformed official opposed his entrance, and directed him to one of the other entrances. Notwithstanding that Mayor Busse, Postmaster Campbell, Post Office Inspector Col. J. E. Stuart, and several other city and Federal officials were within waiting to greet him, Weston, seemingly misunderstanding the opposition to his ingress, turned on his heel and asked the way to the Illinois Athletic Club. He could not be persuaded to enter the building, where a crowd as dense as that in the streets, was waiting to catch a glimpse of the pedestrian.

After some minutes had passed a custodian explained the situation to the Mayor and others, and it was decided to dispense with the reception to Weston.

Nothing, however, interfered with the unofficial welcome of the citizens, or that which took place at the Illinois Athletic Club to which Weston proceeded.

At the athletic club the crowd was so dense that the police heading the procession had great difficulty in opening a way. From the steps of the building Weston made a brief speech, thanking the people for their interest in him.

"Within a week," he said, "I will be ready to repeat this walk, and I challenge the world for such a walk. When I say I challenge the world, I mean that I would like to meet a walker from some foreign country, especially from England, France, or Germany. The foreign countries do not produce athletes like those to be found in the United States."

Weston crossed the State line into South Chicago at 1:05 o'clock this morning.

Three thousand people were present at the border of South Chicago to greet him. Capt. Charles Dorman of the South Chicago police station, commanding twenty-five policemen, kept the crowd from interfering with the walker's feet. A solid line of patrolmen marched twenty-five feet ahead of him, brushing the good-natured spectators out of the roadway. At the outer ends of this bluecoat line two ropes were held which extended back to the following automobile. These ropes formed the sides of a hollow square 6 by 25 feet in size, in which the aged man walked.

The big crowd was joyful. "Marching Through Georgia" was sung throughout the way. The old man plodded on, seemingly unmindful of the attention he was receiving, or, more properly, rather scornful of it, as putting further difficulties and distractions in the way of an already difficult task.

He left the Chicago Beach Hotel, seven miles south of the business district of Chicago, at 9:52 A. M.

Weston reached Drexel Boulevard and Fifty-first Street at 10:12 and struck out northward at a fast gait. The boulevard was packed with a cheering crowd all along his line of march.

When Weston made his appearance at the Chicago Beach Hotel he had discarded his dusty garb, which he had worn during the rough portion of his journey, and wore a new blue suit, polished shoes, black gaiters, and a neat black felt hat and white gloves.

Attended by a noisy crowd he began the finishing lap of his long journey. The procession went south two blocks, thus adding four blocks to the distance Weston had to cover. This was done because of difficulty encountered by the automobiles which were following the pedestrian in passing under a viaduct.

The rest of the distance was covered in the most direct manner possible. Weston, during the final tramp, was preceded by Alderman Badenoch, who carried a banner of the Illinois Athletic Club, with the inscription "Welcome to Weston." Then came a line of twelve policemen. Weston followed closely behind and appeared jaunty and fresh, and kept up a spirited conversation with his guards in front.

In automobiles following Weston, were his judges and members of the Illinois Athletic Club Reception Committee, headed by President William Hale Thompson.

Over a part of the distance, Chief of Police Shippy and Fire Marshal Horan walked beside Weston. They were joked by the aged walker about their ability to keep the pace set by him.

November 28, 1907

Big Pedestrian Events Being Planned

Edward Payson Weston will celebrate his seventieth birthday on Monday, March 15, by starting from this city to walk across the continent. This will be the most arduous effort that the veteran athlete has attempted in his long life of successful walking, but he fully expects to accomplish the unusual task within 100 days. His splendid physical condition leaves little doubt in the minds of his friends that he will make as great a triumph of this transcontinental trip as rewarded his efforts a little over a year ago, when he lowered by nearly twenty-eight hours the record established by him forty years before in walking from Portland to Chicago, traveling 1,288 miles in 24 days and 19 hours.

Mr. Weston's trip as mapped out calls for a walk of from 4,400 to 4,500 miles. He says he will average forty-five miles a day, but this is a conservative estimate for him, for in his recent 1,288-mile walk to Chicago he averaged slightly over fifty-two miles a day, on one day making ninety-six miles. Following his usual custom, which he has rigidly observed from his early years, Mr. Weston will not walk on Sundays. Adhering to his prescribed limit of 190 walking days, therefore, he will enter San Francisco in the afternoon of Thursday, July 8, but he has secret ambitions of arriving slightly ahead of time.

Several alleged walks across the continent have been heralded from time to time, but their accuracy has been so vague as to be valueless for records of bona fide achievements. Mr. Weston will be accompanied by an automobile on the journey, carrying an attendant and official observers, who will be picked up from place to place, but the 70-year-old pedestrian will walk every foot of the way. He has planned his route so that all of the rivers will be crossed on bridges, thus obviating the necessity of using a ferry.

A revival of interest in long-distance walking has been growing for some time, and its culminating features will be exemplified in the coming six-day international go-as-you-please race in Madison Square Garden, beginning at 12:05 o'clock on Monday morning, March 8. This big race will end Saturday night, March 13, and it will be immediately succeeded by Weston's long walk on the following Monday.

Never, perhaps, in the athletic history of the world has such an exhibition of physical endurance been planned by a man so well advanced in years. Were Weston forty years younger it would be a feat worthy of arousing wide attention. Indeed, when Weston, in 1867, at the age of 29 years, essayed to walk from Portland, Me., to Chicago in twenty-six days it was regarded as a remarkable effort, and its success placed him in the front rank of pedestrians and attracted the interest not only of the sporting public, but of eminent scientists and physicians in all parts of the world. Later, when Weston went to England and repeated his triumphs, he was the object of the greatest curiosity to all classes of people and was the recipient of more popular favor than had ever before been lavished upon an athlete.

Now, at the age of 70 years, when a man's active career in athletics particularly, is supposed to be at an end, Mr. Weston is preparing to eclipse all of his other achievements by starting out on what will be, if it succeeds, the most spectacular, as well as the most difficult, task ever attempted by a pedestrian

EDWARD PAYSON WESTON.

Mr. Weston is not taking the shortest route to the Pacific Coast, which would be somewhat less than 3,400 miles to San Francisco. By long detours he is adding fully a thousand miles to the regular transcontinental trip. Starting from New York he will follow the line of the Hudson River to Troy and then strike westward through the Mohawk Valley to Buffalo, following the same route traversed on his two long walks from Portland to Chicago. At Buffalo he will make a detour, going south through Jamestown, N. Y., and Youngstown, Ohio, to Pittsburg, and then turn northward, going through Canton and Massilion, regaining his old route at Bellevue, Ohio, and thence to Chicago, passing through Toledo and South Bend.

One of Mr. Weston's reason's for making this detour is to avoid going through Cleveland. This is the only place, he says, in his entire walk in 1907 from Portland

to Chicago where he did not have proper protection in passing through the city, and, owing to the crowd pressing upon him, he received his only injury of the whole trip, a boy treading on his foot, which caused him severe pain for the following two days.

Leaving Chicago, Mr. Weston will enter new fields in his pedestrian career. While following the main railroad lines, his walking will be done entirely on the post roads, which will add somewhat to his total mileage from the distances by railroad. From Chicago he will go to St. Louis, 285 miles, passing through Joliet and Bloomington. The next stretch will be to Kansas City, 298 miles; along the line of the Union Pacific thence to Denver, 640 miles; to Cheyenne, 107 miles, and on to Ogden, 484 miles. To escape the severe alkali deserts west of Ogden, Mr. Weston will turn southward, following the route of the San Pedro, Los Angeles & Salt Lake Railway to Los Angeles, a total of 781 miles. From Los Angeles he will walk direct into San Francisco along the coast road, 475 miles, the greater part of which he traveled a year ago. By the railroad mileage this brings the total distance up to 4,347 miles, but by the public roads the mileage will be nearer 4,500 when Mr. Weston arrives in San Francisco.

The seventy-year-old pedestrian will not confine all of his duties to walking. He intends to lecture in all of the principal cities and towns through which he will pass, and arrangements will be made in advance for his lectures. This was the method he adopted with great success in England from Nov. 21, 1883, to March 15, 1884, when he walked 5,000 miles all over England, averaging fifty miles a day and lecturing nearly every night under the auspices of the Church of England Temperance Society.

Mr. Weston is carrying along in his automobile no camping outfit, as he believes he will have no difficulty, even in the most-distant parts of his long Western trip, in finding villages or hamlets where he can get a comfortable sleep. He will carry a small stock of provisions, chiefly eggs, tea, and a little meat and plenty of ginger ale. A special contrivance will be ararnged in the automobile whereby a quantity of ice may be carried at all times. He will also take some good blankets, extra shoes, and changes of clothing.

Mr. Weston is as enthusiastic about his big walk as a young man starting off on his first important venture. Barring illness or accident there is little doubt of his success for walking is second nature to him, and he is not deterred by any condition of weather. He is par excellence, the most remarkable and successful pedestrian that the world has ever seen. He is a typical Yankee, having been born in Providence, R. I., March 15, 1839. He was not particularly strong as a boy, and took to walking as a means of healthful exercise. When 22 years of age he walked from Boston to Washington to witness the inauguration of Abraham Lincoln, covering the 453 miles in 208 hours. His walk from Portland, Me., to Chicago, in 1867, when 29 years of age, in 25 days, 23 hours brought him into world-wide fame, and for the next twenty years he took in many professional walks beside long open air trips. In 1874, in Newark, he walked 500 miles in 5 days, 23 hours and 38 minutes, including a 24-hour walk of 115 miles. In 1876 he went to England where his walks drew thousands of spectators. In 1879 he won the famous Astley championship belt by walking a distance of 550 miles in 141 hours and 44 minutes, making a new six-day record. In December, 1893, at the request of a number of gentlemen, including many physicians in New York, to demonstrate that his walking feats had not injured his health, he walked over ice and snow from the Battery to the Capitol at Albany, 160 miles, in 59 hours and 59 minutes. On May 2, 1906, he walked from the City Hall, Philadelphia, to the Fifth Avenue Hotel, 100 miles, in 23 hours and 54 minutes, making but one stop when he slept for thirty minutes at New Brunswick.

February 28, 1909

WESTON AT 71 STARTS 4,300-MILE WALK

Thousands See Veteran Pedestrian Begin Jaunt to San Francisco.

ESCORTED THROUGH CITY

Company B, Seventh Regiment, and Police Lead Way from Post Office—Mr. Morgan Sends Veteran Off.

Daily reports will be sent exclusively to The New York Times by Edward Payson Weston during his walk from New York to the Pacific Coast.

BY EDWARD PAYSON WESTON.

Special to The New York Times.

TARRYTOWN, N. Y., March 16.—I arrived here at 12:30 this morning, feeling in the best of health and spirits.

The reception that was extended to me in New York, at Yonkers, and along the route was the greatest I have ever witnessed, and I am indeed truly grateful to those who appreciated the start of my effort.

Police Inspector Schmittberger and his force are entitled to the highest praise for the manner in which they assisted me in my start. Ben and Dan Rinn, who walked with me, are the best walkers on the New York police force. My old regiment, the Seventh, showed its loyalty in escorting me and my thanks to them cannot be expressed in words entirely, especially to Companies A and B, and John Chalmers and C. A. Joseph Tuck-Berner, who walked with me to Tarrytown. The police of Yonkers were very kind, and their interest was very noticeable. After escorting me to Meadow Hall, the historical building recently presented to the city, where I signed the register, they went with me to the city limits.

Walking with elasticity of step and freedom of action that was the absolute contradiction of age, Edward Payson Weston, the veteran pedestrian, celebrated the seventy-first anniversary of his birth yesterday afternoon by starting one of the longest walks of his career, a walk from ocean to ocean, the start being made from the General Post Office in this city and the finish to be in San Francisco. The total distance approximates 4,300 miles, and Weston expects to reach the Pacific Coast city in 100 days, Sundays not included, for he will, according to his usual custom, take this as a day of rest. Along the route Weston will deliver a number of lectures on the benefits of walking in maintaining health.

Weston will not take the most direct course to San Francisco, making a wide detour that will bring him down to Pittsburg. The first stage of the long journey takes him up the Hudson and then west through the principal cities of Central New York, including Albany, Utica, Syracuse, Rochester, and Buffalo. He will then switch down through Pennsylvania to Pittsburg, and then turn into Ohio and Indiana, touching Canton, Springfield, and South Bend. After that the direction will be north to Chicago, where a big reception will be tendered to him by the Chicago Athletic Club.

After crossing the Mississippi River he will go to St. Louis, and from there to Kansas City, Denver, Ogden, Salt Lake, and Los Angeles, and thence up the coast to San Francisco.

The start yesterday was from the General Post Office, Weston first appearing in the office of Postmaster Edward M. Morgan, where a number of his friends were gathered to bid him farewell and a pleasant journey. The time scheduled for his appearance was 4:15 o'clock, but he was a trifle late in arriving, and there was some anxiety aroused when the scheduled hour passed. Suddenly the swinging doors were thrown wide open, and Weston raced into the middle of the floor, attired in a long linen duster. He greeted a few friends, and a moment later was going down the steps of the building to the street, removing the duster on the way. His walking costume was composed of a blue coat of light weight, riding trousers, and natty mouse-colored leggins, and a felt hat of broad brim that resembled a sombrero in all but color.

The streets around the Post Office were thronged with people who were waiting for the start, and these flocked around him so closely that for a moment it seemed that the police guard would be swept away. His friends of the police force, Dan and Ben Rinn, whom he had asked to be his special guard for the first few miles of the journey, rescued him and he was escorted to the rear of the Post Office, where about thirty of his former comrades of Company B, Seventh Regiment, from 1863 to 1865, were assembled under the leadership of Capt. James B. Schuyler. Together with the Metropolitan Band and a cordon of mounted police these soldiers, who were not in uniform, acted as his escort through the city.

Walking with a springy step and a general jaunty air, Weston crossed Park Row and started the first course of the trip up Lafayette Street. The short cane which he carried gave him a striking appearance as he clasped it with one hand behind his back and the other over his shoulder. The crowd was dense and repeated cheers and shouts of encouragement were called out to him, and he was kept busy doffing his hat. For a great part of the distance through the city streets the crowd trailed behind the pedestrian, those who dropped out being replaced by new recruits.

From Lafayette Street the course led to Fourth Avenue as far as Twenty-sixth Street and then across to Fifth Avenue. All along this thoroughfare he was greeting acquaintances, several times rushing to the sidewalk to shake hands with those he recognized.

At Fifty-ninth Street the members of Company B, many of whom looked as if they had about walked themselves out, lined up and bade farewell, while the band struck up "Auld Lang Syne." From Fifty-ninth Street Weston went up Broadway, the first scheduled stop being at Yonkers, where he delivered a short address before the members of the Y. M. C. A.

Weston took the first refreshment he had had since morning at a restaurant at 125th Street, his trainer bringing him out a hot cup of tea in which a raw egg had been dropped. He looked fatigued at this point, the excitement having drawn heavily on his vitality. This, however, did not prevent him from starting out at a fast clip as soon as he had finished the tea. Last night he went as far as Tarrytown, a distance of thirty miles.

For the trip across the continent Weston will be accompanied by an automobile, which will contain his trainer, Charles E. Hagen, and S. W. Cassells, in addition to the chauffeur. The auto contains all the supplies needed for the trip, and in addition foodstuffs will be taken

aboard in case of emergency.

While this is not the longest walk that Weston has ever attempted it is the hardest. He once covered 5,000 miles in 100 days in England, but the event was over a road course of which many laps counted to make up the distance. This performance, however, is taken as an indication that he will be able to make the 4,500 miles in the scheduled time.

WESTON BEATS SCHEDULE.

Veteran Pedestrian Walks Ahead of His Figures to Yonkers.

Alfred Payson Weston arrived at Yonkers, officially at 9:15 o'clock, with an escorting crowd that grew in size until more than 2,000 spectators filled the streets when he reached the City Hall and there signed the visitors' book.

Only a small crowd met the veteran walker when he reached the city line, but from that time until he left for Tarrytown, at 10:45, after an hour and a half in Yonkers, he was the centre of attention, and a special guard of ten policemen had to be called out to open a way for him when he left the City Hall and started for the Young Men's Christian Association Hall, where he delivered a lecture on walking to a big audience.

He had a light meal at a restaurant before he resumed his walk, declaring that he had walked ahead of his schedule, in arriving at Yonkers, simply because he could not slow down to the figures he had intended to make.

March 16, 1909

WESTON IN BLIZZARD, HALTS IN HIS WALK

Pedestrian Reaches Bergen, Where He Will Stay Until Storm Abates.

DONS HIS OILCLOTH SUIT

Snow and Slush More Than a Foot Deep, with Gale Blowing Fifty Miles an Hour Against Walker.

Written Exclusively for THE NEW YORK TIMES
By EDWARD PAYSON WESTON.
Special to The New York Times.

CHURCHVILLE, N. Y., March 25.—I neglected to state last night that, after leaving Macedon, for the first time during this walk it began to rain very hard, so that I had to don my oilcloth suit and fisherman's hat. The roads were fairly good, but the rain continued all the way to Rochester. After delivering my lecture at the Y. M. C. A. the police officers kindly escorted me, under the direction of Capt. Stein, to the new and beautiful Hotel Rochester, where I was most cor-

dially greeted and became the guest of the manager, W. D. Horstman. A splendid suite of rooms was reserved, not only for me, but for the entire party accompanying me.

Weston's Transcontinental Walk, New York to San Francisco.

Weston is in his seventy-first year, and his task is to walk across the United States in 100 days, (Sundays excepted.)

Post Road Distance, 4,300 miles.

	Miles.
March 15 New York to Tarrytown....	30
March 16 to Poughkeepsie............	46
March 17 to Hudson..................	60
March 18 to Troy....................	39
March 19 to Fonda...................	43
March 20 Utica. (remained Sunday)...	55
March 22 to Syracuse................	60
March 23 to Lyons...................	47
March 24 to Rochester...............	49
March 25 to Bergen..................	16
Total	445

Route for To-day:
Byron, Batavia, Corfu—About 27 miles.

I retired at 11 o'clock and enjoyed a most refreshing sleep until 5 o'clock this morning. On arising I found that it not only rained all night, but was still pouring, and as this is a short day and as I wished to attend to some private business, I deferred the start until 8 o'clock, when my dear old friend John Winsley Breyfogle tried to induce me to be his guest in the same house for this day, as the downpour was so continuous and promised to be so all day. Though the offer was rather tempting I wanted to make extra miles to-day by going to Corfu. There is now a full-sized blizzard raging, which might interfere with the food schedule, so I decided, if possible, to go eleven miles further.

Leaving the Hotel Rochester, on Main Street, under the escort of six police officers, sent by Capt. Stein to Seneca Parkway, I had not gone more than two miles when the rain changed to a snowstorm, accompanied by a gale blowing forty miles an hour. I endured this for a mile, when some ladies from a piazza waved me good cheer, and I thought it a good place to arrange a handkerchief around my neck, the house protecting me from the gale. To my surprise, I found that in changing my coat for the oilcloth suit I had forgotten to take my handkerchief. This house proved to be the home of Mr. C. C. Palmer, 140 Seneca Street, Rochester, N. Y., who insisted upon supplying me with a large handkerchief to protect my neck, and he adjusted it, with the aid of the ladies of his family, who seemed very solicitous that I should not get pneumonia.

Though the gale was the fiercest of the year in this district, the road was so very good for the first eleven miles that I was really enjoying it until the last four miles, which were covered with clay mud and four inches of snow, that consumed one hour and twenty-three minutes, and the usual added miles which do not appear on the schedule, which brought me here at 12:40 P. M.

I have just finished a refreshing nap at Miss Jenny Edwards's cozy home and partaken of a hearty dinner, and shall be on the road again at 4:15 P. M., hoping to reach Corfu, twenty-nine miles, before 1 A. M. Friday, making forty-four miles for the day and making the total 473 miles to date.

The blizzard is far more welcome than the frozen ruts and sticky clay mud, and consequently I am in perfect condition and health.

BERGEN, N. Y., March 25.—On leaving Churchville I found the snow and slush more than a foot deep, with wind and gale blowing directly in my teeth at the rate of fifty miles an hour, so that it took me one hour and twenty-five minutes to reach Bergen, three miles. Several old residents have advised me to stop over, as the gale may subside at midnight. I have taken their advice, as they say it is the worst blizzard of the season.
EDWARD PAYSON WESTON.

March 26, 1909

WESTON STRUGGLES IN GALE AND DRIFTS

Veteran Walker Plods Along and Leaves His Auto Party Far Behind.

CRAWLS OVER SNOWBANK

Only Thing That Bothers Aged Pedestrian Is His Enormous Appetite— Escorts Along the Route.

Weston's Transcontinental Walk, New York to San Francisco.

Weston is in his seventy-first year, and his task is to walk across the United States in 100 days, (Sundays excepted.)

Post Road Distance, 4,300 miles.

	Miles.
March 15 New York to Tarrytown....	30
March 16 to Poughkeepsie............	46
March 17 to Hudson..................	60
March 18 to Troy....................	39
March 19 to Fonda...................	43
March 20, Utica, (remained Sunday)...	55
March 22 to Syracuse................	60
March 23 to Lyons...................	47
March 24 to Rochester...............	49
March 25 to Bergen..................	16
March 26 to Buffalo.................	44
Total..........................	489

Route for To-day:
East Aurora, Chaffee, Machias, Franklinville, Hinsdale, Olean, (remain over Sunday,) about 71 miles.

BUFFALO, N. Y., March 26.—Making scarcely three miles an hour at the end of his day's journey, Edward Payson Weston plodded over the city line to-night at 11:30. The roads traversed to-day were several inches deep in mud.

"I hope that I don't strike anything as bad as this between here and the coast," said Weston.

The old pedestrian covered forty-four

miles to-day. He stopped at Bowmansville, six miles from the city line, at 9:30 for a brief rest. He was urged to remain there for the night, but insisted on making Buffalo to-night and keeping up with his schedule. He will leave for Olean to-morrow morning.

Written Exclusively for THE NEW YORK TIMES
By EDWARD PAYSON WESTON.
Special to The New York Times.

BATAVIA, N. Y., March 26.—"Oh, the snow, the beautiful snow!" And how deep it is and how it blows! There was so much of it here that when I tried to resume my journey to San Francisco this morning at 1:30 o'clock I found it a physical impossibility under the conditions then prevailing. The chauffeur of the automobile which carries the party that accompanies me on the journey went out early this morning and was blown into a snowdrift. I soon discovered it was useless for me to start out in the deep, drifting snow, with a terrific gale still blowing, so I returned to the house until a later hour.

I had breakfast at 6 o'clock, and left Bergen at 7:40 and arrived at Byron at 9:40, wading through some drifts fully four feet deep. The lowest depth of the snow at any point was one foot, and a fifty-mile-an-hour gale swept into my face as I struggled along at a slow pace. At every house I passed a good woman or man came out and offered me hot refreshments and any aid within their power to bestow.

I left Byron after drinking a cup of coffee with two eggs in it. I plodded on, the gale increasing in its velocity and the snow drifting higher and higher each minute. I had not proceeded out of Byron more than two miles before I struck a snowdrift more than six feet high. The automobile meantime was struggling in the smaller drifts far back of me. I tackled the immense drift, and had to crawl through it on my hands and knees, but had lots of fun, with no one in sight except a dog. I did not see a person until I had traveled two miles further, when I began to grow faint. Just then a farmer and his wife came out of their house and gave me a bowl of hot milk, which was a life saver sure enough. The good Samaritans were Mr. and Mrs. Fred Blood. This nourishment provided me with strength sufficient to permit me to wabble into Batavia, near which place I met some of the prettiest girls and handsomest boys on my trip.

Joseph Driscoll, Charles Monroe, Earl Whitehead, and Peter Bernfeld, members of the Sixty-fifth Regiment of Buffalo, came here to escort me to Buffalo, where I have an engagement to deliver a lecture at Shea's Theatre this evening.

Just outside of Batavia I was met by Capt. McCulley and Policeman Blair. The Captain said it was the third time that he had the honor of escorting me through the town in my long walks. In passing through Batavia I received one of the grandest ovations I have met on the road. Ex-Alderman Edward Russell, who accompanied me from Byron forty-two years ago, most kindly offered me the hospitality of his home and a luncheon. When I arrived at his home, at 12:05 P. M., I decided to remain about thirty minutes, and then leave for Buffalo. I expect to reach there about 11 o'clock tonight, unless the roads are in such condition that I cannot possibly do it.

Physically, the only thing that now bothers me is my enormous appetite. I hope to see my chauffeur somewhere between here and Buffalo, if he is lucky enough to drive his car through the drifts. So far I have got him beat.

EDWARD PAYSON WESTON.

March 27, 1909

ON FOOT FROM NEW YORK TO SAN FRANCISCO

Scenes Along the Road

with Famous Walker, Edward Payson Weston, in His Hundred-Day

Sprint Across America

HAVING exceeded the allotted span of threescore years and ten, one's conception of this famous walker would be that of the white-haired veteran of the roads resting before a cheery fire in slippered feet, recounting to a younger generation the deeds that had made him famous, and in a general way bringing to mind the picture of the old soldier who

Wept o'er his wounds, or tales of sorrow done,
Shouldered his crutch and showed how fields were won.

But instead we now see him in his seventy-first year trudging through rain and mud and negotiating more miles a day than the vast majority of half his age could accomplish. The task that he has now set for himself is to walk from New York to San Francisco —a distance of 4,300 miles—and to cover the entire route in 100 days.

It has frequently been observed of Weston that he walks to keep well, and if ill resorts to that method of exercise as a curative agent. There was an illustration of this when the famous pedestrian was engaged in his 5,000-mile walk in England. Early in the journey his left leg became swollen to twice its natural size. Doctors endeavored to dissuade him from continuing his journey. Weston would not listen to them and hobbled on his way, stoutly proclaiming his belief that walking is good for whatever ails you, and continued to preach that gospel with his feet.

✦ ✦ ✦

Weston never makes any preparations for his walks. He believes that training is artificial and unnecessary, and that in the main it is harmful. It creates, he says, a condition which is unnatural, because it is not sustained; that when followed by the usual lapses at the completion of the given task, injures the body very seriously, not to speak of the excessive exercise which one takes in the undue hardships imposed by the athlete upon himself in his preparations. He declares that for the man who takes uniformly good care of himself there is not the slightest need for training, and that in the course of all his long career in which he has engaged in many long-distance walking feats he has never trained for a single day.

The explanation of his superb condition lies simply in the regularity of his habits and the simplicity of the fare that he eats. While not a total abstainer either from liquor or tobacco, he is an excessively temperate man. He has never in his life, he declares, taken a drink over a bar. He uses no stimulants whatever during the contests in which he engages, nor for a brief time before he undertakes a contest, and eats regularly the same food during what would ordinarily be the training period that he eats generally. This consists of two eggs, four slices of bread, and two cups of coffee for breakfast, no luncheon, and a dinner

of meat, about a quarter pound, two potatoes, and such vegetables and fruit as are in season. He drinks at night a single cup of tea. He eats fish and poultry at times, but game rarely, and never lobsters or other rich foods that tend to upset the stomach by giving it extraordinary work to do He especially avoids pastries.

✦ ✦ ✦

He rises in the morning at 8 o'clock and goes to bed at 2, holding that six hours' sleep is ample for any one, that more tends to lethargic action of the bodily functions. He invariably takes an hour and a half nap after dinner. In his life he has had a single illness, an attack of typhoid in 1871, and such minor ailments as he has had, like colds, he has invariably sweated out with exercise and cured in a day. Rain or shine, day by day, he walks from twelve to fifteen miles, except on Sunday, when he never takes exercise. He declares that it is with great difficulty that he shakes off the consequent torpor on Monday morning.

This is the life that Weston has been living always, and he believes it accounts entirely for his condition and exceptional vitality. He says that it costs less in bodily fatigue and is less harmful to walk 100 miles in twenty-four hours than it costs the athlete to run 100 yards in ten seconds. He calls attention to the accelerated heart action and unnatural breathing that succeed such unusual exertion, and declares they are harmful.

Weston, in spite of his gray hairs, gives one the impression of much less an age than he really is, and his vitality and wiry vigor are astonishing. He stands about 5 feet 7 inches in height, weight less than 150 pounds, but is as hard as nails. The usual deterioration which is noticeable in men of 70 years of age, in the tissues and blood vessels, is entirely lacking in him, according to the reports of experienced and well-known physicians who have examined him.

✦ ✦ ✦

Following is a record of the more notable journeys which Weston has accomplished on his pedestrian tours:

In 1867 Weston inaugurated the popular interest in walking by making his famous walk from Portland, Me., to Chicago, Ill., 1,326 miles, in 24 days 22 hours and 40 minutes, between noon of Oct. 29 and 10:40 A. M., Nov. 18.

In October, 1868, Weston made the first record in America of a walk of 100 miles within 24 consecutive hours, by walking the distance over an accurately measured road in Westchester County, New York, in 22 hours and 20 minutes.

In New York City in May, 1870, Weston walked 100 miles in 21 hours and 39 minutes.

Five years later in the same city Mr. Weston walked 115 miles in 23 hours and 40 minutes without a rest.

In June, 1879, Weston won the Astley Belt by walking a distance of 550 miles in 141 hours and 44 minutes, defeating two Englishmen and one other competitor 100 miles at the Agricultural Hall in London.

In 1884, under the auspices of the Church of England Temperance Society, Weston walked a distance of 50 miles per day for 100 days, without walking on Sundays, making a distance of 5,000 miles over the country roads in England.

In January, February and March, 1886, in a contest with Daniel O'Leary, Weston covered a distance of 2,500 miles, occupying 12 hours each day for a period of five weeks, and beating O'Leary 200 miles.

In December, 1893, he walked from the Battery in this city to the Capitol at Albany, a distance of 160 miles, in 59 hours and 59 minutes.

In 1907 he walked from Portland, Me., to Chicago in 24 days and 6 hours, duplicating his walk of forty years before and breaking his old record by 16 hours.

In his own opinion, his star achievement was his 5,000-mile walk in England, when he walked 50 miles a day for 100 days.

ON FOOT AND AT REST.

A Typical Ovation on Line of Veteran's March.

Special Correspondence THE NEW YORK TIMES.
SYRACUSE, N. Y., March 22.—"Here he comes!" In concerted volume the shout arose from a throng massed at the foot of a hill at the city line at 6 o'clock this evening. They had waited there long, with eyes strained to the east, and only reckless, extreme youth ventured beyond this point. For

Edward Payson Weston.

Weston's Reception in a Central New York City.

His Walking Costume

here the asphalt ended and beyond stretched, deep in interminable mud, the old Genesee turnpike that winds eastward from Syracuse to Albany, and from this City of Salt westward to Buffalo. It is the turnpike of the old stage coach days, and in portions it is in such condition that the veteran now "hiking" to far-off Frisco declares that plenty of those same old stage coaches are deep buried in its mire.

"Here he comes!"

The waiting crowd snuggled the more deeply into wraps that served to ward off the blade-like thrusts of a keen March wind and stared ahead at some approaching objects, dim in the gathering dusk. Soon was audible the chugging of a pair of automobiles moving slowly in the wake of a spare, hurrying figure toward which all eyes were turned, tramping stolidly, stubbornly through clinging mud.

Soon the pedestrian had reached the pavement, and with unflagging stride breasted the hill. A mighty cheer arose as the crowd disintegrated at his approach, deploying forward as an uproarious bodyguard. One of the automobiles moved ahead to clear the way, a blue-garbed cordon of policemen fell into step ahead of and beside the old man, who tramped on and on up the hill with the zest of a boy, waving his slouch hat in acknowledgment of the tribute implied in a name shouted by the gathering din:

"Weston!"

At the crest of the hill the marchers met with recruits swarming toward the outskirts, for the pedestrian was charac-

teristically an hour ahead of his schedule. These turned and marched with the others toward the city. It grew darker, the arc lights sputtered and flickered and suddenly gave forth their radiance. Down the easy grade leading toward the centre of the city marched the old man, who is seventy-one years young, silvery head up like a grenadier's white mustache militant, his hat swinging easily in his hand. Right and left he bowed to throngs that had gathered swift as a storm upon the walks, and as he marched his attendant bodyguard grew and grew until the utmost effort was required by those in charge to clear the way, albeit the route he was to take had not been publicly known, and he was escorted down side streets to the Good Will Congregational Church, his destination. Had not secrecy been observed traffic, sadly impeded as it was, would have been wholly stopped.

✛ ✛ ✛

Like a boy of twenty the veteran marched at a pace which soon had university youths, new to the razor, mopping their brows as they kept step with him. Right and left the old man bowed as there sounded in his ears the cries of greeting from men and women, the sharp, staccato crack of clapping hands. Moving freely and gracefully despite a limping leg, eternal youth burning in his dark eyes under the glare of the street lamps, Edward Payson Weston walked on, a rebuke to senility, a triumphant foe of years, the breathing embodiment of iron will.

It was three hours later. A few news-

paper men and two or three personal friends of the walker were standing outside a restaurant on West Fayette Street awaiting the arrival of Weston. He had just delivered his lecture to the audience that thronged the church. An automobile was now bearing him to his dinner and a merited rest.

A little later, surrounded by his friends and attendants at a table in a secluded corner, the old man dropped into a chair and carefully deposited his precious feet upon another that an attendant solicitously drew up. The triumphant zest of his arrival had departed. There were lines temporarily in his ruddy face, for the moment the spur relaxed, he was an old, tired man.

He passed a hand wearily over his eyes. "I ask your pardon for being so 'dopey,'" he said, apologetically. "It's the wind. Fifty-five miles from Utica and wind every step of the way. It makes you drowsy. Ah, how I'll sleep to-night!"

✛ ✛ ✛

They consulted him about the order. "Vegetable soup? You bet. Is there anything like vegetable soup? It puts new

life in you. Yes. And steak? Oh, yes. I'm not very hungry, but I can eat some. I've eaten only six times to-day.

"Would you kindly ask the waiter to bring me a few sheets of paper I've got to write my dispatch to THE TIMES. Don't feel much like writing. I've got to wake up."

"Here's a newspaper man," said some one. "He'll take down your dispatch for you. You dictate to him."

"Say, now, will you? Well, that's kind of you. Sure it won't trouble you? God bless the newspaper boys, that's all I can say. They've always been my friends. One of 'em said to me in Chicago last year, 'Uncle, what can I do for you?' I said: 'Do for me? Good God! You've done everything for me already. What more can you do?' And they're all like that, they're on the square."

His stationery had arrived and he pulled it toward him and produced a pencil. "Just to start it," he explained to the scribe, "and then I'll tell you the rest." He wrote a few lines, then dictated the rest, shading his eyes with his hand.

It is no exaggeration to say that the veteran at this moment was the freshest looking man in his party. The rest of them looked as if they'd like to fall asleep in their chairs. Renewed by the food and his favorite beverage of coffee, the old gentleman looked ready to take to the road again.

"Beats all," he ruminated, "how often, while I'm prowling along at night with my lantern, I'll hear some woman's voice from a door yard: 'Mr. Weston, I saw you pass here forty years ago and I was just seven years old. I shook hands with you.'

"'Did you?' I'll say. 'Well, let's shake hands again, for I like to shake hands with a woman that'll own up to her honest age. God bless you, madam!'"

"Ask him how he likes Chittenango," whispered one of the party to THE TIMES correspondent. Chittenango, by the way, is a place of diminutive size known to Gotham as a burg.

"Chittenango? Oh! it's a good little place, but hang its barbers. They're robbers. I've always been shaved in my room, for such is the free advertising you fellows give me a barber wouldn't have elbow room in his shop. They've never charged me more than 50 cents. But in Chittenango—in Chittenango, mind you— the fellow asked a dollar. Yes, Sir! And he got it. I never haggle. But his conscience ought to trouble him more than his razor did me."

He paused a moment to demolish some more steak, then leaned back with an air of being at peace with the world.

"More people know me every trip," said he. "Tell me by the pictures. Many teamsters stopped their horses to-day coming from Utica through the mud and sung out: 'How're you, Mr. Weston!' Makes a fellow feel good on a lonely road, hauling your hoofs out of mud like mucilage. Bless the people! I've tramped the country over many a time—they've been good to me. When you hear any one hammering at human nature he's a poor old grouch. He probably drinks too much."

"How were those eggs you got at Kirkville, Uncle?" asked an attendant, winking at THE TIMES man.

"Say," impressively replied the veteran, "they were the best ever. After eating some of those eggs I told my chauffeur here that if I ever heard of his running over a chicken I'd kill him!"

"By the way," put in Mr. Wilcox, "you've heard of the I-SAW-YOU-GO-THROUGH-HERE-FORTY-YEARS-AGO Club? It springs up wherever Mr. Weston visits. It remained for a woman to start an Ananias Club, as a sort of offshoot, the other day. She told him: 'I saw you go through here forty-five years ago.' And the point was, she didn't."

"Yes," put in the veteran, a twinkle in his dark eye, "and the worst of it was that by her own admission she tacked five years more on to her age."

The veteran was enthusiastic over the reception he received in Troy and Schenectady, through which cities he has passed five times. "There's a warmer welcome for me each time," said he.

Weston's Start from New York City on March 15.

"They're great people down there."

A messenger boy entered with a telegram for the old-young gentleman. "Pay your wash bill," he murmured as he opened it. But it wasn't. It was a message from a Buffalo theatrical manager in regard to Weston's lectures there passing to the West.

"Say," resumed the veteran, "you have towns through this section with some ungodly names. I came to a place to-day I understood at first to be called Swamproot. I understood later it was Wampsville. Even at that the name doesn't sound promising, but it's a good little town and I ate like a Christian there."

❖ ❖ ❖

Prompted by George C. Ryan, a Syracuse friend of his, he related one of his best stories of the evening. "On my Chicago trip," he said, "I was approach-

now."

"All right. Good night, friends; bless you all."

With a couple of friends, to whom he wished to address some parting words, the veteran climbed the stairs to a dormitory above the restaurant.

And as his friends left the room the veteran's eyes had already closed.

WESTON AS VIEWED BY EXPERTS

His Example and Its Influence on Athletics.

MANY physicians, of this city at least, are watching with close interest the attempt of the veteran walker, Edward Payson Weston, to cross the continent on foot at the average rate of some forty-odd miles a day. Their interest is

of any other of the exemplars of strength, skill, and endurance that now and then excite popular wonder and admiration.

They attribute his extraordinary powers to four factors: a naturally strong constitution; moderation through life in food and drink; long and careful training, so that in covering with his stride a given distance a minimum of energy is expended, and a will of tremendous strength.

Many of them doubt if he will finish, though, having made no examination of the subject, they are unwilling to prophesy. They feel that Weston's last year's walk from Portland to Chicago is a cogent argument in favor of success, yet they attribute so much to his will that they think it may force his body too far, so as to cause a breakdown before the course is done.

The most far-sighted professional inter-

Entering Weedsport, N. Y.

ing Port Byron when along drove a bright little boy in an open buggy.

"'Have a ride?' he asked.

"'Haven't any money.'

"'Ah! come on, it won't cost you nothin'.'

"'Guess I'll walk.'

"'How far you been walkin'?

"'Left Syracuse this morning.'

"'Why, that's twenty-seven miles. Where you walkin' to?'

"'Oh! I thought I'd sort of stroll to Chicago.'

"He looked wild-eyed at me a minute, then grabbed the whip. 'Gee! I've struck a lunatic!' he yelled. 'Giddap!' And up the road they went in a cloud of dust."

Dinner was done and the veteran was plainly weary. His attendant rose. "Come, Uncle," he said. "You know you've got to be up by 5. Better turn in

not excited alone by the nature of the feat, though all hold it marvelous that a man of Weston's age is capable of even attempting it; they are looking deeper, watching for the effect which this example will have in renewing the lost interest in walking as a pastime and an exercise, and for the effect they believe it will have in counteracting the theory they condemn—the theory that at the age of fifty or thereabouts a man is "down and out."

❖ ❖ ❖

Physicians and athletic directors interviewed regarding Weston's walk do not take him for the most part as an example of what many men who have kept in good physical trim might be able to do; they consider him entirely exceptional, as extraordinary an example of physical prowess as Jim Jeffries, Corbett, or Hayes, or

est displayed in Weston's walk by any physician was that of Dr. Frederic Brush, the Superintendent of the Post Graduate Hospital and Medical School on Second Avenue and Twentieth Street. Aside from the admiration with which he views Weston as an athlete, and the interest with which he watches his attempt as an individual feat, he holds of deep significance the example given to men above middle age for all kinds of energy and exertion.

"The garbled statement of Dr. Osler," he said, "has done tremendous harm; I believe it has caused many suicides. The greatest thing about Weston is that he is showing men that at an age where they have begun to think of chloroform they should be energetic and vigorous still.

❖ ❖ ❖

"I look on Weston personally as a

most remarkable man; a man of extraordinary individual equipment. It's absurd to say that he shows only what men who, starting with good physiques, could do at his age with careful training. They can't. Why, he is doing what mighty few young men, young athletes, can do. No man of any age at all has ever come up to his record so far as I know.

"He is not an example for emulation in that way, for he stands alone. It is in a general way that I mean. What he can do should go to convince other men that they are capable of a great deal more than they now think. You know how men so often nowadays begin to let things slip in at about forty-five, and then at fifty give up altogether. That's what I'm talking about. It's a reaction against this that I hope will follow Weston's extraordinary example. It should bring more energy all around; more energy in exercising, more energy in business. It should make these adherents of the misnamed Osler theory—for Osler never voiced that theory—courageous and cheerful. If Weston enterprise can do that, and it certainly tends to, he will have done something greater than to excite the astonishment and admiration of the country—that he had done already.

"In a narrower view the value of his attempt is great—it gives impulse to walking, as a pastime. We have become a non-walking nation. Working down here as I do, among many foreigners, I am surprised to find how readily these people walk ten or twelve miles a day as a matter of course.

"You know what effect the Marathon races had among schoolboys and other people, too. That showed how quickly a thing can be brought into popularity. Marathon running had a bad effect; it was too violent, and many people have suffered from it. But if Weston's walks give the same impulse—if they bring walking back into popularity—he has done untold good."

Dr. George L. Meylan, Physical Instructor of Columbia University, perhaps the best-known man of his line in the country, was most enthusiastic about Weston.

"He is marvelous," said he. "I tried to see him start this last time, but he must have started late. I have followed carefully the accounts of his progress in THE TIMES. Aside from the marvel of a man of that age undertaking such a thing, Weston certainly has a perfect command of the art of walking; he is unexcelled by any man of any age or nationality. Probably his closest competitor would be found in the French Army; that's where they have the best walkers in the world, by and large; they have studied walking there. But they can't beat Weston in spite of his age.

"I wouldn't prophesy as to whether he can finish. If it were not for his walk last year from Portland to Chicago I wouldn't think it possible, but that makes a man ready to believe anything of him.

"He certainly has a marvelous physique. It's hard to tell what factor enters most into his power—natural physical ability, or moderation through life, or nerve, or will, or whatever you want to call it, 'sand,' if you like, or long training which has given perfect command of the art.

"I take him simply as an individual phenomenon, not at all as an example of what other men might do with right care. He is just like Jeffries, or Hayes, or any other great athlete, and his particular branch is as hard to excel in as any other branch of sport.

"He shows us another valuable thing from the athletic point of view. Apparently he doesn't go into training in our sense. He has no fixed diet. So far as I can see he eats about what he pleases, but he eats in moderation, and drinks in moderation. That moderation is one of the secrets of his wonderful strength, and we are coming round to the idea that this, and not strict training, is the thing.

"He is a man in 10,000 or 100,000 or a million if you like. He has the mechanism of walking to perfection—the ability to use just the minimum of energy in covering a given space. Of course he has the "bent-knee" method—that's the French army way—the body forward, and the leg muscles used only in the middle of their range. It's just the natural way to walk; our stiff-legged method, product of high hats, stiff clothes, and canes is purely artificial. But Weston has perfect mastery, perfect balance.

✦ ✦ ✦

"No, no; mighty few, or none at all can do what he's doing. But he is giving impulse to all around energy and impulse to walking as an exercise. He has done that already. A man in just my position hears about those things. I know of many people prompted by his example to try walking; they were delighted when their attention was called to it by him, and though they had almost forgotten how to walk they have kept it up.

"I know, too, of many tramping and walking clubs, the result of his suggestion. There's one in Waltham, Mass., of 75 boys and girls, that cover some fifteen miles or so in one walk.

"It will be a great thing if that becomes popular. It's so simple and easy, accessible to every one up to the age of 80, and quite harmless. Any one at any time can walk. Most men neglect exercise between 35 and 45, and between 45 and 50 they begin to suffer. If Weston's example brings walking into fashion he has done something worth while, even if he takes three or four years off his life. But I don't think he will do that; he is an extraordinary man."

Dr. J. Leonard Corning of 53 West Thirty-eighth Street, the nerve specialist, said that he was opposed to excessive exercise, which was what he believed Weston's attempt to be, as he thought that from the over-cultivation of the physique the mentality suffered. But he said of Weston nevertheless:

"He is certainly an edifying spectacle, a man over 70 attempting such a thing—you can't deny that. I suppose his powers are largely, very largely, inherited. Few, if any, men could be at his age in such a condition of strength. He is an example of remarkable vitality, and that comes generally from inheritance.

"It would be gross folly to say that other men could do such a thing, especially at his age. People fall too often into the way of judging the mass by the individual; of saying so and so can do it, and therefore I can do it. This man is peculiarly fitted for just what he is doing. He is marvelous as an individual, simply that."

Another enthusiastic doctor was Henry S. Pascal of the Strathmore, Fifty-second Street and Broadway. "I think he will succeed," he said. "Judging from his other walk he ought to. What an extraordinary mechanism he must have—a wonderful heart, wonderful digestive organs—it is that rather than muscular strength that is surprising. Think of the little sleep he gets in proportion to his exertion!

"An example to other men above middle age, he certainly is that. Of course he is a natural exception, yet I think he does show to a large degree what other men might be. He has simply, by care and moderation and exercise, kept himself young; that's all. He is now what he was, or nearly what he was, at 40, and other men might keep their prime in the same way—by decent care and moderation. I do not think he will injure his life by it."

March 28, 1909

WESTON RUFFLED OVER MISTAKES

Pedestrian Loses His Temper After a Chapter of Mishaps on the Road.

MONDAY'S TASK TOO HARD

Veteran Rests Poorly and Defers His Start from Bryan Until Afternoon, Making a Short Walk for the Day.

Weston's Transcontinental Walk, New York to San Francisco.

Weston is in his seventy-first year, and his task is to walk across the United States in 100 days. (Sundays excepted.)
Post Road Distance, 4,300 Miles.

	Miles.
March 15 to 20, New York to Utica..	273
March 22 to 26, Utica to Buffalo.....	216
March 27 to April 2, Chaffee to Sharon	243
April 2 to 10, Sharon to Toledo.......	243
April 12 to Bryan...................	71
April 13 to Waterloo................	29
Total	1,075

Written Exclusively for THE NEW YORK TIMES
By EDWARD PAYSON WESTON.

Special to The New York Times.

BRYAN, Ohio, April 13.—It is only when I do some foolish thing that I am made to realize that I am a trifle older than I was twenty-five years ago. Yesterday was one chapter of mistakes. They began when I failed to secure the customary sleep from 5 to 11 o'clock on Sunday evening. Then my taking the wrong

road to Delta, which caused me to walk thirty-six miles before breakfast. Had I not, to some extent, been protected by the hearty supper supplied by Mr. Walton Sunday night I never should have tried to exceed this limit of stupidity. Then when I was led six or seven miles further off my road I lost by temper and "cussed" like the army of Flanders, for which I am very much ashamed, though I was obliged to face the seventy-mile-an-hour gale for three miles.

The climax came when, after enjoying excellent roads all days, the last eight miles between Stryker and Bryan I had to play checkers by passing from one cake of dry clay to another, in danger of falling every minute, and, though for the last three miles I was followed by 200 men and boys cheering lustily, it made me dizzy.

All through Stryker the roads and streets on either side were crowded with men, women, and children, who were most hearty in their demonstrations. The same scenes met me on my arrival in Bryan, though on a much larger scale, and the town band added greatly to the enthusiasm, escorting me to the hotel.

Though I had a sleep of six hours, when I awoke this morning I was made to realize the reaction of the excitement of Monday, and did not feel rested. I arose at 5, breakfasted at 6 o'clock, but was apathetic and dizzy. It was raining hard, so I lay down in my clothes for another hour's sleep. Feeling no better, I decided to make this a short day by going only to Waterloo, twenty-nine miles, and put in the long day to Goshen, fifty miles on Wednesday. Meanwhile a snowstorm set in and lasted until noon. It is now 1:30 in the afternoon, with indications of clearing, and I am starting for Waterloo, feeling quite well after a hearty dinner. I shall arrive at Waterloo by 10 o'clock to-night.

———

WATERLOO, Ind., April 13.—I am inclined to believe that the medical men are right when they say my recuperative powers are wonderful, for that extra seven hours' rest put me once more on "Easy Street."

I left Bryan at 1:30 P. M., and over slippery clay roads I walked to Edgerton, twelve miles, in three hours and forty minutes, and to Butler, nineteen miles, in five hours and twenty minutes, the last four miles over a beautiful road. Then I finished at Waterloo, twenty-nine miles, at 9:50 P. M., making twenty-nine miles for the half day and the grand total 1,077 miles. I am in perfect condition and my left arm is improving, so I will walk a long distance Wednesday.

EDWARD PAYSON WESTON.

April 14, 1909

WESTON WAITS FOR FASTER CHAUFFEUR

Veteran Walker Hopes To-morrow to Get an Attendant Who Will Keep Up with Him.

HIS CHICAGO RECEPTION

Written Exclusively for THE NEW YORK TIMES By EDWARD PAYSON WESTON.
Special to The New York Times.

CHICAGO, April 18.—Firmly resolved that I and the chauffeur driving the au-tomobile which has attended me since I left New York are to part here, my departure from Chicago for San Francisco will be delayed until the time to-morrow when I shall have a substitute driver. I shall, however retain memories of the original to keep me warm when I get into the high altitudes approaching the Pacific Coast. My stay in Chicago since my arrival here Saturday afternoon has been among my most pleasant experiences, in spite of the fact that in planning my route I made Chicago a way station instead of a terminal, as in my walk of 1907.

Weston's Transcontinental Walk, New York to San Francisco.

Weston is in his seventy-first year, and his task is to walk across the United States in 100 days, (Sundays excepted.) Post Road Distance, 4,300 Miles.

	Miles.
March 15 to 20, New York to Utica..	273
March 22 to 26, Utica to Buffalo.....	216
March 27 to April 2, Chaffee to Sharon	245
April 2 to 10, Sharon to Toledo.......	243
April 12 to Bryan.....................	71
April 13 to Waterloo, Ind.............	29
April 14 to Goshen, Ind...............	51
April 15 to New Carlisle, Ind.........	42
April 16 to Hobart, Ind...............	53
April 17 to Chicago..................	30
April 18 (Remained in Chicago.)	
Total 1,253	

———

There were hundreds of automobiles containing ladies and old friends that came out to the city line (16 miles) to welcome my arrival here Saturday and follow me into the city, and from there on through the generous kindness of Inspector Hunt, following instructions from Chief of Police Shippy, an ample police force escorted me to the Illinois Athletic Club. Just as I arrived at Jackson Park I was met by President McCormick, Lieut. E. C. Race, Chairman of the Athletic Committee, and other officers of the I. A. C. and informed that a reception had been arranged in my honor, to take place in the club that evening.

At various corners of the more important streets large numbers greeted me with generous applause. Ex-Alderman Badenoch again cheerily accompanied me as before. Arriving at this hospitable club at 6:30 P. M. I was loudly cheered, and after my walk of forty miles for the day, I immediately retired for a two-hour nap to prepare for the reception, which I took part in at 10 o'clock. It was a rousing welcome the club members gave me, and Vice President Samuel T. C. Loftis made it doubly interesting by presenting me with a valuable gold watch and a fob.

In making a résumé of the last week, I walked not only a longer distance (286 miles) than I had walked before, but under the most uncomfortable conditions I have ever endured. I left Toledo at 12:05 A. M. last Monday, and owing to negligence of the chauffeur, to whom I shall bid farewell, I was allowed to follow the wrong road to Delta. This artist allowed the auto to be stuck in the sand about 2 o'clock.

An hour later I found myself wandering in a woods near a swamp, and at 5 o'clock discovered that I was six miles north of the direct road and had the six miles to walk back. Meanwhile my chauffeur made no special effort to find me, but went on.

The consequence was I had to walk thirty-six miles in nine and a half hours before I got my breakfast. Luckily I had three or four young fellows with me who had followed out of Toledo. As though that was not enough for one day, my chauffeur prevailed upon me to take another road, instead of going through Wausau, which not only added seven miles to the trip that Monday, but the next three miles made me face a fierce gale. Altogether it caused me to lose a half day at Bryan Tuesday.

Wednesday night this interesting chauffeur again retired, and did not show up until Saturday. He retires for good and all to-morrow, and I am forced to lay over here until Monday night awaiting the arrival of another chauffeur.

To date I have walked some 300 miles more than the first quarter of the distance, deducting the one whole day I laid over at Mansfield, Ohio, the half day at Bryan, and three-quarters of a day at Youngstown. In the twenty-seven days of service I have averaged 47 miles each walking day. This gives me 108 miles to the good on the first quarter. From now on I shall make the average 45 miles per day, that is, 40 miles each of five days and 30 miles extra each Monday, unless something should cause me to add 5 or 10 miles on one of the other five days.

EDWARD PAYSON WESTON.

April 19, 1909

WESTON ARRESTED BY NEGRO OFFICER

Brooklyn, Ill., Policeman Thought Pedestrian Was an Escaped Lunatic.

RELEASED, THEN GOES ON

Singular Incident In Veteran's Trip to St. Louis—Guest of Missouri A. C. —Crowds Greet Him.

Weston's Transcontinental Walk, New York to San Francisco.

Weston is in his seventy-first year, and his task is to walk across the United States in 100 days, (Sundays excepted.) Post Road Distance, 4,300 Miles.

	Miles.
March 15 to 20, New York to Utica..	273
March 22 to 26, Utica to Buffalo.....	216
March 27 to April 2, Chaffee to Sharon	245
April 2 to 10, Sharon to Toledo.......	243
April 10 to 17, Toledo to Chicago.....	286
April 18-19, (Remained in Chicago.)	
April 20-25 Chicago to Lincoln.......	170
April 26 to Girard, Ill...............	55
April 27 to Alton, Ill................	49
April 28 to St. Louis, Mo............	32
Total 1,569	

Written Exclusively for THE NEW YORK TIMES By EDWARD PAYSON WESTON.
Special to The New York Times.

ST. LOUIS, Mo., April 28.—I enjoyed a good night's rest after yesterday's walk of 49 miles. I was awakened at 5:30 A. M. to-day, but had to wait for breakfast until 6:20, and I started for St. Louis at 7 A. M. It was cloudy, with a slight sprinkling of rain. An hour afterward the sun was shining and the weather balmy.

A singular incident developed in my walk to-day. When I entered the town of Brooklyn, Ill., inhabited chiefly by negroes, and followed by a crowd, I was arrested by a negro policeman. Upon asking the reason, he said that when a stranger walks through town with such a crowd following him he had a right to have his suspicions aroused. "How do I know but what you may be an escaped lunatic," he said. This was a funny incident, especially when my identity was made known. When the policeman learned who I was he walked away without offering an apology for my detention. On entering East St. Louis, Ill., at 3 P. M. I was greeted by a very large and enthusiastic crowd, which increased as I neared further into the heart of the city, where I was greeted by a committee of twenty-five members of the Missouri Athletic Club of St. Louis.

Here much confusion existed by a

crowd of people making it extremely difficult for the police to make a way for me, but they did grand work, and with the committee I was escorted to the Missouri Athletic Club house, where I will be their guest until to-morrow morning.
EDWARD PAYSON WESTON.

April 29, 1909

WESTON'S LONG DAY ON ROAD.

Walks 66 Miles and Is in Fine Condition—More Milk and Eggnog.

Weston's Transcontinental Walk, New York to San Francisco. Fifty-fifth Day of Walk. Weston is in his seventy-first year, and his task is to walk across the United States in 100 days, (Sundays excepted.) Post Road Distance, 4,300 Miles.	
	Miles.
March 15 to 20, New York to Utica...	273
March 22 to 27, Utica to Chafee.....	250
March 29 to April 3, Chafee to Youngstown	225
April 5 to 10, Youngstown to Toledo.	239
April 12 to 17, Toledo to Chicago.....	276
April 19 to 24, Chicago to Lincoln...	170
April 26 to May 1, Lincoln to Mexico.	246
May 3 to 8, Mexico, Mo., to Topeka..	239
May 10 to 15, Topeka to Wakeeney, Kan.	259
May 17, to Monument................	66
Total............................	2,243

Written Exclusively for THE NEW YORK TIMES
By EDWARD PAYSON WESTON.
Special to The New York Times.

OAKLEY, Kan., May 17.—After enjoying a restful day and a most refreshing sleep, arising at 10:30 P. M., I partook of a substantial meal and hurriedly wrote a short letter to the king of mascots at 60 Wall Street.

I started for Oakley at 12:05 A. M. with a number of ladies and gentlemen accompanying me several miles out of town. Mr. Schwiggert walked with me to Quinteer, a distance of 22 miles, without a stop before breakfast. Arriving at Grinnell, 22 miles further, at 1 P. M., I stopped for a long rest, and arrived at Oakley, 13 miles, at 6:40 P. M.

I am in excellent condition, not having a pain or ache of any kind. I will go to Monument, which is 9 miles from here, although I started out with the intention of remaining here over night. I feel good enough to make this extra distance without injury to myself.

All along the route, whether early in the morning or midday, I am met by enthusiasts who usually have some fresh milk or an eggnog for me, which is very kind and thoughtful of them, and escorting me into the town, where I am greeted by the entire population as I pass through, many going with me for many miles and catching a train going back home.

The weather, the roads, and my own condition are most favorable for walking. I could not wish it better. Total for to-day, 66 miles; grand total, 2,243 miles.
EDWARD PAYSON WESTON.

May 18, 1909

RANCHMAN RESCUES WESTON FROM STORM

Veteran Pedestrian Finds Shelter from a Four-Hour Rain in Kansas.

PRAISES SUN FLOWER STATE

People Hospitable and Country Beautiful—Passes Into Colorado in 56-Mile Walk.

Weston's Transcontinental Walk, New York to San Francisco. Fiftyseventh Day of Walk. Weston is in his seventy-first year, and his task is to walk across the United States in 100 days, (Sundays excepted.) Post Road Distance, 4,300 Miles.	
	Miles.
March 15 to 20, New York to Utica...	273
March 22 to 27, Utica to Chafee.....	250
March 29 to April 3, Chafee to Youngstown	225
April 5 to 10, Youngstown to Toledo..	239
April 12 to 17, Toledo to Chicago.....	276
April 19 to 24, Chicago to Lincoln....	170
April 26 to May 1, Lincoln to Mexico.	246
May 3 to 8, Mexico, Mo., to Topeka..	239
May 10 to 15, Topeka to Wakeeney..	259
May 17, to Monument................	66
May 18 to Sharon Springs............	22
May 19, to Cheyenne Wells, Col.....	58
Total	2,323

Written Exclusively for THE NEW YORK TIMES
By EDWARD PAYSON WESTON.
Special to The New York Times.

SHARON SPRINGS, Kan., May 19.—To Providence and that prince of ranchmen, A. C. Overhott of Lisbon, Logan County, Kan., P. O. address, Winona, Kan., I am surely indebted for saving me from disaster last night, just as I neared the stockyard pens, which is all there is of Lisbon, known as the first terminal of the Union Pacific Railway, and is the point formerly known as Sheridan, where the Indians massacred 3,000 people forty years ago, and also destroyed the entire village.

A furious thunderstorm seemed ready to burst over the country. I immediately took refuge under a temporary platform, which only partially shielded me from the storm. After I got comfortably settled, a wagon containing a gentleman, two ladies, and two young boys drove up to the wire fence, which separated the railroad from the stock pens. They all got out and came to where I was and said they were looking for me all afternoon, as they felt the shower was coming, and they thought they would urge me to go to their home, a half mile distant across the ranch.

They assured me that the storm would be very heavy and that I would have no protection there, so I reluctantly became their guest. The ranchman sent his family ahead with the wagon and we walked to his cozy home together. Just as we got to his gate the storm broke with all

its fury, and I was drenched before I reached the piazza, a hundred feet distant. The storm, which was accompanied by a cold gale, lasted for four hours. If it had not been for the thoughtfulness of my host in coming for and urging me to go to his house I should certainly have been attacked with pneumonia or lumbago. As it was, I enjoyed the perfection of hospitality, retiring at 8 P. M., there being no prospect that the storm would cease before midnight.

Not content with inviting me there, my hosts arose at 3:45 A. M. and prepared a bountiful breakfast, which I enjoyed. At 4:50 A. M., accompanied by my genial host, I returned to the track and made my way to Sharon Springs, where I arrived at 11:40 A. M., a distance of twenty-five miles. After partaking of a hearty dinner, prepared by Mrs. King of the Central Hotel, I shall leave here about 2 P. M. and expect to arrive at Cheyenne Wells, to make my first stop in Colorado, between 10 and 11 P. M.

In leaving Kansas, I want to say that though I have traveled all over England and part of France and a large part of America, thus far I have never yet passed through such a beautiful and health-giving country and such genial and hospitable people as are located in the sunflower State. To me it has been a paradise in every town and village I passed. Some one would invariably appear with some refreshing drink. I want to acknowledge my indebtedness to the Union Pacific Railroad for the assistance rendered me by all the station agents, also to the section men for their extreme kindness and courtesy, and at the same time to congratulate the company on having the finest roadbed I have yet passed over.
EDWARD PAYSON WESTON.

May 20, 1909

WIND BOWLS WESTON OVER EMBANKMENT

Pedestrian Encounters Severe Storms in Wyoming, but Goes On.

ENTERTAINED BY JAPANESE

Expects to Put in Another Big Day's Tramp To-day, Starting from Rawlins, Wyoming.

Written exclusively for THE NEW YORK TIMES
By EDWARD PAYSON WESTON.

Special to The New York Times.
HANNA, Wyo., June 6.—I finally arrived at this town after combating the

wind and heat at 8:30 P. M. yesterday. The Hanna Concert Band awaited me and escorted me to the hotel. Conditions were favorable to continue walking, but as there was no place to stop within the next twenty-five miles, which would cause me to walk on Sunday, which I will not do, I remained here. Last Friday I stopped at a section house run by a Japanese, who gave me the best of treatment and was the soul of hospitality, and which pleased me beyond expectation.

Weston's Transcontinental Walk, New York to San Francisco.
Seventy-third Day of Walk.

Weston is in his seventy-first year, and his task is to walk across the United States in 100 days, (Sundays excepted.)
Post Road Distance, 4,300 Miles.

	Miles.
March 15 to 20, New York to Utica..	273
March 22 to 27, Utica to Chafee......	250
March 29 to April 3, Chafee to Youngstown	225
April 5 to 10, Youngstown to Toledo.	239
April 12 to 17, Toledo to Chicago....	276
April 19 to 24, Chicago to Lincoln...	170
April 26 to May 1, Lincoln to Mexico.	246
May 3 to 8, Mexico, Mo., to Topeka..	239
May 10 to 15, Topeka to Wakeeney..	259
May 17 to 22, Wakeeney, Kan., to Hugo, Col.	219
May 24 to 29, Agate, Col., to Nunn..	184
May 31 to June 5, Nunn, Col., to Wyoming	167
June 7, to Rawlins, Wyo..........	40
Total	2,787

The storm at Medicine Bow, where the plot was laid for the book "Virginian," kept me there several hours after starting at 8:40 A. M. for Hanna. I was blown thirty feet down an embankment without serious injury about six miles out of Hanna. The storm ceased, but too late for me to take advantage of the changed conditions. Coming into Hanna I passed Number A coal mine, where sixty-seven people were killed and suffocated more than a year ago by an explosion.

EDWARD PAYSON WESTON.

June 8, 1909

WESTON IN DISTRESS.

Complains of Lack of Proper Food, Which He Cannot Obtain.

Written exclusively for THE NEW YORK TIMES By EDWARD PAYSON WESTON.

Special to The New York Times.
WAMSUTTER, Wyo., June 9.—The pros-

Weston's Transcontinental Walk, New York to San Francisco.
Seventy-fifth Day of Walk.

Weston is in his seventy-first year, and his task is to walk across the United States in 100 days, (Sundays excepted.)
Post Road Distance, 4,300 Miles.

	Miles.
March 15 to 20, New York to Utica..	273
March 22 to 27, Utica to Chafee......	250
March 29 to April 3, Chafee to Youngstown	225
April 5 to 10, Youngstown to Toledo.	239
April 12 to 17, Toledo to Chicago....	276
April 19 to 24, Chicago to Lincoln...	170
April 26 to May 1, Lincoln to Mexico.	246
May 3 to 8, Mexico, Mo., to Topeka..	239
May 10 to 15, Topeka to Wakeeney..	259
May 17 to 22, Wakeeney, Kan., to Hugo, Col.	219
May 24 to 29, Agate, Col., to Nunn..	184
May 31 to June 5, Nunn, Col., to Wyoming	167
June 7, to Rawlins, Wyo..........	40
June 8 and 9, to Wamsutter, Wyo...	41
Total	2,828

pects for to-day's walk are not very encouraging. The wind is blowing and it is very evident it will rain again. The recent storms have put the roadbed in bad walking shape, and for a few days at least, conditions will not change. These sudden changes and the daily drenching that I get are becoming monotonous.

The lack of proper nourishment, and at the time when I need it most, does not help matters. This can't be helped, because it cannot be had for love or money. Add to this the weather conditions, and nothing short of discouragement could be expected. However this may be, I am not a victim of discouragement, but will fight to the end. I will go to bed at 3 P. M. and leave a call for 9 P. M. and will try to make a long day. My physical condition will permit any amount of walking, and I am only waiting for a chance to show it.

EDWARD PAYSON WESTON.

June 10, 1909

WESTON LAID UP WITH A BAD CHILL

Lack of Proper Care Forces Walker Off Road in Wyoming.

Written exclusively for THE NEW YORK TIMES By EDWARD PAYSON WESTON.

Special to The New York Times.
SPRING VALLEY, Wyo., June 15.—I left Carter at 1:30 this morning determined

to make a long day of it, but you know the old saying, "Man proposes." I arrived at Bridger at 5:15 A. M., where I endeavored to relieve myself of a chill. After a sort of fixing up I left there at 8:30 A. M., arriving at Spring Valley at 12:40 P. M. By this time I was in a frightful condition.

My fears of a few weeks ago are about realized, that is, the want of the much-needed food at the proper times and the

Weston's Transcontinental Walk, New York to San Francisco.
Eightieth Day of Walk.

Weston is in his seventy-first year, and his task is to walk across the United States in 100 days, (Sundays excepted.)
Post Road Distance, 4,300 Miles.

	Miles.
March 15 to 20, New York to Utica..	273
March 22 to 27, Utica to Chafee......	250
March 29 to April 3, Chafee to Youngstown	225
April 5 to 10, Youngstown to Toledo.	239
April 12 to 17, Toledo to Chicago....	276
April 19 to 24, Chicago to Lincoln...	170
April 26 to May 1, Lincoln to Mexico.	246
May 3 to 8, Mexico, Mo., to Topeka..	239
May 10 to 15, Topeka to Wakeeney..	259
May 17 to 22, Wakeeney, Kan., to Hugo, Col.	219
May 24 to 29, Hugo, Col., to Nunn..	184
May 31 to June 5, Nunn, Col., to Hanna, Wyo	167
June 7 to 12, Hanna, Wyo., to Granger, Wyo	205
June 14, to Carter, Wyo......	29
June 15, to Spring Valley, Wyo......	22
Total	3,003

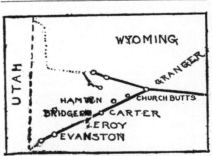

WESTON'S ROUTE THROUGH WYOMING.

He was compelled to stop at Spring Valley beyond Bridger on account of illness.

lack of care have combined to bring about my present deplorable state. Just what the outcome will be I cannot at present determine, but I am doing all in my power to prevent lumbago, and sincerely hope I may succeed. If I am not successful there is only one thing to it— I am here for a long stay.

I cannot now say that I will be able to continue my walk to-morrow.

EDWARD PAYSON WESTON.

June 16, 1909

WESTON'S WALK
ACROSS
THE CONTINENT

Following the Trail of Famous Pioneers of America
Veteran Pedestrian Has Gone Through a Series of
Rare Experiences That Illustrate Country's Progress.

EDWARD PAYSON WESTON has been walking through wonderful and historic country during the past few weeks. It has been to him, in countless places, a land not of milk linked with honey, but a land of milk and eggnog. The combination has been one that has warmed the cockles of the aged pedestrian's heart, imparting a spring to his muscles and a cheerfulness to his countenance which have kept him plodding steadily on, seeing, in his mind's eye, the beauties of the Golden Gate and the triumph of his long-cherished desire to round out his pedestrian career by walking across the American continent.

The residents of Kansas seem to have manifested a peculiar appreciation for Weston's partiality for milk and eggnog. Just before reaching Wakeeney, a good-sized town near the centre of the State, 2,500 feet above sea level and in the midst of a vast prairie, Weston was met by an escorting party of men and women in automobiles bringing milk and eggnog in jars. "It was mighty refreshing," says Weston in recounting his experiences of that day. At still another place an enthusiastic admirer of the aged pedestrian's pluck and vigor drove out twelve miles carrying a supply of the invigorating beverage. No wonder that when traversing the monotonous stretches of the Union Pacific roadbed in Wyoming, exposed to severe storms and with settlements far apart he sighed for the milk and eggnog days of Kansas.

"In all my travels, in England and America," said Weston in referring to his pleasant Kansas experiences, "I never passed through such beautiful and health-giving country and met such genial and

Edward P. Weston and the Route of His Walking Tour Across the United States.

hospitable people as in the Sunflower State."

Weston is now almost within sight of Great Salt Lake and the spires of the Mormon temple. He has been traversing for several hundred miles practically the route of the Mormon pilgrims over sixty years ago, when, inspired by the descriptions given by the "pathfinder," Frémont, they turned their faces westward from Illinois to their Utah home. It is the same trail followed by hundreds of the gold-crazed Forty-niners. Only sixty years ago, and yet what a contrast!

Instead of the long files of prairie schooners wending their way laboriously across the prairies and over the mountain passes, palatially equipped railroad trains cover the distance in an almost incredibly short space of time and without a

suggestion of the physical hardships encountered by the intrepid pioneers of old. Four months from St. Louis to Great Salt Lake and Sutter's Fort, 200 miles beyond, was considered good traveling with fifty or more teams in the pioneer days.

Now five days is easy running time from New York to San Francisco, and the Harriman special, in May, 1906, made the run from San Francisco to New York in seventy-one hours and twenty-seven minutes, a shade under three days. Automobiles and even motor cycles have crossed the continent in what a few years ago would have been considered extraordinary time for any conveyance. So many automobiles have gone across the continent that the trip by motor car is no longer a novelty, although it still possesses hardships in many localities. The record trip is fifteen days two hours and ten minutes, made by the six-cylinder Franklin car, from Stockton, Cal., to New York, in August, 1906, while the fastest motor car trip from New York to San Francisco was made by a Buick car in twenty-four days, eight hours, and forty-five minutes, also in 1906. In September, 1905, W. C. Chadayne traversed the continent by motor cycle from New York to San Francisco in forty-seven days eleven and one-half hours, and in August, 1906, starting from San Francisco, Louis J. Mueller broke that record, covering the distance to New York in thirty-one days twelve and one-quarter hours.

A transcontinental journey, if done in a new way or with a new method of conveyance, has always aroused the keenest interest. There was a time when it was not deemed possible to cross the mountain passes to the Pacific with wag-

ons. Marcus Whitman, the missionary, whose services to save Oregon to the Union have been the subject of much dispute and historical discussion, was one of the first, in 1836, to prove the practicability of taking wagons across the mountains. Additional travel, new settlements, and the explorations of such pioneers as Fremont, Capt. Bonneville, Lewis and Clark, "Kit" Carson, Gen. Ashley, and others whose names and deeds are indelibly associated with much of the country through which the 70-year-old pedestrian is now making his journey, gradually rendered the modes of travel easier, and in 1869 transportation was perfected by the completion of the Union Pacific Railroad. This road follows the famous old trail, and the names of many places on its route recall those earlier days of danger and hardship. For instance, there is Bridger, in the southwestern part of Wyoming, through which Weston passed last Tuesday.

It was formerly Fort Bridger, and commemorates the name of "Jim" Bridger, a famous trapper and explorer who had almost as many deeds of daring as were crowded into "Kit" Carson's life. Indeed, in the village of Kit Carson, in upper Colorado, Weston was entertained at dinner by the boss of the section house, which is practically all there is to the settlement at the present time, and during his night walk in the country round about Weston states with a certain grim humor that he was serenaded by coyotes and prairie dogs.

Heavy storms and unlooked for difficulties of travel have delayed the ambitious pedestrian, but he has not yet given up hope of reaching San Francisco within his scheduled time of 100 walking days. More than four-fifths of the stated time has now been expended, and there are still somewhat over 1,000 miles to go, as the post road distance from New York to San Francisco is estimated at about 4,300 miles. Weston has now covered over 3,100 miles. While following the pathway of the pioneers of old he is really a pathfinder in his own way. He is the first man who has ever attempted to make a bona fide walk from the Atlantic to the Pacific coast, or, perhaps, to be more exact, he is the first one who has carried out his plan on practical lines and with bright assurance of success.

It is a notable triumph for a man in his seventy-first year, and it will probably be a long time before any one will try to emulate his record by following in his footsteps to San Francisco.

As Weston has advanced further and further toward his desired goal, the interest in his walk has grown enormously. Weston himself says that he has been cheered more than once by messages of encouragement from his mascot in Wall Street. The section workmen all along the line of the Union Pacific have extended to him every possible courtesy, but their benefits have generally been slight. Milk and eggs, which were so bountiful in Kansas, were at a premium through the greater part of Wyoming, and even the generous bosses of the section houses were unable to supply his simple wants. He refrained from drinking the water, owing to its alkali ingredients, but once, being unusually thirsty and having a cup of cool water temptingly offered to him in a section house, the pedestrian drank it, with the result that he became very ill an hour or two later; but, finally securing some milk, he drank it hot, and after a short rest was able to continue his journey. Once he walked twenty-two miles without seeing a sign of habitation and without being able to secure anything to eat.

But these casual hardships in the food supply were of minor importance as contrasted with the furious storms that seemed to have a knack of coming up when Weston was well out, away from all possible shelter, and then raining in torrents or blowing with such force that more than once he was literally bowled over, and on two or three occasions was rolled down steep embankments and narrowly escaped painful injuries. "The people east of Chicago," he says, "have no idea of the force and magnitude of these elements of the West. They come suddenly and in torrents. Compared with the showers of the East they are awful and past comprehension." For two weeks after leaving Kansas there was hardly a day that did not witness some heavy storm. Still, with wet clothing, delay in obtaining his baggage for dry changes, and long distances between settlements, Weston pushed sturdily on. The severe conditions did at last react upon his system, and it was only due to his splendid physical condition that he was able to overcome his slight indispositions so readily.

One of his most trying experiences occurred after leaving Greeley, where he had been practically the honored guest of the town. He expected to walk to Cheyenne that day, May 29, about sixty miles. One of the worst storms he ever experienced came on soon after leaving Greeley, and he was forced to stop after going but eleven miles. Then the next day he could cover but eighteen miles, and eventually cut out Cheyenne, making a short cut across country, rejoining the Union Pacific this side of Laramie. As a compensation for his hardships he was gloriously entertained at Senator Warren's 7 XL ranch, the superintendent getting up at midnight to cook a hearty breakfast and then escorting him several miles until he reached the main route.

He arrived at Laramie June 2, very feeble, but the storms and furious rains pursued him all the way to Utah. Most of his walking through the lonely wastes of Wyoming was on the track bed of the railroad, the officials having offered him every possible convenience. The block signals were one mile apart, but noted the coming of a train for a distance of three miles, so that there was no danger of being run down by an approaching engine. He found the towns from fifteen to twenty-five miles apart, a few lonely section houses being the only signs of habitation between, and these frequently occupied by Greek, Italian, and Japanese laborers. There were no Indians to molest Weston, as troubled the pioneers of earlier days, but he did find the modern parasite, the hobo or railroad tramp, a menace to his comfort and peace of mind, and in one of the recent dispatches he says he is carrying a revolver, but he really does not know what he would do with it, for, if attacked by tramps, they would take that as well as anything else they might fancy.

But the tramps have thus far left him alone, perhaps regarding him as a tramper like themselves, but without any distinguishing badge of honor. One marked evidence of the widespread interest that Weston is arousing in the localities through which he passes is the friendly rivalry among the residents to entertain him. Before reaching any fair sized town he is invariably met by an escorting party and is the recipient during his stay of all the honors that can reasonably be bestowed. At St. Louis he was the guest of the Missouri Athletic Club. The Governor of Colorado greeted him as he entered Denver, and he was forced to make a speech to the assembled throng from the balcony of his hotel. At Greeley an enthusiastic admirer gave him a gold seal ring, and he was entertained by two cousins whom he had never seen before.

But above all these honors and public demonstrations one can hear the refrain "eggs and milk," with a half audible sigh for eggnog, for Weston realizes that these aids to his physical well being will enable him to complete his 100 days' walk from New York to San Francisco successfully, if it is within the realms of possibility and provided the elements will only let up on him for a few days of good long distance walking.

June 20, 1909

WESTON CROSSES SALT LAKE.

Pedestrian Makes Best Time of His Walk, Covering 72 Miles.

Weston's Transcontinental Walk, New York to San Francisco.
Eighty-fifth Day of Walk.

Weston is in his seventy-first year, and his task is to walk across the United States in 100 days. (Sundays excepted.) Estimated Distance Revised Schedule, 4,000 Miles.

	Miles.
March 15 to 20, New York to Utica..	273
March 22 to 27, Utica to Chafee......	250
March 29 to April 3, Chafee to Youngstown	225
April 5 to 10, Youngstown to Toledo.	239
April 12 to 17, Toledo to Chicago....	276
April 19 to 24, Chicago to Lincoln..	170
April 26 to May 1, Lincoln to Mexico.	246
May 3 to 8, Mexico, Mo., to Topeka..	239
May 10 to 15, Topeka to Wakeeney..	259
May 17 to 22, Wakeeney, Kan., to Hugo, Col.	219
May 24 to 29, Hugo, Col., to Nunn..	184
May 31 to June 5, Nunn, Col., to Hanna, Wyo.	167
June 7 to 12, Hanna, Wyo., to Granger, Wyo	205
June 14 to 19, Granger, Wyo., to Ogden, Utah	149
June 21, to Hogup, Utah.............	72
Total..........................	3,173

Written exclusively for THE NEW YORK TIMES
By EDWARD PAYSON WESTON.

Special to The New York Times.

HOGUP, Utah, via Ogden, Utah, June 21.—I did not get my usual good sleep last night, due to overjoy over having everything arranged to my entire satisfaction for the rest of the trip. I did, however, get three hours' rest, after which I had a large midnight luncheon in the presence of some fifty residents, who were anxious to see me off at 1 A. M.

I started in company with Mr. J. N. Murray, who will follow me with a railroad velocipede with refreshments. Through the kindness of Vice President Kruttschnitt, General Passenger Agent

Weston's Route Through Utah and Nevada.

James Horsburg, Jr., General Supt. J. M. Davis, and Supt. E. C. Manson, I will now have the best of treatment over the Southern Pacific Railway from Ogden.

I reached Midlake at 1:55 P. M., and stopped one hour, distance 38 miles, going over the greatest and longest trestle in the world. I have made the best time to-day, reaching Hogup, Utah, 72 miles. The remainder of the route, as changed, is as follows: June 22, Tecoma, Nev., 51 miles; 23d, Moore, 53; 24th, Ryndon, 51 25th, Carlinn, 34; 26th, Battle Mountain, 59; 28th, Winnemucca, 59; 29th, Rye Patch, 52; 30th, Toy, 38; July 1, Hazen, 41; 2d, Reno, 47; 3d, Summit, 49; 5th, Clipper Gap, 63; 6th, Sacramento, 43; 7th, Stockton, 48; 8th, Niles, 62; 9th, San Francisco, 60.

EDWARD PAYSON WESTON.

June 22, 1909

SHORT WALK FOR WESTON.

Excessive Heat in Nevada Prevents Pedestrian Making Good Progress.

Weston's Transcontinental Walk, New York to San Francisco.
Eighty-eighth Day of Walk.

Weston is in his seventy-first year, and his task is to walk across the United States in 100 days. (Sundays excepted.) Estimated Distance Revised Schedule, 4,000 Miles.

	Miles.
March 15 to 20, New York to Utica..	273
March 22 to 27, Utica to Chafee......	250
March 29 to April 3, Chafee to Youngstown	225
April 5 to 10, Youngstown to Toledo.	239
April 12 to 17, Toledo to Chicago....	276
April 19 to 24, Chicago to Lincoln..	170
April 26 to May 1, Lincoln to Mexico.	246
May 3 to 8, Mexico, Mo., to Topeka..	239
May 10 to 15, Topeka to Wakeeney..	259
May 17 to 22, Wakeeney, Kan., to Hugo, Col.	219
May 24 to 29, Hugo, Col., to Nunn..	184
May 31 to June 5, Nunn, Col., to Hanna, Wyo.	167
June 7 to 12, Hanna, Wyo., to Granger, Wyo	205
June 14 to 19, Granger, Wyo., to Ogden, Utah	149
June 21, to Hogup, Utah.............	72
June 22, to Tecoma.............	52
June 23, to Moor, Nev.............	53
June 24, to Wells, Nev.	
Total.............	3,287

Written exclusively for THE NEW YORK TIMES
By EDWARD PAYSON WESTON.

Special to The New York Times.

WELLS, Nev., June 24.—The excessive heat of yesterday had its effect. I could not get a restful sleep, and I seemed to be very tired this morning. I got to Wells to-day, a very short distance, and will stop here until midnight and make a long day to-morrow.

I could have gone further to-day, but the heat might have prevented me from reaching a place of rest, which is twenty

miles from here, and yesterday's experience will serve as a warning not to take any chances. The night is very cool, but walking in the dark prevents me from making good time. The nights are very dark, as there is no moon. The distance walked to-day is nine miles.

EDWARD PAYSON WESTON.

June 25, 1909

HEAT BOTHERS WESTON.

Usual Breezes of Nevada Fail to Materialize—Mosquitos Give Trouble.

Weston's Transcontinental Walk, New York to San Francisco.
Ninetieth Day of Walk.

Weston is in his seventy-first year, and his task is to walk across the United States in 100 days. (Sundays excepted.) Estimated Distance Revised Schedule, 4,000 Miles.

	Miles.
March 15 to 20, New York to Utica..	273
March 22 to 27, Utica to Chafee......	250
March 29 to April 3, Chafee to Youngstown	225
April 5 to 10, Youngstown to Toledo.	239
April 12 to 17, Toledo to Chicago....	276
April 19 to 24, Chicago to Lincoln..	170
April 26 to May 1, Lincoln to Mexico.	246
May 3 to 8, Mexico, Mo., to Topeka..	239
May 10 to 15, Topeka to Wakeeney..	259
May 17 to 22, Wakeeney, Kan., to Hugo, Col.	219
May 24 to 29, Hugo, Col., to Nunn..	184
May 31 to June 5, Nunn, Col., to Hanna, Wyo.	167
June 7 to 12, Hanna, Wyo., to Granger, Wyo	205
June 14 to 19, Granger, Wyo., to Ogden, Utah	149
June 21, to Hogup, Utah.............	72
June 22, to Tecoma.............	52
June 23, to Moor, Nev.............	53
June 24, to Wells, Nev.............	9
June 25, to Elko, Nev.............	54
June 26, to Browawe, Nev.............	38
Total.........................	3,379

Written exclusively for THE NEW YORK TIMES
By EDWARD PAYSON WESTON.

Special to The New York Times.

BATTLE MOUNTAIN, Nev., June 26.—The cool breeze which can be counted on here failed to materialize last night, consequently it was sultry and warm all day. Mosquitos of a very rare species,

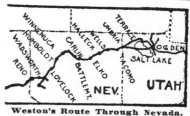

Weston's Route Through Nevada.

and with a bite accordingly, were very annoying.

Early this morning the sun began to pour out its heat at Moleen, twelve miles west of Elko, so I had to stop. I will start at 3 P. M. and try to make Beowawe, thirty-eight miles from Elko. Without the aid of the railroad velocipede and its operator I could not have walked as many miles as the last week shows, for if I make Beowawe, the grand total will be 3,379 miles.

EDWARD PAYSON WESTON.

June 27, 1909

SUN IN NEVADA IS TOO HOT FOR WESTON

Pedestrian Deprived of Usual Sunday Rest by the High Temperature.

WALKS MOSTLY AT NIGHT

His Excellent Physical Condition and Letter from Wall Street Mascot Keep Veteran in Good Cheer.

Weston's Transcontinental Walk, New York to San Francisco.
Ninety-first Day of Walk.

Weston is in his seventy-first year, and his task is to walk across the United States in 100 days. (Sundays excepted.) Estimated Distance, Revised Schedule, 4,000 Miles.

	Miles.
March 15 to 20, New York to Utica..	273
March 22 to 27, Utica to Chafee......	250
March 29 to April 3, Chafee to Youngstown	225
April 5 to 10, Youngstown to Toledo.	239
April 12 to 17, Toledo to Chicago....	276
April 19 to 24, Chicago to Lincoln...	170
April 26 to May 1, Lincoln to Mexico.	246
May 3 to 8, Mexico, Mo., to Topeka..	239
May 10 to 15, Topeka to Wakeeney..	259
May 17 to 22, Wakeeney, Kan., to Hugo, Col.....................	219
May 24 to 29, Hugo, Col., to Nunn.	184
May 31 to June 5, Nunn, Col., to Hanna, Wyo....................	167
June 7 to 12, Hanna, Wyo., to Granger, Wyo..................	205
June 14 to 19, Granger, Wyo., to Ogden, Utah	149
June 21 to 26, Ogden, Utah, to Carlin, Nev......................	252
June 28 to Battle Mountain, Nev.....	59
Total.........................3,412	

Written exclusively for THE NEW YORK TIMES By EDWARD PAYSON WESTON.

Special to The New York Times.

BATTLE MOUNTAIN, Nev., June 28.—Walking at night and in the early morning is the only time that I can devote to this task, without doing myself physical harm. The heat during the day is so intense and houses and hotels are so warm that it is impossible to get a refreshing rest. My long walk on Monday chiefly depended upon the rest I get Sunday, and yesterday I could not sleep

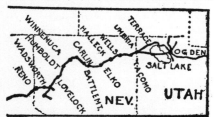

Weston's Route Through Nevada.

until 9 P. M., and at 11 P. M. was up and getting ready for my midnight start. At 12:05 A. M. I started for Battle Mountain, 59 miles, arriving at Beowawe, 27 miles, in 7 hours 40 minutes, without a rest. After resting one hour I walked 15 miles to Mozel, where I will stop until the sun sets, and expect to arrive at Battle Mountain at 10 P. M.

I am in the best of condition and am feeling in fine spirits, especially after hearing from my mascot at 60 Wall Street, which cheered me.

EDWARD PAYSON WESTON.

June 29, 1909

WESTON DEJECTED, BUT WILL KEEP ON

Monotony of Great American Desert Depresses Veteran Pedestrian.

NO DATE SET FOR LAST DAY

Walker's Physical Condition Is Good, Due Principally to Help He Has Received from Westerners.

Weston's Transcontinental Walk, New York to San Francisco.

Weston is in his seventy-first year, and his task is to walk across the United States in 100 days. (Sundays excepted.) Estimated Distance, Revised Schedule, 4,000 Miles.

	Miles.
March 15 to 20, New York to Utica..	273
March 22 to 27, Utica to Chafee......	250
March 29 to April 3, Chafee to Youngstown	225
April 5 to 10, Youngstown to Toledo.	239
April 12 to 17, Toledo to Chicago....	276
April 19 to 24, Chicago to Lincoln...	170
April 26 to May 1, Lincoln to Mexico.	246
May 3 to 8, Mexico, Mo., to Topeka..	239
May 10 to 15, Topeka to Wakeeney..	259
May 17 to 22, Wakeeney, Kan., to Hugo, Col.....................	219
May 24 to 29, Hugo, Col., to Nunn.	184
May 31 to June 5, Nunn, Col., to Hanna, Wyo....................	167
June 7 to 12, Hanna, Wyo., to Granger, Wyo..................	205
June 14 to 19, Granger, Wyo., to Ogden, Utah	149
June 21 to 26, Ogden, Utah, to Carlin, Nev......................	252
June 28 to July 3, Carlin, Nev. to to Lovelock, Nev..............	194
Total 3,547	

Written Exclusively for THE NEW YORK TIMES By EDWARD PAYSON WESTON.

Special to The New York Times.

LOVELOCK, Nev., July 4.—Two weeks on the Great American Desert. Is it any wonder I long for something else than sand, alkali, tremendous heat, mosquitos, and sage brush? There is nothing here that tends to encouragement or induce pleasant walking. The natives themselves

do not spare the unkind words about their desert. One who has never traveled in these parts could not possibly imagine the conditions. Loud complaints are heard from those traveling by rail through this section. What would they say if they walked?

Naturally many unpleasant thoughts are in my mind regarding this country.

Of my supplies, attendants, and good people who live here I have no fault to find, and, while my plans have been

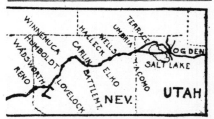

Weston's Route Through Nevada.

shattered, my effort reduced to practical defeat. I am naturally depressed.

Were it possible for everybody who is interested in my effort to know the exact conditions under which I have been traveling, some kind consideration would be shown to me in this task. The fearful conditions cannot be realized by any except those who have experienced something of them.

I started for Lovelock yesterday at 4:10 P. M., and arrived here at 10:20 P. M. without a rest. The conditions were slightly better than at any time in the past week, which would account for the good time I made.

There are still 103 miles of desert, and I do not anticipate any change for the better. My physical condition is perfect, which is shown by my walk of yesterday.

I leave here at 12:05 to-morrow morning, and will walk as far as possible until conditions force me to stop, and will so continue until I arrive in San Francisco. EDWARD PAYSON WESTON.

July 5, 1909

WESTON IN SANDSTORM

But He Struggles On—Too Hot for Rest on Sunday.

Written Exclusively for THE NEW YORK TIMES By EDWARD PAYSON WESTON.

Special to The New York Times.

PARRAN, Nev., via Reno, Nev., July 5.—The heat yesterday afternoon made sleep and rest impossible. Later in the evening it grew cooler, and I got some rest. At 1 A. M. I started for Hazen,

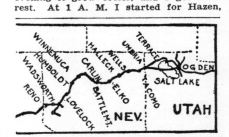

the night being cool and I feeling like taking a good walk. About 7 A. M. a heavy wind blew the sand so hard that I

Weston's Transcontinental Walk, New York to San Francisco.
Ninety-seventh Day of Walk.

Weston is in his seventy-first year, and his task is to walk across the United States in 100 days, (Sundays excepted.) Estimated Distance, Revised Schedule, 4,000 Miles.

	Miles.
March 15 to 20, New York to Utica..	273
March 22 to 27, Utica to Chafee......	250
March 29 to April 3, Chafee to Youngstown	225
April 5 to 10, Youngstown to Toledo.	239
April 12 to 17, Toledo to Chicago....	276
April 19 to 24, Chicago to Lincoln...	170
April 26 to May 1, Lincoln to Mexico.	246
May 3 to 8, Mexico, Mo., to Topeka..	239
May 10 to 15, Topeka to Wakeeney...	259
May 17 to 22, Wakeeney, Kan., to Hugo, Col..................	219
May 24 to 29, Hugo, Col., to Nunn..	184
May 31 to June 5, Nunn, Col., to Hanna, Wyo...............	167
June 7 to 12, Hanna, Wyo., to Granger, Wyo	205
June 14 to 19, Granger, Wyo., to Ogden, Utah	149
June 21 to 26, Ogden, Utah, to Carlin, Nev	252
June 28 to July 3, Carlin, Nev. to Lovelock, Nev..............	194
July 5 to Hazen, Nev.................	57
Total......................	3,604

could not see 100 feet before me. For this emergency I am somewhat protected with sand glasses. The wind brought a cool breeze and made it possible to walk. I arrived at Parran, 33 miles, without a rest. Expect to arrive at Hazen, 57 miles, at 10 P. M.

EDWARD PAYSON WESTON.

July 6, 1909

WESTON LAMENTS HIS MANY MISTAKES

Though He Goes Over Only a Few Days of His Schedule, He Calls Walk a Failure.

WILL FINISH ON WEDNESDAY

Veteran Contends That He Has Walked More Than 2,500 Miles Over Railroad Tracks.

Written Exclusively for THE NEW YORK TIMES
By EDWARD PAYSON WESTON.
Special to The New York Times.

ROSEVILLE, Cal., July 11.—"If any one had told me six months ago that I would undertake to walk over railroad tracks between Chicago and San Francisco for 2,577 miles, and practically without attendance or necessary refreshments for 1,800 miles of that distance, I would have said, 'I am not such an idiot.' I am not saying this to excuse this wretched failure. I am simply stating facts.

"This has been an effort which should be called one chapter of mistakes from beginning to end. In the first place I

Weston's Route Through California.

should not have relied upon a miserable and worthless automobile to convey my attendants, and again, should have gone from San Francisco to New York. Then the tornadoes, gales, and drenching rains invariably coming from the West, would have driven me into New York instead of depriving me of the use of the road for fifteen days out of the 100 days all told.

"This is the most crushing failure I have encountered in my career. When I arrive in San Francisco on Wednesday forenoon I shall have placed to my credit a distance of 3,895 miles, walked between New York and San Francisco. All railway men say I should add at least 200 miles more for crossing and recrossing the tracks during the 2,577 miles I have followed the railroad. Be that as it may, I could never exceed over three and a half miles per hour, and it took a far greater effort to walk that distance on tracks than to walk four miles per hour on a country road, when one is in sight.

"The past week has been excessively trying to one's nerves, walking through snowsheds, averaging two miles per hour,

Weston's Transcontinental Walk, New York to San Francisco.

Weston is in his seventy-first year, and he started out to walk across the United States in 100 days, (Sundays excepted.)

	Miles.
March 15 to 20, New York to Utica..	273
March 22 to 27, Utica to Chafee......	250
March 29 to April 3, Chafee to Youngstown	225
April 5 to 10, Youngstown to Toledo.	239
April 12 to 17, Toledo to Chicago....	276
April 19 to 24, Chicago to Lincoln...	170
April 26 to May 1, Lincoln to Mexico.	246
May 3 to 8, Mexico, Mo., to Topeka..	239
May 10 to 15, Topeka to Wakeeney...	259
May 17 to 22, Wakeeney, Kan., to Hugo, Col..................	219
May 24 to 29, Hugo, Col., to Nunn..	184
May 31 to June 5, Nunn, Col., to Hanna, Wyo...............	167
June 7 to 12, Hanna, Wyo., to Granger, Wyo	205
June 14 to 19, Granger, Wyo., to Ogden, Utah	149
June 21 to 26, Ogden, Utah, to Carlin, Nev	252
June 28 to July 3, Carlin, Nev. to Lovelock, Nev..............	194
July 5 to 10, Lovelock, Nev., to Roseville, Cal.	240
Total	3,787

and crawling on a path twelve inches wide, bordering on a cañon 1,000 feet below for at least twenty-five miles. A single false step or a rolling stone would have plunged me into the great unknown. This is bad enough in the daytime, though the scenery is grand, but when you retire to sleep it's a nightmare. With all this I am in the best of health, but much depressed in spirits.

"I leave here for Sacramento at 5:30 Monday, as the citizens have asked me to come to their city in the daylight. I shall probably go fifteen or twenty-five miles beyond that city, so as to make a shorter distance for Tuesday and a still shorter distance before entering San Francisco on Wednesday. Arriving at Oakland, I shall retrace the track three

miles, and then walk three miles back to the ferry, thus covering the distance. I could not walk over the bay.

EDWARD PAYSON WESTON.

July 12, 1909

WESTON AT END OF HIS LONG WALK

Veteran Walker Arrives on the Pacific Coast Slightly Behind Schedule.

105 DAYS FROM NEW YORK

Walks Extra Miles to Equalize Trips by Ferries in California—In Good Condition.

Weston's Transcontinental Walk, New York to San Francisco.
105th Day of Walk.

Weston is in his seventy-first year, and he started out to walk across the United States in 100 days, (Sundays excepted.)

	Miles.
March 15 to 20, New York to Utica..	273
March 22 to 27, Utica to Chafee......	250
March 29 to April 3, Chafee to Youngstown	225
April 5 to 10, Youngstown to Toledo.	239
April 12 to 17, Toledo to Chicago....	276
April 19 to 24, Chicago to Lincoln...	170
April 26 to May 1, Lincoln to Mexico.	246
May 3 to 8, Mexico, Mo., to Topeka..	239
May 10 to 15, Topeka to Wakeeney...	259
May 17 to 22, Wakeeney, Kan., to Hugo, Col..................	219
May 24 to 29, Hugo, Col., to Nunn..	184
May 31 to June 5, Nunn, Col., to Hanna, Wyo...............	167
June 7 to 12, Hanna, Wyo., to Granger, Wyo	205
June 14 to 19, Granger, Wyo., to Ogden, Utah	149
June 21 to 26, Ogden, Utah, to Carlin, Nev	252
June 28 to July 3, Carlin, Nev. to Lovelock, Nev..............	194
July 5 to 10, Lovelock, Nev., to Roseville, Cal.	240
July 12, to Dixon, Cal..............	39
July 13, to Benicia, Cal.............	37
July 14, to San Francisco..........	32
Total.........................	3,895

Written Exclusively for THE NEW YORK TIMES
By EDWARD PAYSON WESTON.

Special to The New York Times.

SAN FRANCISCO, Cal., July 14.—I arrived at the St. Francis Hotel here, the end of my transcontinental walk of 3,895 miles, at 11:15 o'clock to-night, [2:15 Thursday morning, New York time,] in perfect health, but very hungry. After crossing the bay from Oakland I set foot in San Francisco at 10:50 o'clock.

After leaving Suisun last evening I walked something over ten miles, when a Kansas gale took possession of the track and hurled me around merrily. It put my lantern out and left me in darkness, so after reaching Goodyear I was forced to retire until eight o'clock this morning. A number of San Francisco newspaper men accompanied me from Goodyear to Beniciaa, where I retraced one and a half

miles of the tract to offset crossing the Carquitez Straits in a ferryboat.

The fact that I have walked the last ninety miles between Sacramento and San Francisco in forty-nine hours will convince my friends that I am in perfect health.

EDWARD PAYSON WESTON.

Special to The New York Times.

OAKLAND PIER, Cal., July 14.—Edward Payson Weston arrived here this evening at 9:38, Pacific time, and left on the ferryboat Piedmont at 10:18 for San Francisco. Mr. Weston is in apparent good physical condition, smiling and happy. He read his correspondence standing, refusing a seat crossing in the boat.

WESTON'S LAST DAY ON ROAD.

Starts from Goodyear, Cal., After Being Stopped by Wind

Special to The New York Times.

SAN FRANCISCO, Cal., July 14.—Edward Payson Weston left Goodyear a small railroad station six miles north of Benicia, this morning on what he believed to be the last leg of his journey from New York to San Francisco, five days behind his schedule of 100 days to cross the continent. Weston intended to make Benicia early this morning by indulging in a night walk from Goodyear to Benicia, but a high wind, which blew out his lantern and caused him to stumble in a small hole, made him stop for the night at Goodyear.

Accompanied by two brakeman furnished by the Southern Pacific Railroad Company, who carried his supplies on a gasoline speeder, and an engineer named Brown of the Sparks Division of the railroad, who accompanied him on foot, Weston resumed his journey this morning. The pedestrian started out a trifle stiff, but soon got into his lively stride, and covered the distance to Benicia in about two hours. This time included three miles of retracing his steps to cover the distance which he rode on a ferry between Benicia and Port Costa. At 11:30 o'clock he reached Crockett, thirty miles from San Francisco, and at 1:50 o'clock he arrived at Pinole, twenty-four miles from this city. He anticipated getting into Oakland by 8 o'clock, where he would retrace his steps for five miles to cover the distance across the bay to San Francisco by ferry.

To THE NEW YORK TIMES correspondent who met Weston at Goodyear and kept with him to Crockett, he talked freely of his trip and some of the hardships he has endured. Wyoming left a particularly dark place in his mind, for he was compelled to cross most of that State alone, and many days he was without nourishing food or pure water. He fought off exhaustion, however, and while he lost some of his strength on these hard hikes and through heavy rains in Colorado, which drenched him to the skin, he declared he had quite recovered by the crisp air of the high Sierras and the mild weather in the Sacramento Valley. The roads in this State, too, have aided him, being the best he has walked on since reaching the Plateau. Weston also recently found an abundance of eggs and milk, chief articles of his diet, of which he ate every hour during his walk in this State.

WESTON'S TRIALS ON ROADS.

Hardships Encountered in Far West Almost Unendurable.

Although taking 105 days and some hours for his walk from the Atlantic to the Pacific Coast, five days more than he had allotted for the transcontinental trip, Edward Payson Weston's long walk from this city to San Francisco ranks as one of the most notable pedestrian feats ever accomplished. It is the first time that a bona-fide walk has been made across the American Continent, Weston laying so much stress on this fact that he walked over railroad bridges in the Far West instead of resorting to the ferries, and declared that after arriving at Oakland he would walk an additional five miles to equal the distance across the bay into San Francisco, as he found it necessary there to resort to the boat to reach his desired haven.

When one stops to consider the conditions under which this long walk of 3,895 miles has been accomplished no one can fail to admit that it has been the most remarkable event of this character ever attempted. Here is a man, trained from his early manhood, it is true, to the fatigues and strenuous exertions of long-continued walking on the ordinary roads of the land, starting out on his seventieth birthday to accomplish something that would tax the physical stamina of the sturdiest athlete with muscles hardened for long endurance. It had always been Weston's ambition to make a walk across the American continent, and the fact that he has succeeded in his seventy-first year is a fitting culmination of the long career of pedestrian triumphs with which the name of Weston is associated.

Had Weston ever dreamed of the difficulties he encountered it is possible, as he admits, that he would never have attempted to make it. He left New York, starting from the Post Office Building on March 15. Almost from the start he met bad roads and severe weather conditions. His walk up the State, and, in fact, almost until he arrived in Toledo was a constant succession of battles against adverse weather conditions, with severe snowstorms and cold rains, making the roads at times almost impassable.

He made two long days' walks, however, on March 17 from Poughkeepsie to Hudson, 60 miles, and the same distance on March 22 from Utica to Syracuse. He reached Buffalo on March 26, and the following day fell on a bad piece of road, injuring his left arm, which troubled him considerably for several days.

Going through Pennsylvania and Ohio he found the roads so bad that the automobile with his attendants was unable to keep up with him, and for over a week he was deprived of the changes of clothing and necessary supplies carried along for him. He was obliged to abandon his plan to go through Pittsburg, and from Youngstown, Ohio, went to Toledo, arriving there April 10, making 53 miles on that day from Bellevue, the best walking day, he said, since leaving New York. On April 17 he reached Chicago, where he had an enthusiastic reception, being entertained at the Illinois Athletic Club.

Beyond Chicago he entered upon a new walking country. Going through Illinois by the way of Joliet he arrived in St. Louis April 28. Just before arriving there he enjoyed the humorous experience of being arrested by a negro policeman in the little town of Brooklyn, the constable saying he was sure that any man walking through the town with a crowd of people at his heels must be crazy. Better road conditions were then encountered through Missouri and Kansas, and on May 10 he made his longest single day's walk, seventy-eight miles, from Topeka to Junction City, Kan. On May 17, from Wakeeney to Monument, Kan., he covered sixty-six miles. Denver was entered May 27, and here another big reception awaited him. Then his route led to Greeley, fifty-seven miles, made in one day, and thence to Cheyenne, going through Wyoming to Utah, passing through Ogden and Salt Lake City.

Practically all of Weston's walk from Greeley to Oakland was done on the railroad tracks of the Southern Pacific Railroad. In Wyoming his troubles multiplied to such an extent that had it not been for the timely aid rendered by the officials of the Southern Pacific Railroad in sending along from Ogden an assistant on a railroad track velocipede carrying milk, eggs, and other nourishing foods, it is doubtful if Weston would have survived the heat and storms encountered day after day. Previous to this aid Weston had almost despaired of ever accomplishing the journey.

Towns were far apart, food and water of good quality were impossible to obtain, and for many days he walked hours without proper food and drink. The heat going through the desert beyond Salt Lake City was intense, so that most of his walking was done at night, but even then the miles were reeled off with extreme difficulty. Then came the arduous snow sheds over the Sierras in Nevada, and here the assistance of the railroad was indispensable, for otherwise Weston would have found it a superhuman task.

But his grit and grim determination to reach San Francisco triumphed over all obstacles, and when he entered California the remainder was comparatively easy. He, however, decided to stick to the railroad instead of making the detour to San Francisco direct from Sacramento, which would have meant many more miles and through rough country. For this reason he altered his original programme and set his face straight toward Oakland, and then planned to walk the additional number of miles to equal the ferry trip across the bay.

July 15, 1909

WESTON'S WALK.

San Francisco is not Seattle, of course, nor is 105 days 100, but when a man in his 71st year walks from New York even to the nearer of the two cities and in the longer of the two times, the difference between purpose and achievement constitutes only a technical failure, and EDWARD PAYSON WESTON can console himself with the thought that he is the object of about as much wonder as he would have been had he reached his originally chosen destination on the date fixed by his hopes.

That he did not do so seems to have been due in no degree to a diminution of his pedestrian powers as a result of age. On the contrary, he reaches the coast in a condition apparently as good as that he was in when he started, and his delays were caused by obstacles—storms, excessive heat, failure of supplies, and the like —that were unforeseen accidents of the journey, and would have kept back a younger man, or WESTON himself in his prime, to the same extent.

With all his troubles, and despite what he calls "the worst failure of my career," his average day's walk from start to finish has been 38.1 miles. To make that distance even once would severely strain the energies of most of us, and be beyond the capacity of many who, nevertheless, are far from considering themselves weaklings. WESTON, after 105 such jaunts, over all the kinds of roads

there are, including a few miles of good ones, and with the incidental rest of only fifteen Sundays, is already talking about the ease with which he can immediately retrace his steps and do it in a shorter time. Ninety days are all he thinks necessary for the return journey, and seemingly he could do it if he had what alone he lacked when outward bound, and that is good luck in the matter of weather.

So, though WESTON has not walked quite as far or as fast as he intended and expected, his achievement is nothing less than amazing. Also, he has falsified a large number of lugubrious prophecies, and there's comfort in that for almost any disappointment. The explanation of WESTON's prowess? There is none, any more than for any other display of abnormal ability. The doctor who described him as a "somatic freak" was right, but the term describes; it does not elucidate.

July 15, 1909

WESTON'S ACHIEVEMENT.

Says It Proves Him the Greatest Athlete in the World.

To the Editor of The New York Times:

I have been more than casually interested in Mr. Weston's present walk, as I have seen him in nearly all of his greatest walks, and in his six-day contests with Daniel O'Leary, and in his exhibitions of walking against time, as well as ordinary fancy exhibition walks. I was present with him when he first accomplished the great feat of walking 500 miles in six consecutive days, which he did in the large Washington Street rink in Newark along about 1875.

I have the utmost sympathy for plucky, persevering, and indefatigable Mr. Weston, and he has many thousands of like admirers over the wide domain of this country. They as well as myself wish to acknowledge this feat of Mr. Weston's as the greatest in the walking line (all considered) ever undertaken or executed in this country. It really places Mr. Weston as the one great unapproachable athlete of the world. You will find imitators, and some will spring up who will try to do the same thing and to beat Weston's transcontinental time, but just watch the results. One will walk forty or fifty miles for three or four days, is behind Weston's schedule record, "steps on a rolling stone and sprains his ankles," and gives up the walk and goes back home. Another one "yaps" about it for six months in the papers in advance, starts out, gets about 200 miles, is behind Weston's record, meets some good friends in some John Barleycorn town, and winds up in a Keeley cure or a sanitarium. Another one reverses the route and starts from San Francisco and intends to make the New York population "sit up and listen" when he arrives and look at the greatest "hiker" of them all. But alas! he gets as far as Utah and falls through a hole in the bridge of sighs!

Mr. Weston is in a class by himself. His many great achievements and records in the walking line will stand. His walk to Frisco may take him about six days longer than he calculated on, but if the roads had been more appropriate and even and less deep mud and less strong headwinds and better feed he would, in all probability, have reached 'Frisco over five days ahead of time.

CARL TEMPLE.

Middletown, N. Y., July 13, 1909.

July 16, 1909

WESTON'S FINAL EFFORT.

Veteran Pedestrian Starts Monday to Walk to Minneapolis.

Edward Payson Weston, the veteran pedestrian, with walking records by the score to his credit, has mapped out what he believes will be the crowning effort of his notable career in the walking line, and he will leave New York on Monday, June 2, on a 1,500-mile walk to Minneapolis. The start will be made at 12 o'clock noon from the College of the City of New York, and he plans to reach the grounds of the new Minneapolis Athletic Club on Saturday, Aug. 2. Dr. John H. Finley, President of the College of the City of New York, will be the official starter.

Mr. Weston, now in his seventy-fifth year, has a double motive for undertaking the long walk. The first is that he has long cherished the ambition to take an extended journey at this age, with the belief that he can further spread the gospel of walking, and thereby confer a boon on humanity by interesting others in its possibilities and good results. The choice of Minneapolis as the goal came as a result of an invitation from the Minneapolis A. C. that Mr. Weston lay the cornerstone of its new clubhouse on Aug. 2.

The distance of the long jaunt is 1,500 miles, and the veteran figures that he can cover the route in sixty days. As he never walks on Sunday during these long journeys, he will average about 158 miles per week, or almost 26½ miles per day, in the coming trip. He will follow the Erie Railroad route from New York to Chicago, and at the latter city he will turn to the Chicago & Northwestern Railroad for the last leg of his journey. The first seven and one-half miles to be covered by the veteran, from the starting point, at 139th Street, to the Twenty-third Street Ferry, will not be counted as part of the journey, this walk being offset for ferrying two and one-half miles across the Hudson River. The schedule calls for Weston's arrival in Chicago on Wednesday, July 9, and he is due to reach St. Paul, Minn., on Friday, Aug. 1.

May 26, 1913

WESTON JADED, BUT GAME.

Veteran Walker Makes Suffern— Resumes Chicago Hike To-day.

Special to The New York Times.

MOUNTAIN HOUSE, SUFFERN, N. Y., June 3.—Edward Payson Weston, the famous long-distance walker of America, who started from the plaza in front of the City College on Monday at noon to walk to Chicago over the Erie Railroad, a distance of 999 miles, arrived here this afternoon at 2 o'clock, having covered 40 miles. On account of the hot weather Mr. Weston decided it would not be advisable to go further to-day. He felt somewhat jaded, as he explained always had been the case on the second day after beginning his foot journeys, because of the reaction from the exertion.

Mr. Weston will start to-morrow morning at 8 o'clock for Goshen, a distance of 28 miles, and he expects to reach there by the middle of the afternoon. He is attempting to beat his former record walk to Chicago, which he made over the long route, 1,236 miles, in the Summer of 1909, in 36 days on his journey to the Pacific Coast.

June 4, 1913

WESTON THE WALKER.

That "an old hoss kin run" was vouched for in stirring verse by OLIVER WENDELL HOLMES, who was himself a wiry and spry old fellow, like EDWARD PAYSON WESTON. WESTON the walker is well started on another little cross-country jaunt of 1,446 miles to lay the cornerstone of the Minneapolis Athletic Club's new building. His ocean-to-ocean walk in 1910, at the age of 72, was something of an undertaking, he admits; but the trip on which President FINLEY of the City College bade him godspeed on Tuesday is intended merely as a breather. Dr. FINLEY must care for his college, Mayor GAYNOR is tied to the City Hall, and Mr. ROOSEVELT, who at 25 wrote a book on the joys of walking trips, has been busy of late with politics and litigation. The world is too much with us, getting and spending, but WESTON walks.

"Walking is equivalent to sleep," he says; for it is the "most healthful thing you can do." It earns healthful sleep, a good digestion, and a limber old age. WESTON began to feel rheumatic twinges some fifteen years ago, so he resumed his walking "stunts" and thereafter defied all infirmities. He has still the advantages of youth and the green out-of-doors.

June 4, 1913

E. PAYSON WESTON, HIKER, DIES AT 90

End Comes Peacefully, After He Had Been Rescued From Poverty Two Years Ago.

WALKED 3,895 MILES AT 70

Won Fame as Union Spy in Civil War and Was at Deathbed of Horace Greeley.

Edward Payson Weston, for many years premier long-distance walker of America, died late Sunday night at 205 Taaffe Place, Brooklyn, at the age of 90, which he had set as his goal of longevity. His physician attributed his death to the infirmities of old age.

Relieved of poverty two years ago by the generosity of Anne Nichols, author of "Abie's Irish Rose," who established a trust fund, yielding him $150 monthly, after he had been found dazed and helpless on the streets of New York, Mr. Weston had spent the last two years of his life under the care of Miss Anna O'Hagan, for twenty-one years his secretary, whom he called his "adopted" daughter. Miss O'Hagan explained yesterday that she had not been legally adopted.

Most of the time he had been moved about in a wheel chair, due to injuries he sustained when he was struck by a taxicab two years ago. Since last November he had been confined to his bed.

With Mr. Weston when he died were Miss O'Hagan, her adopted son, Raymond Donaldson, and her sister, Miss Mary O'Hagan. None of his relatives was present. His wife, Mrs. Maria Weston, herself an octogenarian, from whom he had been separated for many years: his daughter, Mrs. Maud Beard, and her two daughters, Ruth and Margaret, live at 85 Fairview Avenue. Other surviving relatives are a daughter, Mrs. Frank J. Hazen, and her son, Richard, who live on a ranch near Lewistown, Mont.

Served as Spy in Civil War.

Mrs. Beard said that she had been notified of her father's illness and had intended to hold a family consultation with a physician yesterday, when she learned that he had died.

Mr. Weston was born at Providence, R. I., on March 15, 1839. In the Civil War he served as a Union spy and developed his propensity for walking as a dispatch bearer when his horses were shot from under him.

Following the war, he attracted attention as a walker, first as an office boy and later as a reporter for The New York Herald. His ability to walk in the days before there were telephones and rapid transit enabled him to score many "beats" against his rivals. He was long a friend of Horace Greeley, and was present at his death-bed.

Mr. Weston had an elastic, swinging stride and legs that never seemed to tire. At the age of 22 he took his

International Newsreel.

EDWARD PAYSON WESTON,
Famous Walker, Who Died Here at the Age of 90.

first long walk, 443 miles, from Boston to Washington, to attend the inauguration of Abraham Lincoln, covering the distance in 208 hours. But the most remarkable walking feats of his career were performed after he had passed the age of 70.

His Boston-Washington walk attracted so much attention that Weston decided to embark upon a career of a professional walker. In 1867 he walked from Portland, Me., to Chicago, 1,326 miles, in twenty-six days. Forty years later he repeated the feat and covered a route nineteen miles longer than the first and bettered his record by twenty-nine hours. He appeared in many exhibitions and contests in America and Europe. In 1879 he won the famous Astley Belt by covering 550 miles in 141 hours and 44 minutes in Agricultural Hall, London.

He was an entrant in the first international six-day walking contest in Madison Square Garden.

In 1909 Mr. Weston made what was regarded as his most remarkable walk. Then 70 years old, he covered the route from New York to San Francisco, 3,895 miles, in 104 days and seven hours.

The next year he walked the return trip over a different route, covering 3,600 miles in seventy-six days, 23 hours and 10 minutes.

His last big hike was in 1913, from New York to Minneapolis, a distance of 1,546 miles, to lay the cornerstone of the Minneapolis Athletic Club. He covered the distance in fifty-one days.

At the age of 85 Mr. Weston gave a demonstration of his unusual physical powers and courage by beating off several intruders who attacked him in his little farm home near Kingston, N. Y., in 1924. He was shot in the leg.

Funeral services will be held by Father Walter Geary at St. Patrick's Roman Catholic Church on Taaffe Place, Brooklyn, tomorrow morning at 10 o'clock. Burial will be in St. John's Cemetery.

May 14, 1929

WESTON ENDS HIS TRAMP.

Escorted Into Minneapolis by Gov. Eberhart—Lays Club Cornerstone.

MINNEAPOLIS, Aug. 2.—Amid the roar of cannon, the clanging of bells and the tooting of whistles, Edward Payson Weston completed his tramp from New York City here to-day. The aged pedestrian, by changing his plans after leaving the metropolis, added 100 miles to his schedule and walked 1,546 miles. Leaving New York June 2, he was due to reach Minneapolis August 2. He reached Stillwater, Minn., July 29, four days ahead of schedule.

Weston arrived at the city limits dividing Minneapolis and St. Paul at 11:15 A. M. From the city line he was escorted by a company of Boy Scouts, several hundred members of the Minneapolis Athletic Club, and a platoon of mounted police, to the site of the Athletic Club's new building. At 12:15 P. M. he laid the mortar on the cornerstone of the new building. Gov. Eberhart walked with the pedestrian from the starting place in St. Paul to the city limits. Mayor Wallace G. Nye of Minneapolis met the party at Midway, walking a part of the way into the city.

August 3, 1913

HIS LAST JOURNEY.

EDWARD PAYSON WESTON, the greatest walker of his day, has made his last journey, this time

> To the undiscovered country
> from whose bourn
> No traveler returns.

He crossed the continent on foot and made other long journeys: from Portland to Chicago, from New York to Minneapolis, and, before all these, from Boston to Washington to attend the first inauguration of President LINCOLN. That was called "a "novel feat" at that time, for the exploits of Indian runners were not then generally known and ROBERT BROWNING had not rescued from mythology the story of how PHEI-DIPPIDES ran and raced from Athens to Sparta, then back to Athens and up to the field of Marathon and back, falling dead at the end of his last "marathon." WESTON'S name has been for a half century a synonym for long-distance walking.

It was said of WILLIAM M. EVARTS that he never walked when he could ride, never stood when he could sit, and never sat when he could lie down. Yet he, too, lived to a ripe old age. WESTON attributed his robust manhood and health, developed from a weak and sickly childhood and a delicate and feeble youth, to his continued exercise and his temperance in all things. He began to walk in order to gain health, and he kept on walking for the joy of it and as a means of interesting the public in it for health and pleasure.

It must be admitted that he had a serious and increasingly powerful competitor in the automobile, which at last pushed him into the roadside. But, thanks to Miss ANNE NICHOLS, who came along the highway like a good Samaritan, he had a "lift," a "hitch-hike" which he would have contemned if his legs had not been lamed, and so was carried to the end of the journey, which he must have so much desired to reach with his feet still "on the quest."

He had been of more cheer and help to others along the way of life than he could have known, even with all the applause along the way. HORACE GREELEY, back in 1869, addressing him as "my kind friend," presided at a meeting in his honor, in order, as he said, that WESTON might not "want for encouragement "to elevate the exercise of walking "in our country." When abroad a little later he made a memorable record and gave example and advice to Englishmen, including the Prince of WALES. It is remembered that when the Washington Arch canvass was sagging, he went about on foot reviving interest and gathering subscriptions, and that he lent his legs to many another good cause.

He has gone at last on what one has called the "perfect walk," the walk for which solitude is essential; but in his pilgrimage across the earth he has led a multitude who will keep on walking till they, too, come to the end of the road which is the longer for going on foot.

May 15, 1929

(An editorial on Weston appears on page 6.)

Chapter Two

COUNTRY WALKING
IN THE UNITED STATES

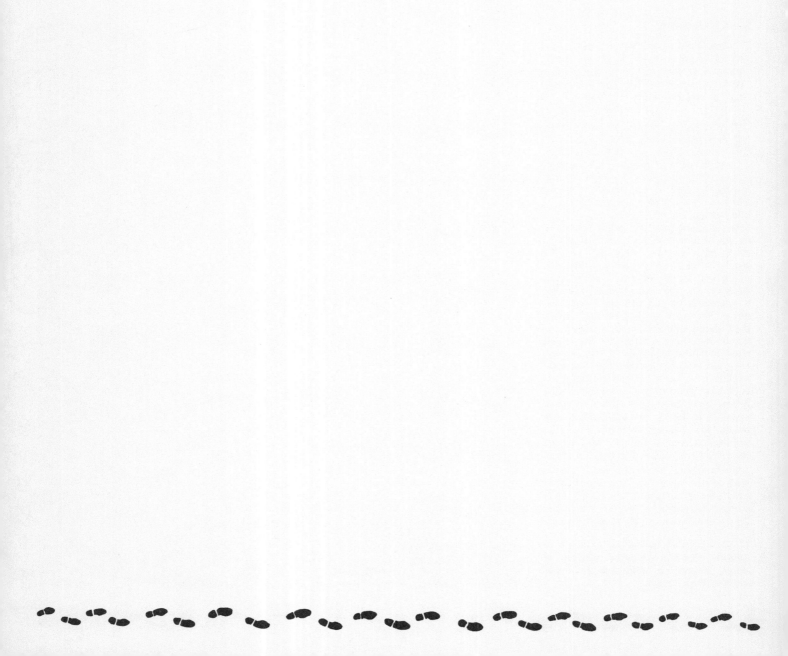

The Back Packing Boom

Backpacking: 'I Go to the Wilderness to Kick the Man-World Out of Me'

By SUSAN SANDS

"Think what a great world revolution will take place when . . . [there are] millions of guys all over the world with rucksacks on their backs tramping around the back country. . . ."
—"The Dharma Bums"

JACK KEROUAC asked us to think about that in the late fifties. Today we can almost *see* it—tens of thousands (if not perhaps millions) of "guys with rucksacks on their backs" hitting the trail in a backpacking boom that has practically revolutionized American outdoor life.

What might have caused even Kerouac to unsling his pack and mop his brow with wonder, however, is that the boom has reverberated in virtually every quarter of American society. In addition to the long-haired spiritual descendants of the Dharma Bums, today's backpacking battalions include their sisters and their cousins and their uncles and their aunts—persons of all ages and from all walks of life. Indeed, so great is their number that an anti-backpacking backlash has set in. Deep ruts have been worn into some trails, others have been hacked and littered, and not a few conservationists, as a result, are finding themselves in the unlikely position of thinking up schemes to restrict the "use" of wilderness areas.

Backpackers must not be confused with less self-sufficient breeds of wilderness trekkers. Unlike campers, for example, backpackers carry everything they need for survival on their backs,

SUSAN SANDS is the editor of Rags, a fashion magazine published on the West Coast.

and unlike hikers, backpackers carry enough to sustain themselves for considerable periods of time. And thus, with food and drink to last a couple of weeks, say, plus whatever protective clothing may be necessary to penetrate a particular terrain, backpackers can plod deep enough into the wilderness to enjoy remote regions still untouched by civilization (although not, perhaps, untouched by other backpackers).

How big is the backpacking boom? Nobody knows for sure, and since practically anyone who totes paraphernalia around in a pack—fisherman, mountain climber, even hitchhiker—can call himself a backpacker if he wants to, meaningful statistics are hard to come by. Still, one survey estimates that in recent years no fewer than 20 million Americans have tried backpacking in the most general sense of the term. That's one in every 10 of us.

The sales figures from the outfitting industry tend to confirm the magnitude of the boom. According to an industry study conducted by the Leisure Group,

"Sales figures from the outfitting industry confirm the magnitude of the boom. Every manufacturer or retailer to whom I spoke reported that sales doubled in the last 3 to 5 years."

Inc., a sporting-goods outfit based in Los Angeles, retail sales totaled $16-million in 1969, up 15 per cent from 1968. The study predicted, moreover, a rise of 25 per cent in 1970.

Camp Trails, in Phoenix, the largest manufacturer of backpacking equipment in the country and the official Boy Scout supplier, has reported astounding sales gains of 500 per cent since 1966. In fact, every major manufacturer or retailer to whom I have spoken, including old-timers like Kelty Pack of Glendale, Calif., Recreational Equipment of Seattle, Colorado Outdoor Sports of Denver and Trailwise of Berkeley, Calif., reported that sales had doubled in the

last three to five years despite competition from dozens of new outfitters.

Hudson's, in Manhattan, which last summer was selling as many as 100 backpacks a week, is often a study in pandemonium, attracting most of the nomadic population of the East Village. Farther downtown, Camp and Trail Outfitters, founded in 1932 and one of the oldest backpacking specialists in the country, is busier than ever stitching together custom backpacks, sleeping bags and other gear for the discerning. Even pets are being equipped to hit the trail these days—Ann Sieck, an outfitter in Berkeley, is offering a nylon pack and wooden frame for canines at

$16 to $25.

What sort of breed are the backpackers? To begin with, despite the fairly widespread notion, they are not exclusively or even mainly hippies, the long-haired people of Harvard Square, the East Village and Berkeley's Telegraph Avenue. They represent every segment of American life. Most backpackers, however, according to the Leisure Group study, are between the ages of 18 and 34, are married and come from families with incomes of more than $7,000 a year. Officials of the National Park Service add that almost all are from urban areas and that more and more are women.

Far From the Madding Crowd

What distinguishes backpackers is their independence. They like to be far from the madding crowd, and since at least 60 million Americans have tried their hand at camping (which is somewhat akin to the madding crowd's transporting itself bodily from congested metropolitan area to not-so-secluded woodland), backpackers have taken to slogging farther and farther into the wilds to put some distance between themselves and the mob.

It pains true and dedicated backpackers to be caught in the same clearing with "outdoorsmen" ensconced in their trailers or camper trucks complaining that their electric blankets are not working. It hurts them to be found on the fringes of the same forest with out-for-the-day hikers who hop into their cars at dusk and head back to civilization for an evening of television. Backpackers consider themselves a breed apart who have outgrown dependence on the machines of an increasingly mechanized world. Deep in the woods, they know the most magnificent part of the wilderness remains the most magnificent precisely because it is available only to determined footsloggers. To the campers or hikers with any sort of motor vehicle at hand, they would say: "If you have brought your car with you, you have brought society with you; you've completely missed the point."

To get away from society, to return to the primitive—this theme invariably emerged when I asked a backpacker why he backpacks. "Because I want to get the hell out of here," one told me. "The urban life style is unbearable," said another. Colin Fletcher, author of "The Complete Walker," which is undoubtedly the best "how to" book in the backpacking field, wrote, "I go to the wilderness to kick the man-world out of me."

Take the not untypical case of Tom, Carl and "Skinflick." Last summer, weary of their lives as Berkeley street people, they turned to the wilderness in a quest for "better vibrations." They pooled resources to buy packs and sleeping bags from a second-hand outfitter, picked up 80 pounds of brown rice and some other essentials and then hitched their way to the Rockies, where they built a lean-to of pine branches. There were problems—rain, bugs, monotony—but, according to Carl, a sort of psychological victory in the end. "Up there with the trees for four months I learned my head," he said to me. As he spoke, his shoulder-length fair hair flapping with every earnest nod, I was suddenly reminded of a note I had once seen scribbled on a signboard deep in California's Los Padres National Forest. "Dear Mother Nature," it read. "Thanks for a wonderful summer. Love, David."

"Natural, Green, Clean"

"Nature," "natural," "green," "clean," "silent," "simple," "unchanging" are words backpackers frequently use when pressed to explain their infatuation with the wilderness. And they speak also of the sense of absolute freedom to be exprienced in the wilds—freedom to crawl under a foaming waterfall or sleep in the fragrant grasses of a meadow with no one about to say "go away" or "keep out." In contrast to the cities, they say, where a terrifying interdependence between man and machines fetters and restricts, the wilderness leaves one existentially free to make one's own decisions and mistakes.

In that phrase—"one's own decisions and mistakes"—lies the second reason for backpacking. To many, the woods and trails become a "proving ground." Robin Way, 30, a seasoned hiker and former administrative assistant to the director of the Sierra Club, the nation's pioneer conservation group, declares: "Hiking is the supreme human challenge. You learn what you're capable of doing and not doing." Adds Don Evers, manager of Sierra Design, a Berkeley outfitter, "By putting yourself in physical jeopardy you must concentrate on all the little things—Did I buy my boots too short? Will my water last?—and drop all 'home' pressures." In this sense, he thinks, backpacking is therapeutic.

Others think it is therapeutic, too—among them Arthur Kovacs, a Los Angeles clinical psychologist and devoted backpacker. Two summers ago he gathered together gear and food and led his first group of 20-odd persons into the Sierras for a long weekend of hiking,

camping, swimming—and group therapy.

"I felt the experience of being out in the wilderness would add another dimension to the psychotherapy experience," said Dr. Kovacs, "for it allows an individual to relate to his body, to cope with cold, fatigue and other simple problems of survival, which simply don't come up in ordinary psychotherapy. In the woods there is a whole new set of rules and obligations: This process of deculturation helps people to relate to each other openly and honestly." He has repeated the experience three times and plans more hikes for this summer. Trip members—clinic patients and interested outsiders—have ranged in age from 18 to 55.

As Dr. Kovacs expected, all the trips have been marked by unusual group cohesiveness. And in one instance the wilderness experience helped a particularly alienated 19-year-old achieve a new sense of himself. Alone, he built a raft by lashing together logs with tent line and, using metal plates as paddles, traveled Huck Finn-style across a lake. Then, said Dr. Kovacs, he came back to the group and met his problems "like a tiger—having demonstrated his competence to himself."

"The Storied Good Life"

Many affluent young Americans appear to have taken to backpacking to seek an alternative to the luxury and ease of the storied Good Life. Backpacking is such an alternative, for hiking 15-or-so miles a day up and down steep and rocky trails with a 40-pound load on your back may be eminently satisfying but it is not "pleasurable" in the sense that other recreations are. "I don't think backpacking should be enjoyable," says Warren Walters, a Forest Service executive, a backpacker and a former ranger. "I think it is satisfying precisely because it is so different from other recreations."

Different it is—especially for the marathon walkers. Last year Ernie Ryback, 18 years old, hiked the rugged 2,313 miles of the Pacific Crest Trail in 132 days. Five feet six inches tall and weighing 120 pounds, he toted a pack that averaged at least 80 pounds. Don Engdahl, a beefy ecology buff, walked 1,200 miles down the beaches of California last summer to draw attention to the fragility of the threatened coastline. Colin Fletcher himself has hiked through the Grand Canyon and down the entire length of the Golden State and written books about his experiences. And no fewer than 55 people have hiked all 2,025 miles of the Appa-

lachian Trail.

Another reason why people are drawn to backpacking is that, unlike tennis or golf, it is not a class sport in which costume and protocol play a large part. A hiker dressed in Levis, a work shirt and boots, as are all men, women and children on the trail, is hard to classify in terms of education, profession or economic position. Anyone who can hike and mind his wilderness manners will

"I felt the experience
of being out
in the wilderness
would add
another dimension
to psychotherapy," said
Dr. Kovacs,
"for it allows
an individual to relate
to his body,
to cope with cold,
fatigue and other
problems of survival."

be accepted into the backpacking fraternity. The woods are open to all, regardless of age, sex or race.

This is one reason why backpacking has become an acceptable and even praiseworthy pastime for hippies, radicals and other members of the "counterculture." It offers equality. It is believed to offer honesty. It even fits in nicely with the counterculture's fascination with Zen Buddhism.

Gary Snyder's "The Back Country," Kerouac's "The Dharma Bums" and other writings have influenced the young by combining backpacking and Zen. Both teach delight in simplicity and silence and the eschewing of the intellectual in favor of the intuitive. Both deplore the Western habit of conquering and exploiting nature rather than harmonizing with it. The wilderness lover sees himself in his mind's eye much as Japanese Zen painters depict a human being—as a dot in the entire landscape, a part of the whole rather than master of all he surveys.

Although hardly a Buddhist, Fletcher describes in suspiciously Zen-like terms that sublime backpacking moment when what is human and what is non-human harmonize:

"... . you know, deep down in your

fabric, with a certainty far more secure than intellect can offer, that you are a part of the web of life, and the web of life is a part of the rock and air and water of pre-life. You know the wholeness of the universe, the great unity. . . ."

For the hippie, the backpack itself has taken on symbolic importance. While a suitcase pinpoints its carrier as a temporary traveler and implies the stability of a permanent home somewhere, the pack signifies transience and an unfettered spirit. "I've got my house on my back," says a bushy-haired girl of 19. "It means perpetual motion," another told me.

In Berkeley, as in other youth-dominated areas, the backpack has become the badge of a certain life style—and a means of identifying kindred souls. "Where you been?" is the inevitable greeting. Then, logically, "Where you going?"

Perhaps the biggest single factor in the backpacking boom, from the technological standpoint at least, has been the development of lightweight gear—in particular, the nylon pack, the aluminum frame and the freeze-dried foods. Backpacking gear is a specialized form of camping equipment, for it must be both tough and, as just indicated, light. A good-size backpack weighs only about four pounds, a nylon sleeping bag about three pounds, a tent with a rain "fly" around five pounds. (Most backpackers do not carry tents. depending instead on plastic ground cloths for sudden rainstorms.) All other gear, including about one and one-half pounds of food per person a day, ensolite or foam pad, gas stove, cooking utensils, first-aid kit, etc., should, for a one-week jaunt, weigh no more than 40 or 50 pounds.

Not surprisingly, equipment and provisions meeting such requirements are expensive — say $350 for a complete first-rate outfit. (Many items, like a tent and cooking equipment, may be shared, of course). But after the initial outlay—and this is a major attraction of backpacking—the spending practically stops, except for food, batteries and the like.

Three items are particularly vital and should be chosen with special care: pack, sleeping bag and hiking boots. Any one of these items—if shoddy—can make a trip miserable.

There are so-called backpacks that sell for as little as $1.50 at some Army-Navy stores, but those made to be of any real use start at about $15. An excellent pack designed for long hikes will run about $50 (or as high as $80)

and it is well worth the money. The pack should be made of rip-stop waterproof nylon and mounted on an aluminum frame shaped to fit the contours of the body. It should also have outside zipper compartment, straps to attach sleeping bags and tents, a mesh back vent, padded shoulder straps and a cushioned waist belt to distribute the load.

Major Improvements

The aluminum frame and the waist strap represent major advances in the development of the modern pack because they so dramatically augment the comfort of backpacking. Most suppliers now offer smaller, less expensive packs for short hikes, and specialty shops sell packs designed for fishing and mountaineering.

A fine sleeping bag (nylon, down-filled baffle-seamed, differentially-cut, mummy-style and good to 20 degrees) will cost anywhere from $60 to $100 (and more). A less expensive bag, even if warm enough, will probably be much too heavy for backpacking.

Good boots are especially important, because blisters can quickly turn a backpacking trip sour. They should have heavily lugged soles (Vibram, Commando), tough leather uppers, good ankle support and foam padding for extra comfort. Cost: $20 to $45.

For those who would like to try backpacking before taking the big financial leap, a number of outfitters are now renting equipment—at weekend rates of about $4 for a pack, $6 for sleeping bag, $6 for tent.

It is possible, of course, to get intensely involved in the equipment phase of the game, and some backpackers do, especially those who regard rugged hiking as a sport rather than a recreation. They can be found at their favorite outfitters debating the relative merits of Bluet and Primus lightweight stoves. They keep their eyes peeled for new developments in backpacking technology—say, the plastic pack and frame made from a single mold. They become weight fetishists—and in this regard no one is absolutely immune: even Fletcher recalls having removed labels from tea bags, and once he pulled out his scale in a department store to compare the weights of two rival pairs of jockey shorts. Within reason, it goes without saying, such ounce-chopping makes sense, for every pound will make itself felt on a long hike.

Today there are literally hundreds of hiking clubs and kindred organizations eager for the backpacker's membership,

"'Dear Mother Nature,'
a scribbled sign
deep in California's
Los Padres
National Forest
reads,
'Thanks for a
Wonderful
Summer.
Love, David.'"

hiking organizations.

Although backpacking may be done almost anywhere, anytime, the most popular locales will undoubtedly remain the lovely back country trails of the national parks and forests, particularly those in the mountains. Mountain trails offer the hiker infinite variety—spectacular views, challenging terrain, the thrill of attaining the summit, and, most important, a sense of privacy. For these reasons the 4,500 square miles of roadless wilderness in the Sierra Nevada is considered America's supreme backpacking country. Over 3,000 miles of trails (with more than 50 trail entrances) weave through the region, which includes large parts of three national parks (Sequoia, Kings Canyon, Yosemite) and five national forests (Sequoia, Inyo, Sierra, Stanislaus and the Toiyabe). At the heart of the Sierra wilderness is the John Muir Trail, which traces the crest of the Sierras for 218 miles from Yosemite Valley to the Whitney Portal.

For those who enjoy marathon hiking, there are the two "supertrails" established by Congress when it authorized a National Scenic Trails System in 1968: the Appalachian Trail, which runs some 2,000 miles from Maine to Georgia, and the still-incomplete Pacific Crest Trail, stretching from the State of Washington all the way to Mexico.

Maps and trail information for every state in the Union may be obtained from the National Park and Forest Services, state and local parks and hiking clubs. The United States Geological Survey offers topographical maps for the expert and the curious. For the most resolute there remains some uncharted trail-less wilderness — where modern

and they range from local outdoor groups to the Sierra Club, with new organizations constantly emerging. In the New York City area alone there are more than 30 clubs that promote backpacking, hiking and camping. Among the largest (see Page 10) are the Sierra Club, the Metropolitan Council of the American Youth Hostel Association, the Adirondack Mountain Club and the more exclusive century-old Appalachian Mountain Club. All are members of the New York-New Jersey Trail Conference (whose publication, "The Trailwalker," gives good, up-to-date trail information) and all share in the maintenance of trails.

The largest conferences of trail clubs in the nation are the Appalachian Trail Conference (which manages the Appalachian Trail), the New England Trail Conference and the Federation of Western Outdoor Clubs. All are excellent sources of information on trails and

Zvi Lowenthal; Tex Griffin

the trees." Some outfitters, like the Ski Hut in Berkeley, have been displaying a heavy interest in ecology of late, but even as conservation-minded staff members of the Ski Hut suggest that you really don't need that paper bag with your purchase, manager Peter Noone shakes his head ruefully. "We're a bunch of hypocrites," he says. "We're trying to save the mountains and, at the same time, sell as many backpacks as possible."

As the backpackers move in force into the interior, Government officials charge that some of the most magnificent areas in the United States are suffering "irrevocable damage." Careless or inconsiderate backpackers leave their marks in dozens of ways. They cut dead or even living trees to build fires. They move rocks to construct fireplaces and, in some instances, even shelters. (Near one lake in California's San Gorgonio Wilderness, officials charge, campers have built "virtual ground-floor apartments" out of rocks. And, inevitably, human beings litter, despite the availability of plastic bags provided by the Park and Forest Services. In addition, officials maintain, even those conscientious backpackers who try to live up to the National Park Service motto, "Take nothing but pictures and leave nothing but footprints," despoil the environment and upset natural cycles simply by being in the back country in such numbers.

In moist areas, for example, the John Muir Trail has already been worn as deep as it is wide. And California's Mount Whitney, the highest peak in the United States after Alaska's Mount McKinley, offers such an alluring combination of challenge and ease that each year some 25,000 pairs of boots tramp its trailside ecology to death. And South Fork Meadows, which serves the heavily populated Los Angeles basin, has come to be known as "Slushy Meadows." One could go on and on.

All the damage to the back country, of course, cannot be attributed to the man afoot—or at least to the man afoot on his own or in a small party. Motorcyclists grind up the more accessible trails, and when the season changes there are the ubiquitous snowmobilers who, according to many backpackers, have positively ruined winter camping in the Sierras. Others reserve their harshest criticism for what might be described as the organized hordes—Sierra Club outings, say, or the "boy scouts" (a generic term among backpackers for any bunch of noisy young hikers).

men can become Lewises and Clarks and exercise otherwise stifled explorer instincts.

Serious Question

This brings us, sadly but inevitably, to a sober consideration—how long can the wilderness, charted or uncharted,

remain unspoiled in view of the increasing hordes encroaching upon it?

"The woods," declares Colin Fletcher, "are overrun and sons of bitches like me are half the problem." Comments a ranger in Los Padres National Forest, "On warm days it gets so crowded around here that they're hanging from

Conservationists Object

The Sierra Club outings, which last year consisted of 26 backpacking trips and numerous other expeditions into the wilds, are under attack by conservationists both in and out of the club who complain that they are too big and that there are too many of them. To this, Norton Myer, head of the knapsacking section of the club's San Francisco chapter, responds: "People see *any* large group of backpackers and say, 'Oh, God, there's the Sierra Club again!'" Club leaders further protest that on their outings they not only enforce camping rules ignored by the majority of backpackers but have also reduced the number of paying members per trip from 20 to 15 in an effort to blunt the impact on the environment.

Sierra Club or not, organized or not, by groups or individually, Americans in ever-growing numbers, it seems. will continue to push into the wilderness. Commenting on this trend, Ronald Mortimer, a National Park Service official, declares: "Five years ago the back country was an area to be let alone. Today it is an area to be planned."

Evidences of the planner's hand are everywhere. In an attempt to assure non-concentration of usage, more and more campsites are being designated for the back country (a trend certain to raise the hackles of any genuine admirer of solitude). At the same time, restrictions on usage are multiplying — last year, for example, in Sequoia-Kings Canyon National Parks, a one-day limit was placed on the most heavily traveled area to reduce damage to fragile vegetation, and, in one particular area, to halt pollution of the water supply, camping was prohibited within 100 feet of any shore. Worse yet, from the backpacker's point of view, are designs to "civilize" the wilderness. Word has leaked out of plans to build "back country chalets" (much like the stone cabins already operated by the Sierra Club) and to utilize monorails, tramways and hydrofoils to provide increased access to certain spots.

Park planners, of course, are merely endeavoring to reconcile a pair of irreconcilable propositions—that the wilderness be *enjoyed* by people today and that it be *preserved* for people in the future.

It would be catastrophic if the wilderness were to vanish or to become so ruined or so tamed as to lose the qualities that make it what it is. The Wilderness Act of 1964 sets aside millions of acres of Federal land as "wilderness," which "generally appears to have been

Photographs by Zvi Lowenthal

affected primarily by the forces of nature, with the imprint of man's work substantially unnoticeable" and which "provides outstanding opportunities for solitude or a primitive or unconfined type of recreation." At present there are about 10.4 million acres of wilderness (a bit more than one-twentieth of an acre per person in the United States) and an additional 4.4 million acres of "primitive" areas under consideration for inclusion in the National Wilderness Preservation System.

To help keep the wilderness wild, the National Forest Service is revising its policies almost from day to day. The previously quoted Warren Walters, chief

"Backpacking
offers equality.
It is believed to
offer honesty.
It even fits in nicely
with the
counterculture's
fascination
with
Zen Buddhism."

of recreation and wilderness planning for the Forest Service's California region, explains the new thinking thus:

"Before 1964 we managed wilderness areas as recreation areas. Now we are managing them as places for solitude. We are removing all those tin potties, those telephone wires, those signs. We are no longer stocking the lakes and streams with fish. In short, we are removing all those imprints of man's work."

Unfortunately, however, man himself will continue to mar the wilderness as long as backpackers continue to backpack and the population continues to grow and our tolerance for urban life continues to wane. And so, if this writer may be permitted to conclude with a point of view, let us, all of us, see to it that our imprints are as transitory as possible and that where we are privileged to tread, others may follow.

Hiking Clubs in the U.S.A.

Hundreds of hiking clubs dot the map of the United States and they range in size from local groups with a handful of members to the Sierra Club with 37 chapters throughout the country. The addresses of major organizations follow:

New England Trail Conference—26 Bedford Terrace, Northampton, Mass.

Federation of Western Outdoor Clubs—P.O. Box 172, Carmel, Calif.

Appalachian Trail Conference—1718 N Street N.W., Washington, D. C. 20036.

Sierra Club—1050 Mills Tower, San Francisco, Calif.

American Youth Hostels, Metropolitan Council, 535 West End Avenue, New York N.Y. 10024.

New York-New Jersey Trail Conference—GPO Box 2250, New York, N. Y.

Adirondack Mountain Club, RD 1, Ridge Rd., Glen Falls, N. Y. 12801

Photographs by Zvi Lowenthal

May 9, 1971

WINTER WOODS PROVIDE A REFUGE FOR WALKERS

Tranquil Paths Where They Need Not Fear Being Run Down By Traffic Afford Effective Stimulant for City Weariness—The Suitable Costume

By HUGH HAMMOND BENNETT.

IF one knows something of the proper way to approach Winter woods—how to get straight to them and to accept unreservedly the fullness of their proffered hospitality—one receives from a leisurely stroll among them an effective stimulant for tired feelings and a wholesome inspiration.

In many localities a short walk—and one must walk in order to see clearly and to feel poignantly the beauties and beatitudes of Winter woods—will take one from the clamor of the city with its contaminated air and the never-ending necessity for watching one's step, into an utterly different world—a place where joyful simplicity and sincerity are the outstanding characteristics and there is nothing to offend one's senses. Here is a place where one walks upon the very bosom of the earth, upon soft loam and deep, spongy forest mold, without fear of being run down from four directions at the same time.

To the uninitiated the Winter leaflessness of deciduous hardwoods has some of the aspects of austerity, it must be confessed, and perhaps even depressing characteristics. Such an impression, even though it may be of piercing cheerlessness in the beginning, usually vanishes after a few attempts at becoming acquainted with Winter woods. Thenceforth one is engulfed in the loving embrace of the most friendly beings on earth, the trees of a living forest. And so, having learned, one plunges ahead as if, after being lost, the right way has been found.

Selecting an Area.

For the perfect woodland jaunt one should use discrimination in selecting an area, if there is any opportunity for such choice; also one should choose proper companions or go alone. Due attention should be given to one's apparel, especially the shoes. As a rule it is best to confine such tramps to upland forests as much as possible, if such lie near, selecting those areas that have been least changed from the virgin condition. It would be disastrous to the aims of a contemplative recreational woodland tramp to go abroad with those who talk incessantly of such inconsequential things as last week's opera, or of such practical things as the commercial value of trees or the soil-building and water-conserving functions of plants and leaf-mold. It is advisable to leave even your dog behind, unless it be one of those rare dogs that understands his master's moods and behaves accordingly. Your stick, if you must carry one, should be without a hooked handle to wrestle with every contrary branch and vine. Your shoes must be heavy-soled and of flexible leather, known by trial to fit comfortably. Your leggings should be of leather and your trousers of strong cloth, closely fitted, but none of these details is so important as the shoes. It will not matter very much about anything else, not even the weather; for under each condition—snow, sleet, rain, wind or sun—the woods will have a different quality to offer—variants that can be understood only through experience.

An excellent choice for such a journey is a cold day, preferably one of those gray, wintry days when cloud seems almost to touch friendly tree top and snow may fly at any moment. If a wind is blowing it will only add to the pleasure, for then there will be song among overhanging boughs and protection from biting gusts in the alluring snugness of the forest undergrowth.

A Middle Atlantic Tramp.

In the Middle Atlantic States, an excellent place for a Winter tramp, is a rolling or hilly area forested with oak, beech, hickory, dogwood and poplar, with here and there a stand of pine or hemlock. The best areas are those diversified by winding ridges from whose crests lateral spurs fall away to enclose enticing hollows or coves. After these come the snug, wooded valleys with meandering streams and overhanging rock ledges splotched with moss and lichen and crannied with fern. In many of these forests there is dense undergrowth of laurel and grapevine and, in places, clusters of ferns tucked away among projecting rocks or growing in leaf-strewn depressions that groove the steeper slopes.

In order to derive the greatest enjoyment from a deciduous forest of Winter the woods must be accepted as they are, without slighting comparisons to sylvan conditions of Spring or Summer. A forest in Winter is an entirely different thing from the woodlands of Spring or Summer, particularly in the case of hardwoods. To some of those who have not yet learned to appreciate Winter woods, leafless trees are but the symbol of bleakness, sadness, even death. The true lover of the out-of-doors, on the other hand, sees not the slightest suggestion of any of these. To him, towering leafless branches outlined against sky or cloud make the most perfect etching and are symbolic of enduring strength. The lover of Winter woodland depths sees in these etchings of Nature the tranquillity of perfect peace—a picture of healthy organisms asleep, undergoing a period of rest and preparation for the activities of Spring-time, when every tree and every sapling and sprout will burst into surging energy of growth and of the task of bearing fruit.

One sees more in a forest of Win-

ter hardwoods on a gray, cloudy day than when the sun is shining. On such days shadow and light, though less sharply contrasted, are still strong enough to paint alluring pictures. As one comes from a densely wooded part of the forest into sparser growth, the misty blueness of the air has the pleasing hazy appearance of smoke. The smallest sapling of holly, cedar or other evergreen stands out in almost startling contrast against the prevailing ensemble of tranquil grays, sober browns and pale yellows. It stands inviting in its friendliness, soothing in the depths of its enduring verdancy. Tiny ground plants, such as wintergreen and lion's tongue, seem to rise above their lowly habitat, nestled among fallen leaves and twigs, to become an integral part of the forest. From the stream bottoms stark white branches of sycamores rise not so much in attitudes of supplication as if to greet the friendly visitor.

On such a day forest plants seem unusually friendly, for the world seems more compact; the horizon has closed in, the clouds have descended to the position of a roof, and dimmed visibility has added to the snugness and intimacy and friendliness of all that the woodland contains.

To those who point to the starkness of the trees and describe them with colorless grays, dead browns and insipid yellows, let them be reminded of the infinite beauties of an ice-sheathed forest in magnificence that cannot be described. But the lover of Winter woods plunges into the inviting depths, knowing full well the pleasures awaiting him and expecting new revelations, such as every forest walk brings.

Once within the forest, nothing must be permitted to deter the tramper. At a patch of batted blackberry, tangled wild grape or a crowded laurel thicket one must not be turned aside. Seek no detours, but plunge through, insensible to grasping claws of bramble or jabs and thrusts of shrubbery wattle.

When the wind is high stop at intervals to enjoy the mystery and beauty of the invisible choir. No voice of man or bird or musical instrument could excel this symphony of Winter winds among leafless hard woods. The message stirs the response of the heart without necessity for interpretation.

The Winter woods are as various as the flavor of as many fine wines. There can be no description of the multitude of varying conditions, each of which impresses itself in some manner or degree upon the character of the forest, and thus, indirectly, upon those who invade its depths. The range is vast—from the deciduous hardwoods of the East to the great stretches of fir in the Northwest and from the monsoon forests of the Tropics to the Alpine types of high altitudes or latitudes.

In the North your Winter tramp

THE PEACEFUL WOODS OF WINTER

Photograph by T. H. Sherrard, United States Forest Service.

A Forest of White Pine With a Snow Mantle.

may take you into dense forests of evergreens. Usually one finds here a more mossy and resilient floor, less openness and reduced light, as compared with deciduous growths. In such woods there may not be the same freedom of movement one finds in the more open forests further to the South. The branches are likely to be lower, and there is in many places more obstructing undergrowth. But these things are as nothing to the forest lover, determined not to be cheated by mere obstacles to travel.

In the Southeastern States one urged on by the perfection of the finds in numerous localities delightful pine woods for Winter jaunts, especially in the Piedmont country and the more sandy parts of the coastal plains. If the sun is shining, there is often a suggestion of Springtime in these Southern forests even in January. On chilly, cloudy days one finds among the Southern evergreens some flavor of Northern woods, but generally they possess individuality. Everywhere there is bird

life, no matter how warm the sun or how cold the north wind. And the floor of the forest is strewn deeply with pine needles, the most perfect carpet of all creation, wherever fires have not run over the ground. Here one's steps swing into buoyant stride, ground, the pineland fragrance, the chatter of birds, the cheerful brightness of scarlet yaupon and smilax berries.

The song of wind among Southern pines is always delightful, whether it be the soft sighing of gentle breeze or the surging of heavy wind, when the music is much like the roar of distant surf, although there is peculiar sweetness in the soft stridency produced by the wind among the long, thin needles of the pines —the choral ensemble of countless Aeolian harps. In sunshine the slender, emerald needles glisten and sparkle, covering the growth with a sheen of loveliness possessed by no other woodlands.

Come to a streamway or to one of the common "bays" or "pocosons" of the region. In many places there are masses of smilax heaped upon lower shrubbery or strung from overspreading branches in great pendants of pale and deep green. Clusters of shining berries. beads of ruby and jet. It is strange that these most beautiful evergreens seldom find their way into the market places for Christmas greens, although they can never be so lovely elsewhere as in their native places.

Passing by the moss-draped forests of cypress, sweet gum, black gum and tupelo that cover many parts of the lower Mississippi Valley—forests that really are dreary at times, although possessing beauty of their own peculiar type—we come to the post-oak and pin-oak woodlands lying between the western extension of the southern yellow pine belt on the east and the prairies on the west. These woods usually are not so attractive either in Winter or Summer as the forests already mentioned, yet one finds them not bad places for woodland adventures.

March 10, 1929

The Appalachian Trail

55 Men, Women and Grandfathers Have Hiked All 2,025 Miles Of the Appalachian Trail

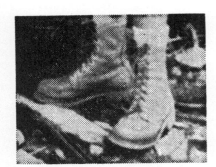

By PEGGY THOMSON

ONE day last October, Edward B. Garvey of Falls Church, Va., a retired government employe, plodded to the summit of Baxter Peak, the 5,200-foot-high topmost elevation of Maine's Mount Katahdin, and photographed the sign there which reads: "2,025 miles to Springer Mountain, Georgia." He had just hiked every last one of those 2,025 miles—the entire length of the Appalachian Trail—and in so doing, Garvey joined a select circle of outdoorsmen.

The "end-to-enders," as these Georgia-to-Maine footsloggers are sometimes called, include a 13-year-old boy, a 67-year-old grandmother, a 69-

PEGGY THOMSON is a freelance based in Washington, D. C., who frequently writes about nature.

year-old Missourian who turned down a White House invitation in order to keep on hiking, and an 80-year-old physician who must be some kind of record-holder—he took 20 years to complete the trek, hiking on weekends and short vacations.

Garvey, much faster but by no means the fastest, took five months to walk the 2,000-odd miles. He was one of eight persons to negotiate the entire Appalachian Trail last year, the 53d person ever recorded to have done it, and the 33d to have completed the trip on a single continuous hike.

After Garvey reached Baxter Peak, Numbers 54 and 55—Margaret and Clifford Smith of Buckport, Me.—crossed the finishing line before the winter set in. They had embarked with a gas-station road map, and spent six months on the trail.

Getting Set for New Season

Today, with spring in the air, stalwarts of the

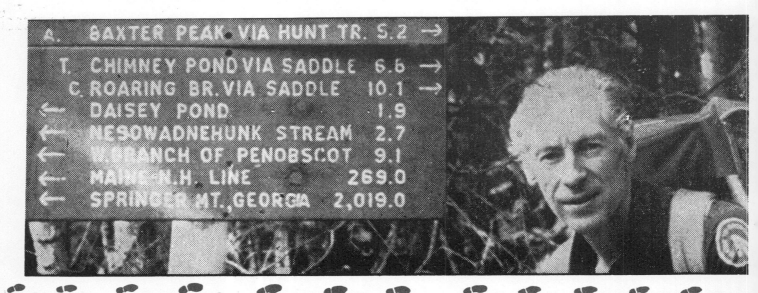

132 hiking clubs affiliated with the Appalachian Trail Conference are oiling their boots for the new season and a good many of them are expected to take a crack at becoming end-to-enders. And with long-distance hiking, or backpacking, as it's now called, becoming increasingly popular, others will try, too. Any who succeed in covering the entire route will have their names recorded at the headquarters of the A.T.C. in Washington, D. C.

The object, of course, is not to see how fast you can do the job, although it is worth noting that the speed record is held by an ex-paratrooper, Branley C. Owen of Knoxville, Tenn., who admits that he moved so fast in completing the trek in 70 days that he will have to hike the route again to really see it. A much more rewarding experience was had by Garvey who started from Georgia in April and followed spring north, keeping pace with the blooming of the May apples and reaching the Balds of the Southern Appalachians in North Carolina-Tennessee in time to look out across acres ablaze with flowering rhododendron and laurel. By mid-June, having traversed the 460 miles of his native Virginia at a comfortable rate of 100 miles a week, he looked over the confluence of the Potomac and Shenandoah Rivers from a point above Harpers Ferry.

Then after having picked up eight letters on the normally mail-less Fourth of July (they were invitations and greetings from local hikers posted on trail-side trees west of Nazareth, Pa.), he crossed the Delaware Water Gap into New Jersey on July 6.

Garvey took his time the rest of the way, maintaining that "like Thoreau, I felt rich in sunny summer days, and I spent them lavishly." He reached Maine just as autumn arrived, and the maples turned radiant with color. About 115 miles from the end of his hike, he deliberately slowed his pace again in order to savor the final 10 days of his journey.

No ordinary hiker, Garvey, who is on the A.T.C. board of managers and trail adviser to the Interior Department, set two tasks for himself along the way. One was to keep a daily log on conditions of the trail, which is maintained jointly by the National Park Service and the Forest Service (where it crosses their territories) and elsewhere by trail club volunteers.

He also noted conditions underfoot (for example, where blowdowns or fallen trees obstructed the path), checked some 270 lean-tos, the three-sided shelters providing sleeping platforms and firplaces for hikers; mapped water sources and inspected signs and blazes painted on trees to identify the trail. In one to two hours of daily paper work, he

noted corrections for future printings of trail guidebooks.

Garvey also assigned himself a daily quota of litter pick-up which, he says, in the densely used sections of New Jersey and New York "somewhat strained my resources. There I was picking up 170 pieces a day, including 15 cans (more soft drink than beer). In Maine I picked up almost nothing."

Garvey's clean-up activities would win more praise than would his feat of walking the entire length of the trail from Benton MacKaye, the Appalachian Trail's still-vigorous 91-year-old founder. MacKaye considers marathon hikers "stunt men" who have confused the trail with a race track. "What MacKaye originally envisioned," says Les Holmes, executive director of the A.T.C., "was a wilderness trail, accessible to the cities of the East Coast, where people could hike in an unspoiled natural environment for an afternoon, a weekend or a short vacation, and that's essentially what it is today. But these stalwart souls who accept the trail as a challenge and persevere to the end deserve some recognition."

To honor them, Holmes has devised a plaque bearing an Appalachian Trail "A-over-T" metal marker, the kind which is supposed to line the trail at quarter-mile intervals but which has proved to be too desirable as a souvenir item. He presented one of the plaques to Garvey in the auditorium of the Smithsonian Institution's Natural History Museum.

Appropriately enough, the first officially recognized end-to-ender was Myron Avery, the A.T.C.'s first chairman. He completed the trek in 1936, the year before the trail officially opened, and he did it an unusually hard way pushing a measuring wheel along a good part of the route.

In 1948, Earl Shaffer, of York, Pa., traveling the recommended south-to-north direction, was the first person to hike the entire trail in a single year. In 1965 he did it again — in the opposite direction—and was impressed that whole areas he had earlier bushwhacked were cleared and marked. (Then as now, the most rugged sec-

tions were the high climbs of the White Mountains and the mile-long boulder-strewn stretch of trail at Mahoosuc Notch, Me., which takes two to three hours to cross.)

The 67-year-old grandmother, who completed the Maine-to-Georgia hike in 1955, was Emma Gatewood of Hurron, Ohio, mother of 11 and grandmother of 23. Her feet swelled from size 8½ to 10, she complained that the solitary trudge was oppressive and she left the trail to eat and sleep as often as possible in homes and motels. But she was sufficiently hooked on the experienced to do it twice over, and on her second go she cut four days off her time.

Two retired New Jersey businessmen spun out their trip in 1959 for over eight months. The following summer two recent theology graduates covered the route in 99 days. A pair of Maryland University students three years later did it in 94, noting afterward that their cushion-foot socks failed to live up to a year's guarantee.

A 44-year-old Texan, Chuck Ebersole, completed the through hike in 1964 with his 17-year-old son and a beagle which backpacked its own food. Ebersole later re-did the trip with a younger son.

Jim Shattuck of New Haven, Conn., starting late from Maine in September, 1967, found himself snowshoeing in February over five-foot drifts on Sinking Creek Mountain, Va. "I was a walking deep freeze, with my drinking water, honey and vinegar all solid cakes of ice despite the motion of my walking," he reported. Shattuck slept out under rock overhangs, in pig pens and under fallen trees four and five days in a row between "pit stops'" in hotels and homes.

In the summer of 1968 a short-term hiker who met four end-to-enders in the course of his 200-mile trip reported in The Appalachian Trailway News: "Good Grief! Congestion!" The first two they met were Everett and Nell Skinner, traveling with their two sheepdogs. (They now travel with two pups as well.) Next he met Howard Bassett, a retired telephone company employe from

Wolcott, Conn., who had gone three weeks without seeing anyone at all (though he picked up signs of people in the form of a $1 bill, a windbreaker and a blanket and was sustained by the sight of "deer—150 of them—wild turkeys, bears, mice, mosquitoes, no-see-ems and flies"). The fourth end-to-ender he met was Elmer Onstott, a 69-year-old grandfather who came down the path with a white Moses-like beard, an evergreen staff and an overloaded pack.

Onstott, a sheet-metal worker from Ferguson, Mo., and an inexperienced hiker set out alone on the occasion of his retirement carrying 54 pounds of gear. He soon mailed home his tent, radio and sleeping bag but carried his camera and tripod all the way. Cooking gear was no problem for him since he lived on peanuts, pecans and raisins, with an occasional treat of wild berries and pumpkin seeds and sunflower seeds mailed to him by his wife. He did buy himself ice cream and cheese and crackers when he reached a store, and for the last 200 miles in Maine he cooked rolled oats for breakfast.

In contrast to some hikers who wear out six pairs of boots on the hike. Onstott found that one pair—a $23.95 mail order purchase from Sears—lasted him all the way and had "several miles of wear left over." He stitched them once

---

" 'Like Thoreau I felt rich in sunny summer days, and I spent them lavishly,' Garvey said, slowing down to savor the final 10 days of his journey from Georgia to Maine."

---

with nylon thread found in a shelter, and he accommodated himself to a 32-pound weight loss by wearing four pairs of socks instead of two.

At one point during his trek, in October, 1968, President Johnson invited him to attend the White House signing of the National Trails System Act, which placed the Appalachian Trail under Federal protection.

The legislation opened the way for publication in the Federal Register 16 months later (this past February) of an official "proposed" route which the states are now authorized to secure by entering into written agreement with private landowners to buying their land. (Until now free passage for hikers has been at the whim of the landowners, some of whom set up barriers routing hikers around the perimeter of their land).

Onstott sent his regrets. He said he was unable to spare three days from the six months he had allotted himself to complete his journey. As it turned out, when he neared the trail's end, the area was socked in and the hiking grandfather had to turn back several hundred yards short of his goal.

In 1969 two 17-year-old end-to-enders passed each other midway. Jeff Hancock, traveling north, had blisters all the way, spent $150 on telephone calls home to Wenham, Mass., and was captured twice by soldiers on maneuvers ("It was rather annoying"). Eric Ryback, from Belleville, Mich., going south, wore a single shirt nonstop from Maine to Virginia thereby inspiring a gift—a second shirt— right off a day-hiker's back.

Eric averaged 25 miles a day and reached Georgia in 80 days, having battled black flies in Maine, dysentery in Virginia which landed him in a hospital overnight—and loneliness all the way. He planned to take 86 days but found he liked to keep walking on bright moonlit nights. A little more than a year later, on Nov. 10, 1970, Eric completed the Canada to Mexico Pacific Crest Trail to become the first "through" hiker for the two coasts.

Speed demon ex-paratrooper Owen, who lopped 10 days off Eric's record of 80 days, set out in April, just five days after his discharge, to do just that. In the interest of speed, Owen early ditched his tent and his stove and cut himself back to carrying no more than a three-day supply of food, supple-

menting his diet with wild greens and cattail roots. He walked sometimes as much as 17 hours a day and complained later of a heavy investment in flashlight batteries. Owen did get a picture of a golden eagle banking in a turn against a New Hampshire sunset, but he admits he was too rushed to savor many sights and that the entire 2,000-wide trail was one fast blur.

A number of the end-to-enders have preferred to spread out the work and cover the course in bits and starts. One man did it in 14 months with time out to get married and travel around the world. The "record-holder" who took 20 years is Dr. Frederick Luehring of Swarthmore, Pa., now 87, who seven years ago completed the final 200 miles, part of it with an 8-year-old neighbor, Marc Boyer, who hiked the entire trail himself by the time he was 13.

Using The Appalachian Trailway News as their forum, the end-to-enders offer to those who would follow in their footsteps a number of practical sugges-

> "Garvey started from Georgia in April and followed the spring north, keeping pace with the blooming of the mayapples and the flowering rhododendron and laurel."

tions on subjects ranging from the preferred type of underdrawers to how to cross the Kennebec River in Maine. (Owen swam it. Garvey, attempting to ford it, was chest-deep in the swirling water before opting for a detour.)

"The really basic how-to-do-it," says Holmes," is to put one foot in front of the other. It takes a tremendous desire to do this thing. After the first three days you think you can't make another step. On the fourth you begin to feel pretty good."

General advice on preparations (in addition to getting physically fit): select equipment with care, test it under trail conditions, and stock up on Appalachian trail maps and the 10 regional guidebooks, ripping out as excess weight the south-to-north portions since these will

Photographs by Tex Griffin

END-TO-ENDER—Edward B. Garvey, on the rocks here, pauses near finish line in Maine

be of no use to you if you're traveling north-south. (For a handling charge of 25 cents, the Appalachian Trail Conference, 1718 N Street NW, Washington, D. C. 20036, sends an information packet including a price list of its publications.)

Garvey's special counsel is not simply to break in hiking shoes but to break them in while carrying a 30-pound pack. It makes a difference.

"The tread wore off fast," he said. "I had more falls in Maine than on the rest of the trail put together. And eight days of rain sent a flow of water from my pants down into the shoes where it had no way to run off. Another time I'd stick to leather boots all the way plus a pair of basketball sneakers."

Garvey's conclusion on rain gear is that none is satisfactory. The water-repellent fabrics that breathe let the hiker become soaked in a downpour. The waterproof fabrics soak him in sweat.

He carried a Kelty pack, goose-down sleeping bag, ground-cloth and foam pad and would recommend in addition an eight by ten nylon tarp for a shelter. There are gaps in the chain of lean-tos and when school closes in June, the hiker may arrive, as Garvey did at Virginia's Elk-Wallow Lean-to, to find 70 Scouts already in residence.

Aside from an initial weight loss of 11 pounds in 12 days, Garvey had no real trouble until he took two weeks off the trail in May. "At home I got leg cramps and my feet swelled up." A return to the trail cleared that up, and snacks of honey and peanut butter laced with powdered milk and garnished with nuts, raisins and dates restored his weight.

Finding Water

Garvey's principal complaint about trail conditions was that the water supply is poorly marked at least 75 per cent of the time. He warns hikers also of domestic dogs which charge pack-carrying strangers and of the depression, the real letdown feeling, that hits the hiker when the trip is done.

As to wildlife, Garvey totted up two rattlesnakes, one bear snoozing beside the trail in Georgia and one moose which paid a midnight call on him in his Maine woods lean-to—"When I shone my flashlight I saw two eyes, seven feet up." He also met on the trail near Sunfish Pond, N.J., where the trail supervisor assured him he never saw anything but an occasional deer, a dungareed lad strolling with his nude and giggling girlfriend.

May 9, 1971

HIKING FOOTPATH TO DIXIE URGED

Proposed Taconic Section of the Appalachian Trail Would Connect New York and New England—Links in the Route South

By RAYMOND TORREY.

OPPORTUNITIES for walking tours along woodland paths far from the bustle of motor highways have been proposed for inclusion in the State park program of New York. Such opportunities would result from the construction of the Taconic section of the Appalachian Trail. The Taconic link would extend from the headquarters of the Harriman section of the Palisades Interstate Park, at the Bear Mountain Bridge, to the Taconic Plateau at the corner of New York, Massachusetts and Connecticut, where the lands for the proposed Tri-State Park are being assembled.

It would cross the territory assigned to the Taconic State Park Commission, Putnam, Dutchess, Columbia and Rensselaer Counties, along the east side of the upper Hudson Valley. A project for a survey for the location and construction of the route has been presented to Franklin D. Roosevelt, Chairman of the commission, by Benton MacKaye, who proposed the idea of the Appalachian Trail, a footpath for hikers and campers, from Maine to Georgia and Tennessee, several years ago.

The Taconic section would be about 120 miles long. It would be accessible at several points by the Harlem Division of the New York Central Railroad and by motor highways. If carried out on the lines that are in effect on New England trails it would include shelters equipped with wood, water and blankets, to be maintained by private or public agencies, at intervals of an easy day's tramp along the route. The system would give the camping hiker readily accessible routes like those provided in New Hampshire and Vermont and in the Adirondacks for week-end or holiday outings with a knapsack.

A Sunday Walking Trip.

Arrangements for quick conveyance of parties leaving the city to hike the trail are desirable. A motor car waiting at some railroad station, by previous plan, saves loss of pleasurable hours on the trail. Food supplies, arranged for in advance with dealers at such points, may also be transported to the trail shelters in the same way. Costs of maintaining camp upkeep should be allotted among members of parties using the shelters. This method has been efficient in the mountain clubs and lowers costs to a reasonable degree.

Mr. MacKaye gives this example as to how such a trail service would work in affording outdoor enjoyment to a party of hikers:

"The party desires, let us say, to spend a Sunday walking on the Appalachian Trail in upper Dutchess County. They leave the Grand Central on Saturday afternoon at 3:20 for Amenia, N. Y., on the Harlem Division, arriving at 5:44. They are met by motor car, with food staples aboard, and are driven directly to Camp 10, where they cook and eat their supper and spend the night.

"Sunday morning after breakfast they start northward on the trail, carrying in their knapsacks enough food for midday luncheon and for supper. They stop for luncheon at some site provided with a rock fireplace for outdoor cooking. In late afternoon they would arrive at the next camp, No. 11. Here they cook and eat supper. Afterward they are met by a motor car which takes them to the station at Millerton, N. Y., whence they return on the 7:25 train to New York, where they arrive at 9:50."

Status of Appalachian Trail.

The accompanying map shows the route of the Taconic section, with approximate camp locations and railway connections. Fourteen proposed sites are shown, placed about the same distance apart as are such camps on trails with shelters in New England. Such a Taconic section would complete the Appalachian Trail from the Maine border to the Delaware Water Gap, a distance of over 500 miles.

The Appalachian Trail project was first proposed by Mr. MacKaye in 1920 at the invitation of a committee on regional planning of the American Institute of Architects, of which Clarence S. Stein was Chairman. About that time a group of members of the New York City walking clubs had begun to make trails in the Harriman

APPALACHIAN TRAIL, TACONIC SECTION

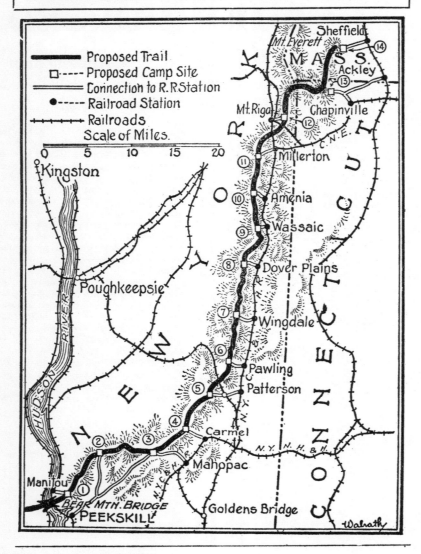

Long Trail southward to the Massachusetts line is considered part of the Appalachian Trail.

Extension to Atlanta.

Passage of a law by the Massachusetts Legislature providing for State trails within State preserves and over narrow strips to be acquired connecting them will permit construction of a trail from the Blackinton State Forest at the Vermont line over Mount Greylock and Mount Everett to the Connecticut line. It would cross Bear Mountain and then enter New York.

The Taconic section, starting at Bear Mountain Bridge, would climb Anthony's Nose and follow the northeast trending ridges past Oscawanna Lake to Boyd Corners reservoir, over Smalley's Hill, thence north past Whalley Pond to Mount Tom, near Pawling; to Bald Mountain, west of Wingdale; to Dover Plains, across the gorge of Turkey Hollow at Wassaic, and would come down to the Harlem Division at Mount Riga. It would climb the western face of the Taconic massif, to Brace Mountain, and cross into Connecticut.

Westward from the Harriman Park, the Appalachian Trail has been scouted over Bearfort Mountain, west of Greenwood Lake, across the Wawayanda plateau to High Point State Park on Kittatinny Mountain, and southwest along that ridge to Delaware Water Gap.

Southward, the route as proposed by Mr. MacKaye crosses Pennsylvania on the Blue Ridge to Harper's Ferry, follows the range on the east side of Shenandoah Valley in the region of the proposed Shenandoah National Park, goes through the Shenandoah and Natural Bridge National Forests and reaches the Tennessee line in the Unaka National Forest. The design is that it shall follow the Tennessee-North Carolina line through the Unaka, Pisgah and Cherokee National Forests and the region of the proposed Great Smoky Mountain National Park. Two branches at the lower end are proposed, one leading to Stone Mountain, near Atlanta, where the great Confederate memorial is being sculptured, the other to the national military monument on Lookout Mountain, at Chattanooga, Tenn.

Would Attract City Tenderfeet.

Here and there along this route many lengths of trail now exist, especially in New England, and from Bear Mountain to Delaware Water Gap. Local trails in the national forests and mountaineers' paths in the Great Smokies could be linked up. Groups in various places along the line are working on the project and had a conference in Washington last year, under the auspices of the Federated

section of the Palisades Interstate Park by invitation of its general manager, Major W. A. Welch. They welcomed the idea of a great trail all the way down the Appalachian ridges and organized the New York-New Jersey Trail Conference, of which Major Welch is Chairman and Frank Place, President of the Tramp and Trail Club, Secretary, to build the Palisades Interstate Park section.

This section, twenty miles long, from Bear Mountain Bridge to Arden, on the main line of the Erie Railroad, is now completed and is much used by hikers. The same volunteer workers also carried the trail westward toward Greenwood Lake, through the Harriman estate, by permission of W. Averell Harriman. This part is known as the Harriman section. Both are marked with white painted copper squares embossed with an A-T mono-

gram.

The Appalachian Trail idea was also taken up by outdoor organizations in Vermont, New Hampshire and Massachusetts through the New England Trail Conference, which affiliates about thirty-five clubs maintaining over 2,000 miles of trails. The Appalachian Mountain Club has a through route from the Mahoosuc Range, just over the Maine border, west via Gorham, Mount Washington, Crawford Notch, Franconia Notch, to Mount Moosilauke, where it joins the trail of the Dartmouth Outing Club and goes south to Hanover, on the Connecticut River. The Dartmouth club has pushed a trail west into Vermont, to Happy Hill, where it will meet a branch path of the Green Mountain Club of Vermont, which joins the Long Trail of that club at Killington Peak, near Rutland. The

Societies on Planning and Parks.

Mr. MacKaye has conceived of the Appalachian Trail as something more than a path for hikers. It is, he says, "a new approach to the problem of living, a development of the outdoor community life, as an offset from the various shackles of commercial civilization. It would encourage vacations in the open and make them accessible to people in dozens of cities along the various sections of the great trail."

Such a trail, as it is built section by section, would provide facilities to encourage those of little experience and make their initiation to the outdoors easier. The resourceful hiker, who has everything he wants in his pack, does not need them so much; he can find a lodging for the night in any wilderness. The Appalachian Trail, built and equipped as Mr. MacKaye suggests, would bring out of the cities the yearning but timid and inexperienced ones and set their feet aright in their first steps on the healing and stimulating paths of nature.

May 16, 1926

FALL TRAILS FOR HIKERS

Appalachian Route From Maine to Georgia Is Adding Sidepaths.

By S. R. WINTERS

AUTUMN days summon the vagabond to tread the woodland path. Then the dirt kicks freer beneath the hiker's boot, there is a pleasant coolness to the air and the sky, bright blue by day, is splashed at sunset with the wildest color.

The American rover finds numerous meandering trails in the East, where a 2,050-mile network known as the Appalachian Trail has been blazed through wilderness. This trail was the vision of a philosophical forester and hiker, Benton Mackaye, who hoped for "an endless trail." The Appalachian network, which extends from Mount Katahdin in Maine to Mount Oglethorpe in Georgia and passes through fourteen States, might well be called endless, for it would take the traveler many arduous months of foot-toil to cover it. Benton Mackaye's call to men-of-the-trail

aroused keen interest among the numerous outdoor club groups along the Eastern coast and units of volunteers set out with axes, scythes, pruning shears and trail-markers to blaze their cooperative footpath. Today years of building have evolved the longest uninterrupted footpath in the world.

Regional Hikes

It is not alone the length of the Appalachian Trail that lures hikers to its paths. It offers gratification of the longing for sylvan peace and beauty, and the primitive love for out-door recreation. Throughout the Autumn months the Appalachian Hiking Clubs, which have become affiliated through their joint venture of building the trail, plan a program of regional Sunday and week-end hikes. These jaunts are mapped out at the seasonal Appalachian Trail conferences held for this purpose.

Although the two termini of the trail have been completed, new side-paths to various points of interest are continually being developed, thus adding new regions for exploration. The Federal Forest Service has added many features for the comfort and interest of the hikers where the trail passes through recently developed national forests and parks. The National Forest Service keeps the Appalachian Trail in good hiking condition and also maintains cabins and shelters along the forest trails for overnight accommodation. Rangers act as guides, and make many helpful suggestions to the travelers concerning good walking routes and interesting sites.

The hikers foot the trail through one great mountain range after another. Starting at Mount Katahdin, in Maine, the northern terminus, a wilderness trail, leading past lake and stream and over a series of disconnected mountain peaks takes the traveler a distance of 250 miles to the White Mountains of New Hampshire. Mounts Madison, Jefferson, Gorham and Carter Notch are popular New Hampshire mountains, but the most frequently visited is Mount Washington. Many hikers spend several days on Mount Washington, for there the Appalachian Hiking Club maintains some of its huts. These huts are run by college boys, who receive as many as sixty to eighty people a day there as overnight paying guests.

From Vermont to New York

The trail continues into Vermont where the famous maples of that

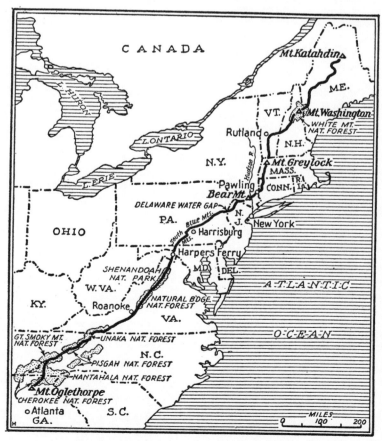

State now glow brilliantly. Near Rutland the trail turns south for 100 miles along the Green Mountains, scene of many historical Revolutionary War battles. In Massachusetts the path leads to the remarkable Mount Greylock, with its impressive war memorial. Leaving the Berkshire and Taconic Mountains, a somewhat indirect route leads to Connecticut, twice crossing the Housatonic River, where the scenic forest preserves of the western part of the State may be viewed.

It is at Shaghticoke Mountain, where the Shaghticoke Indians have their reservation, that the border line to New York State is crossed. There is a steep climb that leads past Lake Hammersley, then down into the Harlem Valley at Pawling. Delightful traveling is afforded by way of old abandoned roads which lead to Mount Tom, and then past Fahnestock State Park, with its beautiful Clear and Mud Lakes, so falsely named.

A precipitous descent to Anthony's Nose takes the wanderer to Bear Mountain Bridge over the Hudson River. The Bear Mountain and Harriman sections are popular walking regions accessible to hikers starting from New York City. The route skirts Greenwood and Waywayanda Lakes and crosses Waywayanda and Pochuck Mountains to the base of the Kittatinny Range.

At High Point State Park the direction heads south to the Delaware Water Gap, where the river is crossed by canoe ferry. The trail passes Deerhead Inn en route to the fire station at Mount Minsi. Near the Lehigh River and in Pennsylvania the Appalachian Hiking Club and other clubs maintain cabins built by their members.

The Appalachian Trail cuts through the Alleghany Mountains, goes across the Cumberland Valley, and finally passes through the Mont Alto State Forest; goes over the Pennsylvania-Maryland line and continues to Harper's Ferry, W. Va., where the Potomac River breaks through the Blue Ridge. The trail follows the crest of these mountains until it reaches the Shenandoah National Park, the newly opened recreation grounds whose interesting focal point is

Mark Taylor, courtesy Appalachian Club.

On Mount Katahdin, northern terminus of the Appalachian Trail.

Skyland, leading to many points of scenic beauty.

Three hundred miles south in Virginia, where the Roanoke breaks through the range, the Blue Ridge forks. One trail leads to the southern portion of the Unaka National Forest, found in the States of Virginia, Tennessee and North Carolina. Wild life abounds in this forest. Travelers who are interested in fishing and hunting often spend several days in the forest, sleeping in the excellent tourist cabins provided by the Forest Service.

A circuitous route leads to the Pisgah National Forest, where it winds to the range of the Little Tennessee River to the Great Smoky Mountains National Park, by its nature reminiscent of the northern country. At the southern end of the Great Smokies a cross-range, the Nantahala Mountains, is traversed, leading back to the eastern rim of the Blue Ridge, which is followed uninterruptedly to Mount Oglethorpe, Ga., the southern terminus of the trail, where the Appalachians end abruptly.

Packs for 850-Mile Walk

Two men, of scholarly bent, C. Bradford, an instructor in English, and Raymond M. Mitchell,

covered recently 850 miles of mountain territory by foot on the Appalachian Trail, traveling northward from Mount Oglethorpe.. From May 6 to June 29, they traveled with their packs on their backs, averaging seventeen miles daily until they reached Shenandoah National Park. For less than $100 each they were able to enjoy one of the most remarkable vacations our country affords.

They journeyed with light packs, weighing between thirty and forty pounds, containing a 6 by 4½ foot tent, an axe, sleeping bags, lightweight sweaters and raincoats, tennis shoes for evening change, underwear, socks, shirts, a frying pan, two small kettles, two tin cups and plates, a canvas water bucket, knives and forks, soaps, scouring mit and food. Dehydrated and non-perishable nourishing foods, plus canned meat and fish, formed the bulk of their diet.

Most hardened hikers carry this type of equipment nowadays. Not many years ago, it was thought that a person had to be loaded like a human "pack-horse" before he could set foot on the trail. Comfort and freedom rather than torturing self-discipline are now the ideal of the American hiker, who prefers to swing along under slight burden and sing his "vagabond song."

October 11, 1936

LONG TRAIL'S LAST LINK

Hiking Clubs to Celebrate the Completion Of Footpath From Maine to Georgia

By DOROTHY M. MARTIN

WASHINGTON — Hikers will find walking aplenty this summer on the 2,021-mile Appalachian Trail, which for the first time in fourteen years will be open all the way from Mount Katahdin in Maine to Mount Oglethorpe in Georgia. Work on the remaining unfinished stretch of the long footpath through the Eastern mountains was completed late last month, and next Sunday a simple ceremony commemorating the painting of the last trail blaze will take place at noon on top of 4,000-foot Priest Mountain about twenty-five miles southwest of Charlottesville, Va.

On hand for the occasion will be members of hiking clubs in Virginia and the national capital and representatives of the United States Forest Service and the National Park Service. Myron Avery, chairman of the Appalachian Trail Conference, will be master of ceremonies, and Ranger B. A. Eger, who supervised the construction of the last link of the trail in the George Washington National Forest, will be the principal speaker.

Spring Project

Throughout the spring, trail crews of the Forest Service were at work clearing brush and building switchbacks on the nine-and-a-quarter-mile stretch which crosses the Tye River valley in western Virginia between Three Ridges and Priest Mountain. Ernest Karger, supervisor of the George Washington forest, reports that the trail up both sides of the valley is a hard climb. Members of near-by hiking clubs, however, have been eagerly waiting for an opportunity to test their skill over the new route.

Next Sunday's ceremonies will have special meaning for serious hiking groups throughout the East, for with the exception of a thirteen-month period in the late Nineteen Thirties, the objective of having a continuous foot trail stretching down through the Appalachian wilderness of fourteen states has remained an unrealized dream.

The Appalachian Trail was first proposed by Benton MacKaye of Shirley Center, Mass., in 1921 in an article entitled "An Appalachian Trail, a Project in Regional Planning," which appeared in the Journal of the American Institute of Architects. Mr. MacKaye had been a forester with the United States Forest Service between 1905 and 1918.

Original Plan

One of his early assignments was to determine what eastern lands the Forest Service should buy to protect the watersheds of navigable rivers, and he knew his mountain country well. He envisaged a footpath extending from Mount Washington in New Hampshire, the tallest peak in the North, to Mount Mitchell in North Carolina, the tallest peak in the South.

Trails already existed that would be a part of this long footpath. The Appalachian Mountain Club of Boston had constructed a network of trails in the White Mountains. The Green Mountain Club had partly completed the Long Trail in Vermont. The Palisades Interstate Park Trail Conference had just been organized to develop trails in the Harriman and Bear Mountain sections of Palisades Park.

The Appalachian Trail, however, did not develop easily. Two false starts were made—in 1922 and 1925—before Mr. MacKaye's dream was well launched. Then early in 1926 Arthur Perkins, a retired lawyer of Hartford, Conn., rallied workers to the project. Assisted by Mr. Avery, who has been chairman of the Appalachian Trail Conference since 1931, Mr. Perkins instigated the building of a trail across Massachusetts and helped route the path in the Delaware Water Gap area.

On Aug. 15, 1937, the Appalachian Trail was finally open from Maine to Georgia. Thirteen months later, in mid-September, 1938, what has come to be known as the New England hurricane roared over the northeastern mountains leaving a tangle of uprooted trees blocking long sections of the trail. Before clearing operations in the North could get under way, construction of the Blue Ridge Parkway in Virginia was begun, the highway following for miles the exact route of the foot trail.

The act establishing the Parkway provided for relocation of the Appalachian Trail on lands administered by the Forest and Park Services, but with the outbreak of World War II and the manpower shortage which followed, the work had to be postponed until the emergency was over.

Crosses Fourteen States

This year, however, the trail again runs unbroken from Maine to Georgia. From north to south the intervening states are New Hampshire, Vermont, Massachusetts, Connecticut, New York, New Jersey, Pennsylvania, Maryland, West Virginia, Virginia, Tennessee and North Carolina.

It is unlikely that many hikers will tackle its entire 2,021 miles this summer. So far only one person is reported to have hiked the whole distance in one trip. In 1949 Earl Shaffer of York, Pa., started north from Mount Oglethorpe in April. Without benefit of the improvements since added to the trail, he reached Mount Katahdin in Maine the following August.

Throughout its entire length the trail sticks to semi-wilderness country, avoiding civilization as much as possible. This atmosphere is protected by an agreement among the Forest and Park Services and the various states, which forbids construction of a parallel road for public use within a mile on either side of the route.

Since it is intended solely for foot travel, the trail consists of a cleared path only six feet wide. Marking is standard—diamond-shaped metal plates attached to trees and white blazes six inches long and two inches wide, except in national park areas where the route is so definite that even the most inexperienced nature lover could not get lost.

For persons making extended

THE APPALACHIAN TRAIL

Foreign visitors, particularly our English friends, are more than likely to observe sooner or later during their stay here that the American people are sure eventually to lose the use of their legs. True enough, if there is a choice between riding and walking we ride—the thought of walking usually doesn't even cross our minds. The kind of footpath for which the English countryside is famous is almost as rare in the United States as is a six-lane superhighway in England. But not quite.

Though it may surprise most foreigners and a great many Americans as well, there are walkers in this country; and there are some mighty fine places for them to walk. One of the most remarkable places of all—in this or any other continent—is the "footpath through the wilderness" that runs more than two thousand miles from Mount Katahdin in Maine to Mount Oglethorpe in Georgia: the justly famous Appalachian Trail.

Originally conceived by Benton MacKaye in 1921, the trail was established as an entity in the summer of 1937, but the hurricane of the following year damaged parts of it. What with various subsequent misadventures, including parkway construction and the Second World War, it is only this spring that it has become a continuous trail for the whole distance once again—thanks to the efforts of local hiking clubs, the Park and Forest Services and the private coordinating body called the Appalachian Trail Conference.

Of course not many people will take advantage of the occasion to hike the whole way from Georgia to Maine—though it has been done; but anyone who has ever walked along one of its breath-taking ridges or through its beautiful woodlands or across its sunny meadows will gain satisfaction in knowing that the Appalachian Trail has at last been restored to its pre-war glory.

June 17, 1951

trips, shelters a day's hiking distance apart are maintained along several sections of the trail. These include the stretch from the Kennebec River in Maine to the White Mountains in New Hampshire, the Long Trail in Vermont, a segment running from southern Pennsylvania through the Shenandoah National Forest, and a section extending from the Pisgah National Forest in North Carolina through the Great Smokies National Park.

To a great extent the trail is maintained by volunteer workers from various regional hiking clubs. Coordinating organization for these clubs and all other persons interested in the project is the Appalachian Trail Conference, which operates without endowment and also on a volunteer basis. Since the

pathway runs for 167 miles through national parks and 538 miles through national forests, both Park and Forest Services also contribute substantially to its care in these areas.

Prospective hikers can direct inquiries about the various sections of the trail to Appalachian Trail Conference headquarters. However, since the organization is not subsidized, there is a charge of 25 cents for the general information packet. This contains pamphlets giving a description of the trail, an outline of the conference's program and a list of maps and booklets on equipment and outdoor life which are available at varying fees. The address of the conference is 1916 Sunderland Place, N. W., Washington 6, D. C.

June 3, 1951

'ROUGHING IT' ON SCENIC RANGES

In Late Summer the Amateur Explorer Heads for Near-By Peaks For an Outdoor Vacation of Hiking, Climbing and Camping

By NATHANIEL NITKIN

LATE Summer finds trains, buses and automobiles carrying mountain campers and their pack sacks into New York's Adirondacks, Vermont's Green Mountains, the White Mountains of New Hampshire and Maine's Blue Mountains. From now well into the Fall amateur explorers will blaze new trails and follow old paths, seeking the higher altitudes where the air is crisp and invigorating.

Mountain climbing and camping gain more recruits each year. Veterans sigh for the time when they logged many miles before they met other camping parties, but now one has company in the wildest and toughest areas of the Northeast.

Mountaineering Clubs

Hiking and mountaineering club members form the majority of mountain campers. Older Boy Scouts and Girl Scouts apply to the trail knowledge gained in their apprenticeships. The most adventurous are the collegiate outing clubs, whose members, bubbling with energy and enthusiasm, cover many hard miles. On Sept. 3 the Intercollegiate Outing Club Association, with girls and boys from two dozen Northeastern colleges, will hike and camp in the Adirondacks.

The mountain region that is the Summer haunt of the average New York mountaineer is the Northeast section of the long Appalachian cordillera, the several regions geologically alike, yet each with its own characteristics and flavor. Here are true mountains, mellowed by age, yet rugged enough to demand hard physical labor of those who tread their long brown paths. Some of them remain as much a wilderness as they were in the time when the Indians roamed the woodlands, yet each of them is within reach of highways and railroad stations.

The Adirondack range is tall and majestic in its purple and green mantle, broken here and there by white and orange rocks, winning the hearts of its visitors at first sight. When the hiker ascends to the higher altitudes, he comes to stunted evergreens and sweet-smelling balsams, with a perfume that is said to be found only in the Adirondacks.

It is in the Northeastern section of this range, where the mountains are more rugged and wild, that hiking trails are most numerous, centering around Mount Marcy, 5,344 feet above sea level. The starting points are Lake Placid Village and Keene Valley, with St. Huberts and Underwood as secondary points. Each trail has its own color scheme for directional marking, and thus finding the way through this wilderness area is made easier for the part-time out-

Edward L. Gockeler, Pinney from Black Star.
Magnificent vistas reward climbers in Northeast. Above, McIntyre and Colden peaks, Adirondacks.

Girl hikers resting on Whiteface Mountain   E. M. Newman, New York Times

door man.

The best and most rugged trail of the Adirondacks is the Range Trail, built and maintained by the Adirondack Mountain Club. This trail extends from the road between St. Huberts and Keene Valley over a series of mountain peaks, such as Wolf's Jaw, Gothic Mountain and Basin Mountain, and ends at Mount Marcy. The shelters of this trail have been built by the Adirondack Mountain Club which maintains a blanket cache at Sno Bird Shelter and is building another cache on the trail between Sno Bird and Mount Haystack.

The New York State Conservation Department recognizes the Range Trail as a blue-blazed one starting from the yellow-blazed John's Brook Trail from Keene Valley and joining the trail proper at Gothic Mountain Shelter. From here it goes on toward Mount Marcy.

Circuit Trail

The Great Circle Trail, which the Adirondack Mountain Club is surveying, will dwarf the Range Trail as an achievement. Starting at Adirondack Loj, it will make a long circuit around Indian Pass, taking a cutaway to Calamity Brook. From here a new trail will run to Opalescent River between Calamity and Adams Mountains, continuing up Flowed Lands and its districts to Mount Marcy. Then it will follow the Range Trail,

swerving at Gothic Mountain Shelter to John's Brook Lodge. The final phase will be the red-blazed Klondike Trail to Adirondack Loj.

Those with a limited time may take the blue-blazed Van Hoevenberg Trail from Adirondack Loj to Mount Marcy, and there are other trails at their disposal.

The Adirondack Mountain Club publishes an excellent pocket guide with a complete map of the Adirondacks. In addition it sells topographical sheets with trails drawn on them.

The Green Mountains of Vermont are unique. This range molded the character of its inhabitants and made Vermont a State of rugged individualists. It gave Ethan Allen and his Green Mountain Boys the singleness of purpose that drove them across tangled mountain wildernesses to capture Fort Ticonderoga.

Trail to Border

The Green Mountains are the culmination of the Taconics and the Berkshires to the south. Through the Vermont hills runs the Long Trail, which starts on the Massachusetts border near Mount Greylock and ends at the Canadian border, following the crests of the range.

Should one wish to follow the entire length of the Long Trail, the best way is to debark from train or bus at Blackinton, Mass., and take the Appalachian Trail.

Exactly at the Vermont border the Appalachian Trail joins the Long Trail and follows it for ninety-seven miles to Sherburne Pass, where it swings to New Hampshire. The Long Trail continues northward to Canada.

The noblest of the Green Mountains is Mount Mansfield. Seen from a distance, Mount Mansfield resembles a man's face turned upward. Running from south to north, the sections are known as the Forehead, the Nose, the Chin and the Adam's Apple. The highest point, the Chin, 4,393 feet, is a bare, windswept summit with glacial boulders, curiously stunted trees having a tang that is different from the Adirondacks' balsam perfume, and alpine plants. A cairn of stones, the Frenchman's Pile, marks the spot where a man was struck by lightning during a storm.

The Green Mountain Club, which not only maintains the Long Trail but also has camps and supply depots conveniently situated on it, publishes a comprehensive booklet and maps of this trail.

Variety in White Mountains

The White Mountains are the highest north of the Great Smokies and east of the Mississippi. For some years they have been set aside as a national park. Where but in the White Mountains would the camper find, much to his consternation, that temperatures

Lunch in a shelter typical of those in the White, Green, or Blue Mountains, or Adirondacks.

sometimes falls from sweltering heat to just above freezing point in less than ten minutes? Where in the East but in the White Mountains is there a beautiful and multicolored alpine garden that is the botanist's delight?

The Dartmouth Outing Club takes care of trails in the western part of the White Mountains, but much credit also goes to the Appalachian Mountain Club, which has done yeoman work. Indeed, the A. M. C. has built and maintains ninety-five trails with an aggregate length of 360.11 miles. The United States Forest Supervisor's headquarters is at Laconia, N. H.

Like the Adirondacks, the White Mountain area is too big to be described in detail. However, the most popular part is the Presidential Range, centering around Mount Washington, standing 6,288 feet in its stockings. To conquer Mount Washington one should respect the weather, for a storm or even a rainfall on this temperamental mountain may be disastrous. A climber needs not only a good map but a trusty compass and plenty of stamina.

Up Mount Washington

Mount Washington is accessible from the comparatively easy Tuckerman Ravine Trail, running from Pinkham Notch Camp, on Route 16 between Glen House and Jackson, N. H. Only experienced mountaineers have any right on the difficult Huntington Ravine Trail, and they steer clear of it in any but the sunniest weather.

The Appalachian Trail follows the crests of the Presidential Range. A favorite itinerary starts at Appalachian Station, a few miles from Randolph, N. H., and follows the trail south, over the Presidential Range to Willey House Station, not far from Crawford Notch. The procedure may be reversed. Either way, it makes a good vacation for a mountaineer.

The Appalachian Mountain Club prints and sells a book on the White Mountains that is a model of its kind. Its 564 pages and maps are crammed with the information that the visitor to this region needs to have, with some chapters on camping and first aid.

No one who claims to be familiar with the mountains of the North-east misses Mount Katahdin of Maine. Reaching 5,264 feet above sea level, it is the most rugged peak of the East, and it is the fitting terminus of the Appalachian Trail. This mountain itself is an imposing sight. A great, irregular-shaped mountain, with its famous dome, Pamola, rises suddenly from a comparatively flat, wooded country. This is the simplest description of Katahdin. Part of this mountain's crests demand real mountaineering technique to overcome.

Some hikers cross 150 miles of Maine's Blue Mountains before reaching Mount Katahdin. It is not necessary now, thanks to the new Millinocket-Sourdnahunk tote road that leads to the foot of the Hunt Trail at the Maine State Camp on Katahdin Stream. One may pick up the Appalachian Trail here and explore as much of the Blue Mountains as one wishes.

Maine's Blue Mountains and Mount Katahdin are well covered in the booklet "The Appalachian Trail in Maine," published by the Maine Appalachian Trail Club, which takes care of this State's 150-mile path.

August 24, 1941

MAGNIFICENT FOOT TRAIL TAKES SHAPE

By HERBERT GORDON

HIGHLAND MILLS, N.Y. —On a recent spring day, when the crocuses were buried beneath six inches of fresh snow, a one-mile section of a new route between New York's smoggy skyline and the green and rugged Catskills was relocated along Schunemunk Mountain's boulder-strewn slopes.

This arduous job of moving the route was undertaken so that travelers atop Schunemunk's windwept summit would have more breathtaking views of the Shawangunk range, to the west, and of the tip of Bear Mountain, to the east.

The new route winds along unscarred corners of the Palisades, and through half-forgotten villages. It skirts tiny jewels of cerulean lakes, climbs high, rocky ridges, crosses streams whose waters splash in almost pristine cleanliness and wanders through valleys that are thick with hardwood forests.

No Speed Traps

Along its entire 130 miles, there are no radar traps, no grim policemen, no complex interchanges, no speed limits and little traffic. For this route, a magnificent foot trail, encompasses the southern third of the developing Long Path of New York State. Eventually, it will stretch some 400 miles—from the New Jersey side of the George Washington Bridge to the 4,867-foot summit of Whiteface Mountain, which overlooks the Lake Placid region of the Adirondack Mountains.

The northern third of the Long Path, completed more than 25 years ago, extends 155 miles from the southern Adirondacks to Lake Placid. Still to be tied into the trail is a 115-mile stretch through the Mohawk Valley; it will link the northern edge of the Catskills with the southern Adirondacks.

When finally completed, the Long Path, whose bordering trees are being marked with splashes of light-blue paint five inches high and three inches wide, will be the third longest foot trail in the United States. It will be exceeded only by the Appalachian Trail, which extends 2,000 miles from Maine to Georgia, and the Pacific Crest Trail, which follows the coastal ranges from Canada to southern California.

Little Known

Although the Long Path has been abuilding for some 40 years, it is still incomplete and surprisingly little known. But in time, because of the 15 million potential hikers who live near it, the Long Path is expected to become one of the best known and most heavily used hiking trails in the nation.

Work on the trail began in the 1930's, but was abandoned during World War II. The Long Path was then left to wither away until the winter of 1960, when it was abruptly brought back to life by Robert Jessen of Brooklyn.

One day, while browsing in a second-hand bookshop, Mr. Jessen, whose hobbies include hiking, came across a 1938 edition of "Guide to the Appalachian Trail — From the Housatonic River to the Susquehanna River." In it, on page 107, he found this intriguing paragraph:

"A larger trail project which connects with the Appalachian Trail is the Long Path of New York, proposed in 1931 by Vincent J. Schaefer of the Mohawk Valley Hiking Club of Schenectady, N. Y. Mr. Schaefer proposed that New York State, like Vermont, should have a Long Trail from New York City to Lake Placid. His group began work at Gilboa Dam on the Schoharie River. Marking has so far been scattered and discontinuous."

Mr. Jessen, a new member of the New York-New Jersey Trail Conference, an organization of hiking clubs and individuals, suggested that the group help to revive the Long Path. After some debate, the conference gave him $25 to get the plan started, and held endless discussions to determine the route.

It was generally agreed that the Long Path should follow existing trails as much as possible. Among those now incorporated, in varying degrees, into the Long Path are the Appalachian and the Northville-Lake Placid Trails through the Adirondacks, plus several lesser-known trails. The latter include Hook Mountain-Tor Ridge, Panther Mountain and Allison.

It was also agreed the Long Path should follow the original routing as closely as possible, although mushrooming suburbs, spreading industries, developed vacation sites and highway systems had battered the Long Path out of its original shape.

For example, the original Long Path route would have headed directly north along the western shore of the Hudson River, following the Palisades and going through the Highlands and over the summits of Bear Mountain and Storm King Mountain. Today, the trail follows the Hudson only to Hook Mountain State Park. Then it swings west through High Tor State Park, more than 20 miles south of Storm King.

Palisades Trail

The first section restored and marked was an old trail running along the Palisades from the George Washington Bridge to the New York Line.

Petty differences developed over specific trail locations, for those who love the mountains have an ardent passion for a particular valley, a certain ridge or a familiar hiking trail. However, these problems were more easily resolved than was that of winning permission from property owners for the trail to cross their acreage.

There were other problems. Money was scarce, and work was performed by volunteers. On any particular job, they would either show up in relatively large numbers, or, for inexplicable reasons, not appear at all.

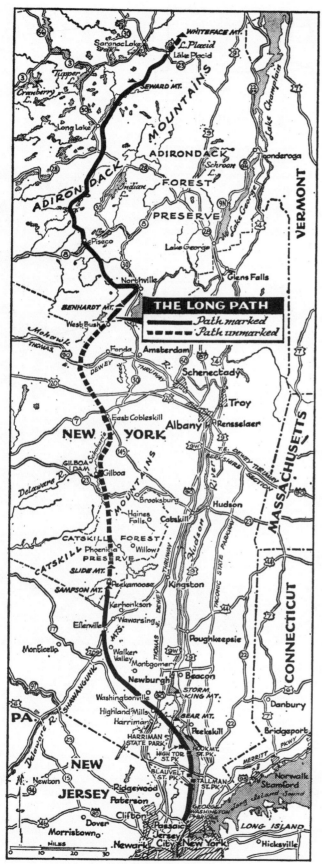

THE LONG PATH
━━━━━ *Path marked*
┅┅┅┅┅ *Path unmarked*

Clearing, marking and maintaining trails is tough, yet delicate, work. The object is to clear only as much land as is essential for hiking, disturbing the remainder as little as possible. Over - cutting and over-clearing are as detrimental to a good trail as is the failure to maintain paths that can be hiked safely by mountain-bound city dwellers.

An ideal work team on the trail consists of at least four persons. The lead-off man swings a razor-sharp machete at any brush within reach. The second man carries brush clippers and a scraper. He cuts brush and limbs that will not yield to the machete, and scrapes a small section of bark from carefully selected trees.

The third man wields the paint brush, decorating chosen trees with blazes of blue. The last man carries the bulk of supplies, which usually include a hand axe, buck saw and folding saw.

When the team is twice as large, the work is half as difficult and four times the fun.

The New Jersey section of the Long Path, which runs along the Palisades, is highly accessible and provides magnificent views of the Hudson River. The trail there is relatively level and ideally suited for a family stroll or for a vigorous walk.

The Long Path becomes gradually more rigorous as it crosses into New York and heads through a series of almost unknown state parks: Tallman Mountain, Blauvelt, Hook Mountain and High Tor. Then, it cuts northwest through the green loveliness of Harriman State Park, following the Appalachian Trail briefly near Island Pond Lake and through the interesting Lemon Squeezer rock formations.

As it leaves Harriman, the Long Path nicks the corner of West Point. It then crosses pas-

toral lands and increasingly higher mountains and ridges, until it reaches the Shawangunk Mountains, parallel to U. S. 209. There for the first time, the trail climbs above 2,000 feet.

After almost 10 miles along the Shawangunk range, the route heads west into the Catskills, where it can provide a rugged adventure. It climbs tough, 3,867 - foot - high Peekamoose Mountain, and then reaches the 4,204-foot summit of Slide Mountain, the highest peak in the Catskills.

3,500-Foot Level

The trail has not been defined as the Long Path through the entire Catskills. Existing trails within this forest preserve will be marked during the spring and summer, carrying the Long Path through country dominated by peaks towering above the 3,500-foot level.

The Long Path will link up with the original section near Gilboa Dam, and then follow Schoharie Creek north to East Cobleskill, near the intersection of State Routes 7 and 145.

From there, the Long Path, when completed, will traverse a region of farms, small towns and rolling hills. Tentative plans call for the trail to follow easy hiking trails and country roadsides until, after crossing the Mohawk Valley midway between Utica and Albany, it reaches the southern boundary of the Adirondack preserve.

The longest of the three sections of the Long Path, the Northville - Lake Placid Trail, runs north through the Adirondacks for approximately 155 miles. It almost bisects the region.

From Lake Placid to the top of Whiteface Mountain is a distance of seven miles. It is now traversed by the Whiteface Trail, but Mr. Jessen expects that the short stretch eventually will be incorporated into the Long Path.

April 11, 1965

The Ramparts That Watch Over the Hudson

By HERBERT GORDON

EDGEWATER, N. J. — The towering ramparts of the Palisades, like the walls of a great fortress, stretch north from here for almost 13 miles along the western bank of the Hudson River. Those who know the Palisades only from the window of a train, or from a car speeding along the eastern bank of the river, will never discover their wildness and forbidding grandeur. That is reserved for people who walk the trails and climb the cliffs within the Palisades Section of Palisades Interstate Park.

There is no lack of travelers. Cars stream along the Palisades Interstate Parkway, at the top of the cliffs, in an almost endless flow, but many facilities that once attracted visitors have vanished.

For example, the Yonkers-Alpine and the Dyckman Street ferries no longer run. All beaches are closed to swimming because of water pollution, and the dozen or so pleasure-boat docks that once dotted this area have dwindled to four.

In addition to the parkway, there is another road for the motorist, Henry Hudson Drive. It meanders along the shore for approximately two-thirds of the section's length—from Edgewater to the Alpine Recreation Area.

Choice of Trails

Two major foot trails traverse the Palisades. One, which follows the water's edge, is overshadowed by the giant wall of rock thrusting upward at a height of between 300 and 500 feet. It wanders through groves of trees, some of which are among the finest specimens of Eastern forests. Of note are some magnificent empress trees, which had been in the gardens of old estates. Around Memorial Day, these trees come ablaze with a profusion of bluebell-like flowers.

The second trail follows the crest of the cliff. It is the first segment of the Long Path, a hiking trail marked with blue blazes. Eventually, it will stretch 400 miles from the George Washington Bridge to the Adirondacks. Within the park, the Long Path offers breathtaking views of the Hudson River Valley.

The two major trails are linked by five main side trails, each of which scales the Palisades. The vertical paths are not dangerous, but they are not recommended for walkers with weak legs or for those who may be susceptible to vertigo.

There is no best season to roam the Palisades. In early spring and late fall,

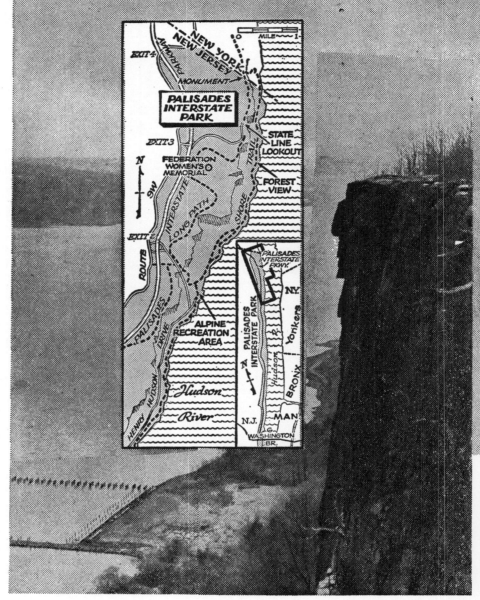

however, the trees are barren of foliage, offering the walker an almost continual view across the Hudson.

Perhaps the most rewarding of the trail walks, and my favorite, is a circular trip of the northern section, where no roadway penetrates the shore area.

High Point of Palisades

The walk begins at the parking lot of State Line Lookout, which is reached from Exit 3 of the Palisades Parkway. This is the highest point within the Palisades Section of the park, an elevation of 530 feet. Looking south, one can see the massive silhouette of Indian Head, stonily staring

IN PROFILE — The massive silhouette of Indian Head in the Palisades staring stonily across the Hudson River.

eastward across the river.

From the parking lot, head north and follow the blue blazes of the Long Path to a marble monument at the New York-New Jersey line. The path dips briefly and goes through a gate in a high chain fence. Slightly beyond the fence, the trail forks. The Long Path continues through the wooded acres of the Lamont Geological Observatory.

Leave the Long Path and begin the descent to the river. The downward trail requires caution, and the hiker will appreciate sturdy clothes and walking shoes.

At the river's edge, the path joins the northern end of the Shore Trail. Turn south. The next mile or so is the most rugged portion of the Palisades Section.

In describing this little-visited section, the "New York Walk Book" says:

"With consummate landscape art, this footway wanders by huge monoliths and giant staircases from one view to another on a course that, in Europe, would be justly famous. The vast wall hangs above one. The river of wonders is at one's feet."

Approximately a mile and one-half to the south is the Forest View Picnic Area, its docks now a line of gray posts and its pavilion only a memory. A side trail, marked by a few red-paint blazes and beginning near some half-rotten picnic tables, leads to the top of the cliff.

At the top, rejoin the Long Path. However, before heading north to the parking lot at State Line Lookout, it is worth taking a few steps south to visit a small stone building overlooking the edge of the Palisades. The building is a memorial to the New Jersey Federation of Women's Clubs, whose efforts during the late 19th century saved the Palisades from destruction by quarrying interests.

If the hiker has the time and the energy, he can continue along the Shore Trail from the Forest View area to the Alpine Recreation Area. From there, follow a Revolutionary War road to the summit, and take the Long Path north along the edge of the cliffs and back to State Line Lookout.

The shorter loop trip covers about three and one-half miles; the trip by way of Alpine is about seven miles long.

Additional Walks

There are less strenuous walks from the parking field at the Alpine Recreation Area, which is reached from Exit 2 of the parkway; from the Englewood-Bloomers Recreation Area, which is reached from Exit 1 of the parkway, and from Ross Dock, which is situated along the southern section of Henry Hudson Drive.

The Palisades offer more than magnificent views. They are also rich in history. They may appear as inaccessible cliffs and inhospitable to civilization; however, when the nation was in its infancy and the Hudson River was a primary source of commerce and travel, many Dutch farmers lived there and prospered from the shad in the river and from the stone building material close at hand.

HERBERT GORDON

A HIKER'S VIEW—Of the Palisades, 'a giant wall of rock thrusting skyward.'

April 14, 1968

111

DEEP IN MOUNTAIN WILDERNESS JUST A FEW MILES NORTH OF THE CITY LINE

I. Herbert Gordon

IN THE HUDSON HIGHLANDS—Looking east from High Tor, the prominent ridge at the left is Little Tor and, beyond, is the Harriman-Bear Mountain Park country.

Exploring the Hudson Highlands

By I. HERBERT GORDON

HAVERSTRAW, N. Y. — South Mountain towers above this Hudson River town like some great, crude Chinese wall. It is a spectacular cliff of mountain encompassing two peaks, High Tor and Little Tor, and it rises almost sheer from the banks of the river.

To the thousands of motorists wheeling along U.S. 9W, at its base, the mountain marks the beginning of the historic Hudson Highlands, even though it is actually a part of the Palisades.

It also is one of the least known of the series of scenic reserves that make up the Palisades Interstate Park system. Locally, it is called South Mountain; in the park system, it is known as High Tor State Park. (Tor is a Gaelic word meaning peak.)

During the past summer, New York made the only improvements in the park in the 25 years that it has owned the land. It developed a small picnic area and an outdoor swimming pool at the southeastern tip.

Spectacular Views

With these exceptions, the park is an arcane retreat that withholds its rugged beauty and spectacular views from all but those who hike its uncivilized trails.

High Tor is richly covered with second-growth hardwoods — maple and oak, beech and hickory — and they are interspersed everywhere with dogwood and cedar. The result is that fall overlays the mountain with a panoply of scarlets, reds, yellows and muted browns.

One major trail winds the length of the verdant mountain, climbing its steep eastern slope and following the ridge line for about three miles within the high, narrow 500-acre park. The trail is now part of the Long Path, a footpath that eventually will stretch 400 miles from the George Washington Bridge to Lake Placid. It is identified by occasional blaze marks of blue paint and an older, now faint, yellow paint.

The trail can be picked up at either end of the great arc of the park, or reached from side trails. But the hiker is warned to wear comfortable shoes that will not slip on an occasionally perilous wall of talus, the rock debris at the base of a cliff. It is also advisable to wear long pants as protection against the ground cover that grew in wild abundance in the rain of the summer. And one should carry one's own canteen.

Unplanned Parking Area

From the southeast, the trail takes off on an abrupt climb from a rather vague and unplanned parking area on South Mountain Road, about one-half mile east of U.S. 9W. The start can be identified by a few blue blaze marks. These are on trees immediately opposite a private road leading to a thunderous conveyer, which, as it hauls rock from a quarry, is chewing up a lovely, small mountain to the south.

From there, it is less than a mile to the summit of High Tor, which has an elevation of 827 feet. The trail winds through thickets of trees, across brief meadows spangled with fall flowers and up steep inclines near the top.

Haverstraw Down Below

The Hudson River opposite High Tor is about four miles wide, its greatest width anywhere. Haverstraw lies, like a Lilliputian village, at one's feet. To the north are the Hudson Highlands, as well as Revolutionary War points of pride and shame. For example, one and one-half miles north is Treason House, where Benedict Arnold met with John Andre, the British major, to plot the betrayal of West Point.

Not far away, jutting into the river, is Stony Point, where Mad Anthony Wayne—so called for his impetuous temper—routed the British with his tough troops in 1779. To the south is the outline of Verdrietige Hook; in Dutch, it means tedious, or troublesome, point. This is exactly what it was to the settlers who had to tack their way around this bend in the river, now the site of Hook Mountain State Park.

To the west lie the Ramapo Mountains, to the southwest, the fertile fields and glistening lakes of Rockland County.

From High Tor, the trail follows the ridge line that arcs to the west. Little Tor, at an elevation of 710 feet, is slightly more than a mile away for travelers on foot.

At Little Tor, an unmarked branch trail drops down to the High Tor swimming pool and picnic grounds. The main trail continues across a new highway, Little Tor Road, which leads into West Haverstraw.

'Escape Route'

For those who desire an easier path than the steep climb up the southern flank of High Tor, the trail can be picked up at either the picnic grounds or the summit of Little Tor Road. It is easily identified by the blue blaze marks on the trees and by a road set aside for the use of fire equipment only. The road runs along the ridge line and is closed to traffic by a heavy chain.

At its intersection with U.S. 202, Little Tor Road is known as Central Highway; at the southern end, however, it bears its own name. The road follows an old, long-abandoned ridge crossing that villagers, fearing a Redcoat invasion during the American Revolution, had built as a possible escape route.

Little Tor was once owned by Archer M. Huntington, who in 1944 gave the mountain to the state for use as a park. The bright new swimming pool stands at the foot of Little Tor, near the location of Mr. Huntington's old mansion. More picnic grounds and an elaborate flower garden are planned for the site.

Not long before World War II, High Tor was threatened by quarrying in-

THE VIEW FROM THE RIDGE—Two High Tor hikers stand just below the summit of the mountain and look north up the Hudson River Valley.

LILLIPUTIAN—From atop High Tor, Haverstraw lies at one's feet like a gleaming toy village stretching away to the Hudson River.

terests. They sought to buy it from Elmer Van Orden, the last in a line of early settlers who had farmed the mountain's lower slopes for generations.

Play Raised a Furor

Maxwell Anderson's play "High Tor," in which two realtors try to force the mountain's owner to sell it so they can "quarry the guts out of it," raised a tide of regional concern. In fact, the furor was comparable in some ways to the uproar created by the recent plans of Consolidated Edison to build a hydroelectric plant at Storm King Mountain, south of Cornwall, N. Y., and also on the west bank of the Hudson. The utility has since shifted the site of the proposed facility a mile and one-half to the south.

Money to buy High Tor for the state was finally raised in 1943.

Only about a mile of the western stretch of High Tor remains in private hands. However, there is uneasiness again among those who love the Tors. They argue, with considerable vehemence, that the state should quickly acquire the remaining stretch of mountain and push the park boundaries farther down the slopes, the reason being to protect the scenic ridge from developers.

Geology Described

"The New York Walk Book" gives this description of the Tors' geology:

"The rocks of the Palisades section of the interstate park are almost exclusively of two kinds—the Newark sandstones and the intrusive Palisade diabase. The diabase was molten rock forced upward through rifts in the sandstones, forming immense dykes and sills, or sheets, 700 to 1,000 feet thick, and now stretching some 40 miles along the Hudson.

"When the molten mass cooled, contraction broke the sheet into great vertical columns; these now form the Palisades. They are less handsome, but less monotonous, than their cousins at Fingal's Cave in Staffa, Scotland, or its continuation, the Giant's Causeway in Northern Ireland.

"The great volcanic sheet ends in Rockland County, in a magnificent curl westward whose highest point is High Tor."

October 22, 1967

NEW MOUNTAIN TRAILS MADE FOR CITY HIKERS

Volunteer Pathfinders in Five Years of Enthusiastic Work Have Crisscrossed Palisades Interstate Park With 100 Miles of Scenic By-Roads

By RAYMOND H. TORREY.

IN the Harriman region of the Palisades Interstate Park, in the Hudson Highlands and the Ramapos, more than a hundred miles of scenic skyline trails, over the hills and through the woods, have been scouted, cleared and marked by volunteer trail makers in the last five years. It was good exercise and good fun and it gave their usual tramps the zest of discovery and of permanent accomplishment. The reward has been the appreciation that walking clubs and other hikers have promptly given to these new paths in making them the routes of their excursions.

This trail-making has been done with the cooperation of the Commissioners of the Palisades Interstate Park, represented by the general manager and chief engineer, Major William A. Welch. Since most the workers were experienced in trail scouting and clearing, as members of the Appalachian, the Adirondack, the Green Mountain and other clubs, with previous knowledge of such work in the mountains of New York and New England, Major Welch left most of the work to them. He provided transportation and shelter when needed, and also the metal markers and painted signs that were the final touch.

Trails Near Town.

Two strong motives prompted this volunteer work. One was a desire for country by-roads not spoiled for walkers by automobile traffic. The other was the ambition to bring trail development nearer to the city, so that such pleasures as vacation hikers enjoy in the Adirondacks, the Catskills and the New England mountains might be available close about home during the Fall, Winter and Spring months. The automobile has made the roads uncomfortable for hikers, but has done them a service by forcing them to explore the old and largely abandoned wood-roads in our near-by hills, relics of iron mining, charcoal burning and timber cutting of half a century ago.

Since the old roads were made to haul heavy loads and followed the valleys and notches, and most walkers want views and climbs and ledges, the next step was the scouting and marking of new trails along the tops of the parallel northeast-southwest ridges of the Ramapos and the Hudson Highlands, in the thirty thousand acres of the Harriman Park and in adjoining forest and hill country open to trampers.

Modern Pathfinding.

The work was begun in the Fall of 1920 by a committee of delegates from the New York City walking clubs, the head of which was Meade C. Dobson, formerly active in the Boy Scouts. It was continued during 1921-24 by the present writer, and is now under the direction of Frank Place, President of the Tramp and Trail Club of New York.

The practice adopted was that worked out through long experience by the Appalachian Mountain Club in the White Mountains of New Hampshire. The working parties were divided, according to experience and ability, into scouting, clearing and marking squads. The scouts were those who knew how to lay a trail to include the highest scenic qualities, directness of route, supplies of water in springs or clean brooks and occasional ledge and cliff climbs to make the routes interesting. They went out ahead of the rest and made temporary small blazes or rock cairns. When every one had argued out the best route it was agreed upon and was primarily marked with a line of cotton string, looped over the bushes and trees along the way.

Then came the "elephant squad," the trail clearers. With hatchets and large pruning shears, the most efficient tool for green stuff, they cleared the route, following the string, on United States Forest Service trail standards, four feet wide, and cleared up high enough of protruding branches so that a man with a pack will not run his face into such obstructions. Larger blazes were made on convenient trees, and the tempo-

rary cairns, on open ledges, were made large and permanent.

The last touch was the placing on trees of metal markers, which were provided by Major Welch. These are three inches square, with symbols and letters in red, a different symbol for each trail, and initials indicating the names of its termini. The earliest were of galvanized sheet iron, enameled white. After two or three years, it was found, the sap of trees containing strong acids, such as the oaks, disfigured the lettering. Sheet copper was next tried and served somewhat better, but further experiments in weathering and sap action are being made by Major Welch with sheet aluminum markers, the lettering stamped with a die and unpainted. Lettered wooden sign-boards are used at termini, road crossings and important junctions.

Tuxedo to Jones Point.

In the first Winter, 1920-21, was completed the principal trail, from Tuxedo, on the Ramapo River and main line of the Erie Railroad, across Harriman Park to the Hudson, at Jones Point station on the West Shore Railroad, at the east end of Dunderberg Mountain. This trail is known as the Ramapo-Dunderberg, and is about twenty-four miles long. Not many make it in one day, for it requires about 3,500 feet of total climbing. The best record, made by George Goldthwaite of the Fresh Air Club, is five hours and a half. Two women, Miss Helen Buck of the Appalachian Mountain Club and Miss Annette Buck of the Green Mountain Club, have made it in just under six hours.

The first part of this trail from Tuxedo is known as the Tuxedo-Tom Jones Trail, as Tom Jones Mountain was the initial objective of the trail makers before their ambitions became more extensive. It leaves the railroad station at Tuxedo, crosses the Ramapo River on a road bridge, and turns in along a terrace at the foot of Horse Pond Mountain, which rises to the east. In about a mile it crosses a brook, turns up the north side of the stream, crosses again to its south side

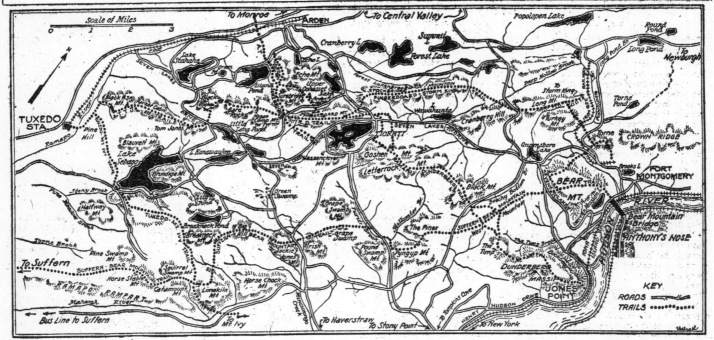

and climbs up to a third crossing, at the outlet of Black Ash Swamp. This is through territory of the Tuxedo Park Association, to which access will probably be permitted as long as no abuses are committed.

After a third crossing of the brook, the trail climbs a hill which, for want of any previous name, the trail makers called Black Ash Mountain, and on the summit enters the Harriman Park. It climbs over the next hill northeast, Parker Cabin Mountain, where there is a fire observatory, descends to the Old Continental Road, a military route in the Revolution, and climbs to Tom Jones Mountain. It then drops steeply down to the Seven Lakes Drive, the main park highway. The markers on this stretch are white galvanized iron squares, bearing a red square and the initials T-TJ.

On the Ramapo-Dunderberg.

Across the drive begins the Ramapo-Dunderberg Trail proper, marked with squares bearing a red dot and the initials R-D. It climbs to the Black Rocks and follows a broad ridge around over open ledges called Bowling Rocks and Ship Rock, to Hogenkampf Mountain, where is another observatory. It descends into a notch, crosses the old Surebridge Mine road and continues along the next ridge northeast, Fingerboard Mountain. About 150 yards northeast of the old road is one of the most notable geological curiosities of the Harriman Park, a large, beautifully smoothed pothole, in hard granite, site of an

abandoned waterfall, now a mile from any stream. It was gouged out probably during a period of different drainage, before the last ice sheet of the glacial period changed the face of these ridges.

Near the north end of Fingerboard Mountain, from which views of the Hudson begin to appear, the R-D trail takes to the Arden Valley road, downhill, right to the Seven Lakes Drive again and Lake Tiorati. It follows the Lake Tiorati Brook Road around the north side of the lake for half a mile and then turns in on a wood road, to make for the top of Goshen Hill. All the rest of the way to the Hudson it is through the woods and over summits, the most scenic part of the trail, with new and finer views of the Hudson on every mountain top. It crosses from Goshen to Letterrock Mountain, climbs along the brink of the cliffs of Black Mountain and descends across the old road over which Anthony Wayne marched his Continentals through Beechy Bottom to storm Stony Point in 1779.

Historic Ground.

The R-D Trail next climbs the rugged side of West Mountain, descends into the narrow notch of Timp Pass, through which Sir Henry Clinton pushed his force to the taking of Forts Clinton and Montgomery in 1777, and climbs the steep Six Chins Trail up the side of the Timp, a cliff which bears the features of George Washington when viewed from Bear Mountain northward.

From the top of the Timp, a famous viewpoint, it runs along the Dunderberg massif, including splendid views over the Hudson Gorge and the Bear Mountain headquarters of the park, from the knobs known as Bockberg and Bald Hill, then to the eastern end. Dunderberg proper and down the ledges to the railroad and the river at Jones Point.

The next trail undertaken by the volunteer workers was the Timp-Torne, the most concentratedly scenic of all. It starts in the Timp Pass, climbs to the northern crown of West Mountain and follows its narrow summit ridge with views east over the Hudson and west over the hundred hills of the park. It descends to the old Doodletown Road which echoed to the tread of American, Tory and British feet in 1777, crosses the Seven Lakes Drive and climbs up a chimney in the smooth cliffs on the southwest face of Bear Mountain. It drops off the west side of Bear, through some curious boulders fallen together to make a tunnel, crosses Popolopen Creek, in the gorge known as the Hellhole, and climbs the bare granite knob of Popolopen Torne, the west side of which is scarred by the shells of the mimic battles of the West Point cadets. Its symbol is a square with the initials T. T.

Fingerboard Storm King.

A fourth trail was the Fingerboard-Storm King, intended to run from the Ramapo-Dunderberg trail on Fingerboard Mountain to Storm King Moun-

116

tain at the northern gate of the Highlands. It descends northward to cross the Arden Valley Road, climbs past the great cave of Bradley Mine to the top of Bradley Mountain, and then turns northeast along the Stockbridge Mountains and Cranberry Hill to the Long Mountain Road. It crosses this road to Long Mountain, which gives one of the finest interior views in the Highlands, and descends at its north end to Popolopen Creek, near the Forest of Dean iron mine.

It will eventually be carried northward, past Long Pond, across the Central Valley-West Point Road, to the Black Rock Forest plateau and Storm King. Obvious routes, not yet marked, will take the hiker there now. The markers for this trail are sheet-copper squares, with a cross and the initials FB-SK.

A short trail connects the Fingerboard-Storm King route with the Timp Torne. It is called the Long Mountain-Torne Trail, is marked with the letters LM-T and crosses from the FB-SK at the north end of Long Mountain, over Turkey Mountain, and across the Popolopen Creek Valley to the Torne.

Next, a crossing of the Ramapo Plateau, in the south end of the park, was made as the Tuxedo-Mount Ivy Trail, from the main line of the Erie to its New Jersey-New York division. It leaves the Tuxedo-Tom Jones Trail about half a mile from the Tuxedo Station and turns sharply to the right up the north face of Horse Pond Mountain. It passes the famous Claudius Smith's Den, the cave where that revolutionary bandit stored his loot, crosses Blauvelt Mountain to the valley of Spring Brook, and a lower ridge to the dam of the new Lake Sebago, the last artificial lake built by Major Welch. It next climbs Halfway Mountain, passes along it northeast to an old road which crosses the plateau and leads downhill to Ladentown and the road to Mount Ivy Station. Its copper markers bear a straight red line and the initials

T-MI.

The Arden-Surebridge Trail leads east from Arden, on the Erie, mostly by old wood roads, to Lake Tiorati, over Echo Mountain, past Island Pond, over Surebridge Mountain, through the "Lost Road," a route long obscured by dense rhododendron and reopened as a narrow trail arched over by these evergreen shrubs, and through the notch between Hogenkampf and Fingerboard Mountains, to the Seven Lakes Drive. It is marked with a triangle and the letters A-SB.

The Appalachian Trail.

The trail workers also built the Interstate Park section of the Appalachian Trail, the great path which is the dream of hikers from Mount Katahdin, Maine, to Stone Mountain, Georgia, and Lookout Mountain, Tennessee. It starts on the Erie Railroad, half a mile south of Arden station; climbs Green Pond Mountain, crosses the Arden Surebridge Trail in the Lemon Squeezer, a remarkable cleft on the south end of Echo Mountain; crosses Surebridge Mountain to the Surebridge Mine Road and the old iron mines, and enters the R-D on Fingerboard.

It uses the R-D to the Arden Road, follows a slightly different route to Goshen, picks up the R-D again over Goshen, Letterrock and Black Mountains, climbs the north crown of West Mountain, uses the Timp-Torne to the top of the southern cliffs on Bear Mountain and follows its own route over the summit of Bear and down to Bear Mountain Bridge. It is marked with copper squares stamped A-T.

The Harriman section of the Appalachian Trail, made by permission of W. Averell Harriman over the Harriman estate, is being marked westward from Arden toward Greenwood Lake, and has been scouted to High Point State Park on Kittatiny Mountain and along that ridge to Delaware Water Gap.

This Winter the trail makers, under Mr. Place, are marking a new trail which will surpass them in all scenic

quality. It runs from Suffern along the Ramapo Rampart to Bear Mountain. It will be ready by Spring and much of it is now completed. It extends along the skyline, northeast over Pearson, Horsestable, Squirrel Swamp and Limekiln Mountains, with fine views over the lowlands eastward, then crosses to the next northeast-trending ridge, Breakneck Mountain, and continues over Big Hill and Jackie Jones Mountain to the Gate Hill Road.

Crossing Irish Mountain, this trail will reach the Lake Tiorati Brook Road, then climb the steep cliffs of Pyngyp Mountain, cross the next elevation, known as The Pines, and reach the Ramapo-Dunderberg trail at the foot of the cliff on the south end of West Mountain. It will then use the Timp-Torne and Appalachian trails to Bear Mountain Bridge.

Boy Scout By-Roads.

The Boy Scouts of America have also made about seventy miles of marked paths, mostly on existing wood roads, in their White Bar Trail, in the form of a wheel, the hub being the headquarters at Kanohwahke Lakes.

The new trails are not yet shown on the trail map published by the Palisades Interstate Park, which does present, however, hundreds of miles of old woodroads which are delightful hiking routes. This map may be obtained at the office of the commission, 25 Broadway, and the writer will be glad to mark in the new trails for any reader of THE TIMES who will send a copy to him, w retui postage.

The Boy Scouts issue a map of their White Bar Trail, which may be obtained for five cents at the New York headquarters, 200 Fifth Avenue, or at the Kanohwahke Lakes camp. The Ramapo, Schunemunk and West Point sheets of the United States Geological Survey are also useful for this region, used with the other maps, and with allowance for errors in early suveys and for recent changes. They may be obtained of the Survey in Washington at ten cents each and of map stores here for fifteen cents.

May 2, 1926

STIFF NEW TRAIL
CALLS TO HIKERS

Footpath From Suffern to Bear Mountain
Takes in Cliffs, Brooks and Woods in
Scenic 25-Mile Course

THE NEW SUFFERN-BEAR MOUNTAIN TRAIL

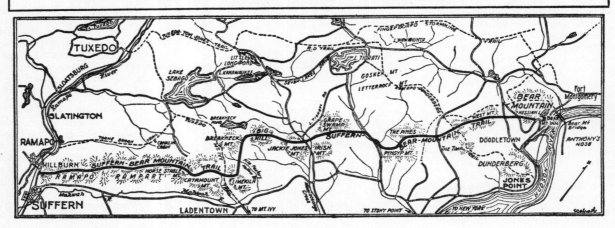

By RAYMOND H. TORREY.

THE Suffern-Bear Mountain Trail, the ninth of such footpaths for hikers made during the last seven years by volunteer workers from the New York City metropolitan district walking clubs in the Harriman State Park, in the Highlands of the Hudson and in the Ramapo Mountains, is now almost complete. It discloses new scenic viewpoints and new aspects of the hills and forests, lakes and streams of this 40,000-acre preserve.

This new trail is twenty-four miles long, following the curves of ridges, dipping into gaps for springs and waterholes, yet pursuing a course intended to combine with scenic values a reasonable degree of directness. It begins at Suffern, on the main line of the Erie Railroad, thirty miles from New York, and follows the Ramapo Rampart, the long straight front of the Ramapo Mountains. Then it angles back to another parallel northeast-southwest ridge and runs north and northeast to the headquarters of the Harriman Park, at Bear Mountain.

It will be a hardy hiker who does all of this trail in one day, for it rivals in ruggedness the Ramapo-Dundenberg Trail, twenty-five miles long, from Tuxedo to the Hudson, which few walk at a stretch; but it offers fine sections from five to fifteen miles in length that can be reached at various points by train or bus.

Suffern is a convenient point to reach by rail from Jersey City, by trolley from Edgewater and Paterson, by bus from Paterson. A second bus line, from Paterson to Haverstraw, runs along the highway at the foot of the Rampart, with several stops, such as Kakiat, Wesley Chapel, the Suffern Community Club and Ladentown, where trails and old roads climb through the ravines in the mountain front and reach the new through trail on the summits.

The Trail Markers.

The new trail is marked as are others in the Harriman Park, with metal squares bearing a symbol and the initials of the termini of the route. On this trail copper squares, with the initials "S-BM" and a diamond are used. A new method of securing lasting qualities for such a marker has been adopted by Major W. A. Welch, general manager of the Palisades Interstate Park, who provides the signs and has encouraged the volunteer workers in this interesting combination of their usual hiking excursions with a definite object in view.

To begin at the south end of the Suffern-Bear Mountain Trail, the hiker should go west from the railroad station at Suffern, past the last of the gasoline filling stations on the left, and turn right, into a little amphitheatre, between two conspicuous granite ledges that abut the highway. The trail climbs up a ravine to a ledge which gives a fine view south over the valley of the Ramapo and the mountains westward toward the Wanaque Valley; then turns right to another viewpoint out east, over the lowlands of Bergen County, N. J., and Rockland County, N. Y.

Just north of the second viewpoint, an old road is picked up, which follows the summit. For the first half-mile the route is marked with cairns and paint blazes, but presently the copper markers begin and may be followed thereafter. The trail drops into a notch in a cutover woodlot; then climbs again up a cliff which the trail markers have called the Kitchen Stairs; then on over a level plateau, dipping into a cattail swamp; then up again, and out to another viewpoint over the Rockland County rolling farmlands, with the Palisades and Hook Mountain in the background.

From this view the trail turns left—westward—to gain a crossing of a rocky notch in the Rampart without descending too much. This notch, filled with boulders of all sizes, has been called by Frank Place, President of the Tramp and Trail Club and one of the chief workers on the trail, the Valley of Dry Bones, a name that has stuck. From this gap the route climbs eastward again to another open viewpoint: a ledge with an interesting geological feature, a curi-

ously branching dike of diabase in the midst of the granite of the summit.

The trail passes on north, through the brush grown fields of a long abandoned farm; then to a rocky ridge heaped with huge boulders in picturesque confusion, some of them twenty feet high and among the largest of those transported by the ice in this region. This boulder field has been called MacElvaine's Rocks, after a member of the Fresh Air Club, who most ingeniously laid out the route here to make it as rocky as possible.

Cliffs and Boulders.

On the next summit northeast the trail climbs past a steep cliff called the Hangman's Rock, which looks much like the setting in the final scene of "Turandot." This mountain gives another view east. Beyond, the trail dips into a gully where there is a spring, and then climbs Pierson Mountain, past a good example of a "propped rock," where a small boulder melted out of the ice sheet that covered the Ramapos 2,000 feet deep, to serve as a prop for a much larger block that dropped later on.

The trail curves around to the west side of the mountain, giving a good view west over the interior alleys of the Ramapo Plateau, including the Mountaineer's Meadow and Conklin's Cabin—the only occupied house in the region—and the ledgy slopes of Halfway Mountain.

On the next descent the trail includes a remarkably polished protruding ledge, known as the Egg, later crossing a brook, which provides another good luncheon place. Climbing Horsestable Mountain, past a clump of cubical boulders, the trail passes along the cliffs of Hawk Rock and enters an old wood road at a large white oak, spared as a corner mark of some property line. The road turns northeast and then to the left, proceeding downhill into a deep gully between Catamount and Panther mountains. The trail route around the

outside of Panther gives many fine "windows" out to the country eastward and presently brings into view the Hudson, over the ridge of the Tors—Haverstraw Bay, with the Westchester hills beyond.

A Westward Turn.

The trail now curves around westward, over a brook hidden by tumbled boulders, crosses the Tuxedo-Mount Ivy Trail, climbs to Eagle Rock, passes over knobs scarred by fires, and descends to use an old path known as the Red Arrow Trail. This trail follows northwest across File Factory Hollow Brook, the Woodtown Trail and Ladentown Mountain, to Breakneck Mountain, which gives views east to the Hudson and west over the lakes and hills of the interior of the park and beyond toward Greenwood Lake. It pursues this ridge northeast to a northern point known as Big Hill, where there is a sort of balcony of open ledges with a splendid outlook to the Hudson.

The S-BM now descends, crosses the Old Turnpike and climbs to the fire observation tower on Jackie Jones Mountain, where one can see the skyscrapers of Manhattan, thirty-five miles to the southeast. It follows a path down to the corner of the Gate Hill Road and the old Lake Tiorati (Cedar Pond) Road, which it uses a short distance north to cross the north branch of Minisceongo Creek. Just beyond the creek at a set of bars the trail turns to cross the pastures northward and passes through another set of bars at the edge of the woods. On the other side is an old road used by the Boy Scouts as the rim of their White Bar Trail and adopted here by the S-BM. This leads over Grape Swamp Mountain and down to the Lake Tiorati Brook Road, with a fine view out northward.

Eastward, to the right for half a mile the road runs past the bridge over Lake Tiorati Brook, and then the hiker turns in to the left to look

for stepping stones over the stream. The trail climbs up the steep, pine-clad cliffs of Pyngyp, for more fine views. It drops into a gap, then climbs the next summit, The Pines; descends again, and crosses the old road over which Anthony Wayne led the Continentals to the storming of Stony Point in 1779.

Soon it reaches the Ramapo-Dunderberg Trail (marked "R-D" with a red dot) at the bottom of the cliffs on the south side of West Mountain; it uses this trail to climb to the summit, where it resumes its own course northward.

Crossing the swampy notch between the south and north crowns of West Mountain, the trail climbs a zigzag route up a cliff called the Fire Escape, and at the top enters the Timp-Torne Trail, marked with a square and the initials "T-T." It uses the T-T a few rods north, then leaves it at an angle and descends to the bottom of the notch, which cuts off from the main mass of West Mountain a high eastern shoulder, with cliffs on its south and east faces; follows the brink of the cliffs, around northward, with views of the Hudson gorge; descends a steep talus slope; enters a cutover area; drops to a pretty brook which comes off the amphitheatre in the centre of the mountain, and follows it on the left side, downhill to a sharp left turn through another notch.

After crossing two more brooks, the way leads up to the old Doodletown Road, over which Sir Henry Clinton sent his flanking body to assault the American forts Clinton and Montgomery in 1777. This it crosses and then makes its way east, crossing the Seven Lakes Drive, the main park motor highway, and descends to the outer curve of the drive, at the foot of Bear Mountain, a few hundred feet west of the park headquarters. A large lettered sign marks the north end of the trail and similar signs have been placed at important points elsewhere along its route.

May 1, 1927

HUDSON HIKING

New York's Stony Point Goal of Walking Tour

By JOHN B. McCABE

STONY POINT, N. Y.—The 184th anniversary of the Battle of Stony Point is as good a reason as any for calling attention to the scenic, historic attractions of this Hudson River region.

One particularly fine way to observe the anniversary, to be marked July 15-16, would be a walking tour of the countryside traversed by Gen. "Mad Anthony" Wayne and his troops in July, 1779, en route to the storming and successful capture of Stony Point from the British during the Revolutionary War.

Such a walk might start at the Bear Mountain Inn, circle through the forested area in back of Bear Mountain and then angle south toward the Hudson, terminating at Stony Point Park. Involving a distance of about 13 miles, this pleasant tour would make an ideal project for metropolitan area hiking clubs, botanists, camera fans or weekend history buffs.

Trail Map

The first move for hikers meeting at the Bear Mountain Inn is to buy one of the trail maps on sale there; each group should have at least one map. There are, after all, still a few areas in Bear Mountain State Park where hikers can test their trail-tracking capacities, a fact that adds the spice of adventure to this walk in the footsteps of General Wayne.

After leaving the inn, hikers should follow the trail that leads along the east shore of Hessian Lake to the traffic circle north of the inn. One should keep to the left along U. S. 9W, crossing Popolopen

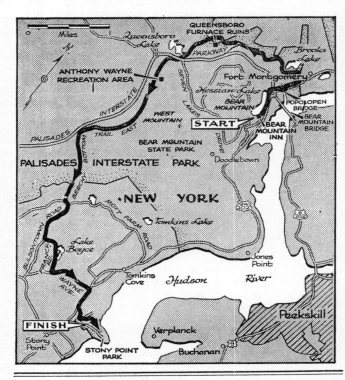

Bridge and then bearing left onto the old 9W route. This area was a battleground in 1777, when the British attacked the twin forts at Bear Mountain and Fort Montgomery.

One now turns left at the old Mine Road, where a marker reads, "July 5, 1779, the light infantry of the American Army under Gen. Anthony Wayne marched over this road to storm Stony Point."

The Mine Road now is paved, but its steep grades and curves are evidence of what the original road was like. One follows the road for about a mile and one-half to the point where, just beyond the last house on the left, a gravel road leads downhill to the ruins of the old Queensboro Furnace.

The structure was dismantled by the British in 1777; it was one of several furnaces built prior to the Revolutionary War as part of an effort to extract iron ore from these hills.

The original road passes the rear of the furnace site and heads down the valley toward Queensboro Lake. General Wayne's troops stopped to eat and rest just beyond this point, and today a metal plaque marks the site.

In earlier days, the old road passed through a Queensboro settlement where a group of mountain people had their homes. Today, a cemetery is all that remains, and change has come to the area in the form of new roads, a recreation area and the Bear Mountain water treatment plant.

Follow Grass Strip

On reaching the main highway, the hiker may have to consult his map in order to find, and then cross, the bridge to Seven Lakes Drive. One should follow the grass strip on the left of the road, keeping in mind the fact that this is not really a pedestrian right-of-way.

From there, the hiker's path leads along the old Beechy Bottom Trail East, which skirts West Mountain and the An-

thony Wayne Recreation Area. One should bear left, ignoring that portion of the Beechy Bottom trail that angles off to the west. Eventually, the explorer emerges on the Bulsontown Road.

Continuing along the Bulsontown Road, past the Mott Farm Road intersection, the hiker arrives at Franck Road. A marker at this junction notes that the road dates to 1770.

The Franck Road leads past Lake Boyce, a pleasant place for the hiker to stop and rest awhile. It was here, too, that General Wayne's men rested and refreshed themselves at the nearby spring. Beside the spring is a rock inscribed with the date of that event.

Letter to Relative

It was also at this site that General Wayne, during the hours preceding the midnight attack on Stony Point, wrote a letter to his brother-in-law. In it he expressed the hope that his wife and children would be cared for, should he not survive the assault.

Just south of this point, Franck Road—or Cricket-town Road, as it was called in earlier days—intersects the old Mormontown Road, now known as Wayne Avenue. Here, General Wayne divided his forces for a north-south attack. The northern approach followed Wayne Avenue, which is the shortest of the two approaches to Stony Point.

If one walks to the end of this road and turns right on U. S. 9W once more, the entrance to Stony Point Park is but a short distance away. The park is open daily until sundown, and the park's history museum is open daily until 4:30 P.M. There is a bus stop south of this point, at the traffic light.

There is bus service from New York City to both Bear Mountain Inn and Stony Point, and accommodations and restaurants are plentiful in the area.

July 7, 1963

WILD HIKING REGION LIES TWO HOURS OUT

Hills Near Greenwood Lake Offer Skyline Ridge Paths—Up-tilted Ledges Provide Climbing Opportunities, Ruins Of Abandoned Settlement, and a Labrador Effect

By RAYMOND H. TORREY.

GREENWOOD LAKE, half in New Jersey, half in New York, only two hours by train or motor from the metropolitan district, is the centre of one of the finest near-by regions for tramping and climbing. It is a sort of miniature Lake George, its surface being about 700 feet above sea level and the hills on both sides of it rising 600 to 700 feet higher. The rugged, heavily wooded ridges about it, quite like the Harriman Park, eastward, have been preserved from development, except n the shores of the lake, and offer one of our best readily accessible bits of wilderness.

Dozens of old roads and trails entice the hiker on either side of the lake, but this article will deal with the paths between the east shore of the lake and the Ramapo River.

Greenwood Lake separates two distinct geological formations. On the east the rocks are part of the ancient Archaean complex found in the Ramapos and the Hudson Highlands, the roots of the continent of Appalachia, the oldest rocks of the section's geological record. On the west are the younger Devonian and Silurian rocks, the red sandstones and conglomerates of Bearfort Mountain, laid down in a long bay or sound on the west side of the ancient continent.

Hills "en Echelon."

The hills on the east side resemble the forms of the Hudson Highlands, made up of great fault blocks, with their long axes trending northeast-southwest, and the cross fault notches northwest-southeast. This gives the formation characteristic of the New Jersey and New York highlands, with the hills flanking each other as they run northeastward. Ebenezer Emmons, an early State geologist of New York, described their formation by the military term "en echelon," which graphically pictures the hills marching northeast like regiments, aligned so that the northwestern flanks of each are overlapped by the next ridge running in the same direction.

As in the Hudson highlands, the effect of these geological influences is to give long, fairly continuous skyline ridge paths, with breaks in the notches, where water may be found in brooks heading in hem. Stretches of granite ledge afford many rods of open walking and many viewpoints

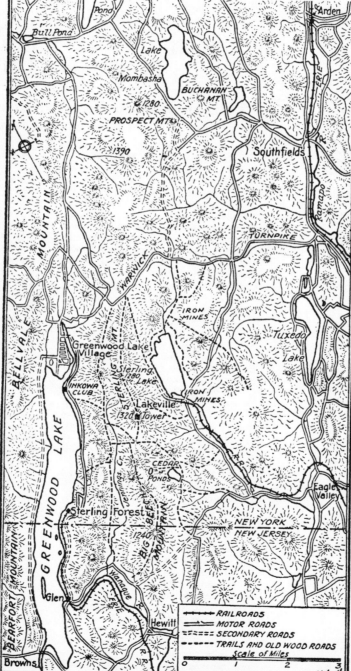

Trails East of Greenwood Lake.

over the hills. The cliffs at the up-tilted southwest ends of the fault blocks provide sometimes a bit of alpine climbing.

Hewitt and Sterling Forest, stations on the Greenwood Lake Division of the Erie Railroad, are convenient points from which to enter the hills east of the lake. They can be reached by somewhat longer approaches from Sloatsburg, Tuxedo, Southfields or Arden, on the main line of the Erie Time can be saved by taking an automobile from these latter stations and going five to eight miles westward into the hills before starting a tramp.

The region is mapped by the Greenwood Lake, Schunemunk and Ramapo sheets of the United States Geological Survey. These sheets, surveyed twenty years ago in the early days of this mapping, have some inaccuracies and in spots need correction, especially in relation to the remoter regions.

The Best Entrance.

For the beginner, perhaps the best point of entrance is from Sterling Forest station. Take a train on the Greenwood Lake Division from Jersey City at 9 o'clock and you will reach Greenwood Lake about 11. Follow the road north on the slope above the lake, about a mile and a quarter, until you pass a brook coming off the hill on the right, climb a steep rise and watch on the right for an old road, now scarcely more than a footpath, going in eastward.

It is the usual route to the fire observation tower on Sterling Mountain, and is fairly well marked under foot. It crosses a brook twice, keeping a little south of east. Beyond the second crossing of the brook, about a mile in from the highway, watch for a path turning sharp left, climbing up over a rocky ridge, and then descending into the valley of Jennings Creek. It soon enters an old road. This was once a route from the north end of Greenwood Lake to Hewitt, and on it were several farms half a century or more ago, but now only the cellar stones and the apple orchards half smothered in wild growth can be found.

Turn north on this road, along the west side of the brook, climbing for half a mile, and watch for a turn east, across the brook, then up a steep slope and through a high notch in the ridge. Follow the old road northeastward until you come to another

road entering from the right. At this point you cross a trail, made in recent years, which extends along the Sterling Mountain ridges for many miles. Follow it north, up a steep cliff, down across a brook and up another steep rise to the 80-foot steel tower on the highest point of the ridge at 1,320 feet. The view from the fire warden's aerie at the top of the tower is one of the finest in our near-by hills, and sweeps all around the New York and New Jersey highlands and northward to the Shawangunks and the Catskills.

The north-south trail may be followed northward to the Warwick Turnpike, which runs from Greenwood Lake Village to Southfields, in the Ramapo Valley. North of that road—to be replaced soon by a modern motor highway on a different location—the Harriman section of the Appalachian Trail begins. It runs along the ridge northeastward over One Cedar Mountain and Mombasha High Point, descends to follow the south shore of Mombasha Lake, and continues over Buchanan Mountain and the hills eastward to the Ramapo River, south of Arden, where it touches the Palisades Interstate Park section of the Appalachian Trail.

Several miles of the Harriman section have been cleared and marked with the copper squares bearing the A-T monogram, from the Ramapo westward to the brook emptying into Mombasha Lake, and along the ridge from Mombasha High Point southwest, although markers in the latter portion have been ripped off by vandals. The name Harriman was given to this section in appreciation of the courtesy of W. Averell Harriman, in permitting the marking of the Appalachian Trail across lands assembled by his father, Edward H. Harriman.

The Sterling Mountain ridge has various local names for its higher points; it may be left at several convenient trail junctions by hikers bound eastward from Greenwood Lake toward the Ramapo. About a mile north of the fire tower an old road leads down to the west shore of Sterling Lake, one of the beautiful lakes within fifty miles of New York. A road along the shore may be followed around the north end, although two bridges across the mouths of brooks and swamps are now wholly or almost gone and one may have to detour back to higher land or wade. At the northeast corner a road that once served the old iron mines and charcoal burnings about the lake runs north-northeast, past forgotten homestead spots to Warwick Turnpike; it is an easy way out to the Ramapo between Tuxedo and Southfields.

One interesting spot along the Sterling ridge is the high valley in which lie the Cedar Ponds, set in a notable stand of evergreens, with red spruce, arbor vitae, Southern white cedar, white pines, rhododendron and mountain laurel. The easiest way to reach it from Sterling Lake is to follow the route to the fire tower as far as the junction where the foot trail turns

north. Continue east on the old road and you will soon pass the north end of the swamp where the lakes stand. Watch for a turn to the right, take it and soon another turn to the right will carry you through the dense evergreen forest out to the quaking shores of Little Cedar Pond, a bog-lined tarn as remote and wild-looking as if it were in Labrador.

The best time to visit these ponds is

in the Winter, when both are frozen and covered with a foot of snow, for then you can explore every nook of them. In Summer their shores are lined for many rods by bog and wet swamp and some parts are inaccessible. The region is worthy of a dozen exploring rambles, and any old road you come to will yield something interesting. The way to enjoy it most is not to worry too much about fixed routes.

September 12, 1926

COUNTRY INDIANS ONCE TROD LURES AUTUMN TRAMPERS

Wyanokie Plateau, Near By, Holds Many Attractions for Devotees of Forest Trails

By RAYMOND H. TORREY.

WITH the coming of crisp Fall days devotees of hiking take a renewed interest in life and begin casting about for new and interesting excursions afield. The tang of Autumn air has a special lure for those who like to tramp over hilly trails through forested countryside, and the problem for residents of the metropolitan district is ever to find accessible such walks as yet untried.

One of the most attractive of these regions of wide possibilities is the Wyanokie Plateau, in Passaic County, N. J. It comprises about forty square miles, in the angle of the Greenwood Lake and Susquehanna divisions of the Erie Railroad, and several stations giving access to it may be reached in an hour and a half from Manhattan. Twenty minutes' walk from any of these stations will take the tramper into the hills and woods, and there he has a hundred miles of well marked trails and old woodroads to ramble over. The hills rise to more than 1,200 feet above sea level, and there are many wide views—east and south, over the valley of the Wanaque River and the Ramapo Ridge; north and west, over the higher hills toward Greenwood Lake and beyond.

"Wyanokie" is the name given to this region by Professor Will S. Monroe, Honorary President of the New York section of the Green Mountain Club. As a teacher in the State Normal School, in Upper Montclair, N. J., a dozen years ago, Mr. Monroe began the construction of an extensive system of trails in the region. It means "sassafras" in the Algonquin tongue, and was evidently given by the Indians in recognition of the

prevalence of this aromatic scented tree, whose roots and bark were highly esteemed for their medicinal virtues. The name is spelled "Wanaque" on modern maps.

Old Indian Country.

The valleys of the Ramapo, Wanaque and Pompton Rivers were of old favorite haunts of the red man, who found easily tilled land in the level bottom of what was once the Glacial Period Lake Passaic. Thousands of bits of their handiwork have been dug up from the fields. Their squaws built fish weirs on the streams, relics of which remain in V-shaped lines of stones, and their hunters left traces of temporary occupation in rock shelters which can be identified to this day in the mountains on either side of the valley.

Since white men entered the region two hundred years ago it has become the scene of iron mining and the attendant charcoal burning. The history of the iron industry was similar to that of the New York field, rising to its peak about the time of the Civil War and subsequently being hard hit by the discovery and exploitation of the Lake Superior region hematite ores, fifty years ago. Iron mining is now carried on at only one place in the district—Ringwood—but there are scores of abandoned mines and prospect holes, and the usual relics of charcoal burning, as well as the old furnaces—one of which, half a mile west of Wanaque-Midvale, is a tall and picturesque ruin. Some of the old mines, such as the Roomy Mine, are worth a visit, and their abandoned chambers may be explored under ground for some distance. Others,

however, are filled with water.

The region is largely a part of the great Cooper-Hewitt estate, which consolidated many separate holdings of iron lands more than half a century ago. It is now well covered with second-growth oak, beech and maple with some hemlock along the streams. The strike of the ridges is mostly north and south, differing a little here from the usual northeast-southwest lines of the highlands of New Jersey and New York.

The Valley Is Altering.

The Wanaque Valley east of the Plateau appears to be along the line of a great fault or break in the earth's crust, though this depression was probably smoothed by the ice that lay there in the glacial period. This valley is being greatly altered by the construction of an immense reservoir for the North Jersey Water Commission, supplying Newark and other cities. When it is filled, in a year or two, a large lake will cover the present meadows from Wanaque-Midvale, ten or twelve miles upstream toward Greenwood Lake, with long arms of brooks reaching into the hills westward. This lake will add to scenic values, but not to recreation, for it is not to be used for bathing or boating.

Entrances to Trails.

The most convenient entrances to the trails in the Wyanokie Plateau are from Haskell or Wanaque-Midvale on the Greenwood Lake division of the Erie. From Haskell, take the dirt road west, up the valley of Post Brook. The road crosses the brook from the south to the north side within a mile and continues to Lake Iosco, an artificial body surrounded by a cottage colony. The trail made by Professor Monroe turns off at a white painted blaze before reaching the lake and goes northwest through the woods to the wing dam of the reservoir. A few hundred yards in it passes a "wahlikamika," or Indian rock shelter, with the remains of the fires of many an Indian hunter in the bottom of the cave. Beyond the dam it follows up the gorge of Post Brook, entering Navasink Ravine. Navasink, or Neversink as it is also spelled, means "Moccasin snake place." This is a very picturesque path, with many rapids and falls, very beautiful in high water. About a mile upstream is the largest, a drop of fifteen feet, called Chikahoki, "the place of the turkey," in Algonquin.

The route over Carris Hill, a 1,200-foot elevation to the north, reaches several high ledges with fine views, descends a little and then climbs to Wyanokie High Point, a sharp peak, mostly bare granite, with a stand of pitch pines, from which there is a

splendid view to the east over the Wanaque Valley and the Ramapo ridges.

A Choice of Trails.

Two routes, one short and steep, the other longer and easier, descend to Wyanokie Lodge, a shelter built by Professor Monroe. It has long been regional headquarters for his friends and for members of the Green Mountain Club. From it trails radiate in several directions—westward, toward the Macopin Lake country; eastward, to some of the old iron mines and out to Wanaque-Midvale; and northward, across the Winfield Road and up the headwaters of Blue Brook, over the rough knobs called the Pine Paddies, through the Wolf Den, a remarkable ledge formation, and out to the West Brook Road. Another trail goes out to the Assiniwikam, a more permanent form of Indian rock shelter, which originally was probably walled in front with bark and logs and has

been similarly treated in recent years by white occupants.

Before Dr. Monroe retired from teaching he and members of the Green Mountain Club kept these trails well marked with white painted blazes and lettered metal arrows. Some of the members continue to give them attention, so that they are yet in good shape. The future recreational uses of this region are dependent to some extent on sanitary precautions entailed by the new reservoir; but if the greater part of these hills remain open to the public as they have been, there is opportunity for a great park here.

The maps required for the Wyanokie region are the Greenwood Lake sheet of the United States Geological Survey—a "reconnaissance" sheet—imperfect as to accuracy of contours; a much better map published by the New Jersey Geological Survey; and a large scale map, showing the trails, printed for the Green Mountain Club.

October 10, 1926

The Magic Season on Old Schunemunk Mountain

By HERBERT GORDON

MONROE, N. Y. — To the motorist hurtling along the New York State Thruway, Schunemunk Mountain, when viewed from the windows of a speeding automobile, might be just another ridge in the Hudson Highlands. But to anyone who has hiked its trails and savored its many pleasures, it is a very special place indeed.

To know the real Schunemunk is to drink from the splashing, clear waters of Baby Brook, to pause in windswept silence atop a high crest and gaze toward the distant Catskills or to thrill to the vast panorama of farmland and village stretched out far below.

Schunemunk, an elongated, hulking mountain nearly 1,700 feet high, is pronounced Skun'—ee—munk, and it extends for more than eight miles between Monroe, to the south, and Salisbury Mills, on the north.

There is no "best time" to explore the trails that crisscross the mountain, but fall is a magic season on Schunemunk. The mountain is thick with second-growth forest

—maple, ash, hickory and oak and a scattering of elm and pine—and it turns aflame at this time of year.

Guardian of Highlands

Schunemunk stands as a magnificent guardian along the western flank of the Hudson Highlands. Although it is part of the Highlands geographically, it is distinct geologically, belonging to a much younger era.

Actually, Schunemunk is a massive upthrust of sandstone, shale and conglomerates extending southwest from Monroe for more than 40 miles. During the Silurian era, this mass was formed at the bottom of the ancient sea that surrounded Appalachia, or Old Land. Today, the area harbors a variety of fossils, ranging from fern roots to shells.

The mountain lies within a bugle call of the West Point Military Reservation, just to the east, and it played a minor role of its own in Colonial history. Revolutionary War troops camped at its base, and its forested slopes provided charcoal for the iron furnaces that once flourished in the Highlands.

But history and geology aside, Schunemunk is a mountain to which hikers have

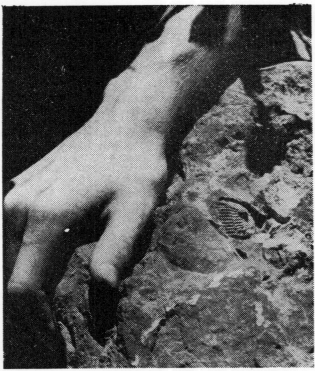

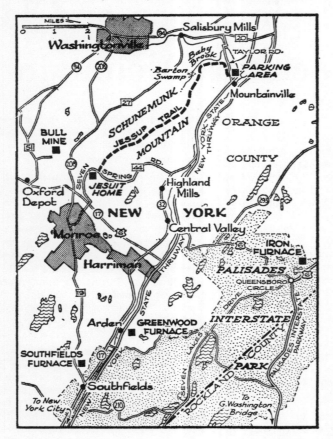

FOSSILS—A rock hound exhibits a choice specimen found in vicinity of Bull and Schunemunk mountains.

long laid special claim. While walking near Arden one time, I stopped at a small, scraggly farm to drink from a creaky hand pump. I asked the farmer, an old man whose face was covered with white stubble and with lines etched deep around his faded blue eyes, if he had any favorite mountain trails.

"When I was a boy," he said slowly, as though thinking back a long time, "I can remember when my big brother first took me climbing around old Schunemunk. I guess if I got a favorite, that's it."

Old Schunemunk. It was the first time I had heard the name, and it fascinated me no end. In fact, I was not content until the day I climbed the long, north slope and hiked for hours among the reddish-purple boulders on the lengthy summit.

Clearly Marked Trail

The major Schunemunk footpath is the Jessup Trail, which runs the entire eight-mile length of the mountain. It is clearly marked with frequent blazes of yellow paint roughly three inches square.

The southern end begins about one-tenth of a mile east of the Jesuit home on Seven Springs Road, near Monroe. The start of the trail is simply that, a path that leads from the road up the mountain, and only the yellow paint marks indicate the beginning.

The northern section of the Jessup Trail is the more interesting. Here, the mountain forms a great V, with Baby Brook tumbling down the trough. The brook springs from the heavily wooded Barton swamp in the high reaches of the cleft.

The northern section of the trail begins on Taylor Road, near Mountainville, at a clearly marked parking site west of the thruway.

From the north, the climb is fairly steep in parts, but not difficult. The trail weaves through heavy timber, passing Baby Brook several times, until, about two miles from Taylor Road, it reaches its highest elevation (almost 1,700 feet).

Magnificent View

The open view is magnificent. To the east is the Hudson River; to the south, Bear Mountain; to the north, the Catskills, and to the northwest, the Shawangunks.

There are loop trails and side trails on Schunemunk, including a stretch of the Long Path, a 400-mile hiking trail that eventually will link the George Washington Bridge with Lake Placid.

For those who wish to leave the yellow-marked Jessup Trail, Hiker's Region Map No. 18 is recommended. It is available through the New York-New Jersey Trail Conference, which maintains the trails; the address is Box 2250, New York 10001.

November 10, 1968

Harvard's Forest Next to West Point

By DOUGLAS V. CLARKE

CORNWALL, N. Y. — Next to the United States Military Academy here in Orange County lies a mountainous forest thick with oak and chestnut, which is owned and operated as a forest research facility by Harvard University. During the Revolutionary War, it was a well-trodden route for General Washington's soldiers; those who tramp along its trails today are hikers and hunters.

The overwhelming majority of the thousands of visitors to Harvard Black Rock Forest, which is in the Hudson Highlands about 55 miles north of New York City, live nearby.

Walking Trails

This 3,600-acre preserve has uncounted miles of well-managed walking trails, as well as 14½ miles of graveled roads; however, visitors are not allowed to drive into the property. It is open throughout the year and entrance permits are not required. In the fall, the forest is busy with deer hunters.

Scientists seeking data for long-term forestry experiments also are attracted to Black Rock, which was willed to Harvard in 1950 by Dr. Ernest Stillman, who had operated it as a privately owned research area.

Organizations devoted to hiking and nature study, as well as those affiliated with the New York-New Jersey Trail Conference, are frequent users of this tree-covered and uninhabited sanctuary.

Forestry Experiments

Over the years, a network of roads has been constructed that provides access to all sectors of the property's six square miles. Experiments in forestry fertilization, esthetic thinning and coniferous planting have been conducted in parts of the forest for more than 35 years.

During the Revolutionary

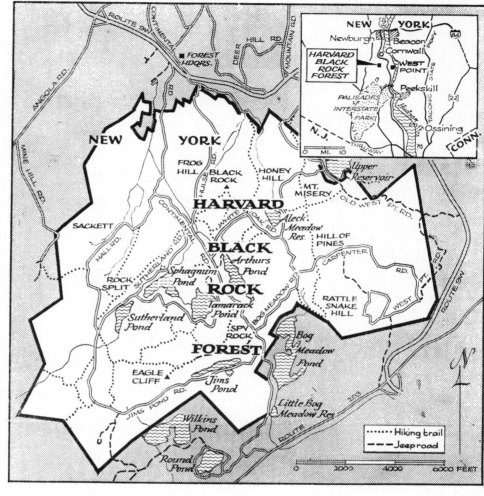

War, when West Point was being fortified to prevent British ships from raiding Hudson River settlements, Washington's soldiers built a north-south route through the forest from Newburgh to the present site of the Military Academy. Washington made his headquarters in Newburgh, and used the route many times on trips southward to the fortifications at West Point.

SS Road

This road, shown on current maps of the forest as Continental Road, was abandoned about 100 years ago, according to local historians. A so-called SS road — the reference being to numerous switchbacks built to enable horse-drawn wagons to nego-

tiate high elevations—was constructed in its place in 1868. The highest point in the forest is 1,500 feet.

Although cars are barred from the SS road, except for the few that enter the preserve on forestry business, it provides an excellent hiking trail.

There are many quaint place names in the forest: Glycerine Hollow, Rattlesnake Hill, Spy Rock, Mount Misery, Frog Hill, Eagle Cliff, Whitehorse Mountain, Bog Meadow Pond and Split Rock. There are seven ponds in the preserve, but six of them are reservoirs and are not used for recreational purposes.

Oak-hickory type of timber predominates, but every tree indigenous to New York State grows in the forest.

Northern red oak is the species most in evidence, followed by chestnut and white oak, red maple and associated species.

Jack J. Karnig, the forest manager, estimates that it has been totally cut over three or four times since the emergence of the white man in North America. In modern times, the timber has been used mainly to supply Hudson Valley brickmakers' kilns and the New York City building industry. Charcoal was made in the forest years ago, there being evidence in the forest of widespread patches where burnings have been undertaken.

Pitch pine is prevalent on the high ground. It grows in lonely solitude in places where the wind blows fierce-

ly during winter storms. Mr. Karnig says that foresters do not know whether this species is "coming or going, since we can't tell whether it's a fossil or a pioneer."

Mr. Karnig frequently entertains visitors from forestry schools in other parts of the world, as well as scientists working on soil or forestry projects.

House for Guests

To accommodate his guests, or extra summer help, Mr. Karnig sometimes opens an 1840 stone house, known as the Chatfield House. There used to be an apple orchard near the building, but in 1933 the orchard was planted in pine, spruce and larch.

Hikers can enter the forest via 10 separate, well-defined trails, as well as by way of the graveled roads.

Guided tours of the forest are organized occasionally by the directors of the Museum of the Hudson Highlands here in Cornwall.

October 13, 1968

PEDESTRIANISM.

THE SHAWANGUNK MOUNTAINS FROM END TO END.

The Shawangunk Mountains are the wildest, the most interesting locality within one hundred, perhaps several hundred, miles of New-York. Many experienced travelers consider them perfectly unique, and one of the most remarkable bits of scenery in the world. They are peculiarly suited to the pedestrian by offering a great many objects of interest in a small compass, and by affording many extensive views—even greater than the eye can master. They give entertainment to the most industrious sight-seer for a whole Summer, or more, if he enjoys the beauties of nature for themselves. At the same time their features are very striking, even at a hasty glance; they therefore give ample returns for money and time to the vigorous man who likes a short run in good mountain air and bold scenery.

The shortest time that one should spend to go, visit them, and return to New-York is three days—say from Friday P. M. till Monday M. The expense of the trip, including railroad fares, is $12.

The Shawangunk Mountains, an isolated spur of the Catskills, run from Rosendale, Ulster County, N. Y., where the Wallkill and the Rondout Creeks join, in a south-west direction to Ellenville. From there they continue their course as hills to the Pennsylvania Mountains, near the Delaware Water Gap. The range, twenty miles long, is about fifteen hundred feet above tide water, and presents a bold front 1,200 feet above the Valley of the Wallkill. The northern end is a rapid rise of abrupt hills and

rocky knolls culminating in the Mohunk or Paltz Point. Farms run up to the summit in smooth, undulating fields. A wide hollow or pass, called the Traps, separates Mohunk Point from the rest of the range, which presents an irregular wall or palisades of rock. The regular strata of quartz, rising southward with an inclination of ten degrees, are frequently broken into perpendicular bluffs and points. The strata dip more decidedly to the westward, with an inclination from twenty to forty degrees, and are broken into bluffs in line with the range as well as across it. From this it can be seen that the Shawangunk Mountains are a ridge of rock 1,500 feet high, where inclined planes, comparatively smooth, end in bluffs forming points, or in walls from 100 to 200 feet high, sheltering hollows and gullies. Stunted pitch-pines, huckleberry bushes, wintergreen vines, and mosses grow in the cracks and cavities on the plains; forests, swamps, streams or lakes occupy the hollows. The rock breaks with singular regularity into right angles, and often forms cubes of immense size, fissures of great depth, and a wonderful variety of details for minute inspection. Excepting the few fields in the hollow of the Traps, and the farms north of Mohunk, the range is a barren, uninhabited wilderness.

The pedestrian leaves New-York at 3:30 P. M., via Erie Road, in a train for Wallkill Valley, and arrives at Rosendale at 7:37 P. M. He sleeps there, and starts early the next morning for Mohunk, distant eight miles, via High Falls and Alligerville. The rolling hills, the busy canal, the Rondout Creek, and the falls are a series of pleasant sights. Half way from High Falls to Alligerville, and on the north side of the Rondout, is a subterranean river. The stream flowing through the farm of Mr. S. Broadhead, leaves its upper bed in dry times and passes underground for a considerable distance. The lower passage has very interesting caves and hollows, washed out of the limestone. It is called Pompey's Hole, in honor of its first occupant, a fugitive slave who eluded his pursuers by hiding in those dark caverns. The road climbs the mountain soon after leaving Alligerville, gives many fine views of the fertile valley of the Rondout with its stone farm-houses and other substantial remains of the old Dutch and Huguenot industry; and beyond this of the front range of the Catskills, including the conical Olive Mountain opposite, and Overlook further off to the right.

If you arrive at Mohunk some time before noon, visit the bluffs and Eagle Cliff, east of the hotel, and row around the lake. After dinner ascend the Point, 300 feet above the lake, and 1,546 above tide. The view is magnificent, both as to foreground and as to distance. About us are numerous bluffs and rocks, the lake below walled in on all sides; below lie the valleys of the Rondout and the Wallkill, checkered with farms and woods, and lighted here and there by the flashing streams. The west is dark with the forest-covered hills of Sullivan County. The Catskills to the north are beautiful at any time, but particularly in a clear day, when clouds and sunshine shade and light their round masses peeping over one another as far away as fifty miles. On exceptional days in the Fall the Green Mountains may be seen, 150 miles north-east. The Hudson River is visible near the City of Hudson, and sails may be seen in the Highlands. The horizon touches five States besides New-York, viz: Connecticut, Massachusetts, Vermont, Pennsylvania, and New-Jersey. As you should leave Mohunk about two hours before sunset, you will probably not have time to visit the Crevice and the Giants' Workshop.

Take a path leading west-south-west from the hotel to the valley below, and then the woods road up the Coxing Kill to the Traps, about five miles. Spend the night with Mr. George Davis. The next morning start early—taking a lunch in your pocket—for the "Steps," a cascade 150 feet high, at the site of a burned saw mill, on the Peterskill, one mile and a quarter from Davis'. Just before reaching the mill you pass on your left one of several caves or partial caves that are occupied as houses by the least wealthy of the native population. Two or three of the walls, and perhaps the roof, are of the natural rock; to these is added enough masonry or woodwork to inclose a space. Barring the absence of sash and glass from the window, of hinges from the door, and of boards from the floor, the habitation is quite endurable. The falls below the "Steps" are

pretty. Ascend the Peterskill one-quarter of a mile above the "Steps" by a road on the right bank—your left hand—to the Minnewaska Falls. The stream leaps seventy feet into a deep basin, at one side of a great amphitheatre formed by high bluffs and wooded hills. Climb to the top of the falls, and ascend the Peterskill one or two hundred yards, to a road crossing it, and leading up the hill, eastward, half a mile to Minnewaska Lake.

The Minnewaska Lake is an oval sheet of water half a mile long. The water is so clear that a white object may be seen thirty feet below the surface. In many places it is blue, with great depth. The cliffs about it rise in one place to 145 feet, and overhang in grotesque forms. Pitch-pines afford shade on the cliffs, and laurel, white birch, hemlock, and some other trees line the south shore. From the highest bluff is to be had a fine view toward the eastern outlook of the range, from the Catskills and Berkshire Hills, past the Hudson, glistening between the Highlands, to the Pennsylvania mountains beyond the Delaware Water Gap. The lake is still without a house or other marring evidences of man.

The Paulymer Gut is a quarter of a mile south-west of the eastern end of the lake. It is a deep gorge, between walls several hundred feet high and so near each other that the sun shines into it but a short time. Large hemlocks rise but a little way out of its depths. The huge rocks, black with lichens, the heavy forest in deep shadow, the damp thick mosses, and the unbroken silence, make this place very impressive. You should resume your route by 11 o'clock.

Those who can follow a course through the woods by compass may proceed south-west from the entrance of the Gut, along the edge of the cliffs for about three miles to Awosting Lake or Long Pond. Those who cannot trust themselves alone on this interesting walk must return by the road across the Peterskill to the turnpike, which follow westward a quarter of a mile to the huckleberry shanties. It is best to get directions there, or perhaps a guide to the lake, which lies four miles to the south-west.

Awosting Lake, one mile long, is the largest and most beautiful of the five sheets of water that surprise the visitor finding them on top of this dry, rocky range of mountains. Probably they are all rain-water basins, as they have neither flowing inlets nor outlets during droughts. The water is perfectly clear and sweet, and in places dark blue with depth. A few trees and shrubs line the shores. East of the north end of the lake high points give a fine view all around. The low eastern shore, pretty with symmetrical bays, is a smooth inclined plain, bearing pines, shrubs, and beds of rich, gray moss; the whole suggests a park of wild, unique effect, the scene of some strange, yet human, romance. Two other ponds lie south-west, but neither they nor their surroundings are very attractive compared with those already passed. Therefore those who do not wish to scramble again over bluffs, through swamps and brush, may linger about the Awosting Lake till an hour or more before sunset, and then descend the eastern side of the mountain to one of the farm-houses for the night. They can return to New-York early the next morning by a train from Shawangunk, nine miles from the foot of the mountain. Those who are more adventurous, and ambitious to see the whole range, will resume their journey not later than 3 o'clock, pass the south end of the lake, and continue south-west, about four miles to Sam's Point. In a swamp, about half a mile from Awosting, is a brook flowing from Mud Pond, a short distance to the west. In the ledge north-east of this swamp is another cave or crevice occasionally inhabited. This region is one of the most remote from civilization. I last visited it alone, on the 30th of November. My Thanksgiving dinner was a sandwich and some frozen Wintergreen berries I found under the snow. A partridge sat hiding before me under a log, and a fox on the top of the bluff looked with contempt at my meager meal and comfortless condition. The only sound was the wailing of the pines in the bleak November blasts. The only brightness under the leaden sky was the great beards of icicles on the frowning crags.

Sam's Point is the southern end and the highest part of the Shawangunk Mountains. The

pond is a shallow basin with low shores. Scrubby pine bushes are the only vegetation on the barren rocks. A very extensive view is to be had from the bluffs. The lower part of the range runs off south-west in a long bow, ending in Pennsylvania. The rolling hills, covered with forests, are picturesque at sunset, and lead the mind to wander in pleasant speculations among the houses scattered over the thousands of square miles between you and the horizon. Ellenville lies under the hill, four miles westward, on the road leading along the foot of the precipice. You stay there all night and return the next morning to New-York. You will wish your visit were longer, and forthwith resolve to camp out next year, for a month or two, in a region so healthful and interesting.

December 24, 1876

NEARBY MOUNTAINS FOR CITY HIKERS TO CLIMB

By HERBERT GORDON

ELLENVILLE, N. Y.— The northern Shawangunk Mountains may be a troublesome and time-consuming obstacle to motorists heading for the southern Catskills via the New York State Thruway and State Route 52, but, to those who know them, this brief mountain chain is an arcane wilderness of magnificent vistas, roaring waterfalls, strange ice caves, abundant wildlife and lakes of unbelievable clarity.

I discovered the charm and remote grandeur of the northern Shawangunks, which rise precipitously above, and parallel to, U.S. 209, while on a recent two-day backpacking trip along the Long Path. This is a foot trail that climbs the heights of the Shawangunks on its 400-mile journey from the George Washington Bridge to Lake Placid.

Until that trip, Sam's Point was but a name on a map to me, and the High Point Lookout Tower simply a landmark to watch for where the Long Path swings to the northwest. Neither Verkeerder Kill Falls, nor a half-dozen other places of

George Zimbel

HIKERS' REWARD—View of Verkeerder Kill Falls awaits those who leave their cars on the road and make the mile-and-one-quarter hike over the well-marked trail.

strangeness or loveliness, existed. Now, each such place name has a meaning all its own.

The lone road that leads from Cragsmoor, N. Y., to the wind-swept summit of Sam's Point is open the year round. Motorists must pay a fee of 75 cents, with the money going to the community of Ellenville.

Beyond the gateway, the road is narrow and steep. The spectacular view from Sam's Point can be reached either by car or by hiking along the roadside trail.

Drop to Valley

Sam's Point is slightly more than 2,250 feet above sea level, and from the summit there is a

drop of almost 1,500 feet to the valley floor. At the summit, the wind whips about the visitor as he looks to the Ramapo Mountains, far to the west and south, or to the upthrust peaks of the southern Catskills, to the north. Spread out below is half of Orange and Ulster Counties.

From Sam's Point, the only road across the plateau of the summit skirts Lake Maratanza as it weaves its way to the High Point Lookout tower, some three miles away.

Lake Maratanza is almost too blue and clear to be real. About a half-mile in diameter, the lake is a reservoir for Ellenville. And, although its crystal waters are closed to fishermen and swimmers, its shores are not closed to picnicking or to enjoyment of the cool breezes that ruffle its waters.

The High Point Lookout tower is a fragile nest of glass and wood perched on spindly steel legs. Those who brave its open steps are warmly welcomed by the fire-watcher on duty. They may ask him questions, peek through his powerful binoculars and marvel at the distances.

Before the visitor leaves, he gets a small card, affixed with his name. It duly attests that, on such and such a date, he did climb this tower and look down with impunity upon the world.

For the tourist who clings to his automobile, this is the end of a brief but lovely tour of the northern Shawangunks. But for those who are willing to continue on foot, the mountains will unveil their most picturesque charms.

Certainly, one of the most inspiring of the trail sights is Verkeerder Kill Falls, a lacework of water that roars over a sheer drop of about 150 feet. (The word "kill" is Dutch for stream, or tributary.)

Easy Trail

The falls lie east of Lake Maratanza. Precisely, they are about a mile and one-quarter from the road, along a clearly defined and easy-to-follow trail that is marked with splashes of red paint. A small spillway from the lake—it is marked with three bright red dots in a triangular pattern and a red arrow—leads off the highway toward the falls.

The Verkeerder Kill, which feeds the falls, is, in turn, an abundance of springs. These are situated on the summits of

George Zimbel

ROOM AT THE TOP—A card is presented to those brave enough to climb the open steps to the tower atop High Point Lookout in northern Shawangunks.

higher hills, about a mile to the north.

The stream gathers in a dozen other springs along the way as it flows, with increasing urgency, toward the cliffs. Then with a roar heard a quarter of a mile away, the waters leap into the air and down to a hemlock-filled valley that is far below.

The Verkeerder trail follows a gentle, but rocky, slope. The casual walker should allow at least 90 minutes for the trip from the lake to the falls and return. The more vigorous hiker can push on farther—

into other seldom-visited sections of the Shawangunks.

Mud Pond

The red-blazed trail leads onward to Mud Pond, whose pristine cleanliness belies its name. The pond is about a mile from the falls. Another mile of trail brings the visitor to the southwestern tip of Lake Awosting.

Like Lake Maratanza, Awosting is as clear as crystal, and its water is pure enough to drink. Although much of the land around the lake is privately owned, swimming is permitted. Two miles to the north of Lake Awosting is another of Shawangunk's waterfalls, Stony Kill.

Neither falls, lakes, vistas nor mountain trails complete the list of the Shawangunks' points of interest. There remain the weird ice caves. And these, also, are to be reached only on foot.

There are two. The larger, and better known, is referred to locally as the "Big Ice Cave," to differentiate it from "Little Ice Cave." Maps and signs point only to the existence of the target.

Big Cave Trail

The trail to the big cave begins at the parking area at

the base of the High Point Lookout Tower. This path is about a mile and one-quarter long, and the casual travel time is 45 minutes to an hour each way.

Big Ice Cave shrinks to a deep depression in the winter. But as the temperature goes up, the cavern goes deeper and deeper, almost straight into the mountain. One inhabitant of the area says that, late in the summer, it is possible to penetrate several hundred yards into the cave.

Inside, the walls are encrusted with frost, and thick with ice. And on hot days, visitors emerge shivering and carrying rapidly melting souvenirs.

We did not visit Little Ice Cave, but it is said to be much the more interesting of the two. This cave is near Sam's Point, and not more than a 15-minute walk from the road. One enters it by climbing down a ladder, as though going into a deep well. The cave is split into side caverns, all eerie with frost and ice. Visitors are not encouraged to prowl this cave.

The trails across the Shawangunks pass through land thick with mountain laurel, huckleberry bushes and May apple. In season, the last named, also known as mandrake, has single, edible, lemon-yellow fruit that has a strawberry flavor.

Spring Was Late

Spring came late to the Shawangunks this year. The May apples did not bloom until the end of May. The mountain laurel was at its peak during June, and huckleberries appeared in July and August.

Now, of course, the countryside is ablaze with fall color. Mile after mile of the Shawangunks is covered with young, wind-twisted "scrub" pine and oak, and slender, new paper birch trees glistening in their white, flimsy bark. This is the kind of growth that, in this area, covers land that has been swept by fires, of which the region is said to have had more than its share.

No one knows definitely how these fires start, but there is a superstition that huckleberries grow best on burnt-over land. In recent times, huckleberry pickers here have become fewer and fewer, and so, too, have the fires.

October 31, 1965

It Is Hiking When You Walk
for Fun in the Mountains

By CECIL E. HEACOX

The author of the following article is the former Deputy Commissioner of the New York State Conservation Department.

MORE than 40,000,000 Americans walk for pleasure. Indeed, a survey by the Outdoor Recreation Resources Review Commission reveals that, in the United States, walking for pleasure is topped only by driving for pleasure in the family car.

In the Northeast, walking heads the list. So, if you have hankered to try walking or hiking, but hesitated because you did not want to be labeled a square, go right ahead and get in step.

Jogging appears to be a current fad, but its benefits are purely physical. Dr. Paul Dudley White, the eminent cardiologist, has said he thinks it rather ridiculous for mature men to jog around indoor tracks. With special praise for outdoor hiking, Dr. White indicates that man would be better off taking a brisk walk in the woods.

Walking can be an outdoor "in" thing — a healthful activity and rewarding physically, esthetically and spiritually.

According to Noah Webster, walking is that form of movement where one foot is put repeatedly ahead of the other. The definition might apply to jogging, although Webster notes that jogging is "to make one's way laboriously."

The difference between walking and hiking? I asked an expert, S. G. Bascom of the New York State Conservation Department, for the distinction. His answer: "When a walker becomes a hiker, he loses his amateur status."

Height of Enjoyment

To the thousands of people who love the outdoors, a hike in a forest setting is the height of walking enjoyment.

Fortunately for them, the New York Conservation Department maintains nearly 200 miles of well-blazed hiking trails in the Catskill Mountain region. Twenty-eight different hiking trails crisscross mountain peaks, dip into rocky ravines and skirt steep ledges high above green valleys.

Last year, more than 12,000 hikers looked out at the same wilderness beauty and were thrilled by the same magnificent views that inspired artists like Thomas Cole and Frederick Church, and writers like Washington Irving, James Fenimore Cooper and John Burroughs, who was to the Catskills what Thoreau was to Walden Pond.

Contrast from City

All this wilderness paradise is just a short drive from Times Square. In a little more than two hours, you can see mountain peaks instead of skyscrapers, sniff balsam-scented air instead of diesel bus exhaust and hear the liquid note of the wood thrush instead of the horns of stalled traffic.

Hiker's Choice

Best of all, hiking does not have to be a complicated recreation. Beginners can start with one-day trips, taking along only lunch and walking a trail in the morning and returning in the afternoon.

The Conservation Department has helped simplify hiking by keeping trails well marked and clear of underbrush. Circular trail markers are in three colors: blue, red and yellow. Blue markers designate trails running north and south; red is for east and west and yellow is for diagonal trails.

Indispensable to the Catskill hiker is "Catskill Trails" (Recreation Circular No. 9) by W. D. Mulholland, direc-tor of Lands and Forests of the Conservation Department. The circular contains a map and describes the chief features of each trail, including point-to-point distances. It can be obtained by writing the New York State Conservation Department at Albany, Catskill or New Paltz.

Basic Kit

Special clothing is not necessary for a hike—only a sturdy pair of slacks, stout shoes high enough for ankle support and a lightweight, waterproof parka. An over-the-shoulder canteen for water and a knapsack for lunch leave hands free for balance and an easy-going stride. Take along an insect repellent for protection from flies and mosquitoes.

Novices should learn to pace themselves and rest frequently. In hiking, one should never hurry. On the trail, one enjoys the luxury of disregarding time.

My wife and I are devotees of the one-day safari. Earlier this spring, ready for some instant therapy, we walked one of our favorite trails to the summit of Slide Mountain. Although we are far from the Mount Everest type, climbing Slide—at 4,204 feet the highest peak in the Catskills—gives us a heady feeling of accomplishment.

Way to Go

After leaving the Thruway at Exit 19 (Kingston), we followed State Route 28, turning off at Big Indian and continuing through Oliverea to Winnisook, the western end of the Wittenberg-Cornell-Slide Trail.

For the neophyte, the climb from the Winnisook end of the trail is the easiest approach to Slide. From the other end, Woodland Valley, the going is more rugged and much longer.

As we climbed the steep trail, two juncos flew along with us. Painted trillium bor-dered the path. Near the summit, patches of pink spring beauty carpeted the woods.

We took advantage of every fallen log and flat rock to rest. Rests are not only a restorative, but also lead to woodland adventures. Sitting quietly for a while by a mountain spring, we were accepted by the forest creatures as part of the landscape.

All around the spring, we noticed deer tracks. Later, rounding a bend, we found a doe straddling the trail; she stood there motionless, staring at us. Curiosity satisfied, the doe bounded into the woods, white tail held high. We resisted a temptation to follow, knowing that an experienced hiker never leaves a blazed trail.

Fine Vistas

During the last part of the climb, fine vistas opened up to the north. As we neared the summit, a group of Boy Scouts came tearing down the trail. A moment later, we met two Scoutmasters who asked how many boys we had seen.

Hopefully, "Did you see six?" Anxiously, "Or was it only four?"

Fortunately, we could reassure them.

There was even more activity at the top. One of the lean-tos had been taken over by a group of college girls. The other was occupied by three veteran hikers who had been two nights out on the Catskill trails, sleeping in Conservation Department lean-tos strategically situated throughout the trail system.

Storm Clouds

As happens so often on mountain peaks, storm clouds began to drift by, and we lost no time climbing atop the fire observatory tower. Before the thick mists closed in, we had a good view of the Catskill Forest Preserve.

As always, there was a

proprietary thrill in looking out at "our" property—250,-000 acres of wilderness that we own jointly with all the other residents of New York State.

We had planned to take the longer Curtis Trail back; however, it began to rain and so we decided to retrace our steps. Although we were rather soggy by the time we reached the bottom, we knew that special exhilaration that comes from a confrontation between man and nature.

This rewarding Slide trip is not beyond the more ambitious novice, but there are other good trails for beginning hikers. As Mr. Bascom says, "The Red Hill Trail near Claryville is good for beginners. It is a loop trail leading to the Red Hill Forest Fire Observatory. The views from the top are terrific. No wonder the Indians called it Land of the Sky."

There are other good trails to limber up on. The Phoenicia Trail to the Mount Tremper Forest Fire Observatory starts at State Route 28 at a point about a mile east of Phoenicia. The trail to the Belleayre Mountain Forest Fire Observatory from the Belleayre Mountain Ski Center, about 11 miles west of Phoenicia, is especially suited to the novice. If the

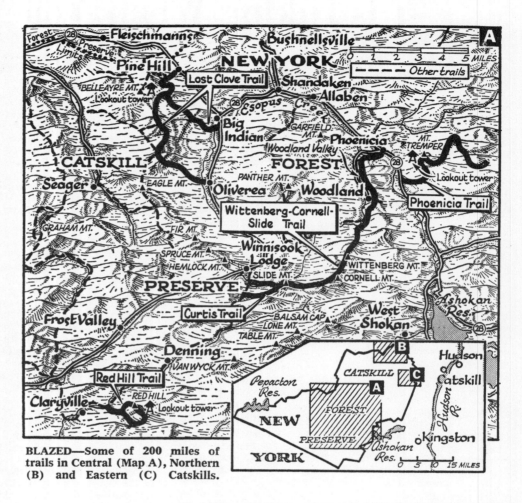

BLAZED—Some of 200 miles of trails in Central (Map A), Northern (B) and Eastern (C) Catskills.

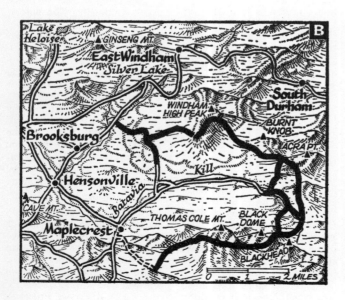

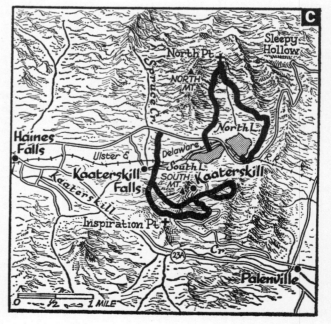

chairlift is operating, you can cheat a little and save your legs.

Easy Height

Little climbing is also necessary on the North Mountain and South Mountain trails, which can be reached from the parking lot (parking fee: 50 cents) at the North Lake campsite near Haines Falls. Both trails wander past picturesque rock formations, and are especially beautiful in June, when the laurel puts on a spectacular flower show.

This is Washington Irving's Rip Van Winkle country. From an escarpment of 1,000-foot cliffs, you can see Palenville, home of the legendary Rip. Directly below is Sleepy Hollow, the locale of Rip's 20-year snooze.

Along the South Mountain Trail, at Inspiration Point and Bellevue, are wide views of the Hudson River. Nearby is the site of the former Catskill Mountain House, where President Grant spent several vacations from the White House.

On Canvas

Although the house is no more, it is preserved in a painting by Thomas Cole, a founder of the Hudson River School. The newly developed Windham High Peak Trail crosses the summit of the 3,940-foot mountain peak named for Cole.

Any of the Catskill trails offers a rare opportunity for communication between man and nature. We like to think of a hiker as more than just a man with a pack on his back. We see him as a walker with the spirit of adventure, taking—as Robert Frost said —the road "less traveled by, and that has made all the difference."

June 9, 1968

FINGER LAKES TRAILBLAZING

A 185-Mile-Long Network of Wilderness Hiking Paths Already Open Between Alleghenies and Catskills

By LOIS O'CONNOR

COOPERS PLAINS, N.Y. About 185 miles of the Finger Lakes Trail have been completed, the Finger Lakes Trail Conference announced at its fifth annual meeting here last weekend.

Reporting to 175 delegates from trail clubs in all parts of western and central New York, Ervin H. Markert, trails chairman of the conference, said that prospects appeared good for completing the trail by 1972, which will be the 10th anniversary of the formation of the conference.

Mr. Markert conceded that difficulties had been encountered in routing the trail through portions of the Catskill Mountains, but added that the various clubs engaged in the project were continuing to submit plot plans and to seek assistance of Federal, state and local governmental agencies.

650-Mile System

When completed, the Finger Lakes Trail will consist of a 350-mile trunk trail and some 300 miles of branch spurs. The trunk trail will link the Catskills with the Allegheny Mountains, and the spurs will lead from the Southern Tier of New York northward into the Finger Lakes region.

From Allegany State Park, western terminus of the Finger Lakes Trail, the Conservation Trail, completed by the Foothills Trail Club of Buffalo, leads north to Lewiston, N. Y., and the Niagara Frontier. There, it connects with the Bruce Trail in Canada.

Eastward, the Finger Lakes Trail will eventually join the Appalachian Trail in the Catskills and, through the Appalachian Trail, will provide a link with the Long Trail in Vermont.

Two major spur trails, in addition to the Conservation Trail, are under way. The Bristol Hills branch runs between Canandaigua Lake on the north and Hammondsport,

at the southern tip of Keuka Lake. The Interloken Trail lies midway between Seneca and Cayuga Lakes, along the Hector Backbone.

A 12-mile section of the Interloken Trail is not an official part of the Trail Conference system. It traverses the 13,000-acre Hector Land Use Area, and is maintained by the United States Forest Service, which administers the tract.

Parts of the completed trail lie far from populated areas, and offer a taste of wilderness atmosphere. The hills and deep valleys, sculptured by glacier action, frame spectacular views and offer glimpses of the shimmering blue expanses of the several Finger Lakes.

Plans call for the entire Finger Lakes Trail to have a three-foot base so as to allow for easy foot travel and prevent use by vehicles. Trail construction follows procedures outlined in "New York State Conservation Trail Standards" and the "Appalachian Trail Manual."

The Finger Lakes Trail gained support six years ago, when Wallace D. Wood of Rochester, who has served as president of the conference, responded to a ground swell of interest and brought various groups together. The conference was organized in March, 1962, to coordinate the work of the hundreds of volunteers who have offered to help build trails, either through their organizations or by individual sponsorship.

The conference receives no public financial support. Trails are being built and maintained through volunteer work and club dues. Each member group of the conference assumes responsibility for a specific section of the trail.

The groups spread from Binghamton, Utica, Syracuse and Ithaca to Rochester, the Genesee Valley, Buffalo and communities in between. They include youth organizations— Scouts, Campfire Girls and

American Youth Hostels—as well as adult clubs.

The building of trails is a slow and difficult process. This applies not only to the chore of trail breaking and marking, but also to the task of locating and mapping routes and obtaining clearance to cross private and public property.

Plane Used

The job was lessened appreciably for the Cayuga Trails Club, headquartered in Ithaca, by the use of a plane piloted by Fred L. Hiltz, a graduate student in the School of Veterinary Medicine at Cornell University. He became an aerial trail-scouter when the Cornell Outing Club, a trail conference member, was asked to locate a trail route over Connecticut Hill, the highest point in central New York. A 10-minute flight over the area, during which time photographs were taken for later study, accomplished the work of several days' walking.

Mr. Hiltz has subsequently assisted in scouting other prospective trail areas. Some knotty problems have also been solved with the aid of aerial photos in the Office of Land Economics at Cornell.

In one situation, ground scouting had produced little of interest. However, by the use of aerial maps, woods roads, hedgerows and an old stage route were pinpointed and led to the mapping of a good route.

Tamarack Lean-to, the first shelter to be built on the trail system, has been completed by the Cayuga Trails Club near South Danby, in Tompkins County. Eventually, shelters will be erected throughout the system and spaced a day's hike apart.

The Bristol Hills branch leads into some of the beautiful vineyard country. There, a completed section of footpath takes one over Italy Hill to Naples, or along Rumpus Hill Road to the hilltop of the High Tor Game Management

Area. The latter offers a sweeping view of lower Canandaigua Lake.

The High Tor area also provides specimens of preglacial flora and fauna. Three lovely glens—Parish, Tannery and Grimes—dot the Bristol Hills section, where the ambitious hiker can also climb to the peak of Gannett Hill and, from Jump-Off Point, get a breathtaking panorama of the Bristol Valley.

Farther west, a hiker can leave Letchworth Park at Portageville and, by hitting a section of the trail at Whiskey Bridge, go along the high escarpment to a view of the oxbow on the Genesee River.

For the history-minded, the trails lead through country rich in Indian and pioneer lore and with an attendant wealth of legend and folklore. Quaint place-names, still in use, spice the imagination—Jubertown Swamp, Cat Elbow Corners, Rinners Knob, Burnt Hill and Panther Gul (a dialect word for gully that is used in the Honeoye area).

Some projects, while not yet a part of the Finger Lakes Trail system, are under way with the cooperation of the trail conference. For example, canal buffs will soon be able to walk the towpath along the old Erie Canal in the Syracuse area. Under a special state permit, the Syracuse Youth Hostel Club is clearing the way through sumac thickets, barbed wire fences and a 300-foot stretch of dense poison ivy.

Picnic Facilities

For visitors to Montour and Watkins Glen, the Hector Land Use Area offers the Blueberry Patch Recreation Site. It has picnic facilities, a limited campsite and several access points to 12 miles of easy trail.

The 13,000 acres of the land use area were purchased during the Depression of the 1930's by the Resettlement Administration. Over the last 20 years, development of the area's resources has been accelerated.

Some sections have been reforested, grazing areas have been established and, in cooperation with the New York State Conservation Department, wildlife projects have been initiated. Too, about 15 ponds have been built to encourage waterfowl and to fa-

cilitate fishing.

A brochure on the Hector Land Use Area, plus a detailed map, can be obtained from the United States Forest Service, 225 South Fulton Street, Ithaca, N. Y. 14850.

New sections of the Finger Lakes Trail system are being completed continuously, and each sponsor group tries to provide updated maps and directions. Inquiries can be sent to Mr. Markert, 5 Cullens Run, Pittsford, N. Y. 14534. A No. 10 self-addressed, stamped envelope should be enclosed.

A comprehensive booklet, "Guide to Trails of the Finger Lakes Region," was published by the Cayuga Trails Club. The first edition is exhausted, but a notification list is being kept for use when the new edition is ready. Names will be put on the list if a request and a self-addressed postal card are sent to the Cayuga Trails Club, General Delivery, Ithaca, N.Y. 14850.

May 8, 1966

The Amazing Adirondacks— On Appreciating the Woods, Their Mystery and Repose

By MARGARET W. LAMY

SARANAC LAKE, N. Y.—Verplanck Colvin, who surveyed the Adirondacks beginning in the 1870's, called them, in his report to the Legislature, "a region of mystery over which none can gaze without a strange thrill of interest and of wonder at what might lie hidden in that vast area of forest covering all things with its deep repose."

Today's city dwellers are more apt to be put off by that sense of mystery than attracted to it. They are sometimes uncomfortable driving along Adirondack highways because the trees are so close to the edge of the road that it is like driving through a green canyon.

Crowded by Trees

All but the very tops of the highest peaks are covered with trees, which crowd the edges of almost every lake and stream.

Long ago, a Mayor of Tupper Lake, Joe Gokey, was asked what was the population of his town. "A little spruce and a little pine, but I'd say about 90 per cent hemlock," he replied.

This lush, green cover adds to the distinctiveness of the Adirondacks and to the air of mystery that Colvin described. But because of it, many visitors are frightened away. They go speeding along the main highways from one civilized oasis to another, looking for ready-made entertainment that resembles what they are accustomed to at home.

With just a slight dash of adventuresome spirit, it is possible to have an altogether different kind of experience on an Adirondack vacation. It is not necessary to qualify as a Mount Everest climber, either. The secret is to tackle the woods in easy stages and to take a little time to find out-of-the-way spots.

'Going to the Woods'

Since the 1840's, visitors, when referring to the Adirondacks, have talked about "going to the woods." In those days, it was the guides who penetrated this "mystery," finding routes first for sportsmen who came to hunt and fish and, later, for tourists eager to rough it.

One of the earliest and most famous guides was John Cheney. He also was one of the most literate. Cheney accompanied the party led by Ebenezer Emmons, the state geologist, who named the Adirondacks on the first climb of Mount Marcy in 1837. Later, Cheney wrote:

'Creation Under Feet'

"It makes a man feel what it is to have all creation under his feet. There are woods there which it would take a lifetime to hunt over, mountains that seem shouldering each other to boost the one whereon you stand up and away, heaven knows where.

"Thousands of little lakes among them so light and clean. Old Champlain, though 50 miles away, glistens below you like a strip of white birch when slicked up by the moon on a frosty night, and the Green Mountains of Vermont beyond it fade away until they disappear as gradually as a cold scent when the dew rises."

There is great satisfaction for the ambitious hiker or climber who tackles a long trek to one of the major peaks here in the Adirondacks. First, there is the sense of accomplishment. Second, there are 10,000 square miles of wilderness spread out in varying views. One can see a few or many of the 2,000 peaks and some of the nearly 2,000 lakes,

ponds and streams that mark the area.

'A Random Scoot'

Another of the colorful guides, "Old Mountain" Phelps of Keene Valley, had a different way of looking at this particular pursuit of pleasure. He would ask his customers whether they wanted to take "a regular walk or a random scoot."

Not all the peaks require a full day's outing or equipment for camping in the woods. Like Old Mountain's "random scoot," a 15- or 20-minute hike can be an introduction to a whole new world.

For example, at Wilmington Notch, in the pass east of Lake Placid on State Route 86, a short but fairly steep climb of about 20 minutes (more with children) leads to Copperas Pond. There are lean-tos there for camping, and enough shoreline to find a spot of one's own for a picnic.

A Family Outing

About eight miles west of Saranac Lake on State Route 3, opposite the trail to Ampersand Mountain, begins a half-mile walk to Middle Saranac Lake, or Round Pond as it is called locally. This is generally level and slightly downgrade terrain leading to a lovely lake with a wide, sandy beach. It is ideal for a family outing.

Farther on toward Tupper Lake on State Route 3 is Panther Mountain. The highway climbs close to the top, passing Panther Pond. From there, it is a short, but again steep, climb to the summit. One can have the same rewards as the all-day climber, but with much less expenditure of energy and time.

A frequent complaint heard from city dwellers is that it is "so quiet" in the woods. Sitting quietly and listening for a few minutes will change that impression.

Forest Sounds

Birds, chipmunks and squirrels chatter, while the wind creates almost constant movement in the leaves and sings through the boughs of evergreens. There are brooks

'GOING TO THE WOODS'—Silver birches at Lower Cascade Lake, one of the passes leading to Lake Placid in the Adirondacks.

Photographs by MARGARET W. LAMY

APPROACHING THE ADIRONDACKS—

at frequent intervals.

Although there are deer and bear in the woods, they steer well clear of man and are happy to go away and leave any intruders they chance to meet.

Maps detailing all types of hikes, long and short, can be obtained from numerous sources, among them the Chambers of Commerce in the various starting areas, gasoline stations and grocery stores, the Department of the Interior in Washington and the State Conservation Department in Albany.

An interesting walk may well be along an old logging road on what was formerly private land. The barber, the gasoline station attendant or the clerk in the grocery store may know where to find a good picnic spot, a favorite bird haunt or a prime berry patch.

Children's Guides

Many parents try to turn their vacation trip into a learning experience for their children and, for them, inexpensive paperback books are available for identifying birds, flowers and trees. A

good pair of binoculars can add to the pleasure.

Good sense should be used in selecting clothing, particularly shoes, which should give adequate support to the foot and ankle.

At the Huntington Wildlife Forest in Newcomb, the Syracuse University College of Forestry maintains a nature trail at which the learning is made easy. Trees, birds and animal signs are identified along an easy half-mile walk and, since it is a preserve, many wild animals can be seen.

July 21, 1968

HIKING MADE EASY IN ADIRONDACKS

By LESLIE D. GOTTLIEB

LAKE COLDEN, N. Y. — Many summer motorists in the Adirondacks are deterred from venturing even briefly into the wilderness on foot by tales that mountain treks can be negotiated only by long-legged, hardy hikers. However, so far as this particular area is concerned, such stories are more fiction than fact.

Lake Colden, a few miles northwest of 5,344-foot-high Mount Marcy, the highest peak in New York State, is the perfect spot for the vacationist who wants to get out into the woods but does not want to be exposed to carrying great loads of foodstuffs and other supplies while adventuring over mountain trails.

The lake can be reached over a short and easy trail from a public parking lot, and it has a number of three-sided log shelters, or lean-tos, available for overnight camping. The swimming is good, although the water is cold, and there are no less than six interesting, well-marked hikes that can be started and finished in one day from its shores. Thus, the only pack-hauling required during an entire stay here is that from the parking lot and back.

Since the lake lies deep in the mountains, there are no stores, and it is necessary for the camper to bring all supplies, such as sleeping bags, packs, food and clothing. Happily, however, it is common practice to leave these supplies in the lean-tos while out enjoying the trails.

The lean-tos are available on a first-come, first-served basis and may not be used by the same party for more than three successive nights. There are thirteen of these at Lake Colden and an adjoining lake that can accommodate more than 130 adults, and there are eight more along the trail from the parking lot to the lake.

Fireplaces Near By

Adjacent to each lean-to are stone fireplaces, latrines, and rapidly flowing streams that provide water for drinking, washing and cooking. There is usually some cut wood stacked near by, and plenty of additional fallen branches and trees

IN THE ADIRONDACKS—Mount Colden, near Lake Colden, towers in background. Philip Gendreau

in the immediate vicinity to keep the fires hot.

It is a good idea to bring along a hatchet to split the wood and cut chips for kindling. Birch bark lying along or near the trails makes excellent tinder, but the Conservation Department requests campers not to peel bark from living trees.

The trail to Lake Colden starts from Adirondack Lodge, a resort operated by the Adirondack Mountain Club that is reached by turning south from State Route 86A, four miles east of Lake Placid Village, at the tiny hamlet of North Elba.

For four of its five miles to the lake, the trail traverses level forest floors, passing Marcy Dam and Marcy Brook. The last mile, along the western edge of Avalanche Lake, is only slightly more difficult to negotiate as the trail crosses several log bridges and

scrambles up, over and around a number of huge boulders alongside the precipitous rock face of Avalanche Mountain. The similarly steep and rocky sides of Mount Colden can be seen across the lake.

The average hiker should not need more than four hours to cover the distance from the parking lot to Lake Colden and the forest ranger's headquarters, where the lean-tos are assigned to campers.

Once the business of settling into a lean-to is over, the problem of deciding on which trail to take first should be discussed. The decision, of course, varies with different campers, and it is not easy to say which is best because of the variety of the trails and the worth-while sights along each of them.

Three of the trails lead up into the mountains, and three meander along the banks of brooks, through mountain passes and across less steeply graded areas. Signposts designate the

point where each trail begins, and the trees bordering the trails are clearly marked with painted metal disks.

Four miles to the east of the lake the summit of Mount Marcy rises, and to the north, one can see the McIntyre chain of mountains, its five peaks, ranging in height from 4,411 to the 5,112-foot-high Algonquin, the only Adirondack peak other than Marcy that tops the 5,000-foot mark.

Up Mount Marcy

The lower trails follow Calamity Brook to the west, the Opalescent River to the southwest and back along Avalanche Lake and Marcy Brook to Indian Falls in the east.

The most impressive and exciting trail—but also the longest and steepest—is that up to Mount Marcy. Named for New York's Governor Marcy in 1837 when the first recorded ascent was made, the peak previously was known as Tahawus, an In-

dian name meaning cloud-splitter. The last 800 feet of its crest rise above the tree line.

At first, the trail follows rock-strewn Opalescent Brook for about a mile. In several places the brook cascades down narrow gorges just a few feet from the trail. Near the half-way point, two lean-tos are passed, and the path continues upward on the shoulder of land above Feldspar Brook.

There is a mile of steep climbing here through a heavily wooded forest of spruce, balsam and birch, and the hiker will be glad to put his pack down again at Lake Colden. After this stiff climb, the trail comes out on the edge of Lake Tear of the Clouds, less than an acre in size and the highest lake source of the Hudson River.

There is an additional lean-to at Lake Tear, and it offers one of the best views of Marcy. Another mile of climbing brings the hiker out onto the mountain's thinly soiled, sloping granite ledges.

From this point upward, the trail is marked with rock cairns and painted rocks. The view from the top of the mountain is truly spectacular, embracing miles of irregular mountain peaks and unbroken forests. Lake Placid spreads out in the north below the cone of Mount Whiteface, and to the east, on a really clear day, it is possible to see Lake Champlain and the Green Mountains in Vermont.

The trips to the top of Algonquin and Colden take less than half as long as that to the top of Marcy, The trail on Colden is the shorter, and it is also the more interesting of the two because it has more lookouts. From the summit of Colden, a splendid view of Lakes Colden, Avalanche and Flowed Lands can be had.

The easier brook trails include two that lead to waterfalls. A little more than two miles southwest of Lake Colden along the Opalescent River is Hanging Spear Falls, so named because it is divided by a long rock resembling a spearhead.

The more substantial and broad Indian Falls is slightly more than four miles distant. To get there, the hiker must back-track over Avalanche Lake to Marcy Brook and then skirt along a branch of the brook for about two miles. Both of these walks are quite leisurely, and the falls are good spots for picnic lunches.

Part of the fun of walking in the woods is keeping an eye out for animals. Tree toads and chipmunks scurry beside the paths, and crickets frequently herald the hiker's approach. The insistent thumping of woodpeckers can be heard and the songs of many other birds.

Enter the Animals

At dusk, the raccoon and hare emerge, and sometimes one may spot a doe nibbling at the grass. There are no poisonous snakes in the area, but occasionally a garter snake will slide across the path. If one happens to see a bear, the best advice to follow is to leave it alone, and it probably will cause no trouble. As for mosquitos, mites and other insects, the ranger at Lake Colden says there are none after the end of July.

Another approach to the Lake Colden-Mount Marcy region is from the east through Keene Valley. An Adirondack Trailways bus goes through this area on Route 86A about twenty miles south of Lake Placid. The bus makes three trips a day north from New York City and south from Massena and Saranac Lake.

The trail starts at Alexander's General Store and follows the paved road west for 1½ miles before entering the woods. From there, it continues along Johns Brook, on an easy and level tract, for three more miles until it reaches the Johns Brook Lodge of the Adirondack Mountain Club. The lodge is open to all visitors for lodging or board by the day or week at reasonable rates. It is far less crowded on weekdays than on week-ends.

Without a Pack

By using the lodge as head-quarters, it is possible to make a number of one-day hikes without having to carry a pack or even bring food or other supplies. There are several scenic approaches to Mount Marcy from the lodge, but it would require a dawn departure for one to make the hike to the mountain and back in a single day. The distance is five miles each way, with approximately a 3,000-foot climb up the mountain.

A detailed map and description of all the trails adjacent to Johns Brook Lodge and to the other trails in the area can be obtained free by writing to the New York State Conservation Department, Albany 1, and asking for Circular 8, "The Trails to Marcy."

August 6, 1961

Northeast to Katahdin

TRAIL TO QUEBEC OPEN TO HIKERS

By RAYMOND H. TORREY.

THE longest single mountain trail in the East for climbers and trampers, and the best equipped with shelters for overnight camps, is the Long Trail, built within the past fifteen years over the summits and ridges of the Green Mountains of Vermont by the Green Mountain Club. From the Massachusetts line it now extends to within a few miles of the boundary of Quebec, its northernmost high point, Jay Peak, overlooking the international border.

Having a total length of maintained trail of more than 230 miles, it exceeds any similar enterprise for outdoor recreation in our Eastern mountains except the admirable system of the Appalachian Mountain Club in the White Mountains of New Hampshire, whose trails have a total of 300 miles, but include no such long through route as the Vermont hiker's highway.

It is kept up almost wholly by private funds, provided by the Green Mountain Club out of dues and gifts, or by private supporters. No State appropriations have been made to build or maintain it, and the only public moneys expended in connection with it were small sums allotted through the Vermont Forestry Department for patrol and custody of shelters by fire wardens. Members of the club, not only of Vermont but elsewhere, notably those of New York City, have contributed largely in money, labor and material to construct the footpath and the shelters and to keep both in good condition and open to public use. The trail constitutes a unique and valuable recreational resource of Vermont, comparable with State parks on which other Commonwealths have expended large sums, and yet it is 99 per cent. the charge of a private organization and of private citizens.

Better Trail Making.

The Long Trail project was started simultaneously with the organization of the Green Mountain Club at a meeting in Burlington, Vt., March 11, 1911. The moving spirit was James P. Taylor, then Principal of the Vermont Academy at Saxton's River. The purpose of the club was to build trails, erect camps and shelters, issue maps and guidebooks, and to make the Green Mountains better appreciated for their recreational value to the people of the State and to visitors.

The making of the trail began in 1911 with the marking of a footpath from Mount Mansfield, highest summit of the Green Mountains, to Camel's

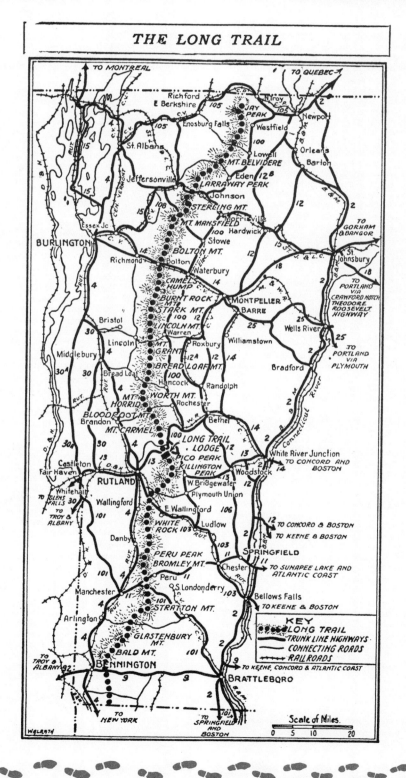

THE LONG TRAIL

KEY
●●● LONG TRAIL
TRUNK LINE HIGHWAYS
CONNECTING ROADS
RAILROADS

Scale of Miles.
0   5   10   20

Hump. In 1912 it was extended north to Johnson. In 1913 it was carried south to Killington Peak, near Rutland, and in 1915 to the Massachusetts line at Prospect Rock. Between 1916 and 1920 the trail from Camel's Hump to Killington Peak was relocated and improved. In 1923 it was extended north from Johnson to Belvidere Mountain and in the past two years to Jay Peak.

Improvement in standards of construction and maintenance was brought about in the years 1916-1920 by Professor Will S. Monroe of Montclair, N. J., who organized a New York section of the club, of which he was ten years President, and enlisted many of its members for sustained volunteer labor in relocating and clearing the section between Bolton and Middlebury Gap. Professor Monroe, a teacher of psychology and pedagogy at the State Normal School at Upper Montclair until his retirement in 1925, established the ideal of a Skyline Trail. It kept to the high peaks and ridges, and descended only to permanent water sources where shelters were located. The portion which he took over and which is still maintained by the New York section, is known as the Monroe Skyline Trail. It includes two summits above 4,000 feet high, Camel's Hump and Lincoln Mountain (with three peaks over 4,000) and several other points above 3,500 feet.

Forty Shelters Along It.

The standards which Professor Monroe demanded, as to scenic quality and general high elevation, and also yearly care as to clearing out blowdowns and removing brush and ferns from the path early in the Summer, have been extended to other parts of the trail. The New York section raises annually from $500 to $800, from dues and gifts, for the upkeep of the Monroe section. Originally the Long Trail had been laid out by Forestry Department agents, who planned it for convenience in fighting fires, and it omitted many summits.

The Long Trail now has about forty shelters where walkers may find overnight refuge at convenient intervals. Most of them are open front cabins with pole bunks covered with spruce boughs, a stove and a fireplace. Fuel is obtained from dead timber, and the ethics of the trail provide that each hiking party shall leave sufficient kindling and firewood for the next group. This code is generally observed.

Other points of shelter are more luxurious, such as the hotel on Mount Mansfield, the Lake Mansfield Trout Club, boarding-houses at Bolton and hospitable farmhouses close to the trail or within a few miles of it. The northern part of the Long Trail, from Johnson to Camel's Hump, can be walked without carrying sleeping blankets, but south of Camel's Hump to Sherburne Pass, near Rutland, the hiker must carry food, blankets and other necessities, although he will find an axe and simple cooking utensils at the shelters.

A Wilderness Lodge.

At Sherburne Pass is the Long Trail Lodge, a remarkable example of adaptation of natural surroundings to a dwelling. This was a gift to the club from Mortimer R. Proctor, now President of the organization, and his mother, Mrs. Fletcher D. Proctor. The architect, Paul W. Thayer of Wallingford, Vt., made such use of boulders and trees on the site that the structure has the appearance of growing out of the mountainside. It contains sleeping quarters and a restaurant.

The Long Trail is approachable at points from ten to fifteen miles apart by railroad or highway. Good entrances are by way of Bennington, at the south end; at Rutland, Brandon and Middlebury, in the middle, and from Burlington via Bolton or Johnson, toward the north. The club has issued a convenient little pocket guide, with maps and directions.

Several new improvements have been made on the Long Trail this season. Mr. Ross has marked the point where the trail touches the Massachusetts line at the border of the Blackinton State Forest near North Adams, with a large sign wired in the trees. It links up with a Massachusetts State forestry trail which will be part of the Appalachian Trail, the proposed hikers' path from Maine to Georgia. The Williams College Outing Club continues this trail southward into Massachusetts over Mount Greylock.

Du Val Approach Trail.

Middlebury College boys built this year a new shelter near Bread Loaf, Vt., called the Boyce Camp, and the Burlington section has erected another in Nebraska Notch, south of Mount Mansfield, named for James P. Taylor, originator of the club and the trail. J. J. Fritz, forester of Middlebury College, is rebuilding Battell Lodge, a camp on Lincoln Mountain, constructed originally by Joseph M. Battell, who bequeathed 10,000 acres of forest to the college. George F. E. Story of the Worcester (Mass.) section of the club is completing the Jay Peak section of the trail this Summer.

Another contribution to the Long Trail this year was the construction of Du Val Trail, the first approach route from a railroad town, running eight miles from Brandon, to the main path at Mount Horrid. This was provided by Guy Du Val, a New York business man long interested in Vermont. It climbs from 700 feet to 2,184 feet, through woodlands, crosses streams by bridge and is well marked with arrows and cairns. Mr. Du Val has published a pamphlet on the subject, including notes on the plant life by Norman Taylor of the Brooklyn Botanic Garden.

Other guides to the Long Trail are: "Trails and Summits of the Green Mountains," by Professor Walter Collins O'Kane of the New Hampshire State University; a series of maps giving details as to grades, springs, &c., by Captain H. W. Congdon of Arlington, Vt., obtainable from the clerk in Rutland, and topographic sheets of the United States Geological Survey, which now cover the main ridges of the Green Mountains as far north as the south end of Mount Mansfield, and which show the route of the Long Trail.

For beginners the Burlington and Monroe Skyline sections of the Long Trail, including Mansfield, Bolton and Camel's Hump Mountains; or the Killington section, centring about the Long Trail Lodge in Sherburne Pass, ten miles east of Rutland, are recommended. The high peaks in these portions give splendid views, eastward over the White Mountains or New Hamphire and westward across Lake Champlain to the Adirondacks. They are accessible overnight from New York, an evening train landing the climber at points from Rutland to Burlington, from which the trail can be reached in the early forenoon.

September 5, 1926

FOUR CONNECTICUT TRAMPS

WHERE THEY WENT AND WHAT THEY SAW IN ONE SHORT WEEK.

From the Central Part of the State They Journeyed Down the Eastern Bank of the Famous Old River to Rock Landing and Thence to Saybrook — Interviews With Curious Natives—Camping Out Under Difficulties—Haddam Academy.

A walking tour for four was planned, and the route as laid out should take them from a point in Central Connecticut, on the eastern bank of the Connecticut River, down that bank to Rock Landing, across by ferry, down the west bank, through Haddam, Deep River, Essex, and Centrebrook, to Old Saybrook; thence across the river to Lyme, returning on the eastern bank to the point of starting. This for the last week of August.

So good an authority as Robert Louis Stevenson has laid it down that when one goes a touring, one should not mince in time with a girl or closely pin to any companion other than one's self; but, with knapsack, pipe, book, and mental quietude, sing along the highways. But these four were strong enough to disregard the master. In point of fact, it was La Philosophe, the wife of the Sketcher, who proposed the tour, and L'Amie said if La Philosophe went she should go also. The Sketcher approved of all his wife did, and the Scribe was pleased with the vivacious determination of L'Amie. So it was that when the sun came with reg-

ular pace over the eastern hills he saw, not alone the two brown hats of the Scribe

"Well, Who Pays for It?"

and the Sketcher heading to the south, but with them the bright-red headgear of La Philosophe and L'Amie. And there were knapsacks and books and mental quietude, and songs by the quartet along the highway; which was much better than soloing.

An early start. This is the first rule of a walking tour, for either pleasure or profit. There is an exhilaration in saluting the sun upon the road which the later hours of the day miss, while to have seen the dew sparkling like a thousand diamonds upon the leaves and cartwheel spider webs before he can dry it with his rays is as sweet a victory as one is likely to achieve. On the day of the start the sun was scheduled to show his face at 7, and the four had been walking briskly for half an hour before the sun, taking advantage of a wide break in the beeches and maples that lined the road, pushed a bar of light across in front of them. Being thus forestalled, he came not as a conquerer, but as a companion; and he was a pleasant fellow for as long as he shone that day.

It is a long hill that leads down to the river at Rock Landing, and sandy underfoot. But overhead there is a bower of leaves through which the sun may not pierce, and the descent was more like wandering by a wood road than marching on a highway. It was on this hill, after two hours of steady marching, that the first natives were met—two girls in a wagon. The Sketcher was some rods ahead with La Philosophe, and the red tam o' shanter enchained the untutored attention of the pair. When they again looked to the front, it was but to see the Scribe and L'Amie, with a companion tam on her head, bearing down upon them. L'Amie is striking in appearance—strong, tall, and supple, with much hair of a cop-

pery glint. The girls in the wagon simply pulled up short at the sight. They watched as the trampers went by, and when, far behind them, a turn of the road was reached and the Scribe daringly looked back, they were still halted on the water bar, staring with their four eyes. L'Amie gurgled a little laugh.

"They're struck mute, silent, and dumb, and they can't say a word," said she. And it did look that way.

Rock Landing was a temporary centre of industry that morning. A boatload of coal had come up the river during the night, and a dozen men, with as many ox wagons, were unloading her, chaffing one another the while. Some wagons had four yokes of oxen; the hill up which the coal was to be drawn warranted as many. The Society for the Prevention of Cruelty to Animals would have insisted upon it. The men who handled the oxen were of the brawny, hoarse-voiced type, with one exception. He was a slim, graceful youth, with blue eye-glasses and a cord attached, which wandered over one ear and lost itself in his hair. He carried his ox goad over his shoulder, like a gun, and he walked with a military air of precision. His commands to the oxen partook of the nature of requests.

La Philosophe, whose specialty is character, put him down for a Yale student working for his health through the Summer, and as no one, on inquiry, seemed acquainted with his antecedents, it was allowed to go at that. He looked like a student, anyway; he was certainly no farmer. L'Amie cast a backward glance after him as he toiled up the hill, but he was occupied with the oxen and paid the party not the slightest attention. This in itself proved he was not to the country born.

As the party trooped down to the water's edge, following the stout waterman who was to set them across, a small boy, fishing from the landing, gathered himself up and surveyed them from beneath his arm. He was such a sturdy little chap, sunbrowned and lithe, that he was the immediate successor of the Yale student in the estimation of the four.

"Well, son, what do you think of us?" asked the Scribe in his best manner of patronage.

"Looks like the Salvation Army," he replied, without a tremor.

"The red tams are to blame for that, but we will forgive them this time," murmured the Sketcher, as he nailed the little fellow where he stood.

The surface of the river was of a silken smoothness. Not a touch of wind ruffled it, and the white mist of morning was not yet completely risen from it. Haddam Island ran a long, green needle into it toward the north, lower and lower till it slipped beneath the surface. Far up the river some buildings in Higganum stood out boldly and aggressively on a bluff, their colors painful to the eye in contrast with

walk till some feature of the country especially pleases you, or till lunch suggests itself. And then you sit and rest as long as may please you. Be assured, if you hurry, you will lose more than half what you started out to attain.

Now, as they sat by the track, the Sketcher made a study of certain old houses in the village of Haddam which showed over the hill, and the Scribe read in Herbert Spencer's dictum concerning the coming slavery. And two men, telegraph repairers, coming up the track, uttered a little laugh at sight of the party.

"All the way from Californy," commented one.

"Like a stranded theatrical troupe," said the other.

The Sketcher was eager for a fight at once, but the Scribe, cool to an unusual degree, counseled moderation, and the two telegraph men, laughing jollily, passed on.

"It's all the fault of those red head gears," said the wrathful Sketcher. "Hereafter you've got to put handkerchiefs over them, or I won't be seen with you on the road." And he put away his sketchbook with a sudden lack of interest. La Philosophe took him in hand. She knows a wife's prerogative. And presently the Sketcher looked around with a half grin, and said to L'Amie, persuasively:

"That hat is very becoming to you."

"Say no more," replied L'Amie. And the party took to the ties again.

A fortunate crossroad tempting them from the ties, they followed it as it led them coaxingly along under old apple trees into the ancient and handsome town of Haddam. It is a good town—a town with an atmosphere. The principal street is dignified—so much so that dog fights never occur in it, even. At Haddam Academy another halt was made to secure a sketch of some quaint old gambrel roofs, and a citizen of repute stopped, talked, and gave such information about the town as here appears.

"Takin' picters, be ye? No? Artist, eh? Well, them roofs now are all right, ain't they?" (He squinted over the Sketcher's shoulder to see what he was doing.) "That house's older'n I be. More'n a hundred an' a half." He paused, then took a new start. "You know this's where David Dudley Field was born? 'Tis. Yes, an' dyin' he left the town a legacy—five thousan' dollars. We hain't got it yit; don't know what we'll do with it when we do git it. Ain't acquaint with th' terms of the legacy. S'pose we'll hev to fight over it in town meetin', some. Eh? Well, Field he done some for the town besides that. He tuk Isinglass Hill up there behin' them houses you're a-sketchin' of, and made it into a park. Set out a lot of trees. What he want t' do that fur? I do'no. We got trees enough, seems to me. I ain't finding no fault, him bein' dead, anyway. But why didn't he take that money an' build a house? I do'no. Wisht he had. We ben long time now tryin' to git a library built, with a lyceum into it. Now, if he'd a-done that— We got trees enough. Why,

The Connecticut Below Goodspeeds.

the tender green and soft white of nature and the new day.

On the west bank, where a landing was made, the Connecticut Valley Railroad runs. And as it was much nearer than the highway, the party took to the ties. A little distance down they stopped to rest, in accordance with their plan.

Make frequent rests. That is the second rule of a walking tour for pleasure. The object of walking is not a test of endurance. You wish to reach your destination in the pleasantest manner possible. So you

we're a-cuttin' of 'em down every Winter! But a library, now, with books—an' a lyceem into it fur debates—now, that would a-suited Haddam to a T!"

There is a very fine blue building stone quarried at Haddam, and several of the more pretentious houses are built of it. All public buildings are of the stone. At the southern end of the principal street is the jail, of bluestone, its grated windows giving upon a green lawn shaded by ancient elms. The Haddamite followed the party to show the

beauties of the place, and, pointing out the jail, said it was as "likely a buildin' as he ever see;" adding, with an air of pride, that "we hev f'om twenty-five to forty prisoners in it all the time"—as one might boast of the patronage bestowed on a hotel.

Haddam is a fine town to spend some quiet weeks in, and has an air of repose and refinement that is lacking in some of the towns along the lower Connecticut that the party tramped through. It is a pity, though, that the finest building site in the peaceful, elm-shaded village should be given over to the jail, with its barred windows, suggestive of crime and restrained criminals. It is out of harmony with the brooding peace and goodwill of its environment.

Below Haddam the road marched on about its business, bordered in many places by tobacco fields. The crop was just being cut, and many wagons, picturesque with their loads of tobacco stalks hanging from a frame, were passed. The highway abounded in picturesque bits, still and active. There were magnificent orchards of old apple trees on sloping hillsides, and wells with curious sweeps and windlasses, wide stretches of meadow, and now and again some curious, subdued face framed in a doorway or window of a wayside cottage to wonder at the spectacle of four young people, apparently happy and in their right mind, who would lade themselves with knapsacks and march so gayly on through these homely scenes. That was one secret of the trip's pleasure—the scenes were homely.

One could feel the honest toil wrought into the erection of the farmhouses, and understand the affection a farmer must have, on these scant New-England acres, for the fields he cultivates. For many of the river farms have been in possession of one family many generations. The original ancestor of the family in this country cleared the fields of trees, his sons helped him, and, in their turn, bequeathed the heritage of land and labor to their descendants. One such farm the party made the acquaintance of at Old Saybrook, which has been in the possession of one family since the settlement of the valley. The old house is still standing, well kept up and quite modern—unfortunately—in white paint and green blinds. The sixth generation now lives beneath its roof, but eight generations have sprung from beneath it.

About noon a halt was made in a small grove below Slaterville, and lunch was eaten. This resulted in materially lightening the knapsacks, for the party had observed closely the third rule for a walking tour of pleasure, which is:

Proceed in light marching order. You will not be going through an enemy's country, and therefore it will be easy to subsist upon it. Put the things you decide upon as indispensable in a pile before starting, divide the pile in half, and take one section. Let that section include a wispbrush, hairbrush, toothbrush, comb, soap, towel—the toilet can need nothing more; a blanket, if you are to camp out, and a change of socks. One can travel luxuriously all over New-England on this equipment, and be everywhere well received.

On again after an hour's rest. The sun warmed up to the highest temperature of the day, but it was not uncomfortable. A breeze fanned the road, and dust rose beneath the tramping feet only to be blown away. By and by the Scribe and L'Amie stopped at a farmhouse for water. It took an unconscionable long time to arouse any one, and at the last a tragedy was exposed. The woman who answered our knock was the caretaker of another woman—an imbecile. The tender heart of L'Amie was touched. She had had several unhappy sidelights on human existence during the march.

"Do you remember," said she, softly, "that up here we stopped to speak with a very deaf old man—how anxious he was to have a word with us—how tired of his unhearing monotony? And at the house where we stopped to ask our way a handsome boy swung himself out of our sight on crutches? And now, in this modern, conventional house we fir! this saddest of all afflictions—a crazy woman, grinning and muttering. It makes me feel as though life was honeycombed through with suffering and sorrow, and I am afraid to speak to another stranger on the road lest I find another tragedy."

"And yet the sun shines and is warm, and the breezes blow, and the earth brings forth her increase," said the Scribe.

"That is true," said L'Amie. And presently she was singing to the time of the tramping feet, setting the pace for the merriment of all.

A long, steep, and sandy hill threatened the party in front, according to an ancient

Old House, Haddam.

woman from whom they sought information. "You had better take the railroad here for a mile," she said, kindly. "It takes you right to the camp meeting grounds. You going to camp meeting?"

That, to her, was the point upon which all interests pivoted. It was a pity to shatter ever so slightly her belief, and so the party said it was its intention to pay at least a call in passing. That pleased her. "The meetings have been well attended, and much good has been done," said she.

A short tramp further on along the ties, and the cottages on the camp meeting grounds came into view on a high bluff to the right of the track. Some were for families through the Summer, others were city headquarters, and bore the name of their city on their front. "Brooklyn" was prominent above all. A mile down the river, on the other side, was Goodspeed's, with its attractive collection of houses, its grotesque landing, and funny scoop of a ferryboat, that made frequent trips across. The sketcher was charmed, and sat him down, with L'Amie, who is herself something of an artist, to make a sketch, while the scribe and La Philosophe went up to the grounds of Camp Bethel to see the place of Summer revivals. What they found of special interest was a restaurant, and when La Philosophe read on the sign that ice cream was to be had she showed no sorrow over the lack for the day of religious services. For La Philosophe is yet much of a girl, and, though she might decline the seductions of ice cream on a Sunday, on Tuesday, with no clergyman to interfere, she surrendered with every sign of joy. The other two were summoned, and Camp Bethel, as a point of supply for ice cream, was declared a success.

At Goodspeed's Station, on the Valley Road, the ties were again abandoned in favor of the highway. For—rule four:

Of two paths to your destination, abandon the more direct, if it is the least pleasant. No one can accuse a railroad of being a good footpath. And, although the road which was found took the party around three sides of a large rectangle, of which the railroad formed the third, it was much to be preferred. The young woman telegrapher at Goodspeed's advised in favor of it, and she knew whereof she spoke.

"I suppose we take this long road so as to get our money's worth," said the Sketcher, wearily, when a halt was made.

"We are bound to get our money's worth on such a path as this," La Philosophe replied, looking with pleasure at the prospect. The road was dusty, but a tiny footpath led beside it in the crisp grass; many gnarled apple trees looked over into the road from their foothold in the garden mold, holding out fruit to the passer-by; at a little distance the road disappeared enticingly behind a jutting wooded knoll; a house or two, old even when the century came in, stood along the way; an old man, digging potatoes in a field above the road,

stopped and leaned on his hoe to contemplate the bright bit of color that had encamped under the trees; afar, on the opposite side of the river, were salt marshes reaching into an unknown valley between the hills. This, and the sun and the air and the entire association of objects and sentiments, made the trip worth while. A vote was taken and passed to that effect, and entered on the minutes of the Scribe.

Then on again. The road marched up to its wooded point, and behind it lay along a bare height many feet above the river. It was a superb view. Some Government craft was at anchor below Goodspeed's, and innumerable small canoes and light-winged craft of the good people at the camp meeting darted about the water like so many dashing, flashing dragon flies. A purple haze hid the extent of the salt marshes. The woods at hand smelled of sweet, woodsy secrets, and wild flowers in the road and yellow shook off the dust of the road's travel in a gust of wind, and appeared freshened. It was the old Middlesex Turnpike, along which the march was made, and the thought of its antiquity pleased the marchers. But a dweller by it, whose sentiment they entertained as completely as he could.

"Oh, this isn't such a very old road," said he. "There's older around here. It was only 1800 when this was put through. My father knew all about it—helped build it."

The last village passed that day was Tylerville. Three miles below it La Philosophe called a halt in an imperative manner. She thought the day's march had been quite long enough. There was an attractive hill, with a grove in which to camp, two farmhouses at which to purchase whatever was needed, a well for water, and the entire river for bathing. It was a happy combination, and one not to be matched in many miles. Her word prevailed. The camp was made.

Forth from one of the two houses issued an ancient man, his face set in white whiskers, and wearing a pervading smile. With honest grace he put his sidehill at the service of the party, first having his curiosity satisfied as to the cause and nature of the measure they proposed. Then he became reminiscent, told of some remarkable walks he had made in his young days, and passed to a discussion of the prevailing "hard times." Strangely, he did not attribute them to the Democratic Party. This old man, a farmer, living out of the world, proved himself something of a student of social and economic matters.

"Times change," he said, burying his hands in the pockets of his overalls and becoming serious. "They're down, then up, then down agin. I was born poor, and I'm poor now. I started life at $2.50 a month. That ain't much nowadays, is it? It was doing well enough then, though. Now, there's little fifteen-year-old girls goes down to the factory at Deep River and makes their $30 a month. Ain't satisfied with any less. But they'll have to come down to my figger yet. They'll have to come down! Half a loaf's better'n no bread'n this world."

"But the laborer is worthy of his hire," interposed La Philosophe, relying on Scripture to pose the old man.

"Yes!" He raised his voice and his hand. "But the one that come at the 'leventh hour got the same penny! Don't forgit that!"

"When they git a little miff nowadays, they go on strike," he resumed. "Perhaps they think they ain't gittin' 'nough wages; they never worked for two-and-a-half a month! Out here in Chicago—there was a lot of property burnt. Who pays for it? That's what I want to know. Every time there's a strike there's property destroyed. Well, who pays for it? I jus' notice these fellers, when they do go back to work after a strike, they're likelier'n not to go back for less wages than they was gittin' when they struck. There's been time wasted and property lost. Who pays for it? I ain't a-sayin' —but I notice they goes back to work for less than they was a-gittin'."

Up on the hillside they built a little fireplace of stone and brick, so that the fire should not run through the dry underbrush. La Philosophe discovered an immense hemlock tree, the opposite sides of which she announced were to be the bedchambers for the night, and she busied herself breaking off small hemlock twigs to form the couches. L'Amie went to the well for

water, and came back with a gift of pears from the friendly old farmer. Her face was serious, for she had found in his house another crippled boy. The Sketcher worked up his portrait of the farmer, and the Scribe went to the other farmhouse to purchase roasting ears. There is a theory, well substantiated, that roast sweet corn should be stolen to bring out its best flavor, but the party disregarded it, and paid for what they got.

This farmhouse had for occupant a solitary man, under forty. He was unkempt, disheveled, needed being taken care of. His house was neat and his garden a model. The Scribe sympathized with him over his lonely condition, and as he picked the ears of corn he reciprocated with a side-light on life as he found it alone on his farm:

"I guess it had to be that way. You see, I couldn't go away; I had to stay at home and take care of the old folks. That was all right so long as they lived, but they was bound to die, o' course, and finally mother she did die, two years ago. And I ben alone ever since. Well—and, you see I was one of them that gets left, anyway. It was just 's well while mother was alive, but it's ben kinder hard sence. Yes, Sir 'Tain't so bad in Summer. Then there' passin' on the road and the river, and get out doors and have my farm to work. But come Winter and I'm shut in here, nothing to do all them long evenings but sit and look at the wall and hear the wind —yes, Sir, that's hard; that's when I'm sorry I was one that got left."

"You have one neighbor, however," said the Scribe.

"Yes; good folks, too. But they ain't my own folks, you know. Now, I ben away to-day, up to Haddam, to dig potatoes for a blind man. I had to get the neighbor to feed my hog and do some little chores while I was gone. I done them, but 'twan't so free as if my own folks was here. If I was sick they'd neighbor willing enough; but I suppose a man's best business 's to home, and they think so."

"Perhaps you won't be alone always. Strong man like you, with a good house and farm—you ought not."

"Maybe not," he sighed. "I did think one while I wouldn't be alone this year—but I be. I got left. I suppose I'll fair get drove to trying of it again, some time. The thought of the long Winter evenings coming scares me. A man can't read all the time, and he can't sleep all the time. He's got to have somebody to talk to."

He charged for the corn at a rate that reminded the Scribe of the prices of New-York corner grocers, showing him to be a "forehanded" man, despite his loneliness and gloom; and he called after the Scribe, climbing the hill with the corn:

"World's kinder out o' jint, ain't it?"

The crying need in every secluded locality the party tramped to seemed to be for "somebody to talk to." It was easy to understand the heart hunger which this uncouth man suffered beneath his sorry exterior.

In the twilight the fire on the hill burned bravely, and the roasting ears crackled before it; then, eaten hot with butter, salt, and pepper, they were something for the gourmand to aspire to. Down in the road a group of three natives hung over the fence, watching the flickering blaze, but not venturing near. After the supper of corn and tea and bread and chipped beef, the hemlock received the four beneath its dense foliage. There was never a sweeter scented room than that—new hemlock twigs

broken beneath the blankets, the tree above, and a multitude of aromatic plants mingling their perfume on the soft breeze. Thus they lay, while the hush and beauty of the night grew about them. The outlines of the farmhouses sunk in the lower gloom; the hills across the river were black and mysterious under the stars and dark-blue sky. No moon shone out. A single light from a farmhouse, hitherto unguessed, was like earth's answer to the eternal glimmer of the stars; and then the crippled boy at the house below took his violin and played the airs he knew—simple and homely, touches of the country dance and of the country religious services. Dance tune and hymn tune followed each other with no sense of incongruity, and when he paused it was as though the silence held its breath. And sleep came under the brooding blackness of the hemlock tree, and the world was at rest.

It was a pity that so idyllic a state should not have continued till morning; but truth must be told, and the truth is that mosquitoes and gnats came close upon the heels of sleep, and did so torment the party that sleep fled, and there was wailing and

"Looks Like the Salvation Army."

execration in the darkness. The pests became unbearable, until the tree was deserted and refuge taken in the farmer's barn. The floor was covered with new hay, and on this the fugitives slept deeply till morning; there was nothing to disturb them there.

The second day dawned pleasantly, and the march was resumed. Deep River was the most considerable town of the day, and it impressed itself upon the party less by reason of its brick factories and hum of

machinery than by its pretty girl. The one girl noted was declared by the Sketcher to be the prettiest he had seen in Connecticut, and ever La Philosophe agreed with him. She was tall and plump, in a muslin gown tied at the elbows with narrow blue ribbons; and she walked along the principal street, looking upon the world through an admirable pair of eyeglasses. Evidently the earth was her footstool and men her abject slaves. "That is quite good enough for the men," said l'Amie.

Just beyond Centrebrook the midday halt was made, although it was no more than 11 by the clock. Centrebrook will long be remembered as the place where the kindly old gentleman to whom application for a dish of dinner was made sent out pork and fried eggs, boiled potatoes, sliced cucumbers, and boiled corn, with all necessary plates and forks, and would take for it—25 cents.

"I won't be hard on you," he said, when the question of payment was broached and the dinner was prepared. "I guess 25 cents will do."

The Scribe uttered an ejaculation of surprise which was taken for one of dismay.

"Oh, not apiece," the old gentleman hastened to add, "not apiece. Twenty-five cents for all."

"But we're not tramps," was interposed; "we can pay, and we want to."

"Oh, bless you, I know that," he laughed. "You are having a good time in your way; I'm having one in mine. We're even."

From Centrebrook to Saybrook was four miles, and they were miles of monotony. The road lost in interest. It was deep with dust and led through alternate wood and swamp, where no houses were found save some huts in which Italians had settled. They looked much like the adobe huts and wattled inclosures of the poorer Mexicans along the Rio Grande, and the sight of the short, dark men, followed by women lugging inevitable babies, did not dispel the likeness; it rather added to it.

Saybrook was gained. It was the end of the tramp—twenty-four miles. The party marched down to Saybrook Point and let the water touch their toes. It was as far as they could go. There was the Sound in front, with the blue of Long Island bounding it.

"Now we've come; let's go back," said the uneasy Scribe.

"No, let's stay awhile," said the Sketcher. "This is the best country I've seen yet."

So they staid—walking and sketching by day, sheltered beneath a hotel ordinaire at night. By and by somebody suggested that it had been proposed to return by walking on the eastern bank.

"Let us have variety of locomotion," pleaded La Philosophe. "We walked down; let us ride back. Let us go by boat."

So they did. And the boat took them the distance they had walked in two days in something less than four hours. But there was not a tithe of pleasure in it.

And at this point it becomes necessary to formulate the fifth and last rule of a walking tour for pleasure. It is:

Don't anticipate economy. Walking tours are expensive. One may go from point to point by rail or boat or wagon much quicker, easier, and cheaper. But just remember that the walking tour for healthful pleasure, whatever it costs, is worth while; and if you consistently observe the rules laid down in this description of a genuine tour, pleasure in walking will surely be yours.

October 7, 1894

WALKING IN THOREAU'S FOOTSTEPS ON CAPE COD

By CAROLINE BATES

EASTHAM, Mass. — October is at its best now and it is at its very best on Cape Cod. The days are fresh and sunny, the nights cool, and the surf still fluctuates between a comfortable 66 and 72 degrees. It was at this time of year in 1849 that Henry David Thoreau, his big, black umbrella unfurled behind him, hiked along thirty miles of Great Outer Beach.

Thoreau preferred and recommended October: "Most persons visit the seaside in warm weather, when fogs are frequent, and the atmosphere is wont to be thick, and the charm of the sea is to some extent lost. But I suspect that the fall is the best season, for then the atmosphere is more transparent, and it is a greater pleasure to look out over the sea. The clear and bracing air, and the storms of autumn and winter even, are necessary in order that we may get the impression which the sea is calculated to make. In October, when the weather is not intolerably cold, and the landscape wears its autumnal tints, such as, methinks, only a Cape Cod landscape ever wears, especially if you have a storm during your stay, that I am convinced is the best time to visit this shore. In autumn, even in August, the thoughtful days begin, and we can walk anywhere with profit. Beside, an outward cold and dreariness, which make it necessary to seek shelter at night, lend a spirit of adventure to a walk."

Most of Cape Cod's eastern shore, from Monomoy Island to Provincetown, is as wild today as when Thoreau first explored the area. Concerned that it might become a fashionable resort, he wrote: "If it is merely a ten-pin alley, or a circular railway, or an ocean of mintjulep that the visitor is in search of—if he thinks more of the wine than the brine * * * I trust that for a long time he will be disappointed here."

Development is now reaching out to this section of the Cape, but if it becomes a National Seashore Recreational Area, as proposed, one of the

Ruth Block

OCTOBER STROLL—An off-season visitor to Cape Cod follows the shore.

country's most magnificent stretches of unspoiled beach will be saved. Few coastal areas have escaped the encroachments of civilization, and even fewer retain the primitive grandeur of the Great Outer Beach. The adventurer in search of wild America visits this coast for the same reason that Thoreau did.

'Atlantic House'

"They commonly celebrate those beaches only which have a hotel on them," he wrote. "But I wished to see that seashore where man's works are wrecks; to put up at the true Atlantic House, where the ocean is land-lord as well as sea-lord, and comes ashore without a wharf for the landing."

Few would want to duplicate Thoreau's long walk and rely on his catch-as-catch-can method of obtaining food and lodgings. Starting out on foot at Nauset Inlet, near Eastham, he criss-crossed the arm of the Cape several times and eventually arrived at Provincetown. On one evening, as was the custom then, he merely knocked on the door of a Wellfleet oysterman s house and asked to be put up for the night. On another, he stayed with the keeper of North Truro's Highland Light. Today, the natives are no less hospitable, but it is customary to check in at one of the local tourist homes or motels.

The average hiker can sample the best of this shore line on a series of one-day jaunts. Three good hikes, certainly, would be in the areas of the lighthouses.

Nauset Light, which has guided mariners since 1839, makes a good point of departure and return for one hike. For this, one should take U. S. 6, the Mid-Cape Highway, to Eastham, and about half a mile north of the Old Windmill (which still grinds corn) turn right on Nauset Road which leads to the light. Here commences the great sand cliff, carved out by glaciers 35,000 years ago, which continues northward for more than twenty miles.

At approximately this point, where this hike begins, Thoreau got his first glimpse of Cape Cod's Great Outer Beach. Far below the bank, the Atlantic surf pounds the shore and the beach stretches endlessly, and invitingly, in both directions. Here, he wrote, "a man may stand * * * and put all America behind him."

If it is at all possible, the hike from here should start on the outgoing tide. As Thoreau observed, a mile on sand is as good as two elsewhere. The wet, hard-packed sand left by a receding tide is easier to walk on, and faster, than the dry sand of the upper beach. The choice of shoes also affects one's comfort and speed. Many wear ankle-high hiking boots or sneakers; some prefer to go barefoot.

Thoreau was content to roast a clam on the beach, but present-day tourists will probably want to take a lunch. A lightweight shoulder bag is handy, and as it becomes empty, it begins to have room for shells and other gifts from the sea.

Although the hiker could cover ten miles or more round trip from Nauset Light, there is little advantage in doing so. Thoreau maintained that walking was an art, and that there was "a genius, so to speak, for sauntering." The visitor who follows this advice will be more likely to find a starfish, sand dollar, or sea treasure cast up by the tide. Although Thoreau walked the beaches primarily to observe and to evaluate, he returned home laden with shells, pebbles, and specimens of seaweed.

Souvenirs Underfoot

Few hikers can resist the collecting instinct. Thoreau also found a barnacle-covered bottle half-filled with red ale. Even this discovery has a contemporary parallel: in May of this year several clam diggers came upon nine unopened bottles of imported champagne, vintage 1920.

All this takes time, and beach walking is, therefore, a leisurely business. These two quotations from Thoreau indicate the proper pace for this kind of life:

"Sometimes we sat on the wet beach and watched the beach birds, sand-pipers, and others, trotting along close to each wave, and waiting for the sea to cast up their breakfast."

"We walked on quite at our leisure, now on the beach, now on the bank,—sitting from time to time on some damp log, maple or yellow birch, which had long followed the seas, but had now at last settled on land; or under the lee of a sand-hill, on the bank, that we might gaze steadily on the ocean."

A second hike might originate in North Truro, turning right off U. S. 6 on Head of the Meadow Road, which leads to the beach of the same name. Two miles south of this point stands the powerful Highland (or Cape Cod) Light, one of several lighthouses that warn ships away from the rocky coast. Few places along the Atlantic seaboard demonstrate as dramatically the erosive force of wind and water. Contours of the beach constantly change, cliffs rapidly crumble away.

When Thoreau stayed at the original lighthouse, built in 1797, the keeper feared the building would topple into the ocean, even though it stood about 300 feet from the edge of the bank. In less than a year, one section of the cliff lost forty feet. The present structure, erected in 1857, then seemed secure on its ten acres of sand. Less than an acre is left today.

Walking With Sandpipers

North of Head of the Meadow Beach the bank begins to shorten into undulating sand dunes. One's walking companions here will include sandpipers scurrying in and out of the tide and herring gulls soaring overhead. All along this stretch, which vies with Cape Hatteras for the title "graveyard of the Atlantic," offshore sand bars have brought destruction to hundreds of ships, many of which still lie in the ocean depths. In about fifteen minutes time, the walker will come upon the rusted hull of one German wreck, which is exposed at low tide and can be reached from the beach.

Thoreau met several natives along here and noted that they were picking up every scrap of wood. In those days on Cape Cod, wood was both scarce and valuable. People comb the beaches today for sea-polished driftwood with which they make table lamps.

If the hiker climbs the dunes and cuts inland about three miles north of Head of the Meadow Beach, he will come to an immense desert of sand which separates the Atlantic Ocean from Pilgrim Lake. Here, at dusk, a blanket of gray and white settles on the sand when the gulls return for the night. South of the lake and just over the dunes from the beach, Pilgrim Springs is hidden among the rolling grass-covered moors.

Water for Pilgrims

This historic point is hard to find because the small tablet, which marks the site where the Pilgrims first drank water in the New World, is partly obscured by foliage.

Perhaps the best hike on the entire shore is the vast wilderness of dunes at Race Point, west of Provincetown. Here, the hiker may wander in splendid isolation except for an occasional passing beach buggy filled with sight-seers.

The walk might start at the Coast Guard station, following the wide dune-backed beach for about two miles to Race Point Light. At almost any point, a short climb to the top of the dunes will offer an excellent view of airplanes taking off from the runway of Provincetown airport. In the distance over miles of dunes and scrub pines, the top of Pilgrim Monument rises above the village of Provincetown.

In these great inland hills of sand, where the roar of the sea is barely a murmur, beach grass holds sway atop the dunes and, along with scattered clumps of beach plum, helps keep Cape Cod from blowing away altogether.

Herons and Yellowlegs

Near the lighthouse, the tide comes in slowly, flooding the salt marshes and sand flats. Here, great blue herons stalk fish and yellowlegs probe the wet sand for food. In this area, a little digging between the dunes will often reveal sun-bleached whale bones.

Monomoy Island also is a rewarding place for a one-day hike, although it is south of the area that might be called "Thoreau's Cape Cod." Monomoy is a National Wildlife Refuge, one of the best places on the Atlantic coast to see birds. Some 300 species, including the rare curlew sandpiper, have been identified here.

When one finally leaves the Great Outer Beach, chances are that, like the Yankee from Concord, one will return home with the sea's roar in one's ears and a "gill of sand" in one's shoes.

October 11, 1959

DARTMOUTH'S MOUNTAIN

WARREN, N. H.—In late June the last of the Winter snows on Mount Moosilauke disappear, the long frost feathers on the summit house melt and the four-man crew of Dartmouth undergraduates have things ready for another season of guests.

The summit house on Moosilauke is situated at an altitude of 4,811 feet, where it has withstood Winter storms for eighty-one years. It is believed to be the oldest standing summit house in the United States, being first opened to the public on July 4, 1860. Extensive improvements and additions have been made over the years, but most of the original house remains. It was built to accommodate twenty-five people and was constructed mostly of rock, with four-foot-thick walls. Today more than eighty people can be taken care of comfortably.

Since 1920 the summit house has been operated by the Dartmouth Outing Club and kept open from June 15 to Sept. 10 for mountain climbers and people wanting to get away from the noise and crowds of the cities. A quiet, comfortable night on the top of Moosilauke is an unforgettable experience. Games

are played outside till dark, and after the sun has set there are songs and a square dance or polka. On stormy nights, with the wind tearing at the eaves and windows, the guests can stretch out in front of the living-room fire with the lights out and listen to a symphony.

Moosilauke is forty miles north of Hanover, N. H., where Dartmouth is situated, and the summit can be reached only by climbing one of the three well-marked trails. Beaver Brook Trail is four and a half miles long and is the most difficult. It starts at Lost River Reservation, taking the climbers up cascades, over wooden ladders, through stands of birch and pine. Another trail leaves the little town of Glencliff and goes up by gradual ascent from 1,200 feet at the start to 4,811 feet at the top. The other trail is Hell's Highway, an old ski trail starting from Ravine Camp, a Winter headquarters for skiers. This offers the climber a precipitous slope and wide views.

June 8, 1941

CITY GIRL ALONE ON A MOUNTAIN TRAIL

By FLORENCE TEETS

I HAVE friends who like hiking. They return from vacations with faces brown, muscles hard, eyes clear. In hearty voices they say: "Walking is the best way to see the world. You meet fine people. You get close to God." Observing my disinterest, they add calculatingly: "It's the cheapest kind of vacation."

This summer I studied their maps, looked at their pictures, read their books, remembered Thoreau. Then I boarded a bus for New Hampshire. I should have known better. For years I have been carrying on a one-sided love affair with nature; the two of us have never reached an understanding. Nature doesn't cooperate.

Breathing deeply of flower-scented air starts my nose running, my eyes watering, my sinus tickling. Merely passing a roadside festooned with poison ivy assures the immediate use of my hospital insurance.

But going to New Hampshire was to be different. The travel booklet said the air was free of pollen and there was no three-leaved ivy. Another leaflet assured me that "the Trail leads not merely north and south but upward to the body, mind and soul of man," and furthermore that it was "fairly difficult for anyone to lose his way since the trail is well marked."

With a pack on my back, two pair of wool socks on my feet, and a grim determination to like climbing mountains, I started from Franconia down the Appalachian Trail, a wooded path which from beginning to end covers some 2,050 miles from Maine to Georgia. I had no idea of covering it all—just a conservative 200 miles. From Franconia I started southward under the stony, sardonic faces of the Old Man of the Mountain and

Indian Head.

Too Tired for Advice

After the first day on the trail I was too tired to listen to the tales of other hikers who gathered in the hut. The muscles of my legs and the bottoms of my feet protested that they were not meant for prowling in the woods.

The next morning, of course, dawned beautiful and clear. Soon after 9 I started across the hills to Kinsman's Notch, resting place of Lost River. About noon dark ominous clouds rolled out of the mountains. It poured. Now, one of the attractions of the Appalachian Trial (Trail, that is), is that no public highway is within a mile of it. In consequence, there are very few buildings near by, and in a storm the only shelters are the trees, which are sieves. Drenched and weary, I sloshed along the muddy passes over slippery rocks, trying hard to remember some useful philosophy pertaining to rain.

For some reason, all that I seemed to be able to recall were pieces written by folk who, sitting by a fire, looked out upon a rain-splashed world.

Mountain Climbing

The next day I went up Mount Moosilake and then down the other side. I saw frogs, snakes, deer, birds, and other hikers, who told me they had seen bear. Even though I stubbed my toe crawling over an old stone fence, bruised my knee on a hidden rock, and wore out leg muscles I didn't know I had, I was happy. At last I was getting close to nature.

At 8 the next morning I hit the trail out of Glencliff. For an hour I swung happily along a winding, shaded path through birch and maple wood. I picked a handful of blueberries. I passed a pond where frogs croaked and birds sang. As I listened I thought I overheard a conversation between the trees. I stretched out on a great rock and

for the first time in my life, "held communion" with nature.

After this short service, I shouldered my pack and continued along the narrow path. Strange, I thought, how narrow it was becoming. Maybe fewer hikers came this way. I slowed my pace and began to worry. It had been a long time since the last trail marker. The path was not only hard to follow, but was becoming wetter underfoot and the undergrowth higher. Still I plodded on.

Suddenly in the middle of a briar patch, the trail stopped abruptly but conclusively. Now Br'er Rabbit could not have been one-tenth as irritated at that tar baby as I was at the Appalachian Trail. I looked, I searched, but it availed me not. After half an hour I admitted I was lost. The woods were behind and in front of me; a thicket of raspberry bushes surrounded me. Across the patch of bushes, I reasoned, the trail was sure to start again.

Marshy Ground

I tried to cross but no barbed-wire entanglement could have been a more effective obstacle to progress. The ground was marshy, and mud oozed around my ankles. Here and there large rocks lay hidden to be stumbled over. For what seemed hours I pushed aside the thorny whips and finally reached the far woods. I was hot and tired, scratched and bruised. My body ached and my face burned. I hated the woods, despised the bushes, and disliked the sun.

I reviewed every "lost in the woods" story I had ever heard or read. I remembered only the peril of "walking in a circle." I was singularly ill-equipped not to do just that. I had no compass.

However, after a meager lunch of berries and a chocolate bar, my search for the trail began again. For one, two, three hours I pursued my quest. I studied the map, and then I looked at the woods. I fell down in unexpected holes, under rotted foliage; I clambered over great trunks of fallen trees. I broke off branches and stamped down the thick undergrowth. I perspired and grew thirsty. Tears threatened once or twice but "crying in the wilderness" somehow seemed ludicrous. I entered another marsh and tangled with more berry bushes. With every pea-sized fruit I garnered, the bush rewarded me with a three-inch scratch. No mother cat could have been so vicious as those thorny bushes.

Thoughts of Home

Again I found a rock and again I rested. I thought longingly of Fifty-second Street and wondered if I would see it ever again. Nature had turned on me again. The enchantment of the forest was gone. I cursed the brambles, the bushes, the trees, and the Trail. Night was not far off, and I had no desire to spend it on a bed of pine needles. Indeed I was most anxious not to. Morale was low.

At this precise point I observed that cattle had recently been in the vicinity. Slowly, carefully, eagerly I followed the winding, crooked path of the cows. Gradually the thicket thinned; an opening appeared, a pasture, and finally a road. I flagged down a passing truck and begged a ride to the nearest town.

"Where you headed for?" the driver, the local breadman, asked as he curiously surveyed my torn slacks, my scratched arms and straggly hair.

"New York," I replied quickly, "as fast as I can get there."

I know with the futility of a discarded lover that come next spring, and as surely as June follows May, a strange compulsion will stir within me. The old affair will begin again. I shall probably lose again.

September 10, 1950

SCALING MT. WASHINGTON

By NATHANIEL NITKIN

MOUNT WASHINGTON, towering 6,288 feet above sea level, the highest mountain east of the Mississippi and north of North Carolina, offers a challenge to countless New Yorkers, who have been preparing for an assault on its summit by hardening their muscles on the lesser mountains within reach of the metropolis.

There is every reason why a veteran hiker should be proud of including this majestic giant in his list of peaks climbed. Of the Appalachians, Mount Washington has the most interesting personality. It cannot be scaled with impunity. Its moods are unpredictable; at one moment calm and smiling, at another raging and bellowing. Woe betide the careless mountaineer caught during this mountain's spasm of fury.

The Appalachian Mountain Club has done its best to warn all would-be climbers of Mount Washington of the risks involved. In fact, since Darby Field and two Indians scaled it in 1642, the mountain has claimed many lives.

Storms on the Slopes

During Summer and early Autumn Mount Washington is reasonably safe for hikers who have passed the novice stage. The long periods of good weather help a great deal. However, even on the hottest days a storm on Mount Washington means ice-covered crags and slopes, heavy clouds that stifle the climber, and severe attacks of mountain lassitude. Suppose the climber reaches the summit on a fine day and is trapped by a thunderstorm. In this case, the Tip-top House on the crest is a refuge worth more than its weight in gold.

This mountain is not easy to climb. Deep ravines are met on all its sides. About 5,000 to 5,500 feet above them are comparatively level stretches, landmarks for climbers. Climbers rest here before the final assault up rock-strewn cones, exceedingly dangerous when covered with ice or water. The summit offers the most sublime view of the White Mountains of New Hampshire and a part of Southern Maine.

To go to the mountain from New York one should have three days at

Mt. Washington roads and trails.

one's disposal. The proper base of operations is Jackson, N. H., although Bretton Woods and Randolph are also close. Trains and bus lines serve these vicinities. The motorist has only to follow Route U. S. 1 to Portsmouth, N. H., and turn northwest on Route 16 to Jackson.

The trails to Mount Washington start at Pinkham Notch Camp, ten miles northwest of Jackson along Route 16. The one recommended to all except really expert alpinists is the Tuckerman Trail, which is doubly interesting because it passes a glacial cirque.

From Pinkham Notch Camp this trail rises by easy grades at first. The first landmark reached is Crystal Cascade, a photographer's paradise. From here, the trail crosses the Raymond Path, perhaps the handiest side trail in this district. The hiker who feels any trace of lassitude, or any threat in the weather, may abandon his original plan of assault and follow the Raymond Path to Glen House for a rest or wait.

On to the Summit

From its junction with Raymond Path the trail circles Hermit Lake and takes one into Snow Arch, the first real danger spot. Any trace of snow here should be considered with a great deal of respect, for a slip at this stage is no joke.

The next phase is the summit. The total distance is about five miles, but it takes a husky mountaineer four and a half hours to complete it.

Then comes the return trip. The total time for both ascent and descent is approximately nine hours.

While the Tuckerman Trail is the easiest and most convenient of all paths, one cannot know Mount Washington until one has tried others also. The most difficult, and exceedingly dangerous, is the Huntingdon Ravine Trail. Maps of the trails may be procured from the Appalachian Mountain Club.

August 4, 1940

'Hi! Hi! Hi, There! Hi, There!'

By WALTER SULLIVAN

MOUNT WASHINGTON, N. H.—"Hello!" said the cheery young lad who, like the dozen or more who had preceded him down the trail, wore a shirt emblazoned "Camp Mugawumpit" or the like.

"Hi!" I gasped, picking my way up the rocky trail into Tuckerman's Ravine. It is a tradition of the mountains that you cannot pass anyone on the trail without a friendly greeting.

This was the fifth camp group that my daughter and I had encountered as we lugged our packs up toward Mount Washington, and, since each child had been extremely polite, I had learned that saying "Hi!" between puffs was more economical of breath than saying "Good morning," or some other elaborate greeting.

But when the sixth contingent appeared, green-sweatered and bouncing with youth and downhill exuberance, I called to Cathy, by dint of special effort, "I'm going to make a sign that says 'Hi' and carry it."

Troops in Formation

Apparently, the counselors leading this tribe heard me, for they passed in grinning silence, although trailed by a succession of gay "Hi's" like troops numbering off in formation.

Despite these and other gentle hazards, my daughter and I reached the crest of the precipitous headwall of Tuckerman's Ravine. This ravine is a classic "cirque"—an amphitheater carved by ice at the head of a glacier-filled valley — and it is a relic of the Ice Age.

A few white rocks at the foot of the headwall proved to be chunks of ice left from the lethal avalanches of last spring. Plaques on nearby rocks commemorated some who had died in such plunges of ice from the headwall.

The summit of Mount Washington was in clouds that licked over the saddle above the ravine. A Forest Service ranger, coming down the trail, warned us not to try for the summit. Instead, we crossed the rock-strewn alpine meadows of the saddle and descended to the Lakes-of-the-Clouds hut which, true to its name, faded from sight every now and then as the clouds blew a bit lower in their sweep over the saddle.

Too Much Noise

When we entered the hut, which is maintained by the Appalachian Mountain Club, I wondered whether or not it might, in fact, be called "Bedlam-in-the-Clouds." Several contingents of campers had arrived, by prearrangement, to spend the night, and the noise level, after the windy serenity outside, was frightening to an adult hopeful of peaceful recovery from tired muscles and sore feet.

The A.M.C. huts along the Presidential Range of the White Mountains tolerate the old, but are geared for the young. Overnighting in one is the highlight of the summer for countless camp girls. Why? Because of the hut boys.

These lads, who run the huts, are largely of college age. They are deliciously glamorous in the eyes of girls in their early teens, and the boys respond with antics that are sophomoric, sometimes hair-raising, and delightful once you get in tune.

The level of the humor is reflected in signs that adorn the walls. In the Tuckerman hut it says, by the door:

"Due to Circumstances Beyond Our Control The World Will Not End Tomorrow.
Thank You
The Management."

The chief performer of the five or six hut boys at the Lakes-of-the-Clouds exercised a studiously carefree manner emphasized by a rather scruffy moustache. He rang a hand-bell for each announcement, bringing brief surcease to the din.

When newly baked gingerbread was passed out at the long tables, he announced there was a cherry inside one piece. The girl who found it, he said, would be allowed to kiss the hut master, and help wash the dishes. There was a bedlam of squeals from the girls, and so many of them washed

dishes later that it was impossible to determine how many of them had won the cherished prizes.

Quiet, But Cold

With lights out and everyone in their bunks (three tiers high for the boys, four tiers high for the girls) it became reasonably quiet, although frigid for those with only two heavy blankets. After breakfast, we started down the mountain before the predicted thunderstorms. It rained much of the way, but we did not mind.

We paused in the Tuckerman hut, where the signs, as up on the mountain, are signed "Da Croo," but at least one is in a serious vein. It is a nostalgic quotation from Henry David Thoreau:

"In the Wilderness is the preservation of the world.

Thank God men have not yet learned to fly, so they can lay waste the sky as well as the earth."

September 1, 1968

Up Mount Washington on Foot

By ALAN JON FORTNEY

TWIN MOUNTAIN, N. H.—Although a great deal of attention is focused on the cog railway and its 100 years of crawling to the top of Mount Washington, it must be remembered that there is another way to get to the top. That is to walk. This, too, is a tradition of long standing.

The first white man to climb to the top of this 6,293-foot peak, the largest in the Presidential Range, did so 327 years ago. And because the range is an old one by geological standards, its time-worn surface is smooth enough to offer a good, but not overwhelming, challenge to the ordinary fresh-air enthusiast.

At Base Station, where the cog railway begins its rack-and-pinion climb to the top, there is a pleasant store that sells, among other things, a detailed map of White Mountain National Forest. The 724,000-acre forest contains most of New England's highest peaks and the greatest number of foot trails to be found in the country.

The map details the trails to the top of Mount Washington, as well as all the elevations, rivulets and mountain huts, and other information necessary for the climb.

The land around Base Station, also called Marsh-Field, is rich with red spruce trees and seems very tame indeed. The beginning of the trail looks, at least for a few hundred feet, like a setting for a quiet stroll in a forest.

Mass of Age-Worn Granite

And, from that same vantage, Mount Washington looks green with vegetation to the summit. But on second appraisal, it becomes obvious that the color comes from rocks covered with green lichen, and that the old peak rises stolidly above timberline. It is a huge, forbidding mass of age-worn granite, and, through the 10-cents-a-glance telescopes, the fragile thread of a trail winds crazily around these rocks and fades from view.

Even though the mountain looks very calm and quiet and the first part of the Ammonoosuc Ravine Trail looks positively subdued, as we set out about 10 A. M. we saw a sign bearing a grave warning to the amateur alpinist that he must be "in top physical condition, well clothed and carrying extra clothing and food. Many have died above timberline from exposure. Turn back at the first sign of bad weather."

It gives one pause. Not much pause, because the area is warm, the trees are friendly looking and the idea that

OVER THE AMMONOOSUC—Railway is laid out on a three-mile trestle up to the top of Mount Washington.

147

anything untoward could happen seems remote.

On we went, undaunted. Barely on our way, we saw another sign commanding: "Stop! This area has the worst weather in America. Many have died from exposure. Do not continue unless you are well clothed and willing to turn back at the first sign of bad weather."

My two companions knew the mountain, and I took it as a matter of course that the signs were for someone else. We were prepared for a two-day hike with the necessary clothing and food and, we assumed, the good sense these signs recommended.

We proceeded up the Ammonoosuc Ravine Trail, one in the network maintained by the Appalachian Mountain Club. We knew from the map that, in the next 2.4 miles, we would rise about 2,500 feet. On the map, it appeared to be a humble achievement.

But after we had gone less than halfway, I noticed a small plaque designed to reaffirm whatever fears were aroused by the first signs. It read: "In memory of Herbert Judson Young, 32, who died near this spot, Dec. 1, 1926. Dartmouth Outing Club."

The trail had not yet got very rough, but somehow signs like that tend to inspire respect for the old mountain. Ammonoosuc Creek tumbled over rocks and through moss on its way down the mountain, and the memory of the forest primeval just below was still too fresh to imagine life and death struggles in this area.

A little farther up the trail is a restful pool fed by a tall slip of waterfall—a thread of white mountain water filling the small pit in the rocks. It is a good place to sit and rest, for just beyond this the climb begins to get steeper and the going rougher. Even though the temperature at Marsh-Field was in the 70's, the water seemed chilled, almost frosted.

About two hours had passed by the time we broke through timber. I turned and saw the valleys that dipped between the dozens of peaks visible in the Presidential Range.

On another flank of the mountain, the cog railway train was visible, puffing white smoke and crawling up the side of the mountain like a small wheezing ant slowly pushing a miniature car ahead of it. It let out a scream on its whistle that rolled over the distance ages after the sharp spear of steam had shot out from the proud brass whistle itself.

From our place above timber, about a mile from the track, we felt a twinge of superiority to those riding to the top. As we walked on, we came to a small

sign from which the wind had erased whatever it once said, a wordless tribute to the effects of weather at this elevation.

From this point on to the Lakes of the Clouds (elevation: 5,000 feet), it was an easy walk among the lichen-covered boulders. The climb to the top from there was really a little more than a slightly graded path. There is little danger there except for sudden changes of weather, which are hard to prepare for.

The hut at the Lakes of the Clouds offers what is described as "mountain hospitality," which means a bunk, breakfast, lunch and dinner and protection from the weather. The capacity of the block-cement house is about 90 persons. It is a good place to rest and buy a cup of coffee, which is refreshing because it is steaming hot.

After resting, we walked the last mile and one-half to the summit by way of Crawford Path. By keeping a regular pace, we were scarcely winded when we arrived on top, where the passengers from the cog railway were milling around and looking at the incredible panorama of peaks. Each train takes an hour to get there and an hour back down, and gives the passengers an hour at the top to visit the weather station, the museum and Summit House, which serves hot coffee to the rugged alpinists and the railway passengers.

After we had reached the top, we discovered there is a road that climbs there from the other side. The only romance about this toll road is that it was once a stagecoach run to the top.

After about an hour at summit, we walked down the other side of the mountain to Pinkham Notch Ravine (elevation: 2,032 feet), which is situated in a mountain valley facing a glacial cirque called Tuckerman's Ravine.

We had taken our time—about four hours—getting to the summit. Another two hours brought us to the valley camp, where we threw out sleeping bags in a three-sided shelter and spent the night.

The following morning, it was a surprising sight to see hikers walking off toward the ravine—hikers looking for all the world like hikers, except for the skis bristling from their knapsacks.

Pinkham Notch Camp, at the entrance to the Tuckerman Ridge Trail, is the headquarters of the Appalachian Mountain Club's huts system; it is on State Route 16, 11 miles north of Jackson. The system consists of eight huts situated a day's hike apart all over the national forest. The huts are manned by students

who bring supplies in on their backs, cook all the meals and do the general caretaking. They work 11 days on and three days off during the summer.

After spending the night in Pinkham Notch, we crawled up the steep wall of the valley. About a half-hour of this was done on hands and knees over rocks and trees, and this was the only part of the climb that felt as if we were "climbing a mountain."

We hiked over the alpine-like meadows at our leisure and returned to Base Station by mid-afternoon, a day and one-half after we had set out. All the signs had been only warnings, not premonitions; we had had no mishaps. As we packed our gear in the back of the car, the cog railway train let out a blast on its whistle. One of my companions turned and asked, "How can you get to know a mountain *that* way?"

July 20, 1969

MT. WASHINGTON CLIMB MADE BY 1-LEGGED MAN

Scales Heights in Normal Time of 4 Hours 15 Minutes.

Special to The New York Times.
MOUNT WASHINGTON, N. H., Aug. 7.—R. E. Welch, one-legged station agent of the Boston & Maine Railway at Northumberland, N. H., realized his boyhood dream today, making successfully and in normal time the difficult ascent of Mount Washington by way of the trackside of the cogwheel railway. He started from the base. The ascent was made in 4 hours 15 minutes.

After a short rest and luncheon, he started down the mountain by way of the carriage road, eight and one-half miles to the Glen House, whence he will return to Northumberland.

Welch had been in training for the event for some time, and the feat marks the climax in the career of a man who, despite his physical handicaps, learned to swim, skate and ride a bicycle.

He seemed none the worse for his accomplishment. The descent was fairly easy over the well-kept road. He was accompanied by his brother, F. E. Welch; Arthur Young, K. J. Unwin of Schenectady, N. Y., his trainer, and G. W. Parkus.

President Henry M. Teague of the Mount Washington railway and Myron C. Witham of the Mount Washington Club welcomed the party and entertained them at dinner.

Welch's walking time was 3 hours 11 minutes, the remaining time being devoted to rest. The average time taken by a normal man to climb the mountain, which rises to an elevation of 6,288 feet, is four hours.

August 8, 1932

Mountains Are For Climbing

By CRAIG R. WHITNEY

TRAVELING by car in surroundings of natural beauty and wildness, as in the mountains of northern Maine, often boils down to stopping now and then for a fresh stock of picture postcards that, in later days, serve only to remind the traveler of what he didn't get to see when he had the chance.

On a hiking trip, however, the traveler knows precisely where he started, how far he went, what the route felt like and smelled like a d who had gone along it before. He knows the scene as no guide-book can tell it.

It is possible to drive across the State of Maine in about six hours, but then the whole state boils down to "six hours," the mountains in it to only a few hours out of the six, and the greatest and wildest of all, 5,267-foot Mount Katahdin, to only a half-hour, or just before the motel in Millinocket.

And Forever

Mountains exist not only in time, but through all time. And they exist in space, in legend and in the lives of all living creatures in the wilderness they rule.

The automobile roads stop three or four miles from the enormous rampart wall of Mount Katahdin, in Baxter State Park; they are narrow gravel routes that really belong to the deer, moose and bear that roam the mountain's mile-high slopes.

From Oct. 15 to May 15, they roam virtually unseen by humans, for the park is closed then. But if the snow is not too heavy, guides are available for hikers who want to chance the mountain during the off season.

In any season, it is humbling for the soft city-dweller to come to the end of a road, look up at the summit, blue and bare in the mists of dawn, and realize that the top is five miles away, including a climb of more than 4,000 vertical feet.

Up and Down

It is a challenge, a test in a strange environment full of beauty, but anyone in average physical condition—that is, overweight and short-winded—can cover the distance in five hours going up, three hours coming down. Up or down, the trip is never worse than strenuous.

The ascent begins easily enough on the Appalachian Trail, penetrating the dark forest along the course of the Katahdin Stream and more or less on the level.

At first, the stream is a guide flowing straight from the mountain slope. Then the trail goes its own way; the hiker and the stream part company, and the noise of the watercourse is lost in the stillness of the woods.

Native Sounds

The silence is broken only by the scrabbling and crunching sounds of the rocks underfoot; occasionally, an angry tree-squirrel will make itself heard to let the intruder know whose woods these are.

Then there is a soft and distant rushing, more permanent than a sudden wind in the trees. With every step, it grows louder and deeper and more comforting. The bass roar is lightened by treble splashes as the trail approaches and crosses O-Joy Brook into the empty wastes above the treeline.

Even up there, the hiker can hear the water thousands of feet below. If he strays off the trail, he is never lost so long as he can follow the sound to the big stream or any of the smaller ones. For the streams lead to the Penobscot River, and the Penobscot leads to civilization.

Beyond the stream, beyond the fragrance of the stands of balsam fir, the going becomes steeper and tougher on the boulder fields above the timberline. The country mile becomes a real and exquisite torture.

Aching Ascent

The soft body has probably forgotten why it was made with sinew and muscle. It protests when the hiker asks it to haul him up almost 4,200 feet — and decidedly "up" it is. Soon, it demands a rest every few yards.

"Who gives you your orders anyway? Move on!" the impatient hiker commands.

But the flesh has a will of its own and stands fast. Fortunately, nature has been understanding; it has provided delicious little blueberries and mountain cranberries along the way

It is painful for a while, perhaps, this reminder of mortal weakness among those awesome boulders and soaring cliffs. The hiker looks up, hoping the weather will not change from hot to sweeping fog or even snow, as it can in these parts.

But the trail is worth enduring to the end. The view from the summit of Katahdin is extra rewarding because it has taken so much toil to get there.

In one trip I took in the rain, the clouds lifted for just an instant as I reached the top. As if in an apparition, I saw the whole spectacular range of surrounding mountains, the lakes and trees far below. Then the clouds closed again, swift and solid.

Nature had suffered me for a moment on her own ground, and then said, "Go, you do not belong here."

But the real meaning of the hike goes beyond the sight from the top. The real meaning is in going there, through nature as she has been since life began and as nature meant mortals to go.

In Thoreau's Words

In 1846, Thoreau climbed Katahdin, the same then as it is now, and he exulted in these words:

"Talk of mysteries. Think of our life in nature . . . rocks, trees, wind on our cheeks! the *solid* earth! the *actual* world! the *common sense!* Contact! Contact!* Who are we? *Where* are we?"

This contact is with the rugged, powerful nature from which Americans have spent 200 years trying to isolate themselves with cities and automobiles and plastic-packaged foods. But the wilderness is the elemental fact of this country.

Travel has always been a test, and to move through the mountains this way today can be a revealing test of one's own power and importance and will.

A mountain is nature at her most spectacular, a monument raised by elemental forces to themselves, ceaselessly being beaten down, eroded, weathered, its face gashed by slides, but softened and salvaged in the end by the green and fragrant mantle of the forest.

The grandeur of nature's efforts, even in these ancient mountains of the Northeast, is symbolic of our own. Nature is the best teacher and, to learn her lesson, one must walk with her.

April 14, 1968

South From New York

Inn Snubs 'Tramps': Udall and 2 Douglases

Sodden Hikers Given Scant Welcome by Proprietor's Wife

By The Associated Press.

WASHINGTON, May 7—"I run this place to make money, not to serve tramps!"

That was the forthright summary a woman innkeeper hurled at a bunch of drenched hikers yesterday—and her targets included Supreme Court Justice William O. Douglas, Senator Paul H. Douglas, Democrat of Illinois, and Secretary of the Interior Stewart L. Udall.

The hikers, about 170 strong, were nearing the end of a sodden, sixteen-mile course along the old C. & O. Canal route from Seneca, Md., to Washington when they stopped at the Old Anglers Inn near the Great Falls of the Potomac.

Justice Douglas and Mrs. Douglas were among the first arrivals and Senator Douglas led another group in a little later. Soon the inn was packed with dripping nature-lovers, many unwrapping lunches and ordering beverages.

Mrs. John T. Reges, wife of the proprietor, came down the stairs and expressed her general position. Then she leveled a finger at Senator Douglas and cried "Get off that rug! Get over there with the rest of the wet ones." The tall, gray-haired Senator meekly complied.

When told whom she had been ordering around, Mrs. Reges pointed at the puddles on the floor and demanded:

"Well, is he going to clean up the mess you make?"

Having tended to the judicial and legislative arms of government, the blunt-spoken hostess next confronted the administrative branch in the person of Secretary Udall as he started to enter the inn. Said she:

"You look like a bum. Get out!"

As soon as Mr. Udall realized

United Press International Radiophoto

Justice William O. Douglas, left, Secretary of the Interior Stewart L. Udall, center, and Senator Paul H. Douglas of Illinois pause during hike along the old C. & O. Canal.

the irate woman was not joking, he withdrew—and ate his lunch outside in the drizzle.

Mrs. Reges was a little shaken by it all when she learned more about her unwelcome guests but defended her position, contending the hikers were making a sodden shambles of her place—and, besides, they weren't buying very much.

Summing up, she said:

"Of course I didn't know who they were—but I'm not even sure if I care."

It was the eighth annual jaunt for the hikers. The trek marked the yearly reunion of conservationists who, in 1954, hiked from Cumberland, Md., to Washington as a protest against a proposal to build a highway along the historic Chesapeake and Ohio Canal.

Now organized as the C. & O. Canal Association, the group is supporting a move to designate the Canal area as a national park.

May 8, 1961

All Quiet Where Guns Once Roared at Bull Run

By VICTOR BLOCK

CENTREVILLE, Va.—The newly completed eight-mile Bull Run Nature Trail is not only a delight for nature lovers but also an introduction to one of the most important battle sites of the Civil War. The trail, marked by swatches of blue paint on trees, follows the banks of meandering Bull Run. It was in this riverside battle that overconfident Union troops broke ranks and fled in humiliating defeat instead of achieving the victory that might have brought an early end to the war.

The nature trail is part of 2,225-acre Bull Run Regional Park, which is near Manassas National Battlefield Park and which is being developed by the Northern Virginia Regional Park Authority. Land acquisition, continuing over the past 10 years, has cost a total of $1.9 million. Plans call for extending the nature trail about three more miles, to a point near the confluence of Bull Run and Occoquan Creek.

The eight miles of completed pathway afford a comfortably paced hike requiring about four hours. Most of the way is easy walking, although there is an occasional climb over shale bluffs or a squeeze around and under an overhanging rock formation.

Birds, Beasts and Bass

The animal and bird watching and the display of Virginia wildflowers are enough to make the hike worthwhile. A recent hiker raised a covey of quail and also spotted a pair of kingfishers noisily flitting along Bull Run. Perch and bass are abundant in the stream.

Visitors who are primarily interested in the historical aspects of Bull Run Nature Trail still have to keep a sharp lookout for landmarks. Plans for the erection of information signs along the trail have not yet materialized.

As the hiker follows the trail eastward from its marked starting point in Bull Run Regional Park, he encounters the spot where the Old Centreville Road (now State Route 616) crosses Bull Run. Nearby is the site of Mitchell's Ford.

About 500 yards west of the Route 616 bridge and an equal distance north of the stream bank are traces of the bed of the first railroad ever built exclusively for military purposes. The military supply railroad, running from Manassas almost to Centreville, was constructed by Confederate troops as a means of bringing supplies and men toward the northernmost front lines.

Newly completed Nature Trail near the Virginia battlefield.

Photograph by WARREN MATTOX

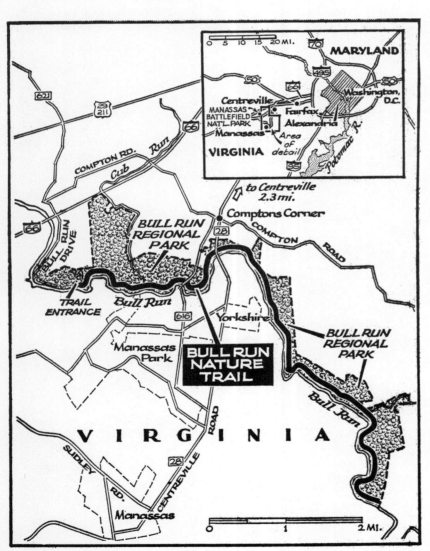

Shallow Trench

Crossing over to the southern shore of Bull Run by means of the bridge along Route 616, the hiker finds remnants of trenches—now only about three feet deep as a result of mudslides and filling—that were hastily dug by Southern soldiers bracing for the expected attack by the Union Army.

It was in this area and at the next bridge along the trail that the first fighting flared on July 18, 1861, in the First Battle of Bull Run (called First Manassas by the Confederates), with Northern troops being repulsed. While the major battle took place three days later and several miles to the west, at the site of what today is Manassas National Battlefield Park, this initial skirmish helped pave the way for the unexpected Union defeat by undermining the Northern troops' confidence in their numerical and tactical superiority.

Continuing eastward, the next historical landmark is the spot where Bull Run crosses under the Route 28 bridge. About 50 feet east of this bridge is the site of Blackburn's Ford.

Nearby, in a field along the north bank of Bull Run, the hiker can see the well-preserved embankments of an earthwork fort erected by Union soldiers between July 18 and 21, 1861, as part of their defense perimeter.

In the Mind's Eye

Gently rolling fields of flowers and the babbling stream are welcome sights and sounds along the trail. The history-minded need only let imagination wander a bit to envision the smoke of cannon and muskets fired across the water, or to hear the cry, as troops of Gen. Thomas J. Jackson withstood the blistering Northern onslaught, "There is Jackson standing like a stone wall."

To reach the starting point of Bull Run Nature Trail, drive westward into Virginia from Exit 9 of the Capitol Beltway on Interstate 66. Turn off at the Centreville or Route 28 exit and pick up U.S. 29-211. Drive west for about two miles, turn left onto Route 621 at the sign to Bull Run Regional Park and follow the dirt road to the last parking lot; this is adjacent to the marked starting point of the trail.

Since no cold drink or hot dog stands have been erected to intrude upon this stroll back into history, hikers departing near lunchtime would be wise to carry a beverage and a light snack.

May 18, 1969

A WALK IN SHENANDOAH PARK

By JOHN T. STARR

FRONT ROYAL, Va. — The 105-mile-long Skyline Drive along the crest of the Blue Ridge Mountains can be negotiated by car in little more than three hours. However, the way to get close to this picturesque part of Shenandoah National Park, and see it at its best, is to park the car and begin hiking.

The Appalachian Trail, which also follows the crest of the Blue Ridge through this part of Virginia, crosses and recrosses the Skyline Drive. There are a number of overlooks along the drive, including some near the trail itself, and there are places to leave the car and get out into the woods.

There are more than 100 miles of trails in addition to the 94-mile stretch of the Appalachian Trail. They reach up to some of the highest peaks in this part of the park, and down to the deep valleys into which the Blue Ridge's waterfalls tumble. One trail goes through a bit of primeval forest, while another dips into an upland swamp. Several are easy-going "nature" trails, and others are more demanding and rugged.

Mountaintop Resort

A good base of operations for hiking is Skyland, 10 miles south of Panorama, where U.S. 211 crosses the Skyline Drive. The Virginia Sky-Line Company, operating under a concession from the National Park Service, has developed a mountaintop resort there. It can accommodate 350 guests.

The Stony Man Mountain Trail is about a 10-minute walk from Skyland. This is a "self-guiding" trail; that is, the things of special interest along the way are marked with small numerals that refer to corresponding descriptions in the guidebook published by the Shenandoah Natural History Association.

This is an easy trail, and it leads to the top of Stony Man Mountain, one of the highest points in the park. The three-quarter-mile-long trail starts at an elevation of 3,680 feet and rises to the

National Park Service

DEEP WOODS—Foliage obscures hiker on the trail in Shenandoah National Park.

mountain's summit, only 330 feet higher.

It leads through a typical eastern forest of red and white oak, white pine, hemlock, black locust and butternut trees. Near the top, the mountain maples almost become shrubs; at the top itself, nearer the timberline, the trees are small, dry and twisted. The magnificent Shenandoah Valley spreads out, more than 3,000 feet below.

On the other side of the Blue Ridge, and not far from Skyland, is another excellent trail, but this one goes down instead of up. It leads deep into Whiteoak Canyon, where there is a series of waterfalls,

six in all, and each of them more than 50 feet high.

But it is two and one-half miles down to the first fall and, of course, a long, hard climb back. At least a half-day should be devoted to exploring this rugged trail.

A less-strenuous trail leads to nearby Limberlost, whose grades are not difficult. The Limberlost is a grove of primeval hemlocks. Each tree is more than 400 years old and not less than three feet in diameter. The grove was named after Gene Stratton Porter's novel, "The Girl of the Limberlost."

The highest mountain in Shenandoah National Park is

Hawksbill, which rises to an elevation of 4,049 feet. There are two trails leading to the top, both starting at a parking area about four miles south of Skyland.

One of these trails takes almost two miles to rise 700 feet, while the other is a good deal steeper, taking only three-quarters of a mile to reach the mountaintop. This makes for a good circuit hike, taking the easy way up and the steep trail down.

Hawksbill Mountain is known for the view that it provides. As at Stony Man, the great wide expanse of the Shenandoah Valley is spread out below. Often in

the early morning, the valley between Hawksbill and Massanutten mountains is filled with a blanket of white clouds. In the evening, the sun sets behind Massanutten in a blaze of color.

The Big Meadows section is 10 miles south of Skyland.

There, the crest of the Blue Ridge widens into open fields in which the people who once lived in the area grazed their stock. The Virginia Sky-Line Company operates a rambling lodge there that can accommodate 200 persons.

An interesting two-mile-long trail starts near the lodge. It is a self-guiding nature trail, part of which follows the Appalachian Trail. The most fascinating part goes through the Big Meadows Swamp, which is usually lush and bedecked with flowers.

The Potomac Appalachian Trail Club in Washington publishes a booklet, "Circuit Hikes in the Shenandoah National Park," which describes 20 hikes varying in length from three and one-half to 15 miles.

August 7, 1966

A NATURE WALK NEAR MIAMI

The Two-Mile Stretch of Lonely Beach on Key Biscayne Leads to Cape Florida Light, Is Popular With Strollers

By JACK STARK

MIAMI — Stepping back into a small area of Florida's past requires only a two-mile walk along the lower extremities of picturesque Key Biscayne to Cape Florida, with its old, abandoned lighthouse at the tip. Key Biscayne, in turn, is but a short drive from Miami and Miami Beach by way of the Rickenbacker Causeway.

Cape Florida is the oldest place-name in the United States since Cape Canaveral became Cape Kennedy. Canaveral and Cape Florida were conspicuous landmarks for explorers long before St. Augustine, North America's oldest city, was founded in 1565.

French, English and Spanish adventurers, silver-laden galleons, pirates, unscrupulous wreckers and freebooters knew the cape. In 1513, Ponce de Leon called there for fresh water and firewood for his ships sailing north from Puerto Rico. Some historians of this area assert that John Cabot sailed far enough south along this coast in 1479 to observe the cape and name it "The Cape of the End of April," as it appears on a map of 1502.

Early Visitor

The name of the key, as well as the bay that it shelters from the Atlantic, may well have been derived, it is noted hereabouts, from that of an early Spanish sea captain, a certain Vizcaino. He was shipwrecked on the cape and lived there with the Indians for several years. When he returned to Spain, he took a young son with him.

The most picturesque and, indeed, dramatic landmark at the tip of Cape Florida is the old lighthouse, which still stands there, although unused. It was erected in 1825, rising to a height of 75 feet and topped with a strong beam cast by a kerosene lantern.

It was originally built of red brick, which was floated to the site by barge, and whitewashed. The whitewash has long since worn away, so that the graceful structure has reverted to its original red color. Even today, the lighthouse is visited by thousands of people annually. This is attributed to its charming appearance, the fact that it is a natural target for any expedition down the beach and its short, but embattled and grisly history.

The old light's first ordeal occurred only 11 or 12 years after it was built. The Seminole Indians, it seems, were rising in fury against their treatment by the United States Government, which was deporting whole tribes of them to the West. After the famous Seminole chief, Osceola, rallied his forces on the mainland, numerous white settlers were murdered; also Maj Francis Dade and 100 of his troops were massacred near Ocala on Dec. 28, 1835.

Indians Attack

Trouble spread to the key in early 1836, when two vagrant whites murdered an Indian, looted his supply of furs and burned his body. Some 50 infuriated Indians from the mainland took to the warpath in canoes and started an attack on the lighthouse.

The Indians nearly caught the lighthouse-keeper, John Thompson, outside the building, but he managed to flee inside under a hail of shots. His Negro helper, called Tom, bolted the heavy wooden door behind them.

Trapped in Lighthouse

While the raiders set fire to the door, Thompson and his companion climbed the wooden stairs inside, hauling up kegs of gunpowder, muskets and water. Each was wounded by bullets as he passed open windows on the way up, and Tom collapsed near the top. Thompson, although hit several times in the feet and legs, dragged his helper to the top platform, where he died.

During the shooting, the light's supply of kerosene exploded, causing an inferno of flame. Thompson, determined "to take some Indians with him," flung an entire powder keg down the fiery shaft. It "blew" like a cannon, destroying the wooden stairs; the explosion was heard 12 miles away by the Navy schooner Motto, cruising in that area.

Thompson lay near death all that night, and most of the next day, on the iron railing circling the lantern. The blast, meantime, had extinguished the fire. The Indians, believing Thompson dead, looted and burned his nearby cottage and then departed in his sloop.

The Motto soon arrived, and the crew fired a line to the top of the tower, which Thompson secured. Two of the Motto's crew climbed up and rescued the keeper. His helper was buried near the burned-out cottage.

Restored in 1866

The lighthouse's days and excitements were by no means numbered, even then. After the Civil War, Union troops occupied the Cape for a time, and the light was restored in 1866. The worst trouble the old light then faced was from hurricanes.

A series of these storms cut away the land almost to the tower, and a seawall had to be built to keep it from toppling into the sea. But its days as an active beacon were drawing to a close.

In 1877, work was begun on a new light five miles at sea. This is a steel, spider-like tower that is clamped on Fowey Rock Reef. Fowey Light was first turned on on June 25, 1878, and the old one ashore, which had been Cape Florida's main shipping beacon for many of the preceding 53 years, was simultaneously extinguished.

Thus, for the strollers who take the two-mile hike from Crandon Park, a public facility on Key Biscayne, to Cape Florida, there is much history and melodrama to ponder as they approach the old tower. But there is also much else to note on the way.

The lonely beach is strewn with driftwood and other flotsam tossed up and changing with every tide. Even more fascinating is the plant life, some of it actually exotic, that

154

flourishes so abundantly on and near this unspoiled strand. The sea birds and other creatures of the shore also make a delightful study.

Underfoot, one discovers the three main tropic seaweeds. The air-bladder, berry-like brownish Sargassum weed that drifts along the Gulf Stream from the Sargasso Sea is blown ashore here by constant southeasterly trade winds. It piles up daily in long windrows

Mixed with it on the shore are two native types, manatee grass and turtle grass. Manatee grass is flat-bladed, one-half inch wide and jade green, with splotches of brown. It is the main sustenance of the manatee, or sea cow, now protected by law.

Turtle grass, so-called because the succulent green turtle feeds on it, is light green, round as a toothpick and stringy, with small hair roots.

Morning glories twist and twine toward the high-tide mark from the sand dunes inland. They root at each joint, and lift their delicate blooms on thick runners and grapelike leaves. Coconut palms rear themselves majestically 50 to 70 feet in the air.

The stroller also passes stands of waving sea oats on slender stalks. They resemble wheat, and offer a sharp contrast to the graceful, whispering Casuarina pines.

The pines were not here when Ponce de Leon's San Cristoval sailed past these shores. They were imported from Australia, and add protective bulwark to the dunes against the strong trade winds.

A gray ghost crab, with swiftly moving yellow legs, scuttles sideways, like a thief on the run, and darts down a hole. A plodding hermit crab lugs its heavy shell with labored effort along the weed line. Both crustaceans leave criss-cross, hemstitched patterns in the sand.

These tracks are mixed with those of shoreline sandpipers as they run along the beach and in and out of the gentle surf. Overhead, a frigate bird soars in the blue, without once moving his jet black wings; he resembles a glider with cantilever wings.

The white-and black-marked terns, with bright orange beaks, fly the rim of the surf, heads downward, to search for small fish. The larger gray sea gulls fly determined courses, slower of wing beat. And a black cormorant goes by with his long neck extended, beating into the wind.

Beach Menaces

There are three menaces to be avoided on a beach walk—a jagged plant called sandspur, which grows thickly above high tide; a plant called the puncture vine, whose bright yellow flowers conceal thorny nuts, and the huge poisonous jellyfish, the Portuguese man-of-war.

The big jellyfish is a purple-hued, gas-filled balloon that coasts along with the Gulf Stream and has tentacles sometimes 40 feet long. Even when this wretched creature has been washed ashore and has died, its tentacles can still inflict a painful sting.

January 30, 1966

A 600-Mile-Long Trail Takes Shape in Florida

By CYNTHIA MEDLEY

MIAMI—Florida is slowly losing many of its natural resources to land development because of the influx of affluent retirees. Oddly enough, one person who is trying assiduously to preserve some of the state's wilderness is a real-estate man, Jim Kern of Miami, who is president of the Florida Trail Association.

Mr. Kern loves to hike and, when he conceived the idea of a Florida Trail, he dramatized his interest by walking about 160 miles—from a point in the Everglades on U.S. 41, known also as the Tamiami Trail, to Highlands Hammock State Park, near Sebring. The resultant publicity prompted hundreds of people to send contributions to help blaze the trail.

Five-Year Plan

Eventually, the Florida Trail will wind from the Tamiami Trail to Panama City, in the northwestern part of the state, a distance of about 600 miles. It will be divided into 26 sections, each about 23 miles long. Thirteen sections have been completed or are under construction, and Mr. Kern hopes that the entire trail will be open within five years.

From its starting point in the Everglades, about 50 miles west of Miami, the trail will cross the Everglades Parkway and lead to Palmdale. It will then run along the north shore of Lake Okeechobee, pass east of Orlando to Ocala National Forest, go through Osceola National Forest and continue westward through Apalachicola National Forest before ending at Panama City, on the Gulf of Mexico.

The longest stretch available for hiking so far leads 53 miles along the banks of the Suwannee River, in the trail's northern portion; by this winter, 200 miles will have been blazed from the Clearwater Campground in Ocala National Forest to Suwannee River State Park, near Live Oak.

State Help Needed

Mr. Kern hopes that a Florida Trail bill will be passed eventually by the State Legislature so as to enable the association to acquire state right-of-way and gain assistance in maintaining the route. The trail cannot survive without state help, he says.

The sections already completed take the hiker through pine woods, cypress stands and savannas. The northern portion is a delight for bird enthusiasts in autumn, when many species are migrating to the South and are seen in flight or taking a breather in the branches of trees. The birds are also seen in spring, returning to their summer homes in the North.

Hikers can swim in the many streams and rivers that meander near the trail.

The route's first chickee, a raised platform with roof but no walls, was opened in Gold Head Branch State Park near Starke, last April. Chickees, providing a place for trekkers to store their gear and sleep off the ground, are planned at 10-mile intervals along the entire 600-mile trail.

Seasoned backpackers hike into regions where extensions of the trail are proposed to cut and clear the way. Boy Scouts are helping with this work.

When the trail crosses private property,

the owner and the association work out an oral agreement under which the owner does not charge for right-of-way in return for a pledge by the association to care for the land.

The association sponsors hikes and canoe trips. In the winter, canoeists ply waters in Everglades National Park; a summer canoe trip is held on the remote stretches of northern Florida rivers, such as the Suwannee and Oklawaha.

The association has more than 1,000

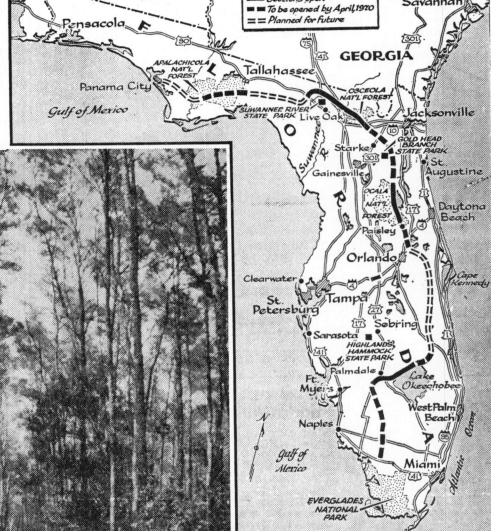

BLAZED SECTION—On trail's route in the Ocala National Forest, at left. Map shows how completed trail will stretch between Everglades and Panama City.

members, and among the topics discussed at the annual meeting each December are conservation and the preservation of the state's scenic areas.

Confident of Support

Mr. Kern believes there is tremendous support nationally for conservation, as well as support in Florida for preserving the state's natural resources. He also observed that, although backpacking and hiking have grown in popularity in other states, they have been almost unknown in Florida because of the few places to hike.

The public is invited to use the blazed sections of the trail, and anyone wishing to become a member of the association should write to its headquarters at 33 Southwest 18th Terrace, Miami, Fla. 33129.

October 12, 1969

Plantation Trails on St. John Run From 'Easy Walks to Difficult Climbs'

By DAVID BIRD

CRUZ BAY, St. John, V. I. — Mention a vacation island in the warm seas, and the first thought is of white, sandy beaches. Usually, the thought ends there, because relaxation alone is enough for most vacationists.

But there is often much more to see and do. For example, take St. John, with its network of trails that lead the visitor inland to reminders of a time when almost every inch of this mountainous island was devoted to the cultivation of sugar cane.

It is difficult to tear one's self away from the beautiful beaches here, but one has to get up and start walking inland to see much of this island, which is what two of us did one recent sunny day.

A Forest Ranger station in this small port village is the headquarters of the vast Virgin Islands National Park, which covers most of the island. There we picked up a trail map and a brochure that described numerous trails ranging from "easy walks to difficult climbs; well maintained to brushy; and short to long—a quarter-mile to six miles."

Old Sugar Mill

We settled on a trip that measured 2.6 miles from the top of a mountain peak to an abandoned sugar mill at Reef Bay, on the island's southern shore.

We started out the next morning, after first heeding the advice that we wear good hiking shoes and cool clothing. Also noted in the brochure was a warning that "water is not available along the hiking trails"; an empty rum bottle filled with water served as our canteen.

The drive to the start of the trail ended near Mamey Peak, 1,147 feet above sea level; after parking our car in a small clearing, we began our walk.

The trail was cleared, but it was so steep at times that we had to place our feet carefully; at other times, the gentle downward slope tempted us to jog along.

Trees and vines shaded the path much of the way, but often the bright sun shone on us. About a mile down the trail, we came to the first of the abandoned sugar cane plantation buildings. Only the stone side walls were standing, and trees grew from the floor and up through where the roof had been.

Indian Carvings

Further along, we came to a bisecting trail that led to the remains of the main plantation house, or, in the other direction, to the site of petroglyphs. These ancient carvings in giant rocks had been made by the Indians who lived on these islands long before the white man.

At this crossroads point, there was also a logbook maintained by the Park Service. The last signers had made their entries two days before.

We decided to continue on to the sugar mill, on the bay about a mile ahead. Large land crabs—some more than a foot wide—skittered away and took shelter in crumbling walls and foundations as we approached on the trail. They looked frightening at first, but they were apparently much more afraid of us than we of them.

Soon, we came to the mill at the water's edge. We poked around the rusting remains of the cauldrons that had been used to boil the cane juice into sugar. An old steam engine that had been used to power the machinery that squeezed the juice out of the cane had been taken over by a swarm of bees. We approached it gingerly.

It was only a few steps to the water's edge, and the beach was completely deserted. We were tempted to go for a swim, but decided against it; without a fresh-water shower afterward, the drying salt on our bodies might have made the return climb up the mountain uncomfortable.

As we looked at the water, we noticed that a large sailboat had anchored in the otherwise empty bay. The boat had lowered her dinghy and three people were heading for shore.

It was a strange sensation. They were the first people we had seen since we emerged from the "jungle," and for a moment we felt like natives waiting to greet some strange adventurers from a foreign land.

Island Cruise

We met them as they stepped ashore, and they identified themselves as the captain of the sailboat and two persons from a party of four from Harrisburg, Pa., who had chartered the boat for a two-week cruise among the islands.

They, too, were surprised to see us because the captain had said, as they pulled into the bay, that he had never encountered anyone on that beach previously.

They invited us to the sail-boat for lunch and refreshments. Two hours later, we returned to shore with renewed vigor for our return climb.

We started off at a fast pace on the fairly level trail near the water, and decided not to try an alternate route back up the mountain because it looked heavily overgrown and had a small sign warning that it was not maintained. But we did take the detour this time, and saw the petroglyphs; the strange symbols are carved into rocks bordering a stream-bed long since dried up.

Steep Climb

Returning to the main trail and heading back up the mountain, we began to be affected by the sharpening rise. We rested frequently to drink from the water bottle. Sweat poured off us and at times we stretched out flat to rest. It was late afternoon when we finally reached the road and collapsed in our car.

On Virgin Gorda, an island in the nearby British Virgins, there are interesting walks to be taken around the huge house-sized boulders that make its beaches unusual. Walking is often the only way to see the best of these formations, because coral reefs make landing a boat hazardous and roads do not run down to the water.

On Buck Island, a United States national monument just north of St. Croix, another of the Virgin Islands, inland trails are opening up the interior. So far, the main attraction of that island is an underwater trail that draws thousands to view the offshore coral reef.

November 3, 1968

Some Westward Touch-Points

DELAWARE WATER GAP HIKES

By JOHN BOHNE EHRHARDT

COLUMBIA, N. J.—A great many people have looked at a great many pictures of a New Jersey peak called Mount Tammany, but few know it by that name. Tammany is the height that forms the New Jersey wall of the Delaware Water Gap; Mount Minsi, on the Pennsylvania side of the Delaware River, is its opposite number. But for all the prominence of the Gap's two mountains in the travel folders, Tammany remains a distinct challenge to the climber. No road goes near its summit and, indeed, up to two or three years ago, the highway from Columbia to Flatbrookville was anything but inviting. Now there is good hard-top pavement at the base but Tammany's summit can only be reached by hard work afoot.

The great advantage of a go at the peak is that the way can be exactly as arduous or as simple as the hiker wishes. There are several approaches to the summit, two of them well blazed. One requires little or no skill or preparation, though any trail that rises 1,600 feet in less than two miles can consume a great deal of energy. The second blazed trail calls for a modest amount of mountaineering but is not particularly hazardous. The third trail, beaten out but unmarked, can be as difficult as the climber wishes to make it.

The simplest and easiest approach to Tammany is from the north face at a point 3.75 miles above Columbia. Dunnfield Creek passes under the road and, immediately after the bridge, the old high road to Blairstown strikes out to the right. The Kittatinny Beach Inn on the left pinpoints the junction.

The old road is passable only on foot and parallels the creek through much of its way. It has been out of use for close to 100 years but it still shows its corduroy of logs underfoot. This route is especially favored in early spring when the creek is full of water, since it provides many picturesque vistas as the stream rushes on through its deep gorge to the river.

Trails Are Only Means Of Scaling Mountain On Jersey Side

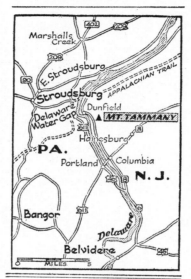

Six-tenths of a mile from the highway, the trail crosses the stream on a log bridge. The main trail (marked with white blazes) continues in the gorge to Sunfish Pond and beyond; the summit trail (marked with red and white blazes) swings right and begins the steep ascent of the mountain.

This route is a sharp climb, but the rocks are largely moss-covered, footing is secure and no particular skill is needed. Snow lingers long on the north face and can usually be found in hollows up to the middle of April. The little basins of snow contain a wealth of deer, raccoon, 'possum and fox tracks.

Near the summit, a blue-blazed (blue dot in a white field) trail swings right to the shelter of the Appalachian trail system and the lookout. This presents a view of the Water Gap from above, with the river stretching north and south. The shelter contains bunk frames for those who may wish to spend the night.

The descent may be made by the same trail, or by the blue-blazed trail down the south face

of Tammany. The blue blazes continue as far as a rock marked: "To Columbia," where the single white blaze of Appalachian main trails takes over. This route is considerably steeper than the north trail but it is not particularly dangerous. There is a 200-yard stretch of loose rock which calls for caution but no great skill.

This south face trail joins the highway about one and a half miles south of Dunnfield Creek. Those who wish to ascend by the south trail can locate its opening by the Appalachian trail insignia nailed to the tree nearest the highway.

The most difficult ascent is through the gorge of the little creek that runs just north of the south trail. This route is not blazed but it is sufficiently well beaten to be followed easily. The beginning of the ascent of the gorge is deceptively easy but the hiker soon finds himself working the sheer face of the gorge wall. In most places, the toe-holds cut by predecessors aid progress, but anyone who wants to practice rope and piton work has ample opportunity. One of the great consolations of this route is the sure knowledge that when the going becomes too arduous the main south trail can always be reached by leaving the gorge and circling a few hundred yards to the right.

In the gorge, rope-soled shoes are desirable but otherwise the only equipment needed for the climb is a pair of strong boots, preferably triple-soled. Those making the climb before mid-May should carry warm clothing. It will not be needed during the ascent, but without proper protection it is impossible to remain long among the wind-blasted trees at the summit.

Motorists from the New York area can best reach the scene by following U. S. Route 46 to the point just south of Columbia where it joins State Route 8. The latter joins the county road that leads past Tammany two blocks east of the covered bridge at Columbia. The county road is not identified in any way, but it is the only paved road northward out of Columbia. There is ample parking space along

an abandoned railroad embankment near the mouth of the south trail. At the north trail entrance, turn-outs at either side of the road will accommodate a total of six cars. Arrangements for the parking of larger parties may be made with the Kittatinny Beach Inn.

Those wishing to use public transportation may use the Delaware Water Gap bus to Portland, Pa., where a short hike across the covered bridge brings the visitor to Columbia and the road leading to the base of the mountain.

Overnight use of the shelter at the summit of Tammany is free. Those wishing hotel accommodations will find a wide range of services in Portland or at Water Gap Village, Pa., five miles to the north. Single accommodations begin at $2.50.

April 6, 1952

A Black Forest of Many Colors

By LOIS O'CONNOR

COUDERSPORT, Pa. — Autumn transforms this area, the heartland of the Black Forest, into a vortex of dazzling color that enmeshes mountain and valley. Here, in northeastern Pennsylvania, in a stretch some 200 miles wide and 40 miles southward from the New York State line, the foliage usually flames to its peak during the first two weeks of October. And no place is it more brilliant than in Potter County, where the dense forest covers more than 500,000 acres.

Coudersport, which is about a six-hour drive from New York City, makes a good headquarters from which to explore this fascinating region. This is not sophisticated resort territory, but it offers superb natural beauty, opportunities to observe animals in their native habitat, excellent camping facilities and motel and lodge accommodations.

To quote one enthusiastic visitor, it has "elbow room," and a visit lasting a day, a week or a weekend can thus be exhilarating.

Most Flaming Foliage

A brochure issued by the Pennsylvania State Department of Commerce, "See Pennsylvania's Flaming Foliage," explains why this state boasts more kinds of tree-leaf coloration than any other in the nation— or, in fact, in the world. The mountain slopes in this northeastern zone flaunt the glowing gold of aspen leaves, of basswood turned to russet and of beech to golden bronze, as well as the deep purple of white ash and the blazing orange-to-crimson hues of the maples.

Six state parks lie within easy reach of Coudersport. One of them, Lyman Run State Park, has a man-made lake with a spacious white-sand beach that can accommodate about 1,500 swimmers. Lacing

The Potter Enterprise

CIRCULAR ROUTE—A family wanders along the 65-mile-long Susquehannock Trail System in Pennsylvania's Black Forest.

through the parkland and between the small villages are hundreds of miles of paved or well-kept dirt roads.

Deer are commonly seen browsing along these highways and byways. The visitor should plan to drop in at Slim Croyle's farm, which is on State Route 144 between Oleona and Cross Fork, in the late afternoon. Anywhere from a dozen to 80 or more deer emerge from the forest when Slim whistles or calls them by name to come and share food. Some will approach shyly to be hand-fed.

Majestic Turkeys

A leisurely motorist may spot one or more majestic wild turkeys among the woodland shadows or come upon beavers building a dam across one of the mountain waterways. Occasionally, a black bear will be seen.

Fire towers manned to protect the forests are situated at Crandall Hill, West Pike, Fox Mountain (near Austin) and Cherry Springs. A climb up one of these steel towers—the one at Cherry Springs rises 80 feet—rewards one with a breathtaking panorama.

It is difficult to believe that these heavily forested mountains were once plundered of their original wilderness and that, by the time of the Civil War, stands of pine in the Potter County area had almost disappeared. The prized white pine was shipped out; later, giant hemlocks were left to rot after the bark was peeled and carted off to flourishing tanneries.

The recently opened Susquehannock Trail System, a 65-mile looping footpath, is said to be unique in that the hiker can walk for several hours or for days without retracing his steps. Shelters and other facilities have not been provided yet, and

hikers must be self-sufficient. No vehicles are permitted on the trails, most of which run through state forestland.

Potter County Recreation, Inc., is developing the trail system with the cooperation of the Pennsylvania Department of Forests and Waters and with volunteer help from the Susquehannock Trail Club. The circular route was formed by connecting existing fire trails that were constructed years ago by the Civilian Conservation Corps. The trails will guide not only hikers, but also the thousands of hunters and trout fishermen attracted to Potter County.

There is much of historical interest in the region—folklore often intermingled with fact, and romantic legend with the grim truth of tragedy. A prime example is the story of a violinist, Ole Bull, and his Norwegian colony. Ole Bull State Park now commemorates his name and marks the site of his disastrous venture.

Dreamed of Colony

From the time of his first concert tour in America in 1843, Ole Bull nurtured a dream of establishing a Norwegian colony in this area. In 1852, with funds accumulated from concerts, he paid for 11,144 acres in the Black Forest and laid out four villages—Oleona, New Norway, New Bergen and Wallhala.

On the crest of a bluff was built a two-story frame cottage called Ole Bull's Castle; the name still designates the crumbling foundation that remains today. It is a spot where visitors can look far over the Black Forest and where the United States and Norwegian flags fly side by side.

The group was destined to lose the property and the log homes they had

struggled to erect, for the land sale to Ole Bull was a swindle. The violinist returned from a South American concert tour to learn of the fraud and find the colony's affairs in chaos.

Many of the sturdy band in whom he had placed such high hopes left for settlement further west, but a few families remained permanently. Ole Bull returned to his concert career and no longer did the wild music from his violin stream through the moonlight and into the dark forest.

Miss Inez Bull of Upper Montclair, N. J., a great-niece of Ole Bull and a musician herself, has conducted a summer school in Ole Bull State Park for several years.

Devastating Flood

It was 57 years ago this fall that a devastating flood swept away the villages of Austin and Costello and brought death to some 80 residents. A huge concrete dam that had been constructed across the narrow valley at a point three miles above Austin —its purpose was to provide adequate water supply for a pulp and paper mill—gave way, and an estimated 400,000,000 gallons of water in a 50-foot-high wall roared down the valley.

Between the oncoming flood and Austin, some 700,000 cords of pulpwood were piled in the mill's woodyard. The water struck the woodpiles and forced them, like battering rams, into the mill and on down to Austin.

For history buffs, the Potter County Historical Society headquarters and museum on Main Street, Coudersport, is worth a visit. It occupies part of a brick house built in the 1890's, and is open from 2 to 4 P.M. on Mondays and Fridays.

September 22, 1968

FORBIDDING—Trail Rider's Pass, a typical stretch of rugged terrain traversed on the hike in the high Rockies.

A Confrontation With Nature

Organized hiking, backpack and horse-back trips into the wilderness areas of the Rocky Mountains each summer are bringing more and more city dwellers into confrontation with a nature more hostile than the one they know from the botanical gardens of Brooklyn and the Bronx. The following is a report of a trip made late last summer by 36 members of the Appalachian Mountain Club, an Eastern organization that promotes hiking and outdoor activities, principally in the mountains of New England. Similar hikes are planned this summer by the American Forestry Association, 919 17th St., N.W., Washington, D. C. 20006; the Wilderness Society, 729 15th St., N.W., Washington, D.C. 20005, and the Sierra Club, P.O. Box 3471, Rincon Annex, San Francisco, Calif. 94120.

By OLIVE EVANS

THE plane landed in Denver beneath a hard blue sky and a metallic noon sun. We didn't suspect then that this would be almost the last sunshine we would feel for two weeks. Purple and black clouds were hovering ominously over that part of the Rockies into which we were about to venture on a two-week, high-altitude hiking and camping trip.

Our group ranged in age from 15 to the 60's, and we were bound for the Elk Mountains, an area where no motor vehicle can possibly get. Holy Cross, Pyramids, Snowmass, Massive, Maroon Bells, Capitol, Bellview and Treasury would be our mountain neighbors and their names would be often on our tongues. Some of them would loom over our campsites.

Carrying Only Day Packs

Our plan was to cover about a hundred miles, moving westward from the outskirts of Aspen and coming out of the Elk range at Marble. We would move camp about seven times, hiking from campsite to campsite.

Our duffel bags containing tents, clothing and eating utensils would be carried by 30 horses and mules. Our leader had contracted with a professional outfitter from Evergreen who would provide crew and wranglers to cook our breakfasts and dinners and handle the animals. On our daily walks, we would carry only day packs filled with raingear, extra sweaters and the lunches we made ourselves each

morning.

Those considering such a trip should be forewarned that the elements at altitudes above 10,000 feet can be merciless, even in summer, and that it is essential to have stout hiking boots, winter-weight clothing, a sleeping bag good down to 20 degrees, a sturdy but lightweight tent and an absolutely dependable rainsuit.

That first night, a bus and then a truck took us up to Half Moon Camp, in the shadow of Notch Mountain. In less than 12 hours, we had gone from sea level to 10,500 feet, and some of the party were feeling the effects.

Dreams at High Altitude

My tentmate and I managed to put up our tiny orange tent without too much discussion, and, after a hot meal in the cook tent, we were glad to crawl into it and into our sleeping bags. My dreams were vivid that night, as they were to be for the next 13 nights. Profuse and often weird dreaming is a common phenomenon at high altitudes.

Acclimatization was supposed to be the plan for the next day, but before the crack of dawn, a party of eight left to climb Mount Elbert, at 14,431 feet the second highest mountain in the United States. We knew then that we indeed had some hardy people along. Before it was over, we all would be more rugged.

None of my own mountain walking had prepared me for the ruggedness of the Colorado wilderness, for the long distances we were to hike, nor for the sense of complete isolation from civilization.

The first few days, we made some fairly easy treks: a level and lovely five-mile walk to Lake Constantine, sparkling under tentative sunshine; exploring Holy Cross City, an abandoned mining town where 75 years ago grubstakers had traded food for gold; bathing in the 100-degree, odd-smelling and delightful water of Conundrum Hot Springs, our only bath for more than a week.

Quick, the Raingear

During those first days, we learned to get our raingear quickly out of our knapsack, and we had it on more often than off. Mercifully, it rarely rained in the chilly dawn, when we rolled up our sleeping bags, gathered gear, folded tents and packed all of it into the duffel bags to be carried by the pack horses. Nor did it rain as we lined up for breakfast, washed our eating utensils or made our trail lunches.

Usually, it rained sometime shortly after lunch, letting up briefly in midafternoon and resuming heavily as we arrived at our campsite. Putting up the tents in a downpour became rather routine. The most valued possession became a dry pair of socks.

But it was in dry, if not sunny, weather and good spirits that some of us started up the trail to move over Conundrum Pass. For me, this was to be the most memorable walk of the trip.

Up we went, moving ever higher through the indescribably beautiful Conundrum Basin. Up beyond timberline, up into the green Alpine meadows, where wildflowers made an endless sea of multicolored splendor. I will always be grateful that the fog did not move in too soon that day. As a result, we were able to see the array of Indian Paintbrush and, higher up, a myriad of miniscule exquisiteness: mountain pinks, primroses, blue alpine phlox, purple pentstemon, moss campion and yellow arnica, all nestled beside the steep trail as it wound over barren rocks and through snowfields.

Alone in the Silent Fog

Two of us had been walking at a slow but steady pace a bit ahead. Suddenly fog and silence descended and, for a little while, we seemed to be the only people in the world. My companion, only a few feet beyond me, was a creature shrouded in mystery.

All awareness of height was blotted out by the fog, but we now knew we should wait for the others, that now was the time to stay close together. All six of us continued slowly, slowly up the remaining 500 feet to the pass. As we came into it, I was just able to make out a sign that read, "Conundrum Pass, 13,050 feet."

The mist cleared, and the feeling of height returned in earnest. I went down the next thousand feet roped to companions in front and back of me, until I wanted to be on my own again.

"I thought it might come in handy," said the man who had the rope. "I would have been disappointed if no one had needed it."

During all our mountain walking, we saw evidence of deer and other animals, but the animals themselves probably fled when they heard our often noisy approach. Not so timid were the marmots and the coneys, which were seemingly unconcerned, even bored, with our presence, as they perched on the rockpiles in which they live and squeaked their special, nervy little squeak. They sounded like toys one squeezes.

Beautifully, and very early, began the day on which we started off on a four-day trek that proved the most frightening adventure of all. It was easy and pleasant at first. From camp in Rustlers' Gulch, we walked around Mount Bellview and through Scofield Pass and another miracle of wild flowers.

Lunch Amid the Lupin

In a blue field of lupin, we ate lunch under a brief, warm sun. Then we were led off the trail, to "flower-whack" across the mountain shoulder, as the trail wound below us.

The idea was to save us some miles of ascent by avoiding the trail, which wound down and then up through the pass. But on the other side of the flower-covered shoulder was a two-to-three-mile slope of gray jagged scree, or fallen rock, climaxing in craggy, far-off and inhospitable-appearing West Maroon Pass. We had to cross it in a driving rain.

I learned about switchbacks when we picked up the trail again at last, for it switched back and forth across the steep slope leading into the 12,600-foot-high pass. "Boundary — Maroon Bells-Snowmass Wild Area," the sign said. "Closed to Motorized Vehicles." The only motorized vehicle that might be up there would be a helicopter!

After one layover day of solid sunshine, the weather turned sour again as we proceeded to our last camp. We ascended once more through West Maroon Pass, followed the trail up over Frigid Air Pass and then down through the Fravert Basin, the longest and most difficult walk of the adventure.

After hiking at least eight miles, we missed a turnoff. Late in the afternoon, we had to ascend another mountain trail in a hailstorm, and lightning flashed as we crossed an exposed field. Another hour's climb and a long slog through deep mud, and we arrived at our camp at Geneva Lake, 11,200 feet up.

That night, the storm broke in earnest, and it snowed. Ice formed in our water bottles. The socks we had optimistically hung on branches to dry were frozen stiff.

The next day, high winds tore through the tenting ground, ripping off the cook tent's tarpaulin. There was no refuge except the little orange tent—if it would only hold. As I lay listening to thunder and howling wind, I longed for my cozy New York apartment.

A Moment of Exaltation

For every valley there is a summit, and such low moments have corresponding moments of exaltation. Next morning, the storm had passed, and the sun rose slowly from behind the sheer wall of rocky Snowmass Mountain, which brooded over our campsite. As it did, the first rays hit snow-capped Treasury Mountain, across the valley.

We ate breakfast in silence, watching the rose-tinted beauty as the sun climbed higher and warmed our coldness. Then we broke camp for the last time.

May 4, 1969

Rocky Mountain Trail
For the Sightless

FOOTBRIDGE— Sightless **girl is about to cross Roaring Fork on bridge built by Forest Service. Note Braille marker on bridge railing.**

By SUSAN MARSH

ASPEN, Colo.—The newest trail in White River National Forest is a little thing. It is about 600 feet long, its design is somewhat circular and it has a parking lot that accommodates only 10 cars.

But small as it is, it is attracting more than ordinary attention. This trail was built for the blind, and inquiries from in and out of Colorado indicate that there soon may be other paths like it.

The Roaring Fork Braille Trail, it is called, and it started taking shape in 1965, or some months after Robert B. Lewis, then a high school biology teacher in Aspen, opened a Christmas package by mistake. The package was addressed to his daughter, Katy, and it was a book about Louis Braille.

Mr. Lewis was fascinated by the account of how Braille's brothers and sisters had taught the blind boy the feel of a bird's egg and the sounds and smells of the farm. It happened that Mr. Lewis had been making field trips into the forest with his students. The book started him thinking about a trail tailored for blind boys and girls.

He selected an area that impressed him as ecologically ideal. It had a glacial moraine, a wet meadow, a rushing mountain stream and placid pools lined with fine and coarse sand, gravel and boulders. Lodgepole pine, fir and spruce grew there in unspoiled abundance.

For some time, Mr. Lewis worked on his own around the trail area. Then he started getting help. Volunteers from a Job Corps camp at Colbran helped clear and construct the trail, Forest Service rangers and other forestry workers lent expert assistance, and the Forest Service built a footbridge across the Roaring Fork.

On Sept. 16, the trail was dedicated. Mr. Lewis, now an educational projects consultant, was there with 12-year-old Katy, while Job Corps youths served as volunteer guides for 15 blind children from the Colorado School for the Deaf and the Blind in Colorado Springs. They and others at the school had made the 23 Braille markers along the trail.

Each marker has a printed version for sighted visitors. Some of the markers suggest that much can be learned by touching, smelling and listening, and the message is not for the blind alone. Tasting is not recommended; it could be hazardous.

Meaningful Words

The trail gives the visitor a chance to feel the meaning of words like slimy, sharp, smooth, sandy, springy or soggy, for it goes through a variety of environments. Dr. Alfred Etter of Aspen, a naturalist and conservationist,

wrote the text for the 23 markers.

They suggest feeling and smelling the difference between the prickly spruce and the flat, blunt-pointed fir, bouncing on the sphagnum bog, listening to and feeling the water in the Roaring Fork, hearing the wind in the trees and listening for birds or squirrels, touching a tree scar caused by a porcupine and counting the rings on a tree stump.

Nylon parachute cords on each side of the trail guide the blind from one podium-like marker to the next. The trail is narrow enough to allow grasping both cords at once and the line of walk is in one direction. It begins and ends at the tiny parking lot.

Although White River National Forest has some of the wildest country in the United States, there are no poisonous plants, insects or reptiles, as one of the markers assures visitors.

Another marker advises, in part: "As you face the wire, reach out before you and feel the foliage of the trees among which you will be walking. This one is a fir."

Still another: "Meet the spruce in front of you. It is not so friendly as the fir. The leaves, or needles, are prickly."

And at the next marker: "Handle the common juniper with care. It is even more prickly than the spruce."

Finally, the message at the 23d marker:

"This is the last station. The largest tree along the Braille Trail stands in front of you. Reach around it. A tree is a remarkable thing, structured to solve many problems, yet somehow attractive to human beings and to many other forms of life besides.

"Some trees stand alone, but most are a part of the forest, as each of us is a part of the community of living things. We are all interdependent. Nature is constantly at work in many ways and in many images to carry on the continuity of life that makes this earth unique and interesting.

"We have many neighbors around us who were here long before we came. In our management of the earth, we must make room for them. In the scheme of things, there is little doubt that they are as important as we."

The trail will become longer, it is hoped. And there will be improvements, such as placing

Susan Marsh

INFORMATIVE—Markers contain raised Braille characters on left and written translation on right. This one reads: 'Welcome to the Braille Nature Trail. It may give you a new experience in nature study and enjoyment. Nylon cords along the path will keep you oriented and will serve as guides between message stations. The entire trail corresponds to about one block's travel. The first message is about 21 feet on your left. Please do not smoke as this is a National Forest area.' Twenyt-three markers are spaced along trail.

stuffed chipmunks in open shelters and perhaps recordings of bird and animal sounds.

About Oct. 23, the forest rangers will tie plastic bags over the Braille signs to protect them during the winter. But visitors are expected until the heavy snows start, which last year was around Thanksgiving. When the roads are free of snow again, probably around Memorial Day, the trail will be reopened.

Road Project

The trail, about 13 miles from the center of Aspen, is at an altitude of 10,400 feet. It is just off State Route 82, a Forest Service road that goes over Independence Pass. Long stretches of the high-

way are unpaved, but the Forest Service expects complete paving within two years.

The forest is administered by the Department of Agriculture, but more than one Washington agency is aware of it. The ceremonies at which the trail was dedicated were arranged by the Denver Federal Executive Board, made up of top officials of Federal agencies stationed in Denver.

Also there was Mrs. Walter Paepke, director of the Aspen Institute. It was her late husband who started Aspen's development as a resort center.

Mr. Lewis, who has set up visual-aid projects at the University of California, Berkeley, and for the

Peace Corps and the United Nations Educational, Scientific and Cultural Organization (UNESCO), has written thus about the trail:

"The Aspen trail is regarded as a prototype or experimental trail, and it is hoped that the lessons learned here can be applied to other trails in other regions. It is not beyond the realm of possibility that there may some day be a network of such trails across the country in woodlands, along streams, in the mountains and even the deserts."

FOREST VENTURE—Blind youth, above, grasps nylon cords to guide himself along Roaring Fork Braille Trail in the White River National Forest.

October 8, 1967

Rockwall Alleyway

Is Hiker's Entrance

To a 'New' Canyon

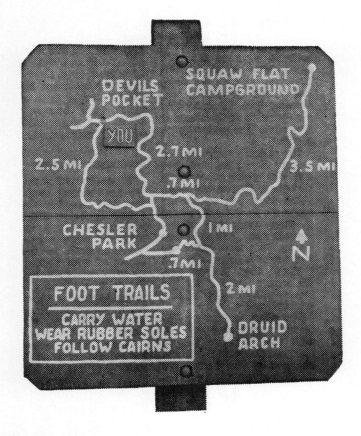

By JOHN V. YOUNG

MONTICELLO, Utah — To my knowledge, a Chesler Park Un-improvement Association has not yet been created, but one should be. Someone ought to start an organization dedicated to the nondevelopment of these canyon hinterlands, and to the nonexploitation of Chesler Park's natural wonders, if for no other reason than to ensure the continuation of the excellent work already begun in that direction by the National Park Service.

I refer to the service's recently announced decision not to build a graded road into Chesler Park, a sequestered "Shangri-La" deep in the heart of new, half-explored Canyonlands National Park. Not only that, but the Park Service has decided that, at some time in the future, all the present trails into Chesler Park will be closed and those who want to visit the area will have to hike in.

Narrow and Unnamed

The hiking trail that leads into Chesler Park, nestled like a gem in a forest of rocky pinnacles, is something quite special. It is often no wider than a door, and is still so new that it does not even have a proper name.

For the time being, it is being called the Joint Trail, because it passes through a natural fissure in the rocks, a phenomenon known geologically as a joint. A joint is nothing more than a fracture in a rock surface produced by subterranean stress.

There are quite a few such joints in Canyonlands National Park. Some are known to old-timers, who once used them as secret paths in and out of hidden valleys like Chesler Park; some are used only by small game and some are still unexplored. Those that are wide enough for a man on foot are not recommended for anyone with claustrophobia.

They are like long alleys, being no wider than an ordinary doorway and running between 10-story buildings with no windows, doors or fire escapes. The sky appears only as a narrow slit high above, where it is not hidden entirely by overhanging rock bulges.

Short of Specifications

Joint Trail falls far short of Forest Service specifications for a proper trail, which require a 10-foot right-of-way with ample views on curves to prevent pack animals from colliding. It is only 30 inches wide in some places, and rarely exceeds five feet.

The sheer rock walls of Joint Trail rise 100 feet along most of its 1,000-foot length. It is quite level and has a nice, sandy floor, and it would be utterly impossible to get lost on it, or in it. One Park Service official remarked that it could serve as a kind of filter against motor-scooters, livestock and fat people.

The Joint Trail is not yet on the map, and the jeep tracks leading to it from the south follow a circuitous, unmarked route. Still another jeep trail, this one from the north and west, is pretty hair-raising in its own right. At one place, it passes through a slot so narrow that it is impossible to open the vehicle's doors.

This is one of the jeep routes to be eliminated when a new conventional road comes up from State Route 95 and the south. The new route will bypass Chesler Park, but will proceed to a parking place at the entrance to Joint Trail, or about a half-mile from a park overlook. From the overlook, an easy trail winds down into the bottom of the park.

The main road into the Chesler Park area from U.S. 160—the cut-off is about 15 miles from Monticello—ends, and will continue to end, at Squaw Flat Campground, a principal gathering place for

visitors and a jumping-off place for jeep tours. Beyond that point, only four-wheel-drive vehicles can negotiate the rock piles and gulches that pass for roads.

After considerable study, the National Park Service decided that any road into Chesler Park itself would "violate the serenity of the Canyonlands country and would be a contradiction of national park purposes." Meantime, the main road to Squaw Flat Campground is being paved; the work reached the halfway point, Dugout Ranch, last fall, and it is hoped that construction will be completed by next winter.

There will, of course, have to be a better name than Joint Trail, lest people think it the entrance to some sort of backwoods honkytonk. Among those suggested to the Park Service are Fat-Man's Misery, Goblin Gully, Aladdin's Alley or the Needle's Eye.

Even Chesler Park's name does not sufficiently reflect any of its fabulous beauty and remarkable setting, having simply been named for a pioneer rancher who used to run cattle in the area. The park lies in a circular, flat-bottomed valley that is perhaps a half-mile across and surrounded on all sides by those sheer, vertical spires of red and yellow sandstone called The Needles.

The Needles rise to elevations of 400 feet above the valley floor. There are a few places where people can scramble through The Needles, and there is only one that will admit a jeep. That passage was blasted out for cattle and horses in the days when Canyonlands National Park was still open grazing land.

Chesler Park is a graben, the term geologists use to describe a type of formation fairly common hereabout. Deep beneath the saucer-like floor of the valley is a thick layer of salt that was laid down millions of years ago, when all of the region was under the sea. Later, surface water from rain and snow leaked down through some fault or joint and dissolved the salt, allowing the entire valley to sink. The process is continuing elsewhere in the area, as Park Service naturalists point out.

Although there are no springs in Chesler Park, the valley usually gets enough moisture to stay fairly green. In some years, it is a haven for wild flowers.

Elsewhere in Canyonlands National Park, things are pretty much as they were when the preserve was opened in May, 1965: Primitive and undeveloped, except for a new store, a service station and an airstrip near the east entrance. Still, upward of 20,000 visitors were logged in last year, and the number could pass 25,000 in 1969.

'NO WIDER THAN A DOOR' — The Joint Trail into Chesler Park, is so narrow that some wags have suggested that it be renamed Fat Man's Misery.

May 4, 1969

AUTUMN RAMBLES
IN THE WESTERN MOUNTAINS

By JACK GOODMAN

HEBER, Utah—Frost has come unusually early to western mountains and valleys this year. As a result, the region's aspen groves are turning a bright, shimmering yellow, mountain slopes covered with oakbrush already are a deep russet, hardwoods in Mormon farmyards are a bright red, and cottonwoods and willows are taking on their yellow-gold hues.

At this season, too, second-crop haystacks dot the low country, lingering snowbanks and the dark blue of pines and spruce stand upon the high skyline, and bright foliage at intermediate altitudes gives the countryside a haunting loveliness that no artist seems to have caught successfully.

Along with much that is Western, part of the region's autumn charm lies in the prevailing contrast of the cultivated and the wild. Hikers, photographers, artists and sightseers can find some scenes reminiscent of New Hampshire and Vermont, but the landscapes now unfolding for foliage-season vacationists in Utah, Colorado, Montana, Idaho, Wyoming and Arizona are more spacious.

On high passes 8,000 feet above sea level, and on trails leading to peaks another 3,000 feet higher, it is possible to see across range after range and valley upon valley for distances of 60 to 100 miles.

Valley Communities

Towns such as Heber, Midway or Park City, tucked away in pocket-handkerchief valleys along the eastern flanks of Utah's Wasatch Range, are pleasant centers for fall foliage trips. Heber, on U.S. 40, is becoming something of an eastern gateway to this country of 11,000- and 12,000-foot peaks. Midway, a few miles off the main road, is inhabited by Swiss emigrants, who find this high country not unlike their fatherland. Park City is a doddering, decrepit silver mining center of considerable charm, with a resort boom in the making.

The region's lone resort is a

Jack White

HITTING THE TRAIL—Hikers climb heights near Mount Timpanogos in Utah.

pleasant, white-porticoed lodge in Midway; there, a slightly sulphurous "hot pot" natural pool is an aid to aching muscles after a day of hiking. There are good motels in Heber and a guest ranch or two near Park City. The rates are pleasantly low.

In addition to valley ranches, in which milch cattle and fat steer browse, some of this Utah countryside is pockmarked with mines and abandoned head-frames, shaft houses and mills. Sheep amble through the high country, and side roads are lined with stone walls and poplar lanes, as well as with the usual barbed wire fencing. All in all, the region is as pleasant for rambling as any in the West.

As for the Wasatch peaks themselves, most acreage above 6,000 feet, and on to timberline, is included in the Wasatch National Forest or Uinta National Forest. Utah's State Park Com-

mission has been quietly purchasing the few sizable tracts still in private hands, making it almost impossible for hikers to stray off the public domain.

One trail favored by autumn foliage viewers zigzags up to the top of Mount Timpanogos, the loftiest peak in the region. Reaching a respectable altitude of 12,008 feet, the mountain is capped by a small glacier, has a pretty lake at about the 11,000-foot level and is easily climbed in a half-day's time by hikers in fair trim.

The "Timp Trail" takes off from the Forest Service camp-site at Aspen Grove. This is on a 6,000-foot-high shoulder of the mountain, at a point halfway round the Alpine Loop. The latter, a paved road that can be used by any standard auto in good condition, links six-lane U.S. 91, on the Salt Lake Valley side of the Wasatch Range, with

the Heber country.

Rising to 8,500 feet during its eight-mile journey between the American Fork and Provo Rivers, the Alpine Loop Highway gives "windshield sightseers" some more than fair views of high peaks and highly colored foliage.

Hiker's Country

Climbers who take the "Timp Trail" find themselves hiking through stands of fresh-smelling pines, traversing aspen thickets and pausing to view a half-dozen unnamed cataracts that dash down the gorges below Mount Timpanogos. Above this series of rocky glens, the trail leads across cool mountain meadows and on to ledges. There, hikers can settle down to lunch, sprawl out to rest and look out upon mile after mile of irrigated valleys, sparkling blue reservoirs and the distant Uinta wilder-

ness country.

After another two miles on the trail, snowbanks remaining from the previous winter, the glacial lake and the tiny glacier itself give footsore hikers a chance to cool or chill their feet while looking down upon the yellow aspen, red oak-brush and yellow cottonwood far below.

Finally, from atop Timpanogos, where a small shelter marks the summit, autumn hikers peer far west across Utah Valley, Utah Lake, the Oquirrh Range and into Nevada.

A dozen other hiking trails fan out from Midway or the Park City country, many of them following the ridges of the Wasatch to the winter ski-slope areas of Brighton and Alta. Pavements through the Wasatch are being improved, and routes once suited only for Jeeps have been graded for passenger cars. However, this situation is being viewed with mixed emotions by the region's hikers and back-country enthusiasts.

This fall, for example, it is easy to drive a standard sedan or station wagon from Park City westward into Guardsmen's Pass and over the 10,000-foot-high ridge into Brighton. At Brighton, a modern manor and on old, log-sided lodge are staying open to house and feed fall foliage seekers. In addition, at least one of Brighton's ski lifts will be operating so as to give lazy Alpinists a boost into the high country.

After jouncing from Park City to Brighton by way of the unpaved Guardsmen's Pass road, motorists may be astonished to find the Forest Service converting its old, winding road from Brighton to the Salt Lake Valley into a veritable boulevard. It will be wide enough for four cars along some of its 15-mile length.

Actually, there is excellent hiking country everywhere in the Wasatch. Six miles below Brighton, a typical old mine road heads south into Cardiff Gulch, passing Doughnut Falls and a dozen abandoned shafts en route. Motorists can drive into the Cardiff country for nearly four miles before the road becomes too rocky and steep for comfort. Parking beside an abandoned mine dump, the hiker can climb out, fill his canteen with crystal-clear water and then ramble uphill for about a mile. There, he can top a ridge

and look down into the Alta country.

Once teeming with miners, the Alta Basin will fill with snow, and skiers, in about two months. At this season, however, its slopes are yellow with groves of aspen, the lodges are closed and there are more deer than people along its trails.

In a week of rambling, or a weekend of motoring, it is possible to see only a small segment of northern Utah's high country. However, a sampling

taken in the Heber-Midway-Park City area, up the ridge in Brighton or almost anywhere between Provo and Logan is likely to bring the foliage seeker back for more in another year.

Mountain Precautions

As in all parts of the West, a few words of warning are in order. Maps are extremely handy, and can be obtained from Wasatch National Forest Headquarters, Salt Lake City, or Intermountain Region Forest

Service Headquarters, Ogden, Utah. This country is pleasant in the daytime but increasingly cold at night, so warm togs and a sleeping bag are recommended for the hiker. One should keep to the trails and tend fires carefully, for the timber is dry at this season.

Check carefully on bow-and-arrow deer hunts, the elk season and the like, and wear clothing that will safeguard you from near-sighted deer-stalkers. And, finally, do not pick those autumn leaves.

October 7, 1962

The Long Trail Into Tribal Lands Of the Havasupai

By SUSAN MARSH

PEACH SPRINGS, Ariz. — While most tribes were being pushed off their lands by the westward expansion of the white man, the Havasupai Indians of northern Arizona managed to remain in the canyon where their ancestors had lived for about 800 years.

The explanation, in part, was the area's inaccessibility. Grand Canyon National Park surrounds the tribe's reservation, and there is no way to reach it on wheels. The Indians live in a side canyon on the western edge of Grand Canyon, at a level about two-thirds of the way down from the rim to the Colorado River.

Visitors have long extolled the serenity and scenery of the area, and my husband and I had heard enough to inspire us to undertake the 22-mile round-trip hike from Hualpai Hilltop in the national park. To reach the hilltop we drove about 60 miles along a dirt road that leaves U.S. 66 near Peach Springs.

The dirt road leads to a turnaround — near Hualpai Hilltop — where the trail down to the Indian village of Supai in Havasu Canyon begins. About 370 Indians live there.

The turnaround was an appalling sight: parked cars lined both sides of the road as far as we could see. People with backpacks were leaving and returning to their cars. We considered giving up the whole idea, for what point would there be to look for peace and solitude in a mob of about 2,000 people? But anyone willing to undertake a backpack of this length couldn't be all bad.

We strapped on our packs and hiked through the maze of parked cars to the trail leading down from Hualpai Hilltop. On the way I estimated there were 250 parked vehicles.

Any contact with Indians, I soon concluded, would be unlikely. The Indians we saw on the trail were too busy guiding tourists into the reservation and seldom noticed or responded to a smile, though one did lean around in his saddle to get a good look at the attractive teen-age girl right behind us.

(Visitors can reserve pack horses through the Havasupai Tourist Enterprise, Supai, Ariz. 86345. Riding in to the village costs $18 and to the national park campground, two miles beyond Supai, $20, round trip.)

The trail starts down from the hilltop, switching back and forth over the face of a cliff. The backpacker is easily distracted by the view of the red and tan formations of eroded rock, whose horizontal strips are punctuated with vertical clefts.

Hikers had plenty of room on the steep gravelly trail, but most of them took the inside track when horses approached. The low stone walls beside the trail are on the inside, where they protect the trail from runoff, not the climber from fall-off.

Utility Poles Intrude

After a descent of about 400 feet the trail turns out on to a broad shoulder, bulging out 500 feet from the face of the cliff. Telephone poles become an unexpected intrusion there, getting in the way of photographing the more overpowering cliffs on the far side of the valley. (One may telephone the village to make arrangements to stay in Supai's new stone lodge, which has four double rooms with private baths; or in the old lodge where nine persons share a bathroom. Both buildings have stoves and refrigerators, used communally; no meals are served.)

The feeling changes as the trail descends—from a sense of immense space between the canyon walls to a cosy feeling as the red walls enclose the trail and afford only an occasional glimpse of those monumental formations.

Although we saw no water in most of the Hualpai creek bed, the bushes and trees must find some, because the vegetation is entirely different from the prickly desert cactus above the canyon walls. The Indians inhabit the broadest, most verdant part of Havasu Creek's watershed.

About a fourth of the Indians' income depends on tourists. Many of the 97 in the work force go outside the reservation to work; but some of the tribe derive income from current construction projects in the village, such as the eight prefabricated homes just begun and the five finished last year, under the Bureau of Indian Affairs.

Indians picked the most beautiful parts of Havasu Canyon for their homes, for they have not only the close, sheer red walls but the distant views of lighter rock. From the far side of the village you can see the two rock spires known as the Wigleeva. Legend predicts that if the spires ever fall the tribe is doomed.

Havasu Creek descends over a series of five waterfalls from an elevation of 3,195 feet at Supai to about 2,750 feet

TURQUOISE WATERS—One of five cataracts in Havasu Valley, part of Grand Canyon National Park.

where it joins the muddy Colorado River.

Most other waterfalls knock off chunks of rock and wear down their stream beds. Havasu Creek, because of the high level of its mineral content, does just the opposite. It builds up a deposit of solid rock called travertine.

A Petrified Look

Eons ago, water flowed over many places now dry. The cliff walls near these cataracts have the same kind of curtains of travertine and look something like petrified waterfalls.

The minerals in the water, which give it a rich turquoise color, have formed dams in the creek, creating a series of wading pools all along the edge of the campground.

Havasu Falls, one of the series of five, is beautiful to watch when the wind blows the white cascade into plumes. Upstream from Havasu Falls is Navajo Falls, and there are two smaller falls, Supai and Beaver. Our goal was Mooney Falls, which at 220 feet, is taller than Niagara by about 60 feet.

Getting to the base of Mooney Falls requires a real climb; the other falls have gradually descending paths around them. Miners devised the route down the nearly vertical cliff from Mooney about a century ago by carving tunnels behind the travertine. Their gouged footholds, metal spikes and chains still provide the hand and foot holds for climbers.

We kept crawling into corners or backing up as we met other climbers, for the scaler has the right-of-way. Long delays occurred when people with backpacks got stuck in tunnels so steep that they are almost like elevator shafts.

The route leads eventually to the Colorado River, a hike that takes at least another strenuous day. We turned back toward Supai after rewarding ourselves with a swim in the pool below the falls.

A bleeding blister I earned on the climb gave me an excuse, late in the day, to get acquainted in the Indian village. I hurried ahead to get to the store before closing, for I'd left my first-aid kit at camp.

The store was out of the only thing I needed: a Band-Aid. The clinic had closed, but men in the store assured me it would be proper to go to the home of Terry Eiler, who is the director of the Head Start program in the village. He gave me a Band-Aid. Eiler enjoyed so much an assignment photographing the village for a national magazine that he and his bride have returned there to work for a year.

He showed me cards he had made to help teach words to the pre-school children. He mounts a photograph taken in the village, then prints a word to describe the picture and attaches a strip of magnetic tape that says the word when the child puts the card in a tape-recorder.

Health Procedures Taught

I also met John Gobert, a Blackfoot Indian from Montana, and his attractive wife, a Sioux. For six years he was a medical corpsman and lost a leg in Vietnam. He takes care of the medical needs of the Havasupai and teaches them better health procedures. He has radio and phone connections with the Health Service doctor in Peach Springs.

After our outing, I phoned the Tourist Enterprise and asked, "What has become of that $1,240,000 awarded the tribe in a land settlement claim?"

"Nothing. Not a cent has arrived yet," was the answer. Nevertheless, a new multi-purpose building is going up. It will have a cafeteria to serve hot lunch to children in the Head Start program, and there are plans to allow tourists who want to buy a noon meal to use it too. If demand warrants, other meals may be served.

This year the village store is barely breaking even in spite of high prices, because almost everything comes by helicopter. Besides canned and packaged goods, there are fresh meats, vegetables, fruit and beadwork, done by village women who have learned the skill from a crafts teacher.

Horses are too busy transporting tourists, mail and bottled gas to supply the store.

Tourists will find that baskets, which used to be important in Havasupai life, are now rare and expensive. The price of the delicate black-on-white coiled basketry was inflated artificially when a wealthy woman offered, in the 1950's, to pay $10 more than the going price for each basket. After she had a large collection and stopped buying, the Havasupai had priced themselves out of the market.

September 27, 1970

Way Stations for Hikers in West's High Country

By JOHNS H. HARRINGTON

YOSEMITE VILLAGE, Calif.—For most of the thousands of visitors who come to Yosemite National Park, gazing at Half Dome, El Capitan and Bridalveil Falls from the valley floor is ample inspiration. For us, however, there is nothing like viewing natural wonders from "the top"—without benefit of wings or a helicopter.

In a 30-mile, three-day hike from Tuolumne Meadows to Yosemite Valley, we met only a handful of people. We found, instead, a panorama of glistening peaks, meadows, lakes and streams that was worth a lifetime of more ordinary sightseeing. And our trip was only a sample, for Yosemite National Park has 700 miles of trails.

Comfortable Camp

To enable us to do our viewing with less strain, we chose to make reservations at several High Sierra camps. This allowed us to travel with only light packs, fishing gear and cameras. The camps provided comfortable accommodations, plus meals so bountiful that they would have satiated a starving lumberjack. The charge for each person was $10 a night.

We arrived a day early at Tuolumne Meadows Lodge so that we could become accustomed to the 8,600-foot altitude and take a few experimental jaunts. Tuolumne, which is about 56 miles by road from Yosemite Valley, is the largest meadowland in the High Sierra.

It is also the most popular starting point for hiking and pack trips into the high country. In addition to the lodge, which is managed by the Yosemite Park and Curry Company, there is a large campground maintained by the National Park Service, a post office, a store and a coffee shop.

Five-Hour Jaunt

With light hearts the next day, we began the five-hour jaunt to Vogelsang, one of the best-known of the high-altitude Sierra camps. Even though our feet and our packs soon felt heavier as we began the climb, our enthusiasm rose as we left the highway and the meadowlands.

The seven-mile journey involves three segments of relatively steep trail. Since it was early in the season, clouds of mosquitoes attacked with the ferocity of suicide pilots until we lathered ourselves with insect repellent. Then they merely buzzed around our ears until the strength of the repellent began to diminish and the process had to be repeated.

Although the avid nature lover will find few unusual sights until he nears timberline, the trip to Vogelsang is essential in order to reach the grandeur of the high country. It is also a great limbering-up exercise for the excursions that follow, even though we reached our destination by 1:30 P.M.

Highest Camp

In the last half-hour of the climb, we began to encounter the scenery we had been waiting for. At 10,300 feet, Vogelsang is the highest of the camps and lies above timberline.

To many visitors, it is also the most dramatic. Fletcher Creek gurgles and splashes through the camp, and towering above it, at 11,576 feet, is Vogelsang Peak. With Fletcher, Booth, Vogelsang, Hanging Basket and Townsley Lakes all nearby, the camp is also popular with fishermen.

Despite these attractions, our first thoughts were of the hot showers available to guests at the camp. Then we relaxed in our tent, which was equipped with a small pot-bellied stove and firewood that had been hauled three miles by pack train.

Good Dinner

I later discovered that the nearby public campground at Fletcher Lake, about a block away, was swarming with Boy Scouts, as well as mosquitoes. They seemed envious of our accommodations, as well as of our meals. Dinner consisted of cole slaw, hot soup, hot biscuits, broiled chicken, spinach, mashed potatoes with gravy and canned fruit. We also had a choice of coffee, chocolate, tea or milk.

For the next leg of our alpine journey, we climbed over Vogelsang Pass, which is about 11,000 feet high, and began a two-day descent to Yosemite Valley. Within 15 minutes after leaving Vogelsang, we reached Vogelsang Lake and passed patches of snow.

Magnificent View

In the pass, the view was magnificent. Granite peaks and jagged cliffs stood out from the gray face of the surrounding mountains, and in the valley emerald lakes sparkled in the sunlight. Our narrow route started a steep descent to the floor of the valley, and along the trail were rocks that had been packed together to prevent erosion.

From almost the moment we came through the pass, the mosquitoes disappeared. We were now on the dry side of the range, and evidently few breeding grounds are there.

Since the insects were scarce and our route was downhill, we thought that the 9.1 miles to Merced Lake Camp would be easy. Certainly, it was not as difficult as it would have been coming the other way, but it was still a challenge because of the roughness and steepness of the trail.

Curious Bear

Shortly before reaching Merced Lake Camp, we encountered a half-grown black bear that probably weighed 200 pounds. It eyed us curiously from a safe distance, evidently noting that we were out of our native habitat.

My first impression of the camp was one of delight. Situated at an elevation of only 7,150 feet, it was neither too cold nor engulfed with insects. The sojourn was blissful, and the fishing was excellent.

During the night, there was some excitement when a bear managed to rip open a camper's pack, even though it had been hoisted to a tree limb 10 feet above the ground.

At the camp, we met the supervisor of the high-mountain facilities. He casually mentioned that he had recently hiked the 10 miles from Merced Lake to 9,400-foot-high Sunrise Camp in three and one-half hours. This was in marked contrast to the report of another camper and his 11-year-old son. They had taken seven and one-half hours to walk *down* from Sunrise Camp.

Expensive Rescue

The supervisor mentioned that helicopters were available at $150 an hour to rescue hikers. Earlier, one of the Scouts had told me it had cost $32 to evacuate one of their leaders by mule.

When a member of our party suggested that we complete the remaining 14 miles to Yosemite Valley without packs, we readily agreed and shipped the packs out by mule train at 15 cents a pound. What we lost in pride was compensated for in comfort.

The third day, therefore, was the easiest, even though the hike was the longest. From Merced Lake to Yosem-

JOHNS H. HARRINGTON

MULE TRAIN—Animals carry packs for tired hikers in Yosemite National Park.

173

ite Valley, the trail follows the Merced River and alternates through great stands of pines and along low ridges that drop to the canyon floor.

Return to Civilization

Our return to civilization was signaled when we reached Nevada Fall, in the vicinity of Half Dome. Park visitors, many of whom had arrived on muleback, were everywhere.

The distance from Nevada Fall to the floor of the valley is only 3.6 miles, but the view along most of this portion is so exhilarating that it is almost indescribable. We continued to sense the amazing emptiness of the wilderness, yet we had no feeling of loneliness. We were close to the thousands of sightseers thronging the valley, but still able to inhale the grandeur of nature and revel in its inspiration.

After nearly seven hours of hiking from Merced Lake, we arrived at the Happy Isles Nature Center, on the edge of the valley. From there, we trudged another mile or two to our lodgings.

Tired Hikers

Dusty and trail worn, we seemed out of place among automobiles, flashily garbed tourists and wandering hippies. But, as we boarded a bus in the morning to retrieve our own automobile at Tuolumne Meadows, we felt rich in the treasure of having followed for a short time the footsteps of John Muir.

Now, more than ever, we could appreciate the words that the renowned naturalist used to describe Yosemite:

"It contains countless lakes and waterfalls and smooth, silky lawns. Here, too, are the noblest forests, the highest granite domes, the deepest ice-carved canyons, and snowy mountains soaring into the sky twelve and thirteen thousand feet."

Despite bunions, blisters and sore thighs, we were glad we had been civilization dropouts for a few days.

August 11, 1968

Chapter Three

CITY WALKING
IN THE UNITED STATES

A WALK IN OLD ANNAPOLIS

Maryland's Venerable Capital, Site of the Naval Academy, Has Preserved Its Fine Colonial Landmarks

By E. JOHN LONG

ANNAPOLIS, Md.—Few cities of historical renown and current interest in this country have been wrapped up in such a manageable package as has Annapolis. Along three sides, tidewater envelops the old town, including the campus of venerable St. John's College, founded in 1696 as King William's School, and the Yard of the United States Naval Academy, all compressed in a few hundred acres. Its tiny size, narrow streets and a dearth of parking places make "Crabtown-on-the-Bay" an ideal spot for walking.

Caution must be urged for the stroller, because most of the sidewalks of Annapolis were built many years ago in a herringbone pattern of red brick on a sand base. Some of these bricks are broken and worn, and some undulate, pushed askew by tree roots. Needle heels are wrong outdoors as well as within the fine old mansions.

Paths With a Past

Annapolis's pavements, however unruly, echoed to the tapping of the gold-headed staffs of Colonial Governors. These walks are still considered part of the charm and flavor of this ancient city and port, which was old more than 300 years ago.

Almost from the start, Annapolis was a planned city, with circles and spoke-like streets branching in many directions. The first State House dominated the chief circle on a low hill. This lofty, manor-like structure overlooked the Severn River, Chesapeake Bay and, beyond, the rich plantations of the Eastern Shore.

The original town had English-flavored street names, such as Prince George, King George, Hanover and Duke of Gloucester, which still prevail today. Beautiful gardens of the more sumptuous mansions were half concealed behind ivied walls, hedges and tall trees.

Life was pleasant and leisurely for their proprietors. Tobacco, the principal source of their wealth, was shipped in square-riggers to England in exchange for fine cloth, furnishings and wine.

While many of these splendid homes and gardens have succumbed to the vicissitudes of time, even more of them have been miraculously saved, or partly kept, and now are being restored and refurbished. Annapolis is preserving some of the finest Georgian architecture in America.

Growing Pains

As Annapolis has grown, particularly since World War II, the commercial values of its downtown areas have risen sharply. Inevitably, this fact has attracted those who want to make profit from it.

Whether it meant erecting high-rise hotels or apartments, or modern office buildings, did not matter. Neither the state nor the city has had the laws or ordinances with the teeth in them needed to prevent such incursions.

The residents of Annapolis now realize that to maintain the original old town will result in greater prestige, and eventually more wealth, than would its replacement by just another hodgepodge modern community. Steps have now been taken in the right direction by such non-profit organizations as Historic Annapolis, Inc., and other civic groups.

With the growing support of Maryland's Governor and Legislature, officials of the county and city, the Naval Academy, St. John's College and other interested parties, the goals may be in sight.

A major step forward was the recent temporary blocking, by court action, of the construction of a seven-story building in downtown Annapolis and of a motel on the historic waterfront. Ordinances have been passed by the City Council so as to give Annapolis a "comprehensive master plan against which to measure all physical change needed to insure the values of the area."

House Reprieved

Meanwhile, the Maryland General Assembly has approved a bill to save the William Paca House, the home of one of the four Maryland signers of the Declaration of Independence. That is, the state has granted a six-month reprieve against the sale of the house for razing in favor of a modern apartment on the site. Instead, historic Annapolis, Inc., has signed a contract to purchase and save the Paca mansion for $125,000, the money to be raised by public subscription.

The National Park Service last week designated the entire old area of Annapolis as a National Historic District exemplifying an American seaport of the Colonial period.

So, somewhat reassured of the immediate future, one may focus on this compact city as it stands today. Most jaunts afoot through it begin at the State House, but the waterfront seems more appropriate. After all, this settlement began at the water's edge, was nurtured by the tidewater seas, and has reared the official sons of the Navy for more than a century.

Thus, a good point of departure is the busy basin of the Annapolis Yacht Club, with its sleek, mahogany-hulled cruisers, and its sails and gay pennants flapping in the breeze from Spa Creek. The tour begins there, going uphill on Duke of Gloucester Street, which is lined with tree-shaded homes.

Name and Address

Over a garden wall, at a point a short way up the street on the left side, rises one of the most notable Colonial homes of the city. It was built by Charles Carroll, the grandfather of Charles Carroll "of Carrollton," the only signer of the Declaration of Independence to add his address to his name on the historic document.

Although the signer was born in this house, the "Carrollton" denoted the manor he owned near Frederick, Md. The Annapolis house, now belonging to St. Mary's Catholic Church, is not open to the public.

Farther on, on the right, as the stroller approaches Church Circle, stands the City Hall. Here, one finds a tablet noting that, in the hall's ballroom, George Washington was feted on the night before he resigned his commission as Commander-in-Chief of the Continental Army.

Duke of Gloucester Street comes to its end at Church Circle, which is appropriately dominated by St. Anne's Episcopal Church, with its graceful spire. The present church was built in 1859, the third to be erected on this site. The first St. Anne's here—Church of England in those days, of course—was founded in 1692.

The original church was supported by an annual tax of 40 pounds of tobacco, levied on every taxpayer. A silver communion service was presented to it by King William III in 1695, and is still preserved here. In St. Anne's churchyard stands the tomb of Maryland's last

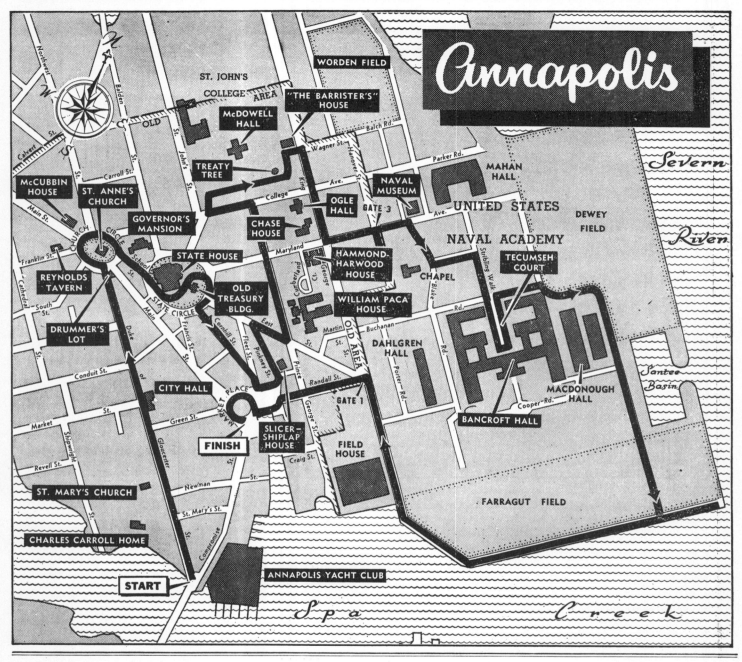

Royal Governor, Sir Robert Eden; he was an ancestor of the former British Prime Minister, Anthony Eden, now Lord Avon.

On the border of Church Circle, where Duke of Gloucester Street joins it, was the Drummer's Lot. There, in earlier times, the Town Crier called the populace together with a roll of drums to hear official proclamations.

Inn into Library

One's course continues clockwise around Church Circle to the point where, at the corner of Franklin Street, the most celebrated of Annapolis's Colonial inns, Reynolds's Tavern, has now been transformed into the public library of Anne Arundel County.

Continuing a block farther, one comes to Main Street as it enters the circle, and here, a few steps along the street, is the McCubbin House. Thomas Jefferson and James Madison lived in the house in 1783-84, during sessions of the Continental Congress in this city.

The stroller, looping to the right around the circle, then enters School Street and thus approaches the most famous and distinguished structure in Annapolis—the State House. On the way toward it, also on the left side of School Street, stands Government House, the home of Maryland's Governors since 1869. Here, a public reception is held every New Year's Day.

The Maryland State House is the real architectural and historical prize of this city. It is the oldest state capitol in continuous use in the United States, and it is actually the third capitol building on this site, fire having destroyed the earlier structures. It stands in State Circle.

The present building was begun in 1772, and its handsome wooden dome, remarkable in these times because it was built entirely without nails, was completed in 1779.

Within its halls, many events of historical significance to Americans occurred. Here, the Continental Congress accepted Washington's resignation from the Army that had won independence from Britain. Here

Jefferson was appointed United States Ambassador to European courts.

Historic Setting

Here, the official declaration of peace with Britain was ratified, and here, too, the so-called Annapolis Convention took place in 1786. This meeting led to the drafting of the United States Constitution.

The original Senate Chamber is still on view, and in the Flag Room is what is described as the oldest official American flag.

Leaving the Capitol building, the stroller follows a winding path on shady, green-lawned State Circle toward the Old Treasury Building. This thick-walled edifice was once the Colony's principal bank; it has been restored, and is now the headquarters of the Maryland Historical Trust.

It is here that the nonprofit organization, Historic Annapolis, Inc., launches its guided walking tours of the city. Its fees from these tours go toward restoration work.

Once more walking clockwise around the perimeter of State Circle, the stroller comes to Cornhill Street, which is lined with some of the most attractive privately restored residences of the early town.

Brassbound

Their window flower boxes are gay, and their door knockers are shiny. These homes are as charming outdoors as they are, when occasionally opened to visitors for charity, indoors. Many of them are the homes of retired Naval officers.

Walking down Cornhill Street, one reaches its intersection with Fleet Street, with Market Square just opposite, and then turns left into Pinckney Street. Here, on the right-hand side, is one of the most interesting of the early Colonial homes, Slicer-Shipley House. It is now restored as the headquarters of Historic Annapolis, Inc.

Visitors can step inside and examine an architect's model of the master plan for the restoration of the city. The model is entitled "Annapolis—Yesterday, Today and Tomorrow," and gives, in three-dimensional form, a fine survey of the city that was, is and will be.

The walk continues on Pinckney Street to where it ends at its intersection with East Street. The next objective is the original William Paca House. To reach it, one takes a hairpin turn to the right into East Street and continues a short distance to Prince George Street, there turning sharp left.

A few steps onward, the Paca House stands on the right; it is now a part of the Carvel Hall Hotel. The old mansion's downstairs parlors and offices are open to viewing.

As has been noted, the prime current project of Historic Annapolis, Inc., and similar organizations is to save the Paca House intact and convert the hotel property into a landscaped garden and plaza.

The next objective is the big, grassy campus of St. John's College, with its several historic relics. The stroller continues along Prince George Street to where it ends; that is, where it is crossed by College Avenue. The course is leftward on College Avenue to St. Johns Street, where one enters the college grounds.

McDowell Hall

A brick walk leads eastward across the campus to McDowell Hall, St. John's principal building. It was originally started as the Governor's residence, but was not finished until 40 years later. When Lafayette made his triumphant return to the United States in 1824, he was entertained there at two banquets and a ball.

The college's venerable history includes the patronage of many eminent Marylanders and others. For example, George Washington sent his two nephews, Fairfax and Lawrence Washington, to St. John's, and Francis Scott Key, author of "The Star-Spangled Banner," was an alumnus.

Continuing eastward across the campus and approaching the college library, one encounters a great and historic tulip poplar tree. It is believed to be 600 years old, and its circumference has been measured at 29 feet. Beneath its branches in 1652, a treaty was signed between the Colonial Government and the Susquehannock Indians.

Another Carroll

Close to the southeast corner of the campus, on King (not Prince) George Street stands an 18th-century mansion that was once the home of Charles Carroll, called "The Barrister" to distinguish him from the other bearers of that famous name. It is now the admissions office of the college.

Within a block en route down King George Street are three of the most impressive homes of the Colonial period. One is Ogle Hall, built in 1742 and now owned by the United States Naval Academy Association. It was the residence of two early Maryland Governors, Samuel Ogle and his son, Benjamin.

At the corner of King George Street and Maryland Avenue is the late-Georgian Colonial Chase House, which is notable for the many fine details of its interior woodwork. It has deeply paneled window shutters decorated with medallions and rosettes of great charm. The paneled doors of the dining room are of mahogany, and their door handles are of silver. Samuel Chase, one of Maryland's signers, started the house in 1769.

Directly across Maryland Avenue from Chase House is the Hammond-Harwood House; like its neighbor opposite, it is an example of great elegance in Colonial craftsmanship. Its window shutters are of similar pattern to those adorning Chase House, thus suggesting that both homes were produced by the same skillful artisan.

Both houses are open to visitors for a small fee. On Sundays, the Chase House is closed.

The stroller now moves on to the Naval Academy "Yard," which is open to visitors daily from 9 A.M. to 5 P.M. The route is along Maryland Avenue to the Yard's Gate 3. Inside, to the left, is Worden Field, where the dress parades of the Brigade of Midshipmen are held on Wednesday afternoons in spring and fall.

Seagoing Relics

The Naval Museum is straight ahead. It contains an engrossing collection of nautical relics, paintings, ship models and other historic mementos. Leaving the museum, the course is

dead ahead—to the chapel, with its great green dome.

Beneath it are the crypt and sarcophagus containing the remains of John Paul Jones, that early Navy hero. The chapel is open daily, and on Sundays visitors can attend the 10:15 A.M. service, to which the midshipmen march in a body.

The next port of call is the enormous dormitory, Bancroft Hall. Entering the main portals, the stroller advances to Tecumseh Court, where the brigade's noon formation is held. Beyond the court, a flight of steps leads to Memorial Hall, with its display of murals of historic Naval engagements, portraits of famous officers and battle flags.

For the Fleet

On leaving Bancroft Hall, the stroller proceeds toward the Severn and Santee Basin, where the academy's fleet of sailboats and other small craft rests. At the southeastern tip of the academy grounds stands a relic of the Spanish-American War —the foremast of the battleship Maine, which was blown up in Havana Harbor in 1898.

To return to the civilian world, visitors skirt the rim of the Yard along the seawall, with Farragut Field, a drill and sports area, on the right. The view beyond the seawall is spectacular, for there the Severn and Spa Creek merge into the broad expanse of Chesapeake Bay.

Turning inland to the right, one comes to Gate 1. This opens onto Randall Street, which, in turn, leads to the picturesque marketplace. This is at the head of Annapolis's inner harbor, and here oysters and clams can be eaten on the half-shell at oilcloth counters. At other stalls, many varieties of fish, as well as crabs and shad roe in season, can be bought.

It is a pretty good place to end a walking tour of Annapolis—a tour of about three and a half miles.

For those who do not want to make the tour alone, guided visits can be obtained for $1.50, from Historic Annapolis, Inc., 18 Pinkney Street.

July 11, 1965

THROUGH BOSTON
IN THE FOOTSTEPS OF HISTORY

By JACK BROUDY

BOSTON — This year marks the tenth anniversary of the Freedom Trail, a foot tour of fifteen historical shrines in Boston. On a stroll of less than two miles, the tourist can visit the Park Street Church, the Old Granary Burying Ground, King's Chapel, the site of the nation's first public school, the statue of Benjamin Franklin, the Old Corner Book Store, the Old South Meeting House, the Old State House, the site of the Boston Massacre, Faneuil Hall, Paul Revere House, the Old North Church, Copp's Hill Burying Ground, the Boston Stone and the Province Steps.

The tour not only is educational and economical, but it also is good exercise. It can be made in one morning or in an afternoon. Some tourists prefer a mid-morning start and then a pause for lunch in one of the many good restaurants in the market district. Only two of the sites charge admission fees. They are the Old Meeting House and the Paul Revere House. The fee is nominal.

For those who want to branch out a bit, there are three "Freedom Paths." One includes the State House on Beacon Hill, Louisburg Square, Boston Common and the Central Burying Ground. The Harrison Gray Otis House in the West End is a separate "Freedom Path" tour, but it is close enough to be included

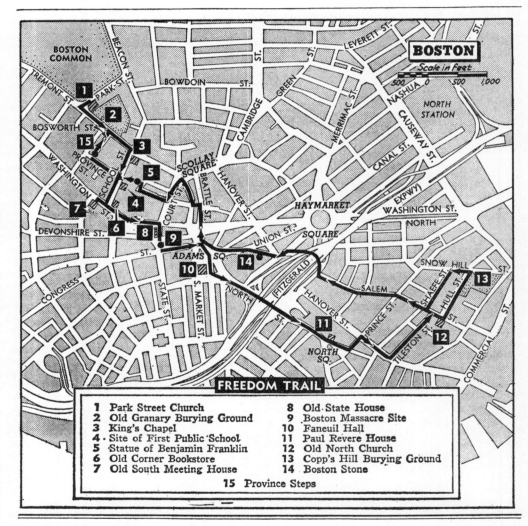

FREEDOM TRAIL

1 Park Street Church
2 Old Granary Burying Ground
3 King's Chapel
4 Site of First Public School
5 Statue of Benjamin Franklin
6 Old Corner Bookstore
7 Old South Meeting House

8 Old State House
9 Boston Massacre Site
10 Faneuil Hall
11 Paul Revere House
12 Old North Church
13 Copp's Hill Burying Ground
14 Boston Stone

15 Province Steps

in the Beacon Hill-Boston Common stroll.

The remaining path leads across the harbor to Charlestown, where the frigate Constitution (Old Ironsides) and the Bunker Hill Monument can be viewed. However, this is too long a walk for the average pedestrian.

Proof of Visit

Visitors who walk the Freedom Trail can prove it. At eight key locations are vending machines that dispense eight commemorative Freedom Trail stamps. These can be pasted on a certificate included in a brochure that is available to tourists. The certificate is signed by Mayor John J. Collins and Richard A. Berenson, chairman of the Freedom Trail Committee. Money from the sale of the stamps goes toward maintenance of the shrines along the trail.

The trail is marked with a sequence of red, white and blue signs. It follows a roughly oval course and finishes at the Province Steps, about a block from the starting point at the Park Street Church.

The idea for a trail originated with a Boston newspaperman only about nine years ago. He suggested a "Freedom Way" to direct tourists to the many historic places they had to search out without help in a city where even a homing pigeon can get lost.

The tour was pedestrian from the start because many of the markers pointed the wrong way down one-way streets. Over the years, maintenance of markers has been a problem for the city. They tend to get lost, stolen or twisted. One tourist complained a few years ago that one marker, indicating Faneuil Hall, actually pointed to a sausage factory.

Some tourists have complained because Faneuil Hall houses a produce market, because the Boston Stone is in an out-of-the-way spot and because the Paul Revere Mall is not always as tidy as it could be. On the whole, however, the response of visitors is enthusiastic.

As for Faneuil Hall, it has its utilitarian purposes as well as historical associations. Beneath the handsome hall are street-level stalls in which meat, cheese, eggs and vegetables have been sold for years.

The Boston Stone is out of the way because the city has enveloped it. Many of the shrines are in the North End, one of the city's oldest and most thoroughly lived-in districts.

The tour starts at the 150-year-old Park Street Church, which overlooks the rolling lawns and tall elms of the Common. Here, William Lloyd Garrison inveighed against slavery, and brimstone for gun powder was stored in the cellar during the War of 1812.

The adjoining Granary Burying Ground, separated by an iron fence from the rush of Tremont Street traffic, contains the graves of three signers of the Declaration of Independence —John Hancock, Robert Treat Paine and Samuel Adams. Also buried here are Paul Revere and Mary Goose, who may have been Mother Goose.

Down Tremont Street

A short way down Tremont Street is King's Chapel, the first Episcopal church in Boston and later the first Unitarian church.

Around the corner, on School Street, is City Hall, a non-historical antique. A school built on this site became the Boston Latin School, the first public school in the country. On the City Hall lawn is Greenough's statue of Benjamin Franklin. One side of the face is considered gay and the other, grave.

At School and Washington Streets, close to the department stores, is the Old Corner Book Store, one of the oldest brick buildings in the city. Here, Longfellow, Emerson, Hawthorne, Holmes, Harriet Beecher Stowe and Whittier used to meet. The book store bearing that name is now in Bromfield Street.

A block or two down Washington Street, on the edge of the city's former Newspaper Row, is the Old South Meeting House, where Colonists held mass meetings when the Revolution was in the making. After the Massacre, Boston citizens met here to demand withdrawal of the British troops.

A short distance down Washington Street, close to the State Street financial district, is the Old State House, which once served as a British barracks. Royal proclamations were read from its graceful balcony. And so was the Declaration of Independence. A circle of cobblestones near-by marks the spot where the Boston Massacre occurred in 1770.

At Dock Square, once waterfront terrain, the tourist reaches Faneuil Hall. The Ancient and Honorable Artillery Company of Massachusetts has an interesting museum in this, the Cradle of Liberty.

The trail bears north here and leads to the Paul Revere House, Paul Revere Mall and Old North Church. The Revere House in North Square is the oldest house in Boston. It was built about 1670, and Revere was living there when he made his midnight gallop to Lexington. Cyrus Dallin's equestrian statue of Revere can be seen on the Paul Revere Mall nearby.

The 237-year-old Christ Church on Salem Street has used up several spires during its history as Old North Church. The present one replaces the steeple lost in a hurricane a few years ago.

A Boston minister recently challenged that segment of history that gives Christ Church the honor of being the Old North Church where two lanterns were hung on April 18, 1775, to warn the patriots that the Redcoats were off to Lexington and Concord. The challenger says that the Old North of that day was the Second Church, which was in the same neighborhood but later was destroyed by the vengeful British. But tourists continue to eye Christ Church with undiminished respect.

Next on the tour is Copp's Hill Burying Ground, where the Rev. Cotton Mather lies, and where British cannons once took a bead on Bunker Hill.

Heading back toward downtown Boston, the Freedom Trail explorer seeks out the Boston Stone, a granite globe once used to grind paint. It was set up as a point of reference in Colonial times to measure distances to Boston.

The Last Stop

The last stop is at the Province Steps, all that remain of the estate of Peter Sergeant. It was the most magnificent private home in Boston late in the seventeenth century, and later served as the administrative center of the province. Its nearest neighbor is a new, elevator-type, non-historical city parking garage.

Promotion of the Freedom Trail as a tourist attraction represents a joint effort undertaken by the Freedom Trail Committee, the Greater Boston Chamber of Commerce and the Advertising Club of Boston. These organizations have been aided in their efforts by the John Hancock Mutual Life Insurance Company, which has prepared a colored brochure on the trail. Copies of the brochure, which contains the certificate to which the Freedom Trail stamps can be affixed, are available free.

May 29, 1960

A WALKING TOUR OF BOSTON

Stroll of Byways Is Rewarding Way to Savor Atmosphere Of Places Where the 'Sons of Liberty' Resided

By LEAVITT F. MORRIS

BOSTON — While every month in the year surely has made history in venerable Boston, April is peculiarly appropriate for reviving its ancient glories because of a spectacular event that was launched there 187 years ago the night of the 18th. That was when, thanks to the signal from the Old North Church, a certain celebrated patriot and silversmith, Paul Revere, commenced his "wonderful ride," as Longfellow called it, to Lexington and Concord, to alert "every Middlesex village and farm" that the Redcoats were coming.

But Boston's Old North is only one of quantities of the city's historic landmarks, and the fact is that the best way to view these sites is on foot. They are fairly close together, and the routes to them have been studiously traced.

By strolling along the narrow, winding streets, literally laid out more than 300 years ago by cows meandering to pasture, exploring the delightful, almost obscured, alleyways, and sauntering between mellowed red-brick buildings, one walks hand in hand with history.

There are several varied walking tours in Boston. But the one which embraces the city's richest historical lore and is the easiest to follow is the Freedom Trail. Indeed, the visitor walking over this route follows in the footsteps of Revere, Franklin, Otis, Hancock, and non-Boston Jefferson. These patriots no longer are just names here but personalities. For instance, it is demonstrated that Paul Revere was not only an eminent patriot, a horseman of rare skill, but politician, soldier, gold-and-silversmith, artist, mechanic, and bell founder.

Decorative pointers mark this tour and the route leading deep into history can be walked in about four hours, including a leisurely pause for lunch at such old-time eating places as Durgin-Park's on North Market Street, with its red and white checkered table cloths, and Ye Old Union Oyster House on Union Street.

Where Trail Starts

The Freedom Trail starts at the corner of Park and Tremont Streets, with the Boston Common in view. In Colonial days, this spacious area was the Village Green as well as a lush pasture for cows. On any warm summer day visitors and inhabitants alike loll in the shade of mighty elms, some older than Boston itself.

Rising in stately fashion at the intersection of Park and Tremont Streets is the Park Street Church, built in 1809. Closely associated with many events leading to this country's complete independence, this church has a cellar where gunpowder was stored during the War of 1812. Immediately, the joining of the two streets became known as Brimstone Corner. Later, Henry Ward Beecher delivered his fiery sermons from the Park Street Church pulpit, further justifying the corner's nickname.

The church stands on the site of the building where the sails of the U. S. S. Constitution, "Old Ironsides," were made. It is open Monday through Friday 9 A. M. to 5 P. M.; Saturday 9 A. M. to 12 noon except during the summer, when it is closed; Sunday 9 A. M. to 1 P. M. and 5 P. M. to 9 P. M.

Moving in a northerly direction along Tremont Street, it is only a short distance to the Granary Burial Ground, dating from 1660. Here the gray headstones probably carry more names known to more people than those of any cemetery in the country. Buried here are most of the great of historic Boston, including three signers of the Declaration of Independence John Hancock, Samuel Adams, and Robert Treat Paine.

Others buried here are Paul Revere, Peter Faneuil, Benjamin Franklin's parents, victims of the Boston Massacre, and the author of the Mother Goose rhymes whose name actually was Mary Goose. It is open daily from 8 A. M. to 4 P. M.

Continuing in the same direction, the Freedom Trail crosses traffic-cluttered Tremont Street to School Street. Here stands King's Chapel, built in 1749. It ranks in historic fame with the Old South Meeting House and the Old North Church.

Oldest Burial Ground

During the siege of Boston, British officers worshiped in the chapel. Adjoining it is Boston's oldest burial ground, containing the remains of Governor Winthrop, John Cotton, and Mary Chilton Winslow. It is open Monday through Friday, 9 A. M. to 4 P. M.; Saturday 9 A. M. to 11.45 A. M. and 12.45 P. M. to 4 P. M.; Sunday 9 A. M. to 4 P. M.

Heading down School Street, the stroller can pause a moment to read a plaque near the City Hall indicating the site of the nation's first public school. Known as the Boston Public Latin School, it was established in 1635. At the same time, the Freedom Trail follower can pause to gaze at the statue of Benjamin Franklin on the City Hall lawn.

Just before School Street merges with Washington Street stands the Old Corner Book Store, once the meeting place of such New England literary lights as Longfellow, Emerson, Whittier and Julia Ward Howe. Built between 1712 and 1715, it is one of Boston's oldest brick buildings.

After the stroller has carefully threaded his way across Washington Street and turned right to the Old South Meeting House, a look down near-by Milk Street will bring into view the bust of Benjamin Franklin on the house where he was born.

The Old South Meeting House, with its conventional Colonial wooden steeple rising 180 feet above the street, is where the outraged colonists held their mass meetings which set off the Revolution. In 1773, these angry citizens gathered there to protest against taxation without representation. This famous protest led shortly thereafter to the historic Boston Tea Party.

The Old South Meeting House is open June 1 to Oct. 1, Monday through Saturday, 9 A. M. to 4 P. M.; Oct. 1 to May 1, Monday through Friday, 9 A. M. to 5 P. M., Saturday, 9 A. M. to 4 P. M.; closed Sunday.

At this point, the visitor must retrace his steps along Washington Street, past Water Street, to State Street, site of the Old State House. It was built in 1713, and rebuilt in 1747. Having the distinction of being the oldest state building in the United States, it is most famous because from its stone balcony the Declaration of Independence was read in 1776. One should note the grasshopper weathervane on its roof.

It is open May 1 to Oct. 1, Monday through Friday, 9 A. M. to 4:30 P. M.; Saturday 9 A. M. to 1 P. M.; Oct. 1 to May 1, Monday through Saturday, 9 A. M. to 4 P. M.; closed Sunday.

Passing the Old State House and moving down State Street, the walker arrives at the intersection of Congress Street where a circle of cobblestones marks the site of the Boston Massacre. Here patriots, protesting against the quartering of British troops in town, fell before the gunfire of the Redcoats.

To Faneuil Hall

Now, the route continues along State Street to Merchant's Row and turns left to Faneuil Hall in Dock Square. Every schoolboy knows that this building is called the "Cradle of Liberty," for here took place some of the earliest and most stirring town meetings of the Boston patriots.

It is open Monday through Friday, 9 A. M. to 5 P. M.; Saturday, 9 A. M. to 12 noon, Sunday 1 P. M. to 5 P. M.

Resuming the tour of the Freedom Trail from a visit to Faneuil Hall, the tourist swings across Market Square, passes under an elevated artery, and takes North Street to Paul Revere House, the oldest house in Boston. The great patriot lived here for thirty years, from 1770

to 1800. It is open Monday through Saturday, 9:30 A. M. to 4 P. M. (closed Sundays and holidays).

On leaving the Paul Revere House, the trail turns left up North Street to Prince Street, goes along Prince Street to Hanover Street, and turns right on Hanover Street to Paul Revere Mall. There a statue of the patriot graces the park. One then walks through the Mall to "The Old North", or Christ Church, Boston's oldest church building.

It was from the original belfry of this church — a hurricane several years ago blew it down and it since has been rebuilt — that the two lanterns sent Paul Revere on his ride. It is open June 1 to Oct. 1 from 9:30 A. M. to 4 P. M. daily. From Oct. 1 to June 1, 10 A. M. to 4 P. M. daily.

From the Old North Church, the Freedom Trail goes straight ahead up Hull Street into Copp's Hill Burying Ground. This was a battery site during the Revolution for the British troops. It was from here that British guns were trained on Charlestown and Bunker Hill across the water.

Now, one continues along Hull Street to Snow Hill and turns left to Sheafe Street. Here it is a one-block stroll to Salem Street on which a right turn is made down to the elevated artery. One crosses to Marshall Street and bears left to see the Boston Stone. This is a granite sphere brought from England in 1700, used for grinding paint by the craftsman, Thomas Childe. A section of the granite trough which also was used in the paint grinding is placed below the stone ball.

At this place — the trip is

almost over — the stroller goes forward to Union Street, past Ye Old Union Oyster House, to Adams Square. Here, the trail crosses to Brattle Street and makes a left turn up any little alleyway to Cornhill. On Cornhill one turns right and walks ahead to Scollay Square.

Old and the New

From Scollay Square, which is a hodgepodge of old and new, a right turn is made on to Court Street which runs into Province Street. Here the walker comes onto Bosworth Street to view the unique Province Steps. In the seventeenth century these steps led to one of Boston's magnificent private homes. All that remains today of the estate is the unusual flight of steps.

It is a quick and easy walk straight ahead from the Province Steps to Tremont Street and back to the Park Street

starting point. There one can step on to the soft green grass of Boston Common and relax under the shade of towering trees.

• There are three other separate walking tours in Boston which lead into the pages of history. They are known as the Freedom Paths and take the wanderer to (A) the State House, Louisbourg Square, Boston Common, and Central Burying Ground; (B) to the Frigate Constitution and Bunker Hill Monument; and (C) to the Harrison Gray Otis House.

The walker who has completed the Freedom Trail can continue on up Park Street to Beacon Street where the gold-domed State House rises majestically on the "Hill" in a surrounding of attractively landscaped grounds. It was built in 1795 and Paul Revere not only laid the cornerstone but later

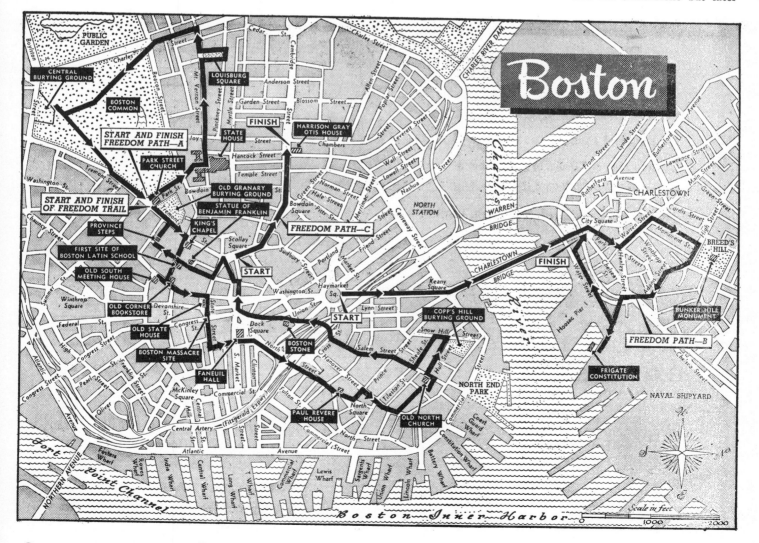

on coppered the dome, now gilded with gold leaf. The State House is considered one of the masterpieces of Charles Bulfinch, called "the first American architect." It is open weekdays from 8:45 A. M. to 5 P. M.

After crossing Beacon Street and swinging left into Mount Vernon Street, the visitor shortly arrives at Louisbourg Square which looks much like some square in London's Mayfair. The central green, which belongs to those living around it, is enclosed by an iron fence with no gate. Famous personages of the past who made their homes in the four-story brick dwellings encircling it include Louisa May Alcott, Jenny Lind, and William Dean Howells.

After sauntering around the Square and savoring this little bit of old England, the Freedom Path continues along Mount Vernon Street to Charles Street, across Beacon Street, and on to the Common and the Central Burying Ground. At this point the Path crosses Boston's new municipal underground garage. This project is nearly finished and the Common and the Freedom Path are being restored to their one-time loveliness.

For the Ambitious

The ambitious walker can, by following Washington Street from Haymarket Square to the Charlestown Bridge and on to Charlestown, see the frigate Constitution and even climb the steep steps of the Bunker Hill Monument. There is subway service from downtown Boston to City Square, from which point the Freedom Path route can be followed with ease. To reach the Monument from City Square, the walker follows Park Street to Warren and swings right on Monument Street to the granite obelisk some 220 feet high, above Breed's Hill.

At the base of the Monument is the statue of Col. William Prescott, who is credited with the famous line: "Don't fire until you see the whites of their eyes." The Monument is open 9 A. M. to 5 P. M., April through September; 9 A. M. to 4 P. M., October to April.

Striding down High Street, the tourist takes a sharp turn into Adams Street and another equally sharp turn to Sea Street which intersects Wapping Street. One steps down Wapping Street to Water Street and walks to the Naval Shipyard where the frigate Constitution is moored. It may be visited daily 9:30 A. M. to 4:30 P. M. The return to City Square is directly along Water Street.

To reach the Harrison Gray Otis House, one takes off from Scollay Square along Cambridge Street, crossing Staniford Street and Lynde Street on the right. The house was built in 1795, and the interior remains about the same today as it was in Colonial times. Its unique architectural features, a Palladian window, third-story fan window and square hipped roof are attributed to Bulfinch. It is open Monday through Friday from 10 A. M. to 4 P. M.

April 8, 1962

New Charter Oak Trail Is Keyed to Hartford

By BERNARD J. MALAHAN

HARTFORD, Conn.—A newly designated Charter Oak Trail has been designed to help visitors find their way to places of special interest in Connecticut. The trail is 500 miles long and winds through 70 communities.

Prominently outlined on the latest official tourist map distributed by the State Development Commission, the lengthy new trail is one of two Charter Oak Trails whose purpose is to facilitate tourist travel in Connecticut. The other trail is a one-and-one-half-mile walking tour through Hartford, the state capital; it was mapped out and marked with directional indicators two years ago by the Greater Hartford Coordinating Committee for the Arts..

Both trails are named for a giant oak tree with a hole in its trunk that served as a hiding place for Connecticut's Royal Charter in 1687, when emissaries of King James II were trying unsuccessfully to reclaim it. The historic oak, its former location marked now by a stone monument in Hartford's south end, was toppled by a storm in 1856.

The Original Trail

Hartford, of course, is a key point on the new Charter Oak Trail. Travelers, therefore, may find it convenient to do some touring by car and then take off on foot over what may become known as the "original" Charter Oak Trail.

It takes about 90 minutes to cover the basic walking route in Hartford, but a visitor may find it well worthwhile to spend additional time at stops such as the Wadsworth Atheneum or the State Library and Museum.

The starting point of the Hartford tour is Constitution Plaza, in the heart

RAY MAINWARING; BERNARD J. MALAHAN

FULL SPEED AHEAD—Phoenix Insurance Company building.

of the downtown business section. The plaza was completed in 1964 on 12 acres of redeveloped land, and is regarded as one of the nation's outstanding urban renewal efforts.

It comprises high-rise office buildings,

a hotel, numerous retail shops, a major television and broadcast facility and an open central area. The open area is closed to vehicular traffic. It is the locale for many of Hartford's outdoor cultural events and is a pleasant place in

ON THE CHARTER OAK TRAIL—The Olde Towne Mill in New London.

which to relax on a summer's day.

A Gigantic Ship

A bridge at plaza level leads to the two-sided headquarters building of the Phoenix Mutual Insurance Company. The elliptical structure, with high glass walls, looks much like a gigantic ship with two bows and no stern. It is called, technically, a lenticular hyperboloid, and it is said to be the first structure of this design in the nation.

Hartford is the home of several of the country's largest insurance companies, and enjoys renown as the "Insurance City." A few hundred feet west of the Phoenix building is the headquarters of the Travelers Insurance Companies.

From the observatory in the tower of the 527-foot-high-Travelers structure,

one can enjoy a panoramic view of Hartford and its environs. The tower is open weekdays from 8 A.M. to 3:30 P.M.

A short distance from Tower Square, the plaza that adjoins the Travelers building, is the Wadsworth Atheneum. Founded in 1842, the atheneum is the nation's oldest free public art museum. Its buildings cover an entire city block and contain some exhibits of exceptional quality.

Among them are the works of Rembrandt, Tintoretto, Caravaggio, Daumier, Copely, Picasso and Mondrian, the Meissen collection of more than 300 pieces of rare 18th-century French and German porcelains, and the Wallace Nutting collection of 17th-century American furniture.

Directly across from Tower Square,

on the west side of Main Street at the corner of Gold Street, is the Center Church and Old Burying Ground. Known as the First Church of Christ, its early history was closely linked to the growth of the colony of Hartford under the direction of the Rev. Thomas Hooker. He was the resolute Congregationalist whose liberal ideas about self-government were embodied in Connecticut's Fundamental Orders, adopted in 1639.

The present church, the fourth to serve the congregation, had been in con-

tinuous use since 1808. To its rear is the Burying Ground, used from 1640 to 1803. A monument lists the names of 100 of Hartford's early leaders buried there.

Among the individual markers are many well-preserved examples of early gravestone art, the work of patient Colonial artisans who laboriously chiseled in stone the ornate designs and lengthy epitaphs favored in those days.

From here, the tour route crosses Bushnell Park, a green expanse of more than 40 acres that gives to Hartford a sense of spaciousness.

Overlooking the park is Connecticut's Capitol. The marble and granite building, topped by a gold dome, houses the offices of the Governor and elective officials, as well as the legislative chambers. It has been in use since 1879.

Museum Hours

Directly across Capitol Avenue, south of the Capitol, is the State Library and Museum. Displayed there is the original Royal Charter, the Colt collection of approximately 1,000 pistols, rifles, machine guns and other weapons manufactured in Hartford, Gilbert Stuart's portrait of George Washington, the table on which Abraham Lincoln is said to have signed the Emancipation Proclamation, the extensive Mitchelson coin collection and many other items associated with Connecticut's long history.

The museum is open Mondays through Fridays from 8:30 A.M. to 5 P.M. and on Saturdays from 9 A.M. to 1 P. M., except on holiday weekends.

The tour route, which includes a number of other stops not mentioned here, leads back to the business center of Hartford and the Old State House. This building, a superb example of Federal period architecture, was completed in 1796 from designs by Charles Bullfinch.

The structure served as the seat of government for many years. Now a historical museum, it is open Tuesdays through Saturdays from noon to 4 P.M. An impressive statue of Thomas Hooker stands at its west entrance on Main Street.

The "new" Charter Oak Trail connects at several points with the already established New England Heritage Trail, a tourist travel route that includes all six Northeastern states. By following either the Charter Oak or Heritage Trail in Connecticut, the visitor can reach virtually every section of the state.

Suggested Stops

The trails include, for example, the shore towns along Long Island Sound; Bridgeport, where the 10-day Barnum Festival gets under way on June 25; Stratford, home of the American Shakespeare Festivale Theater and Boothe Memorial Park, where youngsters find fascination in some buildings of strange design, and New Haven, where visitors can tour the Yale campus or the Peabody Museum of Natural History.

Going east from New Haven, the trail leads to New London, site of the Governor Winthrop Olde Towne Mill and a schoolhouse, built in 1774, where Nathan Hale once taught; to Groton, a bloody battleground of the American Revolution, and to Mystic Seaport, where thousands of visitors each year climb aboard ancient whaling vessels or tour the shops in that restored 19th-century seaport town.

The trails also go through old Connecticut River communities in the central part of the state, among them East Haddam. There, another one-room school house is preserved to honor Nathan Hale, who taught there before entering military service.

Other Points of Interest

To the south, on State Route 63, is Litchfield, which is celebrating its 250th anniversary this year. It is a town with many beautifully preserved early American homes, and is the site of the White Memorial Foundation, a 4,000-acre nature preserve open to the public.

Travelers planning to make use of the Charter Oak and Heritage Trails can obtain a map and other information by writing to the State Development Commission, P. O. Box 865, Hartford, Conn. 06115. The commission can also supply a guide listing hotels, motels and resorts.

RESTING PLACE—Ancient gravestones

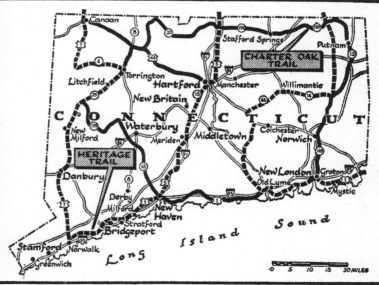

Map at right shows both Heritage and Charter Oak Trails.

April 27, 1969

Strolling in Miami Beach

By JAY CLARKE

MIAMI BEACH — Few people would attempt to walk the length of Miami Beach, but one can obtain a representative sample of this resort city by taking a short walking tour through a midtown section.

The few square blocks around 23d Street show Miami Beach in a nutshell—coconut, of course. Here, one can find just about anything, from seashells to strip-teasers, from plush hotels to fading apartment houses, from brassy bars to quiet museums, from busy thoroughfares to uncrowded footbridges.

Grand Dame Hotel

A walking tour can begin almost anywhere in the area, but a good place to start is Collins Avenue and 23d Street. This is a busy intersection, with the grand dame of Miami Beach hotels, the Roney Plaza, on the ocean side.

This famous pink hotel—it was built in the booming 20's—was supposed to have been torn down last year. However, plans to replace it with a $25-million resort were halted by the tight-money situation.

A block north of the Roney Plaza, on Collins Avenue, is Lake Pancoast, the southern end of Indian Creek. Sightseeing boats leave from a dock there on voyages up Indian Creek, which is lined with millionaires' homes, and out into Biscayne Bay. Tours cost $2.95 to $11.95. Boats can also be rented at the same dock.

Contrasts

A footbridge in the dock area arches over the waterway and leads to a quiet residential apartment section, which contrasts sharply with the bustle of Collins Avenue.

A short stroll takes one to another footbridge, this one over the Collins Canal, a narrow waterway that connects Lake Pancoast with Biscayne Bay.

It is just a block past the footbridge, and past sme older apartment buildings, back to 23d Street.

At the eastern end of the street stand the Roney Plaza and the new Holiday Inn; at the other end are a par-3 golf course and Miami Beach Senior High School.

If one walks west on 23d Street and crosses Collins Canal to Dade Boulevard, he will pass the golf course, a firehouse and the modern high school.

Cross back over the canal at the next bridge, at Washington Avenue. This street goes past the Miami Beach Community Center. At 21st Street, turn east toward the ocean. Along this narrow thoroughfare are Miami Beach's two bastions of culture, both in a park-like setting.

Bastion of Art

The Bass Museum of Art, the first such bastion to be reached, houses numerous paintings and sculptures, including 74 items that have been added since last summer. It is open Tuesdays through Saturdays from 10 A.M. to noon and from 1 to 5 P.M. On Sundays, the hours are 1 to 5 P.M.

Admission is free in the morning, but there is an afternoon charge of 50 cents for adults and 25 cents for children.

Adjoining the museum is the Miami Beach Public Library. An eye-catching feature of the complex, which fronts on Collins Avenue, is the cylindrical tower in front of the main building. Library-oriented programs are presented in this structure,

which seats 100 persons Tourists can borrow books from the 123,000-volume collection if they pay a $5 deposit.

East of Collins Avenue, between 22d and 23d Streets, is the thing that has made Miami Beach famous — the beach. It is one of six public beaches spotted along the oceanfront.

If the city fathers had not retained a few parcels of oceanfront land for public use, it is doubtful whether walking tourists could see much of the Atlantic; highrise hotels and apartment

buildings block most of the shoreline.

'No Two on a Chair'

Beach chairs can be rented for 50 cents a day at this strand, called Collins Park, and signs sternly warn "No Two on a Chair." A coin telescope is/ also available for those who want to get a closer look at ships offshore.

It is only a block or so back to the Roney Plaza, the starting place for the tour, and the entire trip should take about an hour.

June 11, 1967

NEW ORLEANS WALKING TOURS

The Famous Vieux Carre, or Old French Quarter, Contrasts With City's Newer 'American' or 'Garden' District

By ROBERT MEYER, Jr.

NEW ORLEANS, La.—The 18th-century Frenchmen and Spaniards who settled the square mile that is now known as the New Orleans French Quarter, or Vieux Carré, and installed homes, churches and substantial public buildings that are still in use, unwittingly made an incomparable contribution to 20th-century tourism.

True, only a fraction of the area retains reminders of its glamorous, romantic past; yet, what is there is well worth traveling many miles to see, and should be enjoyed in the leisurely manner of a walking tour.

There is a saying in New Orleans that one does not have to stand long at the juncture of Canal and Royal Streets until he will meet someone he knows. Many tourists probably could say "Amen!" to that, because most visitors cross Canal Street from uptown and, like strangers entering a new country, funnel into Royal Street.

For that reason, the intersection of Canal and Royal Streets is a logical point from which to start an unhurried examination of this interesting section.

The First Few Blocks

The first two or three blocks of Royal Street do not contain very much of historic interest to encourage browsing, but antiques stores and a fancy grocery will. No. 121 Royal, once the office of Dr. Antommarchi, who made a death mask of Napoleon, is now shared by a fruit stand and the entrance to a small hotel.

The first carnival ball is reported to have been planned at 227 Royal Street, and the planting of that seed has regularly produced a bountiful harvest.

In 1963 alone, several dozen balls were scheduled between Jan. 6, King's Night, and Feb. 26, Mardi Gras.

The celebrated Shakespearean actor, E. H. Sothern, was born at 709 Bienville Street, just off Royal Street and two thoroughfares below Canal Street. While there is nothing about the building to prompt a pilgrimage, at least one professional guide did his best to give the site an honor it does not deserve.

As his busload of sightseers paused before the wooden structure, he bellowed: "To your right is the place where William Shakespeare was born. You all know who William Shakespeare was. To your left . . ."

Legion Home

The once-majestic Bank of Louisiana Building, which has been at 334 Royal Street, on the corner of Conti, since about 1812, is now an American Legion home. It is badly in need of refurbishing.

The ponderous marble edifice that dominates the river side of the 400 block of Royal Street is actually the center of a full-blown local controversy. Built as a court house in the early 1900's, it became the Louisiana Wildlife and Fisheries Museum a few years ago. The courts, meanwhile, were transferred to a modern civic center a mile away.

Recently, a well-organized group of music lovers launched a campaign to transform the present museum into an opera house. This is something the city has sorely needed since its world-famous French Opera House was destroyed by fire about 40 years ago.

The crusaders contend that it would be more economical to convert the existing building then to build a completely new

opera house. City officials favor a more streamlined structure as part of a proposed cultural center.

On the side of a tavern at the southwest corner of Royal and St. Louis Streets, diagonally across from the Wildlife Museum, is a plaque that states: "In the year 1800 Antoine Amedee Peychaud, founder of Peychaud bitters, originated the first cocktail on this site."

In both the 400 and 500 blocks of Royal Street are some courtyards that thousands of tourists visit every year. Among them, the one that is a part of Brennan's Restaurant has an aura of elegance.

Open to Visitors

The passageway that leads to the courtyard at 520 Royal Street is normally open to visitors free of charge. The attractive old home on the property is now the headquarters of a radio and television station.

Continue along Royal Street to where St. Peter Street divides the 600 block from the 700 block. At 718 St. Peter Street, a popular bar occupies the site where the first theater in the city was erected and where grand opera is believed to have been sung for the first time in America. Nowadays, collegians who frequent the place sing other types of songs.

Turn left at Bourbon Street, walk a block to Toulouse Street and then turn left again without crossing the street. The tourist will then be at the 165-year-old Casa Hove where, for 25 cents, adults can take a self-guided tour of the old house. Hours are 11 A.M. to 5 P.M., Mondays through Fridays, and 11 A.M. to 4 P.M. on Saturdays.

Across the way, at 708 Toulouse Street, is the Gate of the

Lions, a favorite subject for painters and photographers. A few steps from there is Royal Street. Cross Royal and walk one block to Chartres Street, where one can turn right for a block and visit the building popularly known as the Napoleon House. It was intended to become a refuge for the Emperor if he had escaped from St. Helena.

Or, the tourist can turn left and head for the venerable heart of the French Quarter: Jackson Square. The square was the Place d'Armes when the French ruled New Orleans. The Americans renamed it for Gen. Andrew Jackson, hero of the Battle of New Orleans in the closing days of the War of 1812.

Jackson Square, with its familiar equestrian statue, and the buildings on three sides of the park—St. Louis Cathedral, the Cabildo, the Presbytère and the two-block-long Pontalba Buildings, which are believed to be the oldest apartment houses in the nation—are probably the most photographed group of structures in the French Quarter.

Dates to 1794

The cathedral dates to 1794, and the Cabildo and Presbytère, which flank the church, are admission-free museums. In the lower Pontalba Building at 525 St. Ann Street is a handsomely appointed apartment furnished tastefully and completely in the style of 1850. This is an admission-free, state-sponsored museum, where visitors climb graceful, winding stairs to the second and third floors.

The elegant dining room and living room are on the second level, and four French windows separate the living room from a

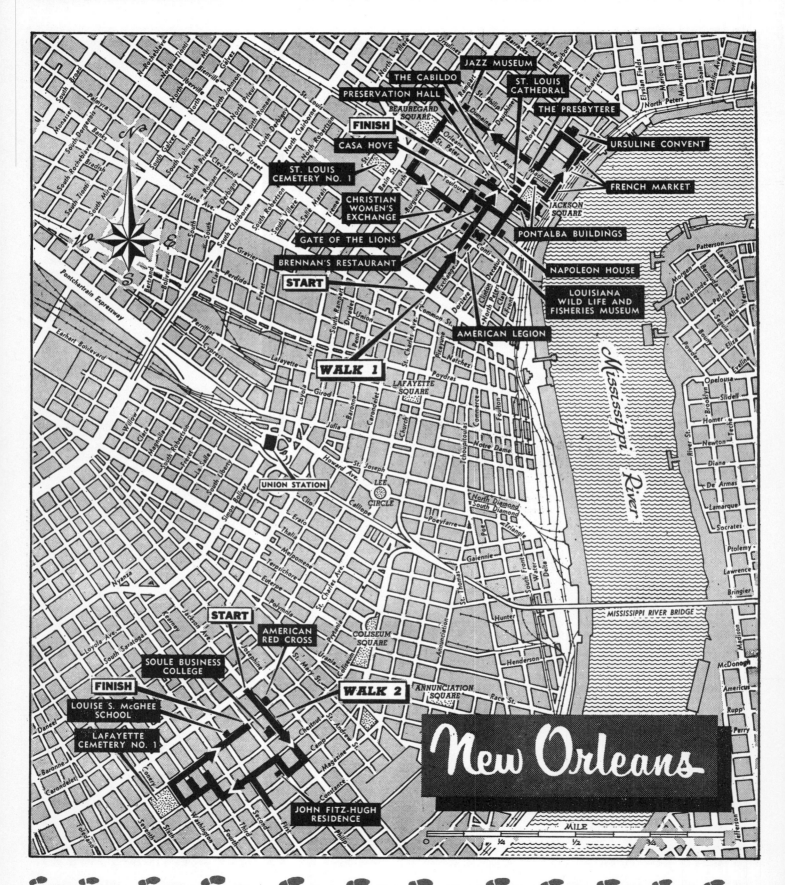

New Orleans

spacious balcony that overlooks Jackson Square. Two bedrooms on the third level also have a view of the park. Near the doorways on both floors are detailed descriptions of the furnishings.

If some warehouses across Decatur Street at the east, or river, end of the square are removed, as they are supposed to be, visitors will have an exciting view of the Mississippi River, the eastern boundary of the Vieux Carré.

Behind the lower Pontalba Building, on Madison Street between Decatur and Chartres Streets, are several splendid examples of how the preservation or restoration of structures can enhance the character of an area. A graceful patrician landmark in the block is a tall, weeping willow tree that grows in the courtyard of the Gallery Circle Theater.

The vaunted French Market, with its well-patronized coffee and doughnut shops, stretches along the river side of Decatur Street for about three blocks—between St. Ann and Ursuline Streets. After inspecting the exotic fruits and vegetables, and probably taking a coffee break, walk along Ursuline Street to Chartres Street and the Ursuline Convent, one of the oldest buildings in the Mississippi Valley.

Here, too, is a 20-year-old replica of the first botanical garden of Louisiana as it was planted in 1731. The original Ursuline School and Chapel was built around 1727-34 on a site close to the river. Its successor was erected in 1745 during the reign of Louis XV, and served as a convent, orphanage and school until 1827. Then it became the residence of the bishops and archbishops of New Orleans until 1899.

The site was designated by the Historic American Buildings Survey as the oldest in Louisiana still devoted to its original purpose.

A dozen blocks separate the Ursuline Convent from Royal and Canal Streets, where the walking tour started. Returning from that point in a roundabout way would be worth the additional effort, because one could visit the newly established Jazz Museum at 1017 Dumaine Street and then saunter across North Rampart Street to voodoo-haunted Beauregard Square and St. Louis Cemetery No. 1. This is the oldest burying place in town, and is notable for its tiers of receiving vaults above ground.

It is about six blocks from the cemetery to Canal and Royal Streets. En route there, at 820 St. Louis Street, is the 132-year-old Grima House, now the Christian Woman's Exchange. This stately brick building, with its balconies of iron lace and two courtyards planted with banana and magnolia trees, fits many a tourist's romantic dream of old New Orleans.

In a completely different way, Bourbon Street after dark has created its own wicked image in the minds of potential visitors. Honky-tonk, tawdry and tired, it is a midnight market place for vicarious thrills.

Less frenetic, and infinitely more indigenous to New Orleans is the jazz music played by old-time musicians at Preservation Hall, 726 St. Peter Street. An hour or so there between 8:30 P.M. and 12:30 A.M. is a truly tuneful way to top off an evening.

Canal Street is the dividing line between downtown and uptown New Orleans. The street named Royal on the downtown side becomes St. Charles on the uptown or, as it had been known for several generations, the American side.

That distinction came into vogue around 1825, some 22 years after the United States purchased Louisiana from France and when the huge Livandais sugar plantation was bought by real estate promoters and converted into the city's first exclusive development for wealthy Americans.

Significantly, the principal east-west thoroughfare in the suburb was named Washington Avenue.

Because the miniature estates were well supplied with sturdy oak and magnolia trees, and semi-tropical flowers and plants thrived there, the area was christened the Garden District.

Today, this aristocratic neighborhood is a 10-cent streetcar ride from Canal and St. Charles Streets. A convenient spot at which to begin a walking tour of the district is St. Charles Street and Jackson Avenues. Almost immediately, one will sense that here is a veritable live museum of capacious, white neo-Greek mansions crowned with mansard roofs, festooned with frilly cast-iron grillwork and enclosed with metal fencing of austere or intricate design.

Strollers can get their first glimpses of this native grandeur one block from St. Charles Street, the actual spot being where Jackson Avenue crosses Prytania, the main street of the Garden District. A towering two-story residence dominates the southwest corner, while across the street, at 2127 Prytania, an exquisite example of the typical raised cottage built in 1849 is now the local headquarters of the American Red Cross.

An imposing two-story mansion—it has porches on the front and sides on both levels—is at 1410 Jackson Avenue, at the corner of Coliseum. It was built in 1856 for Henry Sullivan Buckner, but it has been the Soule Business College since 1923.

Continuing toward the river on Jackson Avenue, the 1300 and 1200 blocks have a few modest samples of traditional area architecture, but more intriguing models are farther uptown. For instance, one block uptown from Jackson Avenue, at 1220 Philip Street, is the 100-year-old John Fitz-Hugh residence. It was built in the 1850's, and for many years was the home of a successful businessman, Isaac Delgado, who gave the city its Delgado Art Museum, the Delgado Trade School and hospital buildings.

Now, its well-tended gardens are noted for a lavish display of red, pink and white azaleas in the spring, and other appropriate shrubs all year. Hearty perennials also beautify the 110-year-old, two-story brick home of classic Greek Revival architecture at 1238 Philip Street.

On the next street uptown, at 1134 First Street, is the stately mansion in which Jefferson Davis, the President of the Confederacy, died. A granite block in front of the house is inscribed: "Here in the home of his friend, Jefferson Davis, first and only President of the Confederate States of America, died on December 6, 1889. A truly great American."

Other places of interest within easy walking distance are at 1239 First Street, 1331, 1415 and 1417 Third Street, 1448 Fourth Street and Lafayette Cemetery on Washington Avenue.

The mansion at 2353 Prytania Street was built in the 1870's; it is now the Louise S. McGehee School. It is customary for the school to sponsor tours of the Garden District on Tuesday and Friday afternoons in February. Also, from October through May, it arranges for private tours of 50 or more persons. Proceeds benefit the school.

The extraordinary architecture that pervades the New Orleans cemeteries has long made them of interest to sightseers. The antiquated St. Louis Cemetery No. 1 on the fringe of the French Quarter, and the Lafayette Cemetery in the Garden District, are so crowded with plots, delapidated vaults and weather-beaten tombs they are remindful of miniature tenements or ghettos.

More modern Elysian fields fan out around the far end of Canal Street, another 10-cent streetcar ride from the business district. Within easy walking distance from the car line are Odd Fellows Rest, a Jewish cemetery, St. Patrick's, Cypress Grove, Greenwood and Metairie.

There is more space around the tombs and graves in the other burying grounds, especially in Metairie. There, many of the final resting places are extravagantly ornate, and some verge on the bizarre. More often than not, they are embellished with sculptured cherubs, angels, weeping widows, lambs caressing crosses, obelisks, urns, fancy fences, and cast-iron garden furniture.

The great day for visiting cemeteries in New Orleans has been Nov. 1, All Saints Day. However, this feast day is not being celebrated as fervently as it used to be.

Ground-Level Burial

At long last, too, Orleansans are able to inter their dead at ground level, something previous generations could not do because of inadequate drainage. No doubt, the cemeteries of the future in New Orleans will look more like those in other parts of the country where mere metal plaques imbedded in a lawn mark a family plot.

Nevertheless, as long as the local tombs withstand the elements and ravages of time, they will continue to be a landmark of New Orleans and attract the curious.

May 19, 1963

WHO WALKS IN CITY STREETS

Infinite Variety of Peopled Places Is His and Contempt of Country Hikers

By M. B. LEVICK

ONCE again comes the season when the hikers flit through town, hastening like migrating birds, yet finding time to chatter of adventure on the way and to finger the anthology of the open road which sticks from the corner of the knapsack. But at the other edge of the sidewalk there passes a fellow who eyes them a trifle dourly from bandana to shoes, noting that like as not the shoes are high-heeled and cut low. This passer-by is the city hiker, who wastes no time over verses about the long white road, but merely sets out and walks.

There are many of him, even yet. He walks far and he walks long, for the sake of the walk, and no one notes him: he has a stride and swings from the hips, and if he does not occasionally sleep in a haystack (with the mosquitos) his road is as long as need be and it is at hand when he puts on his hat.

The walker within the city is not dead. True, he does not compose an army in his coddled age, but there are enough in the city who still cling to the habits of bipeds even though the taxicabs outnumber the chariots of eastern kings. Lately a voice has been raised once more against the decline of walking: Dr. Alvah H. Doty pleads, among other things, for the benefit to the vascular system. One recalls older prophecies of a race which would forget how to cross its legs because of much rush-hour riding, as the Japanese grew short from squatting on the floor; and prophecies also of a new order of centaurs, half man and half motor. But even so, the old model will be preserved, for the city hiker is a hardy being.

And he has his rewards. sometimes even greater than the rewards which fall to those who run to the country to compete with roadsters. For him there is not the monotony of trees, all green, but the infinite variety of the city's strata of architecture; the old sloping roofs with a touch of Dutch about them; the flaking brownstone, to be observed as a ge-

ologist looks at a canyon; the efflorescent brickwork of the 1890s and often the majesty of towers like peaks or the gaunt beauty of stepped skyscrapers against the blue sky. For him there is color as he may desire; if he choose he may walk in yellow streets or in red, and when he comes upon a tree he has no trouble in seeing it because of the forest. The sun's rising arc is lifted above him as the year grows and he tastes the seasons through the changing riverward vista of cross-streets; and after dark, housetops and street lamps only make the blue of the night sky deeper.

You doubt, perhaps, but if you pass the walker at Bowling Green and again by Spuyten Duyvil you cannot see he is the same man. You cannot tag him with a red button, for he is not the sort that likes to walk in parades. He passes unnoted, now here and now there, giving the appearance of two men out of those who ride when the distance is more than half a dozen blocks.

He walks because he likes it. It is no use to ask him why he likes it; if you were not born to walk and understand, you must ride and carry your ignominy in your lap. But if you press him to tell you what of city hiking he likes best, he may take sides and (thinking of the high-heeled shoes beneath the breeches) say, "Well, you're not bothered by any hikers."

For the city walker knows the true companionship of the road, which is silence. The gregarious band palavering as they hoof it—that is not his way. When he walks he gives himself to walking. He does not go in crowds; two at the most, and if he speaks it is at the proper time, in a moment when some aspect of the city's beauty demands the tribute of a pause.

"Then," he may add, "there's good, solid flagstones and cement. Turf is all right, but you can't get a gait on clods. In the city there are no stretches of sand to pull the legs out of you and, as for mud, it doesn't matter if it rains or not."

There is something in that, especially if all the years' use of one's legs has been accustomed to stone.

"And," he goes on, "there are no gates to shut behind you."

Is walking thus made too smooth, a magnified stroll? Watch him now, doing his four miles an hour in a street so crowded there is neither right nor left (even if New York's sidewalk crowds knew one hand from the other). It is helter-skelter all about him, but the city hiker, homeward bound, takes his openings as they come. A swing of a shoulder here, a change of gear where the crowd is packed at the corner, a detour, a sidestep, a clearance of an inch taken as prettily as by an expert chauffeur, and he is through; and then again past the next phalanx, with not a sleeve brushed and hardly a step lost. Beside this, what is mere lumbering up mountain slopes? In such a passage as this a city hiker calls to him the agility of a mountain goat, the litheness of a cat, the judgment of a pilot fish. Exercise? Try it.

These, however, are matters of technique, even though they seem foreign to the cockney, who knows the neighborhood of his home and that of his office and nothing but the subway in between.

There are higher things than mere propulsion.

This city fellow plucks your sleeve. "Rather nice, that, eh?" he says and points to the mellowed red of a perspective of old brick, softened by the falling sun. Or it may be a suggestion of infinity in roof tops looked down upon from such height as Mount Morris Park. He comes upon old porticoed churches, each of which is worth a dozen waterfalls, and on old dwellings that keep within New York a simplicity which has been driven from the villages by gas stations. If he would go in foreign lands, he need only walk south instead of north, and on every hand he comes across the strange beauty that grows in ugliness.

There are things that he misses, of course. This he would not deny, for, as a rule, he has had his experiences in fields and on unpaved roads. In Manhattan one is not likely in the Spring to come upon a ball of infant snakes, writhing just beneath the

earth like a symbol from some half-forgotten old religion of the East, but an ailanthus tree is ample enough to stand for old Mother Nature. The city hiker finds no meadow of flag lilies in a little bay of the Hudson, but here and there, early in the fair months, he sees an equal miracle: the pavements themselves made into a garden at some cross street flower market with its pots and trays, and at times the flowers themselves pursue him on a peddler's cart. And as for the hazards which some regard as adding zest, is the automobile less ferocious than the copperhead?

"Pooh!" says the country hiker, wiping his forehead with his red handkerchief. "Think of the open—distance—ozone!"

But the seasons follow their courses above rooftops as well as above the countryside. The city hiker, indeed is apt to know more of them than the one who journeys further, for those who needs must walk outside the city make it a Summer pleasure, while the city hiker goes his way in one season as in another.

If it is a green walk he wants in Spring, there is a path for him half the length of Manhattan, with few breaks; the narrow parks strung along from Fifty-ninth Street to 200th: Central, Morningside, St. Nicholas, Colonial and the Speedway, one beginning not far from where the other ends. Six miles is not much, but it gives enough green to rest the eye—and the city walker must hunt out his green more than in the days when trees were not uncommon. And beyond the Speedway, northward, it is a step over the hill to Inwood, where the leaves lie thick in Autumn.

Every season is his and Central Park itself is as wild as one wants it when a heavy snowstorm is driving. If the luck is good, one may even see a sleigh there then.

"Yes," says the country hiker, "but this city fellow wouldn't know a cow if he saw it."

"Who wants to know a cow?" says the other. "Besides, cows make poor walking companions."

Much better, he thinks, to be able to recognize a street without the help of the corner signpost. To tell Second Avenue from Third by the character of it, to meet stray little parks as friends with names, to know a street in the Sixties from one in the Eighties and the savor of one neighborhood from another—that, he says, is lore worth having, for streets are not dead, but are the setting for men and by a man's street may you know him. The city hiker thus collects not drooping flowers and butterflies but men.

"But the city is all the same," says the country hiker. "Just houses. Now the country—"

"Listen to him," the city man retorts. "Just houses! My dear man, think of the country; tell me honestly now, isn't it just nothing with maybe a hill in it and —"

And so they come near to blows, forgetting that they are brothers, or cousins at least; and neither related to that androgynous creature the hitch hiker, who pretends to walk when he would ride and pretends to ride when he would walk.

The hitch hiker throws the city hiker into relief, for the former is bent on getting there—where? anywhere, so long as it is there—while the city man hikes for hiking's sake. He is not of the kind that cuts a notch in a stick for every mile. If that sort came to know how swiftly the miles pass when they are measured one to every twenty blocks, the streets would become even more cluttered and the tick of pedometers would silence the elevated.

No, the city hiker is above such things. He has no corps, no handbook, no regimentation. He is unknown, but kit and commissariat give him no worry. He leans against the wind or stamps in slush boots or takes the shady side in Summer (which is best of all, with the heat haze giving the city a charm the country can never attain), but he packs no canteen nor does he have to pretend to chew a pebble to cheat his thirst, for he can always get a drink. Perhaps a heavy walking stick for the swing of it, if the day looks enticing for a long walk, but for the rest he is ready without a dress rehearsal. He does not need to bother with such recondite matters as how to sling a blanket or how the British tramps wind their feet with bandages; he may slip on an extra pair of socks to absorb chafing, and sometimes beneath a park shrub he may change a sock from one foot to another to make it rest easier, but as for paraphernalia, shoes are sufficient and he knows enough to wear in all circumstances the sort of shoes that will stand a good trudging without laming the wearer. Besides, he can always stop.

But when does he walk? That is best of all. He (and she, too, though the women are fewer) walks when he wishes to, as far as work and opportunity permit, and if there is work to do, it is possible to walk to it or home, as far as that goes. Those who use their legs only in the country (says he) must spend half a day getting there and another half getting back, and because it is so far they walk their fill and, being city folk after all, need still another day to rest. But the city hiker, without gear and without time table, can begin his road at his doorstep. Three hundred miles of island streets lie before him, and if he would go exploring there are unsuspected reaches in the boroughs beyond Manhattan. And for him there is never the need to adopt the countryman's form: "How far do you call it?"—a locution far more accurate than "How far is it?" In the country there are miles and hunting dog miles (which are elastic), but in the city the wayfarer can tell where he is and need not push on ten miles more to prove it.

Many miles and many routes, up and down Manhattan and across and beyond. Which of them has the most lasting satisfaction?

"Well," says the city hiker, "coming home, as a rule, I find my feet take me along Fifth Avenue."

May 25, 1924

"A fellow who eyes them a trifle dourly."

UPPER FIFTH-AVENUE FILLED WITH RED-CHEEKED MAIDENS.

Pedestrian exercise has become fashionable within the past few years, and it is a common sight on pleasant mornings to see couples and trios of young ladies taking their constitutional on the avenues in the upper part of the city, or above Thirty-fourth-street, attired in the London style of woolen ulster and hat. It is an admirable costume for outdoor exercise, completely protecting the wearer. These young ladies are generally supposed to be English, but the majority of them are New-Yorkers, and many have never even been across the ocean. Perhaps their ruby complexions, the result of their regular outdoor exercise, induces the conclusion that they are English maidens, whose habit of taking "constitutionale" is well known.

To many of the more robust the inclement weather of the Winter has no terrors, and they go out in all excepting rainstorms, their costume affording ample protection, being warm, yet not heavy or cumbersome. Fifth-avenue, the best cleaned street in the city, is the favorite promenade, especially along the Park. In wet weather, or when there is snow, the Park itself has a damp and chilly atmosphere, and is not therefore as inviting as in the Spring and Fall, when shelter from the sun's rays is sought in the embowered walks. The open region of the Park, with its fresh invigorating air drawn from the Sound on one side and the Palisades on the other, almost too stiff, sometimes, when a northeaster or northwesterly breeze prevails, is the general Mecca to which all the promenades lead, whether the route be "the" Avenue, or Madison-avenue or upper Sixth-avenue.

These groups of pretty pedestrians are becoming quite an incident of social life. The gentlemen who formerly took their strolls in the noontime now go out in the mornings; and those who are not cognizant of the fact would be surprised at the number of those out walking, purely for the exercise. As a rule, these fair pedestrians are in the swim of society, and will be seen later in the day in the Park in the family carriage or sleigh, or at the opera, or at a fashionable reception. These female faces are seldom seen on the popular promenade in the afternoon, which is now Broadway, from Twenty-third to Fourteenth street—a heterogeneous crowd of saints and sinners, and strangers out sight-seeing, that compose the vast floating population of the metropolis.

It is true that in the morning hours the lower promenades in the neighborhood of the popular retail dry goods houses and stores are crowded with ladies out "shopping," who disappear home when the later and miscellaneous frequenters come out; but it is rarely that the fresh and rosy faces of the morning promenade are to be seen in the afternoon, excepting possibly on "matinée" days.

The morning constitutional on the avenue is in vogue only among the wealthy class who can take the leisure from household duties. The delicate, dyspeptic, consumptive beauty is converted by these constitutionals into a hearty, robust, rosy, English-looking girl, who prizes good health and the happy flow of spirits resulting therefrom more than small feet or the intellectual pallor which the poets used to rave about. There is a style among "our girls," that the English prototypes, with their heavy, ungainly shoes and clumsy apparel, do not display, and the natural grace and aplomb of the American, is evinced in her walking.

The light gayety and independence, also characteristic of the American, are conspicuous, especially when a passing school, out for the morning stroll, chaperoned by one of the mentors, is in contrast. The "society reporter," if there is such a thing, would find many names among these morning constitutional takers, and probably conclude that many of them preserved themselves by this regular outdoor exercise from the dissipations of the opera and the dance. The list he would be able to furnish would surprise those who are not cognizant of the fact that the custom of the morning constitutional has become so fashionable on the "upper" avenue. It is to be hoped, however, that no one will invade the sanctity of domestic life to the extent of driving these fair constitutional takers from their favorite promenade by the notoriety he would give them.

January 15, 1887

Lionel Green

Glacial Walk, Central Park, showing rocks polished during the Ice-Age.

HIKERS VISIT THE ICE AGE

Routes in the City Lead To Stone Evidences Of Last Glacier

By JOHN MARKLAND

AMONG the attractions offered by the metropolitan area to the hiker—whose numbers increase in the Fall—are the many glacial vestiges and markings that exist in Manhattan and its environs.

One does not have to be a geologist to read the story of the last visit hereabouts of the great ice fields. Even after the passage of 35,000 years or so, evidences of glacial action may be plainly seen. No section of the country, according to geologists, is richer in glacial markings than New York City and the surrounding countryside.

Perhaps the most dramatic evidences of the last great glacier, which extended southward over the metropolitan district as far as Perth Amboy, N. J., and Prince's Bay, S. I., are the barren exposures of crystalline rock which geologists call "roches moutonnés," or "sheep-shaped rocks." Still showing plainly the markings made by the ice sheets in passing, these exposures are seen to good advantage in Central Park, along Riverside Drive, in Fort Tryon Park, along the Palisades and in other parks and open areas about the city.

Glaciated Stones in Parks

Rearing their huge, timeworn bulks above the land, these grim reminders of the last Ice Age are immediately recognizable. Some are as round and smooth as an igloo; others are rugged and furrowed by time. Parallel grooves or striae, made by stones and other abrasives carried in the base of the ice, are visible on the surface of some of the exposures.

Entering Central Park from Columbus Circle and heading east, the walker comes almost at once upon these rock exposures. The most striking one lies a short distance in from Seventh Avenue. Criss-crossed with furrows and striae and rising to a height of twenty or twenty-five feet, this particular witness of glacial action looks as though it might be the peak of a submerged mountain of stone.

Elsewhere throughout the park, around lakes and playing-fields, along drives and at underpasses, one comes upon many other glaciated stone surfaces. Likewise, one sees them along Riverside Drive, at Fort Tryon Park and at many other points easily accessible to walkers. A famous example is "Mount Tom," the smoothly rounded and deeply furrowed dome of rock at Eighty-third Street and the Drive, which is said to have been a favorite retreat of Edgar Allan Poe nearly a century ago, when he lived at the old Brennan farm near by.

Great "drift" boulders or "erratics," held by geologists to have

been picked up by the ice sheets and carried many miles from their original homes, are likewise to be seen about New York, resting where the ice left them when the slow melting process began. A great cluster of these boulders, some of them weighing many tons, may be observed at the lower end of the south playing field in Central Park. A well-known ice-transported boulder is the huge "rocking stone" in the Bronx Zoological Gardens.

In Near-by Areas

Hikers in Palisades Park, in Westchester County, Connecticut and Long Island will find many glacial boulders, some lying near barren rock surfaces, some in open fields. Like the rock exposures, they are marked with striations and deep furrows. Many of the boulders seen in upper Manhattan and the Bronx originated, according to geologists, in the Catskills and further up-State. Erratics found on the North Shore of Long Island have been identified with rock formations in Westchester, Connecticut and Massachusetts.

November 1, 1936

PEDESTRIAN'S LOT NOT A HAPPY ONE

Motorization of Modern City Has Made Walking a Specialized and Complicated Means of Locomotion—Requires Concentration

By ELIZABETH ONATIVIA.

WALKING is generally considered a simple form of exercise, but with the motorization of cities like New York, it has become a highly specialized means of locomotion. In our crowded streets the methods of transportation provided by Nature and Detroit rank about fifty-fifty.

The day of the hero with the long, careless stride is over. The more careless it is the quicker it is over. Pedestrianism in city streets today involves executive ability, planning and foresight, specialized knowledge and concentration. On the other hand, one seldom takes a taxi except for seating privileges, seclusion or a long haul. The mental anguish is about the same, according to the temperament and temperature.

"Shall we take a taxi or walk?" How many times a day that debate comes up! And most often when the time and the distance is short, the feet win. It's pure paradox that walking is often quicker than motoring. And it's paradoxical that it should be equally complicated.

Lo, the Poor Pedestrian.

It's hard on the pedestrian, for he has to keep turning and craning and stopping and starting. Assuming that he has the right of way, and that no driver wants the satisfaction of running over him, he still has some justification for retaining his timidity. In the first four months of this year, according to recent figures, because motorists refused to grant the right of way, fifty-four persons were killed and 5,152 injured in New York State. How many of these were pedestrians is not specified, but the figures indicate that moral right is no protection.

The crafty New Yorker, therefore, walking for so-called exercise, to save money, to save time, plots his journey like a trip to Europe. He goes crab-like from east to west, say, crossing with the lights. He may even go crab-like down the main lanes, two blocks this side to avoid the débris and boardwalks of construction work, two blocks to the other, to avoid the detour around the excavation. He develops all sorts of unconscious tricks and fancies. His mind is always on the job. If it isn't, the blast of a horn, or the gentle push of a fender, will recall it.

It's destructive to conversation, and if his companion is also traffic-minded, sometimes to friendship. The husband who is accustomed to it all and the wife who is not are a familiar and a depressing sight at busy corners. The back-seat driver afoot. And the most to be pitied in the need for decision and courage are those who are weak from long illnesses and those who are entirely unused to traffic.

In Again, Out Again.

In some places, the arcades and underground passages afford relief, but these take practice. For instance, the new passage from the station to Forty-sixth Street, under the New York Central Building, is delightful, after you have found the entrance, but even then you may end up in the more intimate quarters of the Railway Express. The pedestrian who is an adept at these passages exhibits his knowledge as proudly as if he were driving a new car.

About a hundred years ago, Coleridge wrote:

Like one that on a lonesome road
Doth walk in fear and dread,
And having once turned round walks on
And turns no more his head,
Because he knows a frightful fiend
Doth close behind him tread.

How well that describes the thoughts of a timid soul crossing Fifty-seventh Street! But would the timid soul swap that crossing for the lonesome road? He would not Lonesome roads suggest rural districts, where walking is walking.

Here in New York walking ha become as technical a business a the automotive industry whic' caused the metamorphosis, and you average citizen, though he ma grumble, is secretly pleased an satisfied with these manifestation of modern civilization.

July 7, 1929

Navy Officer Near the End of 4-Year Project of Walking in Every Street on Manhattan

By MEYER BERGER

MEN sometimes set themselves to curious objectives. Cmdr. Thomas J. Keane, 65 years old today, hopes to complete next Sunday afternoon, if the weather is bright, a project he started a little less than four years ago—to walk in every street, avenue, alley, square and court on Manhattan Island.

He intends to start from the northern end of Broadway on Marble Hill around 1 o'clock in the afternoon and do the thirteen miles to the Battery. That will complete his self-imposed task. He thinks that at his normal walking pace, three and one-half miles an hour, he should make it within four hours.

The Navy Reserve officer is a rather short, brisk, blue-eyed man with remarkably good color. He has dropped thirty pounds on his walks, which he took only on week-ends. He was 175 pounds when he started and his health, even in the Navy, was never better.

Even with brow-wrinkling and a decent time for harking back, Commander Keane can't quite remember what started him on his project. He thinks most New Yorkers are extraordinarily provincial, that they don't know much about neighborhoods six blocks from where they live, but he admits that comes as afterthought.

Thomas Keane was born in Galway, Ireland. At 8 he was cabin boy on a tramp sailer that beat up and down Eire's west coast. In World War I he became an ensign in the United States Navy. He was in the U. S. N. R. when World War II took him to Belfast and to Melbourne, Australia, as Base Commander.

•

He formed the Sea Scouts for the Boy Scouts of America. He retired as a Scout national executive ten days ago. If he gets time he may write a pamphlet on his Manhattan walking project, though he doesn't like the idea of tying himself to a desk.

A pocket map guided the commander in his landlubberly rambling. He started at the island's tip, taking all the east-west streets. He had to weave and backtrack a lot in the crooked lanes and alleys in the financial district and in Greenwich Village.

He worked the flanks of Central Park as solid east and west blocks—took them from Fifty-ninth to 110th and then resumed his river-to-river hikes north of that point. The going was roughest where the marginal motor highways block easy access to the rivers' brims.

All told, the commander has covered 3,022 city blocks, which add up to roughly 502 miles. After he had done all the side streets he took the avenues, working from east to west. He left Broadway for the last, because it is the only avenue that runs the island's full length.

•

When visitors have only an hour in town, the commander recommends the walk from Christopher Street on the west, eastward along Eighth Street, as a stroll that offers the greatest variety for the eye and for the ear. "All kinds of people, all kinds of architecture," is the way he sums it. Takes him fifty-five minutes.

One thing that stands out from his island coverage is the city's children. In the richest neighborhoods and in the poorest, he finds, only the children are universally cheerful. Their laughter is the only relieving note in bitter slum surroundings.

The most curious things the commander saw were a goat farm, or stable, at 128th Street near the East River and the shacks on stilts on Harlem River around 223d or 225th Street. He kept no diary and isn't too sure of these locations.

There were little adventures. One day in lower Mulberry Street the commander wandered into a deserted Chinese herb, spice and tea shop, delighted with the heady odors. He lingered twenty minutes, pounded the counter, called with deck-range bellow. No answer.

He says, "Only the Chinese would be that trusting. Leave an open door in a shop like that. The smells put me right back in the Orient."

Another time, on a Saturday afternoon, he fancied a Virginia ham he saw in another Chinese shop (he forgets the street) and found that store deserted, too. He finally looked behind the counter and there he saw six Chinese chaps, shoeless and deep in sleep.

"Never figured that one out," he says. "They looked dead, though I'm sure they weren't. Crazy thing."

December 15, 1954

START, 10 A. M.: Comdr. Thomas J. Keane, 65, checks his watch as he stands in the middle of bridge over Harlem River Ship Canal at beginning of walk down Broadway.

CITY MAN, 65, ENDS MARATHON STROLL

Has Hiked From One End to Other of All Thoroughfares on Manhattan Island

Comdr. Thomas J. Keane, who was 65 years old last Wednesday, has walked from one end to the other of every thoroughfare on Manhattan Island.

He completed the final lap yesterday by hiking thirteen miles in four hours from the northern tip of the island to the Battery. The veteran Naval Reserve officer and Boy Scout executive ended his walk down Broadway at a weathered jetty alongside the Governors Island ferryboat terminal.

When he got there, someone suggested he might like to rest a moment on the stringpiece, with the Statue of Liberty in the background.

"How can I get up if I sit down?" he asked with a laugh. He turned right back toward Bowling Green, and his legs were pumping at the same rhythmic pace when he spotted his son-in-law and daughter in a station wagon on State Street.

Rides Home in Car

"Oh, Sheila!" called the commander, in a voice no offspring could ignore. In a few moments, she was embracing him on the sidewalk. Then her husband, Peter Gibbons-Fly, drove the conquering pedestrian triumphantly back to his home at 69-40 Dartmouth Street, Forest Hills, Queens.

Commander Keane had left there shortly after 8 A. M. At exactly 10 A. M. he was standing in the middle of the bridge over the Harlem River Ship Canal, just south of 225th Street. He took a final look at his watch

The New York Times (by Neal Boenzi)

FINISH, 2 P. M.: The Naval Reserve officer steps cautiously to the tip of a jetty alongside the Governors Island ferry terminal at Battery to complete his thirteen-mile journey.

and headed south.

For all but short portions of his trek, the commander stuck to the west side of Broadway. Briefly, in the low Eighties, he removed his tan topcoat. He ran ahead of his prepared log from the start. He was at 164th Street at 10:48 instead of the estimated time of 11 o'clock. And he crossed Times Square, so as to keep on Broadway, at 12:40 instead of 1. Continuing to gain as the competing foot traffic lessened south of Thirty-fourth Street, he finished a full half-hour ahead of schedule.

During accompanied stretches the commander explained how the plan had formed. When he returned from six years of overseas Navy duty his weight was 175—a little too much for his height of 5 feet 6¾ inches. So he tried walking near his home. But, somehow, a certain variety and flavor seemed lacking.

Then one day in the fall of 1950:

"I had to make a trip to east Fulton Street for a certain type coffee my wife wanted. And I had to pick up some hardware on Washington Street, on the other side of the island. And when I saw the river open up before me I began to think how wonderful the island was and how much there was of it between the two rivers, if only you would care to look."

His intricate criss-crossing began then. It pleased him more and more. "What I'd like to do," he said, "is sell Manhattan to the world—and not because of the skyscrapers or the theatres, but because it's a place where people live."

Incidentally, during 502 miles of walking, he got his weight down to the desired 150.

He traveled in subways to get from his home to the starting points of his walks and from the finish points back home again. The station wagon yesterday was for a special occasion.

December 20, 1954

MAD ABOUT MANHATTAN

Who of us, enamored of Manhattan, does not suffer the pangs of unrealized love? The only one we know is Comdr. Thomas J. Keane. Walking one day back in 1950 from Fulton to Washington Street, Commander Keane was taken with a sudden passion for the island and vowed to cover on foot every mile of its many thoroughfares. Last Sunday he ended his journey when he strolled the length of Broadway from 225th Street to the Battery.

We can't at the moment, office-bound as we are but still in love, imagine many activities more fulfilling than tracking this fabulous twenty-four-dollar rock. To wander from the pathetic and sinister facades of the Bowery to the imposing canyons of Maiden Lane. To saunter through the maddening criss-cross complexity of Greenwich Village, where hundred-year-old houses stand beside towering terraced apartments and footloose young highbrows mingle with the hard-working foreign-born. To pace the triangle of City Hall Park and walk down newspaperless Newspaper Row, through the project-fortified Lower East Side which spawned such opposites as Al Smith and Boss Tweed.

To look among the garages, warehouses and funeral parlors of Hell's Kitchen for the haunts of the long-gone Tenth Avenue Gang. To struggle through the lunch-hour-crowded sidewalks of the garment district, experience the chic bustle about Grand Central and the cool immensity of Penn Station, the business-busyness of Union Square, where radical oratory of the Thirties still hangs in the air, the lushness of Fifth Avenue in the Fifties and the quiet transformation of upper Fifth, where private fortunes have sublet to consulates and institutions, the gray Old-World neatness of Yorkville, the on-the-boulevard aspect of Central Park South, the rhythm and color breaking through the poverty of Harlem, the cliff-like residential hauteur of Riverside Drive, the physical and cultural high ground at Fort Tryon crowned with the incomparable Cloisters.

Oswald Spengler, that professional denigrator of the metropolis, described what he thought was a sickness of city people by saying that they had in them a world-city beat which was not to be denied. We own up to it, as we imagine the Commander does. We just wish we had the Commander's opportunity to make it worse.

December 22, 1954

Bridge Walkers Find Free Way to 'Get Away' From City

Photographs for The New York Times by BARTON SILVERMAN

Brooklyn Bridge offers generous space for those who wish to walk between Brooklyn and Manhattan.

By DEIRDRE CARMODY

It is early morning on the Brooklyn Bridge. The harbor glistens, and overhead thick white clouds are suspended as though giants had splattered spoonfuls of whipped cream against the light blue sky. Far in the distance an airplane's jetstream unfolds behind the Statue of Liberty and, for a startling moment, it seems as though the lady's torch is smoking.

The temperature registers 70 degrees on a nearby Brooklyn skyscraper, and the air is fresh and clear. It is a rare August day and for those who have chosen to walk to work across the bridge that morning, there is no mistaking that New York is a glorious place to be.

Many of them are there because of the magic of the day. But most of them, striding purposefully and swinging their briefcases, belong to that small élite army that regularly marches across many of the 63 bridges of New York.

Most Have Sidewalks

Most of the bridges have walkways for pedestrians. The notable exceptions are the Bronx-Whitestone, the Throgs Neck, the Verrazano-Narrows and the Manhattan. Pedestrians are not allowed on any of the Staten Island bridges nor on the portion of the Queensboro Bridge that crosses from Welfare Island to Queens.

The Verrazano, which was completed in 1965 and is the city's youngest bridge, does not have a pedestrian walkway because an engineering study showed that foot traffic on the bridge that links Brooklyn and Staten Island would be too light to warrant the $3-million additional expense. The same is true of the Throgs Neck.

The Manhattan is closed to

198

pedestrian traffic because the foot promenade is being used for construction, which is not expected to be completed for several years.

Bridge walkers are a versatile lot. In summer they pad barefoot on the warm concrete; in winter they wrap their faces purdah-like in long woolen scarves and lean into the wind. Many with knapsacks hoist bicycles up steep steps on the bridges' approaches and walk their bikes across.

Joggers, Photographers

Some hold hands. Others hold arguments. Many photograph and a few are photographed. Some jog and others stand for hours staring into the water below. Sometimes a pedestrian stares so long he is reported to the police as a potential suicide, but statistics show that bridge suicides are relatively rare.

George Giddish is 67 years old. He lives in Brooklyn Heights and for 12 years he has left his house at 7:40 A.M. and walked with his wife a mile and a quarter across the bridge to the Manhattan side, where she works in the Municipal Building. Then, until his retirement, he would turn around and walk back to Brooklyn and be at his desk at the Consolidated Edison office on Pearl Street by 9 o'clock. Now he walks her across and returns home.

"I do it for exercise," he said, his ruddy face crinkling under his yellow cap as he looked into the sun on that fine morning the other day. "I want to keep physically fit."

Four smiling Chinese girls in cotton sunsuits and sneakers raced across the wide wooden planks that make the Brooklyn Bridge's pedestrian lane so easy to walk on. They carried a large rubber ball, but they did not bounce it for fear that it would go over the railing and splash into the sparkling river.

"I like to look at the sky when it's not polluted," said Jean Seto, a 14-year-old.

At that, her three sisters, Ann, who is 12, and the twins, Edith and Linda, who are 11, burst into giggles. A moment later, still laughing, they ran off toward Brooklyn, four bobbing figures dwarfed by the massive granite arches that stand up against the sky.

A sea gull circled silently. To the south, a yellow ferryboat headed lazily for Staten Island. To the north, the Empire State Building rose high above the skyline like a giant needle pointing toward the clouds.

Although the regular Brooklyn-bound walkers pass the Manhattan-bound ones every day, rarely a nod of recognition is exchanged between them. They are true New Yorkers despite their short daily escape from the city's congestion.

"There's one guy I've tried to say good morning to for a year and now he barely nods," one midtown executive said.

There are three bridges on which vehicles are banned and pedestrians can amble across, free from the fumes and sounds of traffic. They are the Wards Island Bridge over the East River at 103d Street, the Ocean Avenue Timber Foot Bridge over Sheepshead Bay, at East 19th Street in Brooklyn, and the Hawtree Pedestrian Bridge at 163d Avenue in Queens.

A Place for Children

"You've got to understand that most people come here to bring their children," said Norman Gaines as he strolled across the Wards Island Bridge with Lydia Ruth in the late afternoon sun. "It's away from everything here and you can find really secluded spots on the island."

That bridge closes at 8 P.M. every day, but the mile-long George Washington Bridge is open around the clock to pedestrians, and officials say that people walk on it at all hours. They tell about the musician with the tape-recorder who comes out at night when even the incessant singing of tires over the bridge slows down and something close to silence shrouds the structure.

The musician turns up the volume on his machine, cocks a critical ear and listens unselfconsciously to his playing as he never could between the paper-thin walls of his apartment.

Romance and Palisades

Every June, as predictably as the migration of birds, the prom trotters in their fluffy white gowns and stiff-looking tuxedos come from the New York side of the George Washington Bridge in the early-morning hours. They hold hands and the girls shriek a bit at the height of the bridge and the antics of their dates. Then they con-

A morning walk to a Manhattan office starts a day right

tinue on their way to climb to the top of the Palisades and watch dawn come up over the city.

On the high Jewish holy day of Rosh ha-Shanah, small congregations come down from Washington Heights to observe the tash-lik ceremony, which originated in the 15th century. It consists of going to a body of water on New Year's and reciting from Micah: "And Thou wilt cast all their sins into the depths of the sea."

On a warm autumn night a few years ago, a brother and sister arrived at the George Washington Bridge at 3 A.M. They were taken by bridge officials to the lower level of the bridge and there, fulfilling a wish of their deceased immigrant parents, the boy and girl scattered their ashes over the river so that they could drift out to sea and back to Europe.

August 12, 1970

Philadelphia

FOOT-LOOSE IN PHILADELPHIA

Fancy-Free Visitor Finds City Ideal for Aimless 'Walks,' A Relaxed Tourist's Answer to a Planned Walking Tour

By WILLIAM STOCKDALE

PHILADELPHIA — Turn right at the fountain, left at the intersection of Apple and Peach Streets, look for the building with the mansard roof and then follow the trolley tracks three blocks to the monument — at which turn left. These are the customary trappings of the planned walking tour, and they are designed for the shortest number of steps between points of outstanding interest.

But this kind of walking is enough to ruin one's peace of mind, and drive a body back to riding again.

Picture the planned walker at a busy intersection, printed walking guide and maps clutched tightly in hand as he tries vainly to read the fine print, and pedestrians backed up behind him. Picture his arrival at a stone lump in the middle of a street. He knows he is to "turn right at the fountain," but is this stone monstrosity a fountain?

Where's the Water

It looks like a fountain, to be sure, but there is no water coming out of it. Is a fountain without water still a fountain? Will a right turn mean missing the real fountain?

Better to take a deep breath and relax. The answer to the planned walking tour is the aimless walking tour. Equipment? None. Preparation? None. Simply pick an aimless city. This one, for example, is the most aimless place that comes to mind. In fact, it is almost impossible to do any walking in Philadelphia—even to mail a letter—without becoming aimless.

The reason is simple. Philadelphia is so extraordinarily rich in interesting sights that one strikes gold at every turn.

It is like picking up the Bible or Shakespeare and reading at random.

Starting Anywhere

The first delight of an aimless walk in Philadelphia is that there is never any problem of where to start. One can begin any place at all and proceed in the same fashion.

Should a red traffic light interrupt one's travels, he has merely to follow the green with no qualms about missing something. This not only simplifies matters greatly but speeds things up.

If, after walking half a block, one feels like turning back to retrace an enjoyable stretch of scenery, this is the privilege of the aimless walker. It is his inalienable right and part of the master plan of aimlessness.

Sooner or later during this ramble, Independence Hall is bound to turn up. It is inescapable, and rightfully so. But, happened upon aimlessly, this treasure comes as more of a delight than when consciously searched out.

A plaque on the outside of the building proclaims that this is the birthplace of America, since it was here that the Declaration of Independence was signed and the Constitution completed.

What strikes most visitors as the front of this building is very probably the back. Models of Independence Hall, as seen in store windows, show the tower in the front. The tower, a replacement for the one from which the Liberty Bell rang, faces little Independence Square. Most photographs also show this side of Independence Hall.

Many visitors, however, enter from the street side, not from the park, and they are actually using the entrance at the back of the building. The area on the other side of this street —the name of the street is immaterial to the aimless walker — was recently cleared for a mall that provides an unobstructed view of the historic old structure.

Just Push

The visitor may notice that there is no doorknob on the two white doors leading in from the street side. One need only push, aimlessly. Inside, the Liberty Bell occupies the center of the vestibule. A recorded message explains the history of the bell and its significance in American history.

In a separate wing is Congress Hall, where members of our Congress sat during the years 1790-1800. An unusual feature of the Hall is the snack bar where a Congressman — before the days of the coffee break—could mix himself a rum-and-molasses.

A part of Independence Hall has been given over to an information center, where slides, booklets, maps and information are available to the tourist. No doubt, an attendant will mark out a guided walking tour, and politeness requires the aimless walker to keep his intentions to himself. One pockets the map, with its lines and crosses, and then leaves the building in the nearest opposite direction.

Once outside, the aimless walker may well choose to pause and drink in the richness of his surroundings. Across from Independence Square are two similar imposing buildings standing side by side. Our walker may see these as the two most beautiful buildings in America, for it is his privilege to pass any judgment he likes on whatever he sees.

One of these buildings used to house The Public Ledger, a now-defunct newspaper; the other is the home of The Curtis Publishing Company. Inside the Ledger Building, with its richly paneled ceilings, an insurance company maintains a lobby display of Philadelphia memorabilia, including an original "firemark"—a fire insurance plaque.

Status Symbols

These escutcheons — usually about the size of a large dinner plate — were mounted on public or private buildings as a sign that the structures were insured. A green tree was the mark of one popular insurance company; it may be seen on many buildings as one walks aimlessly about. Careful observation also will reveal the firemark on the side of Independence Hall.

The lobby of the Curtis Building is equally interesting, should the stroller's wayward path lead him there, for it holds a gigantic mural formed of tiny pieces of glass put together as a mosaic. Called "The Dream Garden," it depicts trees, flowers, mountains and a waterfall.

As one wanders along the streets, which are nameless to the aimless, he may arrive at a sign indicating that a few blocks away is the nation's oldest hospital. Of course, the aimless walker is free to choose; he can continue on to see the oldest hospital in America, or just take the sign's word for it.

So Much to See, Heigh-Ho

Sooner or later, one may stumble upon Leary's seven-story Book Store; the Atwater Kent Museum, with its history of Philadelphia, and the Old Swede's Church. If not, it matters little, for there are many other things of equal interest to claim one's attention.

The aimless walker might

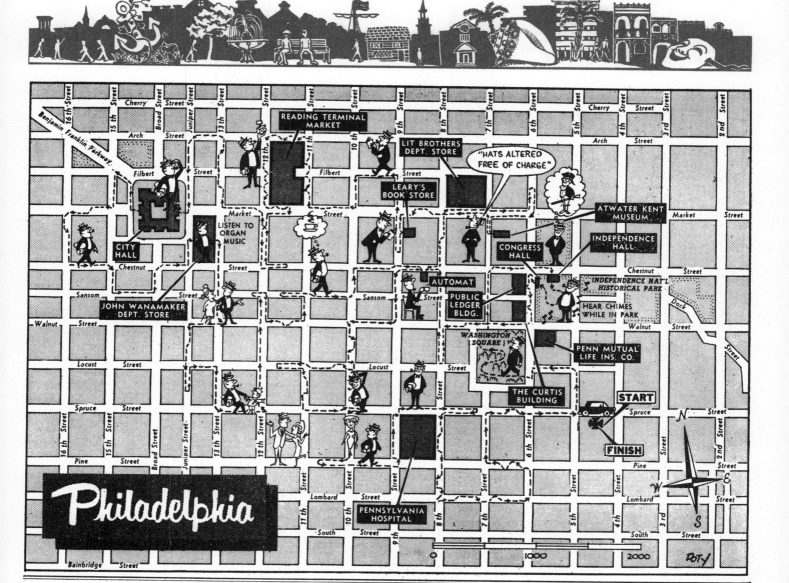

Philadelphia

happen upon Market Street, with its myriad stores. This is Philadelphia's native market, if one can see it in that fashion, with the stalls enclosed in glass and steel.

On this street, the aimless walker may notice the interesting Lit Brothers building. In an age when new buildings look like perforated slabs of concrete or giant peg-boards, with nothing to attract or hold the eye, the Lit Brothers Building is something to be cherished. The eye can caress this intricate design, and the mind can wonder at it.

Free Alterations

This cathedral of merchandise might well be the masterpiece of Market Street. Carved in the building's facade, over the entrance, are the immortal words, "Hats Altered Free of Charge."

An aimless stroll along Market Street might bring one to the Reading Terminal, a sort of half-monstrosity. One has to walk around the terminal to size it up adequately, and the rear is infinitely more interesting than the front. In so doing, one is led quite naturally to the Reading Terminal Market, where imported cheeses, Pennsylvania Dutch foods, strange breads in interesting shapes, and poultry and meat stands all combine to produce a gay atmosphere.

And there is musical accompaniment for the aimless walker in Philadelphia. In the vicinity of Independence Hall, for example, one can hear the tape-recorded chimes that ring from loudspeakers atop a nearby

building at 9 A.M., noon and 5 P.M.

Not far distant, a savings bank serenades the stroller with more chimes, this time on a 15-minute schedule. Or, one might wander into the cavernous Wanamaker store at opening time, noon or just before closing. There, he will hear selections played on the store's majestic organ.

Hither, If Not Yon

As the aimless walker proceeds, he may find one street less rewarding than another, but herein lies his strength. He can dispose of a dull street as easily as he would discard an old shoe, and move on to a more interesting one. No map is his master, nor is his allegiance bound to any series of printed notes. He is free, and

this is *his* declaration of independence!

The aimless walker probably will expend his energy recklessly, rather than hoard it for some future point of interest. He should, therefore, be on the alert for a place of nourishment and rest. In this connection, there is a fair chance that his ramblings will lead him to a historical marker that reads, "This is America's first Automat, established 1902."

Venerable

What a find! In the rear of this venerable institution, plain bulbs illuminate the original food compartments, with their nickel slots, knobs and glass doors. Elaborate mirrored ovals form an intricate pattern along the wall over the items marked "Rolls," "Pastries," "Hot

Dishes" and so on.

The girl in the change booth deftly tosses out the nickels in groups of five, and one can see how the marble has been worn by the touch of countless customers picking up coins over the years. Very historic!

Even the customers have a character that seems in keeping with the "ancient" surroundings. One man sits polishing his silverware with his napkin; another eats a piece of lemon meringue pie for breakfast, and the woman who is cleaning the tables talks to herself—in a loud voice because she is hard of hearing. The original Automat still seems very original.

As one wanders back and forth through Philadelphia's streets, one must sooner or later end up at City Hall, the center of town. No other city in America has such a definite center, so easily recognizable as such.

The massive City Hall building is a monument, a statue and an arch all rolled into one, and all in the middle of a confluence of main thoroughfares. The statue of William Penn at its top is an impressive landmark.

Skyward

Visitors can take a free trip to the tower's observation deck, just below the statue. One rides an elevator to the seventh floor, then boards the cage-like affair that carries him up into the tower.

The observation deck provides a splendid view of the city. The elevator operator, who also acts as guide, remarks that nothing in the city stands higher than "Billy Penn." It was long an unwritten law that no building taller than City Hall could be erected, and now it is a written law.

Someone asks where Independence Hall is, and the operator replies that the building housing the Philadelphia Savings Fund Society blocks the view. The operator also volunteers the information that Broad Street, down below, is the longest straight street. It stretches, he says, for four miles in one direction and for 12 miles the opposite way.

Visiting Hours

The tower is open on weekdays the year around, and seven days a week from May 30 through the summer months. Hours are 9:30 A.M. to 4:30 P.M. It is closed to visitors only when there are high winds.

A booklet given to visitors describes the statue's dimensions in detail. "Billy Penn" weighs 53,348 pounds, stands 37 feet high and has three-inch fingernails.

It is, of course, permissible for aimless walkers to visit observation towers.

Philadelphia is as rich and tasty as a good pie, and it is wise to take it a slice at a time. One would not want to eat too much pie at once — unless, of course, it happened to be breakfast time at the original Automat and the pie were lemon meringue.

June 30, 1963

WALK TOUR OF SAN FRANCISCO

Two Strolls, One Short, One Longer, Savor the Essence Of This 'Most Naturally Beautiful' American City

By GEORGE W. OAKES

SAN FRANCISCO — This city, in many ways the most naturally beautiful of all American cities, has great fascination for the tourist who likes to explore on foot.

Poised on a series of hills between the Pacific Ocean and its vast bay, San Francisco occupies a magnificent position. The visitor will be entranced by the breathtaking views from various high points, such as the wonderful panorama from Lincoln Park toward the Golden Gate Bridge, with the rocky coastline on the opposite shore, and the sweep of San Francisco Bay and its island from Coit Tower on Telegraph Hill.

San Francisco's exhilarating air stimulates a stranger to step out. On a clear day in spring or summer, one feels almost a compulsion to forget driving and take a walk instead.

Those Hills

If the tourist has first driven around the city on the famous forty-nine-mile drive to get his bearings—as he should do—he may be somewhat appalled by the extraordinary steepness of the streets, particularly in the downtown section. This might cause him to shun the thought of walking. But he must put this notion out of mind. There are several delightful strolls easily reached from the business and shopping area that do not involve exhausting climbs.

Let us begin with a very short walk, only a few blocks from Union Square, the heart of downtown San Francisco.

This is planned especially for the tourist who finds himself with an hour to spare in the downtown area. It will provide him with a delightful diversion from Chinatown or the business, financial and shopping center, and yet it is only a few blocks away. It will lead through part of the old Barbary Coast district, so reminiscent of this romantic city.

In recent years, the area has been attractively rebuilt, an interesting example of the reconstruction of old structures, including warehouses, for modern use without destroying the atmosphere of the city's golden past. It will appeal particularly to the ladies because this quarter is now the locale of the interior decorators.

The Old City

One starts out at Clay and Sansome Streets, perhaps after lunching at one of San Francisco's excellent restaurants. Several are located near by. In the old days of San Francisco about a century ago, the water came up to Montgomery Street, one block to the west. As the land was filled in eastward, warehouses were built. Even today the tourist will find fruit and vegetables from California's Sacramento, San Joaquin and Imperial Valleys.

Starting up Sansome Street, the stroller will perceive an awning painted with neckties, a signal that he is approaching the world of interior decorators and makers of fine fabrics. Turning left into Jackson Street, he suddenly finds himself in a charming little tree-lined area. Large shrubs planted in great pots lend a garden-like atmosphere to the wide show windows in the converted low buildings.

Here is an old building that, according to a plaque, used to be a French bank but now houses the representative of a decorating establishment. To the left, again, on Hotaling Place, spice warehouses gave way in the Thirties to artists' dwellings, and recently to agents for manufacturers of textiles and wall coverings.

The visitor should drop in at some of these places just to see how attractively the architects have done over the interiors and the charming courts, secluded from the street.

When back on Jackson Street, and still heading west, the stroller takes a right turn into Montgomery Street. On the right side is a narrow entry next to a fashionable restaurant. Here one can wander into a brick-lined courtyard with an old gas lamppost. Here, the office of a San Francisco lawyer is decorated in the style of the Gay Nineties. Even the counselor's desk is a former bar that was brought from the Mother Lode country in the Sierras.

Another right turn will bring the stroller into Pacific Avenue. In the Eighteen Eighties, this was the heart of the bawdy Barbary Coast, crowded with raucous bars, dance halls and notorious habitués. Looking carefully, one will notice an old firehouse, with the marking "Engine Company No. 1" clearly visible above the entrance.

Fire-House Gallery

The building has been very cleverly transformed into an art gallery that yet retains the atmosphere of the former firehouse. On the outside, the old fire lamps are still in place. As a visitor enters, he will be amused to see the old brass fire pole and spiral stairway—quite an unusual décor for modern paintings.

The technique of retaining the spirit of San Francisco's frontier days gives this little quarter an extraordinary appeal for the tourist, a reminder of the way San Francisco mingles the past and the present. And, if he wishes to visit some amusing, gay cafes in the evening, he will find, near Montgomery and Pacific, several night clubs exuding the spirit of the Gold Rush days. Here ends the short, first walk in old San Francisco.

A little farther from the downtown area, a visitor can combine a highly scenic walk with a ride on one of the city's unique and beloved cable cars. This walk is planned so that there will be only moderate climbs. Most of the route is downhill.

A trip in a cable car is one of San Francisco's most amusing experiences. Sitting on the wooden seat and watching the driver manipulate the long lever, a tourist has a sense of sight-seeing in an urban roller-coaster. The colorful little cars, so gaily painted, demonstrate that, unlike many American cities, San Francisco is proud of its past and will not permit today's skyline to eliminate yesterday's cable-car way of life.

This walk will take the saunterer to one of the city's most attractive residential areas, Russian Hill, only a fifteen-minute ride by cable car from Union Square.

One starts out in the morning by climbing aboard the Powell-Hyde cable car at Union Square. In a moment, it will seem to be rising almost vertically on its way up Nob Hill. From the back, one can see Powell Street disappear below.

The car turns left from Powell Street into California Street, practically at the top of Nob Hill, and proceeds westward to Hyde Street, where it swings north again. Since the start of the stroll is to be at Russian Hill, the rider gets off the cable car at Vallejo Street.

Once Russian Colony

Russian Hill was named for the Russian sailors and traders in California a century ago. Since it has an elevation of 300

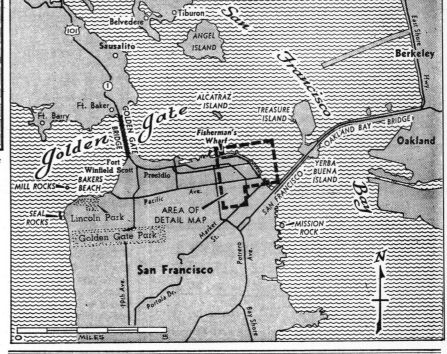

feet above San Francisco Bay, it offers a wide panorama not only of the city and the bay but the hills beyond.

Until San Francisco's Great Fire of April 18, 1906, this hill was the habitat of the city's bohemians, but afterward, its fine views and air made it popular with the richer citizens, and many fine residences were built there. Recently, luxurious apartments have been replacing many of the fashionable mansions.

But artists and writers still linger on Russian Hill, in small cottages. There this combina-

tion of the wealthy and the artistic gives the section a smart caché, unique in San Francisco.

Unique Atmosphere

At once, the visitor will detect that Russian Hill has an air of its own—it seems so far removed from the ordinary. It even has a different atmosphere from other exclusive residential areas. Being on a hill surrounded by drab rows of clapboard houses, it is a world of its own. Its charmingly landscaped dwellings and tastefully planted gardens, with a profusion of shrubs and flowers, make it an ideal area for a stroll. At almost every turning, the visitor will come upon a glorious vista over the city and the bay.

One starts by heading up the hill eastward, crossing Leavenworth and Jones Streets and turning right into the impasse named Florence Street. On the left is a home set back in the trees that once belonged to an old San Francisco family.

In the rather run-down garden the remains of a pear orchard reminds the tourist that not long ago this was a large estate. Now attractive, pastel-colored small homes with flower - lined walks fill the street.

Returning to Vallejo Street, the saunterer turns right a hundred yards or so to the parapet at the end. A marvelous panorama unfolds. In front, Telegraph Hill stands guard over the blue waters of the bay just as it did in the early days, to hoist signals when clipper ships were sighted coming in from the Orient. To the left lies grim and rocky Alcatraz, the Federal penitentiary. A large freighter may be making its way to the Embarcadero or a white sea queen casting off for Hawaii.

Returning along Vallejo Street, one turns north into a short cul-de-sac—Russian Hill Place. The row of houses on the left is a very handsome one.

Bosky Byway

The tourist should now turn north from Vallejo into Jones Street and continue a block to Green Street. Crossing Green Street, a half block farther leads him to one of San Francisco's most delightful byways, Macondray Lane. Overhung with large mimosa trees and enclosed with shrubs, it is a relic of years ago. Its odd little rustic cottages and artists' sheds provide an amazing contrast to the stately homes and modern apartments just above.

It is this unusual mixture, so typical of Russian Hill, that surprises and enchants the stranger. After glancing downhill, one should wander up the lane for a bit, just to savor its unusualness.

Returning along Jones Street, the tourist turns into tree-lined Green Street again. In a moment he will pass a green octagonal house, the last relic of an architectural fad prevalent a century ago.

On the house next door there is an exterior spiral staircase, and across the street, the former firehouse has been remodeled into a residence with a roof garden.

At this point, one reaches Hyde Street again and, turning north, proceeds to Greenwich Street, where a left turn will bring the visitor to a pleasant park planted with pines just below the reservoir. This is a good spot to sit down for a bit and have a rest.

The Steepest

The far side of the park leads into Lombard Street and here the stroller turns eastward to cross Hyde Street. The visitor may think by now that San Francisco's steep streets are amazing, but in front of him is the most extraordinary of all. Lombard Street zigzags downhill in sharp curves, all beautifully landscaped with hydrangeas and palms. Here is the crookedest drive in the city.

After one follows this serpentine road for a few yards, a left turn leads past hillside gardens into Montclair Terrace. Another left turn, this time into Chestnut Street, brings the stroller to No. 944, an interesting Victorian house with a huge bay window overlooking the bay. Next door, fine trees shade an attractively planted garden.

A half block farther westward will bring the visitor back to Hyde Street, where he descends the hill for two blocks to Bay Street. Here on the right, a series of one-room bungalows is built on the side of the hill. Instead of being obliged to climb a path through the garden to reach their separate dwellings, the residents use little caged cars that carry them up the seventy-five-foot incline.

New England Note

At the top stands a delightful New England clapboard house dating from 1849, the days of the California Gold Rush. The entire front of the building was constructed in Salem, Mass., and transported by sailing vessel all the way around Cape Horn.

Next, one walks along Bay Street to Jones, then turns left three blocks to the end. This is colorful Fisherman's Wharf, where the city's big fishing and crabbing fleet ties up. After having a look at the boats, it is time for an appetizer before lunch — a cup of shrimp or crabmeat cocktail sold by vendors in the outdoor stalls, deliciously refreshing.

At other stands, fresh caught crabs are being boiled in huge cauldrons. Along the wharf there are several good seafood restaurants (some overlooking the harbor). One of these is just the place to have a tasty lunch and relax after walking through San Francisco's most interesting and enchanting residential district.

June 3, 1962

WASHINGTON WALKING TOUR

Visitor on Foot Gets a Close-up of the Nation's Past In Its Historic Shrines, and of Its Active Present

By GEORGE W. OAKES

WASHINGTON—The visitor on a walking tour of Washington should put first things first, and in this city that means the White House. For anyone seeking to know the Capital, the office and home of the President of the United States is the place to begin.

But, before taking the morning tour of the White House (10 A. M. to noon except Sunday and Monday), the stroller should look around delightful Lafayette Square and its famous equestrian statue of Andrew Jackson. He will note also St. John's Church, in its simple dignity, at the corner of Sixteenth Street, where Presidents from James Madison to Franklin D. Roosevelt worshiped.

At the northwest end of the square stands Decatur House, the only fine mansion facing the park that has survived, thanks to the National Trust for Historic Preservation.

The house was built in 1819 for Commodore Stephen Decatur, the hero of the war against the Barbary pirates, and is furnished with authentic period pieces. It is open daily from noon to 5 P. M.

Turning right from Jackson Place on Pennsylvania Avenue, the stroller will pass Blair House, the President's official guest house. Here Col. Robert E. Lee was offered, and declined, command of the Union troops in 1861.

These structures, handsome and historic in themselves, are nevertheless subsidiary to the White House in fascination and importance.

The White House

Its façade, centered with a fine Ionic portico, is striking, and its succession of state rooms is rich. Every one of them is evocative of great events in this country's story. Here is a true and living national shrine.

On leaving the White House, the sight-seer should walk down East Executive Avenue opposite the Treasury Department, one of the finest public buildings in Washington. As he swings around the circular drive, he should glance through the iron-rail fence into the White House grounds. In the other direction, a long vista extends to the Jefferson Memorial, which rises over the trees at the far end of the Ellipse.

When the stroller reaches Seventeenth Street, the Corcoran Art Gallery (concentrating on American paintings and sculpture) and the Pan American Union, at the corner of Constitution Avenue, are both worth visiting.

The stroller may be interrested in the museum on the first floor of the Department of the Interior (on C Street), especially the Indian exhibits and craft shop.

To see a fine example of Georgian architecture, a side trip of two blocks north on Eighteenth Street brings one to the Octagon House. This was occupied by President James Madison during the restoration of the White House after it was burned in 1814. It is now the headquarters of the American Institute of Architects, and is open as a museum.

On to "State"

The visitor next should turn right along Constitution Avenue and head for the impressive Georgia marble building of the Federal Reserve Board. It is open 8:45 A.M. to 5:15 P.M., Mondays through Fridays.

From here, it is only a few hundred yards to the vast new headquarters of the Department of State. Visitors can usually tour this building every day at 3 P. M. This is well worth while, especially for one of the finest views anywhere in Washington. The magnificent sweep of the Potomac, with Arlington Cemetery in the background, can be seen from the balcony of the eighth floor.

The saunterer now has ahead of him, at the end of Twenty-third Street, the most inspiring public building in Washington—the Lincoln Memorial. Nearly 2,500,000 tourists visited this shrine last year. Its popularity outranks the White House and is far ahead of the Capitol.

The moving statue of the Civil War president, by Daniel Chester French, and the inscriptions, on facing walls, of the Gettysburg Address and Lincoln's Second Inaugural, never fail to make an indelible impression on visitors.

Spectacular Vista

One of the most striking vistas in Washington is the view from the steps of the Lincoln Memorial, with the Washington Monument mirrored in the reflecting pool. Standing at one end of the memorial's Doric colonnade, the Capitol can be seen looming large behind the monument. In the evening, under floodlighting, this is an unforgettable sight. In the other direction across the Memorial Bridge, the antebellum home of Robert E. Lee can be seen on the crest of the ridge.

On descending the steps of the memorial, the stroller should go down the walk under the luxuriant trees that border the reflecting pool.

Turning past the statue of John Paul Jones at the end of Seventeenth Street the visitor will find himself at the Tidal Basin, famous in spring for the blossoming of the Japanese cherry trees bordering the water.

The Jefferson Memorial, designed in the classic style the former President selected for Monticello and the rotunda of the University of Virginia, lends a distinguished air to this section of the city.

Continuing around the Tidal Basin the walking tour crosses the shadow of the Washington Monument, which was finished in 1884. Most visitors prefer to take the elevator rather than climb 555 feet to its top.

Walking along the Mall, from the Washington Monument to the Capitol, the saunterer passes the Smithsonian Institution, probably the most interesting group of museums in the United States. Nearly 7,000,000 visitors a year tour the several buildings that make up this world-famous institution, which was founded by an Englishman, James Smithson.

The variety of the Smithsonian collection is so extensive that the tourist with a short time in Washington must select his field of interest.

The Hope Diamond

The National Museum contains a collection of animal and Indian groups and a remarkably well-shown collection of gems and minerals, including the world-famous Hope diamond.

In addition, other buildings house an air exhibit that includes the Wright Brothers original successful aircraft and Lindbergh's "Spirit of St. Louis," in which he flew the Atlantic.

Part of the Smithsonian also is the Freer Gallery, which is noted for its outstanding collection of Near and Far Eastern art. The Smithsonian also has one of the world's greatest stamp collections.

On of the left side of the Mall stands the National Gallery of Art, whose stately marble building was donated by Andrew W.

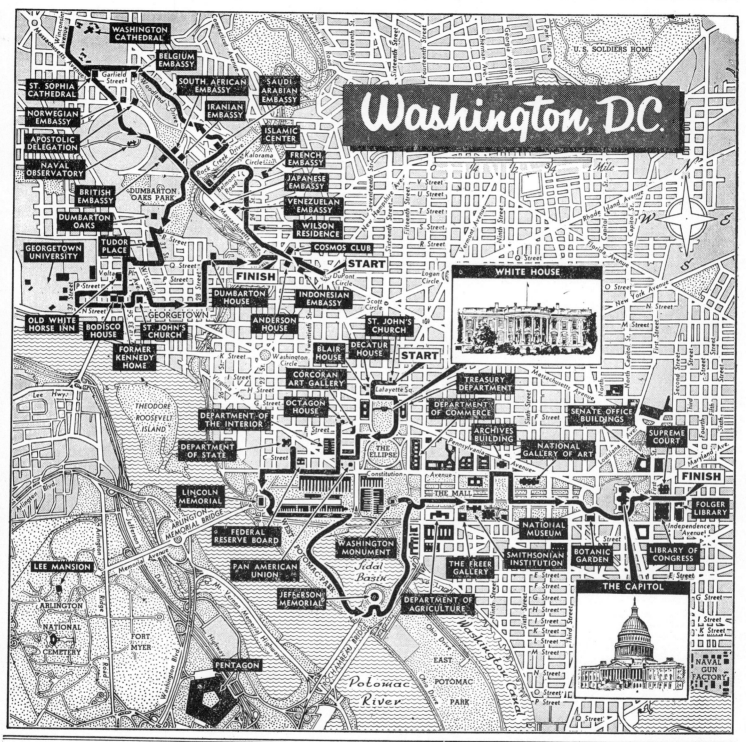

Washington, D.C.

WASHINGTON CATHEDRAL
BELGIUM EMBASSY
ST. SOPHIA CATHEDRAL
NORWEGIAN EMBASSY
APOSTOLIC DELEGATION
NAVAL OBSERVATORY
BRITISH EMBASSY
DUMBARTON OAKS
GEORGETOWN UNIVERSITY
TUDOR PLACE
OLD WHITE HORSE INN
BODISCO HOUSE
FORMER KENNEDY HOME
ST. JOHN'S CHURCH
SOUTH AFRICAN EMBASSY
IRANIAN EMBASSY
SAUDI ARABIAN EMBASSY
ISLAMIC CENTER
FRENCH EMBASSY
JAPANESE EMBASSY
VENEZUELAN EMBASSY
WILSON RESIDENCE
COSMOS CLUB
FINISH
DUMBARTON HOUSE
INDONESIAN EMBASSY
ANDERSON HOUSE
START
BLAIR HOUSE
DECATUR HOUSE
ST. JOHN'S CHURCH
CORCORAN ART GALLERY
OCTAGON HOUSE
DEPARTMENT OF THE INTERIOR
DEPARTMENT OF STATE
LINCOLN MEMORIAL
FEDERAL RESERVE BOARD
PAN AMERICAN UNION
JEFFERSON MEMORIAL
LEE MANSION
ARLINGTON NATIONAL CEMETERY
FORT MYER
PENTAGON
WASHINGTON MONUMENT
DEPARTMENT OF AGRICULTURE
THE FREER GALLERY
SMITHSONIAN INSTITUTION
NATIONAL MUSEUM
BOTANIC GARDEN
WHITE HOUSE
TREASURY DEPARTMENT
DEPARTMENT OF COMMERCE
ARCHIVES BUILDING
NATIONAL GALLERY OF ART
SENATE OFFICE BUILDINGS
SUPREME COURT
FINISH
FOLGER LIBRARY
LIBRARY OF CONGRESS
THE CAPITOL
NAVAL GUN FACTORY
U.S. SOLDIERS HOME

THE ELLIPSE
THE MALL
Tidal Basin
Potomac River
POTOMAC PARK
EAST POTOMAC PARK
THEODORE ROOSEVELT ISLAND

Mellon.

It is probably not an exaggeration to state that no public art gallery anywhere has been more wisely planned or is better maintained for the display of fine paintings, sculpture and other works of art. Many masterpieces are from the collections of the late Mr. Mellon,

of Samuel H. Kress, P. A. B. Widener and also Chester Dale.

If the tourist stops to visit the National Gallery, he should cross Constitution Avenue, before resuming his walk, to inspect the historic originals of the Declaration of Independence and the Constitution of the United States. They are housed

in the Greco-Roman Archives Building.

At the end of the Mall, the tourist, disregarding some of Washington's monstrous Civil War statues with which nearly every public park is afflicted, now commences the ascent of "The Hill"—that eminence where the Capitol stands. The

Botanic Garden, featuring a collection of tropical plants and trees, is on the right. One statue, that of John Marshall, first Chief Justice of the United States, is worth noting at the foot of the steps leading to the terrace along the west front of the Capitol.

The tourist should plan to

take one of the frequent guided tours (daily except Sundays) of the Capitol to see the rotunda, the old Supreme Court Room and other points of interest. Two of the finest pieces of sculpture in Washington are Borglum's head of Lincoln, in the Capitol rotunda, and Jo Davidson's life-like figure of Will Rogers, which is just off the House floor.

House and Senate

The twin hearths of American political life are the Senate and House chambers, where, in session, the visitors' galleries offer the people of the land the right to attend any public debates and to appraise the behavior of the men and women they have elected to represent them.

After an inspection of the Capitol and of its spacious grounds, the visitor will want a glimpse of two other fundamental features of official Washington. They are the Supreme Court and the Library of Congress.

Both buildings require a considerable time to go through on conducted tours. If the Court is in session, the tourist should not miss this intensely interesting experience. The library is one of the world's greatest, reputedly the most complete. Its books, manuscripts, maps and pamphlets are numbered in the millions. It has 414 miles of shelves and extra storage space for 10,000,000 more volumes.

If the strolling tourist still has the desire to return to an earlier age, and wishes to immerse himself in perhaps the world's greatest Shakespearean collection, he should proceed to the Folger Library, just behind the Supreme Court. Its only rival as a Shakespearan treasury is the British Museum.

Up to this point, the faithful walker has seen only official Washington. Now, since he is properly dedicated to absorbing impressions while on foot, he should continue for an hour or two in order to get the atmosphere of a totally different kind of city. Otherwise, he will miss the unusual charm of the capital's residential areas. This includes visiting the embassy quarter that borders Rock Creek Park and leads into old Georgetown.

Transition

To save energy in this transition, and, since his inspection of "The Hill" has set him down at almost the other side of town, he might want to take a taxi or bus, or, if he happens to catch it, the "Silver Sightseer," Washington's sight-seeing air-conditioned streetcar, away from the massive stone fortresses of the American bureaucracy and head as far as DuPont Circle on Connecticut Avenue. The transition is astonishing, for the restful character of the surroundings here is utterly unexpected.

So, at DuPont Circle, after a midday lunch and break, one heads west on Massachusetts Avenue in the direction of Rock Creek Park. In a couple of blocks there is, on the left, a huge mansion at No. 2020. It is now the Indonesian Embassy, although it was built by a mining king, the father of Evalyn Walsh McLean, former owner of the Hope Diamond.

Famous Club

A bit farther along is Anderson House, No. 2118, now the home of the Society of the Cincinnati, an order founded by officers of the Revolutionary War and sometimes used for official receptions. Directly opposite is the stately former residence of Sumner Welles, the diplomat, It is now the Cosmos Club, whose membership includes leading scientists and figures in the world of letters. President Kennedy is currently a candidate for membership.

A block or so farther along the tree-lined avenue brings the stroller to Sheridan Circle, where one of Washington's few fine statues, Borglum's equestrian figure of the famous Gen. Phil Sheridan, stands beneath the overhanging elms. The visitor should take a detour to the right along S Street to see the house at No. 2340 where Woodrow Wilson lived after leaving the White House.

Returning to Massachusetts Avenue, a few hundred yards on the left, and set back from the avenue by an extensive lawn, is the Japanese Embassy, which was built in 1932. Its design is a modification of American Colonial architecture, but an unusual feature of its grounds is a Japanese tea house and garden. All materials used in constructing the tea house, as well as the stones for the garden, were brought from Japan. It is patterned after a seventeenth-century tea-ceremony building and can be seen by appointment on Wednesdays between 3 and 5 P. M.

At this point, the stroller should again cross the avenue and look at the Venezuelan Embassy, a well-designed low building set in artistically landscaped trees and shrubbery. Turning right on Twenty-fourth Street, one will pass several embassies until reaching Kalorama Road. A bit to the right, the residence of the French Ambassador can be seen in extensive grounds.

Some of Washington's finest town houses are situated in this section. One distinguished New England style of house on Kalorama Circle was brought in sections from Massachusetts and reconstructed, to the last detail, on its present site. Walking down Belmont Road, with Rock Creek Park dropping away to the right, one senses the truly rural atmosphere of this section of Washington.

The Mosque

As the stroller returns to Massachusetts Avenue, he finds on his right a lovely and fascinating building, the Islamic Center with its mosque, complete with a graceful minaret, and a museum and library. The center is open to visitors Wednesdays, Saturdays and Sundays. Also, on Fridays, one can observe a noon service and take a tour of the buildings from 2 to 2:30 P. M.

Proceeding along Massachusetts Avenue, the visitor comes to a bridge that crosses not only Rock Creek but a broad section of the famous Rock Creek Park as well. Beyond the bridge, he can turn right and stroll into the park and thus along a trail by the stream. After a few hundred yards, another path to the left will bring him out on Rock Creek Drive.

If the stroller turns into Woodland Drive, which winds its way up from the park, he will pass many sumptuous homes in their suburban settings. Some are embassies, such as the Spanish-style Saudi Arabian residence.

Turning left on Garfield Street, the walker reaches the new Belgian Chancery, one of the better-designed embassies to have been built in the last few years. He can continue up Garfield Street and, at the corner of Massachusetts and Wisconsin Avenues, spend some time visiting the Episcopal Cathedral of Saints Peter and Paul.

President Woodrow Wilson's tomb is in the cathedral crypt, and the cathedral, which calls itself the National Cathedral, also is proclaimed as a "House of prayer for all people."

Descending the hill from the cathedral, along Massachusetts Avenue, the stroller will pass St. Sophia's Cathedral, the largest Greek Orthodox church in this country. A bit farther down on the left are the Norwegian Embassy and the residence of the Apostolic Delegation to the United States.

Naval Observatory

The Naval Observatory, at the corner of Massachusetts Avenue and Thirty-fourth Street, may be visited on regularly conducted tours at 2 P. M., Mondays through Fridays.

A few hundred yards down the avenue, the stroller will reach the imposing British Embassy, with its large garden. On the left are the embassies of South Africa and Iran.

Here, the visitor leaves Embassy Row by turning sharply to the right off Massachusetts Avenue and following a dirt trail which goes through Rock Creek Park and leads, after a ten-minute stroll, to Georgetown.

Close by, just before climbing the slight hill to R Street, Georgetown, lies Dumbarton Oaks Park, one of Washington's smallest and most charming. It is open only on week-ends.

On reaching R Street, the tourist should turn right and, after skirting the brick wall surrounding the Dumbarton Oaks estate, enter its beautifully landscaped gardens on Thirty-second Street.

The visitor should allow at least a half-hour to wander through these magnificent terraced gardens, which are a triumph of the art of landscaping. After touring the gardens, he may want to look around the collection of Byzantine art in the museum.

Tudor Place

Across R Street, one walks down Thirty-first Street past Tudor Place, a mansion of yellow stucco, designed by Dr. William Thornton, who prepared the plans for the Capitol. Tudor Place was built for the granddaughter of Martha Washington and her husband, Thomas Peter, one of whose descendants still lives there.

On reaching Q Street, the stroller should continue across Wisconsin Avenue to Thirty-third Street where one turns left and, just below Volta Place,

comes upon a low, ivy-covered brick house with a fine Colonial fanlight.

This is No. 1524 Thirty-third Street, and in Colonial times it was known as the White Horse Inn. Thomas Jefferson frequented it.

At O Street, the tourist turns right, and on the left he will note some of Georgetown's finest old mansions. Particularly handsome is the Bodisco House, which belonged to a Russian minister.

Three blocks ahead lies Georgetown University, the oldest and one of the leading Catholic universities in this country.

On N Street are numerous Federal period houses of much architectural interest, and here at No. 3307, stands the former home of President Kennedy. It was on the front steps of No. 3307 last December that Mr. Kennedy, as President-elect, announced many of his Cabinet and other appointments.

Going on to Potomac Street and turning north one block to O Street, one finds beautiful St. John's Church, Georgetown, built in 1806. A few hundred yards brings the stroller back to Wisconsin Avenue where there are many fascinating little shops reminiscent of the Chelsea section of London.

It is time to return to downtown Washington, and the way to go is eastward along N Street. Here, are several interesting nineteenth-century homes, including one once owned by Robert Todd Lincoln.

End of the Stroll

At Twenty-eighth Street, one goes left to reach Q Street, where a right turn takes the saunterer past Dumbarton House, the headquarters of the Society of Colonial Dames.

It is open as a museum from 10 A. M. to 5 P. M. on weekdays. The small garden is most charming.

The walk ends when the stroller finds "The Bridge of the Buffaloes" over Rock Creek Park, at the foot of Q Street. Just beyond lie Sheridan Circle and Massachusetts Avenue.

September 10, 1961

Chapter Four

WALKING ABROAD

WALKING TOUR IN OLD VIENNA

By GEORGE W. OAKES

George Oakes began writing walking tours of foreign cities for the travel section of The New York Times in 1961 and continued until 1965, when he was killed, with his wife and son, in a tragic automobile accident in Vermont.

With the exception of the Salisbury walk, all of the walks in this section have been published in a revised form in a book entitled, "Turn Right at the Fountain," published by Holt, Rinehart & Winston. The third edition, brought up-to-date and rechecked for accuracy by Alexandra Chapman, contains 317 pages, with a map of each walk in 20 cities, and is sized to fit the pocket. It is priced at $5.95.

The Salisbury walk, together with 23 other walks through the English countryside and corresponding maps, have been published by David McKay in a book entitled, "Turn Left at the Pub." It contains 174 pages, is sized to fit the pocket, and is priced at $4.95.

VIENNA — This ancient capital of the Hapsburgs and their Austro-Hungarian Empire, of lilting waltz-time and of celebrated coffee houses merits at least two walks.

The first one is through winding streets and obscure little squares. Here are bewitching courtyards and old baroque palaces; here, too, are rooms where Mozart composed and here is the famous St. Stephen's Cathedral, one of the finest Gothic churches in Europe. Here, indeed, is the essence of *Alt Wien,* Old Vienna.

The start is in front of Vienna's world-renowned State Opera House. It stands beside one segment of the Ring, the wide boulevard that circles the inner city where its ancient walls once stood. The opera house was badly blitzed in World War II, but by 1955 it had been reconstructed to become again one of Europe's most eminent music theaters. It was among the first great war-battered Viennese structures to be re-established, an indication of the cultural preoccupations of this capital.

Into the Past

Vienna's main shopping street, Kärntner Strasse, starts here, skirts the side of the opera house and continues northward. It is lined with tempting windows before which crowds of shoppers browse. But in a moment or two, this bustling scene of present-day Vienna disappears, and the stroller is immersed in the atmosphere of centuries ago. This is achieved merely by turning right off the up-to-date thoroughfare and into Himmelpfort Gasse.

Here, on the right at No. 8,

stands the majestic 17th-century palace of the great military leader, Prince Eugene of Savoy. He helped protect Vienna from the Turks and later became the Duke of Marlborough's ally against Louis XIV of France.

The palace is now Austria's Ministry of Finance, and it is open to the public on Saturdays between 3 and 5 P. M. However, custodians are considerate in allowing visitors to have glimpses of at least the entrance hall and the grand staircase on other days.

The ceilings are decorated with paintings, the balustrades are highly ornamented and rococo plaster figures add a gracious period note. The building was designed by a great architect of the day, Fischer von Erlach.

Typically Medieval

Going back a few yards in Himmelpfort Gasse brings the stroller to a narrow, typically medieval street, Rauhenstein Gasse, on the right. Turning into it, another turn to the right leads into winding Ball Gasse and thus to Franziskaner Platz, an ancient square whose fountain fronts on the monastery and church of the Franciscan Order. These are fine examples of the combination of late Gothic and Renaissance architecture.

Lovely baroque houses are to be seen in this square before one swings to the left and into the curving Singer Strasse. There, just beyond Blut Gasse, the Hall and Chapel of the Teutonic Knights appears.

The Teutonic Knights were organized originally during the Crusades, and continued as instruments of German expansion. The 14th-century Hall and

Chapel is rich in mementos of those fiery days of conflict.

Part of the chapel is set aside to display medieval armor, banners and coats of arms of the knights of the order, as well as religious vessels and plate. They combine to make a dramatic historic picture of an era.

On leaving the chapel, a right turn in the Singer Strasse leads quickly back to the busy Kärntner Strasse, at a little square called Stock im Eisen Platz. A block along Kärntner Strasse to the right and Stephenplatz opens out, centered by the great St. Stephen's Cathedral. But before approaching the Platz, it is pleasant to cross Kärtner Strasse, for two reasons.

Iron Tree-Trunk

On the opposite corner, one finds a curious relic rather inconspicuously attached to a building there and for which the little open space is named. This is the Stock im Eisen, the Iron Tree-trunk, the remains of an old stump studded with nails. It seems that, back in the 15th century, local locksmiths were in the habit of driving a nail into the tree every now and then—for luck.

The second reason for crossing Kärntner Strasse is to stroll in the fashionable Graben that branches off there. The Graben is one of Vienna's main shopping streets, and in it also are a number of attractive cafes where the Kaffee mit Schlag—coffee with whipped cream—is practically irresistible.

Proceeding to Stephen's Square, one perceives that the cathedral is enormous. It was built in the 14th and 15th centuries on the site of an earlier Romanesque church. Its spire is stupendous, rising 446 feet,

which is 85 feet taller than the church is long. St. Stephen's interior was burned out during the Battle of Vienna in April, 1945, but was restored by 1952. The art and ecclesiastical aspects are beautiful.

Big Bell

Also restored is the famous Pummerin, the 20-ton bell that was fashioned from Turkish cannon captured during the liberation of Vienna in 1711 and damaged in World War II. One can take an elevator in the bell tower to see it. The view over the city from this high vantage point is quite exceptional.

The stroll continues by searching out, behind the cathedral, a little passage under an arch that leads to Dom Gasse. Here, at No. 5, is Figarohaus, Mozart's home from 1784 to 1787 and where he composed "The Marriage of Figaro." Its little museum has many Mozart souvenirs and manuscripts on display.

A walker retraces his steps under the arch and turns to the right, where he finds another little passageway at No. 6 Stephenplatz, opposite the cathedral. It leads to Wollzeile, across which street another passage leads to Bäcker Strasse. Such a little passage is called Durchhaus, and many of them were in existence when Turkish cannon balls rained on the city two and one-half centuries ago.

On the way along the passage to Bäcker Strasse, however, it might be pleasant to stop at a little Weinstube for a refreshing glass of Heurige, the famous Viennese wine.

Bäcker Strasse is right in the heart of medieval Vienna. At No. 7, there is a picturesque, vine-covered courtyard that is charming to gaze into. Continu-

ing to the right leads to Dr. Ignaz Seipel Platz and Vienna's old university quarter.

The large building on the left —it is in French classic style— is the Aula, or Assembly Hall, of the old university. Here, too, is the baroque Jesuit Church, whose ceiling paintings and fine marble columns should not be missed.

The Basilisk

The walk proceeds along Sonnenfels Gasse for a few yards. Then a right turn is made into the narrow, winding Schönlatterngasse, which is typical of old Vienna. Here, at No. 7, the Basilisk House bears a plaque commemorating the legend of a gallant apprentice. In 1212, he killed a hideous monster that lived in the house's well and poisoned the neighborhood with its fumes.

Just beyond this house, a surprising retreat is encounter-

ed. This is the Heiligenkreuzerhof, on the left, the winter residence of the monks of the Holy Cross Monastery in the Vienna Woods. This large building, which faces an oblong courtyard, has been in the possession of the abbey since 1206.

Leaving by the archway at the far side, the walk continues along the Grashof Gasse. It then turns right on Köllnerhof Gasse and on to the Fleischmarkt, one of Vienna's most ancient streets and now the center of the Greek and Armenian trading community.

Luncheon Break

Next to the Greek Ortnodox Church here is a typical old Viennese restaurant. It is reputed to serve the best beer in town and to have been the place where the popular ballad, "Ach, du lieber Augustin," was composed. Its balconies, fram-

ing a tiny courtyard, give it a delightful air.

If this walk began in the morning, it is probably lunchtime now. One can eat here or around the corner, in the Rotenturm Strasse, at a place established in 1435 and known as the favorite restaurant of Johannes Brahms, the composer. Here, one can lunch in a pleasant garden.

Across the Rotenturm Strasse, one continues along the Fleischmarkt and up a flight of steps to Juden Gasse, the old ghetto, which still retains some of its former character. A right turn leads to the Ruprechtskirche, built on the old walls above the Danube Canal. This is Vienna's oldest church, and it dates from the 13th century. Just to the right stands a synagogue, at No. 4 Seitenstetten Gasse.

Roman Remains

Turning back along Juden Gasse, one comes to the Hoher Markt, the oldest section of Vienna and the center of the medieval town. Beneath the busy square are ruins of the Roman settlement, Vindobona, and excavations at No. 2 Hoher Markt can be visited on Tuesdays, Thursdays, Saturdays and Sundays from 9 A.M. to 1 P.M., and on Wednesdays and Fridays from 3 to 7 P.M.

At the far end of the Hoher Markt, one enters Marcus Aurelius Strasse (the great Roman emperor is said to have died in Vienna in 180 A.D.) and cuts diagonally across it into Salvator Gasse. There, on the left, is the early Renaissance portal of the old Town Hall Chapel.

Just a few yards along stands the lovely 14th-century church of Maria am Gestade, overlooking the Danube Canal. To get a

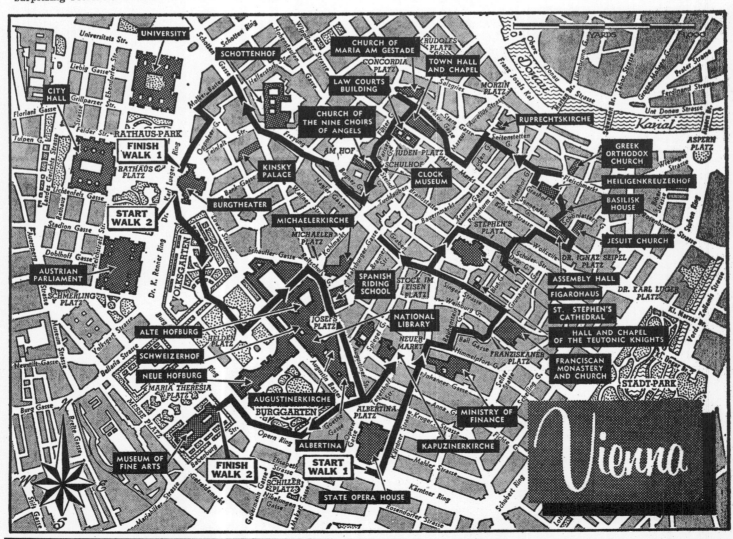

good view of the church and its high tower, it is worthwhile descending some steps to a place where, in earlier days, boats were moored beside that tributary of the Danube.

Returning a short distance on Salvator Gasse, one turns right into Stoss im Himmel Gasse, where, at No. 3, an exceptionally fine baroque house stands. Stoss im Himmel Gasse passes beside the old Town Hall and, at the corner where Wipplinger Strasse crosses it, rises the Law Courts building. This structure houses some of Austria's principal courts; it was another early 18th-century work of Fischer von Erlach and was formerly the Bohemian chancellery.

To the Clock Museum

Crossing Wipplinger Strasse, the walk proceeds along the short Fütter Gasse to Juden Platz. Opposite this square, one wanders down the curving Pariser Gasse into the Schulhof, a little square, where, at No. 2, is Vienna's Clock Museum. Here, thousands of clocks, some dating back 800 years, are on view. The museum is open on Tuesdays, Wednesdays and Saturdays.

The stroller is now in one of the most enchanting corners of Vienna. Just ahead rises the apse of the Church of the Nine Choirs of Angels. Between two buttresses, a tiny watch shop is wedged.

This spot is one of Old Vienna's most characteristic. It is a juncture of four cobblestone streets, and is so narrow that only one car can pass through at a time. The church's high walls are striking. Here is a good, secluded place to pause and muse on the medieval aspects of the city.

Looking in at the little watch shop is an agreeable experience. At one corner, where Steindl Gasse leads off, stands a fine old house, the Pfarhof. It dates from about 1600.

Continuing on Steindl Gasse, the saunterer turns right on Bogner Gasse and presently arrives at Am Hof, a wide square that was the site of medieval tournaments. There are fine baroque façades at Nos. 7 and 12.

No. 10, which used to be Vienna's arsenal, is a good example of 18th-century style. A Turkish cannon ball, a souvenir of that critical siege-time, is lodged over the doorway of No. 11.

Across the bottom of the square, a street called Freyung —so named because it once was a place of sanctuary for fugitives—is the continuation of Bogner Gasse. On the left, at No. 4, is the handsome, late-baroque Kinsky Palace, later an embassy, and just opposite is the massive Schottenhof that Scottish and Irish Benedictine monks occupied in the 12th century. They were later replaced by German Benedictines.

The Schottenhof's tree-shaded courtyard—it is entered by the Schotten Gasse, which turns to the right off Freyung—is a good place for some refreshment.

Continuing on the Schotten Gasse, one soon turns left and climbs some steps to the Mölker Bastei, built on Vienna's old fortifications. On the corner is a delightful rococo house, the Drei Mäderlhaus. It is associated with the three beauties about whom an operetta, "Blossom Time," was produced a generation ago, featuring the music of Franz Schubert.

Beethoven dwelt for a time in the house at No. 8 Mölker Bastei. Now a museum, it is open daily except Mondays.

One continues in the Mölkergasse to a ramp leading down into the Oppolzer Gasse. Thus, a short distance on, the first Vienna walk ends at the Ring.

The second Vienna walk is a contrast to the first. The first, while covering the same scope of centuries, peers at the Vienna of the Viennese. The second looks mainly at their rulers and imperial grandeur.

The places to visit are largely associated with the House of Hapsburg and the Holy Roman and Austro-Hungarian Empires, which that proud, tenacious dynasty ruled successively until the end of World War I.

The start of the second walk is at the Ring in front of the Burgtheater, the national theater, an immense, 19th-century Gothic structure. The walk proceeds, bearing southeasterly, into the beautifully landscaped Volksgarten, a park laid out on the site of Vienna's old fortifications.

In summer, the formal rose gardens throughout this park are particularly attractive. One can gaze to the right across the Ring, beyond the Rathaus Platz, at the big City Hall, and, farther along, at the classic Austrian Parliament building. The last named is about 100 years old.

To the Volksgarten succeeds a large square, the Helden Platz, across the bottom of which stretches the immense Neue Hofburg. This is the newer (late 19th century) section of the former Austro-Hungarian Imperial Palace. The great, sprawling block of buildings to the left is the Alte Hofburg, the old and main part of the palace.

The entire Hofburg is a mixture of architectural styles and shapes because, through the Hapsburgs' nearly 500 years of rule in Vienna, there were frequent alterations, reconstructions and extensions.

In the Helden Platz, one turns to the left on a broad transverse path to enter the great central court of the old palace. Here are many sights to be visited, including the apartments of Emperor Franz Joseph I. They are open weekdays from 9 A. M. to 4 P. M. and Sundays until 1 P. M.

But the most interesting section is the Schatzkammer, the collection of religious and lay treasures. This is reached by entering the oldest part of the palace, the Schweizerhof, which dates from the 13th century. It is closed on Fridays, but open on Mondays, Wednesdays and Saturdays from 9:30 A. M. to 3 P. M., on Tuesdays from 2 to 7 P. M. and on Sundays from 9 A. M. to 1 P. M.

Here are displayed the Hapsburg crown jewels, including the crown of the Holy Roman Empire; the latter is set with precious stones and is reputed to be nearly 1,000 years old. Here, too, is Charlemagne's own book of devotions, and also on view are ancient swords, orbs and scepters of the Holy Roman Empire and the Hapsburg dynasty. Crown jewels, coronation garments, other vestments and royal and religious insignia all conspire to make a sumptuous showing.

Nearby is the entrance to the Burgkapelle, the Imperial Chapel where the noted Vienna Boys Choir sings on Sundays, just as its predecessors have done for 450 years.

Back in the central court, a passage to the right leads out of the old palace to a small public square, the Michaeler Platz. There stands the Michaelerkirche, one of Vienna's oldest churches. It is a combination of Romanesque and Gothic.

Leaving the church and turn-

ing left along Reitschul Gasse, one approaches the Spanish Riding School, whose hall is nothing less than majestic.

Here the famous Lippizaner stallions go through their paces with ballet-like precision, just as has been done for nearly 300 years. This magnificent spectacle is one that no visitor to Vienna should miss.

Even today, the riders never begin a performance without saluting the Royal Box, with its portrait of Emperor Charles VI. He reigned from 1711 to 1740, and ordered the present school building designed and built.

Continuing down Reitschul Gasse, one enters a passageway and emerges in Josefs Platz, an impressive baroque square in which the National Library, with its outstanding collection of books, maps and manuscripts, occupies one side. Leaving the square by Augustiner Strasse, the stroller finds, on his right, the noble Augustinerkirche. Napoleon and Marie Louise were married there in 1810.

Farther on, also on the right, is one of Vienna's finest art galleries, the Albertina, which houses a remarkable group of drawings by Albrecht Dürer. The collection is open Mondays, Tuesdays and Thursdays from 10 A. M. to 2 P. M., on Wednesdays and Fridays from 10 A. M. to 6 P. M. and on Saturdays to 1 P. M.

The stroller continues in Augustiner Strasse to a small square from which Tegetthoff Strasse turns off to the left. The goal here is the Kapuzinerkirche, the Church of the Capucines, whose crypt is the burial place of the Hapsburgs. There are 141 of them here, all laid out in rows in lead and copper coffins.

Turning back in Tegetthoff Strasse, one looks beyond the little square to behold the bulk of the Opera, with the Ring in front of it. Here, a turn to the right leads to the last objective of the second Vienna walk.

The visitor proceeds past the Burggarten, which is as attractively landscaped as the Volksgarten on the other side of the Neue Hofburg, until, on the left, rises the Museum of Fine Arts. Here is an outstanding European collection of great masters of the Italian, Dutch and other schools over the centuries.

It is a fitting backdrop before which to leave the drama of a great city.

November 17, 1963

A WALKING TOUR OF BRUGES

Medieval and Renaissance Traditions Flourish Here, Relatively Untouched by Contemporary Influences

By GEORGE W. OAKES

BRUGES, Belgium — Bruges is unique. The medieval and Renaissance world has miraculously survived in this charming Flemish city, encircled and intersected by quiet waterways. Here the past has been notably preserved.

Although there are a few other relatively untouched medieval towns in Europe, none is quite so accessible to the mainstream of tourist travel. Bruges is only fifteen miles from Ostend on the English Channel and sixty from Brussels.

To cross the outer ring of canals and enter the old city is to be at once transported into the days of Bruges' glory, the fourteenth century. Then Bruges, through its trade both in wool and cloth with England, its status as a Hanseatic town, and its commercial ties with Italy, was one of the great centers of northern Europe. The medieval guilds flourished, and it was the wealthy Flemish merchants who made possible the northern Renaissance.

Today in narrow streets lined with ancient houses and along tree-lined canals, the spirit of old Bruges lingers on. The ivy-covered buildings and tall Gothic towers are reflected in the waters of the canals as they were in the time when Bruges was an important junction of European trade as far as the Mediterranean; was the home of humanism, the city where Italian bankers sat for van Eyck, and where Memling painted his marvelous works.

Concentrated as it is—it is hardly half a mile in diameter —and packed with such fascinating detail, Bruges is perfect for the tourist who wants to do his sight-seeing on foot. In fact, the city cannot properly be seen any other way. By walking, there is time to stop and admire the picturesque corners, medieval towers and lovely facades which abound here.

A prime purchase is a museum-card, giving access to sixteen museums at a reduced rate. It is transferable, and can be obtained at any of the museums or at the Bruges tourist office, in the Government Palace in the Market, or Market Place.

Unless otherwise mentioned, public buildings and museums are open from 9:30 A. M. to noon and from 2 to 6 P. M. from April 1 to Sept. 30.

There are two fairly essential walks in Burges, each comparatively short. Each starts at the great central Market. There, rising above the fourteenth-century Market House, stands its impressive, lofty tower, one of the most magnificent Gothic structures anywhere.

Famous Carillon

One should study it from well back in the square to appreciate the graceful elements of its 280-foot belfry. It is a pleasure to hear the world-renowned carillon, composed of forty-seven bells, played on Monday, Wednesday, and Saturday from 9 to 10 P. M. and on Sunday from 11:45 A. M. to 12:30 P. M. from June 15 to Sept. 30.

From the delightful courtyard, a winding staircase leads up to the treasure room on the second floor where there is an exhibit of medieval charters. Some 400 steps lead upward to the tower's top for a wonderful view of the city and the surrounding countryside.

The stroll proceeds by turning from the southeast corner of the Market Place into narrow Breidelstraat, a short block to the Burg, or Castle Square, named for the moat-surrounded fortress of the Dukes of Burgundy that once rose here.

Here stands one of Bruges' most sacred edifices, the Basilica of the Holy Blood, where, since 1150, has been preserved a vial believed to contain drops of the blood of Christ. The precious relic was given to Derrick of Alsace, Count of Flanders, by the Patriarch of Jerusalem in recognition of Derrick's great bravery during the Second Crusade. Derrick brought the relic to Bruges, where it has been venerated ever since.

The Basilica is open from 9 A. M. to noon and from 2:30 to 6 P. M. This structure is really two chapels. The upper, Gothic in design and rich in coloring, contains the relic. The crypt, below, is Romanesque.

The Burg also contains one of the oldest and finest Gothic town halls in northern Europe. Its turrets are striking and, on the inside, the great hall has a magnificent vaulted fourteenth-century roof and murals depicting the history of Bruges. The Court of Justice, close by, is worth visiting, particularly to see the unusual black marble chimney piece in the court room.

Next to the Government Palace is a vaulted passage, the Blinde Ezelstraat, leading southeast to a narrow bridge that spans a canal. Here is to be found a fascinating aspect of the quiet beauty of Bruges — old houses along the quays, hanging gardens and luxuriant trees shading the canal, donkey-back bridges over it and, overhead, the great Gothic towers and spires soaring to the sky.

Canal View

The stroller proceeds straight on from the bridge, passing the colonnaded Fish Market at the left, to Braambergstraat, making a right turn here into the Rosenhoedkaai, with another memorable view of old houses across calm water. The Rosenhoedkaai soon becomes the Dyver, a quay whose em-

bankment is shaded with linden trees, and here, a hundred yards along and, after a short right-angle turn to the left, is the Groeninge Museum, the city art gallery, with paintings by the great Flemish artists van Eyck, Memling and Gerard David, as well as modern works.

Returning to the Dyver, and a few steps left, brings one to the Gruuthuse Museum, once a palace, now displaying a collection of arts, crafts, lace and pottery for which Bruges is still famous. The palace itself, that of the Lords of Gruuthuse, is a splendid medieval structure, with great fireplaces, beautifully tiled floors and rich wood carving.

Close to it, to the west, stands an imposing church, the Church of Our Lady, in whose south transept is found a marble group, "Virgin and Child," by Michelangelo.

Although these two museums are interesting, the most intensive sight-seeing should be saved for the finest art collection in Bruges, the Hans Memling Museum in St. John's Hospital, across the street from the Church of Our Lady. The Memling masterpieces in the former Chapter Room include "The Shrine of St. Ursula" (perhaps the most notable), "The Mystic Marriage of St. Catherine," "The Adoration of the Magi," and several other of his outstanding works.

On leaving the hospital the stroller turns right along Mariastraat, crosses a canal-bridge and continues on Sint Katelijnestraat to the third turning on the right, Wijngaardstraat, and follows that to the canal again. Before crossing the bridge to enter the beautiful grounds of the thirteenth-century Béguinage, one might well pause a moment to look at the delightful vista on either side.

There probably will be sev-

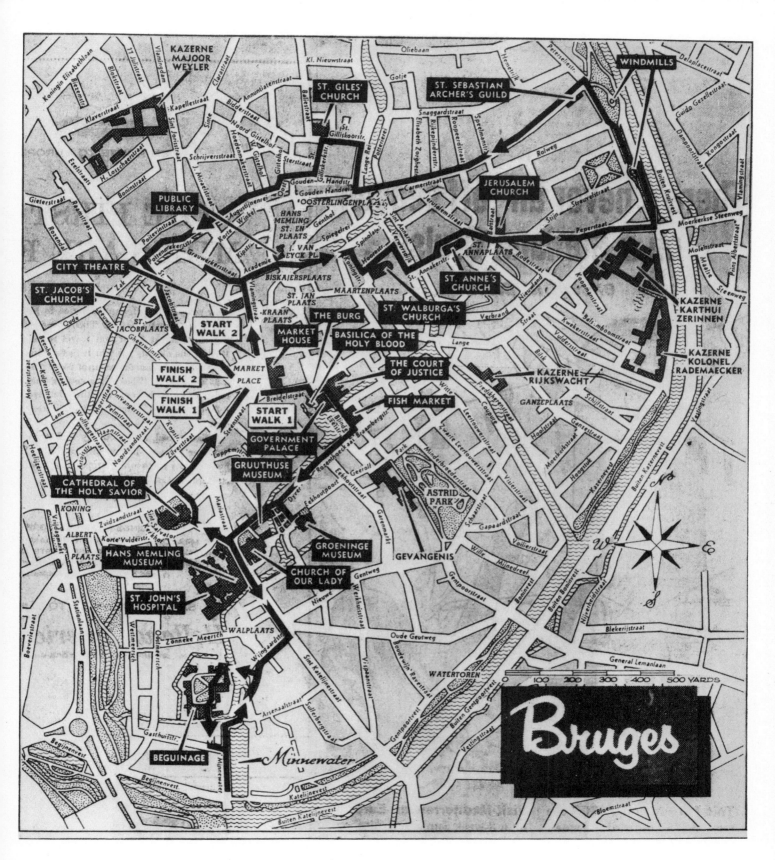

eral swans adding a decorative note to the placid waters of the canal, while black-frocked Benedictine nuns are likely to be passing to and from their home. It is open weekdays between 9:30 A. M. and 12:15 P. M., afternoons 2 to 7 P. M.; and Sundays, 10 A. M. to 12:15 P. M. and 2 to 7 P. M.

The quiet courtyard surrounded by trim white washed houses and the Béguines' House give a charming idea of the meditative life their inmates lead.

One should then leave the delightful grounds by the south gate, cross a bridge, and, after a few yards, turn left to the Minnewater, known as the Lake of Love, which was a harbor during the Middle Ages. From the stone bridge near a fourteenth-century tower, the reflections of foliage in the water make a fascinating pattern. In the background rise the towers of Bruges.

One may stroll beside the Minnewater to enjoy its lovely aspect and then turn back to its top, or north, end. Here, the turn is to the right, again along Wijngaardstraat, to Sint Katelijnestraat and, going left beyond the Memling Museum, one reaches the Cathedral of the Holy Savior, the oldest in Bruges.

Its well-proportioned interior includes a museum with several fine Flemish paintings. But if one has seen enough museums for the day, a walk around the Cathedral leads to Steenstraat, to follow for about 300 yards back to the Market Place.

Lunchtime and Place

If the preceding has been a morning walk, the walker well deserves lunch, and in the great Market Place there are good places to get it. Some of the best restaurants in Bruges are here.

The second basic walk in Bruges can be taken leisurely. As always on a European tour, it is to be hoped that everything need not be crowded into one day. Unobtrusive appreciation of the unofficial, the personal, life of a community, no matter how unhistoric, may have as much ultimate value for a visitor as running through a list of historic and artistic sights and sites, maybe more.

At any rate, one trudges loyally off, after a good lunch, on the second heat of a walking tour, or starts again next day, after some relaxation.

This walk, longer than the first, is less demanding in the field of art observation, but equally rewarding in offering intimate glimpses of the present life and ancient background of this glamorous little city.

Again, one starts charting one's course from the great Market Place, but this time from the northeast corner, by entering Vlamingstraat. Two blocks along lies the Theatre Place, with its City Theatre, or Schouwburg, and, at No. 33, a striking fourteenth-century residence which, in its early days, was the headquarters of Genoese merchants doing business here.

Beurze to Bourse

A few steps farther on lies Grauwwerkerstraat, and here, at No. 35, is a fine house built, long ago, by an eminent family named van der Beurze. In front of it, according to tradition, in the fifteenth and sixteenth centuries, merchants and traders gathered to transact their business. Because of this, the Brugeois deduce that the word bourse, now used to describe commercial exchanges all over the world, derives from "beurze," the old family name. Elsewhere, of course, it is widely agreed that the word comes through the French from the Latin bursa, meaning purse.

Once again, back on Vlamingstraat, a right turn into Akademiestraat leads to Jan van Eyck Plaats, that is, Place, whence one can wander through narrow, picturesque streets in one of Bruges' most historic areas. On the north side of the Place is the Old (fifteenth century) Customs House, now Bruges' Public Library.

A rarity inside is a display of paintings of William Caxton, the first English printer. He lived in Bruges during the fifteenth century.

At the farther side of the square, there is a delightful view of a canal, and one follows its right-hand quay, Spinolarei, until reaching the second street, Koningstraat, where a right turn leads to St. Walburga's Church, a fine baroque structure of the early seventeenth century.

Renaissance Renewal

Hoornstraat runs along the left side of the church, and this the stroller takes as far as Verwersdijk, turning right there, beside a canal to the first bridge across it. Directly ahead rises the Church of St. Anne, once destroyed but rebuilt in Renaissance style with impressive fittings and furnishings of that period.

Immediately behind the church, one turns right in Jerusalemstraat, to the Jerusalem Church whose old stained glass is notable.

One now proceeds easterly in Peperstraat to one of Bruges' fourteenth-century town gates Originally there were seven of them. Four now remain, and this is Cross Gate. Here one turns left through charming gardens where two ancient windmills stand beside the canal. These are the only two out of twenty-five windmills that once rose on Bruges' rim.

This is a very pleasant part of the stroll, and one continues as far as Carmersstraat, leading back leftward into the town. Just after turning off the Garden quay is to be found a sixteenth-century building, the Schutters-Gilde, that is, Archers Guild of St. Sebastian, which houses a collection of paintings and silverware and is open to the public.

Across the Bridge

The saunterer continues along Carmersstraat, to a canal bridge, which one crosses, turning immediately to the right on the opposite side, into the Lange Rei as far as St. Gilliskoorstraat. Turning left there, one comes to St. Giles' Church, dating from the thirteenth century, and possessing several paintings of particular interest.

From the church square, Sint Gillis Kerkstraat leads generally southward, where one makes a right turn in Gouden Handstraat, to reach a canal. Continuing westward, one arrives at Pottenmakersstraat.

Here, the turn is to the left, across a canal bridge into Sint Jacobstraat, where, at the first corner, stands St. Jacob's Church, founded in the twelfth century, completed in 1240. Here are outstanding art treasures, especially paintings, sculptures and brasses.

This is close to the end of the second walk in Bruges. One merely follows down Sint Jacobstraat about 200 yards and then finds oneself in the great Market Place again.

These looping tours will surely convince any appreciative tourist that the small city of Bruges is incomparable, a precious heritage of Western culture.

July 29, 1962

WALKING TOUR OF BRUSSELS

Flemish History Comes Alive in the Ancient Capital And So Does the Anticipation of Excellent Eating

By HARRY GILROY

BRUSSELS—Walking, one gets the feel of Brussels. It comes through the shoes from the cobblestones that are shaped like the good bread of Belgium and as durable as its 2,000-year-old people. The saunterer is up against an old question with sight-seers—is the happiness of feet everything?

The Place Royale is proposed as a starting point, even if it is thankless to tell a walker where to walk. The fun is to go where eyes, ears and nostrils lead. The eyes say, follow that pretty Brussels girl, although one's conscience will recall that the purpose is to look at antiquity.

In the Place Royale, the thing to do is to go up the steps of St. Jacques and turn to look down on the square. This place is a stage of history. The church became a Temple of Reason when Brussels was a part of revolutionary France. On its steps in 1831 stood King Leopold I to take the oath beginning the Belgian dynasty.

But the site has a far older significance. From the steps, the view is down a hill and over the top of the feathery spire of Brussels' Town Hall. This shows that the old center of the city was down on the Flemish plain. The road coming up the hill carried trade goods from the ports of Bruges and Ghent up to the Brabant plateau, at this point, and then it ran on to Cologne and the Rhineland.

Place of History

The Dukes of Brabant built a castle here to control the trade road, and a lot of history flowed from that circumstance. Charles V, that powerful Holy Roman Emperor whose traces are still to be found around Europe and South America, abdicated on this spot in 1555. The historic castle burned in 1731, and Prince Charles of Lorraine, a jolly Governor-General, built the present square twenty years later. So—down the steps after a long look, and turn right.

A short block and another right turn lead into the Place des Palais. On the right is Brussels Palace, where King Baudouin and Queen Fabiola were married last winter. The king does his office chores there as regularly as if he had to punch a clock, and the citizens see him at noon hurrying home for lunch at the residential palace in suburban Laeken.

On the left, a park stretches a sixth of a mile to another palace that houses Parliament and some ministries. The eighteenth century buildings all around the park bring back the picture of the nights before Waterloo when in those palaces "there was a sound of revelry" and "when music arose with its voluptuous swell, soft eyes looked love to eyes which spake again, and all went merry as a marriage bell." (Lord Byron —but surely walkers have a moment for poetry.)

Mounted Royalty

Marching past the Brussels Palace, in step with the guards, the wise sight-seer turns right at the end and heads along the Rue Ducale. One block and a bit more, another half-right past the equestrian statue of Leopold II, and then one should pause a moment to marvel at a city road carrying ten lanes of traffic, and think how clever Brussels is to plan a bypassing road like this, with tunnels and parking lanes.

Clever, yes, because the burghers put up a city wall in the fourteenth century. When it was finally taken down, there was a parkway route. But the sight-seer scorns the automobiles and walks along the Boulevard du Regent, looking at clothes, paintings, rugs and furniture. He crosses the Rue de Namur, where his road changes its name to the Boulevard de Waterloo. Then comes No. 31.

A doorway is open. One walks in. A cobbled alley runs ahead. Some painters' studios are on the right. Then the alley leads into a green gem of a park inside the block. A few minutes stroll to the left around the track will take one under old trees, past flower beds and alongside a funny statue—Peter Pan playing a flute for rabbit critics.

After circling the park, back to its point of entry. A right turn from the alley that led to the park sends one over more cobbles alongside a dancing academy. This is recognizable by the soulful pony-tail types hanging around between their leaps and bounces. Then a left turn opens the way through the courtyard of the old Egmont Palace.

Straight ahead, across the Rue des Petits Carmes, lies a perfect formal garden, the Place du Petit Sablon. Around it are elm trees and an iron fence. Inside are lawns, flowers and statues of beruffed noblemen, dead several hundred years. Egmont and Horn, the Flemish counts who stood against Spanish tyranny, brood over the quiet park.

At the foot of the Petit Sablon runs the Rue de la Regence. A glance left reveals the Palais de Justice, looming overhead as if the dome of the United States Capitol had been put on top of Pennsylvania Station. It is a pity the architect could not have his way. He planned to put an Egyptian pyramid on top instead of the dome.

Late Gothic

Across the street from the Petit Sablon is the Church of Notre Dame des Victoires, flamboyant Gothic, a church started in the fifteenth century by the crossbowmen. On Nov. 3, St. Hubert's day, the Brussels hunting set in elegant riding clothes attends mass.

To the right of the Petit Sablon, but on the same side of the Rue de la Regence as the church is the Museum of Art, with a collection worth looking at. There are dedicated walkers who hold that looking inside museums and churches destroys the marching rhythm, yet it is foolish not to dart into these places and absorb what there is at a glance. Besides, that is how to rest the feet.

Coming back out of the museum and turning left one block, the stroller returns to the Place Royale where the start was made. And now, leaving palaces and culture for the day, one leaves the square to the left to walk down that old trade road. It is marked Montagne de la Cour, and in a hundred yards it opens on a spectacular esplanade, with the spire of Town Hall in the center down below.

On the left, the enormous coffee-cream building is the Albertine Library, connected with the Bibliothèque Royale. On the right, the buildings are the center of the ministerial council of the European Common Market. By going right and then left, under an arch that carries the office building across the street, you can go down the hill on Rue Coudenberg past a row of bright new shops.

Under another office building arch, and then there are two broad streets to cross the Rue Cantersteen and the Boulevard de l' Imperatrice, in order to

get to the other side of a busy intersection. There follows a jog slightly right and another slightly left, keeping the Town Hall's spire ahead. When safely over the roads, it is possible to look right at the Central Station and the Sabena air terminal, big new buildings, and also at the great twin-towered church of Ste. Gudule.

Now Toward Lunch

The church is a trip all by itself, and since the aim of the walk now is to relax, the course continues past enormous parking lots and across another intersection into the Rue de la Madeleine. This is not as hard as it sounds.

Straight ahead is the Rue de la Montagne, lined with cafes, and the stroller inclines left for twenty paces or so and then turns right into a covered arcade called the Galerie de la Reine.

This is an elegant shopping street of two long blocks, with a roof overhead and no vehicles. In the shops are beautiful leather, lace and chocolates. There are cafes and quick lunch counters, bookshops and theatres. This is the city of the future, out of the past. One street, the Rue des Bouchers, cuts across the middle but one goes on into the Galerie du Roi, and then turns left into the Rue de l'Ecuyer.

From then on, the walk goes through eating country. There are little restaurants and big ones. Places specialize in mussels and chicken. There are butcher shops with black and white sausages ornamenting the windows, cheese shops, honey shops, bakeries. Down the Rue de l'Ecuyer one block, the Rue des Dominicains turns off to the left. A few blocks further, the name changes confusingly, but the walker walks on.

The Grand' Place, for which this course is heading, cannot be missed. Skirting it and then standing underneath the Town Hall spire, one is in one of the most spectacular squares in the world. Here trading Brussels grew, beneath that ducal castle on the hill.

More History

Here Egmont was beheaded on June 5, 1568, by order of the Duke of Alva. Here French artillery created an inferno on Aug. 16, 1695, and here the uncowed Flemish burghers built their gilded guild houses again in the next years.

Like St. Gudule, the Grand' Place is a visit all by itself. But a further saunter is suggested. Facing the Town Hall, one should turn right and walk two half blocks to the back of a great stone building, the Bourse or Stock Exchange, continuing past this and across the Boulevard Anspach. This is a shopping and cafe center, where one angles right for one block onto the Rue Devaux. From there, left one block, on the Rue Catherine, and on the right is an old street market.

It runs toward Ste. Catherine's church. A stroll through an open market, full of flowers, fruit, vegetables and jolly old salesgirls, is the right preparation for lunch, and that is the goal of this last bit of the walk. Left from the church is a great open area lined on both sides by excellent restaurants. Let the stroller settle down there for a meal, five good courses, and he will walk no farther. He will not be able to.

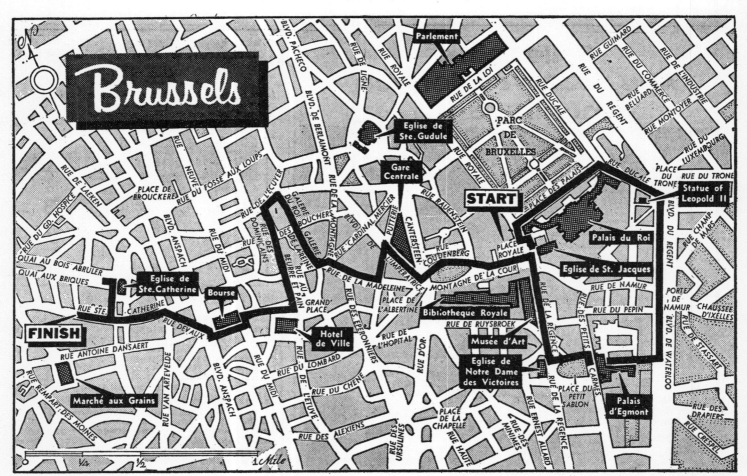

May 21, 1961

A 480-Mile Hike Through Ontario

By GEOFF NIGHTINGALE

OWEN SOUND, Ontario—In the early days of the 19th century, when the white man was settling southern Ontario, it was the custom of the Chippewa Indians around Lake Huron to raid settlements to the south.

The object of the raids, originally made against other Indian tribes and then extended to whites, was to capture slaves and, on occasion, young girls to be the wives of Chippewa braves.

Early one summer morning in 1805, it is said, a marauding band captured a lovely young white girl and carried her to the Huron country. Bimadashka (Laughing Water), they named her. A fitting name, for, as she grew older and forgot her white parents, she was happy with the Indians and became one of them. In time, she married the son of the chief who had led the raid against her people.

Bimadashka's grave can be seen to this day at Frenchmen's Bay; it is on the Saugeen Indian Reserve near Southampton, on Lake Huron's eastern shore. The marker reads "Bimadashka, Laughing Water, wife of Chief Mettawanash."

In those days almost 170 years ago, the Indian raids were carried out on foot or horseback, and the journeys often took the band 400 or 500 miles from home. A favorite route was along the Niagara Escarpment, which winds like a razorback from Niagara Falls northward to Tobermory, on the tip of Bruce Peninsula.

You can still walk this historic trail today, and there are those who say that, in the still of the summer's night, you can hear the hoofbeats of the Indian ponies and the laughter of the braves as they plan their assaults on the villages and settlements to the south.

Spectacular Variety

The Bruce Trail, as it now is known, extends about 480 miles through southern Ontario, and most of it is readily accessible by car. Its familiar marker, an arrow encircled by the words "Bruce Trail—Niagara to Tobermory," directs the hiker through a spectacular variety of country, from the fruit and vine lands of the Niagara district to the wind-swept tip of Bruce Peninsula. The latter separates Lake Huron from Georgian Bay.

In between, the trail cuts through the so-called "golden horseshoe" of industrial southern Ontario, including the steel-making city of Hamilton. It then proceeds northward through Orangeville and the beautiful Caledon Hills, the valleys of the Pretty and Mad Rivers, the enchanting Blue Mountains and the shipyard city of Collingwood, across the delightful Beaver Valley and west to the growing city of Owen Sound. The trail then heads north again up Bruce Peninsula to the popular resort areas of Wiarton, Lion's Head, Cabot Head and, finally, Tobermory, at land's end.

One can hit the trail for an hour's walk or a full day's hike. Or, one can spend an entire holiday sampling

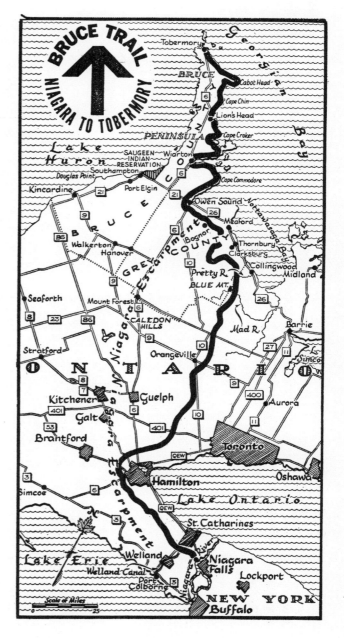

various sections of trail and countryside.

Along many parts of the trail, the tenderfoot is never far from civilization and its familiar sights and sounds. There are other much more rugged sections in which only the experienced outdoorsman should venture. But wherever it leads, the Bruce Trail abounds with scenic

POWER PLANT—Ontario's Douglas Point Nuclear Station lies off northern section of Bruce Trail.

valleys, beautiful vistas of land and water, rugged gorges, laughing waterfalls, chuckling streams and secluded places of quiet charm.

The hiker on the trail for more than a day should take along food and a sleeping bag; meantime, the Bruce Trail Association is endeavoring to provide some simple comforts. Late last winter, plans were made to place some open-faced log shelters every 10 or 15 miles along the trail. The first group of these was built this spring.

The open-front, log cabin-style shelters will be in keeping with the rugged nature of the trail, for all they will do is simply provide shelter from the elements. Nothing will be placed in them; hikers are expected to carry bedrolls and do their cooking outdoors.

Using Telephone Poles

Bell Canada, a telephone company, is aiding the shelter project by giving the Trail Association hundreds of old telephone poles. Dropped off a short distance from the trail, the poles have been dragged by tractor to the first shelter site. It is on a wooded hill near the Grey County hamlet of Bognor, and about five miles south of Highway 26; this is the Blue Water Highway between Meaford and Owen Sound.

This area is drawing increased numbers of summer and winter visitors from southern Ontario and from New York, Pennsylvania, Michigan and other Northeastern states, visitors who want to break away from the turmoil of large cities and commune with natural surroundings.

Perhaps as they lie in their bedrolls at night, they will dream of the days when the trail was trod only by the bare or moccasined feet of Indians, or the unshod hooves of their ponies. Perhaps a whisper of wind will carry a legend to their ears.

It was the custom of nomadic Indians to leave their old people beside the trail to die if they could not keep up with the band. Sometimes, the practice was resented by proud old braves and squaws.

One winter, it is said, a small tribe roving in search of a suitable camp and hunting ground left behind an old woman. As she lay awaiting death under the boughs of a huge elm tree, she cursed the band; all would find death before the snow moons were over.

In the ensuing weeks, famine struck and no food could be found. Rabbits, deer and fish all eluded the hunters.

Then one day, an enterprising hunter cut a hole in the thick ice of a lake and found great numbers of fish. Excited, the whole band scampered onto the ice. It broke with a resounding crack and all were thrown into the frigid water. Not one escaped.

Loon's Cry—Or Laughter?

At night, as the cry of the loon is heard across the stillness of the lake, there are those who say it is the laughter of the revengeful old crone and that the whisperings of the wind through the branches of the trees are the moans of the dying Indians.

Today, the bountiful waters of Bruce County are attracting hundreds of fishermen. This summer, the clear waters of Georgian Bay will also attract Canada's first underwater laboratory, Subliminos I, in which Dr. Joseph B. MacInnes of Toronto and other scientists will

study fish and other marine life. Tobermory is one of the sites being considered for this venture.

The countryside offers year-round recreation. In winter, it draws hundreds of skiers and snowmobile enthusiasts; in summer, campers, fishermen, boatmen and cottage owners increase the population. In the fall, the foliage rivals that of the New England states in brilliance as the leaves burst forth in reds, oranges, golds and yellows.

The region is favored by outdoorsmen, but good dining and accommodations are available in hotels and motels.

Owen Sound, with a population of 20,000, is the largest city in the northern section of the Bruce Trail. It has good shopping facilities. The smaller communities of Grey, Bruce and Simcoe Counties are also worth visiting, for each has its own attraction. Among such stops are Collingwood, Thornbury, Clarksburg and Meaford on Nottawasaga Bay, Wiarton, Lion's Head and Tobermory on the Georgian Bay side of Bruce Peninsula, and Southampton, Port Elgin and Kincardine on Lake Huron's eastern shore.

Between Port Elgin and Kincardine is the Douglas Point Nuclear Generating Station. This plant, owned by the Atomic Energy Commission of Canada, Ltd., and operated by the Ontario Hydro-Electric Commission, now produces 200,000 kilowatts of power. An expansion program that will get under way shortly calls for the construction of a 3,000,000-kilowatt generating plant and of a heavy-water installation. They will cost about $810-million.

Contrasts With Falls Area

Still, this is not industrialized country, but a pleasant contrast to the heavily populated southern part of the Bruce Trail district around Hamilton, Niagara Falls, Welland and St. Catharines. The fruit belt of Niagara, the falls themselves, the garden city of St. Catharines and the Welland Canal are points of interest.

Only a few industries are found in the less populated northern hump of southwestern Ontario. Among them are a small shipyard at Collingwood (where a 750-foot freighter is being built for completion in the fall), china and pottery plants (the much-admired Blue Mountain pottery) and furniture factories.

Tourism is a major factor in the economy of this part of Ontario, and, while the way is clear for industry to come in, a balance is expected to be maintained so as not to destroy the beauty of the countryside, the crispness of the air and the pureness of the water.

The lakes, rivers and streams of Grey and Bruce Counties abound in trout, perch, bass, pike and pickerel. In the fall, deer are plentiful, as are duck, geese and grouse.

The Bruce Trail country is meant to be explored, to be walked and to be "tasted." The air, the water, the cries of birds, the whisper of the wind in the trees, the softness of a summer's morning and the gentle caress of a quiet evening breeze offer surcease to the soul weary of the rush and pollution of city life.

OPEN COUNTRY—Beaver Valley, near Thornbury, is typical of wide-open spaces along Ontario's Bruce Trail. July 27, 1969

Denmark

COPENHAGEN WALKING TOUR

The Ancient and Modern Combine to Give Picturesque Variety to the Capital and Busiest Port of Denmark

By MARION MARZOLF

COPENHAGEN, Denmark —This city, the capital of this oldest kingdom in Europe, lives up to its reputation as a busy, modern center of commerce and culture. But its heart is old. In the center of the city, seventeenth-century town houses stand in the shadow of towering contemporary office buildings and apartment blocks. Broad avenues parallel meandering cobbled streets that follow the same path they did in medieval days.

This comfortable acceptance of the new, while remaining attached to the old, gives Copenhagen much of its charm, a charm best discovered by the walkers who take byways as well as highways.

An excellent field for Copenhagen exploration is the so-called inner city. This was originally medieval Copenhagen, bounded by a wall of earthwork fortifications at its founding at the end of the twelfth century. Just about sixty years ago, the last bit of those old fortifications was torn down to make an avenue and park.

Vanished Walls

All that remains of those walls are the names of the streets that have replaced them —Vester Voldgade, Norre Voldgade, and Oster Voldgade (West North, and East Wall Avenues) and the areas set around the old town gates of Vesterport, Norreport, Osterport, the last being beyond the northeast limits of the accompanying map. Ruins of one watchtower, Janners Taarn can be seen in the intersection of Vester Voldgade and Norre Voldgade.

The Copenhagen of the fifteenth and sixteenth centuries was shaped like a segment of a wheel, with the original fortress (now Christiansborg Castle) at the hub and with streets radiating like spokes out to the gates and the walls at the edge, crossed by other streets parallel to the walls.

The main street, almost exactly the same as the well-known Stroget of today, ran from the West Gate at Halmtorv (Straw Square), now Raadhuspladsen, to the gate which once lay at Kongens Nytorv, the King's New Square. Called "Stroget," or the place where one strolls, Copenhagen's popular avenue of fine shops is actually five streets linked together like a chain.

Raadhuspladsen, the Town Hall Square, is a good place to start the inner city walk. This large square, paved in a pattern of concrete panels and brick stripes, is the present city's center, a meeting place for both people and pigeons, and a popular spot simply to sit in the sun.

Panoramic View

Dominating the site is the romantic town hall, built in 1905, whose 350-degree clock tower offers one of the city's most splendid views, and serves as a means of orienting oneself. Its tower bells chime each quarter-hour and play a night watchman's tune at 6 and 12 o'clock.

Bypassing Stroget (as exploring that street can take a day in itself), one begins the stroll along parallel Vestergade. It is one of the oldest streets in the city and was, in old times, the western end of Stroget.

A few centuries ago, Danish farmers, having brought their straw to sell in Halmtorv, passed through the town gates just along here and shopped on this street, which led directly into Gammel Torv and Ny Torv, the Old and New Squares at the junction of the town's main crossroads. The city's older town halls stood here until 1795, but their only remnant is the "Caritas" fountain, where on March 11, the king's birthday, one may see golden balls dancing on the jets of water.

This was a residential area when Ludvig Holberg, called Denmark's Molière, and later Soren Kierkegaard, the philosopher, lived here. Some of the Empire-style houses remain, but for the most part, newer office buildings have replaced them. The columned City Court building in one corner was the town hall before the present one.

To the Cathedral

Turning left up Norregade, which leads to Norreport, one reaches Copenhagen's Cathedral Vor Frue Kirke, rebuilt in neo-classic style in the Eighteen Thirties after having been heavily damaged in a British bombardment in 1807. Many fine houses in the Latin Quarter, around the Cathedral and Copenhagen's University, were destroyed at this time and the Cathedral's square-topped tower still lacks the spire it lost then. The interior contains a prized group of statues depicting Christ and the apostles by the Danish sculptor, Bertel Thorvaldsen.

A poem inscribed on the Bishop's house, a dark building at the corner of Studiestraede tells that here stood the town hall in 1479, and the Bishop's house since 1537. A statue in the square commemorates the Protestant Reformation in Denmark.

The University of Copenhagen, founded in 1478, has always stood on these grounds which surround the cathedral. Stepping inside its Gate A, one sees a memorial commemorating students who gave their lives during World War II. Across the courtyard a small red brick building with a stepped gabled roof, the Konsistorium, is one of Copenhagen's oldest existing buildings, having survived the city's many fires.

Gothic Origins

From here a gate leads out to Norregade, almost at the foot of the dark brick mass that is St. Petri's, the German Reformed Church. Its choir dates from Gothic times and the churchyard contains some unique tombstones along the wall on Norregade.

Turning east at Krystalgade, one passes the Zoological Museum, part of the university, and reaches Fiolstraede, easily recognized by the yellow half-timbered building at the corner. Here one may take a detour to the left along this street of second-hand bookshops and antique stores. Books are invitingly displayed outside on racks and stands, and the customer is easily tempted to go in and browse.

But, turning to the right into Fiolstraede, one passes the University Library and, just opposite, "Ludvig Holberg's chestnut tree." The top of the tree shows above a yellow cement wall which displays a plaque explaining that Holberg, the great Danish dramatist and historian, lived in a house here until his death in 1754. The house has long since disappeared, but the great tree remains from his time.

Throughout the centuries this "Latin Quarter" has been a popular residence area for both students and professors. Around the corner on Store Kannikestraede, Great Canon's Street, the scientist Ole Romer lived at No. 16; the noted nineteenth-century literary critic and professor, Georg Brandes, once lived near by.

One can stroll through the gate at No. 10 into the courtyard of Admiral Gjedde's Gaard, an ochre-colored half-timbered building. Midday sunshine finds its way into this tidy green garden which the house surrounds on all sides, its wings reaching various heights to peaked tile roofs.

A few moments here will help to re-create the atmosphere that prevailed in the town of the seventeenth and eighteenth centuries. Several such gardens exist behind somewhat modernized street fronts, and the stroller should be alert for glimpses of them through the open gateways.

Three Centuries Old

Admiral Gjedde built this house in 1637, but it burned early in the Seventeen Hundreds and was rebuilt in 1790. It was only recently restored and converted to office use. Leaving the courtyard through a second archway, the visitor continues past the entrance to another of Holberg's apartments. Hereabouts are remains of a tiny alley, only about two yards wide, called Skidenstraede, dating from much earlier times.

Regensen, a dormitory dating from the seventeenth century, for the university's male honor students, lies at the end of Store Kannikestraede. From its courtyard there is a fine view of the Round Tower, which exhibits a gleaming golden seal and is set off by an old linden tree.

A short climb up a corkscrew ramp leads to the top of the tower. It was erected by Christian IV, Denmark's "builder king," as an observatory for the astronomer Tycho Brahe. Although Brahe preferred to work on his island of Hven in the sound between Denmark and Sweden, his museum is here in the tower and the small observatory at the top is still used.

A fine view of the old quarter is available from the platform encircling the observatory. The tower also forms one end of the Trinitatis Church.

Old and New

Descending and stepping out on busy Kobmagergade, originally named for the butchers' shops there, one is again reminded how the old and new are blended in this city. Passing two blocks of bright shop windows and determined shoppers, motorists and cyclists, one then ducks down narrow Lovstraede, along the side of the post office, back into the past again.

Before 10 A.M. there is a flood of color here, as the city's scarlet-jacketed postmen stream through the gates on golden yellow bikes, riding off on their morning rounds. In a few moments they are gone. The stroller quickens his pace to enter sunny Gray Friars Square ahead.

Lying just off Stroget, this serene square with its lilac trees and pastel-colored town houses is often missed by visitors. Nothing remains of the original monastery of the Gray

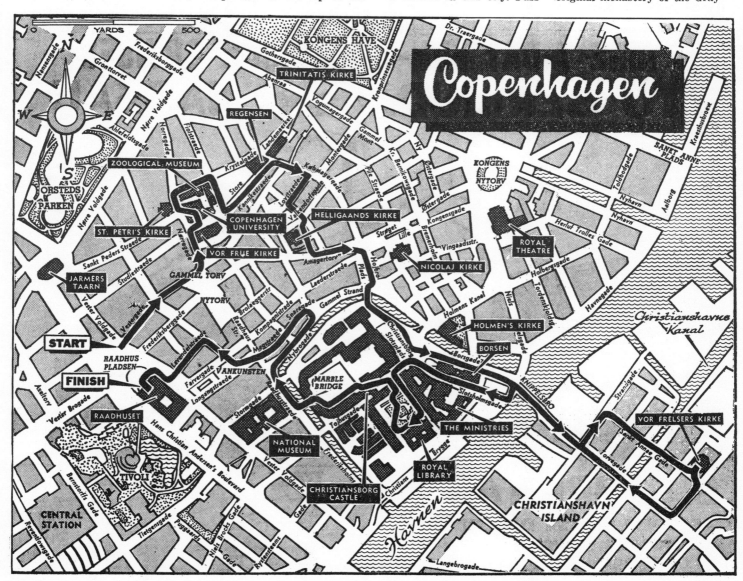

Friars, which was founded here in the Middle Ages.

Fires and bombardment have taken their toll. But several houses have been rebuilt. As one plaque says: "What fire has taken, God has put back." A variety of small shops are found here, and the stroller may unknowingly brush elbows with some of Denmark's screen celebrities who live in this area.

Carillon

Niels Hemmingsens Gade takes one to the Holy Ghost Church, "Helligaands," at Valkendorfsgade. The wing on this north side is said to be the only pure Gothic edifice remaining in the city. The wing has served as a hospital for the poor, and later as a town library. The church tower bells ring out over endless streams of shoppers and traffic, giving a daily afternoon concert.

One can go directly down the front walk to an iron gate leading out onto Stroget, walking to the left on Amagertorv. This square was named for Dutch settlers from the island of Amager who began the outdoor vegetable market which still flourishes here. A stork fountain in the square makes a whimsical contrast to the first view of stately Christiansborg Castle, with its tall misty-green tower.

On days that King Frederik IX is in residence, the picturesque Danish Royal Life Guards march up Stroget at about ten minutes to one in the afternoon and turn north at this square as they return from the ceremony of the changing of the guard.

Maritime Museum

To the right, parallel to Stroget, is Laederstraede, which farther along becomes Kompagnistraede, the streets lined with antique shops of all descriptions. To the left, Nicolaj Church, now a maritime museum, was where Lutheranism was first preached in the city. Just behind the church is an area of cabarets and night clubs called "the mine field."

One strolls past the tempting array of fruits and vegetables in the market to Hojbro Plads at the canal that encircles the island of Slotsholm, the Castle Island. In the square an equestrian statue of Bishop Absalon, dressed in armor, looks out over Christiansborg Castle, beneath which lie ruins of the original fortress-castle the Bishop built when he founded Kobenhavn, "the merchants' harbor," in the twelfth century. There have been five castles on this site through almost 800 years.

From the left along the canal, one sees Holmen's Church (the Navy's church), floating flower markets, the Borsen, or stock exchange, with its tower of three dragons with their tails entwined; the complex of "red brick" Government office buildings, the castle and its church, Thorvaldsen's museum of sculpture, and the canal again on the right. Its near side is lined by town houses, boats, and fisherwives, who sell their fish at the Gammel Strand each weekday morning the year round.

On the promenade in front of the castle is a statue of King Frederik VII, who in 1849 gave Denmark its free constitution, making it a democratic kingdom. Christiansborg, which was the royal residence until 1794, now houses the Danish Parliament, Supreme Court, and royal reception rooms.

The stroller crosses the bridge to examine Holmen's Church more closely, to see the statue of the naval hero Tordenskjold and tombs of various famous seamen. The gable on the canal facade dates from 1563, and the church is one of the oldest examples of Renaissance architecture in the city.

Venerable Stock Exchange

Beside the seventeenth century Borsen, built in Dutch Renaissance style, stands the oldest stock exchange building in Western Europe. A stop on Knippelsbro Bridge allows a broad view up and down the Inner Harbor, where merchant ships of all sizes and from many countries are loading and unloading. From here, too, is a fine view back over Hojbro

Plads, especially on a crisp, sunny morning.

An interesting detour, for the determined walker, takes one across the bridge to the Church of Our Savior, Vor Frelsers Kirke. The spiral staircase curling around the outside of the tower provides an exciting climb for those who do not easily get dizzy. The way to reach it is to take Strandgade to the left, passing merchant houses and warehouses that are typical of this small island of Christianshavn. Going right at Sankt Annae Gade leads directly to the church, passing Christianshavn canal on the way.

A block farther along this street brings one to the earthwork ramparts which border the southern edge of the island and formed the defense lines for this part of the city. An old gatehouse stands at the opening in the ramparts where Torvegade cuts through. By Torvegade and Knippelsbro, one returns to Christiansborg Castle.

Entering the castle at Tojhusgade, by way of a pedestrian archway, one goes left through an arcade into the beautiful gardens of the Royal Library, a favorite sunning and lunching spot for people who work near by. Surrounded by wings of the palace, the garden was formed in 1867 by filling with earth what in Christian IV's days had been a sheltered inner harbor for smaller ships. The wings then served as supply and storage wharves. The Armor Museum with its large collection of uniforms and armaments lies just beyond the west wing.

Riding Hall

The walker can now retrace his steps to the street and cross near the Parliament entrance on the south side of the castle to the riding ring. This is flanked by two curving wings which are the only remaining portions of the eighteenth-century castle that survived the fire of 1794. Stables and an indoor riding hall take up part of these buildings. Here, too, in

one wing is an intimate court theatre trimmed in red plush and gold, now serving as a unique theatre museum.

From the Marble Bridge, also part of the earlier castle, one has a view across to the Prince's Palace, once the residence of the Crown Prince, now the National Museum. To the left along Frederiksholms Kanal are the Army Horse Guard's former barracks. To the right are Nybrogade and Gammel Strand.

Along the canal to the right, on Nybrogade are art shops and offices in the former town houses. A left turn around the corner, down Snaregade and Magstraede, leads to two work-a-day streets that seem to be right out of a comedy by Holberg. The streets are cobbled, and lined with three and four-story combination warehouse-workshop-dwellings, still in use.

Antiquity

Several are in poor condition, but a few have been restored. For example, No. 5 Snaregade with its dark wood half-timbering. Some have been turned into small art galleries or antique shops.

One reaches the corner at the square, Vankunsten, named for the well that provided water to the castle, and the water mill that stood there. In this square, Danish citizens held off the attacking Swedish army which had penetrated the city's walls in the war of 1659. Crossing the square one takes Hestemollestraede and Lavendelstraede to the Town Hall Square.

Whether it is afternoon or early evening, one is just in time for a stroll through Tivoli, the famous amusement park which is just across Hans Christian Andersen's Boulevard from the Town Hall. Fine restaurants, a concert hall, variety outdoor shows and a pantomine theatre, flower gardens and lakes (remnants of the fortifications), and countless amusements and refreshment stands entertain thousands of visitors nightly in a fairyland of gaiety.

June 10, 1962

France

A WALKING TOUR OF PARIS

Searching Out the Mystique of This Great City Leads One On an Eight-Mile Stroll Away From the Boulevards

By GEORGE W. OAKES

PARIS—Instead of strolling along Paris' wide boulevards to shop or watch the crowds on a clear, sunny spring or summer morning, it is more fun to set aside several hours for a real walk. This not only is the best way to absorb Paris' unique beauty but it also puts one in sharp condition to make the most of Paris' renowned *haute cuisine* afterward.

It should be noted at once that the walk here proposed is quite a long one—a matter of practically eight miles, including the occasional turn-offs for special sight-seeing. This means that the stroller would benefit by taking it slowly and easily, with an occasional pause, perhaps at some agreeable cafe terrace, or in any of a number of parks that will be encountered.

Or, indeed, one could divide it up into several separate strolls, since the route actually covers various different phases of Paris, some comparatively modern, some ancient, some elegant, some bourgeois or working-class.

The Take-Off

A start, then, might be made from the Place de l'Alma on the Right Bank, almost in the shadow of the Eiffel Tower. The course would be along the embankment of the Seine in the direction of the Place de la Concorde.

Along here in springtime the alley of carefully pruned chestnut trees on what is called the Cours Albert I—after Belgium's heroic king in World War I—will display their cone-shaped blossoms, flowering through the green leaves. Or, in midsummer, the trees will be turning slightly rust-color. In any case, the long vista of the triple row of chestnuts along the river bank arouses the proper mood for soaking up the *mystique* of Paris.

Approaching the Pont des Invalides, the stroller sees below him, moored to their wharves, the *bateaux-mouches,* those Seine pleasure steamers with glass-enclosed decks on which he probably will cruise one night between the Ile-St.-Louis and the Bois de Boulogne, to see the many artistically illuminated monuments and buildings along both shores.

The Cours la Reine

Crossing the Place du Canada leads to the Cours la Reine, also beside the Seine and also shaded by chestnut trees. It was laid out by Marie de Medici in 1616 so that she could take drives in her Florentine import, the revolutionary sprung carriage that drastically altered seventeenth-century transportation.

The Pont Alexandre III, the most highly decorated and only single-span bridge over the Seine in Paris, is worth a moment's pause. Across the river, beyond the bridge's gilded statues that gleam in the sunlight on top of four stone pylons, lies the broad sweep of the esplanade in front of the Hotel des Invalides. Here, under a great dome, is the tomb of Napoleon. Here is also a military museum.

In the other direction—that is, on the Right Bank side—stand the glass-roofed, ornate Grand Palais and Petit Palais, built in flamboyant style for the Paris Exposition of 1900, and still used for exhibitions. From this point of the walk, a glance backward in the direction from which one has come offers a fine view of the handsome, modern Palais de Chaillot, on the crest of its flowered hill. Then, looking ahead once more, beyond the Pont de la Concorde, the bulk of the Louvre looms in the distance.

To the Tuileries

The Cours la Reine ends at the Place de la Concorde. Crossing this most magnificent Paris square, one must navigate carefully, because of the mass of traffic, but the reward is to reach the Tuileries Gardens. The eastern boundary of the Place is a high terrace and parapet framing the end of the Gardens, and one reaches the terrace by climbing a flight of steps near the small but elegant museum of the Orangerie.

The stroller should stop at the terrace's balustrade for a look at the splendid Place. In its center rises the obelisk from Luxor, flanked by spectacular fountains. Along the north side of the Place are huge twin mansions, colonnaded, designed by the eighteenth-century architect, Gabriel. Between them, the Rue Royale commences, to end at the Madeleine. Directly opposite the viewer on the Tuileries terrace, the Avenue des Champs Elysées commences, broad and beautiful and climbing to the Arc de Triomphe at the Etoile.

At the opposite side of the Tuileries terrace stands the museum called the Jeu de Paume. In it is perhaps the world's greatest collection of Impressionist paintings, but this treat should be saved for another day and another visit. This is a walk, and not a gallery tour.

Midway between the two galleries, eastward of the terrace, is a spacious octagonal fountain, a good place to halt and gaze along the tree-lined Grande Allée of the Gardens to a great arch, that of the Carrousel, or Merry-go-round, beyond which is the Louvre. Once the palace of the Tuileries—the Tile Yards —rose here, but it was destroyed in the Paris uprising of 1871.

Children at Play

The Tuileries Gardens, formal in lay-out, have distinct charm. Children are always playing there, sailing boats in the pond, having a ride on the (child-size) merry-go-round, which has nothing to do with the arch or the bridge called the Carrousel. Or they may be simply sampling an ice at one of the stands under the trees.

Sauntering along the gravel walks brings the tourist to flowerbeds laid out by the seventeenth - century landscape architect, Le Nôtre, who planned the great gardens at Versailles. Under the arch, which was a Napoleonic reproduction of the Arch of Severus in Rome, one sees, directly ahead, the vast Louvre, former royal palace, now museum.

But, since again this is not a museum tour but a walk, one swerves here to the left, retraces one's steps a short distance and leaves the Gardens to emerge at the Place des Pyramides on the Rue de Rivoli, for a look at the mounted, gilded statue of Joan of Arc there. A few hundred yards eastward are the Place du Palais Royal and the Palais Royal itself. This was built by Cardinal Richelieu in the seventeenth century and inhabited for a short time by Louis XIV.

During the eighteenth century, the Palais Royal's gardens and galleries were the favorite promenade of Parisians. After the Revolution, gambling houses flourished there. The long, symmetrical arcades on either side of the gardens are now lined with shops.

Les Halles

Now one leaves the Palais Royal, finds the Rue du Colonel Driant close by, and follows it eastward to Les Halles, an enormous, bustling area that has been Paris' central market since the twelfth century. Al-

though the peak of excitement at Les Halles is in the early morning, there is still plenty of activity in the daytime in the old, high, cast-iron and glass pavilions that were the peak of modernity in the era of Napoleon III.

In one section, porters will be wheeling huge cheeses from Switzerland's Emmenthal, or crates of Brie cheese, produced just east of Paris, and neatly packed in straw. In another pavilion, hundreds of quarters of beef will be hanging, to be bought by the local butchers.

The next stage of the walk is through a very old part of Paris called the Marais because of the marshes thereabouts in ancient times. Now, much of the quarter is commercial, but there are notable hold-overs from the past, some medieval, some Renaissance, some eighteenth century.

In the Marais

One crosses the busy Boulevard de Sebastopol—a sort of Parisian Fourteenth Street—and goes along the Rue Rambuteau past the Archives Nationales, a combination of record office and museum of France's great historical documents, also containing magnificent murals. One enters the Rue des Francs-Bourgeois, with its many old mansions, the heart of the Marais. Here is the Musée Carnavalet, the museum of the City of Paris which contains, in addition to many prints and models of the old city, including the evolution of the streets just traversed, a collection of seventeenth, eighteenth and nineteenth century costumes.

A couple of hundred yards beyond lies the oldest large square in Paris and one of the most enchanting, the Place des Vosges. King Henri IV, who reigned from 1589 to 1610, ordered that all the buildings of this first "royal place" should be harmonious, the roofs and facades and design uniform. Today, the rose-colored brick and peeling white stone of these classical buildings and their arcades are practically unchanged since the times (quite a while apart) when Cardinal Richelieu lived at No. 21, and Victor Hugo at No. 6, now a Hugo museum.

Time for Lunch

By this time, and after the distance traversed, a stroller is probably hungry for lunch and also would welcome a short rest. There is a nice little cafe for an apertif at one corner of the

Place, and also, at the opposite end, a fine restaurant, not inexpensive. For less costly eating, there are many cafes in the neighborhood.

Fortified by lunch, the dedicated saunterer starts out again by finding the Boulevard Henri IV and turning to the right and southward there for the fascinating Ile St.-Louis. This small island in the Seine, a quiet haven from the bustle on either bank, retains much of the sleepy atmosphere of old Paris and has thus become the home of many artists and writers.

The best way to appreciate the quality of the Ile St.-Louis is to walk along the Quai d'Anjou to the Hotel de Lauzun, a typically rich private mansion of the seventeenth century (when the Ile was actually built out of smaller islands and swamps there). It was named for a famous Don Juan of that period and is used now to entertain distinguished guests of Paris.

Turning right into the Rue Poulletier, the explorer comes to the Ile's main thoroughfare, the Rue St.-Louis-en-l'Ile which bisects the narrow little island lengthwise. Here is the Church of St.-Louis-en-l'Ile, from whose tower protrudes an old clock.

At the west end of the island, an iron footbridge over a narrow arm of the Seine leads to the other famous, and larger, Seine island, the Ile de la Cité, the heart and cradle of Paris. The bridge debouches on a small park behind the Cathedral of Notre Dame. Here one has a close-up view of the cathedral's famous flying buttresses. This view is only a start on the visual treasures of the Ile de la Cité—the cathedral's West Front—the twin "salt-shaker" towers of the fabled Conciergerie, the superb Sainte Chapelle.

But the stroller now is about to plunge into Paris' Latin Quarter, by crossing to the Left Bank by the Pont de l'Archevêché, thus reaching the narrow Rue des Bernardins and presently the Rue de la Montagne Ste. Genevieve—named for the earliest of Paris' patron saints.

Hereabouts practically every street, many buildings and monuments are sacred to the memory of early Paris, including the Paris of the Romans, still preserved in the Roman baths in the park of the Musée de Cluny; and to the Paris of scholarship since the thirteenth

century when Louis IX's confessor, Robert de Sorbon, set up a theological college there. It is hard to choose among all these wonders.

Medieval Paris

The Church of St.-Etienne-du-Mont, close to the Place Ste.-Geneviève, is a most attractive combination of late Gothic and Renaissance. It is worth entering especially to inspect the elaborate and beautiful rood screen, unique in Paris.

From the Place Ste. Geneviève, one enters the Rue Clothilde, flanked by the rear of the Panthéon and the Lycée Henry IV and proceeds a short distance to the Rue de l'Estrapade where a turn to the eastward leads to the delightful little square, the Place de la Contrescarpe. From this shaded spot, five narrow streets stem in various directions, the most fascinating of them being the Rue Mouffetard as it twists down a rather steep slope.

This is a lively street filled with the energetic residents of the quarter darting into and out of its many shops — the green grocer's with heaps of vegetables on display; the bakery, with its long, crusty *baguettes* and other shapes of delicious bread. Near by, a bearded student strums a guitar in a wine shop. The Rue Mouffetard is rich in local color and movement.

"Temple of Fame"

The stroller swings to the right into the Rue du Pot de Fer — the Street of the Iron Pot — and right again by the Rue Lhomond for that national shrine, the Panthéon. The great cruciform church was put up by Louis XV over the site of the original tomb of Saint Geneviève, but during the French Revolution it was converted into a secular Temple of Fame.

Here repose many of France's greatest men, philosophers, poets, leaders, among them Jean-Jacques Rousseau, Voltaire, Victor Hugo, and such modern personages as Jean Jaurès. He was the eminent French socialist who, it has been said, might have been able to avert World War I because of his close association and influence with the German socialist movement, had he not been assassinated at its outbreak. Here lie Emile Zola, Sergeant Maginot, of the celebrated Maginot Line of defense

that failed so markedly in World War II, and the novelist and Academician, Anatole France.

A short walk down the Rue Soufflot takes the stroller to the romantic and symmetrical Luxembourg Gardens, where, also, the palace of the same name houses the French Senate. The Medici Fountain here is noted and impressive. The scene in this finest Left Bank park is animated and charming, with many children at play and many elders at ease. Its walks are shady and its flower beds colorful.

On emerging from the Gardens, one crosses the Rue Vaugirard, Paris' longest street, and proceeds down the Rue Férou to the Place St. Sulpice and the church of the same name, the second largest in Paris and designed, unlike most of Paris' churches which are Gothic, in basilica style. St. Sulpice appears occasionally in French literature and even in the opera, "Manon."

From here, it is only a short walk by the Rue Bonaparte to the Boulevard St. Germain and the famous Abbey of St. Germain-des-Prés, Paris' oldest church, with its eleventh century tower, a pleasant sight from the famous cafe there, the Deux Magots. Passing the church, one comes to the Rue de l'Abbaye where, close by, stand a little corner garden and the Abbot's residence. Thence, it is only a few steps to the tiny Place Furstenberg, one of the most charming spots in Paris.

Four Magnolias

This delightful square is noted for its four magnolia trees and old-fashioned, ornate lampposts. Here, the artist Delacroix had his studio at No. 6. The narrow Rue Cardinale leads out of the square, and is lined with picturesque houses in various shades of gray, with window boxes on the upper balconies beneath slanting roofs and crooked chimneys.

Across the Rue de l'Echaudé at the juncture of the Rue de Seine and the Rue de Buci, one finds oneself in the midst of a neighborhood market place. Patisseries, grocery stores, vegetable stalls, fish and meat markets cater to the many customers who crowd street and sidewalks. There is a pleasing corner bistro from which to watch this gay scene.

From here the Rue Dauphine leads down to the Seine and

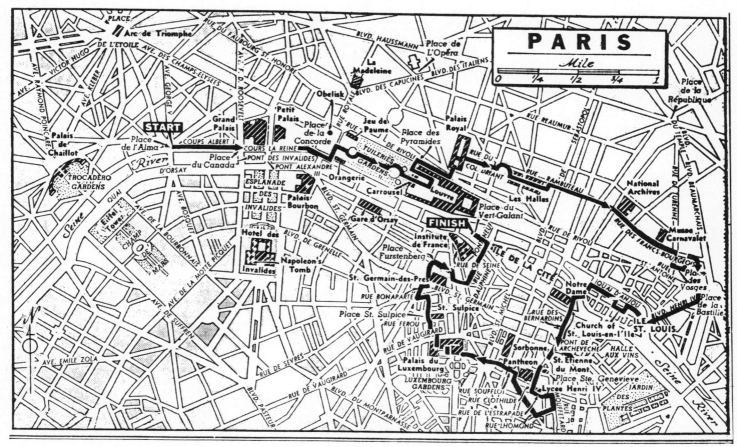

the Left Bank bridgehead of the Pont Neuf which, despite its name, is the oldest bridge in Paris. The Pont Neuf's history and legends are arresting. It was always a popular bridge once lined with houses, frequently the site of fairs and shows. Here, for example, a noted entertainer called Tabarin —hence, doubtless, the title of the famous bar-dance-hall-cabaret, the Bal Tabarin up in Montmartre—performed in the seventeenth century. Jugglers,

songsters and clowns attracted crowds of Parisians. It was then the city's most engrossing playground.

At the Pont Neuf

As a fitting close to a day full of artistic and historic diversity, one might well cross the half of the bridge to where it touches ground on the Ile de la Cité. Here, close to the equestrian statue of Henri IV which dominates the bridge at that point, a flight of steps descends

to a small, wedge-shaped park, the Square du Vert-Galant (as Henri IV had been nicknamed by his loving subjects.) This triangular garden is the western tip of the Ile de la Cité, where the Seine, divided by the island, comes together again.

Looking downstream into the late afternoon sun, several bridges are in view, as well as the noted structures that line the river's banks. On the right, the Louvre extends its bulk. On

the left, are the Institut de France, home of the French Academy; the neo-classic Gare d'Orsay, and the Palais Bourbon, site of the French Assembly.

All these buildings are impressive. But there is something else, too. To stand at the tip of the little square, beneath the trees, and to observe the hopeful Seine-side fishermen placidly watching their floats bobbing in the stream is to find the perfect finish for this walking tour of Paris, old and new.

April 2, 1961

BRITISH ENJOY ART OF WALKING WITHOUT A HITCH

By PATRICK CATLING

LONDON—Britain likes to think of herself as a nation of walkers. Wordsworth wandered lonely as a cloud in the Lake District to see some daffodils. More recently, Dr. Barbara Moore, accompanied intermittently by half the reporters and photographers of Fleet Street, marched more than 1,000 miles from John O'Groats to Land's End to call attention to her theory that vegetarianism and celibacy have given her unusual powers of endurance at the age of 56.

The poet was the nearer to the romantic tradition of walking in Britain, a way of getting close to nature; but the dietitian, although she was born in Russia, was expressing a very British belief that mortification of the flesh, by walking it around in all sorts of foul weather, is good for the character and even for the health.

Dr. Moore inspired Billy Butlin, the proprietor of Britain's popular low-price holiday camps, to sponsor a mass walk over the same route for £5,550 ($15,400) in prizes. The money and publicity attracted all sorts of unfit people to the competition, and the proportion of starters who fell out, cold, exhausted and lame, was high.

About a quarter of the families of Britain today own automobiles, and at last the Ministry of Transport actually has begun to provide some stretches of highway built to twentieth-century specifications. Yet Britons still tell themselves with pride that they are not like those softies across the Atlantic who prefer to drive instead of walk, even on the golf course.

All Walks of Life

Sometimes, it is true, some Britons' enthusiasm for walking seems more theoretical than practical. Some avid talkers about walking became obviously nervous when the National

British Travel and Holidays Association

SUMMER SOLITUDE—A country road winds over the fields of Wiltshire.

Union of Railwaymen recently threatened to go out on a national strike. But there are many thousands, in all walks of life, so to speak, who, given a choice of using wheels or their own feet, gallantly demonstrate that perambulation is not a lost art on these islands.

One of Britain's most celebrated walkers is the Minister of Transport himself, Ernest Marples, who, with his wife, frequently escapes into the countryside for long walks. In a recent interview, Mrs. Marples commented that she and her husband often walk or ride bicycles in London "because driving a car in London traffic these days is absolute hell."

"We keep our car in the garage all week and use it only on Sundays to get out of town to walk in the country," Mrs. Marples said. "We leave early before most Sunday motorists are on the roads, drive out in any direction for about an hour, and then walk for ten or fifteen miles, getting back to the car in time for tea."

"Whenever we come across a place where a farmer has illegally ploughed up a public footpath or closed it," Mr. Marples added, "you may be sure that something is done about it." He said that one of his few unfavorable observations during his recent tour of the United States was that so few people seemed to walk there and that provisions for pedestrians so often seemed inadequate.

Many British commuters elect to walk the part of their workday journey that American ex-

urbanites normally cover by car. The walkers claim that the exercise accomplished between home and the railroad station refreshes the liver and clears the brain and so enables them to enjoy with an easy conscience that protracted period of eating, drinking, smoking and gossiping—the British business-lunch.

The black bowler hats of government and finance may be seen, usually with umbrellas, among the nursemaids' frilly caps in London parks at midday. And many young couples, when weather conditions are unsuitable for amorous dalliance in the parks, spend some of their leisure time strolling through them instead.

Certainly the best way for a visitor from abroad to see Lon-

don is by walking in the footsteps of such celebrated peripatetic diarists as Dr. Samuel Johnson and James Bone. Many of the sights they fondly observed at walking pace and recorded in their books may still be seen in the parts of London that have not as yet been "improved."

London Transport, the organization that operates the capital's buses and Underground trains, has published a booklet intended to encourage people to use the public transportation facilities to get out of town for some fresh air and exercise. This guide, called "Country Walks," which costs the equivalent of 51 cents, can be very helpful to visitors who might waste time if they had no explicit instructions to follow.

Twenty walks, covering 230 miles of London's countryside, are described in detail, with historical notes, photographs and sections of the appropriate Ordnance Survey maps (1 inch to 1 mile). These are as indispensable as strong legs for long-distance walkers.

Protecting Public Rights

The walker's best friend in Britain is the Ramblers' Association, 48 Park Road, London, N. W. 1, whose assiduous lobbying in Westminster for fifty years finally helped to persuade Parliament to pass the National Parks and Access to Countryside Act of 1949. This act preserves places of natural beauty and protects public rights of way along the elaborate network of footpaths that enables walkers to get off the well-worn tracks of tourists in a hurry.

Walkers see the quiet, secluded, unspoiled parts of rural England that travelers in trains, buses and automobiles nostalgically dream about. For a minimum subscription of seven shillings and sixpence ($1.07) the Ramblers' Association will make you a member, plot your course, lend you maps from its library and give you a list of 3,000 clean, economical rest houses.

The Ramblers' Association points out that anybody who wants to do any serious walking should be sure to dress and equip himself for the occasion. The most important item, of course, is footwear. The association recommends "stout, but not heavy, boots or shoes," in which there is room for the toes to move but not for the heels to slip.

Before walking, soft feet can be toughened in a hot footbath containing a lot of common salt and a little sodium bicarbonate. Because a blister can be "as bad as a puncture to a cyclist, and takes longer to repair," the danger of chafing should be reduced further by wearing thick woolen socks dusted with boracic powder.

The Compleat Rambler, according to the association, should carry on his back a large rucksack containing a flashlight, a compass and a first-aid kit that includes adhesive plaster dressings and an antiseptic. A compactly rolled raincoat is also a useful thing to take along.

Another organization that faithfully serves the interests of walkers in Britain is the Pedestrians' Association. Its main objects are "to promote the safety of pedestrians and other road-users and the amenities of pedestrians on the highways and elsewhere." T. C. Foley, the secretary of the association, recently pointed out that the public was becoming alarmed at the continually increasing numbers of killed and injured on British roads. The toll last year was 330,000—30,000 more than in 1958.

From his headquarters at 45 Fleet Street, London E. C. 4, Mr. Foley conducts a vigorous campaign to improve conditions for walking along and across all classes of roads, to reduce speed limits where casualties are numerous or seem probable and to make the legal penalties severer for driving offenses. Any pedestrian who encounters hazards or unreasonable restrictions in the course of walking around this country is urged to tell the association so that it may take the appropriate action.

Where should the tourist begin walking? The answer is almost anywhere except the great, ugly, smoky industrial conurbation of the Midlands and the mining areas of South Wales and Northern England. The Lake District, the moors of Devon and Yorkshire and the Scottish Highlands are probably the most popular regions, but are big enough not to become crowded.

Peter ffrench-Hodges of the British Travel and Holidays Association said one could walk almost continuously along footpaths around the shore of Britain, with few minor detours inland. He suggested two slightly less ambitious tours in the Shakespeare country and around the Smugglers' Coast of Cornwall, near the mild southwestern extremity of England.

The association has published detailed descriptive and historic itineraries. Back numbers of the association's monthly magazine, "Coming Events," may be obtained from association headquarters, Queen's House, 64 St. James's Street, London S. W. 1.

Listed in Guidebooks

Further suggestions are plentiful in the guidebooks of the National Trust for the Preservation of Places of Historic Interest and Natural Beauty. The trust offices are situated at 42 Queen Annes Gate, London S. W. 1. Planning a walk that reaches at least one of Britain's great houses that are open to the public can enhance one's pleasure and give one a sense of added achievement.

The flat terrain of East Anglia is rather boring, some people feel. But in very few places does the walker in England suffer from monotony, partly because, as G. K. Chesterton wrote, "The rolling English drunkard made the rolling English road."

Perhaps it is the compact variety of the landscapes that moved the British Travel and Holidays Association to claim, in a manner bolder than usual, that "Britain is probably the best country in the world for walking in."

March 27, 1960

Hikers in Britain Open Trail For 250 Miles Along Pennines

By JAMES FERON
Special to The New York Times

LONDON, April 24—Britons who cherish their footpaths opened the nation's longest today, the 250-mile Pennine Way in Northern England and Scotland.

The Pennine Way, inspired by the 2,000-mile Appalachian Trail, which enables hikers to go from Maine to Georgia, is the first route of its kind in Britain.

The idea of a long-distance route for hikers was conceived 30 years ago by Tom Stephenson, then and now secretary of the Ramblers Association. Mr. Stephenson, who is in his seventies, has walked the Pennine Way, in parts, many times.

"A couple of American girls wrote to me in the nineteen-thirties," he said, "and asked if there was anything in Britain like the Appalachian Trail. They wanted to do some walking here."

He said there was not, but wrote an article in a London newspaper suggesting a route along what is called the backbone of England.

The response was enthusiastic, especially from the large segment of serious walkers who are painfully aware of the limited hiking space in their densely populated island.

Mr. Stephenson won Government endorsement for his plan in 1947 and a legal foundation through the National Parks Act of 1949. Parts of the trail, which traverses three national parks, had only to be cleared and

The New York Times   April 25, 1965
The heavy line denotes the "Pennine Way" in Britain.

marked. Other sections crossed jealously guarded private land.

The Pennine Way, which starts about 15 miles west of Sheffield, takes in the moors of the Bronte country in its southern section. It takes the hiker across the summit of the highest point in the Pennines, the 2,930-foot Cross Fell just north of its half-way point, and leads him past the most impressive section of Hadrian's Wall, one of the most impressive remains of the Roman occupation.

Most of the trail runs above 1,000 feet, covering fairly easy terrain. There is no rock climbing and, for most of the way, accommodations can be found within a mile or so of the route. These include 15 youth hostels.

The trail begins in industrial England and although the grimy Midland cities of Manchester, Huddersfield and Bradford are never far way, they do not impose on the route.

April 25, 1965

By JOAN MORRISON

WINCHESTER, England—One day last summer, our American family of five shouldered our rucksacks and set off in the footsteps of Chaucer's pilgrims, following the "Pilgrims' Way" from this ancient seat of kings to the holy shrine of Canterbury. In our party were Susie, Jimmy and Bobby (7, 10 and 12, respectively), my husband and I.

We had "done" London and the tourist sights from Buckingham Palace to Carnaby Street—and we had loved it. But now we wanted to be out in the countryside and get the feel of old England.

Pilgrims began flocking to Canterbury 800 years ago, following the martyrdom of Thomas à Becket. The footpath they took through the centuries still exists, protected by common law rights-of-way. Here and there, it has been paved over or covered with new construction, but much of it is still as it must have been in the 12th century.

Like most good footpaths, it seems to prefer the easy way, clinging to the sunny southern sides of the ridges, avoiding steep climbs, crossing the rivers where a shallow ford is available.

Good Family Vacation

We found a walking trip along the "Pilgrims' Way" to be a particularly pleasant sort of vacation to take with children. There is an objective every day, there is plenty of activity and the history is absorbed in easy, comfortable doses, well interspersed with picnics and wading in brooks. Somehow, the youngsters don't seem to squabble as they do when packed in the back seat of a car and motoring from one landmark to the next.

In our rucksacks were only a change of underwear and socks, drip-dry shirts and blouses and toilet articles. My husband and the boys wore tweed jackets, sweaters and flannel trousers, and Susie and I wore plaid two-piece walking suits—sturdy but respectable looking. Each of us carried his or her own necessities to minimize packing time and complaints on uphill climbs.

We spent the night at inns along the way, so no camping or cooking gear was required. The only extras were a canteen, a camera, a bird guide, a traveling chess set, maps and a compass.

Our journey began traditionally at St. Dunstan's Hospice near Winchester, where the good monks still serve the "Wayfarers' Dole"—free bread and ale —to all would-be pilgrims. After re-

In the Footsteps
Of Chaucer's Pilgrims

Joan Morrison

tree that must have started growing in Chaucer's day. While the boys played chess and Susie dabbled her feet in the clear water, my husband and I studied the maps. A fox peered out at us from a thicket, then vanished in a red blur.

That first night was spent at a tiny inn near the river, a place apparently unknown to foreigners. The innkeeper's buxom, blond wife served us a delicious steak and kidney pie, then bustled off toward the kitchen.

"I'll make the coffee extra strong," she told us, "because that's the way I've heard Americans like it." The coffee was good, but very strong. Perhaps she was thinking of South Americans.

After we left the Itchen, the Pilgrims' Way was paved over for a distance, so we hopped on one of the delightful red double-decked buses that crisscross England's rural areas. We were surrounded by shoppers laden with market baskets and by uniformed schoolchildren, all politely curious about our journey.

"Fancy following the old pilgrims," said one boy.

"It sounds like fun. I wish I could go with you," commented another, wistfully eyeing our rucksacks. English children go to school until the end of July, and we must have looked like a symbol of freedom to him.

At Guildford, we left the bus and set off once more on foot. At nearby Shalford, the way led through the shadowy "Chantries Wood," a dense copse of beech and yew that supposedly is named for the chanting of the monks who once walked there. It was still and cold in the wood, and I must confess that I felt a small shiver of relief when we stepped once more onto the sunny downs.

Picnicked in Meadows

For the next few days, we followed the Pilgrims' Way as it meandered eastward across the quiet countryside. At noon, we picnicked in buttercup-spangled meadows and watched skylarks as they rose singing into the air. Every so often, we would pass a half-timbered cottage with a thatched roof and the inevitable rose garden.

Sheep grazed about us as we walked, and once we were lucky enough to come upon a farmer shearing his small flock. Our children watched in fascination as two competent sheep dogs separated the unshorn ewes from their anxious lambs and escorted them to and from the pen. Farmer, dogs and the surrounding meadow were white with wool before the process was over.

Where the subsoil was soft chalk, our path was depressed two or three feet

ceiving our rations (the children passed up the ale), we toured the lovely cloisters and watched the monks working in the nearby fields. Then we set off as the first pilgrims did, on a footpath along the willow-lined banks of the

Itchen River.

Pause by the River

We crossed the river at a grassy shallows known as "Pilgrims' Ford" and rested awhile beneath a giant beech

below the level of the surrounding farmland. How many feet must have trod this way before us to leave such a trace! As we followed the Way's erratic curves, I often found myself thinking of Chesterton's vivid line: "The rolling English drunkard made the rolling English road."

Night Stops at Inns

We spent each night at an inn in one of the hamlets where the original pilgrims stayed. We found it wasn't really necessary to make advance reservations at such small, unfrequented places. In the morning, we would telephone ahead to the village we planned to reach that night. If the first place we called couldn't accommodate us, the second one always could.

These country inns provide good simple food, much of it homegrown. We happened to be making our trip during the brussels sprout season and were served them so often that Susie once mistakenly identified a gooseberry tart as "brussels sprout pie." Venison, domestic rabbit and fresh-caught trout also frequently appeared on the menu.

Rates at these inns run from $4 to $6 a day for bed and breakfast. Dinners average another $2.50.

For lunch, we bought our bread, cheese and fruit from the village shops. These small emporia provide a pleasant experience for the American visitor. Cheese is sliced with a wire, bacon is cut by hand and everyone is extremely unhurried and polite. A sign on the door of a greengrocer in Shere especially delighted us: "Dogs are kindly requested not to enter nor to approach the produce."

We supplemented our lunches sometimes with the small, sweet wild strawberries that grow on every English hedge in early summer, and in the late afternoon we occasionally stopped at a roadside stand for cool drinks or ices.

There are a number of interesting side trips to make while following the Pilgrims' Way. We especially enjoyed exploring the spectacular Roman ruin near Wrotham. This fine villa, with its mosaics and wall paintings, has recently been identified as one of the earliest sites of Christian worship in Britain.

We were received with friendliness everywhere we went. The small villages along the Pilgrims' Way are so far off the usual tourist track that the inhabitants seem pleased to be visited by the outside world. The baker from whom we bought our supplies in Charing pressed a loaf warm from the oven against Jimmy's cheek so that he could feel "how fresh our bread is."

Shelter From Rain

During a sudden shower one afternoon, we took shelter on the porch of a tiny 11th-century church near the village of Harrietsham. We were joined by an elderly Englishwoman, tweed-clad and flower-hatted, who might have stepped from the pages of an Agatha Christie book. My husband remarked that the church seemed inconveniently far out of town, and she agreed.

"So it is," she said. "So it is. But that isn't the way it was planned. Three times the builders set the foundation stones down in the center of the village, and three times the stones were moved at night to this spot. The fairies didn't want the church in town, they wanted it here, and here is where the builders finally put it."

Our children looked around a bit uneasily at the stones that had been moved three times by the fairies. There was nothing like that back in New Jersey.

When we lost our way near Chilham, an aristocratic woman took us into her drawing room to give us directions. We exclaimed over the beauty of her house, and she told us apologetically the place, although mentioned in the Domesday Book, "wasn't really old because it was rebuilt in 1539."

Modern-day pilgrims can reduce their walk to any desired length by hopping a bus at one of the many places where the Way crosses a highway. We did so several times, thus making the 140-mile trip in six days, rather than the two weeks it probably would require on foot. Others may wish to begin their walking trip in Charing, about 28 miles from Canterbury, or Chilham, about half that distance. This last (and loveliest) part of the trip can be made on foot in only two or three days.

Trip Nears End

We spent the last night of our journey at the tiny Inn of the Flying Horse near Boughton Lees, only seven miles from Canterbury and a good starting point for a one-day walk.

The next morning, we climbed to the top of Soakham Down and caught our first sight of Canterbury's white tower shining in the distance. From the very spot where we stood, the early pilgrims were supposed to have glimpsed their journey's end. Following in their footsteps, we walked down the hill, jumped over a brook, passed under the ancient town gate and entered the cathedral at dusk.

The incomparable stained glass windows glowed like jewels, and the boys' choir was singing Evensong. May all good pilgrimages end as well!

May 3, 1970

234

A New Walk in Old Wales

Last month saw the official opening of a 167-mile footpath that has been established around the coast of the county of Pembrokeshire in southwest Wales. Much of the trail runs through Pembrokeshire Coast National Park. The author spent three days hiking on one section of the path.

By NIGEL BUXTON

ST. DAVID'S, Wales—It is uphill where I started. Up the steep lane out of Goodwick, by Fishguard. Up the path where rain drips from the hedges and the breath comes short and blackthorn is in bloom. Up on the headland where the meadows are near emerald green and black and white cows graze in sodden fields and a farmer's wife whose complexion is all peaches and cream confirms the direction.

"Just you keep right on then," she singsongs in her vaudeville Welsh voice. "You mind the boggy bits now, or your feet'll be soaked before you've gone far."

For those who have created the path, it has been uphill all the way. The route was approved by the Ministry of Housing and Local Government in 1953, then bounced back and forth from committee to committee. In 1959, there remained 31 miles where even public right of access had not yet been obtained.

Premature Hopes

A year later, it was hoped that the path would be completed "before very long." Today, 10 more years of bureaucracy on, we have it at last: the triumph of dedicated individuals fighting for a dream; the beauty that man might mar but never could have made.

There is a wind up here on the path. It whips and slaps the skirts of the long cape against the legs. It catapults the gulls up over the edge of the gray, slate cliff, and they soar and wheel and dive and cry their wild cries over the gorse and the stone walls and the young wheat.

There is salt on the lips of the wind, and the walker tastes it and laughs and does not mind the flurries of rain. There is a smell of the sea and recently turned earth.

The path is truly a coastal path. Rarely on its route from St. Dogmaels, in the north of the county, to Amroth, near Tenby in the south, does it stray far from the edge of this westernmost county of Wales. There, by force of circumstances (the nature of the terrain, long-established rights of way, occasional refusal to grant new ones), it faithfully, at times, almost perilously follows the contour of the meeting between the land and the Atlantic.

In places, an unguarded or overdaring pace or two would lead to the long drop to the rocks, to the depths of dark fissures in the gray-black, igneous cliff, to far-down, narrow pebble beaches secret except from the ocean and the sea birds and a few men whose business it is to know of them. Seldom is the walker out of earshot of the waves.

It is not a metaled path, except where it traverses outcropping rock. It is not of stone or macadam or concrete laid by road engineers. But manmade it is, by the custom of many feet over the centuries or by the more recent baby bulldozer, often in defiance of gradients that sternly test the lungs and muscles of the heavy-laden traveler.

Healing the Wounds

So new are parts of it that there are brown, disfiguring wounds across headland and hillside. But already the snakeheads of the new bracken are pushing through, and bluebells are appearing where the blade of the bulldozer necessarily stripped away the brambles and heather and low gorse.

In a year or so, there will be little to distinguish the work of the Roads and Bridges Committee of the County Council from that of sheep and foxes or the ancient Welsh.

Other than native feet have been here. From Scandinavia, the Vikings came and left their memorials in placenames ending with "holm" and "wick." For *holmen* meant island and *vik* meant a haven. Hence Skokholm Island, on the far side of St. Brides Bay; hence Goodwick.

From France, the Normans came and left their mark in the architecture of village churches. And from France again in 1797, during the Napoleonic Wars, came two frigates and more than 1,000 men for an ill-advised, ill-conducted invasion around Carregwasted Point. The going must have been hard for those soldiers who clawed and stumbled up the gullies and cliff tracks.

Not a Tough Task

For today's walker along the coast, the going is not especially demanding, provided there is soundness of wind and limb. Mostly, the path is adequately signed or obvious. Sturdy oak stiles bear further witness to the labors —though inadequately financed—of those who made it. Rude bridges cross most of the streams or swampy ravines.

So, spared serious preoccupations with map and compass—unless a heavy coastal mist envelops the cliffs, unless the foghorn sounds its dismal caution to shipping—one is free to stroll or trudge steadily on, watching the sea birds, the ravens and buzzards and all the ever-moving, ever-busy life of this near-sanctuary.

Wide are the views, good is the air, and now—now that early summer presses hard upon the heels of a late spring—glorious are the sight and smell of the primroses and acres upon acres of full-flowering, full-scented gorse.

And so, sun or no sun, to walk here now for the first time is to make a memory for as long as one lives and, for all I know and hope, thereafter. A memory of gray and yellow and pink and white and blue. A possession of lichen-covered rock and gorse and thrift and daisies and bluebells. A joy of freedom and solitude, of time to loll against a great boulder, out of the breeze, eating cheese and biscuits, reading, gazing, undisturbed by anyone by day or night.

Thus go three days and two nights. All I need I have in my pockets or on my back or get at a spring.

On the first evening out from Fishguard, after seven or eight miles as the coastal path goes, the rain comes on again. I am cold and tired, and the red triangle on my one-inch Ordnance Survey map suggests easy refuge of a kind in a youth hostel. But is it open, and do they welcome nonmembers and bona fide travelers of any age?

It *is* open, and empty of visitors as yet, so neither age nor nonmembership bars the door. Near a fire, wet boots and stockings slowly dry, and the traveler sits and basks and looks out at the dark sea far below.

Later, he cooks his dinner in the well-appointed kitchen, then unrolls

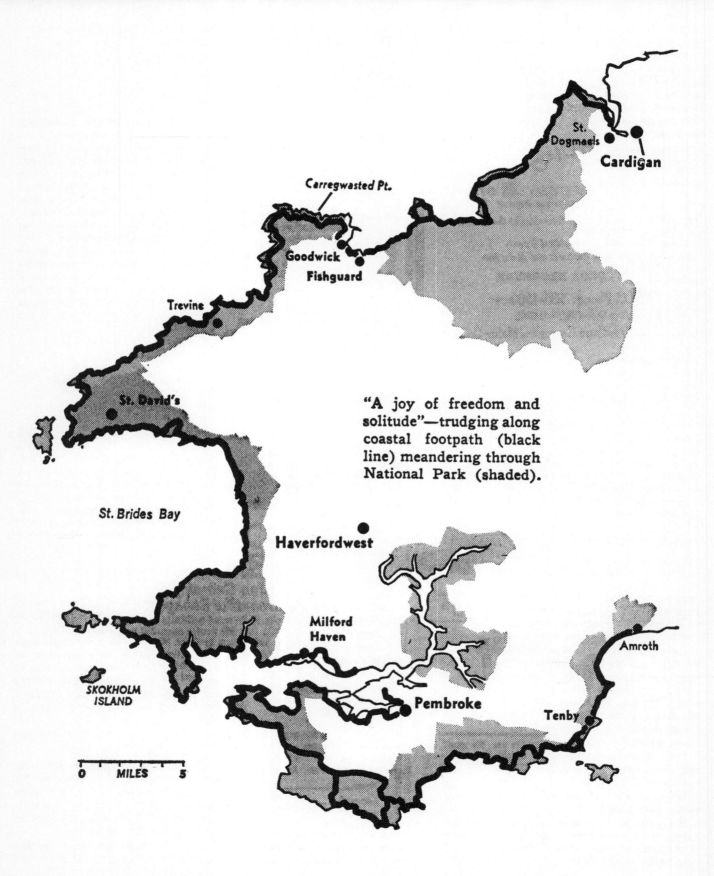

St. Dogmaels

Cardigan

Carregwasted Pt.

Goodwick

Fishguard

Trevine

St. David's

"A joy of freedom and solitude"—trudging along coastal footpath (black line) meandering through National Park (shaded).

St. Brides Bay

Haverfordwest

Milford Haven

Amroth

SKOKHOLM ISLAND

Pembroke

Tenby

0   MILES   5

his sleeping bag in a dormitory shared with two Canadians and falls asleep to the sound of rain against the window panes. There are milk and eggs from the neighboring farm for breakfast, and 6 shillings (72 cents) to pay for lodging. Then it is back to the path with energy renewed and the sun trying to shine.

A Night Outdoors

On the second night, there is no temptation to soft-lying, for the youth hostel at Trevine is passed and 6 P.M. finds me on the headland above Porthegr, nearly three miles on. Cautious as a frontier scout, I seek a hollow out of the wind—level-bottomed, soft but not sodden, as near as I dare to the cliff so that I may sleep within sound of the sea.

Then off comes the 30-pound pack, up goes the four-pound nylon tent that I bought in California, out come sleeping bag and cooking stove and two miniature bottles of whisky by courtesy of British European Airways. When the feast is finished and the camp

candles have expired, I lie for what seems a long time and certainly is long after dusk, listening to the breakers and the birds.

And remembering. Scotland, Brittany, the Canadian Rockies, the Sussex Downs. Remembering other nights like this and other days of walking in country that seemed at the time to have no equal, let alone any peer. And now this Welsh coast—as beautiful as any other, more beautiful than most, safe for all time unless all trusts are repudiated and all society becomes mad.

Scent in the Sun

Next day, the sun shines full for a while and is never darkly clouded. It is warm up here and the scent of the gorse is supreme. But now, when the stride is easy and no hill is formidable and nothing seems more desirable than to walk on to the end of the path, comes the time to leave it. So beyond Penberry, the walker turns inland and goes by farm track and lane and road to the town of St. David's, as many a pilgrim has done before.

Friend, this Cathedral open stands
*   for thee*
That you mayest enter, rest, think,
*   kneel*
And pray.
Remember whence thou art and
*   what must be*
Thine end. Remember us. Then go
*   thy way.*

So runs the exhortation on the first page of the shilling (12 cents) handbook of St. David's Cathedral, which was founded by the Welsh saint in the fifth or sixth century. And so I came through the old gate and down where the new-cut grass was as much of summer as the gorse had been.

On the porch, I left the pack before entering the cool shade of the noble building. In a pew, I rested and thought of many things, and said a kind of prayer for Britain and Wales and the goodness of the earth — and for the survival of the sort of men and women who willed and worked for the path.

Adapted by courtesy of The Sunday Telegraph, London.
June 21, 1970

A CAMBRIDGE WALKING TOUR

England's 'Junior' University, Its Stately Colleges, Its 'Backs' and Gardens Offer an Absorbing Stroll

By GEORGE W. OAKES

CAMBRIDGE, England — Oxonians are inclined to refer disparagingly to Cambridge University as "the other place," thus inferring that in their opinion Cambridge is somewhat inferior.

However, the "junior university's" locale is by no means so, in a city that is almost rural in contrast to Oxford's situation in its big, industrialized community. Cambridge is, if anything, superior from a scenic point of view and thus lends itself particularly well to strolling amid lovely surroundings. The famous "Backs," those sweeping, carpet-like lawns between the backs of various colleges and the languid little River Cam, as well as Cambridge's luxuriously colorful college gardens, provide

a parklike spaciousness hardly to be matched at Oxford.

The several colleges whose rear lawns border on the stream seem to merge into one another. One is not conscious of the walls that separate them. Standing on one of the many picturesque bridges, one senses the calm, restful, unhurried and contemplative atmosphere of the place. The beauties of elegant and ancient buildings and carefully tended grounds mark the ideal university community.

The Big Picture

The stroller in Cambridge should first absorb its unique mood as a whole before exploring the byways of the varied college quadrangles. To do so, on arrival he should enter the

main gate of King's College and walk to the left down the path that leads to King's Bridge over the Cam. Pausing on the bridge and facing the town, he should look to the left, over the close-cropped greensward to where the pointed Gothic pinnacles of King's Chapel loom.

Close at hand, leftward along the Cam, the seventeenth-century stone arches and balustrade of Clare Bridge, without doubt one of the most graceful anywhere, leads to the Fellows' Gardens. Behind the bridge, on both banks, rise stately and luxuriant trees with a green richness that only the moist English climate can create.

In the opposite direction, the half-timbered and deep red brick of Queens' College strikes

a remarkable color contrast against the sloping, turfed banks of the river.

On the river, beneath overhanging trees, the famous punts, filled with undergraduates, and often undergraduettes, are being propelled by long punting poles from the rear decks. The punts are like thin, very elegantly cushioned and appointed shallow scows.

After a few minutes in which to sense the spirit of Cambridge, one wanders back into the main court of King's and approaches Henry VI's glorious chapel.

Inside, the visitor is at once struck by the lofty lace-like fan vaulting of "the loveliest chapel in England" completed by Henry VIII in 1515. The Tudor heraldic carving is a

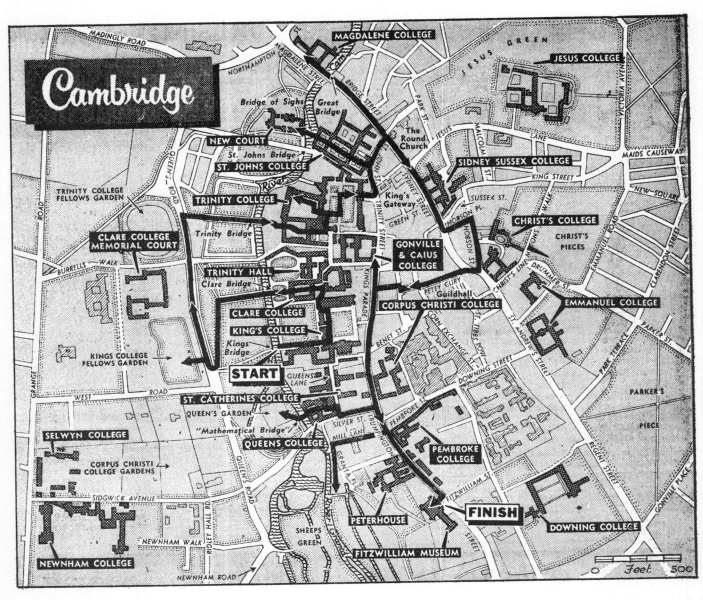

highly decorative characteristic. The stained glass in the great sixteenth-century windows was made by Flemings in England and by Englishmen working under Flemish inspiration and from Flemish designs. The rood screen, one of Europe's finest pieces of woodwork, carries the arms of Anne Boleyn.

Famous Choir

The visitor should inquire when the next service will be held, and return, if possible, to hear the renowned voices of King's College Choir in this unmatched setting.

Leaving King's by the gate on the north side of the chapel,

the stroller turns left into Clare College and proceeds through the old court to Clare Bridge. He will admire the eighteenth-century wrought-iron gates before reaching the river. Crossing the stream—but stopping for a moment at least to enjoy a still different view of the "Backs"— the saunterer might see whether by chance, Clare's Fellows' Garden is open before leaving the park by the back gate on Queen's Road. If it is, no garden is lovelier for a stroll.

A few hundred yards down on the left are two more extensive and delightful gardens, King's Fellows Garden and Trinity Fellows Garden. They

are usually open. The variety of the flowers, shrubs and trees in these well-planned and beautifully cared-for gardens is quite unusual. One should wander around them at leisure or find a secluded spot and sit for a while.

Crossing Queen's Road, the stroller heads toward Trinity Bridge, from which he gets an excellent view of St. Johns College. Directly ahead, in the grounds of Trinity College, is the Avenue, one of the finest walks in Cambridge. It leads to New Court. On the left lies the magnificent classic façade of Sir Christopher Wren's library, built with cream and

pink stone over a covered piazza.

The visitor should proceed into the cloisters of Nevile's Court and enter the library at the far end. It is usually open from 1 to 4 P. M. Wren's interior design of the beautifully proportioned room "touches the very soul of any one who first sees it." So wrote Roger North in 1695.

The walls and shelves exhibit the best examples of Grinling Gibbons' wood carving. The library also contains the private collection of Sir Isaac Newton, one of Trinity's most distinguished sons. Perhaps the manuscript of Milton's shorter po-

ems in his own handwriting will be on display among the library's many treasures.

The Dining Hall of the college, one of the most magnificent Elizabethan halls in England with its carved oaken beams, is just off a passage above Nevile's Court and is generally open between 1:30 and 3 P. M.

Opposite the entrance to the Hall, a colorful portrait of Henry VIII hangs on the fine paneling immediately above the high table. Among other interesting pictures is a contemporary portrait of Francis Bacon, done on wood. Overhead is the Minstrels' Gallery.

Emerging from the Hall, one now should stand at the top of the stone steps to admire the Great Court, the largest of any college in Oxford or Cambridge. All the buildings are in the Tudor-Gothic style except for one section.

Newton's Study

On the left is Trinity's medieval clock tower decorated with armorial crests, and in front stands Nevile's lovely stone fountain. Near the chapel at the far end are the rooms in which Sir Isaac Newton worked out the proofs of his great scientific discoveries.

In Merton Corner of the court is the turret where Lord Byron kept a tame bear while a student at Trinity. After wandering around the court, the visitor will find that to stand by the sundial near the fountain allows the best view of the noble Great Tower before leaving the college through the Tudor archway.

Just a few yards to the left along Trinity Street stands the imposing stone and brick gateway to St. Johns College, bearing elaborately painted and gilded arms of Lady Margaret Beaufort, the foundress. The visitor should inquire whether he may be permitted to see the Combination Room in the Elizabethan brick second court. This paneled gallery, one of the most stately in England, is nearly a hundred feet long with a decorated plaster ceiling worked in 1600.

Beyond the third court, the "Bridge of Sighs" over the Cam (somewhat like the famous one in Venice) leads to the delightful cloister in the New Court. From here one may wander into the college grounds and back across the old bridge through the courtyards to the main gate.

A few minutes walk along Bridge Street brings the stroller to Magdalene College to see the fascinating library of Pepys exhibited in the original bookcases he had built for it. The manuscript volumes of his diary are also in his collection there.

Earliest Round Church

Returning along Bridge Street a visitor should look in at the Round Church, built during the twelfth century and the oldest of the four round churches in England. After glancing around the ivy-covered walls of Sidney Sussex College, he should turn down Hobson Place to the delightful gardens of Christ's College, regarded by many as the most lovely in Cambridge, usually open in the afternoon.

Along the old buildings of Petty Cury one comes to Market Hill, a shopping center since medieval days. Open stalls display colorful flowers, fruit and vegetables. A few steps further is King's Parade opposite the Senate House of classic design, where the chief university functions take place. Just to the right rises the lovely old Gate of Honor of Gonville and Caius College (pronounced "Keys").

Turning left past King's the tourist shortly reaches Corpus Christi College to visit one of Cambridge's treasures, the old court, built in 1377 and considered the earliest example of a complete medieval academic quadrangle still standing.

Across the road, down Silver Street, the stroller will come to Queens' College, whose fifteenth-century mellow dark red brick construction lends a distinct and picturesque quality to its several small courtyards. Queens' has the most complete set of medieval college buildings in Cambridge. The embattled towers of the gateway appear particularly impressive.

The visitor should go into the cloister court to look at the old half-timbered President's Lodging with its bay windows supported by wooden columns, surely one of the most charming places in Cambridge. The large sundial in a near-by court below a sloping red roof adds an attractive touch.

Erasmus' Court

Returning through these delightful courts, in one of which lived Erasmus, one will cross the famous "Mathematical Bridge." It is so called because of the careful calculation of strains upon it, figured out by scholars long ago. It leads to the college gardens.

Returning to Trumpington Street, the saunterer can stop in at the oldest college of all, Peterhouse, founded by Edward I. The Hall and Buttery are the original late thirteenth-century buildings. Prof. Denis W. Brogan, well known to American readers for his many books and encyclopedic knowledge of both the United States and France, is a distinguished Fellow of Peterhouse.

Just beyond Peterhouse the visitor will find the Fitzwilliam Museum, an extensive and outstanding collection of all forms of art. The paintings, including examples of English as well as most Continental schools, are well shown in light and spacious galleries.

As a suitable end of the day's tour, the walker will enjoy having tea or dinner at a delightful hotel whose gardens go down to the river. There he might decide, if he can, which spot in Cambridge is the most fascinating of all.

July 2, 1961

WALKING TOUR OF EDINBURGH

Capital of Scotland Is Scenic and Full of Historic Interest —Old Town, High on a Ridge, Delightful for Stroller

By GEORGE OAKES

EDINBURGH — This, the capital of Scotland, is a delightful city for the stroller, for it not only is scenically beautiful, but also full of historical interest. The old town, perched high on a long, rocky ridge, sits in a dramatic position overlooking the newer section of the city, which spreads northward toward the Firth of Forth.

The dividing line between the old and the new (late 18th and early 19th century) sections of Edinburgh is Princes Street, whose reputation as one of the most striking avenues in Europe owes a great deal to its location. Seen across the gardens from Princes Street, the old town's battlements and spires contribute to a view both memorable and unique.

It is the old town that will concern us during this walk in Edinburgh. We begin at the West End terminus of spacious Princes Street, in full view of the old section. Immediately to the right are the gardens. High on the cliff overhead stands Edinburgh Castle, the first objective of this walking tour.

Landscaped Gardens

One can enter the beautifully landscaped Princes Street gardens at a point just opposite Charlotte Street. As one strolls along, the lawns and flower beds provide an attractive foreground for the turreted castle, stone houses and church steeples of the old town above.

Take a few minutes to wander through these charming gardens, which were built on the site of a former lake. Midway down the main garden walk, below and parallel to Princes Street, is the impressive Scottish-American War Memorial. It is a soldier in kilts, and it was erected by Americans of Scottish blood in memory of Scotsmen who were killed in World War I.

Nearby is the city's colorful floral clock, the oldest of its kind in the world. Each quarter-hour, a cuckoo appears to sound the time. During the festival season, generally in late August and early September, band concerts are held in the garden amphitheater. At night, the floral displays are beautifully floodlit.

At the top of the steps leading out of the western part of the gardens, one should pause for a moment and look at the impressive skyline of the old town. On leaving the gardens, turn right and start up the Mound, the street that winds up Castle Hill into old Edinburgh.

Classic Buildings

On the left stand two large buildings in the classic style. The first is the Royal Scottish Academy; the second is the National Gallery of Scotland. The Academy holds special showings of contemporary works of art from April to mid-September; it is open weekdays from 10 A.M. to 9 P.M. and Sundays from 2 to 5 P.M.

The National Gallery houses a fine selection of Italian and Dutch masters, as well as the most complete collection anywhere of Scottish artists, including that of Sir Henry Raeburn. It is open weekdays from 10 A.M. to 5 P.M. and Sundays from 2 to 5 P.M.

Continue to bear right along the Mound and then up the hill into Mound Place. Turn left into Ramsay Lane, and then bear right again and enter the large Esplanade, the parade ground of Edinburgh Castle.

Admission Is Free

Admission to the castle precincts is free. From June to September, the castle is open from 9:30 A.M. to 6 P.M. on weekdays and from 11 A.M. to 6 P.M. on Sundays. Admission to the state apartments is limited at other times of the year, and an advance inquiry may help to avoid disappointment.

A ticket to the apartments costs about 20 cents for adults and 7 cents for children. Included in the ticket price are Argyll Tower, St. Margaret's Chapel, the Crown Room, Queen Mary's Room, Banquetry Hall and the United Services Museum.

The castle site is so steep on three of its sides that it was an almost impregnable fortress. Statues of two Scottish heroes, Robert Bruce and William Wallace, flank the gateway and serve to remind the visitor that he treads on historic ground. Kilted soldiers stand guard outside the entrance.

Soon one reaches a terrace, where a battery of old cannon are still in their original emplacements and where one is rewarded by a magnificent panorama of the city, the wide Firth of Forth and the hills of Fife on the horizon.

Tiny Chapel

At the summit, a little farther along, stands the tiny, nonsectarian Scottish - Norman chapel of St. Margaret's, the most ancient building in Edinburgh. Founded in the 11th century, it was restored about 100 years ago. Some of the original gray stone is still visible in the walls. The flowers in the chapel are changed every week by a group of Edinburgh women, all named Margaret, under the patronage of Princess Margaret.

In front of the chapel, on the ramparts, is Mons Meg, a huge 15th-century cannon. One of Europe's oldest artillery pieces, it was designed to fire a 400-pound stone ball a distance of more than a mile.

The Scottish National War Memorial is situated inside the castle yard. In the Hall of Honor is the deeply moving Central Shrine, with banners, campaign flags and regimental panels in memory of the Scots who fell in two world wars. A display of Scottish military uniforms and an exhibit devoted to the Scottish-born John Paul Jones, "the father of the American Navy," are on view in the nearby United Services Museum.

On the south side of the quadrangle is the great Banquetry Hall, which is decorated with crests of past governors of the castle. The hall, with its fine hammerbeam roof, was where the early Scottish parliaments met; it now houses a collection of armor and weapons.

In the Royal Apartments, also off the courtyard, one can visit the tiny bedroom where Mary Queen of Scots gave birth to her son, later to become James VI of Scotland and James I of England.

A fascinating display of Scottish regalia — including the crown, scepter and sword of state, last carried in state on Queen Elizabeth's coronation visit in 1953 — is on view in the Crown Room.

After wandering around the castle long enough to absorb some of its memorable history, return by the Argyll Tower portcullis to the Esplanade. One now stands at the head of the renowned Royal Mile, so named because it descends from the Royal Palace on Castle Hill down through the old town to the Royal Palace of Holyroodhouse. It is one of the most renowned walks in Europe. An extensive and gradual program of restoring the old buildings along the Royal Mile, many of which have become dilapidated, now is under way.

Ancient Projectile

On leaving the Esplanade, the visitor may notice a cannon ball embedded in the wall of the first house (1630) on the right, just above the central window. This projectile is said to date from the Rebellion of 1745.

A few yards farther along on the left stands Outlook Tower, an old building that is particularly fascinating for children. At the top of the tower is a "camera obscura" — or viewing device—which yields, on a clear day, panoramic views of the new town and surround-

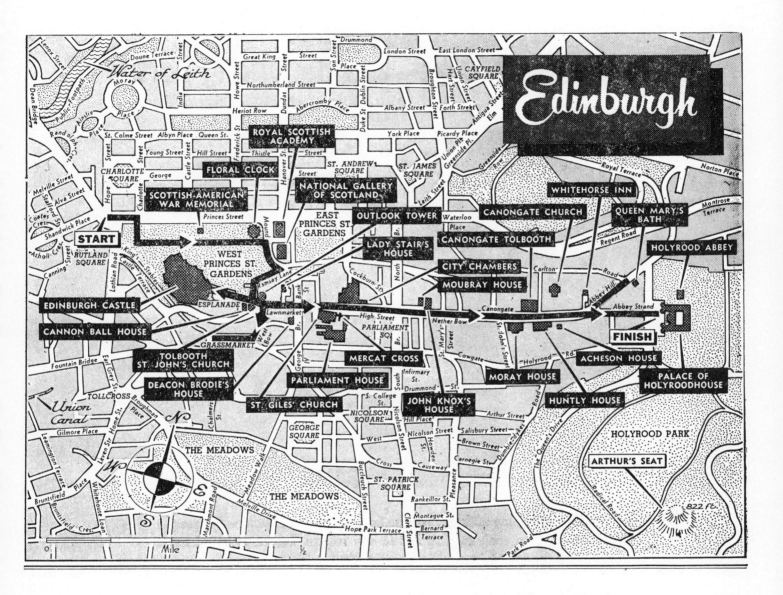

ing countryside. The tower is open during the summer months from 10 A.M. to 6 P.M. on weekdays and from 12:30 to 6 P.M. on Sundays. Admission is about 20 cents for adults and 7 cents for children.

The stroller now enters the wide street known as Lawnmarket, so named because the booths of lawn (or cloth) merchants once were situated there. On either side of Lawnmarket are narrow alley-ways known as

"closes," where many distinguished figures have lived.

In Milne's Court, on the left, the stroller might take note of a balustrade with curved bars; it was built for the convenience of 18th-century women and their wide crinoline skirts.

Dwelling Restored

The old houses in the closes deteriorated into slums during the 19th century, when the new town became fashionable. In recent years, many of these multi-

storied dwellings have been restored to something resembling their former glory.

After a look at Milne's Court, cross the Lawnmarket and turn right, down the steps in front of Tolbooth St. John's Church, to ancient West Bow. Down this steep street, lined with tall houses, have passed royal processions, plus condemned prisoners on their way to the execution block.

At the foot of West Bow, beyond the old shops, one comes upon a large square called the Grassmarket where, for several hundred years, cattle and grain were sold. Returning by West Bow to the Lawnmarket, our stroll along the Royal Mile continues.

In James's Court, on the left, lived the 18th-century Scottish historian and philosopher, David Hume. In 1773, Dr. Johnson stayed in James's Court with his host and biographer, James Boswell. In Lady Stair's Close, also on the left side of Lawnmarket, lived the poet, Robert Burns, in 1786. There, too, is Lady Stair's House, a restored 17th-century dwelling that is now a museum.

Tablet Worth Noting

Note the tablet under the archway from the Lawnmarket. It records that "in a Tavern of 1717 Sir Richard Steele gave supper to a company of eccentric beggars."

Several houses in and around the closes of the Royal Mile have special stones, called "marriage lintels," over their doorways. These stones bear the date and initials of the original owner, and are something to watch for during one's stroll.

Opposite Lady Stair's House is the close where, during the 18th century, a certain Deacon Brodie lived. A town councilor by day and a footpad by night, he is believed to have been the inspiration for Robert Louis Stevenson's "Dr. Jekyll and Mr. Hyde."

Now the Lawnmarket opens into High Street. On the right are Parliament Square and St. Giles' Cathedral, whose tower is in the shape of the crown of Scotland. If the stroller looks carefully in the square outside the west end of the church, he will see a heart-shaped mark in the cobblestones. This mark is the site of the old Tolbooth, or prison, popularized in the opening scene of Sir

Walter Scott's novel, "The Heart of Midlothian."

Founded in the 11th century, St. Giles' Cathedral is known primarily as the Mother Church of Presbyterianism. John Knox, the reformer, who clashed bitterly with Mary Queen of Scots, was its first minister. He is buried in the courtyard near the cathedral, and the site is marked by a cobblestone inscribed "JK 1572."

St. Giles' small Chapel of the Thistle—Scotland's highest order of chivalry—is marked by its exquisitely carved stalls bearing the coats of arms of the knights. It is an elegant, though relatively recent, addition to the church, and its fine nave is hung with old battle flags and regimental standards. Admission to the Thistle Chapel is about 7 cents.

At the east end of Parliament Square stands the Mercat Cross, in days gone by the center of the city's life, as well as the scene of burnings and beheadings. Today, the cross is the forum for official proclamations. The administrative offices of the City Chambers are on the opposite side of High Street.

Parliament House

Also in the square is Parliament House, where the Scottish Parliament met from 1639 until Scotland's union with England in 1707. It is open weekdays from 10 A. M. to 5 P. M. and Saturdays 10 A. M. to 1 P. M. The square also is the site of the Signet Library, which is open weekdays from 10 A. M. to 4 P. M. and Saturdays from 10 A. M. to 1 P. M.

Proceeding down High Street past several other closes — including Anchor Close, where the first edition of the Encyclopaedia Britannica was printed in the 18th century — one crosses busy North Bridge and arrives at the picturesque house where John Knox died in 1572. The house is open weekdays from 10 A. M. to 5 P. M., and the admission fee is about 14 cents. Inside are exhibits relating to the fiery reformer.

Moubray House, next door, is considered to be the oldest private dwelling in the city. An interesting historical collection of toys can be seen for a token admission fee in the Museum of Childhood, just opposite in Hyndford's Close. The museum is open weekdays from 10 A.M.

to 5 P.M.

Smoky Fog

An occasional glance down some of the narrow alleys on the right will afford the stroller glimpses of industrial Edinburgh, often almost obscured by a smoky fog. In fact, Edinburgh won the name, "Auld Reekie," because of the pall of smoke that used to hang over the city in the morning.

After passing what was once Nether Bow, or the East Gate to the old city, one enters the street called Canongate. A lintel dated 1677 can be seen over the doorway at No. 185.

A few hundred yards farther on, the turrets and projecting clock of Canongate Tolbooth come into view on the left. A 16th-century courthouse and prison, this old chateau-like structure reflects the French influence on Scottish architecture. Today it is a city museum with an interesting Tartan collection. It is open weekdays from 10 A. M. to 5 P. M.

Adam Smith, whose inquiry into "The Wealth of Nations" profoundly influenced 18th-century economic theory, is buried in the adjacent Canongate churchyard.

In the 17th century, Oliver Cromwell used Moray House, on the opposite side of Canongate, as a temporary residence. A few doors away stands the restored Huntly House, which is open weekdays from 10 A. M. to 5 P. M. A timbered 16th-century dwelling, it now serves as a city museum. The local history of Edinburgh is shown in displays that occupy several oak-paneled rooms. The exhibits include a copy of the National Covenant and John Knox's Psalter.

A right turn just beyond Huntly House leads into Bakehouse Close, the best restored of the many closes in the Royal Mile. Of the buildings there, Acheson House (1633), home of the Scottish Craft Centre, is particularly attractive.

At this point of the stroll, Arthur's Seat, the rocky crag that looms above Edinburgh, can be seen in the distance. At the bottom of Canongate, in Whitehorse Close, is Whitehorse Inn, an artistic corner of old Edinburgh.

Queen's Residence

Just beyond, Canongate en-

ters Abbey Strand, at the end of which stands the Palace of Holyroodhouse, the Queen's official residence when visiting Edinburgh. Built about 1500 by James IV, it was for years the Scottish Royal Palace.

Before entering its historic grounds, take a turn down Abbeyhill to the left to see Queen Mary's Bath, an odd little building that dates from the late 16th century. It was originally a postern gate in the palace's wall. According to legend, Mary Queen of Scots is said to have bathed there — in wine.

Holyroodhouse is best known for the period 1561-67, when Mary Queen of Scots resided there, but the palace, as it stands today, dates mainly from the reign of Charles II. He had it rebuilt and enlarged in 1671. It is open weekdays from 9:30 A. M. to 6 P. M. and Sundays from 11 A. M. to 6 P. M. from June to September. Hours vary during the rest of the year, and it is wise to check in advance. Admission is 20 cents.

The long Picture Gallery and State Apartments are furnished with a wealth of paneling, paintings and tapestries. The smaller rooms have a lived-in quality, unlike many other palaces. Holyroodhouse is closed to the public whenever the Royal Family is in residence.

Secret Staircase

The most fascinating apartments in the palace are those connected with the tempestuous days of Mary Queen of Scots. In the main tower — the oldest part of the palace — are the secret staircase and the tiny apartment where the bloody murder of the Queen's secretary, David Rizzio, took place. A brass marker in the floor of the audience chamber marks the spot where, on March 9, 1566, Rizzio was found stabbed to death.

After touring the palace, one can visit the ruins of 12th-century Holyrood Abbey, on the left of the central courtyard, and stroll around the beautifully landscaped grounds where, each summer, the Queen holds a garden party. The flowers border carpet-like lawns, and towering trees lend a country atmosphere to the palace park, which seems to nestle so comfortably beneath the high green slopes of Arthur's Seat at the end of Edinburgh's Royal Mile.

June 2, 1963

A WALKING TOUR OF LONDON

Two Routes Are Suggested for Leisurely Inspection Of Its Ancient Grandeur and Contemporary Grace

By GEORGE W. OAKES

LONDON—The way to see London is on foot rather than by bus, taxi or private car. For one thing, it is not done by most American tourists, so it is a bit unusual. Then it will win applause from British friends who enjoy walking but are convinced that most Americans have lost the use of their legs.

An even more practical reason is that London traffic has become so jammed, especially during the tourist season, that one makes better time on foot than any other way. Finally, the walker sees a lot more, because walking is the only way to avoid missing all those little nooks and crannies of old London which a car rushes past before its occupants realize that they were there.

Let us take the case of an average visitor with a few days in London. After he has toured the main sights—St. Paul's, the Tower of London, Westminster Abbey, the Houses of Parliament and the National Gallery—why not have a stroll for an hour or two and visit those fascinating out-of-the-way spots that give London its historic, colorful and intimate character?

Precautionary Umbrella

The tourist might start out after lunch at Piccadilly Circus —London's Times Square—on a one-hour walk. Carrying raincoat or umbrella, just in case the blue skies disappear all of a sudden (as they do too often in London) and a bit of rain descends, he heads down Lower Regent Street towards the Duke of York's Column facing the Athenaeum, London's club for the intelligentsia. There he may spot a bishop, or a don on his way from his London headquarters back to Oxford or Cambridge.

In a moment, the stroller will be on his own way down the wide Duke of York's Steps, flanked by Nash's stately mansions on Carlton House Terrace. Thence, he crosses London's most majestic boulevard, The Mall, with imposing Buckingham Palace at one end and the Admiralty Arch leading to Trafalgar Square at the other.

Now, he suddenly finds himself for fifteen minutes in a country atmosphere in perhaps the most charming and pic-turesque of London's public recreation areas, St. James's Park.

Named in the thirteenth century for a female leper hospital, the Sisters of Saint James in the Fields, this oldest of London's parks was taken over by Henry VIII in 1532 but not opened to the public until the reign of the Stuarts. Patterning his idea after Versailles, the Stuart Charles II cleaned up the swamps and ponds and put in trees and new lawns. But St. James's Park, as one sees it now, dates from the period of George IV.

To the Pelicans

There is a small suspension bridge over the sizable lake in the park from which one gets an unusual vista both of Buck-

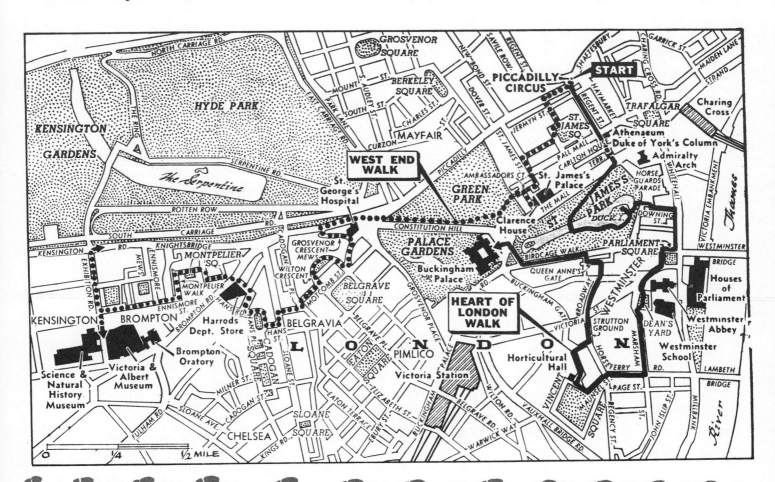

ingham Palace, at one end, and the Foreign Office at the other, rising above the tops of the weeping willows. One of the fascinating sights on turning left, past some of London's finest herbaceous flower beds, is Duck Island, a bird and wildlife sanctuary. About 4 o'clock in the afternoon is probably the best time to see the three species of pelicans parading near the old Birdkeeper's Lodge on the island for their daily fish ration. Twenty species of colorful wild ducks and geese also inhabit the island and are usually swimming in the lake.

After this excursion into country life, the strolling tourist should cross the road by the Horse Guards Parade and wander into Downing Street past the British Prime Minister's official residence at No. 10, and so into Whitehall. A right turn leads one in a moment into Parliament Square with its impressive statue of Abraham Lincoln.

Quiet Cloisters

Perhaps the visitor has already toured Westminster Abbey (consecrated under Edward the Confessor in 1065) and visited the magnificent Gothic Henry VII Chapel as well as the countless memorials to Britain's heroes of the ages—king and poet, Unknown Warrior and noted statesman. Then a turn around the Abbey's quiet cloisters and a look-in at the little known but fascinating waxworks in the Norman Undercroft is still a worthwhile extension of Abbey sight-seeing.

This extraordinary museum contains, for example, the effigy of Admiral Lord Nelson, commissioned in 1806, a year after his death, to provide a counter-attraction to St. Paul's Cathedral, where he was buried. The figure of Nelson, dressed mostly in his own clothing, was regarded by contemporaries as more lifelike than paintings for which he sat. One also can see the death mask of Edward III, victor of the Battle of Crécy, shown as he died in 1377 with his mouth and left cheek affected by the muscular contraction that ended his life.

The remarkable death mask of Henry VII is so perfect in detail of bone structure and facial characteristics that it might have been made yesterday. The plaster around the ears has retained small tufts of red and gray hair that may

actually have belonged to the dead king.

The Original Britannia

The full-size figure of Charles II in his splendid robes of the Order of the Garter stands in a glass case resplendent in all details. The effigy of Frances, Duchess of Richmond and Lennox, who died in 1702, represents one attractive woman who supposedly succeeded in evading the advances of Charles II and who sat for the original figure of Britannia on the coinage of Great Britain.

On leaving the Cloisters, the stroller should take a quick look at Dean's Yard, and, through Little Dean's Yard, at the grounds of Westminster School where, in term-time, students will be dashing in and out of the ancient buildings. From a small garden just off the center quadrangle there is the most striking view of the Victoria Tower of the House of Lords, rising beyond the garden's old walls. This tower, by the way, is higher than Big Ben.

To Horticultural Hall

Now, one makes one's way along Marsham Street, Horseferry Road and Maunsel Street, with its charming little houses, and so, skirting Vincent Square, where the Westminster schoolboys have their playing field, to Horticultural Hall. If lucky, the stroller will be on hand for one of the frequent flower shows of the British Horticultural Society.

To get back to Buckingham Palace, one wanders down Greycoat Street and the busy street called Strutton Ground, one of London's many tiny shopping thoroughfares, crosses Victoria Street and proceeds along London's Broadway to Queen Anne's Gate. There are found some of London's best preserved examples of eighteenth-century red-brick houses, each one an architectural gem or historic site. Finally, a left turn along Birdcage Walk brings the tourist in a couple of minutes to the Palace, perhaps at a time to see the Queen driving out.

There is another delightful walk of about forty-five minutes, which keeps a stroller out of the heavy traffic and which leads through some of London's most charming tiny squares and streets lined with Georgian houses. This walk, from Piccadilly Circus through Belgravia to Kensington, is a special fa-

vorite with West End Londoners.

Starting from Piccadilly Circus, the sight-seer goes along Jermyn Street with its many old shops, turning left into Duke of York Street and so to St. James's Square, and along King Street to St. James's Street, Lock's, the world-renowned hatter, with plumed helmets from the days of the Duke of Wellington on display in the window, occupies the oldest building in the area, except, of course, St. James's Palace. Almost next door there is a very narrow passageway, Pickering Place, cut between two houses and leading a scant hundred feet or so to one of London's picturesque courts. This was the city's last dueling ground, where Georgian gentlemen settled their disputes with the rapier.

The Ancient Palace

Crossing over to St. James's Palace, and going under the arch and past the sentries, brings one to the quiet of Ambassador's Court, only fifty feet from the noise of St. James's Street. As the tourist strolls around the courtyard and notes on the doors the brass nameplates of member of the royal household, such as the Lord Chamberlain, he can see the turrets of the fine Tudor clocktower against the sky. The clock was put out of commission by a Nazi block-buster that tore a vast hole in Pall Mall, close to the palace, late in World War II. It was quickly restored to service.

Walking toward the Mall through Stable Yard leads one past Clarence House, the home of Queen Elizabeth, the Queen Mother.

Now the sight-seer retraces his steps to Lancaster House and enters Green Park. There he should walk up Constitution Hill to Hyde Park Corner with its imposing Quadriga Arch. Crossing Hyde Park Corner by foot is almost like tackling the Etoile in Paris, but London bobbies are on hand there to stop the crush of cars and give pedestrians a chance.

Vine-Covered Cottages

About fifty yards along Knightsbridge past St. George's Hospital one comes to Old Barrack Yard down which one can go to explore the old houses and vine-covered cottages in Grosvenor Crescent Mews. Perhaps it will be an hour when the Grenadier, a celebrated pub, once the rendezvous of coach-

men but later of elegant West Enders, will be open.

Now the stroller makes his way along the stone façades of Wilton Crescent through Motcomb Street, across Sloane Street, to Hans Place and thus past Harrods, the department store, where there is a luxurious food shop frequented by Belgravia's gourmets. Crossing Brompton Road, it is fifty yards to Trevor Square, whence it is just a step to one of London's smallest, most picturesque and fashionable spots, tranquil Montpelier Square.

Bread, Cheese and Bitter

There is an old Georgian pub just off the Square where one can have lunch, or simply bread, cheese and a glass of bitter. Exploring the Square, one notices an old sign forbidding street musicians to annoy the residents.

Like most London squares, large or small, Montpelier Square is tastefully planted with flowers, shrubs and trees. It is a delightful place to sit quietly on a bench, read, or look around at the distinguished small Georgian houses with their large windows. Montpelier Walk, at the northeast end of the square, has unusual front gardens and flower boxes that the residents have most carefully cultivated.

Not many yards to the west through a passage in a brick wall there is a little cul-de-sac lined with pastel-colored houses. Going along Ennismore Street, the stroller passes through one of Kensington's small classic arches into Ennismore Garden Mews. There the blue and pink cottages, once stables and now town *pieds-à-terre,* face on the back gardens of Brompton Oratory, a distinguished Roman Catholic Church whose high dome is a dramatic sight against the late-afternoon glow. Often, along here, photographers are seen posing London's models for the fashion magazines.

Three or four minutes further on, one comes out on Exhibition Road, after passing Prince's Gardens. Now the sight-seer can either turn left and visit the Victoria and Albert Museum or cross the road and roam through London's Science and Natural History Museum. When satiated with knowledge there, he can walk up to the top of the street along Kensington Gardens and hop on a No. 9 bus that will bring him back to Piccadilly Circus.

April 9, 1961

A WALKING TOUR OF OXFORD

Antiquity and Elegance of Gardens, Halls and Cloisters Capture Imagination of the Leisurely Stroller

By GEORGE W. OAKES

OXFORD, England — The purpose of a stroll in Oxford is to sense the beauty and distinction of this ancient seat of learning, to immerse oneself in the antiquity and elegance of the dreaming spires, the cloisters, halls and gardens of its colleges.

The best place to start such a walk is at a bridge, the bridge over the River Cherwell beside Magdalen College—not to be confused with Cambridge's Magdalene College, with an e. This is where the London road enters Oxford, and from it one beholds tnat college's memorable, slightly tapering and extremely graceful Bell Tower, with its pinnacled turrets soaring above the college and the tree-lined banks of the river.

After glancing up and down the stream and passing beneath the late fifteenth-century tower, the stroller enters the college grounds through the main gate from High Street, known in Oxford as "The High."

Climbing the Tower

For the strong and adventurous, wishing to view Oxford from its loftiest perch, permission should be asked of the college porter at the entrance lodge to climb the 144-foot tower. From its battlements, the whole panorama of the university spreads out below. The vantage point affords a unique sight of the varying patterns of the colleges and their gardens.

On the left of the gatehouse is the picturesque seventeenth-century Grammar Hall, and on the right, the only open-air pulpit surviving in England. After looking around the chapel, the saunterer should follow the passageway beneath the Muniment Tower to the cloisters. Ascending a flight of steps at the right corner, he will find himself in the distinguished dining hall, noted for its lovely linenfold paneling, on which hang portraits of famous old members of the college.

Addison's Walk

As the stroller leaves the side of the cloisters opposite the dining hall, he will note a small stone bridge leading to Addison's Walk, named for the great essayist, a former member of the college. Beneath the bridge, trout are frequently feeding.

A stroll around the meadow —only a few hundred yards from the traffic-clogged High— will transport the visitor into a completely rural atmosphere. While walking along the paths beside the stream, he will often notice cattle grazing in the field.

After returning from this twenty-minute excursion, the visitor should wander past the New Buildings, which, despite their name, were constructed in the eighteenth century, to Magdalen's deer park. There, in a grove of tall and luxuriant trees, the sight of the college deer herd adds a special old-world touch to these academic surroundings.

Near by, the visitor will spy a garden on raised ground from which he can obtain an unusual view of Magdalen Tower, rising above the college buildings.

As the walker leaves Magdalen and proceeds up the High, recognized as one of the finest streets in Europe, the famous and graceful sweep of Queen's and All Souls Colleges comes into view, with the spire of St. Mary's Church in the distance. A bit farther on, one should stand at the corner of Queen's Lane and study the college buildings on both sides of the street.

Founded in 1340

The stroller ascends a few steps to enter The Queen's College, founded in 1340. Pausing under the dome at the gate, he will be struck by the stately proportions of Hawksmoor's (an associate of Wren) eighteenth-century front quadrangle cloistered on three sides.

Directly in front, beyond the velvet-like lawn, stands the classic chapel and hall, surmounted by a clock tower. The view of the cupola from the outside steps outlined by the entrance archway is particularly effective against the sky.

The magnificent façade of Queen's, one of the finest in Oxford, is the west front of the library, overlooking the Fellows' Garden and surmounted by a stone eagle, the insignia of the founder. The superb proportions of the library's interior, with its exquisitely carved dark woodwork and highly decorated white plaster ceiling, have few rivals in England in classic nobility and dignity.

The Nuns' Garden

The stroller should wander along a narrow passageway into the old Nuns' Garden, a restful spot beside Drawda Hall, whose gables rise over apple trees and rose bushes. After viewing the college dining hall, one should ask to see the collection of silver, including the founder's ancient drinking horn. During term, a modern trumpet is blown each evening to announce dinner, in accord with the founder's instructions.

Turning left outside Queen's, the visitor walks along the winding Queen's and New College Lane below high stone walls, spiked to discourage students climbing in or out after the college gate is closed.

After passing through the entrance to New College, the tourist should turn sharply to the left to reach probably the most peaceful spot in Oxford, the college cloisters. Rising above these wood-vaulted cloisters stands the crenelated bell tower, once part of the city wall. As one pauses at the far edge of the perfect lawn dominated by a single venerable ilex tree, one senses the calm, meditative air of the scholarship of the Middle Ages that in this place has survived the centuries.

New College, founded in 1379 by William of Wykeham, Bishop of Winchester, is the first college whose founder planned the buildings, most of which still stand, as a college.

On leaving the cloisters, one should visit the chapel, to see the original fourteenth-century stained glass windows. Then, the stroller should proceed through a superb iron gate to the college's spacious garden, open 2 to 5 P. M.

In its center is a high mound covered with trees and shrubs, and around the lawn the battlements of the original medieval city wall look down on an exquisitely planned herbaceous border. Here is a perfect spot to sit for a while on a summer day.

Having seen several of the leading colleges, the tourist now should have a look at the finest buildings of Oxford University, as distinguished from its colleges. Most buildings in academic Oxford belong to the colleges individually, while those belonging to the University provide special facilities for use by all colleges.

A Wren Masterpiece

Passing under Hertford College bridge, the visitor will see ahead the Sheldonian Theatre. It was designed by Sir Christopher Wren, and there university ceremonies, such as granting of degrees take place. The flat, highly decorated ceiling, apparently unsupported, is one of Wren's great mathematical achievements. Outside the theatre, the weatherbeaten stone heads of Roman emperors face "The Broad," Oxford's term for spacious Broad Street.

The world-renowned Bodleian Library stands next to the Sheldonian. The main gateway to the Bodleian quadrangle through the Tower of the Five Orders of Architecture (Tuscan, Doric, Corinthian and Composite) is only opened on ceremonial occasions.

The library, dating from the

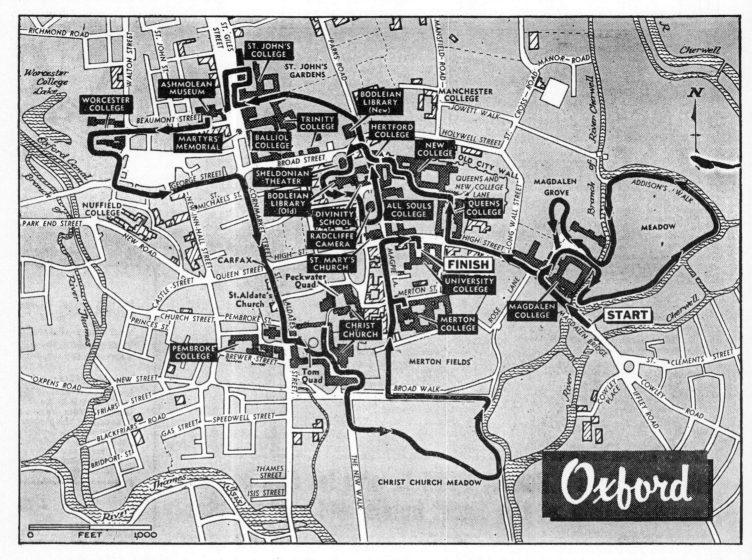

early seventeenth century, was built to house the books Sir Thomas Bodley began to collect, when in 1602 he refounded the former University library which had become dispersed. The visitor should look around the fifteenth-century Duke Humphrey's library. He will note the painted ceiling, oak beams and shelves which contain old books still arranged in their seventeenth-century classification by size and subject (Theology, Medicine, Law and Arts).

Following Bodley's instructions, a bell is still rung when the library opens, and closes. Upstairs are reading rooms with decorated freizes and ceilings. Near by is the Divinity School with a fine stone-vaulted ceiling. The House of Commons met there is 1655 after having been driven from London by the plague. Just to the south stands the Radcliffe Camera. From the gallery that circles the dome there is one of the finest views over Oxford.

No Undergraduates

Just a few steps back to The High brings the stroller to All Souls College—the only college without undergraduates, only Fellows. It is open from 2 to 5 P. M. The resident members here are Research Fellows. Hawksmoor's twin towers in the north quadrangle are a familiar feature of the Oxford scene. One should also ask to see the lofty Codrington Law Library, an extremely well-designed room.

Retracing one's steps along Catte Street and past the new Bodleian library, erected largely through a Rockefeller Founda-tion grant, the saunterer crosses The Broad to enter the extensive grounds of Trinity College. During term-time, visitors have enjoyed watching members of Oxford's dramatic society rehearsing Shakespeare under the trees. Trinity's ornamental chapel with its elaborate woodcarving is quite outstanding.

Balliol's Architecture

As the visitor passes Balliol, noted more for its academic excellence than for its monstrous architecture, he turns right along St. Giles Street and passes on the left the Martyrs Memorial commemorating the burning of Latimer and Ridley in 1555, Protestant reformers, condemned during the reign of the Catholic Queen Mary, and subsequently Archbishop Cranmer, during the same reign.

St. John's College should be included on any tour of Oxford mainly because of its unusually attractive garden, the largest in Oxford, laid out by Capability Brown. Its extensive lawn, rockery and groups of trees, as well as attractively arranged herbaceous border, make it one of Oxford's most delightful havens of repose. Canterbury Quad, named after Archbishop Laud who built it, is perhaps the finest example in Oxford of early seventeenth-century architecture. Its Italian colonnades are unusually lovely.

Celebrated Museum

Emerging from St. John's, the tourist crosses St. Giles (known in Oxford as "The Giles") to visit the Ashmolean Museum, the University's important art and archaeological collection.

Straight ahead down Beau-

mont Street, the stroller will see Worcester College. Inside the gate on the left is a row of relatively untouched medieval cottages. These were originally separate houses and the ancient shields over the doorways show the different abbeys with which they were connected. Passing through an archway, the visitor finds himself in a delightful large garden with noble trees. Its unique feature is Oxford's only lake.

On leaving Worcester, the visitor should make his way along George Street and the Cornmarket (Oxford's main shopping thoroughfare) to Carfax, the center of the city. A few hundred yards down St. Aldate's he will see the familiar Tom Tower of Christ Church on the left.

Before entering the college grounds, the most extensive of any in Oxford, one should step back from St. Aldate's a few yards along the lane leading to Pembroke College and study the details of imposing Tom Tower. It was completed by Sir Christopher Wren in 1682 after the lower part had been begun by Cardinal Wolsey, Christ Church's founder.

Every evening the great bell tolls 101 times at five minutes past nine, once for each of the original 101 scholars. After

passing through the huge gateway, one is spellbound by the grandeur and size of the tremendous Tom Quad. Walking around the stone terrace to the far side, the stroller will notice the arches built in the walls, indicating that Wolsey intended to construct a cloister around the Quad. In the center of the perfect lawn is a small pool.

Fine Staircase

The visitor should now inspect the magnificent staircase in the southeast corner of the quad with its beautiful fan-tracery stone roof. The Great Hall at the top of the stairs, with its elaborately carved oaken roof and superb paneling is the largest and finest in Oxford.

Many interesting portraits adorn the walls. These include Holbein's painting of Wolsey, and portraits of Queen Elizabeth I, "Lewis Carroll," a former canon of Christ Church, and William Penn, an old member of the college. In this hall, stage scenery was used for the first time in England to produce a play before Charles I in 1636. Outside the Hall is Wolsey's kitchen, the oldest part of the building, still in use and worth seeing. The Hall and kitchen are open from 2 to 4 P.M.

The stroller will find Oxford's Norman and early English cathedral only a few steps away, and adjoining it the fifteenth-century Cathedral Cloisters.

At the other end of Tom Quad a towered gateway leads to Peckwater Quad and the college library.

Returning through Tom Quad, the visitor should make his way through several passageways of the newer buildings into Christ Church meadow. It is a few minutes walk down to the river Isis where the gaily colored college barges are tied up.

The saunterer can wander along the tree-covered banks of the Cherwell (which joins the Isis near by) back to the Broad Walk. As he strolls along this avenue of fine trees, he will have on his right a distant view of the Towers of Merton and Magdalen.

Proceeding up the path to Merton Street, past its massive tower, the tourist will find the entrance to Merton College on the right. The College's fourteenth-century Mob Quad is the oldest surviving quadrangle in Oxford.

The medieval library on one side of this simple quad is one of the most fascinating in England (open 2 to 5 P.M.) It has an intimate air with its old

fittings and paneled ceiling Built in 1371-79, this relic of early Oxford still retains an original bookcase with chained volumes.

As the visitor leaves Merton, he should stroll along Magpie Lane with its odd little houses. Up ahead, the spire of St. Mary's looms at the end of the narrow street. Once again in The High, a right turn leads to University College, founded in the thirteenth century.

Shelley "Sent Down"

Although the poet Percy Bysshe Shelley was "sent down," that is, expelled, from University College as an undergraduate for publishing a pamphlet entitled "The Necessity of Atheism" in 1810, the college later repented by erecting a memorial to him. University College is the first Oxford college ever to elect an American as its head, Prof. A. L. Goodhart, its present Master.

As the visitor approaches Magdalen Tower, where he began his walk, pondering the beauties of the quads, halls, chapels and gardens he has seen, he realizes that such a walking tour as this has only served to whet his appetite to spend many more days in the inimitable atmosphere of Oxford.

July 23, 1961

A Walking Tour in England
From Salisbury to Wilton House

By GEORGE OAKES

The following walk, from Salisbury Cathedral to Wilton House, first appeared together with 23 other walking tours of the English countryside in a book entitled "Turn Left at the Pub," published by David McKay Company, Inc.. It contains 174 pages, is sized to fit the pocket and is priced at $4.95. This article is reprinted here with permission of the publishers.

SALISBURY, England—To walk from Salisbury Cathedral to Wilton House is to move from the spiritual world of the 13th century to the gay, amus- ing life of an English country house in the days of the Tudors and Stuarts. When you stroll around the tranquil cathedral close, still a haven of meditation and repose as it has been for 700 years, and look up at the glorious spire soaring above the magnificent mass of gothic architecture, you sense that the inspiration

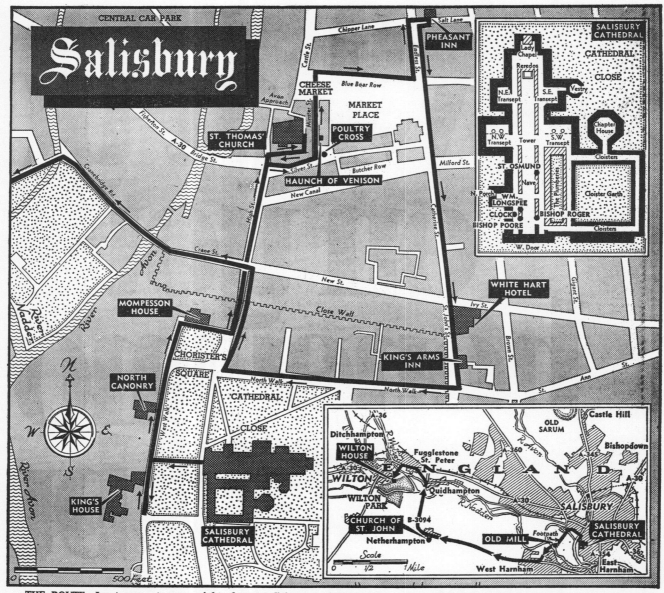

THE ROUTE—Inset map at upper right shows Salisbury Cathedral, where the walking tour begins. The large map depicts Salisbury itself, and the map at lower right shows the route along the River Nadder from Salisbury to Wilton House.

which created this superb structure lives on.

Nowhere in England has the spirit of the Middle Ages survived more successfully the violent vicissitudes and changes of seven centuries than here in the close of Salisbury Cathedral. Salisbury is the only one of the great English cathedrals that is set in such lovely and extensive grounds that you can stand from afar—as did the artist John Constable—and appreciate its full glory.

The walk from Salisbury to Wilton is thoroughly delightful.

You stroll through the long meadows by the River Nadder, with the towering cathedral almost always within view. The distance is roughly two and one-half miles and can be covered leisurely in a few hours.

When you reach Wilton, you will visit one of the most interesting country houses in England, one that is located in one of England's most beautiful parks. This walk combines Salisbury Cathedral, several interesting places in Salisbury itself, an excursion into pleasant country and the fasci-

nating Wilton House.

You can easily reach Salisbury by road or rail from London, about 80 miles to the northeast. It is quickest to take the train from Waterloo (most carry restaurant cars), and you will be in Salisbury in about an hour and three-quarters.

Near Southampton

Should you be touring southern England, Salisbury is likely to be on your route. If you are arriving at or sailing from Southampton, Salisbury is only 22 miles away.

When you are driving to Salis-

bury, the cathedral's lofty spire, a famous landmark in this part of the country, will be visible for miles around, as it is the focus of the city.

On arrival in the town, go directly to the cathedral close, where there is a parking area. Pause for a few moments by the green to absorb the mood of this lovely scene—the lines of the great gray gothic cathedral, its lofty spire that rises over 400 feet (the highest church spire in England), the broad expanse of lawn encircled by a 14th-century stone wall and the charming Georgian brick houses that surround the spacious close.

The most perfectly proportioned example of early English gothic style, Salisbury Cathedral is an architectural classic. The only English cathedral of uniform design, it was begun in 1220 and completed 38 years later. The tower and spire are 14th century.

After strolling about the close to view the cathedral from different angles, enter through the north door. At once you will be struck by the somber effect of the interior—perhaps due to the dark Purbeck marble.

Antique Clock

Turn to your right, on entering the cathedral, to view the great west window. It contains some of the finest and oldest glass in the cathedral, much of it 13th century. Stop on the right of the door to see the clock, made about 1386. It is believed to be the oldest working clock in England and perhaps in the world.

In the center of the cathedral, directly below the spire, you will find in the stone flooring a brass tablet indicating that the spire leans 29½ inches to the southwest. Nearby, you will note a pillar bent under the weight of the tower. There is a fine view of the nave and west window from the choir. Also of interest are the inverted, or scissor arches, and the Lady Chapel, with its 13th-century glass window.

American 'Souvenir'

In the transept opposite the choir, you will find a great cope chest that dates from the 13th or 14th century and is still used. Overhead is an American flag, a souvenir of the American troops in the Salisbury area during World War II.

Turn left in the south transept

past an interesting alabaster tomb on the left. The entrance to the library is through a doorway on the left, just before you go out into the cloisters. Unfortunately, the library is open only on Mondays and Fridays from 2 to 3:30 P.M.

Here you will see the most perfect of the four originals of Magna Carta. (The one with the actual signatures no longer exists.) Also on exhibit is the autographed survey of the cathedral by Sir Christopher Wren, whose recommendations saved the spire.

Rare Old Books

Other treasures are a remarkable 10th-century psalter in old English, books from William Caxton's 15th-century press, a description and map of Virginia by Capt. John Smith (printed in 1612), and William Harvey's book on the circulation of the blood (1628).

Stroll from the cathedral into the exquisite 13th-century cloisters, the largest and perhaps the most beautiful in England. Two tall, magnificent cedars of Lebanon in the center of the lawn contribute to the monastic atmosphere.

Continue around the cloisters to the octagonal Chapter House. The vaulted roof springs from the central pillars in keeping with its late 13th-century style. Be sure to study the remarkable sculptures illustrating scenes from the Books of Genesis and Exodus. These sculptured groups are among the most unusual to be seen in any gothic cathedral.

On returning to the cathedral, wander along the south aisle of the nave, stopping here and there to look at several interesting tombs. On your right is the reclining mailed figure of William Longspee, one of the witnesses to Magna Carta and a founder of the cathedral.

A bit farther along is the 11th-century shrine of St. Osmund, founder of the cathedral at Old Sarum, the great prehistoric fortress two miles north of Salisbury and the forerunner of the present city.

Leaving the cathedral near the clock, cross the close for a better view of the great west front. A few minutes' stroll to the left along West Walk will enable you to see the cathedral and spire from still another angle. On your way back along West Walk, you pass several charming Georgian houses, including the 14th-century King's

House, now a teachers' training college.

Four Rivers Meet

Just beyond, opposite the cathedral's west front, is the North Canonry. Go under the arch of the old stone house. At the rear, you will come to a magnificent herbaceous border that runs down to the banks of the Avon, one of four rivers that meet in Salisbury. The others are the Nadder, the Bourne and the Wylye.

Back on the West Walk, saunter past more attractive red-brick houses, with white windows set back behind flower-filled gardens, to the circular green, or Chorister's Square. Here is the most elegant house of all, Mompesson House. Built in 1701, the interior of this exquisitely decorated and furnished home (open Wednesdays and Saturdays, May to September, from 2:30 to 6 P.M.) is quite exceptional. The splendid paneling, lovely plaster work and beautiful furniture make this home (which is still lived in) one of the most tasteful examples of an 18th-century house.

Turn left from the close and walk under the decorative stone arch leading into High Street, which is lined with old curio, book and antiques shops. When you reach Bridge Street, cross over and go right on the far side of Silver Street. Through a passageway on your left, you will come into the small churchyard of St. Thomas's Church, which is largely of 15th-century construction. The great fresco above the chancel arch is quite an unusual 15th-century painting of the Last Judgment.

Returning to Silver Street, go left a few yards on Minster Street. You will see on your right the 600-year-old Poultry Cross, which is shaped like a crown. Just a few doors farther on Minster Street will bring you to the Haunch of Venison Inn, Salisbury's best restaurant, where you dine in the old timbered rooms of a building that is believed to be 14th century.

About 75 yards beyond here is the Market Square on your right. (Market days are Tuesdays and Saturdays.) Cross to the far side, turn left on Endless Street past the bus station and then go right into Salt Lane.

About 50 yards beyond here, you will come to the Pheasant Inn, an attractive old pub in a stucco and timbered Tudor-style house dating from 1445.

Brass utensils on the walls, as well as pewter mugs and measures, give the bar an attractive air. Ask the proprietor to show you the interesting shoemakers' oak-timbered Guildhall upstairs. For over 400 years, the Salisbury shoemakers guild has been meeting here.

Return along Salt Lane to Endless Street, which runs into Queen Street. No. 8 is one of Salisbury's fine old buildings, the "House of John A' Port." This early 15th-century half-timbered house is now a shop specializing in pottery, china and glass. Go upstairs to see the decorative 17th-century paneling in the front room. In the other rooms, you will find paneling taken from old ships.

Continue along Queen Street and cross Milford Street. Queen Street now changes its name to Catherine Street and then to St. John Street. After passing the White Hart Hotel, perhaps Salisbury's best, you come to the King's Arms Inn, a half-timbered building that is probably Salisbury's oldest inn. You may want to stop for a bitter in its attractive old bar.

Cross St. John's Street and return through the arch to the North Walk for a final view of the cathedral and close before starting your walk to Wilton House at the corner of Crane and High Streets, which is reached from the close.

Turn left on Crane Street, cross the stone bridge and go left on Mill Road to the Queen Elizabeth Gardens, an attractive public park. Keep to the left and cross the far footbridge, from which there is a fine view of the cathedral spire. Stroll along the paved footpath through the meadows, and in about five minutes or so you will reach a weir. The ancient flint and brick building is the Old Mill in West Harnham.

This fascinating inn, with three arches bridging the River Nadder, may be a modified version of the building known to have been there in 1235. The muniments from Old Sarum Cathedral were stored here during the construction of the cathedral at New Sarum, or Salisbury.

Ask the proprietor to show you the old millrace and the original beams and rafters upstairs. The ancient ford, still in use, the millpond, the cattle grazing in the nearby fields and the pointed cathedral spire rising in the distance are straight out of a Constable painting.

About 50 yards from the Old Mill, turn right on Middle Street. Where the road makes a sharp left, keep ahead on the footpath marked Bemerton. You will be walking along the willow-lined banks of the Nadder. The path continues over a little footbridge and along the meadows, and again the ever-present spire looms above the fields to your right.

At the end of the path, turn left along a paved road past thatched-roof cottages. Soon, you will come to a tiny church on the lower road, which then runs along the river.

Turn right at the main road and follow the high wall of Wilton Park to Route A30, where you bear left. In a few moments, stop in to see the parish church of Fugglestone St. Peter, with its double row of trimmed yew trees. Just beyond here, there is a traffic circle, or roundabout, where you turn left, cross the River Wylye and go past the village bowling green to the stately stone gateway of Wilton House.

The house is open Tuesdays to Saturdays from April 1 to Sept. 30, and on Sundays in August and most of September. The hours are 11 A.M. to 6 P.M. on weekdays and 2 to 6 P.M. on Sundays.

The home of the Earls of Pembroke and Montgomery for some 400 years, Wilton House was built by Inigo Jones during the mid-17th century to replace an older house destroyed by fire.

Wilton is one of the most notable country houses in England, not only because of its fine design, both exterior and interior, but also because of its historic past. It is said that Hans Holbein prepared designs for the pre-Jones house built in the early 16th century. The present central tower is all that remains of this structure.

Queen Elizabeth I visited Wilton in 1574; Sir Philip Sidney wrote "Arcadia" while staying there; Ben Jonson, Edmund Spenser and Christopher Marlowe were some of the literary figures who came there. According to tradition, Shakespeare and his theatrical company presented the first performance of either "Twelfth Night" or "As You Like It" at Wilton about 1601.

The visitor gets just a taste of the magnificent grounds on his way to the house from the gateway, and once inside, he finds that the house is, in effect, an unusually fine art gallery. The rooms are distinguished both for their classic proportions and their collection of historic memorabilia and original works of art.

Although guides are available to show you around and explain the significance of the furnishings, a brief summary of the more outstanding rooms may be useful.

The large smoking room on the ground floor contains a unique set of 55 gouache paintings of the Spanish Riding School in Vienna. The suite of state rooms on the first floor are outstanding among English country houses.

The great double cube, designed by Inigo Jones, and considered one of the best-proportioned rooms in England, is most elaborately decorated with its painted ceiling and paneled walls, on which hang some of Van Dyck's finest paintings. Chippendale settees and chairs are among the furnishings.

The single cube, another Inigo Jones room, is equally distinguished in its decoration and works of art. In the upper cloisters, showcases exhibit such interesting pieces as Napoleon's dispatch box from the Russian campaign of 1812 and a lock of the hair of Queen Elizabeth I with a poem by Sir Philip Sidney.

After visiting the house, spend some time strolling around the beautiful park. Great cedars of Lebanon and copper beeches dominate the broad expanse of lawn. Lofty yews harmonize with the Italian gardens.

The 18th-century Palladian bridge over the Nadder adds a fitting classical touch to the luxuriant trees that arch the stream and line the peaceful hills beyond. Opposite the entrance to the house, a wide walk leads to a secluded rose garden. Wherever you wander in this natural yet superbly landscaped park, you will admire the original planning and the perfection of its maintenance.

Before leaving Wilton House, you can have tea or a snack near the entrance gate. Wilton is also the home of the Royal Carpet Factory, in existence for 300 years. The factory is open from 9:30 A.M. to 12:30 P.M. and from 1:30 to 4 P.M., Monday through Friday. Buses leave at frequent intervals from the village or near Wilton House for the 15-minute return trip to Salisbury.

August 18, 1968

A WALKING TOUR OF ATHENS

The Old Quarter of the Grecian Capital, Called Plaka, Has Air of Country Town in Heart of Modern City

By GEORGE W. OAKES

ATHENS—This is an unusual walking tour through the Greek capital, since it omits the Acropolis.

The visitor to Athens will probably spend most of his time on the world-renowned rock in order to explore the most exciting and dramatic ruins of ancient Greece. What he may not do, however, is to wander around Plaka, the fascinating old quarter of the city.

Aside from the remains of the Greek and Roman periods, Athens, now boasting nearly two million people in its metropolitan area, is almost entirely a modern city whose great expansion occurred after World War I.

Age of Quarter

Plaka, largely built just over a century ago, is now the oldest inhabited part of Athens. Its name appears to be derived from the Albanian word "pliaka," meaning old.

The quarter has the air of a country town in the heart of a bustling city. It consists of narrow, winding, cobblestoned streets; low, whitewashed houses with flower-filled inner courtyards, and tiny shops displaying bizarre oriental wares.

Here, hawkers astride little donkeys sell bread or vegetables from baskets. And here, too, are numerous *tavernas* where, in the evenings, one can sample typical Greek dishes and local wines and hear Greek songs to the accompaniment of a guitar.

Touring Plaka, the traveler senses the days of the Turkish occupation, the Athens that Byron knew and even the influence of the Byzantine civilization.

Pepper Trees

The visitor should begin his stroll through Plaka in Constitution Square. Starting from the Grande Bretagne Hotel, he circles the broad esplanade, which is shaded by pepper trees and, in good weather, crowded with tables and chairs for the patrons of nearby cafes.

At noon and late in the day, Constitution Square is so jammed with people that it seems like a giant beehive. On the far side, the stroller turns right along Mitropoleos Street, in the business district.

After a couple of blocks, the street opens into a large square. Directly ahead is the rear of the New Cathedral of Athens, built between 1840 and 1855 from the material of 70 demolished churches and chapels.

Although one may wish to look around the cathedral, the real treasure in this square is the Little Cathedral, or Metropolis. It is just a few yards to the left of the Great Metropolitan Church.

Byzantine Treasure

The Little Cathedral, which dates from the 12th century, is set just below the level of the square and is surrounded by grass and shrubs. It is perhaps the finest example of Byzantine architecture in Athens. Built of marble turned golden with age, it is cruciform, with a dome only 39 feet above the floor.

One should carefully examine the frieze, dating from the fourth century B.C., which depicts the 12 signs of the Zodiac. It shows the major festivals and seasons of the year—an Attic calendar in pictures. Each period is illustrated by a man dressed according to the temperature of the month.

Byzantine bas-reliefs are also set in the church's facade. And

there is an amusing modern touch—a telephone just inside the entrance.

The stroller leaves the square by passing in front of the New Cathedral to enter Evaghellistrias Street. After one block, a left turn on Ermou Street will lead to the Kapnikarea Church.

Island of Peace

This small 11th-century church is surrounded by offices and shops, some in Byzantine style, and stands beneath two tall cypress trees, like an island in the center of busy Ermou Street. It is built of unevenly cut stone and brick, with a dome of fine proportions and a spacious interior.

King Ludwig I of Bavaria, an ardent Hellenophile, was responsible for saving the church in 1834, when town planners wanted to pull it down. Today, it is considered one of the finest of the Athenian churches.

From the church, Kapnikareas Street leads for two blocks to Pandrosou Street, Plaka's most colorful thoroughfare. Venders may be selling roasted chestnuts or sesame-seed rolls in the street. Perhaps an accordion player will be adding to the gaiety of the scene. There is plenty of street life in Plaka.

Turning right into Pandrosou Street, one passes shops selling twine and cloth. The street narrows and suddenly becomes an oriental bazaar, with brass, copperware and bric-a-brac on sale. Here is a cobbler making shoes; dozens of pairs are hanging in bunches inside the shop and out. A nearby shop displays antique ikons and silverware.

A few doors away is still another shop containing all types of Greek national costumes. Besides gay, embroidered blouses or bright scarves, red and black leather sabots with pompons

make attractive souvenirs for the tourist. Craftsmen, sitting at their workbenches and laboring over jewelry or silverware, are typically picturesque.

On this street, too, is the shop of one of the more notable antique dealers in Athens. It features handmade silverware produced by its own craftsmen. Old Greek coins of the fifth century, B.C.—the age of Pericles—may also be on sale.

Perhaps the visitor might want to buy a *lycithos*, a small antique vase (about six inches high) that was used for perfume in the sixth century, B.C. Permission to take these antique pieces out of the country usually requires two or three days.

At the end of Pandrosou Street is the Museum of Decorative Arts, which is open from 9 A.M. to 2 P.M., except Wednesdays. The museum is situated in a former 18th-century Turkish mosque. Its collection includes an exhibit of embroidery of the second century A.D. Coptic cloths, as well as contemporary work from the Greek islands, Greek jewelry, Byzantine pottery, ikons, gold and silverware.

One returns along lively Pandrosou Street, then turns right into Eolou Street. Hadrian's Library (open 8 A.M. to sunset) is about 10 yards on the right. Not much remains of this Roman building except for the portions of the wall, a few facades and several columns.

After wandering about the ruins, the visitor might like to rest on a bench under the trees in the delightful little square opposite. About 50 yards farther along Eolou Street, one will see the marble Tower of the Winds in the Roman Agora (open 8 A.M. to sunset).

This is one of the most in-

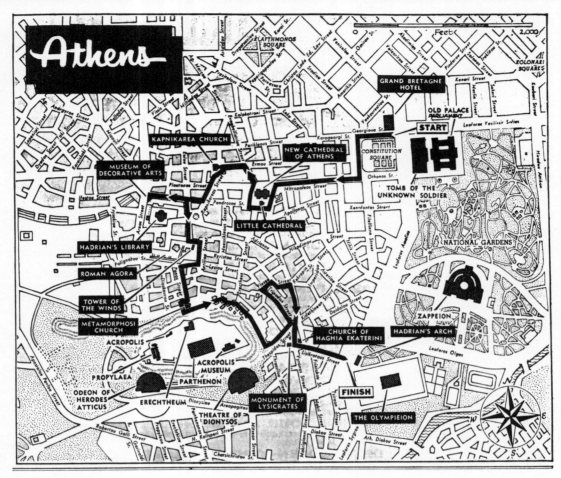

teresting remains of the Roman period. Built in the first century, B.C., the tower displays a water clock, a sundial and a weather vane It was erected as an octagonal, so that each side faces a point of the horizon from which winds may blow.

Carved in Stone

Each wind is represented by a figure carved in stone. For example Boreas, the north wind, is depicted as a bearded man dressed in heavy clothing and blowing into a conchshell. Zephyr, the west wind, is shown as a youth throwing flowers into the air.

The water clock is believed to have operated by the flow of water into a cylinder. The changing water level showed the passage of the hours. The tower itself is one of the earliest architectural examples of an octagonal plan.

From the Tower of the Winds, the stroller should walk around the Roman Agora, keeping it on his right until he is on a curving street above it. After

following this for about 50 yards a right turn leads into a very narrow street between whitewashed houses.

The first little street to the left will lead, after a short distance, to a flight of steps just below the Acropolis. A palm tree sways in a garden to the right of the steps.

Rural Slopes

Just along here—right beneath the precipitous rock — is one of the most rural parts of Plaka. A goat may be grazing along the rocky slope, or chickens are likely to be feeding outside a shack. There is an interesting little church here, the 14th-century Metamorphosi. As the stroller follows the hillside, he will come shortly to a narrow, winding street. On the left is an orange tree on a terrace and, just above, a grape arbor decorates a white house.

After a climb up a flight of steps on the right, a left turn leads past one of the quarter's popular *tavernas*. A bit farther

along is an open slope, and a small olive grove nestles against the sloping hillside. At this point, the stroller finds himself just below the observation terrace at the northeast corner of the Acropolis.

The first narrow street to the left, Thespidos, goes down the hill to a lively vegetable market. At this point, a left turn into Tripodon Street brings the wanderer past fascinating little shops and to Flessa Street.

A right turn here, and then another right at the corner where five streets intersect, lead into Adrianou Street. This is one of the principal thoroughfares of the quarter. It is usually crowded with people and throbbing with much going-and-coming in and out of its many and varied stores.

From one, comes the strong aroma of coffee. Another sells seafood fresh from the Aegean.

Market Tumult

No. 96 Adrianou Street is believed to be the site of one

of the oldest houses in Athens. Outdoor market stalls add to the tumult.

In a small garden at the end of Adrianou Street, the visitor will find a marble monument to a certain Lysicrates, a leader of the Dionysiac festivals of the fourth century, B.C. A circle of six graceful Corinthian columns support a bronze tripod that a chorus, under the patronage of the wealthy Lysicrates, won in musical and dramatic competition.

Notable Icons

Almost opposite the monument is the 13th-century Church of Haghia Ekaterini. Its ikons are noteworthy.

After passing this square, a couple of minutes along Lisikratous Street will bring the stroller to Leoforos Amalias, the broad avenue opposite Hadrian's Arch and the Olympieion. From this point, one can catch a bus or a taxi and be back in Constitution Square in a few minutes.

May 3, 1964

A WALKING TOUR THROUGH OLD AMSTERDAM

By HARRY GILROY

AMSTERDAM—A walk in the center of this big Dutch city becomes a study in contrasts, old and new. One's course is plotted through a maze of little streets and beside canals lined with gems of ancient architecture, the mansions of the city's merchant-princes of the seventeenth century. One discovers vistas down the tree-bordered canals to quaint bridges and old churches. The great Dutch painters painted scenes like this three hundred years ago.

Yet this old part of town is also a busy, modern port and rail center. It is bounded on the north by the River Ij (pronounced Eye) which carries much shipping up from the North Sea, in fact, from all seas, and here it is lined with docks. Here, too, stands the Central Railroad Station, where freight trains can be loaded direct from the docks themselves.

Thus, there is a continuous and developing history here. The earlier Amsterdam merchants and traders dug canals from the river right up to their big houses, which were also their warehouses. The rich argosies from the East could unload at their own front doors. The canals are still here, looping in roughly parallel half-circles down from the Ij and back again, or flowing into another river, the Amstel, for which Amsterdam was named and which runs up through the town from the southeast.

Well Preserved

The great houses are still here, too. Most of them are not privately owned any more but have been converted into office buildings for today's merchants. Such conversions have been lovingly and considerately done. The exteriors are much as they were when first built. In the interiors, too, Dutch business firms have preserved much of the original elegance and beauty.

Amsterdam's continuity and simultaneous development are illustrated in such a detail as the city's coat of arms. The city had civic rights as early as 1300 A. D. Its coat of arms was established hundreds of years ago—a shield in red and black with three X's, looking like windmills, vertical in a central panel, all surmounted by a crown in red and gold. But, although all this was established so long ago, it was recently altered, thus changing with the times as the city does. That was in 1945 when Queen Wilhelmina added the three words in Dutch for "Heroic, Steadfast, Compassionate" in scrolls beneath the shield. This, of course, was in honor of Amsterdam's heroism in World War II.

So much for the background of this great port, and the central portion of it whose streets, canals and history can be so easily explored in a pleasant stroll. The buildings and canal scenes are marvellously quaint and charming.

From the Station

The Central Station is a convenient place to start. From it, a walker can cross a wide canal by any of three bridges, moving south into the old town. Over the bridge, one turns left toward St. Nicolaas Church, which dominates the area. The church is on Prins Hendrik Kade. Turning right from the church steps, the route is along Prins Hendrik Kade — Kade means quay—around a bend that gives a mixed-up view of water, wharves, sails and funnels.

Right around the bend is an old stone tower, at the junction of two canals, Oude Zijos Kolk and Gelderse Kade. Its name, Schreierstoren, can be translated as Tower of Tears. The legend is that sailors' wives and children wept there, watching their men-folk's ships put out to sea. But philologists say the name shows merely that the tower once straddled the town wall and the Oude Zijos Kolk.

It often occurs to a pensive pedestrian that scholars specialize in destroying legends. An old stone in the tower shows a tearful woman looking at a passing ship, so the legend has been believed for centuries. The tower was built in 1482. A plaque put on it by the Greenwich Village Historical Society of New York in 1927 notes that Henry Hudson sailed the Half Moon past the tower on April 4, 1609, outward-bound to discover Manhattan Island.

Past and Present

Behind the tower are little streets and canals that preserve the character of the time when Hudson put out to sea. Circling the tower to Geldersche Kade, one should pause on the right side of the canal, back to the tower and facing along the Kade, for a glimpse of a strange old world. But one must not drift too completely into the past, or contact with the present world may be short. Trucks, cars and cycles press through these narrow roadways, and it seems there must be a town bounty on pedestrians.

Bearing these perils in mind, and also being careful not to back into the canal while looking for the characteristically ornamented tops of the buildings, a walker can get many glimpses of the past. Even the pavement and house walls are evidence of a law passed after a great fire of 1452. It required that everything be built of brick. The brick is a cheerful red brick, a good color above snow, or under blue sky, or when it is seen wetly gleaming in fog.

Before departing from the neighborhood of the Schreierstoren, the wise sight-seer will take long looks along the two canals joining there. Along the Oude Kolk, the Oude Kerk (old church) raises its graceful sixteenth century spire, while, along the Gelderse Kade the fifteenth century Nieuw Markt is seen — two vistas running back in time.

With these glimpses of a couple of the objectives of the day, one starts along the Gelderse Kade. The gables of the tall houses on both sides of the canal are worth studying. The oldest kind looks like two sets of steps, four on each side, running to a fifth common step on the top. The next type of gable that came into use looks like a single wide chimney. Then, for broader houses, a gable that looks like a bell, and another like a little Roman temple, were devised.

Stone Menagerie

A stroller will discover variations in the ornamentation of these old gables. Some display animals looking down on the street. Often there is a date of 200 or 300 years ago, showing the year when the house was built. Most of the houses have a beam projecting just beneath the gable. There will be a hook or block for a pulley, used long ago, and even today, for hauling things up from boats in the canal.

At the head of the Gelderse Kade, a look around the Nieuw Markt is advisable. The heavy tower in its center was originally a gatehouse, called St. Antoniespoort, in the fifteenth century town wall. It later became the Weighing House.

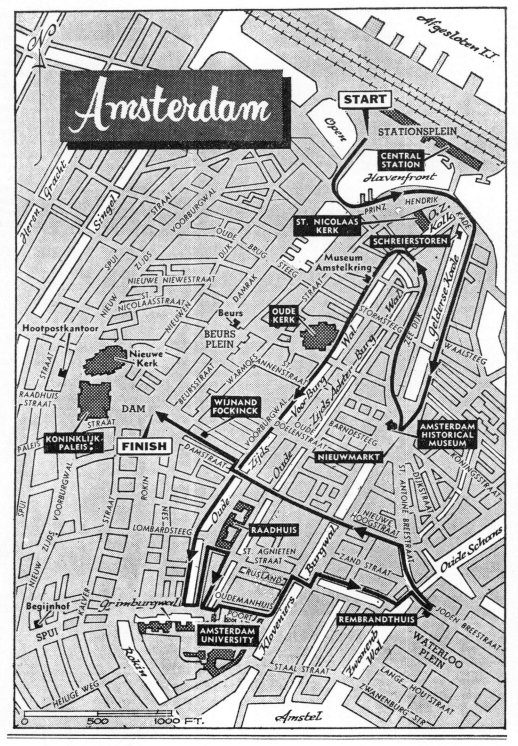

Amsterdam map labels

START · STATIONSPLEIN · CENTRAL STATION · Havenfront · Open · Afgesloten IJ · PRINZ · HENDRIK · O. Z. KADE · SCHREIERSTOREN · ST. NICOLAAS KERK · Museum Amstelkring · Geldersche Kade · STORMSTEEG · ZEE DIJK · WAALSTEEG · WAAL · Zijds Achter Burg · Voor Burg · OUDE KERK · STEEG · Beurs · BEURS PLEIN · DAMRAK · DIJK · BRUG · OUDE · ZIJDS · VOORBURGWAL · NIEUWE NIEWESTRAAT · ST. NICOLAASSTRAAT · NIEUWEN · NIEUW · Hootpostkantoor · Heren Gracht · Singel · STRAAT · SPUI · Nieuwe Kerk · WARMOES SANNENSTRAAT · BEURSSTRAAT · ST. · WIJNAND FOCKINCK · DAM · RAADHUIS STRAAT · STRAAT · KONINKLIJK PALEIS · PALEIS · FINISH · DAMSTRAAT · Zijds · Oude · VOORBURGWAL · OUDE DOELENSTRAAT · BARNDESTEEG · NIEUWMARKT · AMSTERDAM HISTORICAL MUSEUM · ST. ANTOINE BREESTRAAT · DIJKSTRAAT · KONINGSSTRAAT · ROKIN · NES · LOMBARDSTEEG · RAADHUIS · ST. AGNIETEN STRAAT · RUSLAND · OUDEMANHUIS · POORT · Klovenicrs · Burgwal · ZAND STRAAT · NIEUWE HOOGSTRAAT · REMBRANDTHUIS · JODEN BREESTRAAT · Oude Schans · Begijnhof · Grimburgwal · SPUI · AMSTERDAM UNIVERSITY · KALVER · NIEUW ZIJDS VOORBURGWAL · STAAL STRAAT · Zwanenb Wal · WATERLOO PLEIN · HEILIGE WEG · Rokin · Amstel · LANGE HOUTSTRAAT · ZWANENBURG STR · 0 500 1000 FT.

---

tells the history of the Nazi destruction of this community.

When one comes out of the museum, an interesting path to take is along the Zeedijk. This actually is on a dike built to keep out the sea, and today it is the seamen's delight, a street of cafés and dance halls. But these institutions are in fine, old gabled houses, so whether gaiety or architecture is being sought, this street should be visited.

To the Old Church

Just after the Zeedijk crosses the Oude Kolk canal, a left turn brings the stroller into the Oude Zijds Voorburgwal, which is again a canal with roads on both sides of it. Three blocks along this picturesque canal, on the stroller's right side, is the Oude Kerk.

It is not an especially beautiful church, but it has a wonderfully settled, peaceful look. It was built about 1300 and the distinctive tower was added a couple of centuries later. A look inside is worth while, if only to observe the great size of the church and to look at the old stained-glass windows.

Meandering on to the end of the Oude Zijds Voorburgwal, the walker comes to an intersection of three canals, the Grimburgwal and the Oude Zijds Achterburgwal. A house sits in this intersection, as extraordinary a location as can be imagined. A stone set in the facade says "Fluwelenburgwal"—meaning "Velvet Town Wall"—in other words, this was the border of the old town, where the rich, velvet-clad people lived.

Going back on Oude Zijds Voorburgwal on the opposite side of the canal, the route leads to the old Town Hall, and there right into St. Agnietenstraat. One continues to the Oude Zijds Achterburgwal, there turning right again. Coming back to the House of the Three Canals, the stroller should turn left across Oude Zijds Achterburgwal and enter a narrow alley called Oudemanhuispoort. This alley opens on the left into the campus of Amsterdam University.

Rembrandt's House

While in this part of town, there is one more institution that should be visited—Rembrandt House. To get there, one continues from the University on Oudemanhuispoort to

---

As one door, marked "Theatrum Anatomicum." shows, it also was the place where doctors dissected bodies of executed criminals. Rembrandt painted his famous picture, "The Anatomy Lesson" here, thereby bringing off a news

scoop, since this kind of medical research was not supposed to be allowed in those seventeenth century days.

Now this building is an attractive setting for the Amsterdam Historical Museum. On the top floor is the fascinating

collection of the Jewish Historical Museum, including pictures and sacred objects from the large community of Jews who for hundreds of years were among the mainsprings of Amsterdam's greatness. A documentary record in one cabinet

Kloveniersburgwal and turns left along the canal. At the street called Rusland, a right turn on to the bridge over Kloveniersburgwal canal leads to the left side of the Raamgracht, a little canal in front of the bridge.

A sign giving assurance that this is the right track reads: "Museum Rembrandthuis — Jodenbreestraat 4-6" and sketches the route thereafter.

The museum shows not only how Rembrandt lived but also contains a most interesting collection of almost all of his etchings and some of his drawings.

This must be about all the walking and pacing around that any traveler wants for a day. But certainly many things must have been seen off one way or the other from the suggested route that will lead to further exploration. For the present, a fairly direct route back to the Dam, the tourist's usual base of operations, is proposed: back over the bridge to St. Anthoniesbreestraat, left through Hoogstraat and its continuation, Oude Doelenstraat.

Then, after the bridge over the Oude Zijds Voorburgwal canal, comes the moment for relaxation and a typical Dutch drink, which ought really to be Dutch gin, or *jenever*. Color-

less, and served in a small tulip-shaped glass, it is in flavor entirely different from English gin.

Pause That Refreshes

There are several important brands of Dutch gin, but the place most convenient for the stroller at this point is the tasting house of a famous distiller, Fockinck, a firm that makes numerous liqueurs and an unexcelled *jenever,* and has been in business since 1609.

The Wijnand Fockinck establishment is a small bar, which can be reached from the bridge by turning right for a short

block and then left into narrow Pijlsteer. The bar is on the right hand side, in the middle of the block.

Drinking Dutch gin has its ceremonious side. The little glass is filled to the very brim, so that the liquor seems to bulge over the rim. One takes one's first sip without lifting the glass, by bending ceremoniously down to the counter.

Then, the stroller, refreshed, has only a few more steps to go to bring him back to the Dam, the center of Amsterdam, with its hotels and restaurants, and facing the Palace. On this walk, he has really strolled through the past.

June 11, 1961

Ireland

WALKING TOURS OF DUBLIN

Two Strolls Through the Irish Capital Reveal City's Rich Historic, Literary and Architectural Heritage

By MORRIS GILBERT

DUBLIN — To walk through this fine city is to trace three golden strands of human endeavor. They are the strands of Ireland's long-enduring, ardent political story, of Dublin's dazzling literary heritage and of her notable architecture. And the strands are as tangled together as bits of yarn and thread in a sewing basket, so that, in pulling out a piece of one, pieces of the others come tumbling out, too.

Since it is impossible to disentangle these strands of the Dublin story, a stroller in this city should take them as they come, and never mind a hop of centuries. And it is well to note that Dublin's spaces are large, with plenty of mediocre areas, as is true of New York or London or Paris. Hence, in making two fairly compact walking tours, a visitor seeking to bring the city's history and culture into good focus should be prepared to loop out from main routes, now and then, for special sightseeing.

One such loop, for instance, would run to Dublin's western edge, to Phoenix Park, called the biggest civic park in Europe. It is about three square miles in extent, richly planted with playing fields, picnic grounds, paths and flowers, Dublin being a flower city. All Dublin flocks to Phoenix Park on a pleasant Sunday or holiday.

Llamas and Lions

Here stands, in its enclosed private grounds, the official residence of Eamon de Valera, the New York-born President of the Irish Republic. Phoenix Park also has a notable zoo, with llamas and wallabies ruminating placidly by its road-sides, and a reputation for breeding lions, a rather rare accomplishment in zoos. Cattle and sheep graze on the park's broad acres, and there, too, stands the United States Embassy residence, in spacious grounds and gardens. President Kennedy stayed there when in Dublin recently.

But to get to Phoenix Park from mid-Dublin is a bus or taxi excursion. It can be a field day for park-strollers, but it should not, of course, supplant the two principal Dublin walks.

The first of these walks leads the stroller north of the Liffey, the river flowing eastward through the heart of Dublin into Dublin Bay and the Irish Sea. The place to start is at the north end of the O'Connell Bridge, Dublin's finest, a lovely span decorated with imposing floral baskets.

'Street of Statues'

Here, O'Connell Street, a "street of statues" which embodies much Dublin history, starts its northward course. Many statues age quicker than the stories they commemorate, and O'Connell Street's collection is more impressive as history than as art. The first statue is dedicated to Daniel O'Connell himself, he being chiefly remembered as the statesman who brought emancipation in 1829 to Ireland's Catholics. This vast majority of the population, until his day, had had no right to sit in Parliament or hold any public office or military commission.

O'Connell's bronze figure stands 12 feet high on a massive pedestal with winged figures personifying Patriotism, Eloquence, Justice and Fortitude, which were considered the "Liberator's" principal attributes.

Succeeding O'Connell along this central mall come monuments to an eminent priest, Father Theobald Mathew, Ireland's "Apostle of Temperance"; to the statesman Parnell, the work of the American sculptor, Saint-Gaudens, and to Sir John Gray, engineer of Dublin's water supply.

Towering above all is the Nelson Pillar, the tallest thing in Dublin. It stands all of 134 feet high and gives, for sixpence to those who care to climb its interior, a panoramic view of the city, countryside and sea.

Hereabouts, Dublin's story begins to flower in actuality rather than monuments. Here stands, on the west side of O'Connell Street, a symbol of Ireland's struggle for independence, going by the stolid name of the General Post Office. Padraig Pearse and other leaders of the rising of Easter Week, 1916, chose the G. P. O. as headquarters.

The G.P.O. Story

Here, on that "fine and sunny" Easter Monday, a small, determined body of men took over. Here, from the portico, Pearse proclaimed freedom for Ireland. And here, too, on the following Saturday afternoon, Pearse, with his followers falling around him, formally surrendered. British artillery and machine gun fire had reduced the G. P. O. to a smoldering shambles.

Today, the General Post Office has been restored. The populace goes about buying its stamps there as blandly as if nothing unexpected had ever happened in those precincts. But in the middle of the spacious public area there is a statue of the dying Cuchulainn, hero of Irish legend, and out-side is a plaque recalling the Proclamation of the Republic, with memorials to the men who launched the Rising and were shot when it failed. For here, the ending began.

Farther north on O'Connell Street stands the Rotunda. An 18th-century auditorium, originally built as a set of assembly rooms to support a maternity hospital, the Rotunda today is plastered with billboards. Once, Dublin wits and statesmen gathered here, and an Irish constitutional convention met in the Rotunda in the late 18th century.

The Lane Collection

At the head of O'Connell Street, one arrives in Parnell Square. At its top stands Charlemont House, a great 18th-century mansion, now the home of the Municipal Gallery of Modern Art. The collection here recalls its extraordinary founder, Sir Hugh Lane, art lover and benefactor, who established it in 1907.

Lane's bequest, mostly works by the French Impressionists, was blocked for decades by rival claims by Dublin and London's National Gallery. A recent settlement divides them, with transferral of the halves from one to the other gallery every five years. So, in Dublin, Renoir's notable "Les Parapluies" is now on view, along with oils by Manet and others. Also to be seen are Whistlers, an Epstein bust of Lady Gregory, and works of Augustus John, Sickert, Picasso, Vlaminck and others.

On emerging from the gallery, a stroller who is a James Joyce addict or a student of Ireland's struggle for freedom can embark on a special side trip that would add half an

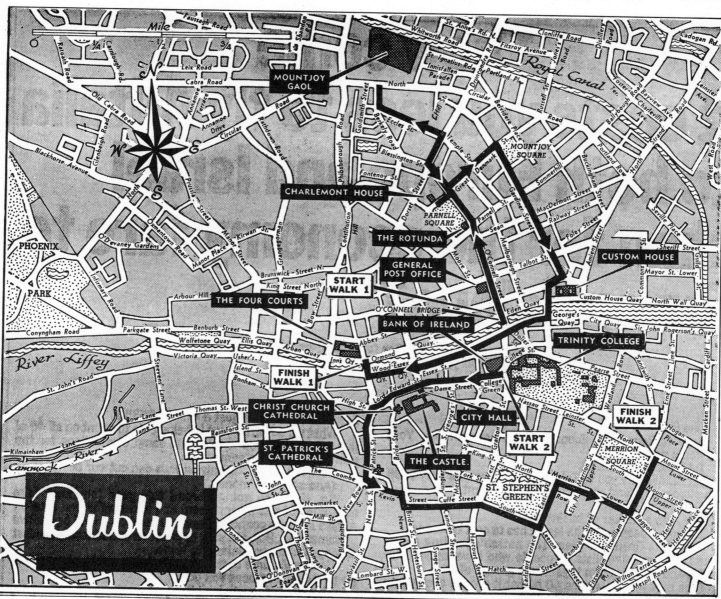

hour to his walk. He would continue north from Parnell Square into Dorset Street, and north along Dorset Street to where Eccles Street leads off to the left.

This is almost a sanctuary for admirers of Joyce's "Ulysses," for in Eccles Street lived Leopold and Molly Bloom on that immortal single day, June 16, 1904, when the full "Ulysses" chronicle unfolded. Today, Eccles Street is a fairly doleful one, with little interest for the strolling tourist except his own sentimental literary associations.

Joyless Mountjoy

The student of Ireland's wars of independence has his day when he turns right from Eccles Street into Berkely Road and comes to the North Circular Road. Here stands the historic and ominous Mountjoy Gaol. This was the place of imprisonment of many an Irish patriot in the 1916 Easter Uprising and the subsequent, eventually successful, clashes ending in 1922.

Those who decline to make this side trip can continue their walk from the northeast corner of Parnell Square, strolling eastward along Great Denmark Street to the square that also bears the name of Mountjoy.

The surroundings here are mostly down at heel nowadays, but once they were elegantly Georgian, having been laid out as a fashionable development by a notable builder of the late 18th century, Luke Gardiner, who became Lord Mountjoy. Typical Georgian fanlights and facades commemorate him.

Mountjoy Square itself is still spacious and runs cheerily downhill, and will have, for Sean O'Casey's disciples, a mel-

ancholy, nostalgic charm. There is interest here for the Joycians, too, for close to the square stands Belvedere, the Jesuit school that young Joyce attended and later depicted in "A Portrait of the Artist as a Young Man." Farther eastward—no use seeking it now, for it is all cleaned up—was the "Nighttown" of Joyce's Walpurgis Night sequence in "Ulysses."

The Custom House

From the square, the walker turns southward toward the Liffey, moving down broad Gardiner Street to one of the

great architectural triumphs and historic hubs of Dublin, the Custom House.

The Custom House is regarded as the finest of Dublin's 18th-century buildings, the masterpiece of the gifted architect, James Gandon. It is monumental, extending along Custom House Quay for 375 feet. Its central portico is upheld by four Doric columns, and a graceful dome rises behind it. Arcades flank the portico on either side, culminating in pillared pavilions.

The Custom House's exterior is best viewed from across the Liffey, on George's Quay. Its details of ornamentation, the high-relief statues in the portico's tympanum and other decorations are all striking. It is a reminder that Dublin is a deepwater port, carrying on overseas trade.

The final leg of this first Dublin walk takes the stroller a scant mile upstream. The south side of the Liffey probably affords the best views of the bustling river, its balustraded quays and placid swans. The objective is the Four Courts, for which one must recross the river.

This great structure also is mainly Gandon's work. Begun in 1785, its 450-foot river frontage even exceeds that of the Custom House. Its central, pillared tower supports a fine dome.

The Four Courts was and is Ireland's legal center. It was designed, to serve its various special purposes, in a cloverleaf pattern. Here, too, the Troubles took their toll, and many valuable historical documents at the Four Courts were destroyed. But this striking edifice, like the Custom House, has been restored. It is an appropriate end for the first walk through Dublin, and leaves one not far from the starting point, O'Connell Bridge.

The second walk is more varied and more elegant than the first. It shows the city in its most gracious guise. In the course of it, one views the oldest of all Dublin monuments, Christ Church Cathedral, reputedly erected on the site of a church built by a Danish ruler of the region in the early 11th century.

From College Green

The walk starts at Dublin's hub, College Green, the great traffic crossroads of the city. There is enough here to hold the visitor for a long time. On one side stands a huge 18th-century building that once housed Ireland's Parliament and is now the Bank of Ireland. As one scholarly Dublin chronicler, Stephen Gwynn, observes, it marks "the tender spot where we keep our overdrafts."

The old Parliament House was erected in two stages, the earlier having been commenced in 1729. This was supplemented after 1785 by a recessed front, colonnaded and fenced with a series of Corinthian columns—again the work of James Gandon. Extensions were added a few years later.

Parts of the building are preserved in museum-like integrity. One such is the old House of Lords Chamber, with great tapestries depicting the victories of William of Orange and his followers—the Siege of Derry and the Battle of the Boyne — and busts of later Hanoverian monarchs.

Trinity College lies across College Green from the bank building. Where College Green itself, with its tangle of bus lines and converging traffic arteries, has all the aspects of a highly urban center, Trinity, with its lovely facade and brilliant lawn, is the reverse.

A broad stretch of lawn runs the entire 300-foot width of Trinity's front, behind a high iron fence. On the lawn are statues of two great Irishmen, Edmund Burke and Oliver Goldsmith, both Trinity men.

Great Campus

One enters Trinity's huge campus through a central archway. The quadrangle is wide and long, framed by a succession of beautiful college buildings, mostly classic and Georgian. None of the buildings is Elizabethan, although Queen Elizabeth founded Trinity in 1591. Here are a beautiful chapel, a massive examination hall, a theater and a campanile.

Trinity's first pride, however, is the great library, finely proportioned and containing Ireland's greatest treasure of antiquity, the Book of Kells. This extraordinary illuminated manuscript of the Gospels dates from the Eighth Century. Its intricate, artful workmanship and glowing colors are obviously the creation of a master craftsman.

Hundreds of other early manuscripts, some dating from the Fourth Century, can be seen in Trinity's library. There also are ancient Egyptian papyri, scrolls in Latin and Greek, and a quantity of Queen Elizabeth's letters, plus Shakespeare folios and other rarities.

The Dublin stroller next turns west from College Green into old Dame Street, his destination the City Hall. This building was originally built as the Royal Exchange in the 1770's. Here, too, in the Muniment Room, are ancient historic documents. They include a Royal Charter, dated A.D. 1171, which blandly granted possession of Dublin to the city of Bristol, across the Irish Sea.

The stroller proceeds next to a massive reminder of British rule in Ireland, adjacent to the City Hall. This is the Castle, the seat of English viceroys.

Here is the great drum shape of the 14th-century Bermingham Tower. Here, too, are the exquisitely designed and furnished state chambers of the viceroys, which are open to the public, and the former Chapel Royal. Clustered about the castle's two courtyards are other buildings now utilized for various functions of the Irish Government.

Dame Street now becomes Lord Edward Street, and one soon reaches Dublin's oldest church, Christ Church Cathedral. The church's exterior is plain; its interior is beautiful, with graceful pointed arches and much delicate stonework in the nave and aisles. In the crypt, the oldest part of the church, is the tomb of its 11th-century founder, Strongbow.

The Great Satirist

The walker's next destination, reached by turning south from Christ Church into New St. Patrick Street, is intimately associated with Jonathan Swift, the mordant Irish satirist. Here, at St. Patrick's Cathedral, Swift was dean from 1713 to 1745. It was here that he poured forth his vitriolic protests in defense of the Irish people, and here that he wrote "Gulliver's Travels."

The great dean's tomb stands in the south aisle of the nave, and a fine marble bust of Swift is close at hand. Over the vestry door can be read his own misanthropic epitaph: "He lies where savage indignation can no longer rend his heart."

St. Patrick's has gone through many vicissitudes, including fire and Cromwellian vandalism, but it is now solid and historic. The church, even apart from its historic associations, is most impressive. The Lady Chapel behind the high altar is notable for its stained glass. A lovely little park lies beside it.

Now the stroller enters the most charming phase of his Dublin walk. By turning left into Kevin Street, below St. Patrick's, and proceeding on into Cuffe Street, one arrives at a fine public park. This is St. Stephen's Green, a quarter of a mile square and laid out with groves, lawns, flower beds and artificial lakes dotted with miniature islands.

Stately Homes

Eighteenth-century houses, among the finest in Dublin, rise beside the park. Many of these houses are identified with Dublin history and personalities. Robert Emmet, the Irish patriot, was born at No. 124 in 1778. Several Dublin clubs are situated here, and anyone fortunate enough to be a guest at one of them will be able to view interiors which are the cream of Irish classical decoration.

The final phase of this walk continues its charm. It consists in visiting the unique half-mile of fine Georgian town houses along Fitzwilliam Street and around Merrion Square. One enters Merrion Row from the northeast corner of St. Stephen's Green, proceeding eastward into Lower Baggot Street and on to Fitzwilliam Street, there turning north.

There they stand, in a long, unbroken row of classic facades and doors with elegant fanlights. None of these houses seems very spectacular, like some in London's Queen Anne's Gate, or Boston's Louisburg Square, but still the Fitzwilliam Street - Merrion Square houses have a homogeneity and balanced decorum that is unequaled.

But anyone wishing to view these 18th-century beauties had better hurry, because the state-run electricity corporation has plans to knock down a long row of them to make room for a huge, modern structure. Already, private ownership has in many cases given way to business of-

fices, but these firms have left the exteriors unmarred.

Other strands of the Dublin story happen to be prominent here. Oscar Wilde was brought up in the house of his father, Sir William Wilde, at 1 Merrion Square. Daniel O'Connell lived at No. 58. George Russell, the "AE" of the Irish literary revival, lived here, and so did William Butler Yeats.

Much has been left out of these Dublin walks, for one cannot assimilate a venerable metropolis in a day or two. Numerous sites are not within walking distance. For instance, the famous Martello Tower, where "stately, plump Buck Mulligan" stood in the opening moments of Joyce's "Ulysses," is a long taxi trip to Sandycove, on the coast to the southeast. The Tower is now the Joyce museum.

More 'Ulysses'

To visit the scenes of Paddy Dignan's funeral, that central episode of "Ulysses," calls for trips beginning far out in Irishtown and Ringsend on the city's east border and ending at Glasnevin, Ireland's best-known cemetery, far to the north.

Glasnevin Cemetery, for other reasons, may well be of interest to American visitors whose roots go back to Erin and her turbulent history. For here are the graves of generations of Irish patriots. Here rest many of the "Fenians," members of the brotherhood of that name, including Americans of Irish descent or origin, whose uprising against English rule in 1864 was crushed. Here lie Daniel O'Connell and Charles Stewart Parnell and many leaders of the 1916 Uprising.

July 28, 1963

Israel

Walking the Walls Of Old Jerusalem

By JAMES FERON

JERUSALEM—The walls of this ancient city have seen much over the centuries. They have witnessed the travail of Jerusalem's 16 wars, more than a dozen of which virtually destroyed the city. And now, three years after the last "declared" war, the walls are becoming a means of seeing the city as it has never been seen before.

Teddy Kollek, the Mayor of Jerusalem, is completing the installation of railings, reinforced stairways and other safeguards on top of the walls for visitors who want a new view of the historic Old City. (The walled Old City was for centuries the whole of Jerusalem. Jewish settlements outside the walls grew and spread west until the Six-Day War, when the Israelis took control of the entire city. The Israeli expansion had to be westerly because until June, 1967, the eastern boundary of the Israel-Jordan border was Jerusalem.) Most of the crenelated exterior of the walls is already open, and a walk around them can be a stunning experience: a rear-window view into Old City life.

Perhaps the strongest argument for a walk around the walls is that they provide a strikingly comprehensible guide to the city—something like the view from a Monorail—and in a singularly uncrowded manner. Furthermore, the walk, which is open at all times and can be navigated with great ease, remains unadvertised and therefore largely undiscovered by casual visitors.

Some Words of Advice

A few words of advice before describing the tour in detail: Take plenty of film (the vistas are splendid) and don't try to do the whole two and one-half miles at once (we spent five hours at it, but lingered over everything). A hat and comfortable shoes are also recommended.

There are many points where the walker can reach the top of the walls, and therefore many places to start (or quit). My advice is to begin at Dung Gate, an inauspicious entrance to the Old City but one that offers several practical advantages.

1 DUNG GATE is the recommended starting point for those taking a tour atop the crenelated wall that surrounds the Old City.

260

Starting at Dung Gate, a southern entrance to the city, enables the visitor to see several of the Old City's most noted sites soon after beginning his walk. The gate is also a good place at which to end a tour because it is easy to find a taxi there for those who will welcome a ride back to their hotel. Similarly, ending the tour at Dung Gate means walking the last few hundred yards sharply downhill, a pleasant surprise for the footsore.

The Dung Gate lies at the lowest point in the walled area and, as its name implies, has been used for the removal of rubbish and waste for centuries. Below it, outside the walls, stands Ophel, the City of David. This is thought to have been the original city of Jerusalem thousands of years ago.

Today the low, stone houses of Arabs scattered over the hillside and in the valley below Dung Gate are ignored by tourists overwhelmed with the beauty, color and tradition of more spectacular sites just inside the walls.

Golden and Silver Mosques

Dominating the area immediately to the east of Dung Gate are two mosques, the golden-domed Mosque of Omar (or Dome of the Rock) and the silver-domed Al Aqsa. Both are within a walled compound—a compound filling the southeast corner of the walled Old City—that is sacred to Jews as well as Moslems.

Moslems revere the Mosque of Omar as the place where Mohammed is believed to have ascended to heaven. The sacred compound for Jews is the Temple Area, the place where David and Solomon built their great temples. The western ("wailing") wall of this compound, its huge stones representing the only known remnants of the temples built nearly 2,000 years ago, has been a scene of Jewish prayer for centuries.

It is this mixture of traditions, the intermingling of history, that provides the key to Jerusalem's uniqueness. Thousands of Jewish worshipers visit the "wailing" wall each day. There are the black-hatted Orthodox men of Jerusalem's Mea Shearim area, the large North African families visiting Jerusalem from cities and villages around the country, and the visitors from abroad, many of them feeling a long-buried Jewishness for the first time here at the wall.

Near the "wailing" wall is a path leading up to the Moslem compound. There is no entrance fee, but the gates are closed sometimes by the Moslem guards, generally during times of prayer, and the wall walker should discover the time for prayer before he starts his trip. If his way is barred he can simply begin the circumnavigation in the opposite direction, heading west from Dung Gate.

The mosques themselves are closed to visitors even when the compound is open, which is a pity. There is no way to describe the interior mosaic work, the centuries-old religious symbols, the feeling of Middle Eastern splendor. One gets a hint of it through the barred windows, however, and in the exquisite tiles of the exterior.

The mosques were closed to non-Moslems after Michael Rohan, a Christian religious zealot from Australia, set fire to part of the Al Aqsa mosque several months ago. Rohan, tried and convicted by an Israeli court, is now in a Jerusalem mental home.

Proceeding north through the quiet Moslem compound, the visitor should leave through a gate at the northeastern corner and ascend the wall walk by climbing a stairway just outside the gate. Less than 100 yards to the north atop the wall he will be passing over St. Stephen's Gate, where legend has it that Suleiman the Magnificent ordered the construction of the walls. They were built in both directions and completed a decade later—in 1542—at Jaffa Gate.

St. Stephen's Gate marks the site, again according to tradition, where Jesus entered the city on his final journey. It leads to the Via Dolorosa, with its Stations of the Cross, and finally to the Church of the Holy Sepulchre and Christ's tomb. St. Stephen's Gate played

2 WAILING WALL, its huge stones representing remnants of temples built nearly 2,000 years ago, has been the scene of worship by the Jews for centuries.

Photographs by James Feron

3 AL AQSA MOSQUE was set afire by a religious zealot from Australia several months ago. It is closed to visitors.

4 MOSQUE OF OMAR, in the Moslem Quarter, is revered by Moslems as the place where Mohammed ascended to heaven.

5 ST. STEPHEN'S GATE marks the site where Jesus entered city on His final journey.

a role in more modern history, too. It was there that the Israel Defense Forces penetrated the Old City to bring the three days of fighting in Jerusalem to a close during the 1967 war.

From atop the Old City's eastern walls, the visitor can see the Mount of Olives less than a mile away. To his left, within the city, is the Moslem Quarter. Here he will find rustic scenes out of place in a crowded city. The fields, goats, Arab children and sparse olive trees represent a more biblical than contemporary image.

Railings at Narrow Spots

Walking the walls will appear dangerous to some, but railings have been installed where the path seems to get too narrow for comfort.

Turning the northeastern corner, the visitor faces the Rockefeller Museum, a storehouse of the region's archeology. Its striking stone tower is pitted with bullet and shrapnel holes, another reminder of the Six-Day-War fighting.

Israeli units captured the museum, a Jordanian stronghold, and then came under fire from Arab Legion soldiers on the very walls that now seem so peaceful. Jordanian soldiers recaptured the building temporarily in one of their few successful counterattacks.

To walk along the northern wall of the Old City is to walk a line between decades of Arab Jerusalem. On the outside there is modern life, a bustling street lined with hotels and tourist shops and filled with visitors and residents. On the inside there is something more traditional, and much older.

Tiny gardens behind splendid homes are shaded by ancient trees whose branches reach out and, in some places, cover the city walls themselves. Narrow lanes open into wider streets with shops and open stalls. Men sit sipping coffee, fingering their prayer beads or just talking. Women squat in the shade of inner courtyards, sorting beans—and talking.

The visitor passes over Herod's Gate, also known as Flower Gate or Sheep Gate. This entrance was sealed for centuries until the British conquest of Jerusalem during World War I. It is used little by tourists, who tend to enter the Old City from Arab Jerusalem through nearby Damascus Gate.

At Damascus Gate the wall walker must descend into the streams of Arabs and Jews who pass through this Saracenic archway. Access to the wall between Damascus Gate and New Gate (an undistinguished portal opened in 1887) is barred by the Franciscans,

whose property dominates this sector of the Christian Quarter. Mayor Kollek said a few weeks ago that he hoped to reach an agreement with the Franciscans that would lead to removal of the spiked barriers closing the sector.

Damascus Gate, according to legend, marks the center of the world (so does the Church of the Holy Sepulchre and the Dome of the Rock, according to other legends). The Romans measured the distances from Jerusalem at a pillar behind the gate, thus providing the Arabic name for it—Bab al-'Amoud (Gate of the Pillar). The gate itself, representing a good example of classic Islamic architecture, has an inscription above the arch reading "There is no God but God and Muhammed is His Prophet."

It is easily the busiest of the entrances to the Old City. Arab venders move in and out, leading donkeys or carrying goods themselves, pushing through the crowds of tourists, many of them Israeli.

Saturday, the Jewish sabbath, is the busiest day of the week in the Old City, with families arriving from all over Israel to add to the normal traffic. Railings of the small span leading into the gate are usually lined with young men —the Arabs on one side and the Israelis on the other—ogling the miniskirted Israeli girls.

Walking outside the wall to New Gate takes the visitor uphill along a broad and still unfinished mall. It is part of the green belt Kollek is building around the city, and is itself part of a national park the Israelis plan for a wider belt around the walls.

From New Gate to Jaffa Gate, on top of the wall again, the walker passes behind several convents and churches, and past schools built before the turn of the century, but with basketball courts of more recent vintage. A nun hanging clothing on one of a dozen lines is surprised to look up and see a line of visitors walking past the crenelations, but she shyly returns a wave and continues her labors.

Back to Street Level

The visitor must drop to street level again at Jaffa Gate, this time because a low crenelated wall that once connected the tower on the northern side of the gate with the Citadel on the other side was torn down at the end of the 19th century, reportedly to enable Kaiser Wilhelm to enter the city without dismounting.

The Citadel, or the Tower of David, was apparently built on the site of a Herodian fortress, three of whose bul-

6 THE ROCKEFELLER MUSEUM is a storehouse of the entire region's archeology.

7 DAMASCUS GATE, a typical example of classic Islamic architecture, is the Old City's busiest entrance.

8 JAFFA GATE marks the beginning of the road to Jaffa, which was the port of Jerusalem for thousands of years.

9 TOWER OF DAVID, a fortress-like enclosure at Jaffa Gate, has been made into a museum of Jerusalem's history.

warks were left standing (and are being unearthed by the Israelis) by the Romans when they sacked the city 1,900 years ago. According to some historians, the Romans left those portions of the fort as evidence of the grandeur of the city they had conquered.

The Citadel, a fortress-like enclosure, which was used as a prison by the Turks, a museum by the British and a military position by the Jordanians, has now been reconverted by the Israelis into a museum that depicts the history of Jerusalem. The entire structure is open for inspection, and its topmost tower is worth a visit if for no other reason than its commanding view of the entire city.

Sound and light shows are presented at the Citadel. The show, called "A Stone in David's Tower," is given three times each evening—in English, French and Hebrew.

The performance lasts 50 minutes and admission costs $1.

The wall walker must make another detour at the Citadel, stepping into the Armenian Quarter and then rejoining the wall about a hundred yards south of the tower. (The Mayor has promised to open this portion soon, too.) Reaccess to the wall is through a gate diagonally opposite the Armenian Archbishopric. If this gate is closed, proceed to the southwestern corner of the Old City—another few hundred yards—where there is another stairway to the top.

The outer western boundary wall of the Old City represented the Jordanian edge of no-man's-land in the two decades between the 1948 and 1967 wars. Jordanian soldiers patrolled this portion of the wall, just as earlier soldiers had done against earlier enemies.

Jewish squatters lived in partially demolished houses, since removed, on the Israeli side and occasionally came under Jordanian sniper fire. The Israeli soldiers manning positions at this spot learned to live with their Jordanian counterparts atop the walls.

The southern wall of the Old City contains Zion Gate, which is at one of the highest points in the Old City, and this site—Mount Zion—has held structures holy to Jewish, Christian and Moslem worshipers. They include the tomb of David and the room said to have been where the Last Supper was held by Jesus and His disciples.

Extensive Redevelopment

Inside the southern walls, especially after the visitor passes Zion Gate, is the Jewish Quarter, now undergoing extensive redevelopment by the Israelis. The area was badly damaged during and after the 1948 fighting and then occupied by Arab squatters, many of them

HISTORIC TUNNEL—Visitors walk within the wall, in an area that "embraces origins of much of the world's religious history."

10 ZION GATE, at one of the highest points of the Old City and final stop on the tour, is the site of David's tomb.

refugees from what had become Israeli Jerusalem.

The Arabs were removed after the 1967 war to make way for reconstruction of the ancient religious and secular buildings. New housing, in the style of the old quarter, is also being built. One of the first to move into the area was Yigal Allon, the Israeli Deputy Premier, who occupies a handsome new stone structure near the bottom of the hill leading to Dung Gate.

The view from this portion of the wall is one of the most extraordinary in Jerusalem. The golden- and silver-domed mosques of the Moslem Compound loom up to the east, and beyond them the Mount of Olives. Below and to the south are Arab villages, their soft outlines nestled in the hills. Within the walls, to the north and west, there are the rebuilt Jewish institutions and, beyond them, the towers and domes of the city's Christian shrines.

It is a city that has embraced the origins of much of the world's religious history. It has also seen its share of mankind's more dramatic moments. The sites recalling these events can be seen and, in some cases, inspected throughout Jerusalem, but they can best be appreciated within the context of the city from atop the ancient walls surrounding it.

August 2, 1970

WALKING TOUR OF FLORENCE

A Mile-Long Stroll Through Ancient City on the Arno Unveils a Panorama of Renaissance Art and History

By GEORGE W. OAKES

FLORENCE, Italy — A walk through the center of Florence—which, although filled with historic and artistic interest, will cover only perhaps a mile at most—should start at the magnificent Duomo or cathedral and its graceful Campanile or bell tower.

This walk is designed to take the tourist to those palaces, squares, churches, art galleries and other scenes that any visitor to Florence must see, even if he has only a few hours—the Bargello, Piazza della Signoria, Palazzo Vecchio, Ponte Vecchio, the Uffizi and Pitti Palaces. In the course of visiting these wonderful sites and collections, the stroller will, as well, be wandering through narrow streets past medieval buildings that will put him in the mood to appreciate all the more the many great works of Renaissance art and moments of history with which Florence abounds.

"Mary of the Flowers"

Second in size only to St. Peter's in Rome among Italian churches, the Duomo was built mostly during the thirteenth century. It is formally named Santa Maria del Fiore, from the lily in the city's coat of arms, which in turn derives from the tradition that the city was founded in a field of flowers.

Before entering the cathedral, one should halt at one side of the square in front of it to view its multicolored marble facade, Brunelleschi's large and lovely dome and, beside the west front, Giotto's graceful Campanile, an architectural triumph of perfect proportions. Michelangelo considered the dome such an achievement that, more than a century afterwards, when designing the dome of St. Peter's in Rome, he remarked that it would be "larger but not more beautiful" than Brunelleschi's in Florence.

Masterpieces

The wanderer in old Florence will be impressed by the immensity of the interior of the dome, where Savonarola preached. But even more impressive are the masterpieces to be found in this vast church—the unfinished Pieta by Michelangelo, bas-reliefs by Ghiberti, frescoes by Ucello and the one by Michelino of Dante explaining "The Divine Comedy."

If the tourist feels energetic, he should climb to the summit of the dome where he will be rewarded by a fine panorama of the city. The ascent of the Campanile, nearly a hundred feet lower, is a more artistic experience on account of the superb details of its classic design as seen from the stairway.

Opposite the Duomo stands the Baptistry, Florence's oldest building, dating from about the year 1000. Octagonal in shape, it is constructed of green and white marble in Romanesque style. Here, indeed, is one of the great artistic treasures of Florence. These include its world-renowned bronze doors with their gilded bas-reliefs. On Ghiberti's East Door, which Michelangelo called "worthy to be the gate of Paradise," is a marvelous group of panels representing scenes from the Old Testament.

This superb piece of sculpture took the artist twenty-seven years to finish (1425-52). After studying the details of these unique doors, a visitor enters the Baptistry, where the thirteenth - century pavement and fourteenth-century mosaics in the cupola are noteworthy.

Early Charity

One leaves the cathedral square by the Via dei Calzaiuoli (named for the stocking-makers in the sixteenth century). Just before starting along the street, a small building with Gothic arches, on the corner, should be scrutinized. This is the lovely Loggia del Bigallo, at one time the home of a Florentine benevolent society for abandoned children. After a stroll down this extremely busy street for about two blocks, the tower-like Church of Or San Michele appears on the right.

This was originally built as a grain market, and is remarkable for the marble statues placed by various trade guilds in the niches of the outside wall, works of such great Florentine sculptors as Donatello, Ghiberti and Verrocchio. One should also note, in the interior, the great Gothic Tabernacle by Orcagna.

Now, a left turn almost opposite Or San Michele brings the stroller along the Via Dante Alighieri to the Casa Dante, the house where the poet is supposed to have been born. In a few moments one comes to the Via del Proconsolo. Here, a half block to the left leads to the Palazzo Pazzi Quaratesi, one of Florence's finest fifteenth-century palaces. Retracing one's steps for a block or so leads to the medieval Palazzo del Bargello (open 9:30 A. M.-4:40 P. M. week days; Sundays 9:30 A. M.-1 P. M.; closed Tuesdays). Its battlemented thirteenth-century tower rises above this urban fortress which as a prison, place of execution and residence of the city's chief magistrate, and later, its police chief, was the locale of some of the bloodiest scenes in Florentine history.

Great Collection

The Bargello Palace is now a national museum, particularly renowned for its unrivalled collection of Tuscan sculpture.

The spacious courtyard is enclosed by a colonnade. On climbing the grand staircase, the colorful coats of arms of Florentine chiefs of police are visible on the wall overhead. On the "great balcony" there is an exhibition of some of Donatello's finest work, especially his wonderful figures of the young David and St. George.

Art lovers will be interested to find here Giambologna's famous statue of Mercury. On other floors there are examples of such great Florentine art as sculptures by Michelangelo, Cellini and Verrocchio, terracottas by the della Robbias, and frescoes by Giotto.

From here, one might well make one's way briefly into modern times again, with a visit to the Mercato Nuovo, the "new market," Florence's main market for flowers, lace and straw goods, always a bustling, lively place. To reach it, the route is to the right from the Via del Proconsolo into the Via Condotta, and along this street and across the Via dei Calzaiuoli, continuing a block farther in the same direction in the Via Porta Rossa. It is a pleasant change to wander among the market stalls with all their bright flowers and their other merchandise on view.

Old Palace

Then one heads for Florence's best-known landmark, the fortress-like Palazzo Vecchio which dominates the splendid Piazza della Signoria. To reach the Piazza, the stroller goes back to the Via Calzaiuoli, where the objective is only a few steps to the right.

The Piazza was the center of political and social life in medieval and Renaissance Florence. The bitter struggles between Guelphs and Ghibellines are associated with this square. Here Savonarola was executed, as is noted on a bronze plaque near the Fountain of Neptune.

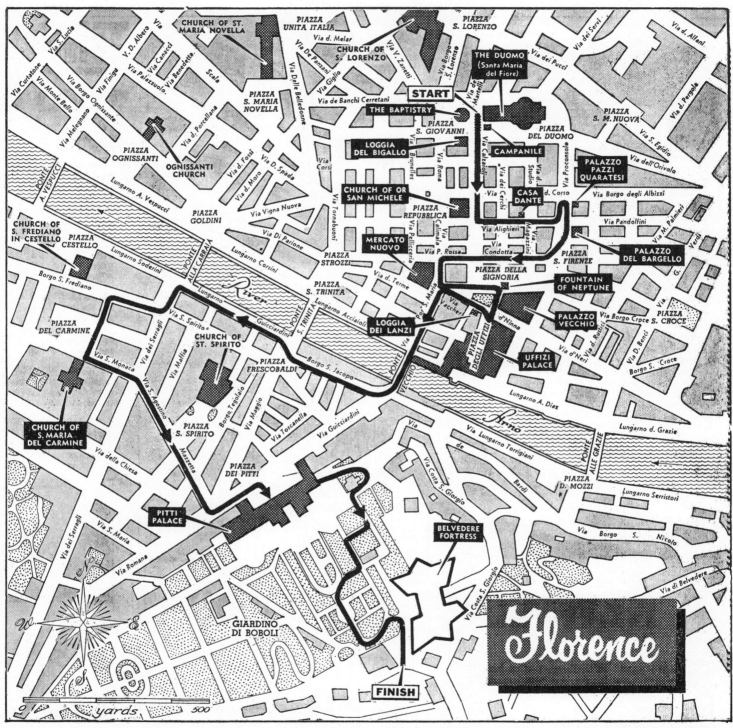

The Palazzo Vecchio is now the seat of Florence's municipal Government. It used to be the residence of the presiding magistrate during the Florentine Republic. Later it was the seat of the Medici dukes. So, much history clusters around it.

The bell in the thirteenth-century tower called the citizens of Florence to arms or to conclave. To gaze at the Palazzo's severe façade is to reflect on the extraordinary contrast between the two great towers of the city, the warlike Palazzo and the spiritual Campanile.

A Medici Palace

Great halls and sumptuous apartments, furnished with fine works of art, give a visitor an idea of the palace as it was in the days of the Medici. On entering, he should linger for a few moments in Michelozzo's beautiful courtyard. The huge Hall of the Five Hundred on the upper floor is one of the most splendid in all of Italy.

Almost next to the Palazzo Vecchio stand the three high semicircular arches of the Loggia dei Lanzi. Built in the fourteenth century as an assembly place for public meetings, the Loggia contains the greatest outdoor exhibit of Renaissance sculpture to be seen anywhere in the world.

Here, Cellini's masterpiece, Perseus, and Giambologna's Rape of the Sabines are two

of the great works that adorn this unusual open-air vaulted arcade.

The visitor is now at the entrance to the narrow Piazza degli Uffizi, between the Loggia and the Palazzo Vecchio. The Uffizi Gallery, one of the world's finest collections of paintings, is very tempting, but probably should be saved for another occasion when one has not been satiated with intensive sight-seeing. However, to view the Botticellis, Leonardos, Raphaels and many other masterpieces of Italian art in this gallery is imperative for anyone visiting Florence.

Leaving the Loggia, the stroller turns left into the Via Por Santa Maria to the Ponte Vecchio. This unique fourteenth-century bridge is the oldest in Florence and characteristic of the old city because of the jewelry shops that line it and overhang the Arno.

Approaching the bridge and gazing upstream, the stroller has a fine view of San Miniato on the crest of a hill above the city, surrounded by groves of cypresses. The Cellini bust in the bridge's piazzetta reminds one that the Ponte Vecchio has always had a goldsmith's shop. One should notice the enclosed passageway above the shops that connects the Uffizi and Pitti Palaces.

View of Ponte Vecchio

After crossing the bridge, the stroller's route is to the right, on the Borgo San Jacopo as far as the Ponte San Trinità. From this new bridge, built since the war, there is a good view of the Ponte Vecchio. Now, one continues downstream on the bank of the Arno along the Lungarno Guicciardini to the next bridge. Here one turns left about fifty yards and then right on the Borgo San Frediano about a hundred yards. A sharp left will lead into the Piazza del Carmine to visit the Church of Santa Maria del Carmine.

Masaccio Influence

The purpose of this little excursion is to see great masterpieces of Masaccio, who revolutionized the art of painting as a forerunner of the Renaissance by introducing three-dimensional concepts and thus influencing Raphael, Michelangelo and artists of all succeeding ages.

Masaccio's series of remarkable early fifteenth-century frescoes in the Brancacci Chapel of the life of St. Peter ranks among the finest examples of Florentine art.

On leaving the church, a right turn leads along the Via Santa Monaca, across the Via dei Serragli into the Via San Agostino, and on to the end of this street. On the left is the massive Palazzo Pitti (open 9:30 A. M.-4:30 P. M.).

Although not as great a collection as the Uffizi, the Pitti possesses a number of Raphel's works, as well as sixteenth and seventeenth century Italian masters, a gallery of modern art, lavish royal apartments and a museum featuring fine workmanship in silver, ivory, porcelain and enamel.

Nature vs. Art

Since by this time the visitor has done considerable sight-seeing, he should postpone visiting the Pitti. Instead, he should enjoy the delightful experience of sauntering leisurely through the luxuriant sixteenth-century Boboli Gardens (9 A. M.-6:30 P. M.). Permits to enter are obtainable at a gate at the left side of the Pitti Palace.

Strolling about the Boboli's hillside, the walker will discover many splendid fountains, statues, grottoes and secluded nooks, as well as beautiful flower beds, formal terraces and a profusion of oleander, ilex, and pines.

The famous May music festival takes place here. The path to the amphitheatre beside an alley of cypress is particularly scenic and there is a splendid view over the city.

If one goes farther, to the Belvedere, the hills of Fiesole are visible in the distance. This beautiful park is the appropriate spot for a tourist to end his walk by contemplating many of the artistic glories of Florence as they lie before him in a panoramic vista.

May 20, 1962

A WALKING TOUR OF MILAN

Italy's Most Modern and Bustling City Also Preserves Much Medieval and Renaissance Grandeur

By ROBERT DEARDORFF

MILAN, Italy — Although Milan appears as one city on a tourist's map, it is really two. And it is so unlike any other city in Italy that many of the people who were born here prefer to think that they are not Italians at all—or, better, that they are the only Italians. They cultivate the notion that they are living in a brisk oasis of 1,500,-000 busy people, an oasis that is surrounded by a financial and cultural wasteland that makes up the rest of the country, all of which is hopelessly lost in the past, while they alone plunge into the future.

In this attachment to their city and to tomorrow in general, the Milanese resemble many ardent New Yorkers when they stroll along their western outpost of civilization, Riverside Drive, and gaze across toward the mysterious and not-worth-bothering-about badlands that stretch from the Hudson to the Pacific.

A tourist who talks to a native Milanese about the local way of life, or one who walks about noting the buildings, coffee bars, stores and the articles for sale, will see for himself that this is an unusual city to find in Italy. For one thing, it is rich, and, for another, it is modern. Milan is the home of Italian skyscrapers, and progress is its watchword.

In the last fifteen years, the skyscrapers have created a second Milan with a distinct and bustling center of its own. Often, when local people speak of it, they give the impression that they are prouder of these slender structures of reinforced concrete than they are of their traditional tourist attractions— the Duomo, Leonardo da Vinci's painting of The Last Supper and La Scala Opera.

Two For One Price

An American not unused to skyscrapers at home may take a different view. But even so, here he has two cities for the price of one, and he can easily stroll between them—from the Middle Ages into what local residents like to call tomorrow, even though it exists today.

The Duomo is the center of the medieval city. It is a huge fourteenth-century cathedral that is the largest church in Italy after St. Peter's in Rome. Whenever Milan's boosters have to concede this fact, they point out that theirs is far different from the Roman church, with many more spires and lots of intricate stone carving. The best way to start a walk through these two Milans is here, not in the cathedral itself, but on its roof.

One takes the elevator, whose entrance is from the street at the back of the nave. From the front of the church roof, the visitor will see the solid, compact houses of the old city just ahead, and, from the rear, the soaring towers of the new city in the distance.

The square in front of the Duomo is marked by an equestrian statue of Vittorio Emanuele II, the king who took the city from Austria and added it to modern Italy in 1859. To the

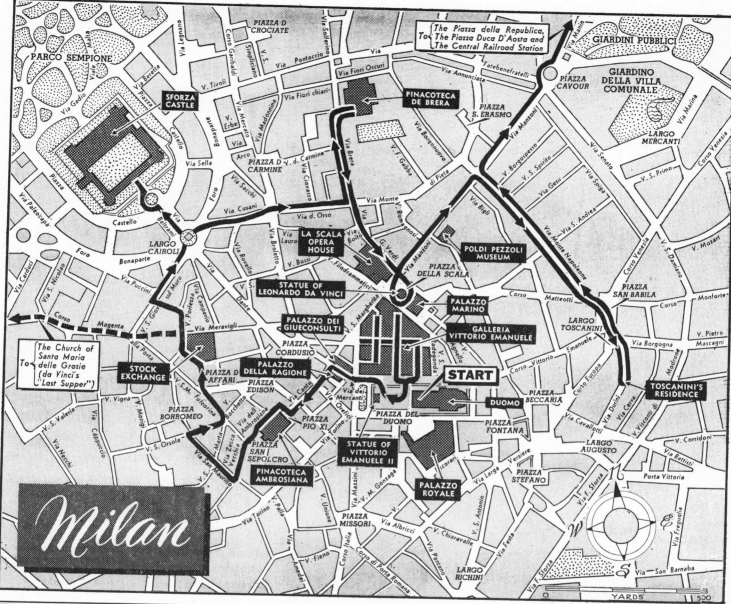

Milan

left is the former royal palace; to the right is the Galleria Vittorio Emanuele, a long, covered arcade lined with shops, cafes and restaurants.

Split Personality

If a stroller, back on the street, glances at the cafe to the right of the Galleria entrance, he will see a symbol of the split personality of this non-Italian Italian city. Inside, especially just before mealtimes, it resembles a New York cafeteria. People are standing up and eating as fast as they can in a rush to do something else. Outside, it is a Continental sidewalk cafe in which other people sit for hours over a cup of cof-

fee.

Many of the latter are tourists and Italians from the rest of Italy, who are clinging to their customs in defiance of the bustle of the north. Many, but not all, for the Milanese think of the Galleria as their drawing room. And, whenever they are inclined to forget their pellmell rush to make money, they, too, like to come here and linger over a drink or an excellent meal.

The visitor should step into the Galleria for a moment and proceed past the cafes, book shops, clothing stores and travel offices. At the far end of it, framed by its round arch, he

will see a reminder of the intellectual bustle that was the Renaissance—a statue of Leonardo da Vinci. Milan's passion for the future is no modern phenomenon.

Back in the Piazza del Duomo, it is best to plunge immediately into the Middle Ages by turning right and walking straight ahead into Via dei Mercanti. Immediately on the right, at No. 2, is the Palazzo dei Giueconsulti, which was constructed in 1562 around the tall, slender tower that dates from the thirteenth century.

Renaissance Skyscraper

It was one of the skyscrapers of its day. In the beginning,

this building was a college that trained young men in jurisprudence. Today, it houses the Milan Chamber of Commerce.

Opposite it stands another handsome building, which also was begun in the thirteenth century. This is the Palazzo della Ragione, or Palace of Justice. Its ground floor consists of two broad, open aisles that once were used for public meetings.

Turning left at the end of this structure, the stroller meets an abrupt surprise. He is standing in Piazza dei Mercanti, a medieval square that is quiet, remote and far removed in time from the insistent rush of traffic just behind him. There is an

ancient well in the center and, back of it, two more beautiful buildings. They are the black and white marble Loggia degli Osii, built in 1316, and the Palazzo delle Scuole Palatine, which was put up after a fire in 1644.

Crossing the square and Via Orefici outside it, one should go straight ahead into Via Cantu, a narrow street on which gold and precious stones have been bought and sold for centuries. It leads to Piazza Pio XI, another reminder of the fact that Milan's enthusiasm for progress is firmly rooted in the past, skyscrapers notwithstanding. At No. 2 stands the first library in Europe—it was founded in 1609—and also Pinacoteca Ambrosiana, a small museum that is worth a brief visit. The museum contains several Renaissance paintings, including works by da Vinci and many of his sketches, as well as some architectural studies for the Duomo.

Old Section

At the end of the museum building, the stroller should turn left along Via dell'Ambrosiana cross Piazza San Sepolcro, continue along Via Zecca Vecchia and veer right into Via San Maurillo, which leads to Piazza Borromeo. These streets are old and narrow and are lined with solid, handsome buildings whose high, spacious entrances lead into tree-shaded courtyards. These, in turn, enclose the tranquility of another era.

Turning right along the piazza and left at Via San Maria Fulcorina, the street at the end of it, one passes Piazza degle Affari (Square of Businesses). This is the home of many merchandise markets, including that of the silk trade, and of the stock exchange at No. 4. Milan is the center of the commercial and banking life of Italy.

Ancient and Modern Mixture

For a few moments, the stroller emerges from medieval surroundings, crosses bustling Via Meravigli into Via Giovanni sul Muro and comes to huge Largo Cairoli. This is a mixture of ancient and modern, with sturdy Sforza Castle, with its dry moat and crenelated walls, to the left behind a maze of unmedieval, whirling traffic.

Begun in 1358 and considerably enlarged since, the castle was once part of the defensive wall that surrounded the city. It now contains a museum that is filled with ancient sculpture, armor, tapestries, furniture and paintings. Stretching out behind it is a spacious, shady park, at the end of which stands the Arch of Peace. This was begun by Napoleon in 1807, when Milan briefly belonged to France.

Leaving Largo Cairoli by way of Via Cusani, the stroller soon comes to Via Brera. If he turns left into it, he will notice still more evidence of the twin poles of past and future that govern life in this split-personality city. The street contains a number of picture galleries, all of which sell modern art. The more modern the art, the better, for art is a popular highway along which many well-to-do Milanese race into tomorrow. Since it is modern, the collector considers it a good investment, and for that reason modern galleries in Milan are as plentiful as antique shops in Florence.

Sharing this street with them is the Pinacoteca de Brera, a huge sprawling museum that is crammed with Renaissance art. Without wasting time on modesty, local residents say that it and the famous Uffizi in Florence are the best in Italy. True or not, it is worth a special visit.

Retracing his steps along Via Brera, the visitor continues to Piazza della Scala, where a statue of Leonardo da Vinci by a nineteenth-century sculptor faces the famous opera house. Since there is a cafe here and others are available in the Galeria across the square, this is a convenient place to pause for a rest and a drink and to prepare for the stroll into the city's future.

Before setting out for there, however, one should take a very brief detour and walk toward Palazzo Marino, a sixteenth-century palace that stands opposite the opera house. This is Milan's Town Hall. It has a magnificent courtyard and, on the ground floor, Sala dell'Alessi, a room richly decorated with stuccos and paintings.

Major Shipping Street

To leave Piazza della Scala, the stroller follows wide and busy Via Manzoni, one of the major shopping streets of the city. He is putting the past behind him now, but, since this is a very old city in spite of its modern tone, it is difficult to escape completely from antiquity. As a result, it is not surprising to arrive almost immediately at the Poldi Pezzoli Museum at No. 12. Formerly a private mansion, it contains collections of tapestries, furniture, statues and Renaissance paintings.

Visitors will discover that it is worth stopping here for a few minutes, not only to see these things but to inspect the building itself.

Its series of handsome, quiet rooms symbolizes the wealth that all the rest of Italy associates with Milan, the solid, substantial wealth that has built, and is building, the skyscrapers that lie ahead.

The museum is not the only building along this street that recalls the money for which this city is famous. Via Manazoni is lined with elegant shops, their windows displaying fashionable merchandise from Italy and the rest of Europe. The local elite come here to buy the best Italian silks, the best Italian leatherwear, the most expensive French perfumes, the finest Swiss chocolates, Italian candy, pastry and ice cream. And here they come to visit more galleries selling modern art.

At Via Monte Napoleone, the stroller detours briefly to the right. Once an old road, this is now another aristocratic shopping street. In a few moments, one arrives at Piazza San Babila, a square of the old town that has been almost completely rebuilt. At No. 20 Via Durini, one of the streets leading out of it, Arturo Toscanini lived.

Milan's Central Park

• Returning to Via Manzoni, the visitor turns right and continues to Piazza Cavour, another bustling intersection. Crossing it, he will find on his right the Giardini Pubblici, a shady landscaped garden that looks a bit like Central Park, complete with playing children and a small zoo. He continues along the edge of it, keeping to Via Manin. Lined with new buildings, it, too, contains a reminder of the past — a beautiful fountain dedicated to St. Francis. Not far ahead can he seen the famous skyscrapers.

Once the stroller reaches the end of this street and enters the immense square, Piazza della Repubblica, he can see the skyscrapers even better. They stretch along Via Vittor Pisani, a broad boulevard-canyon that leads to Piazza Duca D'Aosta, with the central railway station at the end of it.

Since the best way to look at a skyscraper is to view it from a distance, the conscientious stroller may want to pause here before the panorama of tall buildings and whizzing traffic. Then, having paid homage to the new city, he can take a taxi back to the cramped streets and patrician buildings of the old one around the Duomo.

Before leaving Milan, one also should ride along Corso Magenta to the Church of Santa Maria delle Grazie to see da Vinci's The Last Supper. This, of course, is included on all conducted tours. Although this painting is blurred by time, it is still one of the world's memorable works of art and no doubt will continue to be so long after the pride in skyscrapers has passed.

March 25, 1962

A WALKING TOUR OF ROME

Colorful Old Trastevere, Visited for Its Restaurants At Night, Is Equally Exciting for Daytime Tourists

By GEORGE W. OAKES

ROME — Across the Tiber, away from the main part of this ancient city, is Trastevere, a section that few tourists visit in the daytime. This has long been one of the poorest quarters of the city. It is an area of narrow streets crowded with people, of street venders shouting their wares, of old houses and winding alleys, and of colorful restaurants that are popular with residents and tourists alike during the evening hours.

A rewarding daytime walk through Trastevere can start at the oldest bridge over the Tiber, the Ponte Fabricio, near the Theater of Marcellus. Before crossing the span, one might wander along the embankment and examine the bridge's high, graceful arches.

The Ponte Fabricio is said to date from the days of Julius Caesar. It leads to the Isola Tiberina, a small, boat-shape island, which has a pleasantly quiet atmosphere. To the left, one sees the gardens on the island, with the Aventine Hill in the distance. Tall trees stand like sentinels at the tip of the island. Behind, on the embankment, one can see the dome of Rome's main synagogue, in the old Ghetto section.

Left to Santa Cecilia

After crossing the Ponte Cestio from the Isola Tiberina to the far bank, turn left and walk along the river for about 50 yards to the Via dei Vascellari. Following this route, one comes to the intensely interesting Church of Santa Cecilia. Just before the church, however, there is a most fascinating house on the left. It is a remarkable building because so many different architectural styles are superimposed on one another.

A few yards past the house, there is a square on the right. From this point, one can see the church's 12th-century campanile, leaning slightly, above the medieval houses. Opposite is a popular and lively restaurant, where one can dine outdoors and listen to strolling singers.

Priests in the church will show visitors the crypt (open 9 A.M. to noon, 4 to 7 PM.) Here one can view the remains of several rooms of an early Roman residence. In the third century, when St. Cecilia lived here an attempt was made to kill her by scalding; however, she survived, only to be executed later.

The artistic treasures of the church are the ninth-century mosaics in the apse and the group of 13th-century frescoes on the ceiling of the sacristy. There also is a lovely statue of the saint below the altar. The fine cloister adjoining the church is said to be the oldest in Rome.

Turn right from the front of the church down the Via di San Michele, then turn right on the Via di Maddalena dell Orto and left on the Via Anicia to the Piazza San Francesco d'Assisi. Saint Francis stayed in the church in this square when he visited Rome in 1219.

Past Shops and Cafes

At this point, turn right along the Via di San Francesco a Ripa, past typical Trastevere shops and cafes. Cross the broad Viale Trastevere, filled with market stalls, to the Piazza di Santa Maria in Trastevere. A fine fountain brightens the center of the square.

The facade of the 12th-century Church of Santa Maria in Trastevere (open 6:30 A.M. to noon, 4 to 7:30 P.M.), with its Ionic columns from Egypt and its colorful mosaics, is one of the most impressive in Rome. Magnificent mosaics of the 12th and 13th centuries are over the apse and great arch.

From the church, take the Via della Paglia on the left to the Piazza di San Egidio; it is the second turning on the right. Then veer left on the Via della Scala, a delightful old street. The walker is now in a colorful old section of Trastevere. Continuing on the Via Lungara beyond the arch, one arrives at the Villa Farnesina, on the right-hand side of the street at No. 230.

This graceful Renaissance villa (open 10 A.M. to 1 P.M., except Sunday and Monday) was built in the 16th century as a summer residence for the art patron and banker, Agostino Chigi. His sumptuous fetes and banquets were famed for their luxury and gaiety.

Frescoes by Raphael

The quiet gardens planted with high cypress trees provide a suitable approach to the gallery where Raphael painted some of his loveliest frescoes. There, in the long gallery with the large windows, is The Story of Psyche, whose lifelike figures on this superb fresco were designed by Raphael, and painted by him and his pupils.

In an adjoining room is an exquisite fresco of the graceful Galatea, which was executed by Raphael in 1514. There is a story that Michelangelo, curious to see Raphael's work, slipped into the room in disguise and, when the custodian was not looking, drew a lovely black-and-white charcoal head on the wall at the north end. This sketch is clearly visible today, and it is probably one of the most unusual and valuable calling cards ever left by a visitor.

Interior Bright

The large windows of the villa brighten the interior, so that these magnificent frescoes can be seen in the radiant colors which have survived so remarkably over more than four centuries.

Before leaving the villa, wander around the delightful gardens with their tall cypresses, oleanders and little fountain. It is an ideal spot to rest for a bit.

After visiting the Villa Farnesina, return to the Piazza di Santa Maria in Trastevere to lunch at one of the square's moderately expensive trattoria (informal restaurants).

From here, one can wend his way out of Trastevere and up to the Janiculum. From the Piazza di Santa Maria, keep left on the Via della Paglia to the Via Venezian, then right on Via Luc. Manara and up the steps to the Via Garibaldi, leading to Janiculum hill.

Climb the hill to the church of San Pietro in Montorio; its terrace affords a breathtaking view over Rome. In the small courtyard of the adjoining monastery is Donato Bramante's Tempietto (temple). If one rings the bell in the far corner, an English-speaking monk will show the visitor about.

'Finest Example'

This tiny, domed building of the early 16th century rests on 16 Doric columns. Its circular construction is such a perfect example of the finest Renaissance architecture that it has been copied in countless

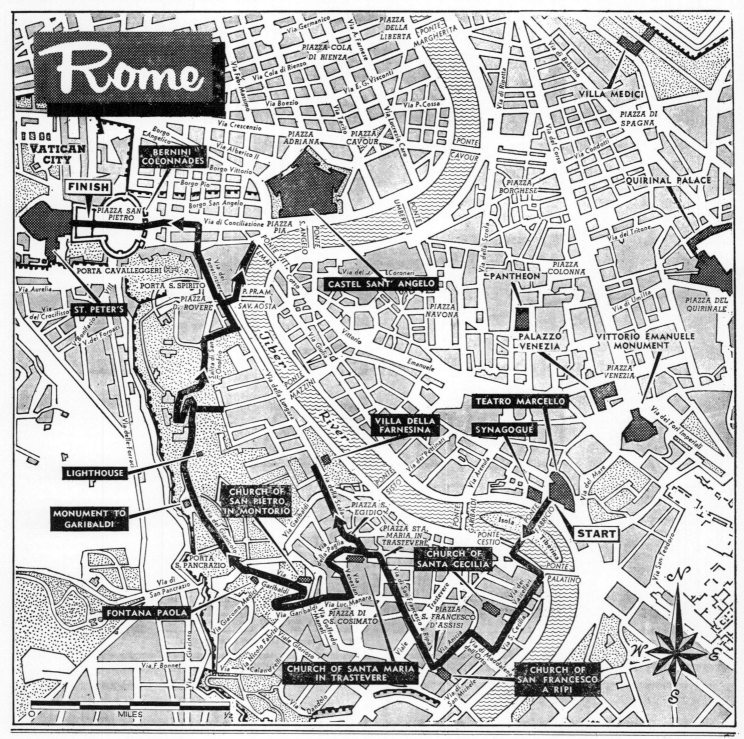

Rome

VATICAN CITY

FINISH

BERNINI COLONNADES

PIAZZA SAN PIETRO

PORTA CAVALLEGGERI

ST. PETER'S

PORTA S. SPIRITO

CASTEL SANT' ANGELO

PANTHEON

VILLA MEDICI

PIAZZA DI SPAGNA

QUIRINAL PALACE

PIAZZA DEL QUIRINALE

LIGHTHOUSE

MONUMENT TO GARIBALDI

CHURCH OF SAN PIETRO IN MONTORIO

VILLA DELLA FARNESINA

TEATRO MARCELLO

SYNAGOGUE

PALAZZO VENEZIA

VITTORIO EMANUELE MONUMENT

FONTANA PAOLA

PORTA S. PANCRAZIO

CHURCH OF SANTA CECILIA

START

CHURCH OF SANTA MARIA IN TRASTEVERE

CHURCH OF SAN FRANCESCO A RIPI

MILES

churches, including the Chapel of the Sacrament in St. Peter's. The dome of the Capitol in Washington was also strongly influenced by Bramante's design.

From this point, continue along the Via Garibaldi to the large Fontana Paola, whose water is carried by a subterranean aqueduct built by the Emperor Trajan. On the right, through a gateway, one approaches the crest of the Janiculum ridge. As the tourist strolls along the path, under a double lane of sycamores, the sweep of the Seven Hills of Rome unfolds below. Farther along, palm and cypress trees shade the walk.

In a few minutes, one will reach the statue erected to the Italian patriot, Garibaldi. One should pause at the terrace and try to pick out the more prominent features of the landscape — the Capitol, the Pantheon, the Quirinal Palace the Villa Medici, the Pincian gardens, and the Alban hills in the distance.

A walk here, in the late afternoon, with the soft light of the setting sun falling on the ocher-colored buildings, is particularly dramatic.

Rome seems more remote from the Janiculum than from

the Pincio and, perhaps for that reason, more alluring. The view is more encompassing and the walk along the ridge more varied. Then, too, the vistas are frequently framed by the swaying branches of palms. The Eternal City seldom seems more artistic and beautiful than from the Janiculum.

View of St. Peter's

Stroll a couple of hundred yards beyond the Garibaldi monument toward the light-house for the finest view of all — the glorious dome of St. Peter's.

If one wants to end the walk here, a bus at the Garibaldi monument goes to the bottom of the Janiculum.

Otherwise, continue beyond the lighthouse and descend the steps on the right. From the terrace below, there is a fine view of the Castel Sant' Angelo on the Tiber. Turn right into the Salita di San Onofrio and, after about 50 yards, go down a long flight of steps on the right to the avenue along the river.

Just to the left is the Piazza della Rovere. Cross over to the bridge. At this point, one can obtain another striking view of the Castel Sant' Angelo a huge circular structure that was originally Hadrian's mausoleum. It is interesting to note the architectural contrast between this massive fortress with its parapets and the modern buildings just to the right.

End of Walk

Return to the Piazza della Rovere and, at the far side go under an archway into the Via S. Penetinziere. From there, take a half-right turn into Via Cav. S. Sepulcro to the wide Via di Conciliazione. A couple of blocks to the left and one will reach the stupendous Square of St. Peter's, about a 15-minute walk from the Piazza della Rovere.

One should make a special visit to St. Peter's, the Sistine Chapel, the rooms of Raphael and the Vatican Museum, for these are among the world's great treasures. These sights require at least half a day in themselves. Meanwhile, where could one find a more magnificent place to end this stroll, than this square surrounded by Bernini's majestic semicircular colonnades?

June 14, 1964

CLIMBING THE SEVEN HILLS OF ROME

ROME—A good way to see Rome from its beginning days to the spectacular present is to travel along the seven hills on which the city was founded more than twenty-five centuries ago. It is an easy, rewarding itinerary and, unlike the usual hill-climbing, is not tiring.

The only thing to guard against is getting lost in the hills. Their original contour has been changed by layers of civilization and by history's builders. Most of them, although holding their ancient monuments, have been criss-crossed with modern streets. As a matter of fact, the twentieth century explorer frequently will not realize he has moved from one classic summit of the city to another.

The Palatine and the Capitoline remain isolated from the swirling events of today. The Aventine, too, has been slow in losing its identity. But the others—the Viminal, Esquiline, Quirinal and most of the Caelium—are almost lost in the crowd of Roman landmarks.

An ideal starting-point is on the Aventine, at the southern side of the city, near the Tiber. From the Aventine the route leads eastward and follows a small circle until the river is again reached on the north.

Actually there are two Aventine hills, the Great and the Little. The Little Aventine shelters monuments of the past and present: the ruins of the Baths of Caracalla and the headquarters of the United Na-

THE HILLS OF ROME—Shaded pathway indicates general route recommended for sight-seers.

tions Food and Agriculture Organization. Several ancient churches, including St. Sabina, are on the Great Aventine.

The Caelium Hill, adjoining the Aventine, extends from the Colosseum to the old city walls. At its base is the basilica of St. John Lateran and at the very top is the Villa Celimontana, a beautiful park of ancient Rome.

Ancient Race Course

In front of St. John Lateran is Rome's tallest obelisk, more than 135 feet high. At one time it was part of the Circus Maximus, the ancient race course near the Aventine. Pope Sixtus V (1585-1590) had it moved to St. John's. In recent centuries about a score of obelisks have been installed in various parts of Rome for decorative purposes.

After the Caelium, the trip through the hills of Rome begins to get engulfed in city traffic. The Via Merulana, a wide busy street filled with shops, connects the Caelium with the Esquiline on which the Basilica of St. Mary Major rises. From St. Mary Major, the Via Depretis skirts across the top of the Viminale, where the Ministry of the Interior and the Rome opera house are found, and leads the way to the Quirinal Hill, site of the presidential, formerly royal, palace.

The Viminal-Quirinal hills, nowadays, are crowded with a splendid medley of modern shops, ancient buildings and unusual views. This is the introduction to Baroque Rome. A fascinating view in this zone is from the intersection of Via del Quirinale and Via Quattro Fontana. In three directions, distant obelisks can be seen: those in front of St. Mary Major, the Quirinale Palace and the Trinita dei Monti Church atop the Spanish Steps.

Another view, toward the

northeast from this intersection, is without an obelisk but nonetheless magnificent. That is because the Porta Pia, a mile away, is sharply silhouetted. The Porta Pia was a gate of Rome in other days, and the part of its facade facing the Via Venti Setembre was designed by Michelangelo.

Rome's most famous hills is the Capitoline, rising near the Piazza Venezia. Foundation stones of the temple to Jupiter are in the Via del Tempio di Giove, behind the handsome City Hall, the Campidoglio, and also in the museum there.

One spot on the Capitoline that cannot be visited without special permission is the City Hall tower. Permission is obtainable from the municipal Antiquities and Fine Arts Department, Via della Tribuna di Campitelli. From the tower there is a dramatic view of all Rome spread out in a giant circle. The tower itself is of interest, too. One gets a close view of he mechanism of its great clock and of its nine-ton bell, the

patarina. The *patarina* is the only bell in Rome which is not in a church tower. It is tolled rarely.

Mountain of Steps

Next to the City Hall is the Ara Coeli Church, with its mountain of more than 100 white-marble steps. Just how old the church is, no one knows. In the sixth century it was already considered ancient. During the Middle Ages, the church was used as a kind of public forum, and the Senate met in it.

One other spot with an unusual view is the little garden on the Via del Tempio di Giove. The staircase, at the right of the City Hall, leads to it. The garden is a unique setting for viewing the Tiber and the nearby Palatine Hill with its Roman Forum.

The Palatine is ranked as the city's most important hill because it marks the beginning of Rome. Romulus is said to have used his plow to line out the boundaries of the Rome-to-be along the slopes of the Palatine.

Several huts, dating to the time of Romulus, are among the hill's guarded treasures.

At its base lie the remaining outlines of the Forum. The belief is that the original Romans lived on the seven hills and used the Forum as a public meeting place. An admission fee of 200 lire (35 cents) is charged to visit the Forum. Atop the Palatin is a small Renaissance-style park, set among the imperial ruins. It looks down on the Tiber and across to the Vatican, and is an ideal spot to pause after crossing over the city's Seven Hills.

Actually, modern Rome has more hills than ever. With its constant expansion, it has reached out to include in its boundaries hills like the Janiculum and the Vatican on the west side of the Tiber, which used to be beyond its original circle of seven.

Parioli Hill, in the far northwestern section of Rome, is now the city's smart residential area, with modern apartment houses and handsome villas. Monte Mario, also in the northwest but

across the Tiber, is the city's highest hill—500 feet.

Besides the natural hills that Rome has added to its collection, there are artificial ones. They generally are the sites of ancient ruins on which fortresses were built in the Middle Ages, and later palaces. Among these artificial hills are Monte Citorio, near the Piazza Colonna, the site of Parliament; Monte Savello, near the Piazza Venezia, now a Renaissance palace atop an imperial Roman theatre, and Monte Cenci, near the Tiber.

The most artificial of all the hills of Rome is Testaccio, just beyond St. Paul's Gate in the southern part of the city. It is a fairly green-covered hill over 150 feet high, built up over the centuries from ancient rubbish and broken pottery discarded there. The mountain of debris grew and grew. Until recent times, Testaccio was a popular center for festivals. Helping to keep alive its popularity, no doubt, are the wine cellars in the hill.—D. M.

March 19, 1961

A WALKING TOUR IN VENICE

Despite the Tradition of the Gondola, Strolling Remains Best Way to Study the Historic Adriatic Port

By GEORGE W. OAKES

VENICE — Every visitor looks forward to touring Venice, the city of canals, by water, preferably in a gondola. But the way to explore enchanting byways and really feel part of this unique community, built on more than a hundred islands and so little changed today from its proud past, is on foot. After all, Venice is a pedestrian's world, as well as a gondolier's.

A walker can stroll through tiny streets, linger by a bridge over a back canal, discover fascinating bits of the old city, away from the tourist crowds —in other words, lose himself in the atmosphere of this "Queen of the Adriatic." A walker is his own guide. He can take his

own time. He has the unusual experience of not being harassed, as in practically every other great city of the world, by motor traffic.

Even in midsummer, Venice is not too hot to spend a couple of hours in strolling. The strong Italian sun beats down only on the *piazzas* and *campos*—plazas and open spaces. The streets and alleys are so narrow that, most of the time, they furnish shade.

Here, then, are two separate routes for walking tours, neither one very long, since Venice herself is fairly compact. The first might be called a glimpse of the "classic" Venice, with its splendid historic buildings and monuments as well as its present workaday activities. The second is through a

leading residential district, although there, too, lovely baroque churches and sumptuous *palazzos* dating back over the centuries are to be seen, rich with history.

From the Great Piazza

The first walk starts, the best time for setting out being about four in the afternoon, from the center of Venetian life, the Piazza San Marco. It is assumed that the visitor has already inspected that glorious public square, with its campanile, the magnificent and glowing Byzantine-influenced church of St. Mark; the Ducal Palace—once the Doges' Palace when Venice was a republic; and its other picturesque wonders.

At the northwest corner of the Piazza, a passageway leads

into the Bacino Orseolo, the Orseolo Basin. This small, open body of water is a livery-harbor for gondolas, bobbing up and down, waiting for customers. Beyond lies the Rio Orseolo, with a crowded street alongside. Here the stroller will brush past porters with crates of provisions, notably tomatoes, on their heads.

Straight ahead, over a bridge, the Calle Goldoni commences, reaching in a few hundred yards the Campo San Luca, lined with antique shops. One turns to the right here for a single block to find the Calle dei Fabbri, which, leftward, leads directly to the Grand Canal.

A short distance away looms the famous Ponte Rialto, a name known throughout the world since Shakespeare's day. This

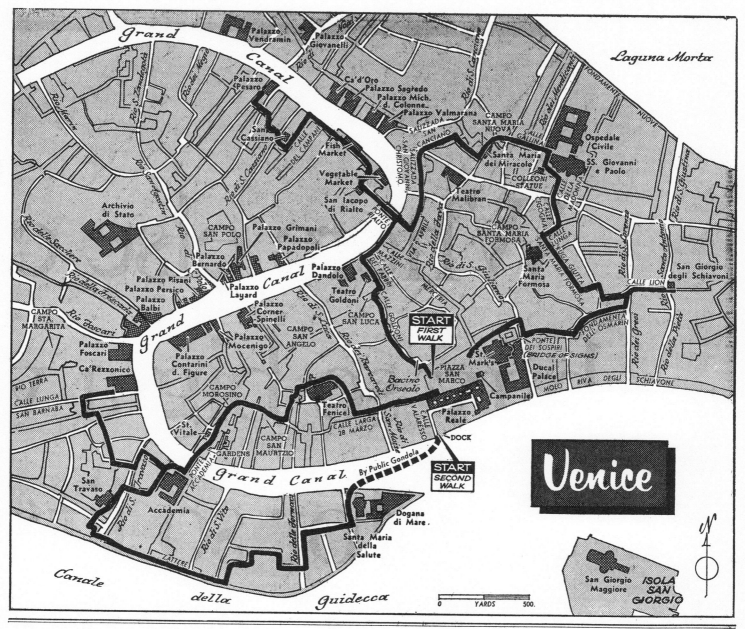

On the map:

Grand Canal · Laguna Morta · Palazzo Vendramin · Palazzo Giovanelli · Palazzo Pesaro · Ca'd'Oto · Palazzo Sagredo · Palazzo Mich. d. Colonne · Palazzo Valmarana · CAMPO SANTA MARIA NUOVA · Ospedale Civile · San Cassiano · Fish Market · Santa Maria dei Miracolo · Il COLLEONI STATUE · SS. Giovanni e Paolo · Vegetable Market · San Iacopo di Rialto · Teatro Malibran · Archivio di Stato · Rio di S. Cassiano · PONTE RIALTO · CAMPO SANTA MARIA FORMOSA · San Giorgio degli Schiavoni · CAMPO SAN POLO · Palazzo Grimani · Palazzo Papadopoli · Santa Maria Formosa · CALLE LION · Palazzo Bernardo · Palazzo Dandolo · Teatro Goldoni · Palazzo Pisani · Palazzo Layard · CAMPO SAN LUCA · Palazzo Persico · Palazzo Balbi · Palazzo Corner Spinelli · START FIRST WALK · PONTE DEI SOSPIRI (BRIDGE OF SIGHS) · CAMPO STA. MARGARITA · Rio Foscari · Palazzo Mocenigo · CAMPO SAN ANGELO · St. Mark's · FONDAMENTA DELL'OSMARIN · Palazzo Foscari · Ca'Rezzonico · Palazzo Contarini d. Figure · PIAZZA SAN MARCO · Ducal Palace · RIO TERRA · CAMPO MOROSINO · Bacino Orseolo · Campanile · MOLO · RIVA DEGLI SCHIAVONE · CALLE LUNGA · SAN BARNABA · Teatro Fenicel · Palazzo Reale · St. Vitale · CAMPO SAN MAURTZIO · CALLE LARGA 28 MARZO · GARDENS · DOCK · By Public Gondola · START SECOND WALK · Grand Canal · San Travaso · PONTE ACCADEMIA · Accademia · Dogana di Mare · Venice · Santa Maria della Salute · ZATTERE · Canale · della · Guidecca · YARDS 0 500 · San Giorgio Maggiore · ISOLA SAN GIORGIO

great stone landmark was designed in 1588 by Antonio da Ponte, and its approaches rest on 12,000 piles.

On the Rialto Bridge

One should pause for a moment while crossing the Rialto bridge and look down at the Grand Canal, teeming with ferries, launches, motorboats and gondolas. The spectacle is diversified and exciting, and on either side of the canal stretches the line of great *palazzos*, those ornate and beautiful private palaces of Venetian nobility and wealth in other days.

Across the bridge, one plunges into a hive of activity, the city's main food markets. Swerving to the canal-side beyond the church of San Iacopo di Rialto, one approaches the vegetable market and then the big fish market. There, on open tables, are all kinds of sea food. James Morris, in his excellent book on Venice, describes the scene:

"A glorious, wet, colorful, high-smelling concourse of the sea . . . its stalls are lined deliciously with green fronds, damp and cool: and upon them are laid in a delicately tinted, slobbering, writhing, glistening mass, the sea creatures of the lagoon."

Another five minutes' walk, weaving inland around the church of San Cassiano and then zigzagging back to the canal, brings the sight-seer to the Palazzo Pesaro, now an international gallery of modern art, in which nineteenth and twentieth century works, not only European but American, are assembled.

Via 2 Aprile

Now one retraces one's steps to the Rialto, crosses it, and goes, turning left in the Via 2 Aprile — April 2 Street — past the central post office. Along the way, street vendors will be shouting, and even singing, their wares.

Here, over a bridge lies the busy Salizzada San Giovanni Crisostomo, the saint known in English as John Chrysostom, "John of the Golden Mouth." The objective here is a gem of Venetian Renaissance architecture, the Church of Santa Maria dei Miracolo, built toward the end of the fifteenth century.

This church is reached by turning off the Salizzada San Giovanni Crisostomo, beyond a bridge, to the right into the

Salizzada San Canciano, and right again, past the Campo Santa Maria Nuova. The Church of St. Mary of the Miracles is small and stands off by itself, one side being washed by a canal.

It is an example of lovely design and exquisite ornamentation. Porphyry and serpentine —the first dark red and purple stone, the second mottled green —light up its exterior. Within, the walls of the nave are precious marble. The choir stalls and the vaulted ceiling are equally fine.

Beyond the church is a little bridge. It produces one of those inimitable vistas with which this city is so notably endowed and which give Venice its painters' quality: the russet-brownish houses, the ivy-covered terraces, red awnings overhanging a tiny tree-lined garden and, just ahead, another graceful, iron-railed bridge. In the canal below lie barges filled with freight. A lavishly decorated gay gondola slips past with a wedding party, bride, bridegroom and family.

Swinging to the right again, and then straight on, one approaches one of Venice's greatest basilicas, the Church of SS. Giovanni e Paolo, Saints John and Paul. In front of it stands what has been called the greatest equestrian statue ever sculptured, Verrocchio's Bartolomeo Colleoni.

Dynamic Equestrian

Colleoni was a famous fifteenth century *condottiere*, or soldier of fortune who eventually became the generalissimo of Venice. Dynamic in his saddle while his battle charger practically prances off his pedestal into the canal ahead, Colleoni is the epitome of ruthless, controlled force.

Here is a good place to pause. One can sit at a cafe on this big *campo*, take a cooling drink and study the details of the militant and arresting statue.

This is the turning place of today's walk. One is to return, with a side trip or two, to St. Mark's Square, leaving the *campo* by the Calle della Madonna and the Calle Cigogna and turning into the Calle Lunga to find the Campo Sta. Maria Formosa, passing the great church of that name, and a colorful fruit and vegetable market.

One proceeds southeast into the Ruga Giutta Santa Maria Formosa, then eastward across a couple of bridges and through the Calle Lion to the furthest east point of the afternoon's expedition on foot.

The objective is a small church, San Giorgio degli Schiavoni where there are much admired paintings by the late fifteenth-century Venetian painter Vittore Carpaccio. They are rich in color, luminous and animated. But since the lateness of the afternoon may hamper the best views of these works, another expedition, a special one, might be a better answer.

Follow the Crowd

At any rate, to return to the Piazza San Marco, one retraces one's steps along the Calle Lion, turns left when across the second canal, and proceeds along the quai to the Fondamenta dell' Osmarin. Turning right along this curving route, one will perceive other wayfarers bound for St. Mark's and a stranger will not go wrong by following the crowd. It is neither a long nor a difficult stretch, and just before one comes to a canal behind the Ducal Palace there is a fine view of the historic Bridge of Sighs.

Arrival at the great Piazza San Marco will be just in time to relax at one of the celebrated cafes there, to listen to the music, and to contemplate the late sunlight illuminating the multicolored mosaics of the portals of Saint Mark's. High above them, the four world-renowned gilt-bronze horses, that date from the time of Alexander the Great, will also be bathed in the sun's glitter.

Thus ends the first Venice promenade, back where it started.

The second recommended Venice walk is through a less famous part of the city, directly across the Grand Canal at its mouth. One takes a *traghetto*, a public gondola, generally used by Venetian citizens, from the foot of the Calle Valaresso to the dock close to the church of Santa Maria della Salute. Inside this massive seventeenth-century baroque church, so widely visible from across the canal, are several Titians and Tintorettos.

Outside again, one discovers that this area is filled with small parks and attractive houses. One makes one's way across this peninsula which is bounded by the Grand Canal on the north and the Canale della Giudecca to the south. A generally southern course brings the stroller to the Zattere or embankment beside the broad Giudecca Canal.

Several hundred yards on, walking westerly, a glance to the right reveals the church of San Travaso with its fine lawns in front. From here, a few steps lead to one of Italy's greatest art galleries, the Accademia, largely devoted to the Venetian school.

The Grand Canal has no quais along the water. The great palazzos line the canal-side. Therefore, to inspect such a splendor as the Ca' Rezzonico, a majestic, late baroque structure designed in the seventeenth century by a very eminent architect of the day, Longhena, one has to wind one's way through several streets and over several small canals.

Where Browning Died

The Ca' Rezzonico is considered by many the most splendid residence in Venice. Now open to visitors, it contains an exceptional collection of eighteenth-century paintings, furniture and tapestries, as well as frescoes by Tiepolo.

It was here that the English poet Robert Browning, that lover of Italy, died in 1889 (although his tomb is now in Westminster Abbey). Complete rooms in the palace have been restored to portray Venetian life among the patricians of the eighteenth century.

Verdi's Opera House

By way of the Accademia Bridge one can cross the Grand Canal and the walk continues beside a delightful garden, with views of other fine palazzos.

Beyond the garden, one turns right from the Campo Morosino in search of the Teatro Fenice, one of the most exquisite opera houses in the world, where the young Verdi had some of his most spectacular triumphs—and a failure or two.

Next door is one of Venice's best restaurants where, in propitious weather, one can lunch or dine under a grape arbor. From here, any one of several byways that lead generally eastward will return the stroller quickly to the Piazza San Marco.

April 30, 1961

CAMPING OUT IN HIGH STYLE

Expeditions on Foot From Katmandu to Mount Everest Offer Modern Conveniences in Primitive Surroundings

By ELIZABETH KNOWLTON

BOSTON — A very good friend wrote me last winter that "three of us are off to Nepal next week, to trek to the foot of Mount Everest. Why not meet us in Katmandu when we get back?"

"This," I thought, "is obviously the time for me to go to Nepal."

I happen to be a mountain-lover and climber. Hence, Nepal has always fascinated me, not only as a primitive and exotic country, but as the land with the highest mountains in the world. Everest, the greatest of all, stands astride Nepal's Tibetan border.

I used to read about earlier Everest expeditions by way of Tibet, because Nepal was closed to foreigners. Now Tibet has been taken over by the Chinese, and Nepal has been opened. So, Nepal's capital, Katmandu, has become the gateway to Everest.

The Outdoor Type

My friends were a pediatrician, a biochemist and a school superintendent. They were all active, outdoor women, experienced in mountain walking and climbing. But it was quite a trip they had in mind.

The round-trip distance between Katmandu and Everest is more than 300 miles, and the trail crosses a series of mountain ranges. It frequently climbs and descends 3,000 to 5,000 feet in a day, at altitudes of between 4,000 and 14,000 feet.

My friends' time was strictly limited. To make their objective, they had to walk steadily for a month, with no days off, averaging 10 miles a day. The youngest member of the party was in her 50's; the other two were over 60.

I flew to Katmandu from New Delhi. In India, the hot season had begun, and the parched plains were already swimming in the red heat-haze of summer.

Ahead of Schedule

In Katmandu, a British tour organizer brought me word of the trek. "They're a day ahead of schedule," he reported. "I'm going out in my Jeep to the end of the road to meet them tomorrow morning."

The organizer, a former colonel of Ghurka forces, was stationed in Katmandu for many years. He is an experienced mountaineer, having led three Himalayan expeditions.

Now he arranges treks of 20 days or more—to explore the villages, valleys and passes of Nepal. He provides everything but personal clothing; in other words, the tents, provisions and an English-speaking Sirdar, or leader, of the expeditions.

Since African safaris are now completely motorized, this is probably the last chance in the world to tramp and camp in a country so primitive that virtually all travel and transport are still on foot.

Bright as a Daisy

The next morning, about two hours before my friends were expected, I heard familiar voices in the garden court. There they were, in shorts and freshly laundered cotton shirts, and with rucksacks on their backs. They looked as bright and blooming as the proverbial daisy, and were full of enthusiasm about their trip.

"How did you ever get back so soon?"

"We allowed two days for delays and emergencies, and only used one. That day it was snowing on the high passes, and our porters were barefoot."

"You must be pretty tired now."

"We're feeling simply wonderful! Worse luck, we didn't even lose any weight.

"It was the most luxurious camping you ever imagined. Individual tents you could stand up in! Cots with sponge-rubber mattresses! Aluminum folding armchairs!

Afternoon Tea

"And when we got in, afternoon tea was always ready for us. And such good meals. There was even some fresh food, including chicken, eggs and vegetables, from the villages. I never ate so much in my life."

"Any trouble anywhere?"

"None. Just a perfect trip!"

After my friends left, I arranged a little Himalayan trip of my own—an overnight excursion with two porters for a glimpse of the people and mountains. From the very top of Nawakot, a 9,000-foot ridge on the east side of the Katmandu Valley, it is possible to see the whole dramatic sweep of the main range of the Himalayas—200 magnificent miles of it. The ridge is 18 miles from Katmandu.

I woke to a clear, sparkling day. As our Jeep honked its way through the little villages of the Katmandu Valley floor, I saw all their inhabitants enjoying the sun and moving about the village streets.

After an hour or so, the car began to climb Nawakot, in long loops and switchbacks. Well below the top of the ridge, the road ended at a gate guarded by soldiers, since there is a military post on Nawakot.

My two porters proceeded to pile the entire contents of the Jeep on their backs. These included, among other things, two tents with poles, sleeping bags, pads and blankets, food, big cooking pots and dishes, a container with a gallon or two of water, all our warm extra clothes and a large kerosene lantern.

Thus loaded, we started up the trail to the higher parts of the ridge. Soon, we could look over the other side. There were ranges and ranges of bare and eroded hills, with great valleys between, one or two miniature villages and little threads of trails. But an afternoon curtain of clouds was closed across the snow peaks.

Back in America, I had dreamed of an overnight camp in the Himalayas. I had hoped to find an open grassy knoll on some mountaintop on the very edge of the world, with a screen of trees and bushes behind me for privacy, and in front the great snow mountains. Here, my dream came true.

Near sunset, the curtain of clouds began to open here or there, affording tantalizing glimpses of one or another incredibly high point of shining whiteness.

When I woke at dawn the next day, the giants were out clear. They stood along the whole line of the horizon, and even the tiny points of Everest, Lhotse and Nuptse—tiny at a distance of more than 100 miles—were easily identifiable.

Indescribable

I shall not attempt to describe the indescribable. All that morning, I walked along the summits of the long ridge. There was a foreground of rhododendrons with dark green leaves and scarlet blossoms, or a screen of bare slender branches, or just a sheer drop beside me. And always in the sky were the snows.

I found it hard to leave that place. Already, I am thinking of plans for going back.

September 5, 1965

Puerto Rico

A STROLL IN OLD SAN JUAN

Heritage of the Spanish Main Prevails in the Restored Streets of Puerto Rico's Historic Colonial Capital

By ROSELLEN CALLAHAN

SAN JUAN, P. R. — This island metropolis, with its unsurpassed climate and galaxy of famous resort hotels, has another special attraction — its gaudy, grim, swashbuckling history that goes back more than 400 years.

A good deal of that history of bloody conquest, piracy and international rivalries revolved around what is now called Old San Juan, the narrow islet that guards the entrance to the city's splendid harbor, San Juan Bay.

It was Ponce de Leon who first established a Spanish settlement on the Puerto Rican mainland. That was in 1508. But in 1524, the Spaniards moved across the bay and began fortifying the rocky barrier—actually a little island—opposite.

Today, the "Historic Triangle," occupying the western end of the island, with eight streets stretching east and west and about as many intersecting them, is so concentrated that it is one of the most convenient in the world for a sightseeing stroll through history.

Restoring Old Spain

After four centuries of history, there has been a decade of painstaking restoration of crumbling, deteriorated landmarks here. Although the Spanish heritage prevails in the ancient fortifications, which even those English sea rovers Hawkins and Sir Francis Drake could not take, United States Army and Navy installations are to be found. But old Spain lingers on in the fine old mansions and churches and vistas.

A narrow channel separates this islet from San Juan's luxury beachfront hotels, high-rise apartments and bustling office buildings to the east, but a visitor will find that more than a blue ribbon of water sets it apart.

In Old San Juan, walks are narrow, and the hilly streets, paved with blue cobblestones brought as ballast in Spanish galleons, are shared with good humor by snail-paced cars and unhurried pedestrians. It is a place of tiny tree-shaded plazas, of faded 18th-century Spanish Colonial houses, of central patios ablaze with bougainvillaea and of a concentration of art galleries, museums, restaurants and shops.

After dark, the old city becomes a blend of Montmartre and Bohemia. From the courtyards and second-floor balconies of attractive small bars and night clubs, the beat of African voodoo singers, Spanish guitarists, flamenco dancers and steel bands can be heard until dawn.

It is a city in renaissance. Ten years ago, visitors to Puerto Rico avoided the area as they would a plague. Longtime residents had moved out to the suburbs. Slumlords took over their town houses, and subdivided spacious rooms into little apartments for a dozen families.

Conservators

Happily, a group of civic-minded citizens formed a society for the conservation of San Juan Antiguo. Through their efforts, legislation was passed to provide financial assistance to restore the old quarter and establish the Institute of Puerto Rican Culture to direct the program. Today, a walk through the old city is a most rewarding experience.

A convenient place to start is the Plaza de Colon, which can be reached from the Condado section of beachfront hotels by taking the No. 10 bus. Directly up the hillside street—Calle Norzagaray—from the plaza is Castillo de San Cristobal, built by the Spanish in 1633 to protect the land approach to the island. It is open daily from 8:30 A.M. to 4 P.M.

The view from the deep embrasures at the top of the fortification is panoramic. To the east appears the dome of the white marble capitol and, farther on, the outlines of "Hotel Row." To the west, the old city wall roughly scallops the ocean side, and the green roofs of La Perla, one of San Juan's few remaining slums, cascade down the cliff to the ocean's edge.

The Missing Sentry

By leaning over the parapet, one can see "Garita del Diablo," a "haunted" sentry box projecting out over the boiling surf. Legend has it that a soldier assigned to this lonely duty disappeared one night and was kidnapped by the devil. But historical researchers believe that a beautiful slave girl captured his fancy and he went A.W.O.L.

From Cristobal, it is a 12-minute stroll along the breezy Boulevard del Valle to the entrance of Fort Brooke, the site of El Morro Fortress, which was built in the 16th century to protect the city from sea attacks. On the right, there is a close-up of La Perla, which is scheduled to be razed and replaced by a park as restoration progresses throughout the area.

On approaching the gate to Fort Brooke, one finds on the left a building that serves as United States Army headquarters. It was erected in 1523 as a monastery of the Dominican friars, and is a superb example of Colonial Spanish monastic architecture.

The walk from the Fort Brooke gate to El Morro, for centuries Puerto Rico's chief defense, bisects an unusual golf course. Fairways dogleg around ancient walls; the moats and arches serve as hazards, and the "greens" are mocha-brown soil. A stroller may have to dodge a golfer's occasional slice or hook, but the walk under the shade of the breeze-bent pines lining the road is one of the pleasantest of the day.

Free Tours

Free guided tours through the fort leave at 9:30 and 11 A.M. and at 2 and 3:30 P.M. They take about 45 minutes. If one's schedule does not conform to these times, the park guide will supply the San Juan National Historic Site brochure; this gives the needed background for a do-it-yourself tour.

The panorama from the topmost level of El Morro is worth the climb up the steep canyon ramps. On the harbor side lies Goats Island, once a leper colony and now a park. In the distance is Caparra, where Ponce de Leon founded the original Spanish settlement in 1508.

At the entrance to the harbor is the disturbing sight of a freighter that missed the narrow channel and impaled herself on a reef. On the left, one will glimpse Casa Blanca, the ancestral home of the Ponce de Leon family, and La Fortaleza, the fortress-residence of the governors of Puerto Rico for the last four centuries.

Architectural Gem

Returning to the Fort Brooke gate, one turns to the right in Calle Cristo (Cristo Street), where, just ahead, stands the Church of San Jose. This is one of the real architectural treasures of the Western Hemisphere, and one of the oldest.

The church was begun by Dominican friars in 1523 on land granted them by the Ponce de Leon family, and is a rare example of Isabelline gothic architecture. It houses numerous religious and historical relics.

Cristo Street is the heart of the Old San Juan restoration

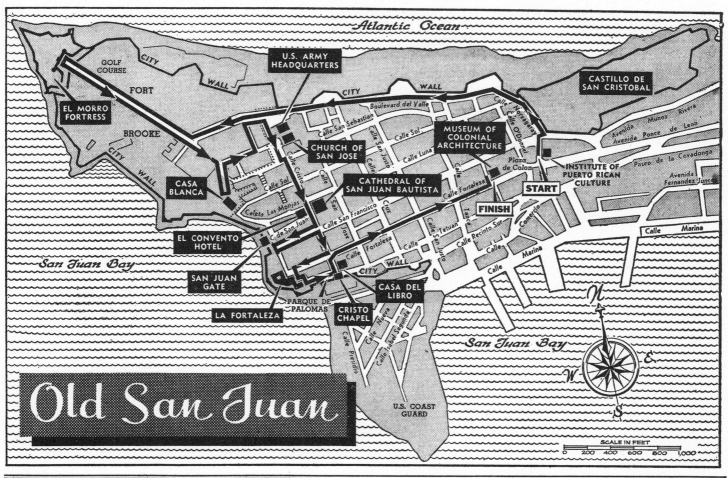

Old San Juan

movement. Here are excellent restaurants, and it is a good idea to reach this point at lunch time.

A favorite meeting place of San Juaneros and visitors is the patio, shaded by a níspero tree, of El Convento Hotel, two blocks downhill from the plaza. In the 17th century, the hotel building was a Carmelite convent; it was later abandoned, and then deteriorated into a garage for trucks. An American man of wealth saved the structure from demolition, and spent $3.5 million to turn it into one of the most unusual hotels in the hemisphere.

Many of the convent's original architectural features have been imaginatively utilized. What was once the chapel is now a spacious dining room with a 50-foot vaulted ceiling. Leaded glass windows, patterned in colorful Spanish coats of arms, tint the room with a muted glow. Rising above the outdoor dining patio are tier upon tier of vine-covered clois-

tered galleries, off which are guest rooms and suites.

There is a great deal more to see in Old San Juan than can be covered leisurely and thoroughly in a day. At this point, it is a question of how much time is to be divided between looking at historic treasures and shopping. Cristo Street, with short detours to the left and right, offers the perfect combination.

Across the street from El Convento is the Cathedral of San Juan Bautista — St. John the Baptist — where Ponce de Leon's remains are entombed. On request, visitors are shown the cathedral's collection of treasures, which include a rare Renaissance statue of the Madonna and a 16th-century chalice.

Gate of the City

Opposite the cathedral, Caleta de San Juan — San Juan Lane, as it were—branches off Cristo Street. A short walk along the lane brings one to the

San Juan Gate, which was once the main entrance to the city from the sea. Here, conquistadores debarked after the long voyage from Spain, and climbed the hill to the cathedral to offer thanks for their safe arrival.

Back in Cristo Street, one finds a concentration of the finest examples of the restoration program. The buildings stand out from their grubby neighbors because of their fresh coats of pastel paint, their intricate ironwork and their balconies with gleaming mahogany balustrades. Many of the restored structures are shops offering Puerto Rican handicrafts and art works for sale.

The Institute of Puerto Rican Culture has been responsible for restoring many of these buildings. It also has inspired and assisted owners of other houses in the area to join the movement of repairing, adapting and restoring.

The institute, in many cases, has provided the means for do-

ing this at cost. For example, it has supplied antique tiles and hardware, mahogany shutters and even great beams of the heavy West Indian timber called ausubo, which formed the rafters of the original houses. The institute has also supplied architectural designs to follow, and trained artisans to help in returning dilapidated houses to their original Spanish Colonial elegance.

There are numerous fine shops. They deal in local ceramics, sand and wood sculpture and other handiwork; antiques, such as "santos," or carved figures of the saints, and, of course, modern, high-style couture.

Continuing down Cristo Street, the stroller turns right on Fortaleza Street and goes one block onward to La Fortaleza. This is the oldest governor's mansion in continuous use in the Western Hemisphere; it has housed 170 governors over a period of more than 400 years.

The Fortaleza's history is en-

grossing. The first fort built here to defend San Juan, it was started in 1533, burned by the Dutch in 1625, restored and then enlarged several times.

The structure still has two 16th-century towers, and a stretch of walls that are among the earliest examples of military architecture in the Americas. Also, it commands a magnificent view of San Juan Bay.

Instead of returning to Cristo Street by way of Fortaleza Street, a pleasant variation on leaving the Governor's mansion is to turn off to the right and climb the flight of stairs some hundred yards ahead. At the top of the stairs one comes upon a secluded little park, the Parque de Palomas; there the visitor can rest on a tree-shaded bench and watch the ships sail into San Juan harbor.

The park's far end joins Cristo Street, and here is the Cristo Chapel, an 18th-century oratory with a magnificent hand-wrought silver altarpiece. The chapel was erected by the friend of a young horseman, in thanksgiving for his miraculous survival after he had raced his steed over the cliff at this spot.

Back in Cristo Street again, one views the Casa del Libro, the House of the Book. It is another early restoration. Here, in the cool of the breeze-swept galleries, are exhibits of the printing arts, and documents dating from the time of Queen Isabella of Spain.

Next, one should turn eastward on Fortaleza Street to encounter still more handsome restorations. Here, too, fine shops occupy what once were elegant Spanish town houses. In their quiet patios women visitors may grow ecstatic over the showings of colorful Caribbean fashions and art.

Farther along Fortaleza Street, still going eastward, the Museum of Colonial Architecture can be the last stop on the tour. Only a block farther lies the Plaza de Colon, from which one has made a circuit of the principal sights of this compact and historic area.

May 9, 1965

BARCELONA WALKING TOUR

The Ancient Quarter of the Great Catalan Metropolis, Called the 'Barrio Gotico', Evokes Dramatic Past

By MARI DE OLIVA

BARCELONA, Spain — To the visitor eager to combine the whirl of today and the peace of yesterday, wide-screen cinema and Gothic cathedrals, Barcelona is an answer.

Modern Barcelona combines industry and commerce, luxury shops, new hotels and restaurants. Flower stands line the Ramblas where the Barcelonese, their wives and children, love to stroll. Buses and trams are jammed. Motorcycles and scooters in special parking lots look like horses at the starting post. There is an international "feel" to Barcelona. But it is old Barcelona, the area called the Barrio Gotico, the Gothic Quarter, that is ideal for a half-day stroll.

Roman ruins are frequent in the Barrio Gotico. Old Roman walls are found here and remnants of an antique esplanade surrounded by pedestals. An Augustan Roman Temple, of which four columns remain, was on the once highest pinnacle of Barcelona. Around it, the town, entirely walled in, spread out.

The Cathedral

We can start at the thirteenth-century cathedral, one of the finest examples of Gothic Catalan architecture. The buildings encircling it shade the light and give it a mysterious air. Noteworthy are the upper galleries where women sat during the services, separated from the men in the nave below.

The church's thirty-two chapels were, and are still, kept up by various *gremios* (guilds) which supply flowers and their suitable decorations. The visitor will be struck by the many wax hands, faces and dolls hanging at the gates of each chapel. These are *ex-votos*, symbols of gratitude for some favor received.

The visitor descends to the fourteenth-century crypt and admires the baptistry in which, tradition says, the first American Indians brought to Spain by Christopher Columbus were baptized. Then he emerges on the narrow street of the Condes de Barcelona, facing the Palacio Real Mayor, the Great Royal Palace of the eleventh century.

The cathedral's wall here shows a small door by which the Spanish kings entered it. A museum, called the Museo Mares, also has its entrance on this small street and houses a superb collection of polychrome wooden carvings and other early works of art.

Aura of the Past

All is romantic in this area. Twentieth century noise and bustle are left behind and forgotten. The aura of the past stirs the imagination when one rounds the building of the Archivo de la Corona de Aragon. Bearing left, one arrives at the beautiful Plaza del Rey, the Square of the King.

On the right the Gothic church of St. Agatha, originally the Royal Chapel, has one entrance leading into the great royal palace. One facade belongs to the Salon del Tinell, one of the most beautiful rooms in Europe. Until 1940, when the Town Hall bought it from the Religious Order of Santa Clara, it was a private and little-known place of worship for the nuns of that Order.

Roman Ruins

Under the Plaza del Rey, a new series of excavations has recently been undertaken, and Roman ruins have been brought to light as a result. The corner stairs to the right of the Tinell Facade witnessed Christopher Columbus' return to Spain after his first voyage to the New World. Here the navigator presented the Catholic Kings with gifts from across the "Ocean Sea." These included Indian hostages or slaves, gold, precious stones and native art.

To the left, El Mirador del Martin, a seven-story tower, watches over the square. Out on the Calle de los Condes de Barcelona, one perceives the patio of the Archivo de la Corona de Aragon. Its staircase and wood-panelled ceiling should not be missed.

Behind the cathedral, where one passes the windows of many antique shops, one enters the Calle de la Piedad, passing the Home of the Canonigos and arriving at the Door of Piety, (the Puerta de la Piedad) through which one enters the cathedral cloister. Above the door appears the unusual polychrome wooden carving of the "Pieta" by Lochner; it is probably one of the few wooden sculptures, if not the only one, to remain unruined after exposure for centuries to the inclemency of the weather.

Now, the visitor enters the cathedral cloister. Peace pervades everything here. A garden adorns its center and three fountains play crystalline music while white geese quack softly around them.

Barcelona's Geese

Geese have been intimately related to Barcelona and its tradition, but never has anyone been able to find when or why they first made their appearance. On Corpus Christi Day—which this year was on Thursday, June 21—an old tradition goes on year after year for the joy of young and old. An empty eggshell balanced on a water spray on the main fountain dances happily all day long. The fountain is decorated with carnations and cherries and the sentimental Barcelonese delight at the sight.

On the left side of the cloister one comes to an arch leading into the Romanesque chapel of Santa Lucia, and emerges at the front entrance facing the Casa del Arcediano (now the Historical Archives). The cloister here merits a look.

Coming out, one leaves the Palacio de Obispado, the Bishop's Palace, on the right and proceeds to the Plaza de Garriga from where one follows the small street of Montjuich del Obispo to emerge onto the Plaza San Felipe de Neri.

The house immediately on the left as one enters the plaza is that of the Guild of Shoemakers. One should note the coat-of-arms over the balconies, bearing shoes, boots and shoelaces.

Pursuing the street of Felipe de Neri, one comes out on the Calle San Severo and bears left. More antique shops line this street, which leads the visitor back on to the Plaza de Garriga.

A stop should be made, before entering the plaza, at the small and wonderful Church of San Severo. There is no way for cars to reach its door, and, so, bridal processions have to walk more than a block to the entrance, to the delight of curious onlookers.

Many Styles

At the Plaza de Garriga, a right turn leads to the Street of the Obispo Irurita. Here one faces a modern Gothic-style bridge connecting the Diputacion (Provincial Council) with its dependencies. A visitor should observe the Diputacion's facade which changes its style from Baroque to Renaissance to Gothic, and includes an image of St. George, the patron saint of Catalonia, and several

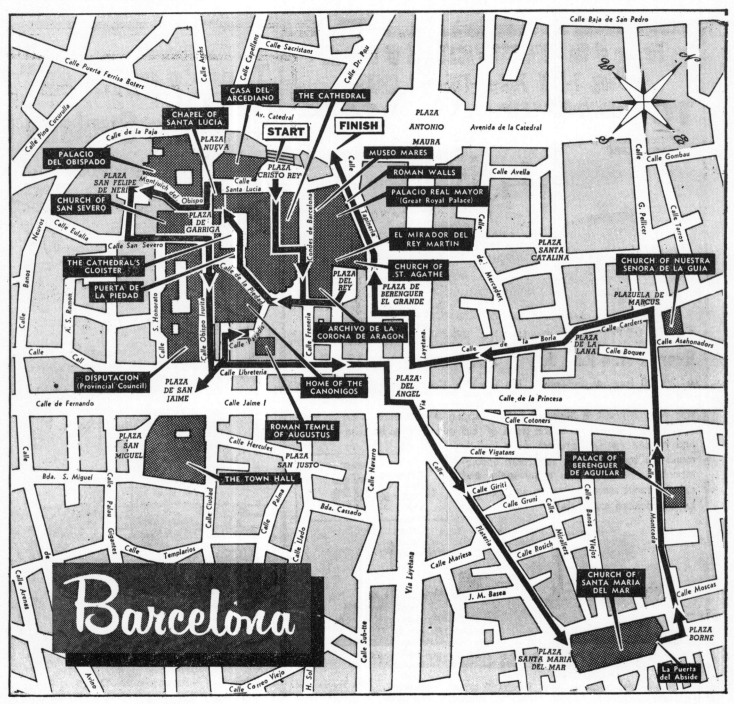

Map labels:

CASA DEL ARCEDIANO
THE CATHEDRAL
CHAPEL OF SANTA LUCIA
Av. Catedral
PLAZA NUEVA
START
FINISH
PLAZA ANTONIO MAURA
Avenida de la Catedral
PALACIO DEL OBISPADO
PLAZA CRISTO REY
MUSEO MARES
ROMAN WALLS
PLAZA SAN FELIPE DE NERI
Calle Santa Lucia
PALACIO REAL MAYOR (Great Royal Palace)
CHURCH OF SAN SEVERO
PLAZA DE GARRIGA
EL MIRADOR DEL REY MARTIN
THE CATHEDRAL'S CLOISTER
Calle San Severo
CHURCH OF ST. AGATHE
PLAZA SANTA CATALINA
CHURCH OF NUESTRA SENORA DE LA GUIA
PUERTA DE LA PIEDAD
PLAZA DEL REY
PLAZA DE BERENGUER EL GRANDE
PLAZUELA DE MARCUS
DISPUTACION (Provincial Council)
ARCHIVO DE LA CORONA DE ARAGON
PLAZA DE LA LANA
PLAZA DE SAN JAIME
HOME OF THE CANONIGOS
PLAZA DEL ANGEL
Calle de la Princesa
PLAZA SAN MIGUEL
ROMAN TEMPLE OF AUGUSTUS
PLAZA SAN JUSTO
PALACE OF BERENGUER DE AGUILAR
THE TOWN HALL
CHURCH OF SANTA MARIA DEL MAR
PLAZA BORNE
PLAZA SANTA MARIA DEL MAR
La Puerta del Abside

Barcelona

gargoyles. Entering the Diputacion, the visitor is impressed by the beauty of the patio.

This patio, each St. George's day, April 23, witnesses the sale of thousands of roses that sons buy for their mothers, husbands for their wives and *novios* for their *novias*—suitors for their loved ones—following an old tradition. The color of the roses that are offered tell the degree

of passion which the donor feels.

"If shy at the start of a courtship, he will send pale roses, but if his passion is as fire, red roses will be sent," goes an old song.

The Diputacion's staircase leads to the gallery through a double arch. A short stop at the Chapel of St. George should be made to admire the unique tap-

estry of the saint in which the geese, once more, make their appearance. On leaving the chapel, at the right, seen through a Gothic door, is the irregularly shaped Orange Blossom Patio, enchanting and typically Barcelonese.

'Salon de Ciento'

On leaving the Diputacion, a right turn leads into the Plaza

de San Jaime and the face of the Town Hall. This merits a visit if only to see its famous "Salon de Ciento" where 100 counselors, constituting the municipal parliament, held their medieval meetings. Here also is "El Salon de Sert," decorated with murals of the late Catalan artist, Jose Maria Sert.

The visitor can now take the Calle Paradis, a small narrow

street, leading to the Roman Temple of Augustus, within the building of the "Centro Excursionista de Barcelona" (a predecessor of tourism). Four huge Roman columns stand erect here.

Retracing his steps back to the Plaza de San Jaime, the visitor can take the Calle Libreteria to the Plaza del Angel, known also as Jaime I, to cross the Via Layetana and take the Calle Plateria, the Silversmiths' Street. Here he enters a zone of days gone but unwilling to perish completely. On both sides of the street, narrow passages tell of the past.

Here is a treasure of medieval corners, doorways, coats of - arms and flowered balconies. So narrow are the streets that even a burro with a load would have difficulty in moving through them. The visitor comes out onto the Plaza Santa Maria del Mar (St. Mary of the Sea), also known as Santa Maria de las Arenas (St. Mary of the Sands). It was so called because it was built on what then was the beach from donations of the port stevedores.

Gothic Masterpiece

The Church of Santa Maria del Mar is the second most important Gothic building in Barcelona. The visitor will enjoy its peace and repose. Passing slowly through the church, one leaves by the back door, La Puerta del Abside, and continues on to the Borne, taking the first right, the Calle Montcada.

Now the visitor enters a section inhabited, until the end of the nineteenth century, by great "seigneurs." Every doorway tells of past opulence and the leisurely life of the Spanish nobility. Each stone could recount tales of families settled there for centuries, of loyal servants, fathers and sons in succeeding generations. But this quarter has to be "felt." The pen cannot completely evoke the character of the Calle Montcada. Visitors should look into every doorway and peek into every patio. Doors are open to all who feel a nostalgia for the past.

Halfway down the street is the old Palace of Berenguer de Aguilar, which, after its restoration, will become the Picasso Museum. Here the artist's gift to Barcelona, consisting of an undisclosed number of his works plus his works now on exhibit at the Museum of Modern Art, will be assembled in permanent exhibition.

During the restoration of the palace, some magnificent thirteenth century murals depicting the camp of King Jaime I as he was leaving for the conquest of Mallorca were uncovered. These will remain by themselves in one hall, while the rest of the walls will play host to Picasso's masterpieces.

Postmen's Church

Following the Calle Montcada, the visitor reaches the Plazuela de Marcus, which takes its name from the Romanesque church built in 1116 and restored in 1860. It is dedicated to Nuestra Señora de la Guia (Our Lady of the Guide), the patroness of postmen. Here, the Calle Carders (Combers Street) leads to the Plaza de la Lana,

the Wool Plaza.

Streets here are still named as in old times according to the trades which until the end of the eighteenth century settled there. The Calle de la Borla (the Tassel) leads out to the Plaza del Angel. Here one crosses the Via Layetana and turns right to the Plaza de Berenguer el Grande. There the visitor can admire the main facade of the Church of St. Agathe and the Roman walls on its sides.

This church, previously seen from the back facade of the Great Royal Palace, offers a unique piece in its interior: the Retablo of the Epiphany by one of the best medieval Catalan artists: Jaume Huguet.

Slowly following the facade of the Church and the Roman Walls, the visitor continues along the Calle Tapineria, which will lead him back to twentieth century civilization.

In front, at the Hotel Colon terrace, Catalans and foreign visitors sip drinks, thus savoring the best of the present while contemplating the glories of the past.

July 1, 1962

A WALKING TOUR OF MADRID

The Proud, Historic Capital of the Hispanic World Affords Vistas of Varied Dynastic and Architectural Splendor

By MARI DE OLIVA

MADRID—This romantic and ancient city, this year celebrating its 400th anniversary as the capital of Spain, is made for the foot-wanderer. Motor transport is, of course, available, but the local taxis, while plentiful and cheap, seem possessed by demons as they hurtle, swerve, dodge, shuttle and career through traffic. The buses are frequently so crowded that one cannot bend to see out the windows, or so engulfed by inky exhaust fumes that visibility is nil.

Walking, therefore, is the best way to see Madrid. It also is the friendly way to savor this capital of 2,000,000 ebullient Spaniards, who spend most of their time out-of-doors, who stroll the boulevards and throng the old narrow streets, who talk, laugh and gesticulate like all Latins, who sing or argue, declaim or quarrel with an abandon fascinating to the visitor.

Three hours any morning or afternoon on a sunny, clear day in Madrid will provide a wealth of impressions. And when the impressions come crowding in too fast, there are many little bars or sidewalk cafes where beer, wine, sherry and shrimps can be had with a snap of a finger or a nod to the friendly white-coated *mozos*, or waiters.

Two Walks

There is so much of Madrid to see, it is so diverse in its manifestations, and history crowds in so richly, that a tourist should not try to hurry through all of it at once. Therefore, this short walking tour is divided into two parts. Either one of them is entrancing for a visitor desirous of saturating himself with the atmosphere of this city. But to do both of them, at leisure, is more than doubly rewarding.

For the first walk, a good starting point is the Puerta de Alcala, which until 100 years ago was the edge of Madrid; everything beyond it was sheep-grazing countryside. The Puerta, or Gate, was built in honor of Charles III, King of Spain who died in 1788, and designed by the architect Sabatini. Through its five arches one gets a splendid view of the start of the Calle de Alcala and the famous fountain of the Goddess, Cibeles driving her lion-drawn stone chariot through the spray.

Through a fine iron grille gate off the Plaza one strolls into the Parque del Buen Retiro, "The Good Retreat," begun by the haughty Philip II who reigned from 1556 to 1598. He was once in theory King of England and he built here for his wife Mary Tudor of England, who never came to Spain, a Norman-style castle.

Old Palace

In 1631 the powerful Count-Duke de Olivares transformed the Retiro into a beautiful park and had the royal palace of El Buen Retiro built. Until the reign of Charles III, the friend of the American revolution, the Retiro was, for most of the year, the residence of the kings of Spain. But during the Napoleonic period it was transformed into a public park, and in 1869 was given to the city. To this day this beautifully kept park remains the property of Madrid, not of the nation.

283

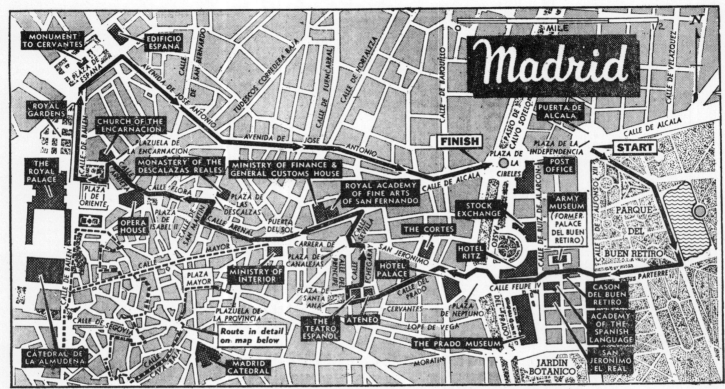

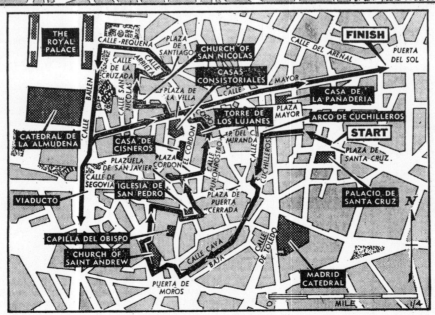

Leaving the Retiro by the broad "Parterre," the visitor comes out on Alfonso XII Street, where it is joined by Philip IV Street. On the right, one sees the remains of the the back of the long unfinished royal palace of El Buen Retiro; on the left the Cason del Buen Retiro, once the reception wing of the palace. To the right is Felipe IV, one emerges at the Plaza de Neptuno, a colossal fountain dedicated to the god of the seas. It is the work of the eighteenth-century sculptor Juan P. de Mena. On opposite sides are the two most celebrated hotels in town, the discreet Ritz and the bustling Palace. Crossing the boulevard straight ahead, one enters the the Army Museum, formerly the palace's residential part. Strolling on, one passes on the left the church of San Jeronimo el Real, an old monastery built in 1503. Below it is the world-famous Prado Museum and across the road stands the Royal Academy of the Spanish Language.

Continuing down the Calle Carrera de San Jeronimo, where, on the right, stands the neo-classical Cortes, or Parliament of Spain. The two lions on the entrance stairs were cast from melted cannons captured from the Moors in the Spanish-African War of 1859-60.

This is the quarter of writers and poets. Here the streets bear names of the celebrated in Spanish letters: Cervantes, Moratin, Lope de Vega, Ventura de la Vega and others. One continues up the Calle del Prado, where are clustered all the antique shops of the capital.

In the same street stands the Ateneo de Madrid, favorite meeting place for the intellectuals of the country. The building was finished in 1835 and boasts one of the best libraries of Spain, not solely for the number of volumes (300,000) but also for their meticulous arrangement. The Calle del Prado leads now into the Plaza de Santa Ana, where on the right stands the Teatro Español. On its stage have been represented works of all the most important Spanish authors, as well as some internationally famous. The American Theatre Guild played here last March.

Both sides of Echegaray are lined with little bars recalling all the fifty provinces of Spain. They offer glasses of white or red wine for 50 centimos (just under 1 cent) and *tapas*, or appetizers, ranging from *angulas*, baby eels, to *tortilla de patatas*, Spanish potato omelette, plus such Spanish specialties as *calamares en su tinta* which is squid cooked in its own ink, *chorizo, sobreasada, butifarra*, which are various types of seasoned sausages, and all tempting enough to persuade the visitor to halt, rest and enjoy himself.

Going along the Calle Echegaray, one comes out at the top of the Carrera de San Jeronimo, by the Plaza de Canalejas. There, one can take the Calle Sevilla and emerge on Calle de Alcala, the Wall Street of Madrid. All the big banks are found on it.

At 13 Alcala is the Royal Academy of Fine Arts of San Fernando. It was originally designed in the late seventeenth-century ornate baroque style of José Churriguera but was modified by Diego Villanueva in a neo-classic manner more in accordance with the eighteenth century. It was inaugurated in 1774. It is both an academy of the fine arts and a museum.

Among its treasures is one of the best collections in existence of José Ribera's paintings. Its double staircase, designed by the famous artist, is notable. Beside it, on the way toward the Puerta del Sol—the Sun Gate — is Spain's Ministry of Finance and the General Customs House.

The Puerta del Sol is the center of this capital, the Piccadilly Circus or Times Square of Madrid, the most popular meeting place for all visitors, from abroad or the Spanish provinces.

Official Time and Space

Kilometer 0, from which all distances from Madrid are measured, can be seen, fixed in the pavement in front of the Ministerio de la Gobernacion, the Ministry of the Interior; and on top of this building is the clock that tells all Spain the official time of the day.

Proceeding, one enters the Calle Arenal and follows it to the Calle de San Martin, which leads into the Plaza of Las Descalzas Reales. Here is the monastery of the same name, founded in the sixteenth century by Dona Juana de Austria, daughter of the Holy Roman Emperor Charles V, who was also King Charles I of Spain.

The front of the building, patios and some of the rooms are still kept as in the times of the Emperor; it is probably the only mansion of that epoch still existing in Madrid. Within its walls a number of members of royal households retired and devoted their ways to the spiritual life. Among them were the Empress Maria, Queen of Hungary and Bohemia, widow of the Emperor Maximilian; and her daughter, the Archduchess Margarita.

Royally Endowed

In the seventeenth century, the daughter of Rudolf II of Germany, the daughter of Juan José of Austria, and others of royal birth brought with them to the convent as dowry a number of works of art. These, now organized and supervised by the Patrimonio Nacional, can be seen any day from 10 A. M. to 1 P. M.

Leaving the monastery, the stroller takes the Calle Flora which comes out on the Plaza de Isabel II. This is directly at the opera house. This house, which once heard such voices as Caruso's, has been under reconstruction for nearly thirty years, but in this land of *mañana* still awaits completion.

On the right, one enters Calle Arrieta and continues to the Plazuela de la Encarnacion. There, the baroque façade of the church of the same name is fronted by a romantic garden. The convent, in the same style as the monastery of El Escorial, was founded in the sixteenth century by Philip III, and designed by Gomez Mora. Its lovely interior is the work of Ventura Rodriguez.

Leaving the church, the visitor finds himself on the Plaza de Oriente, perhaps the most beautiful in all the capital. Semicircular in shape, it has on one side the Royal Oriente Palace; on another, the main façade of the opera house and in the center, the gardens topped by a fine equestrian statue of Philip IV.

The royal palace requires a full morning really to inspect its rooms, its furnishings and its galleries. Suffice it to say that it was begun in 1734 by Philip V. Reared in the magnificence of Versailles, this great grandson of Louis XIV of France, and thus the first Bourbon King of Spain, determined to quench his homesickness by building the finest palace in Europe. He failed notably, although the palace thoroughly merits a visit.

Moorish Influence

Attached to the Oriente Palace are the Royal Gardens. They are known to this day as El Campo del Moro, because there, in the year 1109, the Emir Ali-Ben-Yussuf, ruler of the Islamic hosts which were conquering Spain, established his camp. With a view over the Gardens, the street of Bailen takes the tourist out to the Plaza de España where the modern buildings make a striking contrast to what has just been seen.

Two of the tallest buildings of Europe look down on the Plaza de España with its celebrated statues of Cervantes' Don Quixote and Sancho Panza. The Edificio España is one and the Torre de Madrid the other.

Here the walk could end, but a visitor with unquenched energy and time to spare, might continue down the Gran Via, today named Avenida de Jose Antonio and to many Americans a combination of the shopping delights of New York's Fifth Avenue with the moving picture palaces and cheerful hoopla of Broadway.

This walk could well end by going along the Calle de Alcala to the Plaza de la Cibeles.

Although much of Madrid that has been observed in the first walking tour is ancient, this second one can be even more properly described as a visit to Old Madrid. It is the Madrid of the Hapsburgs, of medieval times. It leads through scenes that call up many Madrid legends of romantic meetings between kings and lovely commoners, of plots, secrecy and duels.

The end of the day is perhaps the best in which to stroll this south side of the town. The sunset light lends a special effect, and around the corner of any street one almost expects, as if quite normal, to encounter a booted cavalier wrapped in his cape, his collar up and his plumed hat well down, hurrying silently toward a secret rendezvous.

For Nobles Only

Let us start in front of the door of the Palacio de Santa Cruz, a building of baroque façade which once was a prison for recalcitrant nobles, later the Palace of Justice and today the Ministry of Foreign Affairs.

From there one enters the Plaza Mayor, or Great Plaza, through one of its nine arches, the arch of Gerona. This plaza of pure Herrera style is about 600 feet long and 300 wide. The sixty-eight houses around it have been limited to a uniform height of five stories. Out of its 477 windows, 50,000 spectators used to watch bullfights, autos-da-fe, jousting, and the like.

Continuing on the left, under the arcades half way down and across the way, one can see the Casa de la Panaderia, the House of Bread, with two typical Madrilene towers adorning its sides. At one of the entrance arches one will see a small balcony under the arch and on the side of it. The story goes that Philip IV, in love with La Calderona, a famous actress of the time, had the balcony built so she could see all the activities in the square from her own private box, since she could not be in the royal box.

Farther on, one reaches an arch with stairs leading on to a street below. This is the Arco de Cuchilleros, or Arch of Cutlers, the most sung-and-written-about corner of the town. An *organillo*, hand-organ may be heard chiming one of those tunes. Down the stairs to the Calle Cuchilleros, the streets take the names of trades which once settled there.

Around the right-hand corner one finds curiously shaped houses, built so as to hold the weight of the floor of the Plaza Mayor just above. The second floors on the Calle Cuchilleros are at street level in the Plaza.

One descends Cuchilleros Street to the Plaza de Puerta Cerrada, or the Closed Door. Two boys are playing bullfight, with a piece of red cloth and a wicker bull's head. This was the end of the plaza. On the other side was the place where country folk in medieval times waited for the gates, which had been bolted for the night, to open. Now one pursues the Cava Baja, or Low Ditch, so called because before becoming a street it was below the level of the rest of the town and carried water.

On both sides of the street one still sees famous *posadas*— inns—with names that recall pages of history and legend. These include Posada San Isidro, Posada de la Villa, Posada de la Merced, Meson del Segoviano. Wall paintings and tiles adorn the entrances to the main courts surrounded by running balconies from which the rooms were, and are still, entered.

One reaches the Puerta de Moros, the Moor's Gate, and, turning right, passes the ruins of the church of Saint Andrew. Following its walls to the right, one reaches a small square. Here, some steps lead into the Capilla del Obispo (Bishop's Chapel) whose interior has an altar-piece considered among the finest in Spain.

Once a Mosque

Continuing right, one arrives at the Iglesia de San Pedro, built in the sixteenth century over what had been a mosque. Many details emphasizing its

Islamic origin are obvious. Going around it, one comes to steps leading to the Calle Segovia.

Crossing the street and taking the small narrow street of El Cordon, The Twisted Cord, one gets, on the left, a glimpse of the tiny Plazuela de San Javier, whose houses are full of legends and whose roofs are red tiles, tarnished by the years. Here old women sit at the window sills, making lace and watching the world go by.

Back at the Cordon, one comes out at the Plazuela of the same name, a square of lovely proportions. Here are palaces of rare beauty, with ironwork on the windows, carved doors and stone coats of arms that give the stroller a good idea of what this residential section once was.

One palace offers five different coats of arms on its facade. The church here is the Pontifical of Saint Michael, and on its left, the Calle Puñonrostro, or Fist in the Face, leads to the Plaza del Conde de Miranda with the accompanying Convent of Las Carboneras, The Coal Women, so named because a religious image now in the church was found in a coal bin.

Passing this peaceful and dreamlike section through the Calle del Codo, named the Elbow, because of its shape, one comes out on to the Plaza de la Villa. Here a small wooden door shows where King Francis I of France was kept prisoner in the Torre de Lo

Lujanes by Emperor Charles V after the battle of Pavia. In these buildings, one of which is the remarkable Casa de Cisneros, the Town Hall has offices, where plans for the beautifying and preservation of Madrid are drawn up.

Lovely Church

Having admired this unique spot, one goes next across the Calle Mayor to Calderon de la Barca Street to take the first left, named for the builder of the Escorial, Juan de Herrera; then on to the little Plazuela de San Nicolas, with its lovely church, which has a remarkable wood paneled ceiling.

Through the archway down the Calle San Nicolas, one finds the Calle de la Cruzada, which opens on the Plaza de Santiago. One proceeds down steps to the Plaza de Ramales, where Velazquez is buried. To the left, one goes down the Calle Requena, which comes out on the Calle Bailen, opposite the Royal Palace.

The first walk passed in front of the Royal Residence, too. But this time one turns left, and before going down the Calle Mayor to reach the central Puerta del Sol, advances to the bridge known as El Viaducto. Here, in recompense for his labors, the visitor can stand, breathe in the fine air of the Sierra and let his eyes wander over gently rolling plains to the far-off snow-capped peaks of the Sierra Guadarrama in the distance.

November 12, 1961

A WALKING TOUR OF SEGOVIA

Excursion Takes the Traveler Back to Medieval Spain —A Romantic, Enchanting Mood Pervades City

SEGOVIA, Spain — An excursion to this town takes one back several centuries to medieval Spain. Segovia is only 90 minutes by car from Madrid, and thus can be visited in a one-day trip.

The fairyland quality of the turrets and towers of Segovia's Alcazar expresses the roman-

tic, enchanting mood that pervades the place. This is a quiet town, not crowded with tourists like Toledo, and, aside from the Alcázar, there is not too much intensive sightseeing to do.

Wandering around the crowded, narrow streets and into the little squares, where

so often a magnificent Romanesque church and quaint houses are to be found, one senses the atmosphere of the Spanish Middle Ages. Little has changed in Segovia since then, and it seems relatively untouched by modern civilization.

Ancient Walls

Perched on a long, narrow,

rocky eminence, Segovia is surrounded by ancient walls dating from Roman times. At various points, there are striking vistas over the countryside and the valley beneath the town.

Walking is delightful in Segovia, and there is an artistic scene to be encountered at every turn. There is little motor

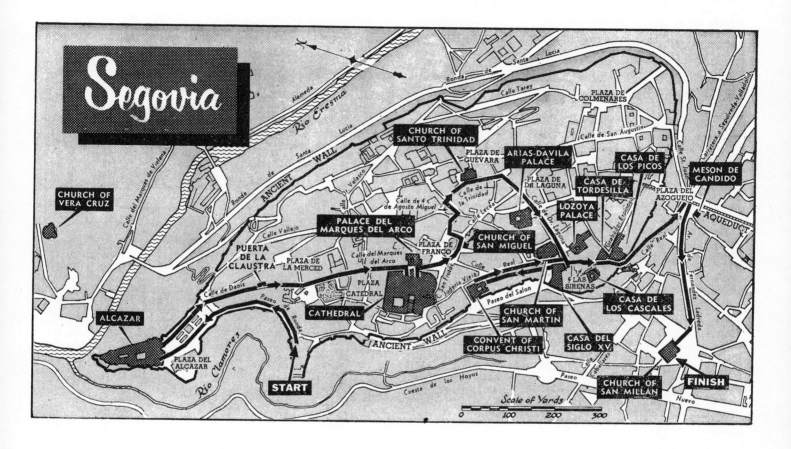

Segovia

traffic; in fact, many of the streets are too narrow for cars.

One's stroll through Segovia begins at the Alcázar, the most dramatic and interesting building in the town. However, before crossing the drawbridge over the moat, a visitor should walk along the curving terrace, the Paseo de Ronda, to get a full view of the castle.

The Alcázar—it is open daily from 10:30 A.M. to 7:30 P.M.—is one of the most famous fortress-castles in Spain. Founded in the 11th century, the present building dates mostly from the 13th and 14th centuries.

Both gothic and Moorish influences are observable on visiting the great halls and magnificent chambers. Lovely Romanesque arches, elaborate gold-leaf ceilings and Mudejar friezes in plaster—the latter are Moorish modifications of earlier Renaissance styles—are among the Alcázar's artistic attractions.

In the throne room, Isabella was proclaimed Queen of Cas-

tile. Columbus made out his will in the Alcázar in 1505; he had his king, Ferdinand, as a witness.

Panorama of Valley

One should walk out on the battlemented terrace, both to look up at the Alcázar's towers, and for a wonderful panorama of the valley. Also at hand is a view of the Knights Templars Church of Vera Cruz, which was built in 1208.

From this point, the castle appears like the prow of a ship. Here, that fairy-like quality, so characteristic of the Alcázar, is most evident.

The Alcázar's small armory contains a collection of medieval artillery, including one of the first cannons in Spain— a 14th-century piece. On the way out, a pause should be made for a few minutes in Clock Court, a charming patio.

After leaving the Plaza del Alcázar, one should bear to the right along the narrow Calle de Daoiz. Segovians call it the

Canonjía de Velarde because its tiny houses, with iron grillwork and tile roofs, belonged to the canons of the cathedral.

A halt at No. 32 allows a view into its patio and the flowers, plants and trees on its terrace. The crests carved in stone over the Romanesque doorways are notable. In a moment, one will pass the arch of the Puerta de la Claustra once the gateway to the canons' quarters.

Just beyond the Plaza de la Merced, the stroller enters the Calle del Marqués del Arco. At No. 6, on the left, he should step inside to see the attractive patio belonging to the palace of the marqués.

The cathedral — it is open from 9 A.M. to 1 P.M. and 3:30 to 6 P.M.—is a fine example of 16th-century Castilian gothic architecture. One is impressed by a feeling of light and space in its beautifully proportioned interior, which is distinguished by graceful vaulting and fine, stained-glass windows.

The baroque wrought-iron gates of the chapels and the carved choir stalls are examples of artistic workmanship. Before leaving the cathedral, a tourist should stroll around its gothic cloisters.

The Plaza de Franco, Segovia's main square, faces the cathedral. To wander under the colonnades to the Church of San Miguel, on the far side, is rewarding.

On the way, the stroller passes some interesting old streets that radiate off the square. From the church's steps can be seen the towers, buttresses and pinnacles of the cathedral.

One should now take the Calle del 4 de Agosto Miguel, at the same end of the square, and then the Calle de la Trinidad, beneath a high wall. In a few moments, the Romanesque Church of Santo Trinidad appears.

The graceful arches of its porch, its bell tower and its beautifully restored interior

make the church among the most beautiful in Segovia. Continuing along the Calle de la Trinidad, the visitor will pass attractive gardens and tall cedar trees.

On the left side of the Plaza de Guevara is a fine building with massive wooden doors. In its patio, one comes upon a bubbling fountain and a superb iron gate with grillwork.

Following the Calle de Doctor Laguna leads one into the Plaza del Doctor Laguna. On the far side of the little park is the battlemented tower of the Arias-Davila Palace, the finest of its kind in Segovia. After passing the tower, a few yards farther down some steps brings the walker to the Church of San Martín.

Here is Segovia's finest Romanesque church. Its exterior galleries, portal and porch are quite exceptional. Indeed, this magnificent church is worth studying from different angles.

The outer porticoes, which distinguish so many of Segovia's Romanesque churches, are a regional characteristic. In the summer, they offer protection from the sun; on cold, clear winter days, they are often warmer than the churches' interiors.

From the 15th Century

Just below the church is the little square of Las Sirenas. The high, square-topped tower rising behind the statue of Juan Bravo is the 15th-century Casa de Lozoya, one of the finest residences in Segovia. Bravo was a leader of a revolt against Emperor Charles V about 1520.

A stroll along the Calle Real toward the Plaza de Franco is indicated here. A turn to the left just before reaching the square leads to the Convent of Corpus Christi, which is open from 10 A.M. to noon and 4 to 6 P.M. Before 1410, this was the principal synagogue of Segovia's important Jewish community.

Here, the stroller retraces his steps to the square of las Sirenas, where, on the right, several interesting and fine Segovian residences are to be found. One, the Casa del Siglo XV, is on the Calle Real. Another, the Casa de lós Cascales, is a few yards down a little lane.

A third one is the Casa de Tordesilla at No. 3 on the Calle Real. It has a decorative facade and graceful arches above the portal.

Farther along the Calle Real rises the fortress-like facade (about 1500) of the Casa de los Picos. A century ago, this was a fortified mansion whose role was to defend this gate of the city.

Continuing down the Calle Real, one soon perceives the majestic arches of a great aqueduct. Dating from the days of Trajan, this remarkable construction is one of the best-preserved Roman aqueducts in Europe.

It is hard to realize that these tremendous blocks of granite have stood for 2,000 years without any mortar to hold them together. The well-proportioned tapering pillars of the highest row of its arches, 93 feet to 102 feet up, give an extraordinary effect of lightness and slenderness to the entire structure.

In Working Order

The conduit above the double tier of arches still carries water to the city. The structure is 2,400 feet long.

On reaching the Plaza del Azoguejo, a walk under the arches for a short distance provides a view of the aqueduct from beneath, and from a different angle on the other side. It is particularly effective to stand on the side away from the sun to observe the design created by light and shade.

By now, it is probably time for a late lunch, as is the custom in Spain. The Méson de Candido in the Plaza del Azoguejo, an attractive medieval house full of Castilian atmosphere, is one of the best restaurants in Segovia.

After lunch, a further stroll in the square leads to the Avenida de Fernandez Ladreda, on the left on coming out of the Méson de Candido. Keeping to the right at the fork, where another street branches off, and continuing under the arcades on the right side of the street for a short distance brings the sightseer to the Church of San Millán.

The exterior of this pure Romanesque church is particularly beautiful, especially the arcaded gallery, portal and apse. Inside, are examples of Mudejar decoration—the carved roof and carved columns of the nave.

March 21, 1965

A WALKING TOUR OF TOLEDO

Spanish City Has Figured Prominently in Nation's History —Home of Largest Collection of El Greco's Works

By GEORGE W. OAKES

TOLEDO, Spain —This city is so much the essence of Spain that it has been declared a national monument. It is perhaps the most characteristic of all Spanish cities, and it embodies the country's turbulent and varied past.

From the days when it was a Roman settlement to the siege of the Alcázar in the Spanish Civil War, Toledo has figured prominently in the great movements of Spanish history. Christian and Arabic cultures are intermingled, because Toledo was Moorish for 300 years.

Too, it is a city of artistic treasures, and it was the home of El Greco for most of his life. The largest collection of the artist's works, including perhaps his finest masterpieces, are on exhibit here.

Dramatically perched on a rocky bluff, Toledo is encircled on three sides by the deep gorge of the Tagus River. It is a walled city with ancient stone gateways, and there is a mysterious air of the past in its tiny, tortuous streets. They wind, like deep ravines, beneath high buildings and walls.

City a Day's Trip

Most tourists make Toledo a one-day trip by car from Madrid, a distance of 43 miles. An early start should be made so that the visitor can stop en route at Illescas to see the five superb El Grecos, especially the painting of St. Ildefonso, in the 16th-century chapel of the Caridad Hospital.

Toledo is ideal for the walker; in fact, it is the only way to explore the city, for many of the cobblestone streets are too narrow for wheeled traffic.

The visitor can definitely tour Toledo's outstanding historic and artistic monuments in a single day. A good place to start is the magnificent cathedral in the Plaza del Ayuntamiento.

The cathedral is the seat of the Primate of Spain, and it dominates the city architecturally and artistically. It is certainly one of the finest cathedrals in Spain and ranks among the great ones of Europe. It was finished in 1493, it is French-Gothic and it took more than 250 years to build.

Before entering the cathedral, the visitor should walk to the far side of the plaza, where he can view the decorative exterior and the impressive 295-foot tower.

The cathedral is open from 11:30 A.M. to 1 P.M. and from 3:30 to 5 P.M., and one enters it through the Puerta del Mollete, at the foot of the tower.

The vast interior is filled with an unusual number of artistic and religious treasures. For example, the choir stalls of carved walnut are considered the finest in Spain, while the sacristy possesses an unusual collection of paintings by El Greco. Included is "Christ Being Stripped of His Garments," one of the artist's greatest works.

On the way out of the cathedral, one should linger for a

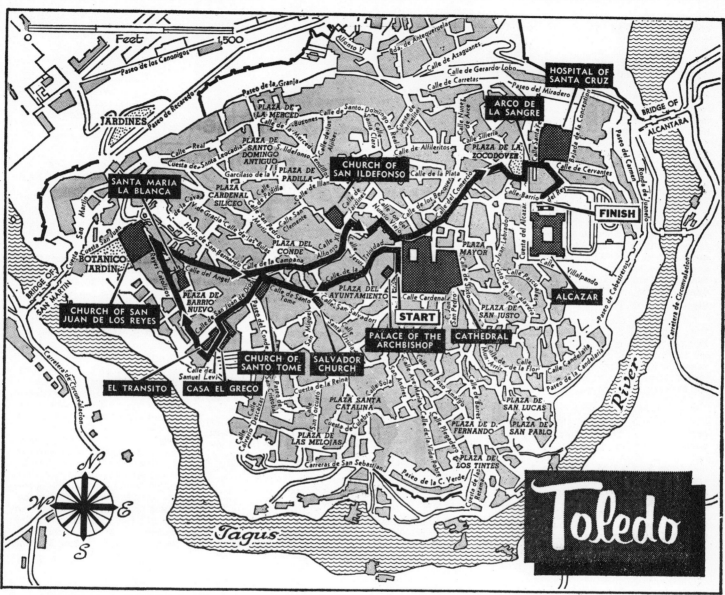

few minutes in the two-storied cloister. This is a delightful courtyard with flowers and trees.

From the cloister, turn right past the Palace of the Archbishop, across from the cathedral, and then go left along the Calle de la Trinidad, following the signs pointing to the Casa El Greco.

Convent Is Next

There is a convent on the right, on the way up the hill. Along the narrow street are faded red-brick buildings and a high bell tower, a frequent sight in Toledo.

At the end of the street stands the Salvador Church. Here, the visitor can see remains of the days when the Visigoths occupied the city. Visigothic sculpture on the marble columns next to the altar dates from the sixth century.

After visiting this church, bear right and follow the signs along the Calle de Santo Tomé. On the left is an interesting old house with big bay windows; on the right is a pleasant little square.

Further down on the left, one can see the Mudejar bell tower of the Church of Santo Tomé, which is open from 10 A.M. to 1 P.M. and 3 to 6 P.M. Mudejar style is an architectural mixture of Christian and Moorish.

Inside the church is a masterpiece by El Greco, "The Burial of the Count of Orgaz." The artist himself is included among the group of Toledans in this painting, one of El Greco's greatest.

After visiting this church, the tourist proceeds along Calle de San Juan de Dios. The shop opposite the Church of Santo Tomé has on display an interesting collection of Toledan metal work. Here, one can watch the craftsmen at work.

Eventually, a left turn, as indicated by the marked route, leads into the Calle de Samuel Levi. Immediately on the left is the building known as the House of El Greco. Although there is considerable doubt whether the artist lived there, he probably resided nearby.

The house was built in the 14th century by Samuel Levi, Pedro the Cruel's Jewish treasurer and chief landowner of this Jewish quarter. It is open from 10 A.M. to 2 P.M. and from 3:30 to 6 P.M., and it has been restored as a 16-century Toledan residence. It contains an interesting collection of paintings by El Greco and other Spanish masters, as well as furniture of the period.

Subject of Painting

For example, one can see the original writing table shown in El Greco's painting of San Ildefonso at Illescas. The 16th-century kitchen, with its large fireplace surrounded by cooking utensils and colorful pottery, also, makes the house well worth visiting.

Adjoining the house is a small museum containing many

unusually fine paintings, including one of El Greco's famous views of Toledo. Opposite the museum's entrance is a chapel decorated with ancient Moorish tiles and frieze.

Just a few yards from the House of El Greco is the ancient synagogue of the Jewish aristocracy, El Transito. It was built in 1366 for Samuel Levi, and later was converted into a Christian church after the expulsion of the Jews from Spain in 1492.

The interior of the synagogue is richly decorated. Oddly enough, the original Hebraic inscriptions on the frieze remain, as do some old Jewish tombstones. The row of Moorish arches above the frieze, and all around the building, is a fine example of the ornamental Andalusian style.

Sign Marks Route

On leaving the synagogue, turn right and follow the sign marked Church of San Juan de los Reyes, on the street of the same name. Shortly after crossing a large square, one will see the entrance to Santa Maria la Blanca.

Before being converted into a church, this was the oldest synagogue in Toledo, having been founded in 1180. It is open from 10 A.M. to 1 P.M. and from 3 to 6 P.M. Note the lovely Moorish horseshoe arches and the carving on the stone pillars.

The Church of San Juan de los Reyes is open from 10 A.M. to 6 P.M. It is one of the most elaborate in Toledo, and was originally planned by Ferdinand and Isabella as their last resting place. They are buried in Granada.

The interior of the church is unusually bright for a Spanish one. However, it is the double cloister that makes this church so remarkable. In florid Gothic design, its exquisitely carved stone arches, doorways and pillars make it one of the finest in Spain.

After visiting the church, one should pause on the terrace to enjoy the fine view over the old city wall, the river below and the Tagus Valley beyond.

From the terrace, keep the church on your right and, a few yards beyond it, opposite a school, bear left on the Calle del Angel. After passing a red-brick gate in Moorish style, the street goes up a slope and beneath an archway. Do not miss the overhanging tiled roofs.

Just ahead is the Tower of Santo Tome. About 20 yards before reaching the tower, look carefully on the left for a tiny alleyway — the Callejon de la Soledad. This is one of those fascinating corners of Toledo that makes wandering around it so delightful. Here are to be found an old house with iron grillwork and an ancient lamppost that has a mysterious air of the past — so prevalent in old Toledo.

Streets Are Narrow

Opposite the Tower of Santo Tomé is a narrow cobblestone street, Calle de la Campana. Have a look at some of the tiled patios on either side. At the top, bear right, and then left on Calle Alfonso XII.

On the right side of a tree-planted square facing the Church of San Ildefonso, take a narrow street — Calle Jon del Nuncio Viejo — down a slope. At places, this street is only three or four feet wide. After about 50 yards, turn right; shortly, one comes out on the cathedral square.

It is only about a 10-minute walk from the cathedral to Toledo's main square, the Plaza de la Zocodover, where one can find simple hotels and restaurants for a late lunch.

Scene of Bullfights

The three-cornered Plaza de la Zocodover is the center of Toledan life, and was the scene of bullfights in centuries past. Iron-grill balconies decorate the buildings around the square, and it is amusing to wander down the two arcades and stop in at one of the crowded cafes.

On leaving the main square the tourist should go through the high archway beneath the clock — the Arco de la Sangre of Moorish design. Cervantes, the great Spanish novelist, lived a few yards from the bottom of the steps below the arch.

The Hospital of Santa Cruz on the left is Toledo's most interesting museum and art gallery. It is open from 10:30 A.M. to 1:30 P.M. and from 3:30 to 7 P.M.

Once a Hospital

Founded as a hospital during the 16th century, and built in the form of a Greek cross, it is considered one of Spain's finest Renaissance buildings. The entrance facade is particularly elegant. In addition to an archeological section in its spacious and richly decorated halls, there is, on the second floor, a wing of El Greco paintings, including the "Assumption of the Virgin."

After leaving the hospital, climb the flight of steps opposite it, pass through a gate and continue up the hill to the Alcázar, Toledo's historic citadel. From the terrace, there is a wonderful view over the Tagus and the surrounding countryside.

The Alcazar is open from 9:30 A.M. to 1:30 P.M. and from 3:30 to 6 30 P.M. It is situated on the highest point in the city, and is perhaps the most famous fortress in Spain. Its last great siege was during the Spanish Civil War in 1936.

Turning Point

From the Alcazar, it takes only a few minutes down the Cuesta del Alcázar to return to the Plaza de Zocodover.

Before returning to Madrid, the tourist should be sure to see the dramatic views of Toledo from overlooks on the road that circles the hillside on the opposite side of the river. Cross the Tagus on the new bridge below the Alcázar, and return to the Madrid road by way of the 14th-century bridge of San Martin.

March 1, 1964

To Walk the Mountains

By WALTER SULLIVAN

TO walk the mountains with someone you love is a joyous experience. To do so with a group of kindred souls is fun. But to walk them alone is a special kind of adventure.

In our urbanized lives, we are rarely alone for any length of time. The constant presence of others wears upon us, as does a constant droning noise, unnoticed until it stops.

And so, when one turns to the mountains, with all of their promise of beauty and excitement, one feels a burden lifted. One walks with a light step. So it was with me a few weekends ago, when I got off a small, local train at the Swiss resort town of Pontresina and headed up the Roseg Valley along a dirt road that paralleled a torrent.

Glaciers Ahead

The water, chalky with rock flour, testified to the presence of glaciers ahead, and indeed they could be seen, dropping into the head of the valley from various directions. Beyond them, snow fields rising to the crest of the Italian border were already aglow in the newly risen sun, but here in the deep valley it was shaded and cold.

The meadows were white with frost so heavy that, on distant slopes, it looked like snow. I stopped, unslung my pack and drew from it a heavy army sweater, leaving inside my overnight things, sandwiches and a bottle of Dôle, a delightful red wine of the Valais district of Switzerland. I would have enjoyed it later to the last drop, but, with the lower external air pressure at higher elevations, the bottle blew its cork (quietly) in my pack,

and what I took to be the sweat of my back proved to be good red wine.

Expert Advice

I had walked into the Geneva chapter of the Swiss Alpine Club to ask advice on possible routes, explaining that I had a free weekend on the eve of a scientific congress in Zurich. I explained that I was a walker, not a climber, but loved the drama of the high Alps.

All agreed that the place, this late in the year, was the Engadine, near the Italian border and close enough to the Mediterranean to be under its climatic influence. As a loner, I was determined to be careful on the trail, but took the extra precaution—a wise one under such circumstances—of leaving my planned itinerary at the Geneva office of The Times.

My goal was the Coaz Hütte, a mountaineering hut at the head of the Roseg Valley from which ascents of various peaks could be made. After spending the night there, I planned to cross a pass—it is known as the Fuorcla Surlej—that leads into the valley where St. Moritz lies; a total of 25 miles.

A train had brought me to St. Moritz the night before, and it was only a short ride to Pontresina in the early morning. As I marched up the valley, the sunlight slowly marched down the slopes to my right until it touched the tips of the pines along my trail.

Sun, Stone and Steam

Then the promised warmth arrived. In the sparkling sunlight, stone walls steamed copiously, as though trying to convert this heaven into an inferno.

The meadows, thus cleared of frost, soon glowed lush green, but the trees still cast white shadows

where the frost remained.

Once an hour, I stopped to nibble a few squares from a chocolate bar—Swiss chocolate, of course—and another time I halted to eat an apple. The trees thinned as I neared the spot where my map showed a "hotel."

'A Fine Walk'

At this rather dilapidated structure, the trail forked, one route climbing to the Fuorcla Surlej and the other following the valley. In German, I asked the hotelkeeper if the pass was clear of snow (for guidance the next day), and was told, "Yes, it is a fine walk."

A sign pointed up the valley to the Coaz Hütte, and a crudely lettered one nearby pointed to the "new" Coaz Hütte.

As I passed the last scraggly pines at timberline, I noticed a man and his son crouched behind a huge boulder. The man had binoculars to his eyes and a rifle leaning on his shoulder. He was scanning the heights, obviously looking for mountain goats.

Soon afterwards, a shot rang out behind me. It was open season on goats but, I hoped, not on walkers.

As the trail rose higher and higher above the valley floor, and Pontresina shrank far down the valley, I tried to slow my pace to compensate for the altitude, but found many rests were needed. These gave me time to marvel at the glacier cascading down from the Piz Bernina, the highest mountain in the area. I was already well above the lower part of the glacier; it had obviously shrunk a great deal in recent years, leaving the remarkable lateral moraines clearly evident in the photograph below.

Not Man-Made

Each was a dike of loose rock

tapering to a knife-edge summit. All of it was so neatly uniform that it seemed hard to believe it was not man-made. Yet, for man to build anything on so massive a scale would have been a feat.

The trail worried me. It was little used and almost completely unmarked. Occasionally, in soft spots, I saw a fresh boot print, but it was always the same. It said that one man, possibly a hunter, had passed that way since the last rain.

Something Amiss

At last, I saw the hut, but clearly something was amiss. It had been built snugly under a towering cliff, presumably as protection against avalanches, but part of the cliff had fallen and reduced the hut to a shambles. The roof was partly gone, and the interior was splintered wreckage. The shutters, gaily painted with blue chevrons, swung forlornly at crazy angles.

I looked in vain for signs pointing to the new hut, and searched for a trail to carry me there. What I found was little more than a grazing trail left by pasturing animals. Slowly, I worked my way higher up the steep slope, sometimes grassy, sometimes rocky.

Now I was above the glaciers draining the ice fields at the head of the valley. Where two of them flowed together, they gnawed at the giant crags separating them.

The rocky debris that they thus collected was carried down on the central back of the combined rivers of ice —what is called a medial moraine. Not long ago, the glacier extended far down the valley, but now it had melted back, leaving this moraine on the valley floor.

The previous extent of the glacier was obvious. Above the former high tide of ice, the rocky slopes were tinted green. Below, they were barren gray.

Much as I hated to turn back, I knew the time for decision had come. It could well be fatal to be caught out overnight on those frigid slopes. Either I must find the hut within a few minutes, or return to that little hotel.

Faint Hammering

Luck was with me. Far up the valley, the faint sound of hammering echoed from the walls of rock and ice. Looking long and hard, I finally saw a stone hut atop a crag that rose above the lateral moraine of the glacier.

Then, a few hundred feet above me, I saw hikers, obviously on a trail. A bit of breathtaking scramble to climb within shouting range, and they confirmed that the hut was in operation.

From then on, it was easy going. The hut, wonderfully dramatic in its setting, was just what I had sought. I was able to write home that I had spent Saturday night in bed with two women and five men, for it had a *Matratzenlager*, or mattress loft, with mattresses cheek by jowl.

All was new, neat and clean in the Swiss manner. The mattresses tapered toward the foot end, and so they formed a fan when laid side by side. Lighting was by gas lamps, food was delivered by helicopter and there was a microwave telephone connection to the outside world.

$1.20 a Night

For members of the Alpine Club and its affiliates, the overnight charge was the equivalent of 60 cents. For me, it was twice that, with extra charges for food, "light" and the "wood tax." The wood was used, after the overnight guests had begun to shiver in unison, to heat a small stove.

The guides who usually stand ready at such huts to lead climbers to the summits were all gone. New snow was on the peaks and glaciers, making them doubly hazardous. I had crossed a

Walter Sullivan

SURROUNDED BY PEAKS—The view that greets the hiker's eye from the Fuorcla Surlej, or The Pass Above the Lake, in the Swiss Alps.

small, semi-permanent snow-field on the way up, plus new snow hiding in the crevices. The hut was to shut down for the winter two nights hence.

There were a group of young men from Basel, a Bavarian couple (he was a lieutenant colonel in the West German Army) and a Swiss couple. We sat in a communal room, rounded to fit the curve of the crag on which it rested. At one end hung a portrait of Dr. H. C. J. Coaz, for whom the hut is named. Dr. Coaz, an *Oberforstinspektor*, or chief forest inspector, had made the first ascent of the Piz Bernina in 1850.

Calm and Clear

Someone remarked that, a few days earlier, three men working their way along a knife-edge linking the Bernina to the next peak had been lost when high winds swept them off. Tonight, it was calm and clear and, over our beer, we speculated on whether the weather would hold. Out on the terrace, we looked at the snowy heights, still aglow in sunlight, and the veterans pointed out that they were not a deep rose.

"That is good," one of them said. "When they are rose, the weather will be bad."

As night came on, we saw a strange sight. Far below, on the valley floor just past the tip, or snout, of the glacier, was a small lake, and on it we saw a light. We were told the light appeared frequently, although presumably no boat had ever ventured onto the lake's waters. Above, in the sky, was a bright planet. Could it have been a réflection?

On the upper floor of the hut, we found three blankets and a pillow neatly piled at the foot of each mattress. I did not sleep particularly well, and heard others stirring. Someone complained that the altitude made sleeping difficult.

I arose at one point, opened the heavy front door and went into the frigid night in my heavy socks. The moon was up, and the snowfields were magic in its light. There were brilliant stars overhead, but a cloud hid those over the lake. And the light had vanished.

The next day, in gaining the pass, there were a few spots where a false step could have been fatal—a hazard of no concern to an experienced mountaineer but, for me, enough to impart special zest to achieving the summit. There, new mountain panoramas opened out, and far below two lakes were stretched along the valley floor, forming the headwaters of the Inn River. The name of the pass, Fuorcla Surlej, means "Pass Above the Lake" in Romansh, the ancient language

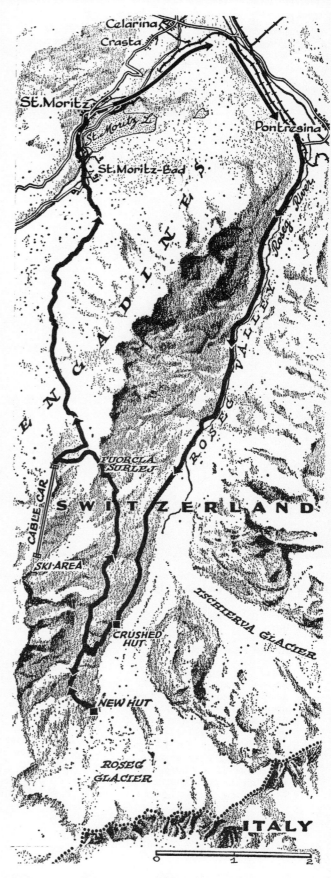

ALPINE 'FOOTPATH'—The map at top shows the author's route in Switzerland—by train from St. Moritz to Pontresina, and then on foot to the mountaineering hut at the head of the Roseg Valley and then across the pass known as Fuorcla Surlej. The total distance covered on foot was 25 miles.

FROM THE TRAIL—The Tschierva Glacier flows between the Piz Bernina, top left, and the Piz Roseg. Glacial action has created knife-edge dikes of loose rock, called lateral moraines, visible above. Edge of the footpath can be seen at lower right.

still spoken in those mountains.

In the Real World

Far up the valley, the massed hotels of St. Moritz awaited me. I heard the drone of a plane overhead, and realized that I was back in the real world.

Not once in the Roseg Valley did I hear a plane. Not once did a contrail intrude on the clear blue overhead. I saw almost no one except hunters and mountaineers.

Once in a while, on my approach, a marmot shrilled his loud whistle of warning, then stood on his hind feet to watch for a moment before plunging among the rocks. Sometimes, too, dark birds arose in a flock and circled, crying like miniature vultures disturbed at their meal.

The most awesome sounds in the valley were the occasional rumblings from the glacier at its head. Apparently, rock slides broke loose from time to time as the glacier, slowly and silently, gnawed at the cliffs.

This thundering was a reminder that man is not alone in being mortal. Not even the greatest mountain lives forever. The fresh moraines, the signs of recent ice retreat and the reverberations of falling rock all testified to the fact that only change is eternal.

November 12, 1967

A Walk Through the Alps From Switzerland Into Italy

By WALTER SULLIVAN

GENEVA—There has always lurked in my restless soul a yearning to walk across one of the Alpine passes from Switzerland into Italy, to climb toward that saddle in the sky, breast it and look down into the Po Valley, as Hannibal and his weary elephants did in 218 B.C.

There is a glamour in these passes that is unmatched. They have seen the tides of history sweep back and forth—the march of tyrants with their hordes, the flight of the oppressed in search of sanctuary.

The opportunity finally came to satisfy this desire: I was in Geneva with a few free days. The map showed what seemed a promising route into Italy, a pass that could be hiked without climbing over glaciers and yet was not traversed by a highway. The route included a hut of the Swiss Alpine Club for an overnight stop.

The pass was the Col de Fenêtre, east of the Great St. Bernard Pass. The St. Bernard has been the traditional route of conquerors; at least 20 medieval emperors marched across it and, in 1800, Napoleon led 40,000 men across it into Italy, the troops dragging their cannons through the snow.

The Geneva office of the Alpine Club said that the Chanrion Hut near the Col de Fenêtre was open, although the caretaker had left for the winter, and that there was ample bedding, probably some firewood but no food.

The main problem was weather, for Europe was sodden after a summer of rain. However, the advice of the forecaster at the Geneva airport was: "Go tomorrow! It will get better. After that it will get worse."

It was drizzling as I left the hotel in the evening and walked, knapsack on back, to the railroad station, where I bought a ticket to Le Châble, 93 miles southeast of Geneva. The plaques on the sides of the coaches said they were bound for Rome via the Simplon Tunnel, but at Martigny I changed to a bus for the half-hour ride to Sembrancher, and there to a rail car that snaked up a valley wall to Le Châble.

Since it was dark after the two-hour journey from Geneva, I found an inn; it was crowded with Swiss soldiers relaxing after a training exercise.

In my pack were wurst, cheese, chocolate bars and a bottle of wine. The innkeeper said there was a bakery next door, but it was closed when I stepped out into the brilliant sunshine the next morning to catch an 8 o'clock bus. The bus was about to leave, and there were no more bakeries this side of Italy.

The innkeeper hurriedly led the way up a steep street to the baker's home; there, beyond a courtyard fragrant with baking smells, stood baskets of fresh loaves. I quickly paid for one and ran down the hill, pack bouncing on my back. Fortunately, the bus left 20 minutes late.

As the bus zigzagged up toward the great Mauvoisin Dam—an hour's journey—it stopped on one of the hairpin turns, and the other passengers got out with the driver to peer over the brink. Far below was a frightfully smashed car. A gash on a pine, some 20 feet above its base, showed where the car had hit after missing the turn and flying through the air.

Crashed in Fog

"When did that happen?" I asked in horror.

"Last night," the driver replied. "Incredibly, the man walked away uninjured. Said it had been foggy."

The bus route ended at the foot of Mauvoisin Dam, a somewhat smaller twin of the Grande Dixence Dam in the next valley. The Dixence, 930 feet high, is said to be the tallest in the world, and the Mauvoisin is almost equally awesome.

They form part of the most ambitious engineering effort ever undertaken by the Swiss—a gargantuan plumbing system that carries water from far-flung Alpine valleys

into lakes in this region. The impounded water then turns power-generating turbines all year, even when watersheds are frozen.

I turned my back on the bus and, with an eagerness I knew would not last, I leaned into the first climb of the day—to the rim of the dam. Its construction is like that of a dome lying on its side.

The dam is roughly as high as it is wide. It bulges to counter the pressure of the water, and its rim presses against the vertical rock walls on either side, as well as on the floor of the ravine. The top of the dam overhangs in a manner that is breathtaking as you walk across it.

Roads Above Lake

Lake Mauvoisin, a long, narrow body of milky-blue glacier water running north-south, is flanked on both sides by single-lane roads carved out of the cliffs. The altitude is about 6,500 feet. The roads were built to reach the tunnels bored to bring extra water into the lake. From the dam, one can see water gushing from tunnel outlets in the cliffs on the lake's two sides.

My route southward on the western side of the lake was up a dirt road, the beginning of which was tunneled into the cliff. The tunnel was just large enough for one car, and I listened carefully to give myself time to find a niche if one came along. Water rained from the naked rock overhead. A few openings had been cut through to the face of the cliff, affording a glimpse of the lake hundreds of feet below.

A roaring noise recalled the hero of the fairy tale, "Curdie and the Goblins," who made his way through the bowels of a mountain by following the sounds of underground torrents. The explanation came when the road tunnel met another one carrying a torrent that had flowed under the mountains west of the lake. This tunnel, four miles long, brought water from the northern slopes of the 14,164-foot-high Grand Combin.

The torrent raced under the road, burst into the open from the cliff and then fell out of sight to the lake.

Once out of the tunnel, the road followed the steep shoreline to the head of the lake. A small car overtook me slowly. The driver would stop, scan the heights above with his binoculars and then drive on. A chamois hunter! I saw several of them that day.

Snowcapped Peaks

Beyond the head of the lake, the valley was savagely stark and flanked by craggy peaks topped with snow. The rugged, treeless terrain reminded me of Hemingway's descriptions of the Pyrenees. The road bridged a stream, and in the churning water lay the wreck of a motorcycle. Someone had taken the bridge too fast.

My corduroy pants, Norwegian fisherman's sweater and light windbreaker were sufficient—the temperature was in the 40's—and the moist ground was firm under mountaineering boots.

The trail left the road, climbing steeply around some cliffs. It crossed humpy pastures and passed a tiny lake before the Alpine Club hut, a sturdy, stone building, came into view. Several hunters were lounging in front of the hut, which stands at an altitude of 8,071 feet.

The hike of about 12 miles from Mauvoisin Dam had taken six hours.

One of the hunters was cooking a marmot for dinner. The marmot looks much like a woodchuck. I had seen a few on the

Photographs by WALTER SULLIVAN

COL DE FENETRE—This is the hiking trail through the pass from Switzerland to Italy. At this point, the climber begins the descent toward Aosta, Italy, deep in the Italian Alps in the background.

WALTER SULLIVAN

ITALIAN-ROMAN BASTION—To hold the southern approach to the Great St. Bernard Pass against invasions from Switzerland, the Romans built towers like this one still standing remarkably intact at Aosta.

way up: they were standing tall on their hind legs for a quick look before dropping out of sight among the rocks.

Suddenly, the young man who had been preparing the marmot dashed out of the house and over a crag, plate in hand, as though the Devil were after him. I heard a greeting behind me, and turned to see an elegantly uniformed officer with a small pistol on his belt. He went inside, then soon came out and continued on his way.

Marmots, it seemed, were out of season.

I was allocated a spot on the wood-burning stove to heat my dehydrated soup. Then, after sampling my wine, wurst, bread and cheese, I explored the bunk room upstairs. There were mattresses for 55 visitors —each had a pillow that felt like a bean bag—and blankets hanging overhead.

Even with five blankets—one below and four above—I was cold that night, for the temperature dropped well below freezing.

When I arose at 6:30 A.M. the next day, the hunters had gone and the weatherman's ominous predictions seemed to be coming true. Charcoal gray covered the sky to the north; beyond the Fenêtre Pass looming high to the south, low clouds seemed to be moving in.

After making some instant coffee and noting my intentions in the hut log, I slipped the equivalent of $2 through the slot of a payment box to cover lodging and firewood, shouldered my pack and started down into the steep ravine lying between me and the pass.

Welcome Footprints

Footprints lay in the snow as I neared the pass. They were welcome, for the snow had concealed the trail. Twice I paused to rebuild cairns with the flat, shale-like rock typical of this region. It is used to roof the cattle shelters in the high pastures.

The thrill of the 9,200-foot-high pass matched my most romantic hopes. It was not a gradual denouement: Italy burst into view as the fruit of a few bounding steps at the summit. It was not the fruited plains of Lombardy or the rich Po Valley that lay beyond; rather, it was a whole new panorama of mountains.

All the way up, I had been looking at one part of the Alps. Now it was like turning a page. The Italian Alps presented a broad array of peaks poking furtively into a lowering overcast.

The pass was a gravelly saddle. The glacier that once flowed down the Swiss side had withered until only fragments remained. A small, but intact, glacier dropped steeply to a tiny lake on the Italian side. It overhung the water, and every now and then circles of ripples showed that bits of ice had fallen.

I wondered what history had been witnessed by this savage place. The Great St.

Bernard Pass to the west, 8,100 feet above sea level, was the route of invading armies. The Fenêtre, more inaccessible and 1,100 feet higher, was more likely used by those seeking seclusion—bandits, smugglers and refugees.

20th-Century Exile

John Calvin, after failing to convert the Italians to Calvinism, had fled along this route more than four centuries ago. But now I found dramatic evidence of a much more recent flight. On a rough stone monument was a plaque in Italian that translated:

On Sept. 23, 1943, when the "fatherland lay under the tyrant's heel," Luigi Einaudi crossed this pass and went into exile in Switzerland. The Valley of Aosta "hails the man whom five years later the newly founded Republic of Italy elected its first President."

An economist and member of the Italian Senate when Mussolini rose to power, Signor Einaudi became a leading anti-Fascist and finally fled, only to return and become his country's Chief of State in 1948.

As I started down from the pass, sleet was falling, despite sunshine and a patch of blue overhead. The true depth of the giant valley ahead was concealed, for the slope dropped in a series of steps so deep that the valley floor, more than 4,300 feet below, was hidden.

Unlike going up, when your face is to the slope, a descent keeps the panorama constantly before you. The Alpine scenery rises and envelops you as you descend, almost as though you were lowering yourself hand-over-hand. From the barren, other world of the heights, where one feels he is an intruder, I dropped back gradually into the inhabited world.

The first outpost was a broad shelf, covered with what in summer must be an extraordinarily rich pasture. There was a stone cow barn with evidence that the cattle had left for lower pastures only a short time before. The valley resounded with the roar of streams cascading down cliffs.

Lunch Among Flowers

This was such a delightful meadow that I stopped for a meal, finished the wine and refilled my canteen from a stream. Although the pastures were more brown than green, this only served to make the blooming wildflowers stand out with greater brilliance.

Over the rim of this shelf, the first scattered trees came into sight—arolla pines that shed their needles in winter to confound those who think all conifers are evergreens. Finally, far below, I could see the thin ribbon of a paved road. The civilization from which I had fled was now a welcome sight.

With leisurely halts for food, photography and relaxation, I had been on the trail from the hut for about nine hours and covered 12 miles or so to the head of the road. From my research in Geneva, I knew that a bus to Aosta was due to leave Valpelline, six miles down the valley, late in the afternoon. The last bus left at about 10 P.M.

On the road, two lads with packs on their backs were approaching a parked car. I asked if they would drive me as far as they were going toward Aosta.

The result was a typically warm welcome to Italy. They had fished one of the ponds higher up, and proudly unwrapped a cloth from around seven fine trout. They insisted that I visit their farmhouse home, where their mother brought out wine, bread and cheese. The boys drank bouillon laced with red wine. "Full of new energy," they explained.

Then the older boy drove me to Aosta, about seven miles farther south.

Aosta, at the southern approach to the Great St. Bernard Pass, has well-preserved Roman walls and watchtowers, a giant gate and theater. Obviously, it had been a bastion against invasions over the pass. My walk had led from the neat, precise, chalet world of the Swiss to the turbulent, earthy, romantic world of the Italians. The streets of Aosta were alive with Alpini, the Italian mountain troops who wear Robin Hood hats topped by dashing feathers.

Next day, I completed the three-day journey, returning to Geneva via the St. Bernard Pass, a journey of 130 miles. Some of the buses run through the tunnel under the pass, but I took one that went to the summit so that I could visit the hospice and its St. Bernard dogs. A myth exploded: The dogs *do not* carry casks of cognac around their necks.

November 10, 1968

SUGGESTED ADDITIONAL READING

The Magic of Walking, by Aaron Sussman and Ruth Goode. Simon and Schuster, New York, 1967. A comprehensive discussion of the whys and wheres of walking, but of particular worth for its vast section of literature on the subject. Here are the basic classical essays, William Hazlitt's "On Going a Journey," Henry David Thoreau's "Walking," Robert Louis Stevenson's "Walking Tours," and John Burrough's "The Exhilarations of the Road." There are later essays by Christopher Morley, John Kieran, Joseph Wood Krutch, Lewis Mumford, Max Beerbohm and others. (It also includes three articles from *The New York Times Magazine* printed in our own book: "The Joy of Walking," by Donald Culross Peattie, "To Own the Streets and Fields," by Hal Borland, and "The Gentle Art of Walking," by H. I. Brock.)

Joys of the Road. A Little Anthology in Praise of Walking, compiled by Waldo Ralph Browne. Books for Libraries Press, Freeport, N. Y., 1970. Reprint of a 1911 edition by Browne's Bookstore, Chicago. Contains the essays mentioned above by Hazlitt, Stevenson, Thoreau and Burroughs, plus the following poems: "The Joys of the Road," by Bliss Carman, "The Vagabond," by Stevenson, "Afoot," by C. Fox Smith, and "On the Road," by Arthur Symons.

The Art of Walking, an anthology of writings edited by Edwin Valentine Mitchell. Loring & Mussey, New York, 1934. In addition to some essays mentioned above, includes "Traveling Afoot," by John Finley, "In Praise of Walking," by Leslie Stephen, "Night Walks" and "Tramps," by Charles Dickens, "Walking Experiences," by George Gissing, "Walking," by George Macaulay Trevelyan, and "A Note on Walking," by J. Brooks Atkinson. (The Trevelyan essay and Atkinson's introduction to it may be found in an individual 1928 edition published by Edwin Valentine Mitchell, Hartford, Conn.)

The Footpath Way, An Anthology for Walkers, with an introduction by Hilaire Belloc. Sidgwick & Jacobson Ltd, London, 1911. The usual Hazlitt, Thoreau, Stevenson, Burroughs contributions, but textured additions by Sidney Smith, Izaak Walton, Sir Walter Scott, William Wordsworth, Thomas de Quincey, George Borrow, Walt Whitman ("Song of the Open Road").

Excursions, by Henry David Thoreau. Illustrated by Clifton Johnson, Thomas Crowell Co., New York, 1913. This is the volume of essays which contains "Walking," plus such others as "A Winter Walk," "Autumn Tints," "Wild Apples," "Night and Moonlight." (There is a 1962 edition by Corinth Books, in paper and cloth, with an introduction by Leo Marx.)

The Gentle Art of Tramping, by Stephen Graham. D. Appleton and Co., New York, 1926. The why and how of the gentle art, refined by personal and poetic reflections.

Tramping With a Poet in the Rockies, by Stephen Graham. D. Appleton and Co., New York, 1922. The poet is Vachel Lindsay, the tramp is in Glacier and Waterton Lakes area, the writing both humorous and philosophic.

Walking Essays, by A. H. Sidgwick. Edward Arnold, London, 1912. In the mainstream of English walking and literary tradition.

A Thousand-Mile Walk to the Gulf, by John Muir. Houghton Mifflin Co., Boston and New York, 1916. His trek through Kentucky, Tennessee, Georgia and Florida in the fall of 1867. (There is a 1969 reprint by Norman S. Berg, Dunwoody, Ga.)

The Harvest of a Quiet Eye, by Odell Shepard. Houghton Mifflin Co., Boston and New York, 1927. A contemplative tramp through northwestern Connecticut.

Turn Right at the Fountain, by George W. Oakes. Holt, Rinehart and Winston, New York, 1971. A completely revised and updated edition, with additional research material by Alexandra Chapman. Walking tours in European cities. (Several of these were first printed in The New York Times, and reprinted in our own book).

Turn Left at the Pub, by George W. Oakes. David McKay Co., New York, 1968. Tours in British cities and towns.

A Walk Through Britain, by John Hillaby. Houghton Mifflin Co., Boston, 1969. A backpack trip from Land's End to John O'Groats, with sensitive observations of people, of nature, of historical and literary associations along the way.

New York Walk Book, by the New York-New Jersey Trail Conference and the American Geographical Society. Pen sketches by Robert L. Dickinson and Richard Edes Harrison, with a geological introduction by Christopher J. Schuberth. Doubleday/Natural History Press, New York, 1971. The last edition of this book (which has a special section in our own) was in 1951.

The Appalachian Trail, by Ann and Myron Sutton. J. B. Lippincott Co., Philadelphia and New York, 1967. This is not a guide book, but a most pertinent description of the famous trail from Maine to Georgia and its related regional and natural history. (A listing of the major trails associations and hiking clubs in the United States, to which one could write for information on trail guides and membership data, may be found at the conclusion of Susan Sands article on the backpacking boom, page 90.)

The Thousand-Mile Summer in Desert and High Sierra, by Colin Fletcher. Howell-North Books, Berkley, Calif., 1964. A backpack trip north from Mexico along the backbone of the state of California, with the lowest and highest elevations in the original 48 states.)

The Man Who Walked Through Time, by Colin Fletcher. Alfred A. Knopf, New York, 1968. A walk along the rim, and occasionally in the depth, of the Grand Canyon, for the entire length of the Grand Canyon National Park.

The Complete Walker, by Colin Fletcher. Alfred A. Knopf, New York, 1970. This is "it" as the latest and most comprehensive handbook on the equipment and techniques of backpacking.

INDEX

Absalon (Bishop), 226

Adams, Samuel, 181, 182

Adirondack Mountain Club, 30, 87, 90, 106, 115, 135, 136

Adirondack Mountains: 27, 30, 105-110; M. W. Lamy article, 132-134; L. D. Gottlieb article, 135-136

Adirondak Loj, 106, 135

AE. *See* Russell, G. W.

Aiken, George D. (Sen), 38

Albee, Allison, 47

"Alcoholics Anonymous," 37

Alcott, Louisa May, 184

Algonquin Mountain, 135, 136

Ali-Ben-Yussuf, Emir, 285

Allegany State Park, 131

Allegheny Mountains, 102, 131

Allen, Ethan, 106

Allenby, Edmund, 44

Alps, 291-298

American Geographical Society, 32-34

American Legion, 48

Ammonoosuc Ravine Trail, 147, 148

Amsterdam, Netherlands, 253-255

Amundsen, Roald, 2, 44

Anderson, Maxwell, 114

Andre, John, 112

Animals, Society for the Prevention of Cruelty to, 139

Annapolis, Md., 177-179

Antaeus, 5

Antarctic Regions, 45

Apalachicola National Forest, 155

Appalachian Mountain Club: 29, 31, 87, 100-103, 107, 115, 137, 145, 146, 148; O. Evans article on Rocky Mountain wilderness trip, 161

Appalachian Trail: Editorial suggesting extension of trail principle, 19; national scenic trail designation, 27, 28; "End-to-Enders" noted, 85; P. Thomson article on them, 94-99; special section on trail, 94-104; maps, 95, 100, 101; marking, 96, 103; history, 99-101, 103, 104, 117; R. H. Torrey article on Taconic section, 99-101; S. R. Winters article, 101; D. M. Martin article on 1951 reopening, 103; editorial on reopening, 104; Palisades Interstate Park section building, 117; trail inspires Pennine Way development, 232; other refs, 32, 33, 87, 106-109, 122, 138, 144, 145, 149, 153, 154, 158

Appalachian Trail Club, Maine. *See* Maine Appalachian Trail Club

Appalachian Trail Conference, 87, 90, 95, 99, 103, 104

Appalachian Trailway News, 96, 98

Architects, American Institute of, 99, 103, 206

Arden-Surebridge Trail, 117

Arnold, Benedict, 112

A-SB. *See* Arden-Surebridge Trail

Ashley, William Henry, 72

Astley, John (Sir), 56

Astley Belt, 56, 57, 60, 63, 78

A-T. *See* Appalachian Trail

Athens, 251, 252

"Athletics Anonymous," 37

Atkinson, Brooks, 34

Atticus, 22

Audubon, John James, 7

Austin, Penna., 160

Avery, Myron, 96, 103

Awosting Lake, 126, 128

Backpacking. *See* Walking—Backpacking

Bacon, Francis, 3, 239

Bailey, Liberty Hyde, 4, 5, 32

Baker, Russell, 25

Barcelona, Spain, 281-283

Baruch, Bernard M., 39

Bascom, S. G., 129

Bassett, Howard, 97

Bates, Caroline, 142

Battell, Joseph M., 138

Battell Lodge, 138

Baudouin, King of the Belgians, 219

Baxter Peak, 94

Baxter State Park, 149

Beaches, 110, 142, 143, 157

Bear Mountain (NY), 33, 116-120

Bear Mountain Inn, 120

Bear Mountain Section of Palisades Interstate Park. *See* Palisades Interstate Park

Beard, Daniel Carter, 46

Beard, Maud (Mrs), 78

Beaufort, Lady Margaret, 239

Beaver Brook Trail, 144

Becket, Thomas a, 232

Beecher, Henry Ward, 182

Beechy Bottom, 116, 120

Beerbohm, Max, 26

Beethoven, Ludwig van, 215

Belleayre Mountain, 130

Belloc, Hilary, 19

Bennett, Hugh Hammond, 91

Berger, Meyer, 196

Berkshire Mountains, 102, 106
Bernini, Giovanni Lorenzo, 273
Bible, 43, 200
Billings, Josh, 3
Bimadashka (Laughing Water), 221
Bird, David, 157
Black Care (Atra Cura), 22
Black Forest (Potter County, Penna.), 159
Black Hawk War, 36
Black Rock Forest. *See* Harvard Black Rock Forest
Blackinton State Forest, 100, 138
Blair, William M., 27, 28
Blauvelt State Park, 109
Blind, Trails for the, 163-165
Blisters, 40, 86, 97, 231
Block, Victor, 151
Blue Mountains (Maine), 105, 107
Blue Ridge Mountains, 102, 153, 154
Blue Ridge Parkway, 103
Bluhm, Lester W. (Dr), 40
Bodley, Thomas (Sir), 246
Boleyn, Anne, 238
Bone, James, 231
Bonneville, Benjamin Louis Eulalie de (Capt), 72
Boots. *See* Walking—Outfit: Shoes
Borglum, Gutzon, 208
Borland, Hal, 11
Boston, Mass., 180-184
Boswell, James, 242
Botticelli, Sandro, 268
Bourglay, Jules. *See* Leather Man, The
Bowman, Isaiah (Dr), 32
"Boy Scouts" (Generic Term), 88
Boy Scouts of America, 37, 39, 40, 43, 46, 78, 84, 88, 99,
    105, 115, 117, 119, 129, 131, 155, 172, 196
Boyer, Marc, 98
Bradford, C., 102
Brahe, Tycho, 225
Brahms, Johannes, 214
Braille, Louis, 163
Braille Trail, Roaring Fork, 163-165
Bramante, Donato, 271, 272
Brandes, Georg, 224
Bravo, Juan, 288
Brennan, William J. Jr., 38
Bridger, Jim, 72
Bridges. *See* Walking—Bridge Walking
Bristol Hills Trail, 131
British Travel and Holiday Assn, 231
Britons as Walkers. *See* Walking—Britons as Walkers
Brock, H. I., 1
Brogan, Denis W. (Prof), 239
Broudy, Jack, 180
Browning, Robert, 79, 276
Bruce, Robert, 240
Bruce Trail, 221-223

Bruce Trail Assn, 222
Bruges, Belgium, 216-218
Brunelleschi, Filippo, 266
Brush, Frederic (Dr), 66
Brussels, Belgium, 219, 220
Bryant, William Cullen, 9, 19
Bryce, James, 4, 19
Buck, Annetta, 115
Buck, Helen, 115
Buck Island, 157
Buckner, Henry Sullivan, 191
Bulfinch, Charles, 184, 187
Bull, Inez, 160
Bull, Ole, 160
Bull Run Nature Trail, 151, 152
Bull Run Regional Park, 151, 152
Bunion Derby (1920s), 38
Burke, Edmund, 258
Burns, Robert, 242
Burroughs, John, 7, 26, 129
Butler, B. T. (Prof), 30
Butlin, Billy, 48, 51, 230
Buxton, Nigel, 235
Byrd, Richard Evelyn, 45
Byrne, James, 43
Byron, Lord, 219, 239

C. & O. Canal, 27, 150
C. & O. Canal Assn, 150
Cabot, John, 154
Callahan, Rosellen, 278
Calvin, John, 299
Cambridge, England, 237-239
Camel's Hump, 30, 137, 138
Camp and Trail (New York City Outfitters), 84
Camp Trails (Phoenix Outfitters), 84
Campfire Girls, 131
Canterbury, England, 232-234
Canyonlands National Park, 166, 167
Cape Cod, 142, 143
Cape Florida, 154, 155
Cape Florida Light, 154
Cape Hatteras, 143
Carlyle, Thomas, 19
Carman, Bliss, 9
Carmody, Deirdre, 198
Carpaccio, Vittore, 276
Carr, Peter, 19
Carroll, Charles, 177, 179
Carroll, Lewis, 247
Carson, Kit, 72
Cascade Range, 27, 28
Catling, Patrick, 230
Catskill Forest Preserve, 129, 130
Catskill Mountain House, 131

Catskill Mountains: C. E. Heacox article, 129; other refs, 27, 32, 108, 109, 131
Caxton, William, 218, 249
Cayuga Trails Club, 131, 132
Cecilia, Saint, 271
Cellini, Benvenuto, 266-268
Central Park, 2, 50, 194, 195
Century Club, 46
Cervantes, 285, 290
Chadayne, W. C., 71
Champlain, Samuel de, 30
Charcoal Burning, 115, 122, 123, 125
Charlemagne, 215
Charles I, King of England, 247
Charles II, King of England, 242-244
Charles III, King of Spain, 283
Charles V, Emperor, 219, 285, 286, 288
Charles VI, Emperor, 215
Charles of Lorraine, Prince, 219
Charter Oak Trail, 185-187
Chase, Samuel, 179
Chatfield House, 126
Chaucer, Geoffrey, 4, 5, 232-234
Cheney, John, 132
Cherokee National Forest, 100
Chesapeake & Ohio Canal. See C. & O. Canal
Chesler Park, 166, 167
Chesterton, G. K., 231, 234
Chickees, 155
Chigi, Agostino, 271
Chiropody, 25
Christian IV, King, 225
Christy, Bayard H., 5
Church, Frederick, 129
Churchill, Winston, 37
Churriguera, Jose, 285
Cicero, 22
City College (College of the City of New York), 30, 43, 46, 77
City College Alumni Assn, 46
Civil War (US), 151, 152, 154, 160, 207
Civilian Conservation Corps (US), 160
Clark, George Rogers. See Lewis and Clark
Clark, Tom, 38
Clarke, Douglas V., 125
Clarke, Jay, 188
Claudius Smith's Den, 117
Cleveland, Grover, 44
Clinton, Henry (Sir), 116, 119
Clubs, Walking. See Walking—Clubs
Coaz, H. C. J. (Dr), 293
Cog Railway (Mount Washington), 147, 148
Col de Fenetre. See Fenetre Pass
Col du Grand St. Bernard. See St. Bernard Pass
Colden, Lake, 135, 136
Colden, Mount, 135, 136
Cole, Thomas, 129, 131

Coleridge, Samuel Taylor, 195
Colleoni, Bartolomeo, 276
Colorado Outdoor Sports (Denver Outfitters), 84
Columbus, Christopher, 281, 287
Colvin, Verplanck, 132
Compasses, 3
Congdon, H. W. (Capt), 138
Connecticut Hill (New York State), 131
Connecticut River Valley, 138-141
Conservation. See Walking—Conservation Problems From
Conservation Department, New York State, 106, 129, 131, 132, 134-136
Conservation Trail, 131
Consolidated Edison Co of New York, 114
Constable, John, 248
Continental Divide Trail, 27
Continental Road, 125
Coolidge, Calvin, 4, 37
Cooper, A. N., 26
Cooper, James Fenimore, 129
Cooper-Hewitt Estate, 123
Copenhagen, Denmark, 224-226
Cornell Outing Club, 131
Cornell University, 131
Corning, J. Leonard (Dr), 67
Corns, Evan (Doc), 40
Costello, Penna., 160
Cotton, John, 182
Couching Lion, 30
"Counterculture," 86
Cows (Alice and Tomboy), 38
Crandon Park, 154
Cranmer, Thomas (Archbishop), 246
Crawford Path, 148
Cromwell, Oliver, 242, 258
Cross Fell, 232
Croton Aqueduct, 2
Cuchulainn, 256
Curtis, "Father Bill," 30
Curtis, Ormsbee, 30
Curtis Trail, 130

Dade, Francis (Maj), 154
Dale, Chester, 207
Dante, 44, 46, 206
Dartmouth Outing Club, 100, 107, 143, 148
David (Biblical), 261, 264, 266
David, Gerard, 216
Davidson, Jo, 208
Davis, Jefferson, 191
Deaf and Blind, Colorado School for the, 163
Deardorff, Robert, 268
Decatur, Stephen, 206
Delacroix, Ferdinand Victor Eugene, 228

Delaware Water Gap: J. B. Ehrhardt article on trails to Mount Tammany, 158, 159; mention as point on Appalachian Trail, 95, 99, 100, 102, 103, 117

Delgado, Isaac, 191

Del Norte State Park (California), 28

Dench, Ernest A., 31

De Oliva, Mari, 281, 283

De Quincey, Thomas, 19

Derick of Alsace, Count, 216

de Valera, Eamon, 256

Dickens, Charles, 19, 24

Dobson, Meade C., 115

Dogs, 84, 91, 96, 97, 298

Donatello, 266

Doty, Alvah H. (Dr), 6, 20, 192

Douglas, Paul H. (Sen), 150

Douglas, William O. (Justice), 12, 38, 150

Drake, Francis (Sir), 278

Dublin, Ireland, 256-259

Duffus, Robert L., 18

Dunderberg Mountain, 115, 116

Dürer, Albrecht, 215

Du Val, Guy, 138

Du Val Trail, 138

Eberhart, Adolph O., 78

Ebersole, Chuck, 96

Ecology: Depiction in braille trail, 163-165. See also Walking—Conservation Problems From

Eden, Robert (Sir), 178

Edinburgh, Scotland, 240-242

Edward I, King of England, 239

Edward III, King of England, 244

Edward VII, King of England, 56, 79

Eger, B. A., 103

Egmont, Count of, 219, 220

Ehrhardt, John Bohne, 158

Eiler, Terry, 171

Einaudi, Luigi, 298

Einstein, Albert, 1

Eisenhower, Dwight David, 37

Elizabeth I, Queen of England, 247, 250, 258

Elizabeth II, Queen of Great Britain, 240

Elk Mountains, 161, 162

Emerson, Ralph Waldo, 6, 7, 9, 23, 32, 181, 182

Emmet, Robert, 258

Emmons, Ebenezer, 121, 132

"End-to-Enders," 85, 94-99

Engdahl, Don, 85

English People as Walkers. See Walking—Britons as Walkers

Erasmus, 239

Erie Canal Towpath, 132

Erlach, Fischer von, 213, 215

Etter, Alfred (Dr), 163

Eugene of Savoy, Prince, 213

Evans, Mervyn (Sgt), 48, 49

Evans, Olive, 161

Evarts, William M., 79

Everett, Mount, 34, 100

Everglades, 155, 156

Everglades National Park, 156

Evers, Don, 85

Eyck, Jan van, 216

Fahnestock State Park, 102

Faneuil, Peter, 182

FB-SK. See Fingerboard-Storm King Trail

Feet. See Walking—Feet

Fenetre Pass, 295-298

Ferdinand, King of Aragon, 287, 290

Feron, James, 232, 260

Field, Darby, 145

Fifty-Mile Walk (US fad, 1963), 35-40

Fingal's Cave (Scotland), 114

Finger Lakes Trail, 131, 132

Finger Lakes Trail Conference, 131, 132

Fingerboard-Storm King Trail, 116, 117

Finley, John Huston (Dr): Quoted in H. I. Brock article, 1; Finley article on Sainte Terre medal, 4; editorial mention of his 70-mi walk in 24 hours, 20; comment on Finley as a true walker, 23; his walks around Manhattan, 24, 36, 43, 45, 46; 70-mile walk on 70th birthday cited, 40; section on Finley as famous walker, 43-46; Finley to start Weston on his walk to Minneapolis, 77

Finley Walk, 46

Fitz-Hugh, John, 191

Fletcher, Colin, 85, 86, 88

Florence, Italy, 267, 268

Florida Trail, 155, 156

Florida Trail Assn, 155, 156

Foley, T. C., 231

Foote, Leroy W., 47

Foothills Trail Club, 131

Ford, Henry, 32

Forest Service, National (US), 85, 87, 88, 90, 95, 101-104, 107, 115, 131, 132, 146, 163, 164, 166, 168, 169

Forestry, 125, 126

Forestry Assn, American, 161

Forestry Department, Vermont, 137, 138

Forests and Waters, Pennsylvania Department of, 160

Fort Clinton, 116, 119

Fort Montgomery, 116, 119, 120

Fortney, Alan Jon, 147

Fossils, 123, 124

Fowey Light, 154

France, Anatole, 228

Frances, Duchess of Richmond and Lennox, 244

Francis, Saint, 270, 271

Francis I, King of France, 286

Franck Road, 120

Franklin, Benjamin, 19, 181, 182

Franz Joseph I, Emperor, 215

Frederik VII, King, 226
Frederik IX, King, 226
Freedom Paths, 180, 183, 184
Freedom Trail, 180-183
Fremont, John Charles, 72
French, Daniel Chester, 206
Fresh Air Club, 29-31, 115, 119
Fritz, J. J., 138
Frost, Robert, 131
Fuorcia Surlej, 292-294

Gabriel, Jacques, 227
Gandon, James, 258
Garibaldi, Giuseppe, 272
Garrison, William Lloyd, 181
Garvey, Edward B., 94-96, 98, 99
Gatewood, Emma, 96
Gaynor, William J., 77
Geological Survey, New Jersey, 123
Geological Survey, United States, 87, 117, 121, 123, 138
Geology: Hudson Palisades, 114; Greenwood Lake area, 121; Schuneumunk Mountain, 123; Chesler Park, 167; glacial effects, NYC area, 194, 195
George IV, King of England, 243
George Washington National Forest, 103
Ghibellines, 266
Ghiberti, Lorenzo, 266
Giambologna, 266, 267
Giant's Causeway (Northern Ireland), 114
Gibbons, Grinling, 238
Gilbert, Morris, 256
Gilroy, Harry, 219, 253
Giotto, 266
Girl Scouts, 105, 131
Glaciers, 194, 195, 292-294, 297
Gleason, Herbert W., 20
Glen House, 107, 148
Gobert, John, 171
Gokey, Joe, 132
Gold Head Branch State Park, 155
Goldberg, Arthur J., 38
Goldsmith, Oliver, 258
Goldthwaite, George, 115
Gomez Mora, 285
Goodhart, A. L. (Prof), 247
Goodman, Jack, 168
Goose, Mary, 181, 182
Gordon, Herbert: Articles; Long Path, 108; Hudson Palisades, 110; High Tor and Little Tor, 112; Schunemunk, 123; Shawangunk Mountains, 127
Gottlieb, Leslie D., 135
Gould, Symon, 49, 50
Grand Canyon, 85
Grand Canyon National Park, 169
Grant, Ulysses S., 131
Gray, John (Sir), 256

Great Circle Trail, 106
Great Outer Beach, 142, 143
Great Smoky Mountains National Park, 31, 100, 102, 104
Greco, El, 288-290
Greeley, Horace, 78, 79
Green Mountain Boys, 106
Green Mountain Club, 20, 30, 31, 100, 103, 106, 115, 122, 123, 137, 138
Green Mountains, 19, 30, 31, 100, 102, 105-107, 137, 138
Greenwich Village Historical Society, 253
Greenwood Lake Region, 121, 122
Gregory, Augusta, Lady, 256
Greylock, Mount, 100, 102, 106, 138
Grundy, John, 48, 51
Guelphs, 266
Guggenheim, Daniel (Mrs), 30
Guide Books. See Walking—Trail Information
Gwynn, Stephen, 258

Haddam, Conn., 138-141
Haddam Academy, 139
Hadrian, Emperor, 273
Hadrian's Wall, 232
Hale, Nathan, 187
Hamilton, Alexander, 19
Hancock, Jeff, 97
Hancock, John, 181, 182
Hannibal, 296
Hapsburgs, House of, 213, 215, 285
Harriman, Edward H., 122
Harriman, Edward H. (Mrs), 30
Harriman, W. Averell, 100, 122
Harriman Section, Palisades Interstate Park. See Palisades Interstate Park
Harrington, John H., 172
Hartford, Conn., 185-187
Harvard Black Rock Forest, 125, 126
Harvard University, 125
Harvey, William, 249
Havasu Canyon, 169-171
Havasupai Indians, 169-171
Hawkins, John (Sir), 278
Hawksbill Mountain, 153, 154
Hawksmoor, Nicholas, 245
Hawthorne, Nathaniel, 181
Hazen, Frank J. (Mrs), 78
Hazlitt, William, 6, 19, 20, 22, 26, 31, 32
Heacox, Cecil E., 129
Hector Land Use Area, 131, 132
Hell's Highway, 144
Hemingway, Ernest, 296
Henri IV, King of France, 228, 229
Henry VI, King of England, 237
Henry VII, King of England, 244
Henry VIII, King of England, 237, 239, 243
Heritage Trail, 187

Herrera, Juan de, 286
Hessian Lake, 120
High Point State Park, 100, 102, 117
High Tor, 112-114
High Tor (Play), 114
High Tor State Park, 108, 109, 112-114
Highland Light, 143
Highlands Hammock State Park, 155
Hiking. *See* Walking
Hiltz, Fred L., 131
Hippies, 85, 86
Historic Annapolis Inc, 177, 179
Hitch-Hiking, 8
Holbein, Hans, 247, 250
Holberg, Ludvig, 224, 225
Holmes, Les, 96, 98
Holmes, Oliver Wendell, 77, 181
Holy Cross Mountain, 161
Holy Land, 4-6
Hook Mountain State Park, 108, 109, 113
Hook Mountain-Tor Ridge Trail, 108
Hooker, Thomas (Rev), 186, 187
Horace, 46
Horn, Count of, 219
Howe, Julia Ward, 182
Howells, William Dean, 184
Hudson, Henry, 253
Hudson, William Henry, 7
Hudson Highlands, 32, 108, 112, 115-119, 121, 123-126
Hudson Highlands, Museum of the. *See* Museum of the Hudson
    Highlands
Hudson Palisades. *See* Palisades (Hudson River)
Hudson River School, 131
Hudson's (New York City Outfitters), 84
Hugo, Victor, 228
Huguet, Jaume, 283
Hume, David, 242
Hunt, Elliot Baldwin, 47
Hunt Trail, 107
Huntington, Archer M., 113
Huntington Ravine Trail, 107, 146
Huntington Wildlife Forest, 134
Hurricane (1938). *See* New England Hurricane

Ice Age, 194, 195
Ice Caves (Shawangunks), 128
Illinois Athletic Club, 57, 58, 68, 76
Indians, American, 72, 79, 102, 105, 122, 123, 130, 132, 135,
    145, 154, 169-171, 179, 206, 221, 222, 281
Inkowa Club of America, 30
Inkowa Club of New York, 30
Intercollegiate Outing Club Assn, 105
Interloken Trail, 131
Inyo National Forest, 87
Iron Mining, 46, 115-117, 120, 122, 123
Irving, Washington, 129, 131

Isabella, Queen of Castile, 287, 290
Ixion, 46

Jackson, Andrew, 189, 206
Jackson, Thomas J. (Gen), 152
Jackson Whites, 46
Jaime I, King, 283
James I, King of England, 240
James II, King, 185
James IV, King of Scotland, 242
James, Henry, 32
Jaures, Jean, 228
Jay Peak, 30, 31, 137, 138
Jaywalking, 18
Jedidiah Smith State Park, 28
Jefferies, Richard, 7
Jefferson, Thomas, 19, 178, 182, 206, 209
Jerusalem, 260-265
Jessen, Robert, 108, 109
Jessup Trail, 124
Jesus Christ, 261, 264
Job Corps, 163
Jogging, 129
John, Augustus, 256
John Muir Trail, 87
John's Brook Lodge, 30, 106, 136
John's Brook Trail, 106, 136
Johnson, Ben, 250
Johnson, Lyndon Baines, 27, 28, 97
Johnson, Samuel, 231, 242
Joint Trail, 166, 167
Jokl, Ernest (Dr), 39
Jones, Inigo, 250
Jones, John Paul, 179, 206, 240
Joyce, James, 256, 257, 259
Juana de Austria, Dona, 285
Jug End Mountain, 34

Karger, Ernest, 103
Karnig, Jack J., 125
Karpovich, Peter (Dr), 39
Katahdin, Mount: 27, 94, 101-104, 107; C. R. Whitney article,
    149
Keane, Thomas J. (Comdr), 196, 197
Keats, John, 9, 17
Kelty Pack (Glendale, Calif., Outfitters), 84
Kenison, Andrew Jackson, 25
Kenison, Nehemiah, 25
Kenison, Parker, 25
Kennedy, John Fitzgerald, 28, 35-40, 208, 209, 256
Kennedy, John Fitzgerald (Mrs), 36, 38
Kennedy, Robert F., 35-38, 40
Kern, Jim, 155, 156
Kerouac, Jack, 83, 86
Key, Francis Scott, 179
Key Biscayne, 154, 155

Kieran, John, 8, 34
Kierkegaard, Soren, 224
Kings Canyon National Park, 87, 89
Kittatinny Range, 100, 102, 117
Klondike Trail, 106
Knowlton, Elizabeth, 277
Knox, John, 242
Kollek, Teddy (Mayor), 260, 263, 264
Korobkov, Gabriel, 39
Kovacs, Arthur, 85
Kress, Samuel H., 207
Krock, Arthur, 35

Lafayette, Marquis de, 179
La Guardia, Fiorello, 43
Lake. See lake names inverted
Lake Mansfield Trout Club, 138
Lake Placid (NY) Region, 105, 106, 108, 109
Lakes-of-the-Clouds Hut, 146-148
Lamont Geological Observatory, 110
Lamy, Margaret W., 132
Land and Water Conservation Fund, 28
Lane, Hugh (Sir), 256
Latimer, Hugh, 246
Laud, William (Archbishop), 246
Lawrence of Arabia, 44
Leather Man, The, 47
Lee, Robert E., 206
Leisure Group Inc, 84, 85
Lenotre, Andre, 227
Leonardo da Vinci, 268-270
Leopold I, King of the Belgians, 219
Leopold II, King of the Belgians, 219
Levi, Samuel, 289, 290
Levick, M. B., 192
Lewis, Katy, 163
Lewis, Meriwether. See Lewis and Clark
Lewis, Robert B., 163-165
Lewis and Clark, 72, 88
Lewis and Clark Trail, 27
Limberlost, 153
Limmer, Peter, 12
Lincoln, Abraham, 13, 23, 25, 35, 36, 60, 78, 79, 187, 206, 208, 244
Lincoln, Robert Todd, 209
Lincoln Mountain, 138
Lind, Jenny, 184
Lipsyte, Robert M., 39
Little Tor, 112-114
Livingstone, David, 1
LM-T. See Long Mountain-Torne Trail
Lobb (of London), 12
London, England, 17, 243, 244
Long, E. John, 177
Long Mountain-Torne Trail, 117
Long Path, 108-112, 124, 127

Long Trail (Vermont), 20, 30, 31, 100, 103, 104, 106, 108; R. H. Torrey article on development, 137
Long Trail Lodge, 138
Longfellow, Henry Wadsworth, 181, 182
Longhena, Baldassare, 276
Longspee, William, 249
Los Padres National Forest, 88
Louis XIV, King, 213, 227
Louis XV, King, 228
Ludwig I, King of Bavaria, 251
Luehring, Frederick (Dr), 98
Lyman Run State Park, 159
Lysicrates, 252

Macaulay, Rose, 26
MacInnes, Joseph B., 222
MacKaye, Benton, 96, 99-101, 103, 104
Madison, James, 178, 206
Madrid, Spain, 283-286
Magna Carta, 249
Mahoosuc Range, 100
Maine Appalachian Trail Club, 107
Malahan, Bernard J., 185
Manassas National Battlefield Park, 151, 152
Manet, Edouard, 256
Mansfield, Mount, 30, 106, 137, 138
Maps. See Walking—Trail Information
Marcus Aurelius, 214
Marcy, William Leonard, (Gov), 135
Marcy, Mount, 27, 105, 106, 132, 135, 136
Margaret, Princess of Great Britain, 240
Margarita, Archduchess, 285
Maria, Queen of Hungary and Bohemia, 285
Marie de Medici, 227
Marie Louise, 215
Marines. See United States Marines
Markert, Ervin H., 131, 132
Markland, John, 194
Marlborough, Duke of, 213
Marlowe, Christopher, 250
Marples, Ernest, 230
Marsh, Susan, 163, 169
Marshall, John, 207
Martin, Dorothy M., 103
Marx, Karl, 17
Mary, Queen of Scots, 240, 242
Mary I, Queen of England, 246, 283
Marzolf, Marion, 224
Masaccio, 268
Massanutten Mountain, 154
Mather, Cotton, 181
Mathew, Theobald, 256
McCabe, John B., 120
McIntyre Range, 135
McKinley, Mount, 88
McLean, Evalyn Walsh, 208

McNamara, Robert S., 38
Mead, Nelson P. (Dr), 43
Medical Association, American, 25, 40
Medici Family, 267
Medley, Cynthia, 155
Mellon, Andrew W., 206, 207
Memling, Hans, 216
Mena, Juan P de, 284
Mendes France, Pierre, 37
Meras, Phyllis, 17
Mercier, Desire Joseph (Cardinal), 44
Meyer, Robert Jr., 189
Meylan, George L. (Dr), 67
Miami Beach, 188
Michelangelo Buonarroti, 216, 266, 268, 271, 274
Michelino, 266
Michelozzo, 267
Middlebury College, 138
Milan, Italy, 268-270
Milton, John, 238
Minneapolis Athletic Club, 77, 78
Minnehikers (Club), 31
Minnewaska Lake, 126
Minsi, Mount, 158
Missouri Athletic Club, 68, 72
Mitchell, Raymond M., 102
Mitchell, Mount, 103
Mohammed, 261
Mohawk Valley, 108, 109
Mohawk Valley Hiking Club, 108
Mohunk, 126
Molony, Patrick (Sgt), 48, 49
Monomoy Island, 143
Monroe, Will S. (Dr), 30, 122, 123, 138
Monroe Skyline Trail, 138
Mont Alto State Forest, 102
Moore, Barbara (Dr), 48-51, 230
Moosilauke, Mount, 100, 143, 144
Moratin, Nicholas Fernandez de, 285
Morgan, Anne, 30
Morris, James, 275
Morris, Leavitt F., 182
Morris, Wright, 13
Morrison, Joan, 232
Mortimer, Ronald, 89
Mother Goose, 181, 182
Motorcycles, 71, 88
Mount. *See* mountain names inverted
Mount Washington Club, 148
Mountjoy, Lord (Luke Gardiner), 257
Mozart, Wolfgang Amadeus, 213
Mueller, Louis J., 71
Muir, John: 7, 174. *See also* John Muir Trail
Mulholland, W. D., 129
Murphy, Edward F., 26
Museum of the Hudson Highlands, 126

Musgrave, Jim, 51
Mussolini, Benito, 298
Myer, Norton, 89

Nansen, Fridtjof, 44
Napoleon I, 17, 189, 215, 227, 250, 270, 295
Natchez Trace, 27
National (Headings). *See* key inversions, eg, Forest Service, National; Park Service, National; Scenic Trail System, National
National Trust (Great Britain), 231
Natural Bridge National Forest, 100
Nature Trails: Bull Run, 151, 152; Big Meadows, Blue Ridge, 154; Roaring Fork Braille Trail, 163-165
Nauset Light, 142
Nelson, Lord, 244, 256
Nepal, 277
Neville, Thomas, 238, 239
New England Hurricane, 103, 104
New England Trail Conference, 87, 90, 100
New Orleans, La., 189-191
New York City: As place to walk in, 2, 5; J. H. Finley's walks around Manhattan, 5, 43, 45, 46; pedestrian problems, 15, 18, 195; New York Walk Book, 32-34; Central Park, 50, 194, 195; special section on city, 192-199; M. B. Levick article, 192-193; Riverside Park, 194, 195; society girls constitutionals, 194; Comdr Keane walk of all streets, 196, 197; bridge walking, 198, 199
New York Herald, 78
New York Hiking Club, 30
New York-New Jersey Trail Conference, 30, 87, 90, 100, 108, 124, 125
New York Ramblers, 30
New York State Conservation Department. *See* Conservation Department, New York State
New York Times: Dr. J. H. Finley assns, 43-46; E. P. Weston reports exclusively to Times on his 1907 New York-San Francisco walk, 60-77; trail map marking service, 117; Geneva office, 292
New York Walk Book, 32-34, 111, 114
Newton, Isaac, 238, 239
Nichols, Anne, 78, 79
Nightingale, Geoff, 221
Nitkin, Nathaniel, 105, 145
Noone, Peter, 88
North, Roger, 238
North Cascades National Park, 28
North Country Trail, 27
North Mountain Trail, 131
Northern Virginia Regional Park Authority, 151
Northville-Lake Placid Trail, 30, 108, 109
Nye, Wallace G., 78

Oakes, George W.; Articles; Athens, 251; Bruges, 216; Cambridge, 237; Edinburgh, 240; Florence, 266; London, 243; Oxford, 245; Paris, 227; Rome, 271; Salisbury and Wilton

House, 247; San Francisco, 203; Segovia, 286; Toledo, 288; Venice, 274; Vienna, 213; Washington, 206
Ocala National Forest, 155, 156
O'Casey, Sean, 257
O'Connell, Daniel, 256, 259
O'Connor, Lois, 131, 159
Officer, Keith, 36
Ogle, Benjamin, 179
Ogle, Samuel, 179
Oglethorpe, Mount, 101-104
O'Hagan, Anna, 78
O'Kane, Walter Collins, 138
Old Angler Inn, 150
Old Man of the Mountain, 144
Old Saybrook, Conn, 138, 140, 141
Ole Bull State Park, 160
O'Leary, Daniel, 56, 57, 63, 77
Olivares, Count-Duke de, 283
Onativia, Elizabeth, 195
Onstott, Elmer, 96, 97
Oppenheim, Beatrice, 25
Orcagna, 266
Ordnance Survey (Great Britain), 235
Oregon Trail, 27
Osceola (Seminole Chief), 154
Osceola National Forest, 155
O'Shea, William J. (Dr), 43
Osler, William (Dr), 66, 67
Osmund, Saint, 249
Ossining Historical Society, 47
Otis, Harrison Gray, 183, 184
Otis, James, 182
Outdoor Clubs, Federation of Western, 87, 90
Outdoor Recreation Resources Review Commission, 129
Outfit, Walking. See Walking—Outfit
Owen, Branley C., 95-97
Oxford, England, 245-247

Pacific Crest Trail, 27, 28, 85, 87, 97, 108
Packs. See Walking—Outfit: Packs
Paepke, Walter (Mrs), 164
Paine, Robert Treat, 181, 182
Palisades (Hudson River), 2, 108-114
Palisades Interstate Park, 29, 30, 46, 99, 100, 102, 103, 108-119
Palisades Interstate Park Trail Conference, 103
Palestine, 45
Paris, France, 17, 227-229
Park Service, National (US), 85, 87-89, 95, 103, 104, 153, 154, 157, 166, 167, 172, 177
Parker Cabin Mountain, 116
Parnell, Charles Stewart, 256, 259
Pascal, Henry S. (Dr), 67
Paterson Ramblers, 30, 31
Pattison, Robert B. (Rev), 47
Pearse, Padraig, 256

Peattie, Donald Culross, 7
Pedestrian Problems. See Walking—Pedestrian Problems
Pedestrianism. See Walking
Pedestrians' Assn, 231
Pedometers, 3, 16, 17, 39, 43
Peekamoose Mountain, 109
Pembrokeshire Coast National Park, 235-237
Penn, William, 202, 247
Pennine Way, 232
Pepys, Samuel, 239
Perkins, Arthur, 103
Peter, Thomas, 208
Pets, 84, 91, 96, 97
Pheidippides, 79
Phelps, "Old Mountain," 133
Philadelphia, Penna., 200-202
Philip II, King of Spain, 283
Philip III, King of Spain, 285
Philip IV, King of Spain, 285, 286
Philip V, King of Spain, 285
Phoenicia Trail, 130
Physical Medicine and Rehabilitation, Baruch Committee on, 39
Picasso, 186, 256, 283
Pilgrim Springs, 143
Pilgrims (American), 143
Pilgrims Way, 232-234
Pinkham Notch Camp, 107, 146, 148
Pisgah National Forest, 100, 102, 104
Place, Frank, 100, 115, 117, 118
Placid, Lake, 106
Planning and Parks, Federated Societies on, 100
Plato, 7, 23
Podiatry, 25, 39
Podiatry Society, New York State, 25, 39
Poe, Edgar Allen, 195
Pollock, Frederick, 19
Ponce de Leon, 154, 155, 278, 279

Ponte, Antonio da, 275
Poore, Charles, 33
Popolopen Torne, 116, 117
Porter, Gene Stratton, 153
Potomac Appalachian Trail Club, 154
Potomac Heritage Trail, 27
Potter County (Penna) Historical Society, 160
Potter County (Penna) Recreation Inc, 160
Prairie Club, 30, 31
Prairie State Park (California), 28
Pratt, George D., 30
Prescott, William (Col), 184
Presidential Range, 145-148
Price, Thomas J., 47
Priest Mountain, 103
Proctor, Fletcher D. (Mrs), 138
Proctor, Mortimer R., 30, 138
Prospect Park, 34
Puerto Rican Culture, Institute of, 278, 279

Putnam, Harrington, 30
Pyle, "Cold Cash," 38
Pyramids Mountain, 161

Quarrying, 111-114

Race, Mount, 34, 100
Race Point Light, 143
Raeburn, Henry (Sir), 240
Ramapo-Dunderberg Trail, 115-119
Ramapo Mountains, 32, 46, 113, 115-119, 121
Ramapo Rampart, 117-119
Ramblers' Assn, 231, 232
Range Trail (Adirondacks), 106
Raphael, 268, 271, 273
Raymond Path, 146
R-D. *See* Ramapo-Dunderberg Trail
Recreation Assn, National, 40, 43
Recreational Equipment (Seattle Outfitters), 84
Red Arrow Trail, 119
Red Cross Commission to Palestine, 45
Red Hill Trail, 130
Redd, Lucille (Mrs), 38
Redwood High School (Larkspur, Calif.), 39
Redwood National Park, 28
Reges, John T. (Mrs), 150
Rembrandt van Rijn, 186, 254, 255
Renoir, Pierre Auguste, 256
Reston, James, 37
Revere, Paul, 180-184
Revolutionary War (American), 111-113, 116, 117, 119, 120,
    123, 125, 180-184, 187, 208
Ribera, Jose, 285
Richelieu, Cardinal, 227, 228
Ridley, Nicholas, 246
Rip Van Winkle, 131
Riverside Park, 194, 195
Rizzio, David, 242
Roaring Fork Braille Trail, 163-165
Robbias, della, 266
Robinson, David, 48
Rocky Mountain Club, 30
Rocky Mountains, 161, 162
Rogers, Roy (Sgt), 49
Rogers, Will, 208
Rohan, Michael, 261
Rome, Italy, 271-274
Romer, Ole, 224
Romulus, 274
Roosevelt, Franklin Delano, 37, 99, 206
Roosevelt, Theodore, 35-40, 77
Rousseau, Jean Jacques, 19, 26, 31, 228
Rusk, Howard A. (Dr), 38
Russell, Bertrand, 26
Russell, George William (AE), 259
Ryback, Eric, 85, 97

Sabatini, Francisco, 283
St. Bernard Pass, 295, 298
Saint Cecilia, 271
Saint Francis, 270, 271
Saint-Gaudens, Augustus, 256
St. John, V. I., 157
St. John's College (Annapolis), 177, 179
Sainte Terre Medal, 4, 5
Salinger, Pierre, 37, 38, 40
Salisbury, England, 247-250
Salvation Army, 139, 141
Sam's Point, 126-128
Sandburg, Carl, 23
Sands, Susan, 83
San Francisco, 203-205
San Gorgonio Wilderness, 88
San Juan, Puerto Rico, 278-280
Santa Fe Trail, 27
Saugeen Indian Reserve, 221
Savonarola, Girolamo, 266
Sawyer, Grant (Gov), 38
Scenic Trail System, National, 27, 28, 87, 97
Schaefer, Vincent J., 108
Schubert, Franz, 215
Schunemunk Mountain, 108, 123, 124
Scott, Walter (Sir), 242
Sea Scouts, 196
Sebago, Lake, 117
Segovia, Spain, 286-288
Sequoia National Forest, 87
Sequoia National Park, 87, 89
Sergeant, Peter, 181
Sert, Jose Maria, 282
Shaffer, Earl, 96, 103
Shakespeare, William, 9, 200, 208, 250, 258, 274
Shattuck, Jim, 96
Shawangunk Mountains, 32, 109, 126-128
Shelley, Percy Bysshe, 247
Shenandoah National Forest, 100, 104
Shenandoah National Park, 100, 102, 153, 154
Shenandoah Natural History Assn, 153
Sherburne Pass, 30, 106, 138
Sheridan, Philip Henry, 208
Shoes. *See* Walking—Outfit: Shoes
Shore and Mountain Club, 30
Shore Trail (Hudson Palisades), 111
Shoup, David M. (Gen), 35
Sickert, Walter Richard, 256
Sidney, Philip (Sir), 250
Sieck, Ann, 84
Sierra Club, 85, 87-90, 161
Sierra Design (Berkeley, Calif., Outfitters), 85
Sierra National Forest, 87
Sierra Nevada, 27, 28, 85, 87, 88, 172-174
Silver, George (Dr), 39
Sixtus V, Pope, 273

Ski Hut (Berkeley, Calif., Outfitters), 88
Skinner, Everett and Nell, 97
Skyland, Va., 153
Skyline Drive, 153, 154
Sleeping Bags. See Walking—Outfit: Sleeping Bags
Sleepy Hollow, 131
Slide Mountain (Catskills), 27, 30, 109, 129, 130
"Slush Meadows," 88
Smith, Adam, 242
Smith, John (Capt), 249
Smith, Margaret and Clifford, 94, 97
Smithson, James, 206
Smythe, F. S., 26
Snowmobiles, 88
Snyder, Gary, 86
Socrates, 7, 23
Solomon (Biblical), 261
Sothern, E. H., 189
South Fork Meadows, 88
South Mountain Trail, 131
Spengler, Oswald, 197
Spenser, Edmund, 250
Springer Mountain, 27, 94
Stanislaus National Forest, 87
Stanley, Henry Morton, 1
Stark, Jack, 154
Starr, John T., 153
Staten Island Bird Club, 30
Steele, Richard (Sir), 242
Stefansson, Vilhjalmur, 51
Stein, Clarence S., 99
Stephen, Leslie, 19
Stephenson, Tom, 232
Sterling Forest, 121, 122
Stevenson, Robert Louis, 6, 7, 19, 20, 138, 242
Stillman, Ernest (Dr), 125
Stockdale, William, 200
Stony Man Mountain, 153
Stony Point, N. Y., 113, 116, 119, 120
Stony Point Park, 120
Storm King Mountain, 114, 116, 117
Story, George F. E., 138
Stowe, Harriet Beecher, 181
Strongbow, 258
Stuart, Gilbert, 187
Suffern-Bear Mountain Trail, 117-119
Suleiman the Magnificent, 261
Sullivan, Walter, 146, 291, 295
Sunday Tramps, The, 19
Susquehannock Trail Club, 160
Susquehannock Trail System, 159, 160
Suwanee River State Park, 155
Swift, Jonathan, 258
Swinburne, Algeron Charles, 9
Swiss Alpine Club, 291, 292
Syracuse University, 134

Taconic Mountains, 32, 99-102, 106
Taconic State Park Commission, 99
Taft, William Howard, 37
Tahawus (Indian Name for Mount Marcy), 135
Talese, Gay, 46
Tallman Mountain State Park, 109
Talmage, T. De W., 53
Tammany, Mount, 158, 159
Tannhäuser, 57
Taylor, James P., 137, 138
Taylor, Norman, 138
Tear of the Clouds, Lake, 136
Teets, Florence, 144
Tennyson, Alfred, 9
Thayer, Paul W., 138
Thomson, James, 9
Thomson, Peggy, 94
Thompson, John, 154
Thoreau, Henry David: Cape Cod 1849 walk retraced in article
    by C. Bates, 142; other refs, 4-9, 19, 20, 23, 24, 32, 95, 129,
    144, 147, 149
Thornton, William (Dr), 208
Thorvaldsen, Bertel, 224
Tiepolo, Giovanni Battista, 276
Timp-Torne Trail, 116, 117, 119
Timp Trail (Wasatch Range), 168
Timpanogos, Mount, 168
Tintoretto, 186, 276
Titian, 276
T-MI. See Tuxedo-Mount Ivy Trail
Toiyabe National Forest, 87
Toledo, Spain, 288, 290
Tom Jones Mountain, 116
Tompkins, Rathvlyn McClure (Brig Gen), 36, 37
Torrey, John, 30
Torrey, Raymond H.: Articles; hiking clubs, 29; Taconic sec-
    tion of Appalachian Trail, 99; trail making in Palisades Inter-
    state Park, 115; Suffern-Bear Mountain Trail, 118; Green-
    wood Lake area, 121; Wyanokie Plateau, 122; Long Trail,
    137
Torrey Botanical Club, 30
Toscanini, Arturo, 270
Trail Conferences. See Walking—Trail Conferences. Confer-
    ence names, eg, New York-New Jersey Trail Conference
Trail Information. See Walking—Trail Information
Trail Making. See Walking—Trail Making
Trailwise (Berkeley, Calif., Outfitters), 84
Trajan, Emperor, 272
Tramp and Trail Club, 100, 115, 118
Tramps (Vagrants), 47, 150
Treason House, 112
Tremper, Mount, 130
Trevelyan, George Otto, 20
Truman, Harry S., 11, 36, 40
T-T. See Timp-Torne Trail
T-TJ. See Tuxedo-Tom Jones Trail

Tuckerman Ravine, 146, 148
Tuckerman Ravine Trail, 107, 146
Tupper Lake, N. Y., 132
Tuxedo-Mount Ivy Trail, 117, 119
Tuxedo Park Assn, 116
Tuxedo-Tom Jones Trail, 115-117

Uccello, Paolo, 266
Udall, Stewart L. (Sec), 150
Uinta National Forest, 168
Ulysses, 2
Unaka National Forest, 100, 102
United States. For headings not here, *see* key inversions, eg,
    Forest Service, National (US); Geological Survey (US); Park
    Service, National (US)
United States Marines, 35-40
United States Naval Academy, 177, 179
United States Naval Academy Assn, 179
'Updegraff's Law,' 34

Vanderbilt, William Henry, 54
Van Dyck, Anthony, 250
Van Hovenberg Trail, 106
Van Orden, Elmer, 114
Vega, Lope de, 285
Velazquez, 286
Venice, Italy, 274-276
Ventura Rodriguez, 285
Ventura de la Vega, 285
Verdi, Giuseppe, 276
Verrocchio, Andrea, 266, 276
Vienna, Austria, 213-215
Villanueva, Diego, 285
Virgin Gorda, 157
Virgin Islands, 157
Virgin Islands National Park, 157
Virginia Sky-Line Co, 153-154
Vizcaino (Spanish Sea Captain), 154
Vlaminck, Maurice de, 256
Voltaire, 228

Walden Pond, 129
Walking—
    Art of: H. I. Brock article, 1; unsigned article, 3; editorial
        on thoughts of Weston and others, 6; D. C. Peattie article,
        7; H. Borland article, 11
    Backpacking: S. Sands article on US boom, 83
    Blind, Trails for the: 163-165
    Blisters: 40, 86, 97, 231
    Boots: See Walking—Outfit: Shoes
    Bridge Walking: C. Carmondy article, 198
    Britons as Walkers: editorial on Victorians and organization
        The Sunday Tramps, 19; John o'Groats to Lands' End
        walks (Dr Moore and others), 48-51; New York society
        girls looking like English walkers, 194; P. Catling article,
        230

Celibacy Factor: 230
City Walking and City vs Country Walking: J. H. Finley
    comment, 5; D. C. Peattie comment, 8; R. Baker article,
    25; M. B. Levick article, 192; E. Onativia article, 195.
    See also Walking—Pedestrian Problems
Clubs: R. H. Torrey article, 29; editorial, 31; major US
    clubs discussed in S. Sands article on backpacking, 87;
    list of major clubs, with addresses, 90
Compasses: 3
Conservation Problems From: 83, 88-90
Decline in: Editorial, 20
Definition: 21, 23, 129
Diet: See Walking—Food
Dogs: 84, 91, 96, 97, 299
English People as Walkers: See Walking—Britons as Walkers
Equipment: See Walking—Outfit
Feats: E. P. Weston and others, 52-79
Feet: E. P. Weston on care, 6, 57; W. Morris article on walk-
    ing in bare feet, 13; B. Oppenheim article on use and care,
    25; P. Catling on care, 231
50-Mile Fad (US): 35-40
Food: Vegetarians as walkers (Dr. Moore), 48-51, 230;
    Weston's diet, 56, 62, 63, 70, 72, 76; other refs, 97, 102
Gear: See Walking—Outfit
Guide Books: See Walking—Trail Information
Health Effects: 6, 20, 38, 39, 52, 60, 79, 85, 129, 192, 230
High Altitude: 162
Hippies: 85, 86

Kinds of Walks: J. Kieran article, 8
Maps: See Walking—Trail Information
Matches: See Walking—Sport
Motivation: H. I. Brock comment, 2; J. Kieran article, 8;
    W. O. Douglas article, 12; editorials, 19, 26; comment,
    24; H. E. Heacox comment, 129
Nature Trails: Bull Run, 151; Big Meadows, Blue Ridge,
    154; Roaring Fork Braille Trail, 163
Outfit: General, 3, 21, 99, 102, 129, 231; backpacking gear,
    86, 99; compasses, 3; high altitude, 162; outfitters, 84;
    packs, 86, 99; pedometers, 3, 16, 17, 39, 43; shoes, 12,
    40, 86, 91, 97, 99, 143, 231; sleeping bags, 86, 99; win-
    ter, 91
Pedestrian Problems: Editorial Have Pedestrians Rights?
    15; R. L. Duffus article, 18; definition of pedestrian as
    one who has been hit by an automobile, 23; E. Onativia
    article, 195
Pedometers: 3, 16, 17, 39, 43
Pets: 84, 91, 96, 97
Posture: 21, 40
Quotations: E. F. Murphy compilation, 26
Records: See Walking—Feats
Road Walking: 22, 23
Sport: 52-54
Technique: H. I. Brock note, 1; editorial quotes Weston,
    6; D. C. Peattie comment, 8. *See also* Walking—Art of;
    Walking—Posture
Thinking While Walking: Editorial, 19

Trail Conferences: 87; list of major US conferences, with addresses, 90

Trail Information (Guides and Maps): New York Walk Book, 32-34; how obtained, 87; list of major US walking clubs and trail conferences, with addresses, 90; Appalachian Trail in Maine, 107; Catskills, 129; Finger Lakes Region, 132; Trails to Marcy, 136; Green Mountains, 138; Shenandoah National Park, 154; summer wilderness trips, 161

Trail Making: 109, 115-119, 129, 131

Vegetarians: Dr. Moore, 48-51, 230

Weather: 21, 22

Wilderness, Impact on: 83, 88-90

Winter: 91-93

Women: Dr. Moore, 48-51; other refs, 53, 85

World War II Effects: H. I. Brock comment, 1; D. C. Peattie article on US going off wheels, 7; editorial, 20; other refs, 104, 108

Wallace, William, 240

Walters, Warren, 85, 90

Walton, Izaak, 7

War of 1812, 181, 182, 189

Warren, Earl, 38

Wasatch Hiking Club, 30

Wasatch National Forest, 168, 169

Wasatch Range, 168, 169

Washington, George, 116, 125, 177, 179, 187, 206

Washington, Martha, 208

Washington, D. C., 206-209

Washington, Mount, 30, 100, 101, 103, 107, 145-148

Way, Robin, 85

Wayne, Anthony, 113, 116, 119, 120

Webster, Noah, 129

Weddell Sea, 45

Welch, R. E., 148

Welch, W. A. (Maj), 100, 115, 117, 118

Welles, Sumner, 208

West Mountain, 116, 117, 119, 120

West Point Military Reservation, 109, 112, 123

Westchester County Historical Society, 47

Westchester Trails Assn, 30

Weston, Edward Payson: Editorial on his concept of walking, 6; editorial mention of 100-mile walk in 22 hrs, 20; special section on Weston as famous walker, 52-79; Portland, Me., to Chicago walk, 1867, 52; repeated, 1907, 55-58; Philadelphia to New York walk, 1906, 55; physical condition, 56, 60, 62, 63, 66, 67, 79; feats reviewed, 56, 57, 60, 63, 78; editorial on feats, 79; diet, 56, 62, 63, 70, 72, 76; feet care, 57; New York City-San Francisco Walk, 1909, 59-77; New York City-Minneapolis walk, 1913, 77, 78; death, 78

Weston, Maria (Mrs), 78

Whistler, James Abbott McNeill, 256

White, Byron R., 38

White, Gilbert, 7

White, Paul Dudley (Dr), 40, 129

White Bar Trail, 117, 119

White Mountain National Forest, 147

White Mountains, 29, 31, 100, 101, 103-107, 115, 137, 143-148

White River National Forest, 163-165

Whiteface Mountain, 106, 108, 109

Whiteface Trail, 109

Whitman, Marcus, 72

Whitney, Craig R., 149

Whitney, Mount, 88

Whittier, John Greenleaf, 181, 182

Whittington, Banning E., 38

Widener, P. A. B., 207

Wild Scenic Rivers System, 28

Wilde, Oscar, 259

Wilderness, Human Impact on, 83, 88-90

Wilderness Act of 1964, 89

Wilderness Preservation System, National, 90

Wilderness Society, 161

Wilhelm II, Kaiser, 263

Wilhelmina, Queen of the Netherlands, 253

Wilkins, Hubert, 45

William of Orange, 258

Williams College Outing Club, 138

Wilson, Alexander, 7

Wilson, Woodrow, 208

Wilton House, 247, 248, 250

Windham High Peak Trail, 131

Winslow, Mary Chilton, 182

Winters, S. R., 101

Winthrop, John, 182

Wittenberg-Cornell-Slide Trail, 129, 130

Wolfe, Thomas, 40

Wolsey, Thomas (Cardinal), 247

Women's Clubs, New Jersey Federation of, 111

Wood, Wallace D., 131

Woodtown Trail, 119

Wordsworth, William, 9, 10, 19, 32, 230

World War I, 215, 228, 240, 262

World War II, 213, 224, 228, 244, 249, 253, 254, 298. *See also* Walking—World War II Effects

Wren, Christopher (Sir), 238, 245, 247, 249

Wyanokie Lodge, 123

Wyanokie Plateau, 122, 123

Yeats, William Butler, 259

Yosemite National Park, 87, 172-174

Young, Herbert Judson, 148

Young, John V., 166

Youth Hostel Club, Syracuse, 132

Youth Hostels, American, 87, 90, 131, 132

Zacharie, Isachaar (Dr), 25

Zen Buddhism, 86

Zola, Emile, 228